The Hidden Places of
SCOTLAND

By
James Gracie

Published by:
Travel Publishing Ltd
7a Apollo House, Calleva Park
Aldermaston, Berks, RG7 8TN

ISBN 1-902-00774-3

First Published: *1994*
Second Edition: *1997*
Third Edition: *1999*
Fourth Edition: *2002*

Hidden Places Regional Titles

Cambs & Lincolnshire
Cornwall
Devon
East Anglia
Heart of England
Highlands & Islands
Lake District & Cumbria
Lincolnshire & Nottinghamshire
Somerset
Thames Valley
Chilterns
Derbyshire
Dorset, Hants & Isle of Wight
Gloucestershire & Wiltshire
Hereford, Worcs & Shropshire
Kent
Lancashire & Cheshire
Northumberland & Durham
Sussex
Yorkshire

Hidden Places National Titles

England
Scotland
Ireland
Wales

Printing by: Scotprint, Haddington

Maps by: © Maps in Minutes ™ (2001) © Crown Copyright, Ordnance Survey 2001

Editor: James Gracie

Cover Design: Lines & Words, Aldermaston

Cover Photo: The cover photograph is Port of Mentieth, Lake of Mentieth, Perthshire © James Gracie

Text Photos: Photographs throughout the book have been kindly supplied by Britain on View © www.britainonview.com or by the author James Gracie © James Gracie

Foreword

The Hidden Places is a collection of easy to use travel guides taking you, in this instance, on a relaxed but informative tour of Scotland – a country which has been inhabited for thousands of years and is rich in history and culture. Scotland is blessed with some of the most impressive mountains in the British Isles and finest coastlines and offshore islands in the world. It is also full of "hidden places", which can enrich the visitor's historical knowledge of Scottish heritage and provide landscapes that astound the eye with their sheer beauty.

This is the fourth edition of ***The Hidden Places of Scotland*** which, for the first time is published ***in full colour.*** All ***Hidden Places*** titles are now published in colour which ensures that readers can properly appreciate the attractive scenery and impressive places of interest in Scotland and, of course, in the rest of the British Isles. We do hope that you like the new format.

The ***Hidden Places*** series of guides contain a wealth of interesting information on the history, the countryside, the towns and villages and the more established places of interest throughout the British Isles. But they also promote the more secluded and little known visitor attractions and places to stay, eat and drink many of which are easy to miss unless you know exactly where you are going.

In this guide you will find hotels, b&bs, guest houses, self-catered accommodation restaurants, public houses, teashops, historic houses, museums, ancient monuments and sites, gardens, and many other attractions throughout Scotland, all of which are comprehensively indexed. Most places are accompanied by an attractive photograph and are easily located by using the map at the beginning of each chapter. We do not award merit marks or rankings but concentrate on describing the more interesting, unusual or unique features of each place with the aim of making the reader's stay in the local area an enjoyable and stimulating experience.

Whether you are visiting Scotland for business or pleasure or, in fact, are living in this wonderful country we do hope that you enjoy reading and using this book. We are always interested in what readers think of places covered (or not covered) in our guides so please do not hesitate to use the reader reaction forms provided to give us your considered comments. We also welcome any general comments which will help us improve the guides themselves. Finally, if you are planning to visit any other corner of the British Isles we would like to refer you to the list of all our titles to be found at the rear of the book and to the Travel Publishing website at www.travelpublishing.co.uk.

Travel Publishing

Note: International Calling

All telephone numbers throughout the book are shown with local dialling codes. Please note that callers outside the United Kingdom should first dial the country code of 00 44 followed by the number shown with the leading zero dropped.

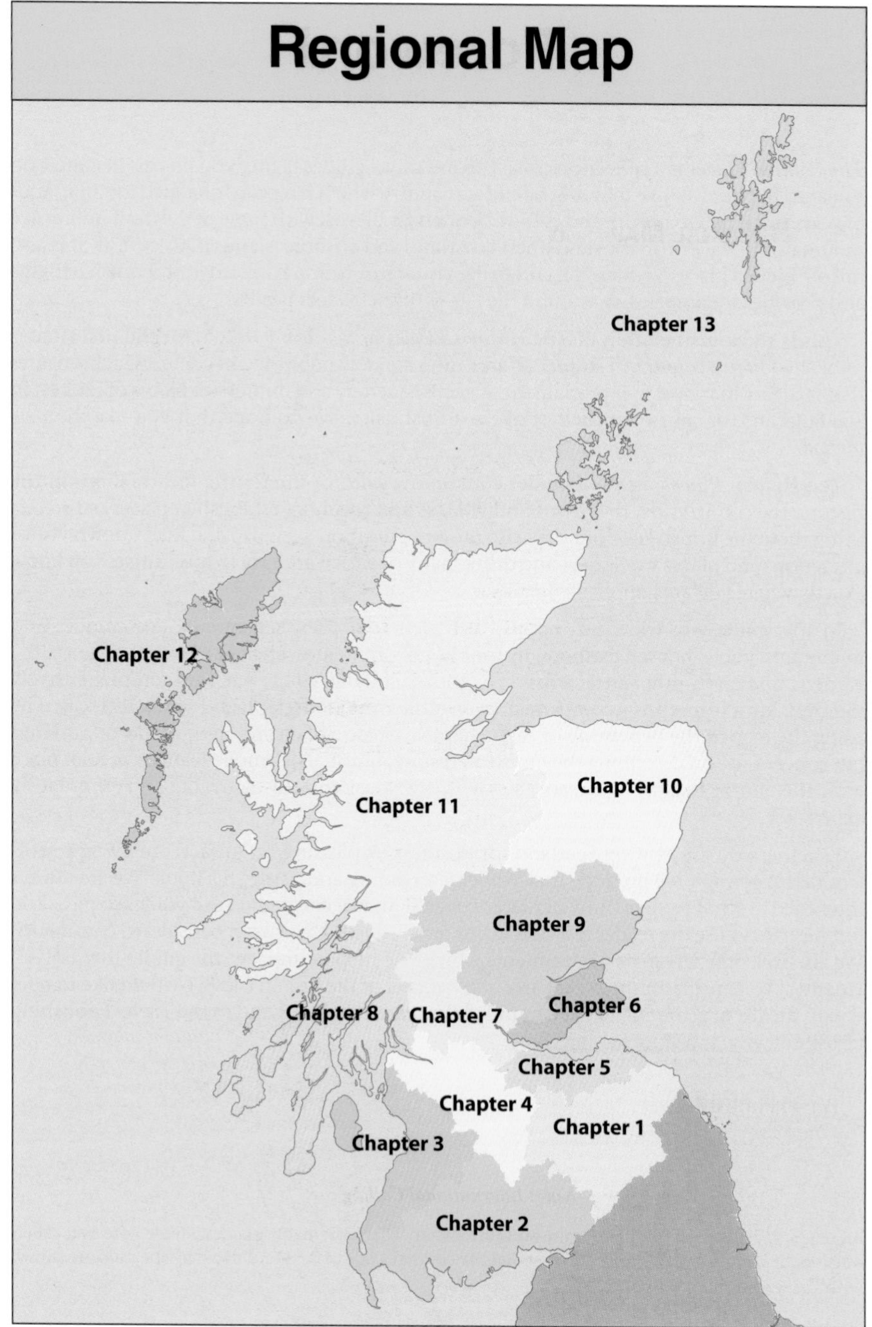
Regional Map
Chapter 13
Chapter 12
Chapter 10
Chapter 11
Chapter 9
Chapter 8
Chapter 7
Chapter 6
Chapter 5
Chapter 4
Chapter 1
Chapter 3
Chapter 2

Contents

Foreword III

Regional Map IV

Contents V

Geographical Areas:

Chapter 1: The Borders 1
Chapter 2: Dumfries and Galloway 22
Chapter 3: Ayrshire and Arran 61
Chapter 4: Glasgow and West Central Scotland 95
Chapter 5: Edinburgh and the Lothians 117
Chapter 6: Fife and Kinross 136
Chapter 7: Stirling and Clackmannan 160
Chapter 8: Argyllshire and the Inner Hebrides 183
Chapter 9: Perthshire and Angus 228
Chapter 10: Aberdeenshire, Kincardineshire, Banffshire & Moray 253
Chapter 11: The Highlands 280
Chapter 12: The Western Isles 321
Chapter 13: Orkney and Shetland 337

Indexes and Lists:

List of Tourist Information Centres 345
Index of Towns, Villages and Places of Interest 352
List of Advertisers 376

Additional Information:

Order Form 383
Reader Comment Form 385

1 The Borders

Of all the regions in Scotland, the Borders has the bloodiest history. It was here, in bygone days, that the constant bickering between Scotland and England boiled over into bloodshed and occasional outright war.

This was the land of the reivers, or "moss troopers" - men from both sides of the Border who raped, pillaged, burnt and rustled their way into the history books. People nowadays tend to romanticise their activities, but in fact they were nothing more than upper class thugs and bullies, and no one was safe from their activities. They even gave the word "blackmail" to the English language.

Talla Reservoir, Borders

But it was also the land of the Border ballads and tales of high chivalry. Sir Walter Scott was a Borders man, and was steeped in them. It was he who, almost single-handedly, invented Scotland's modern image, which depends not on his native heath, but on Highland scenery, skirling bagpipes, sword dances and kilts. This has not been lost on the hardy Borderers, who know there is more to Scotland than that.

The Borders are not as well known as they should be. People driving north to areas they perceive to be more historic and romantic pass through a region that is as beautiful as the Highlands in its own way, and probably has more historical associations than anywhere else in the country. The area stretches from the North Sea in the east to the borders of Dumfriesshire in the west, and contains four former counties, Peeblesshire, Selkirkshire, Roxburghshire and Berwickshire. Their scenery is less rugged than the Highlands, and their hills are rounded and green, with fertile valleys, quiet villages and cosy market towns to explore. That flat area of Berwickshire known as the Merse, roughly between the Lammermuir Hills and the English border, is one of the most intensely farmed areas in Britain.

St Abb's Head, Borders

There are castles and old houses aplenty, from Floors Castle just outside Kelso, home of the Duke of Roxburgh, to 10th century Traquair House in Peeblesshire, said to be the oldest continually inhabited house in Scotland. Mellerstain too, is worth visiting, as is Paxton, Manderston, Thirlestane and Abbotsford.

But perhaps the area's most beautiful and haunting attractions are its ruined abbeys. Again and again they were attacked by English soldiers, and again and again, as Scottish soldiers crossed the border bent on revenge, the monks quietly got on with rebuilding and repairing them. Now the ruins at Melrose, Kelso, Dryburgh and Jedburgh rest easy under the care of Historic Scotland, and their charm and peace can be easily visited and appreciated.

Melrose Abbey, Borders

The area's other great icon is the River Tweed, which, for part of its length, forms the boundary between Scotland and England. Then, just east of Kelso, the border turns south, and the river is wholly Scottish. It's fame rests on salmon, though not as many are caught nowadays as there used to be. But it is still a river that in some ways defines the region, and most of the larger settlements, from Peebles to Coldstream, are to be found on its banks.

Kelso, Borders

A series of themed trails has recently been laid out which takes you round many Borders attractions. The Ballads Trail (103 miles) takes you to many of the places associated with the Borders ballads; the Poets of the Scottish Borders Trail (118 miles) takes you to places of literary interest; the Berwickshire Car Trail (72 miles) explores the "mysteries of the Merse"; the Sir Walter Scott Trail (66 miles) follows the footsteps of the poet and novelist; the James Hogg Trail (62 miles) takes you to places associated with the writer known as "The Ettrick Shepherd", and the John Buchan Trail looks at places associated with the man who wrote "The Thirty Nine Steps".

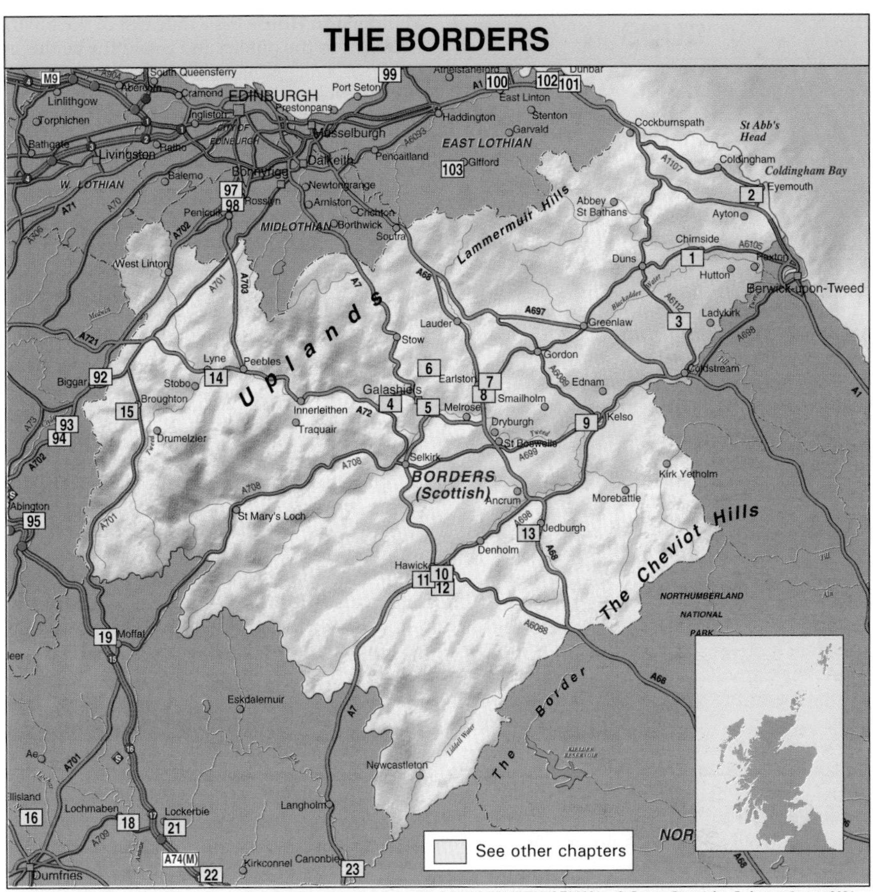

PLACES TO STAY, EAT, DRINK AND SHOP

1	Chirnside Hall Hotel, Chirnside	Hotel	Page 5
2	The Ship Hotel, Eyemouth	Hotel	Page 6
3	Little Swinton Farm, Swinton	Self catering	Page 7
4	Clovenfords Hotel, Clovenfords	Pub, accommodation and restaurant	Page 8
5	The Ginger Jar, Galashiels	Café and tearoom	Page 9
6	Over Langshaw, Langshaw	Bed and Breakfast	Page 9
7	White Swan Hotel, Earlston	Hotel	Page 11
8	Birkenside Farm, Earlston	Bed and Breakfast	Page 12
9	Cobbles Inn, Kelso	Pub with food	Page 12
10	Robbies, Hawick	Bar and restaurant	Page 15
11	Mansfield House Hotel, Hawick	Hotel and restaurant	Page 16
12	Sergio's, Sandbed	Restaurant	Page 16
13	The Caddy Mann Restaurant, Mounthooly	Restaurant and craft shop	Page 17
14	Lyne Farmhouse, Lyne Farm	B&B and self catering	Page 20
15	Laurel Bank Tea Room, Broughton	Café and tearoom	Page 21

DUNS

Berwickshire is an unusual county, in that the town which gave it its name has been within another country since 1482. So Greenlaw, and then in 1853 Duns, was chosen to be the county town. It is a quiet, restful place with a wide and gracious market square.

On its outskirts is **Duns Law**, which gives a magnificent view of the surrounding countryside. The Cheviot Hills to the south and the Lammermuir Hills to the north can be seen on a clear day, as can the North Sea, 12 miles away. In 1639 a Covenanting army, which opposed the imposition of bishops on the Scottish church, set up camp here under General Leslie, and a **Covenanters Stone** commemorates this. On the west side of Duns Law is a cairn which marks the original site of the town.

It was in old Duns that **John Duns Scotus**, known as the "subtle doctor", was born in 1266. He was a Franciscan monk who become one of the greatest theologians and philosophers of his time. His followers were known as Scotists, and his influence is still felt within the Catholic Church today. However, his opponents had another, less flattering, name for them - "Dunses" - from which we get the word "dunce". He eventually died at Cologne in 1308. In 1991, the Pope made him "Venerable", the first step on the ladder to sainthood. In Duns Public Park there is a bronze statue of him, and in the grounds of **Duns Castle** a cairn to his memory was erected in 1966 by the modern Franciscan Order.

Within the town there is a memorial to a famous man who lived in more recent times. Jim Clark, the racing driver, was born in Fife, but from the age of six lived on a farm near Duns. He was killed in Germany in 1968, and the **Jim Clark Memorial Trophy Room** in Newtown Street is dedicated to his memory. He was world champion in 1963 and 1965, and motor racing enthusiasts from all over the world make the pilgrimage to view the trophies (including the two world championship trophies he won) and mementoes on display. He is buried in Chirnside Parish Church cemetery, about five miles east of Duns.

On the west side of market Square is the **Tolbooth House**, once the town house of Sir James Cockburn, who owned most of the land surrounding Duns in the 17th century.

Manderston House lies a mile east of the town. It is open to the public, and is said the be the last great stately home built in Britain. It was built between 1903 and 1905, and incorporates the only silver staircase in existence. Nowadays Manderston House is the home of the Palmer family, of the famous Huntly and Palmer biscuit empire, which explains why it houses a large collection of biscuit tins.

AROUND DUNS

ABBEY ST BATHANS

5 miles N of Duns on a minor road off the B6355

The pretty village of Abbey St Bathans lies in the valley of the Whiteadder Water, surrounded by the Lammermuir Hills. It is truly a hidden gem, and sits on the **Southern Upland Way**, the coast to coast footpath that transverses Southern Scotland. It was here, in 1170, that Ada, Countess of Dunbar, set up a priory, and the priory church was eventually incorporated into the present **Parish Church**. The tombstone of a former prioress, which touchingly shows her pet dog, is preserved in the church.

To the south, at **Cockburn Law**, is the Iron Age **Edinshall Broch**, one of the few brochs (a round, fortified stone tower) to be found in Southern Scotland. It is named after Etin, a legendary giant with three heads who is said to have terrorised the area in olden times.

COCKBURNSPATH

11 miles N of Duns just off the A1

The **Parish Church** is partly 14th century, and close by is ruined **Cockburnspath Tower**, dating from the 15th and 16th centuries. In its time it has been owned by the Dunbars, the Homes, the Sinclairs and the Douglases. The village sits close to **Pease Dean**, a Scottish Wildlife Trust reserve. **Pease Bridge** was built in in 1783 and at the time was the highest stone bridge in Europe.

COLDINGHAM

11 miles NE of Duns on the A1107

The village of Coldingham, which is no more that a mile from the coast, is visited mainly for the remains of **Coldingham Priory**. It was founded in 1098 by King Edgar, son of

St Abb's Head Nature Reserve

Malcolm Canmore, and he gifted it to the monks of Durham. It suffered badly during the Scottish Wars of Independence, and was finally blown up by Cromwell in 1648. Only the tower and a couple of walls were left standing. In 1854 the remains were restored, and today it is the village's parish church.

One mile to the east, on the coast, is the picturesque fishing village of **St Abbs**. The whole coastline here is rugged and spectacular, one of the most magnificent parts being **St Abb's Head**, to the north of the village. The cliffs are over 300 feet high, and are riddled with caves once haunted by smugglers. A monastery for monks and nuns was established on the clifftops in the 7th century, and St Ebba, sister of Oswy, King of Northumbria, eventually became a nun here. An old legend recounts that the nuns, instead of living a life of austerity and prayer, spent all their time eating, drinking and gossiping. The whole area is now managed by the National Trust for Scotland, and is a National Nature Reserve. Offshore is one of the best diving sites in the country.

CHIRNSIDE

5 miles E of Duns on the B6355

Chirnside sits on a low hill with wonderful views of the surrounding countryside, and nearby is where the Blackadder Water and the Whiteadder Water meet. During World War I the peace of the village was shattered when a Zeppelin bombed it by accident. The **Parish Church** is partly Norman, and an impressive Norman doorway can be seen at its west end. Within the cemetery is the grave of Jim Clark the racing driver.

Three miles west of the village is the smaller village of **Edrom**, which has a fine church with Norman details. Within it is the Blackadder Aisle, containing a tomb dating from 1553. A burial vault in the graveyard incorporates a Norman Arch.

HUTTON

8 miles E of Duns on a minor road off the B6460

Close to the village stands **Hutton Castle**, one time home of Sir William Burrell, shipping magnate and art collector, who donated the Burrell Collection to the city of Glasgow in 1944 (see also Largs). **Hutton Parish Church** dates from 1835, and has an old bell of 1661.

AYTON

9 miles E of Duns on the B6355

Ayton, a mile or so from the A1, is a pleasant village that sits on the River Eye. Close by is **Ayton Castle**, a fantastic froth of fairy tale pinnacles dating from the mid 19th century. It is reckoned to be one of the best examples in the country of that style of architecture called "Scottish Baronial". It is open on Sunday afternoons or by appointment.

Eyemouth Village

PAXTON

9 miles E of Duns just off the B6460 and close to the Tweed

Near the village stands **Paxton House**, built in 1758 by Partick Home, later the 13th Laird of Wedderburn, in anticipation of his marriage to the illegitimate daughter of Frederick the Great of Prussia. Alas, the marriage never took place, though a pair of kid gloves given to Patrick by Frederick's daughter is on display. The house was designed by John and James Adam, with plasterwork by their brother Robert, and it is reckoned to be the finest Palladian mansion in Britain. It houses a fine collection of Chippendale furniture, and the art gallery is the largest private gallery in Scotland. It now houses paintings from the National Galleries of Scotland.

Close by is the **Union Suspension Bridge** across the Tweed, connecting Scotland and England. It was built in 1820 by Sir Samuel Browne, who also invented the wrought-iron chain links used in its construction. It is 480 feet long, and was Britain's first major suspension bridge to carry vehicular traffic.

Two miles north of Paxton is **Foulden**, which has an old tithe barn.

EYEMOUTH

12 miles E of Duns on the A1107

Eyemouth is a picturesque little fishing town standing, as the name suggests, at the mouth of the River Eye. At one time it was a smuggling centre, and some of the harbour-side houses still have old cellars and tunnels where contraband was stored. The centre of the trade was at **Gunsgreen House**, to the south of the harbour. Every year in July the **Herring Queen Festival** takes place, when a gaily bedecked fishing fleet escorts the "Herring Queen" into Eyemouth harbour.

Eyemouth Museum records the history of the town and its fishing industry. Perhaps the most poignant exhibit is a 15 foot long tapestry sewn in 1981 which commemorates "Disaster Day" - October 14, 1881. A great storm wrecked the whole of the town's fishing fleet, and 189 fishermen, 129 from Eyemouth alone, perished in sight of the shore.

LADYKIRK

7 miles SE of Duns on a minor road off the B6470 and close to the Tweed

The **Parish Church of St Mary** dates from 1500, and is built entirely of stone in case it was ever burnt by the English. It is supposed

Little Swinton Farm

Swinton, Coldstream, Berwickshire TD12 4HH
Tel/Fax: 01890 860280
e-mail: suebrews40@hotmail.com
website: www.littleswinton.co.uk

A selection of three comfortable and cosy self catering cottages are available at **Little Swinton Farm**, close to most areas of the beautiful Scottish Borders. The Courtyard sleeps three in two bedrooms, and is specially adapted for the disabled, while Cotoneaster sleeps six or seven in three bedrooms and Honeysuckle sleeps four in two bedrooms. All cottages have well appointed kitchens, sitting rooms or lounge/dining rooms (complete with TVs, videos and telephones) and bathrooms with electric showers. There is ample parking space, and children are most welcome.

to owe its origins to James IV, who had it built in thanksgiving after he was rescued from drowning while trying to cross the Tweed.

COLDSTREAM

9 miles S of Duns on the A697

The town is famous as being the birthplace of the **Coldstream Guards**. It sits on the north bank of the Tweed at a point where the river forms the border between Scotland and England. **Coldstream Bridge**, joining the two countries, was built in 1766, and replaced a ford that had been a natural crossing point for centuries. On the bridge is a plaque which commemorates the fact that Robert Burns entered England by this route in 1787. In the 19th century, Coldstream rivalled Gretna Green as a place for runaway marriages. At the Scottish end of the bridge is the **Old Toll House**, where, in a 13 year period during the 19th century, 1466 marriages were conducted.

General Monk founded the Coldstream Guards in 1659. It is the only regiment in Britain to take its name from a town, and within **Henderson Park** is a memorial stone which commemorates the regiment's foundation. The **Coldstream Museum** in Market Square houses extensive displays on its history.

A mile north of the town is **The Hirsel**, home of the Earls of Home since 1611. Sir Alec Douglas Home, the British prime minister, lived here. Though the house isn't open to the public, the grounds can be explored.

Thilestane Castle, Lauder

GREENLAW

6 miles W of Duns on the A697

Greenlaw was the county town of Berwickshire from 1696 to 1853, when Duns took over. The tower of the **Parish Church** date from 1712, and was originally a jail. Three miles south are the impressive ruins of **Hume Castle**, captured by Cromwell in 1651 and partly restored in 1794. They sit 600 feet above sea level, and make an excellent viewpoint.

LAUDER

16 miles W of Duns on the A68

To the east of the town is **Thirlestane Castle**, which is open to the public. It's a flamboyant place, with turrets, pinnacles and towers, giving it the appearance of a French chateau. It was originally built in the 13th century, but was extended and refurbished in the 16th century for the Maitland family, whose most famous member was John Maitland, Earl and later Duke of Lauderdale. He was a close friend of Charles II, and a member of the famous "Cabal Cabinet". So powerful was he that he was soon regarded as the uncrowned king of Scotland. His ghost is said the haunt the castle.

Lauder Parish Church was built in the 17th century in the form of a Greek cross. The medieval church formerly stood in the grounds of Thirlestane Castle, and legend states that the Duke had it removed in the 17th century to improve his view. He instructed a bowman to fire an arrow westwards from the castle steps. Wherever the arrow landed the Duke would build a new church. That is why the church now stands within the town of Lauder itself.

GALASHIELS

Galashiels (known locally as "Gala") sits on the Gala Water, and is a manufacturing town at one time noted for its tweed and woollen mills. As a reflection of this, the motto of the Galashiels Manufacturer's Corporation was "We dye to live and live to die". The **Lochcarron of Scotland Cashmere and Wool Centre** is located within the Waverley Mill in Huddersfield Street, and offers tours which explain the processes involved in the manufacture of woollens and tweeds.

However, the town goes back centuries (the first mention of cloth mills is found in 1588), and every year, in July, it holds the **Braw Lads Gathering**, which celebrates its long history. On the coat of arms of the old burgh appears the words "soor plooms" (sour plums), which refers to an incident in 1337, when some English troops were killed after crossing the border and stealing plums in the town. In 1503, the betrothal of James IV to Margaret Tudor, Henry VII's daughter, took place at the town's old **Mercat Cross.** It's successor dates from 1695.

Old Gala House dates from the 15th century, with later additions, and at one time was the town house of the Pringles, Lairds of Gala. It is now a museum and art gallery, surrounded by gardens, and is well worth a visit. In front of the town's war memorial (described by H.V. Morton as "the most perfect town memorial in the British Isles") is a reminder of the area's bloody past - a bronze

Clovenfords Hotel

1 Vine Street, Clovenfords, Selkirkshire TD1 3LU
Tel/Fax: 01896 850203
e-mail: clovenhotel@barbox.net
website: www.clovenfordshotel.co.uk

Set amid the wonderful scenery of the Scottish Borders, the **Clovenfords Hotel** is an olde worlde hostelry that was formerly a coaching inn. It dates from around 1720, and with its whitewashed walls, it presents an altogether delightful picture. It was frequented in the past by such famous people as Sir Walter Scott and William Wordsworth, and with its cosy and atmospheric interior, it is now your turn to discover the undoubted charms of one of the best inns in the area! It is popular with the locals, which is always a good sign, and is a family run hotel owned by Hazel and John Robertson. The bars serve a fine range of beers, real ales, lagers, wines and spirits, with soft drinks always available should you be driving.

The food is outstanding, with both bar lunches and evening meals available. You can choose from the printed menu or from a daily specials board, and all the dishes are prepared from the freshest ingredients wherever possible. Why not try one of the inn's juicy steaks with all the trimmings? Or beef and ale pie, which is always a favourite? But beware - so good is the cuisine that you are advised to book evening meals at weekends. There are also five en suite rooms available on a B&B basis, though longer stays can be arranged. There is a family room, two twins and two doubles, with the rooms being both comfortable and spacious. Children are more than welcome, and holiday packages that involve activities such as golf, fishing, mountain biking or hill walking can be arranged. In July of each year the Clovenfords Inn organises a beer festival. If you would like details, you are invited to telephone.

statue of a border reiver, armed and on horseback.

Two miles south of the town, on the banks of the Tweed, is **Abbotsford**, the home of **Sir Walter Scott**, writer and lawyer. Scott had it built between 1817 and 1822, and he lived in it until he died. At this point, the monks of Melrose Abbey once had a ford across the Tweed, so Scott decided to call it Abbotsford. It is built in the Scottish Baronial style, and is crammed with mementoes and objects that reflected his passion for Scottish history, such as a tumbler on which Burns had etched some verses, a lock of Charles Edward Stuart's hair, and a piece of oatcake found in the pocket of a Highlander killed at Culloden. Inside there is more than a hint of the Gothic about the place, especially the panelled hallway, which contains a carriage clock - still keeping good time - once owned by Marie Antoinette.

Abbotsford House

The main focus of the house is Scott's austere study, where many of his books were written. A gallery runs round the room, and in one corner is a door with a stairway behind it. Scott, early every morning, descended these stairs from his dressing room to write for a few hours before heading for the courthouse in Selkirk.

Perhaps the most poignant room in the house is the dining room. Having returned from a trip abroad in September 1832, he knew that his end was near, and called for his bed to be set up at the window, so that he could look out towards the Tweed. On September 21 he died. He had never got over the death of his wife in 1826, and at about the same time a publishing firm in which he was a partner went bankrupt. He decided to pay back everything that was owed through writing, even though he still had his duties at Selkirk Sheriff Court to attend to, and it eventually ruined his health. He now lies beside his wife among the ruins of Dryburgh Abbey.

The Southern Upland Way passes through Galashiels, and you can also join the **Tweed Cycle Way**, which passes close by. Three miles west of the town, at **Clovenfords**, is the **School of Casting, Salmon and Trout Fishing**.

AROUND GALASHIELS

STOW

7 miles N of Galashiels on the A7

Stow (sometimes called Stow-in-Wedale) is a delightful village on the Gala Water. The imposing **St Mary of Wedale Parish Church** has a spire over 140 feet high. To the west of the village are the lonely Moorfoot Hills, and to the east is some further moorland which separates it from Lauderdale. The B6362 leaves Stow and climbs up onto the moorland, reaching a height of 1100 feet before descending into the small town of Lauder.

GORDON

11 miles NE of Galashiels on the A6105

This pleasant village is the cradle of the Gordon clan, which moved north into Aberdeenshire in the 14th century. To the north are the well preserved ruins of **Greenknowe Tower**, built in 1581 by James Seton of Touch and his wife Jane Edmonstone. It is a typical L-shaped tower house, built originally as a fortified home. It was later acquired by the Pringles.

Mellerstain sits three miles south of the village, and is a grand mansion originally designed by William Adam in the 1720s, with later work being done by his son Robert. It is one of the grandest Georgian houses in Britain, and holds a collection of fine furniture and paintings by Van Dyck, Naismith, Gainsborough and Ramsey. The Italian terraces were laid out in 1909 by Sir Reginald Blomfield, and give excellent views towards the Cheviots.

MELROSE

3 miles E of Galashiels just off the A6091

Melrose sits in the shadow of the triple peaks of the **Eildon Hills**, which have a waymarked path leading to their summits. Legend states that **King Arthur** and his court lie buried under them.

This quiet town, which is on the Southern Upland Way, is mainly visited nowadays to view the ruins of **Melrose Abbey** (Historic Scotland), surely the loveliest of all the Borders abbeys. It was founded in 1136 by David I, and rose to become one of the most important in Scotland. The ruins that the visitor sees nowadays date mainly from the late 14th and early 15th centuries, thanks to the troops of Richard II's army, which destroyed the earlier buildings. It was here that the heart of Robert the Bruce, Scotland's great hero during the Wars of Independence, was buried. After his death it had been removed and placed in a casket so that it

Melrose Abbey

Priorwood Gardens

might be taken for burial in the Holy Land by Sir James Douglas. But Sir James was killed, and the casket found its way back to Scotland and Melrose. In the late 1990s, during some restoration work on the abbey, his heart was rediscovered, and reburied within the abbey grounds. A cross now marks its resting place (see also Dunfermline).

On a bend in the Tweed, two miles from the town, is the site of **Old Melrose**, where, in about AD650, Celtic monks from Iona first established a monastery in the area. It was near here that a young shepherd, who was later to become **St Cuthbert**, was born. In AD651, following a vision, he entered the monastery to train as a monk. He eventually became Prior of Lindisfarne, and is now buried in Durham Cathedral. A 62 mile walking route called **St Cuthbert's Way** now links Melrose and Lindisfarne.

Close to the abbey ruins is **Priorwood Gardens** (National Trust for Scotland). It specialises in plants which are suitable for drying and arranging, and classes are organised to teach the techniques involved. **Harmony Garden**, also run by the Trust, is close by. It is set around a 19th century house which is not open to the public, and has excellent views of the Eildon Hills.

A mile east of Melrose is **Newstead**, where there are the remains of **Trimontium Roman Fort**, covering 15 acres, and named after the three peaks of the Eildons. At its height it housed 1500 Roman soldiers, and supported a large town which covered a further 200 acres. A **Trimontium Exhibition** can be found at the Ormiston Institute in Melrose's Market Square.

EARLSTON

5 miles E of Galashiels on the A68

The small town of Earlston is dominated by **Black Hill**, which gives a good view of the surrounding countryside. One of Scotland's earliest poets, **Thomas Learmont of Earlston,** was born here. Also known as Thomas the Rhymer, Thomas of Erceldoune or True Thomas, he lived in the 13th century, and attained an almost mythological status. It didn't take much in those days for a man to

WHITE SWAN HOTEL

High Street, Earlston, Berwickshire TD4 6DE
Tel: 01896 848249
e-mail: annedavin@aol.com
website: www.whiteswan-earlston.com

In the small. picturesque town of Earlston you will find the **White Swan Hotel**. It dates back to the mid 1700s, and offers superb food, drink and accommodation. There are five comfortable twin booms upstairs, two en suite, and the place has a fine reputation for its food. You can enjoy a full dinner in the evening (for which you have to book) or a superb bar lunch in its warm and cosy bar, which boasts lots of old wood, pewter and prints on the wall. This makes the ideal stopover when heading north or a base from which to explore the beautiful and historic Scottish Borders.

BIRKENSIDE FARM

Earlston, Berwickshire TD4 6AR
Tel: 01896 849224

Birkenside Farm is a working farm that offers superb B&B facilities to the discerning tourist. The farmhouse is a substantial Victorian building with three guests rooms (two twins and a double), two of which are fully en suite. The guest lounge is stylish and comfortable, with views over some very attractive countryside. Full Scottish breakfasts, with hearty portions, are served, though Continental breakfasts are available if required. This is the kind of quality establishment that does lots of repeat business, and where children are more than welcome.

have the reputation of having supernatural and prophetic powers, and no doubt Thomas's many trips abroad accounted for the stories of him going off to live with the fairies under the Eildon Hills for years at a time. His accurate prophecies included Alexander III's death and the victory of Bruce over the English.

SMAILHOLM

9 miles E of Galashiels on the B6397

Smailholm Tower (Historic Scotland) seems to grow out of a low, rocky outcrop, and is a four square tower surrounded by a wall. Within it you can see a collection of costume figures and tapestries connected with Scott's Minstrelsy of the Scottish Borders. Scott, as a child, spent a lot of time with his grandparents at the nearby farm of Sandyknowe, and he knew the tower well.

KELSO

14 miles E of Galashiels on the A698

Kelso is a picturesque, gracious town with a large, cobbled **Market Square** which would not look out of place in France. It is bounded by imposing 18th and 19th century buildings, with the supremely elegant **Town House** of 1816, which now houses the tourism information centre, at its core.

The town sits at the junction of the Tweed and the Teviot. **Kelso Abbey** (Historic Scotland) was founded in 1128, after David I, who had founded the abbey at Selkirk, decided that Kelso was a much better place for it. It was the biggest of the border abbeys, and during a siege by the English in 1545, it was almost totally destroyed. Now all that remains of the church are the transepts, part of the tower, two nave bays and part of the west end. But the ruins are still dramatic enough to make a solid impact.

In July every year the **Kelso Civic Week** takes place, with many events that echo similar ceremonies in other Borders towns. On the banks of the Teviot, three miles south west of the town, once stood the proud **Royal Burgh of Roxburgh**. This was a thriving walled town in medieval times, but nothing now survives above ground, thanks to the repeated attentions of succeeding English armies.

Where the Teviot and the Tweed meet is a high defensive mound, the site of **Roxburgh**

COBBLES INN

7 Bowmont Street, Kelso TD5 7JH
Tel: 01573 223548

With the emphasis firmly on superb and imaginative food, the **Cobbles Inn** is one of the most popular establishments in the Scottish Borders, with an ever changing menu that includes such dishes as juicy steaks, rack of lamb, pan-fried venison, roast pork fillet or pan-seared salmon. There is also a comprehensive wine list that is sure to have something on it that will complement you meal. So popular is this establishment that you are well advised to book at weekends. You can also enjoy a quiet drink in the cosy bar, or attend one of the inn's monthly folk music concerts held upstairs.

Castle. It was during a siege of the castle that James II was killed outright when a cannon accidentally blew up in his face.The place has been suggested as yet another possible site for King Arthur's magnificent capital of **Camelot** (see also Ayr). To the west of Kelso, within parkland overlooking the Tweed, stands the equally magnificent **Floors Castle**, Scotland's largest inhabited house. It is home to the Duke and Duchess of Roxburgh, and has a huge collection of works of art and furniture.

Kelso Race Course hosts national hunt horse racing netween September and May.

EDNAM

15 miles E of Galashiels on the B6461

The village stands on the Eden Water, and was the birthplace of two famous men. The first was **James Thomson**, born in 1700, who wrote the words to Rule Britannia, and the other was **Henry Francis Lyte**, born in 1793, who wrote Abide with Me. A memorial to Thomson has been erected at Ferniehill, to the south of the village, and the bridge over the river has a plaque commemorating Henry Francis Lyte.

DRYBURGH

6 miles SE of Galashiels off the B6356

The ruins of **Dryburgh Abbey** (Historic Scotland), because of their setting, must be the most romantically situated in Scotland. It sits on a loop of the Tweed, which surrounds it on three sides. Nothing much remains of the great abbey church, except for the west door and parts of the north and and south transepts. However, the other abbey buildings can still be explored. Within the south transept chapel is buried Sir Walter Scott and his wife Charlotte, as well as **Field Marshall Earl Haig of Bemersyde**. He was Commander-in-Chief of the British Expeditionary forces in France and Flanders during World War I.

The Premonstratensian abbey was founded in 1150 by Hugh de Morville, Constable of Scotland. The site had already been a sacred one, as it was here that **St Modan**, a Celtic monk, set up a monastery in the 6th or 7th century. In 1322, during the Wars of Independence, Edward II's retreating army, after a successful invasion of Scotland, set fire to the place. This was the first of many sackings of the abbey, which now forms part of the 55 mile long **Abbeys Cycle Route**, taking in the other three great Borders abbeys of Melrose, Kelso and Jedburgh. A short walk from the abbey is the 22 feet high **William Wallace Statue**. He spent a lot of time in the Borders hiding from the English in the Ettrick Forest.

Dryburgh Abbey

North of Dryburgh is **Scott's View**, which gives an amazing view of the Eildon Hills. Sir Walter Scott used to ride up to it to get inspiration, and when his funeral cortege was making its way to Dryburgh, his hearse stopped here for a short while. It is best accessed from the A68, where it is signposted from the Leadfoot Viaduct that spans the Tweed.

Close by are **Mertoun House and Gardens**. Though the house is not open to the public, the 26 acre gardens can be visited on Saturdays, Sundays and Bank Holiday Mondays. **Mertoun Kirk**, in the grounds of the house, is open on Sunday for church services.

ST BOSWELLS

6 miles SE of Galashiels on the A68

This village is named after St Boisil, who was an abbot of the Celtic monastery at Old Melrose in the 7th century. The centrepiece of the village is its green, which hosts a fair on July 18 (St Boisil's Day) each year. In past times, this fair was one of the largest in the country, and attracted people - especially gypsies - from all over the Borders and beyond.

SELKIRK

5 miles S of Galashiels on the A7

Scott's Monument, Selkirk

Once the county town of Selkirkshire, Selkirk is now a quiet royal burgh on the edge of the Ettrick Forest. It was the site of the first abbey in the Borders, which was founded in 1113. However, 15 years later, before one stone was laid, the monks were moved to Kelso by David I, and they established their abbey in that town instead. The Ettrick Water, a tributary of the Tweed, flows to the west of the town, and it is joined a couple of miles out of town by the Yarrow Water. The Vale of Yarrow is very scenic, with the hamlet of **Yarrow** itself, about eight miles west of Selkirk, being very picturesque. Scott's great-grandfather was once minister of **Yarrow Parish Church**.

In Selkirk's High Street, outside the **Old Courthouse** in which he presided, there is a statute of Sir Walter Scott, who was sheriff here until his death in 1832. Within the courtroom is an audio visual display telling of his associations with the area. Another statue in the High Street commemorates **Mungo Park**, the explorer and surgeon, who was born in Yarrow in 1771. The oldest building in the town is **Halliwell's House**, where there is a small museum and art gallery. **Robert D. Clapperton Photographic** is a working museum and photographic archive. Here, the good citizens of Selkirk posed stiffly in Victorian times while having their photograph taken. At **Selkirk Glass**, just off the A7, you can see glass paper weights being made.

In common with many Borders town, Selkirk has its **Common Riding Ceremony**, held annually in June, when over 500 riders regularly set out to patrol the marches, or boundaries, of the town lands. But the ceremony also commemorates the darkest day in the town's history. In 1513, Selkirk sent 80 of its bravest men to fight alongside James IV at Flodden, taking with them the town flag. The battle was a rout, and on that day the flower of Scottish manhood was wiped out, including the king himself. Only one Selkirk man, named Fletcher, returned, without the Selkirk flag but bearing a bloodstained English one. A memorial to the fallen can be found outside the Victoria Halls in the High Street.

A couple of miles out of town is **Bowhill**, the Borders home of the Duke of Queensberry and Buccleuch. It is a fine Georgian mansion, and in its grounds is **Bowhill Little Theatre**, which presents many professional plays. At **Aikwood Tower**, home of Sir David Steel, and once the home of Michael Scott the legendary wizard, is a small exhibition about James Hogg.

ST MARY'S LOCH

16 miles SW of Galashiels on the A708

St Mary's Loch

The loch is in a truly beautiful setting of rounded, green hills. Its praises have been sung by both Scott and **William Wordsworth**, but no words can describe this delightful sheet of water. A narrow spit of land separates it from the smaller **Loch of the Lowes**, and situated on the spit is **Tibbie Shiel's Inn**, now an angling hostelry. It was opened in 1824, and is named after Isabella Shiels, the woman who ran it until 1878. Her visitor's book is still in existence, and records such names as R.L. Stevenson, Gladstone and Thomas Carlyle. It is a favourite stopping point on the Southern Upland Way, which passes close by.

James Hogg, nicknamed "The Ettrick Shepherd", was also a frequent visitor. He was born nearby in 1770, and wrote Confessions of a Justified Sinner, one of the great books of the 19th century.

HAWICK

Hawick is the largest town in the Borders, and sits in picturesque Teviotdale. It is famous for the quality of its knitwear, and names like Pringle and Lyle and Scott are known world-wide. The **Hawick Common Riding** takes place in June each year, and commemorates yet another skirmish between the English and the Scots. This occurred in 1514, when some young Hawick men beat off English soldiers camped near the town, and captured their banner. A disagreement of a different kind took place in the mid 1990s, when two women riders tried to join what had traditionally been an all-male occasion. Their participation provoked hostile opposition, even from some women. It took a court case to establish that women had the right to join in, though even today some people still tolerate their presence rather than welcome it.

St Mary's Parish Church was built in 1763, and replaced an earlier, 13th century church. The town's oldest building is **Drumlanrig's Tower**. In 1570 it survived a raid by English troops which destroyed the rest of the town., and was once a typical moated L-shaped Borders tower before the area between the two "legs" was filled in. At one time it belonged to the Douglases of Drumlanrig, in Dumfriesshire, and it was here that Anna, Duchess of Queensberry and Buccleuch, and wife of the executed Duke of Monmouth, stayed. The basement was later used as a

ROBBIES

8 High Street, Hawick, Roxburghshire TD9 9EH
Tel: 01450 370868

Situated right in the heart of the historic town of Hawick, **Robbies** is an excellent bar/diner that serves the best in food and drink. It is popular with both tourists and locals, and has a fine selection of lagers, beers, wines and spirits. Food is served between 10.30 and 14.30, with Robbie Watt himself being the chef. It's cuisine is traditional Scottish, with all the dishes representing amazing value for money. It seats 30 in comfort, and children are always welcome. You can choose from a printed menu or from a daily specials board, with a roast being available every day. This is the ideal place to stop for a lunch or snack as you tour the lovely Borders area of Scotland.

prison, and finally a wine cellar when it became a hotel. Now the tower has been restored and houses an exhibition explaining the history the of Borders.

The award-winning **Wilton Lodge Park** sits by the banks of the Teviot, and has 107 acres of riverside walks, gardens, and recreational facilities. Within it is the **Hawick Museum and Scott Art Gallery**, which explains the history of the town and its industries. Many of the mills, such as **Peter Scott and Company** in Buccleuch Street and **Wrights of Trowmill**, have visitor centres and guided tours. The **Hawick Cashmere Company**, based in Trinity Mills, has a viewing gallery and shop. And if Duns has its Jim Clark Memorial Trophy Room, Hawick has the **Jimmy Guthrie Statue**. He was a local TT rider who was world champion in the 1930s.

Mansfield House Hotel

Weensland Road, Hawick TD9 8LB
Tel: 01450 360400 e-mail: ian@mansfield-house.com
Fax: 01450 372007 website: www.mansfield-house.com

Situated in ten acres of grounds on the outskirts of Hawick, the **Mansfield House Hotel** is a superior family run hotel that boasts twelve outstanding bedrooms, all fully en suite. The sizes range from family to twin, and all are beautifully decorated and extremely comfortable, with TVs and tea/ coffee making facilities. You can book in on a B&B basis or a dinner B&B basis, though special break deals for longer stays can also be arranged. The house was originally built in 1870 for a local family of auctioneers, and many period features have been retained, making it a place of distinction, comfort and great service - ideal for the discerning tourist. Ian and Sheila MacKinnon have owned and run the place for many years, and have created an establishment that is so popular it has a lot of repeat business - always a good sign.

The restaurant has been tastefully refurbished and decorated to create a warm and welcoming ambience, and is especially popular with locals and visitors alike. It serves some of the best and most imaginative food in the area, and in fact, the hotel is a member of Taste of Scotland. Only the finest and freshest local produce is used, creating a cuisine that is renowned world wide. The wine list is excellent, and is sure to contain something that will complement your meal. The bar is spacious yet cosy, and it is here that you can relax and order a quiet drink (there are over 100 malt whiskies alone to choose from) or have an informal meal, such as a delicious bar lunch. In fact, the hotel has recently been awarded the 'Best Promotion of Local Food and Drink' in the Best Eating out Places competition in the Scottish Borders.The newly developed Thornwood Suite is the ideal location for a special function such as a wedding, business seminar or party, and the hotel would be more than happy to discuss your individual needs. This is the ideal base from which to explore the picturesque Scottish Borders, and should you visit, you will, like lots of other people, surely return once more!

Sergio's

Bridge House, Sandbed, Hawick, Roxburghshire TD9 0HE
Tel: 01405 370094 & 01405 370701; Fax: 01405 370701

Sergio's is a superior Italian restaurant that advertises itself as offering 'authentic Italian cooking with the best Scottish meat'. It seats 60, and its menu contains many popular and beautifully cooked Italian dishes. The adjacent café/bar seats 40, and serves delicious home baking, snacks and sandwiches. Both make ideal eating places when travelling north or exploring the beautiful Scottish Borders. In addition, Sergio's also offers first class accommodation in six en suite rooms, either on a B&B or room only basis. The rooms are comfortable, cosy and well appointed, and represent amazing value for money.

AROUND HAWICK

DENHOLM

5 miles NE of Hawick on the A698

This pleasant village, with its village green, was the birthplace of John Leyden, the 18th century poet and friend of Sir Walter Scott. The **John Leyden Memorial**, which stands on the green, commemorates the great man. Also born in the village was **Sir James Murray**, who undertook the tremendous task of editing the Oxford English Dictionary. Two miles to the eat of the village, atop Minto Crags, sits the curiously named **Fatlips Castle**, built in the 16th century for the Lockhart family.

JEDBURGH

9 miles NE of Hawick on the A68

The route of the present day A68 was at one time the main route from Edinburgh to England, and so Jedburgh saw many armies passing along its streets when Scotland and England were at war with each other. It is a attractive small town with gaily painted houses, especially in the Market Place and the Canongate, and it regularly wins awards in "Beautiful Scotland in Bloom" competitions. **Jedburgh Abbey** (Historic Scotland), on the banks of the Jed Water, was founded in 1138 by David I. It was destroyed nine times by the invading English. Each time, save for the last one, it was patiently rebuilt by the monks. A visitor centre explains its story.

Not far away is the **Mary Queen of Scots House**. Here, in October 1566, Mary Stuart stayed when presiding at local courts in the Borders. When she was held in captivity by Elizabeth I, she declared that she would have preferred to have died in Jedburgh. Now it is a museum and visitors centre. **Jedburgh Castle Jail**, in Castlegate, was a 19th century reform prison which now houses a display about the history of the town. Four miles north east of Jedburgh are the **Monteviot House and Gardens**, which has a pinetum and a riverside garden linked by bridges.

Jedforest Deer and Farm Park is five miles

THE CADDY MANN RESTAURANT

Mounthooly, near Jedburgh, Roxburghshire TD8 6TJ
Tel/Fax: 01835 850787

Situated beside a golf driving range which it owns, the **Caddy Mann Restaurant** is the ideal place for a meal in the Scottish Borders. Owned and run by Alastair Stewart, it serves beautifully cooked food, which is prepared by Ross Horrocks, an experienced chef who uses only the best and freshest of local produce wherever possible. Alastair also part owns a nearby farm, plus a butcher's shop in Kelso, so you know that the meat is always of the best quality! The restaurant seats 50 in absolute comfort, with lunches being served between 12.00 and 15.00 daily and dinners between 19.00 and 21.00 on Friday and Saturday evenings.

If you require a meal on Friday or Saturday evening or Sunday lunchtime, you are advised to book, as the place is very popular, and won the 'Best Eating Establishment in the Borders 2000' award from VisitScotland. The speciality of the house is slow baked Border lamb, though everything - including the bread - is made on the premises, so you will be spoiled for choice. The restaurant also sells a wide range of country style antiques and bric-a-brac at very competitive prices. The adjacent driving range offers the opportunity for golfers to practise their swing. It is open between 10.00 and 21.00, and admission is by purchasing a number of golf balls. PGA tuition is also available by appointment.

The Caddy Mann is only a mile or so from the centre of Jedburgh, and there is plenty of parking space.

Carters Bar, Jedburgh

south of Jedburgh, just off the A68. It is a modern working farm with a deer herd and rare breeds. There are also birds of prey demonstrations using eagles, owls and hawks. Four miles beyond the Farm Park, the A68 reaches the English border at **Carter Bar**, which is 1370 feet above sea level. From here there is a wonderful view northwards, and it almost seems that the whole of Southern Scotland is spread out before you. In the 18th century herds of sheep and cattle were driven over this route towards the markets in the south.

On the A698, five miles north east of Jedburgh are the **Teviot Water Gardens**, which cascade down to the River Teviot. They are on three levels, and lead to a riverside walk.

ANCRUM

10 miles NE of Hawick on the B6400

Ancrum is a typical Borders village, to the north of which was fought the **Battle of Ancrum Moor** in 1545. It was part of what was known as the "Rough Wooing", when Henry VIII tried to force the Scots into allowing the young Mary Queen of Scots to marry his son Edward. 3000 English and Scottish horsemen under Lord Eure were ambushed by a hastily assembled army of Borderers. During the battle, the Scots horsemen changed sides when they saw that the Borderers were gaining the upper hand, resulting in a total rout.

Two miles east of the village is the **Waterloo Monument**, erected by the Marquis of Lothian in 1815 to commemorate a much later battle. **Harestanes Countryside Visitor Centre**, close to the village, has countryside walks, activities and organised events.

MOREBATTLE

17 miles NE of Hawick on the B6401

This little village sits on the Kale Water, and the surrounding area was once a hiding place for Covenanters fleeing the persecution of Charles II's troops. To the north of the village is **Linton Church**, which has Norman details, a fine Norman font and a belfry dated 1697. The ruins of **Cessford Castle**, which surrendered to the English in 1545, lie two miles to the south west.

KIRK YETHOLM

21 miles NE of Hawick on the B6352

This village is at the northern end of the **Peninne Way**, and St Cuthbert's Way passes close by as well. It, and to a lesser extent its twin village of **Town Yetholm** were famous at one time as being where the kings and queens of the Scottish gypsies lived. The most famous queen was Esther Faa Blyth, who ruled in the 19th century. In 1898 Charles Faa Blyth, her son, was crowned king at Yetholm. Though the title had lost much of its meaning by this time, the coronation was attended by an estimated 10,000 people. A small cottage is still pointed out as his "palace".

NEWCASTLETON

15 miles S of Hawick, on the B6357

Newcastleton, in Liddesdale, is a planned village, founded by the Duke of Queensberry and Buccleuch in 1793 as a hand loom weaving centre. The border with England follows the Liddel Water, then, about three miles south of Newcastleton, strikes east along

Cross Kirk Ruins, Peebles

the Kershope Burn. This is the heartland of the great Borders families of Kerr, Armstrong and Elliots, and was always a place of unrest when Scotland and England were independent countries. At **Kershopefoot**, where the Kershope Burn meets the Liddel Water, the Wardens of the Marches of both Scotland and England met regularly to settle disputes, and seek redress for crimes committed by both sides. Disputes were settled by a jury of 12 men, with the Scots choosing the six English, and the English choosing the six Scots. However, even these meetings were known to result in violence, and many a Scottish or English warden and his men were chased far into their own territory if redress was not forthcoming.

The **Liddesdale Heritage Centre Museum** is in the old Townfoot Kirk in South Hermitage Street, and has attractive displays about the history of the area and its people. Five miles north of Newcastleton is the massive bulk of **Hermitage Castle** (Historic Scotland). It dates from the 14th century, and its imposing walls and stout defences reflect the bloody warfare that was common in this area before the union of Scotland and England. While staying in Jedburgh, Mary Stuart covered the 50 miles between there and Hermitage and back again in one day to visit the Earl of Bothwell, whom she later married. During her journey, she lost a watch, which was recovered in the 19th century.

PEEBLES

Though Peebles, attractively situated on the banks of the Tweed, looks peaceful nowadays, its history is anything but. It was burnt to the ground by the English in 1545, occupied by Cromwell in 1649, and again by Charles Edward Stuart in 1745.

In June each year the Town holds its **Beltane Week**, with the crowning of the Beltane Queen. The ceremony's origins go right back to pagan times, though the present Beltane Week celebrations date only from the 19th century, when it was revived. Within the **Chambers Institute**, named after the Chambers brothers of publishing fame who were born in the town, is a museum and art gallery. On Innerleithen Road, opposite the Park Hotel, is the unusual **Cornice Museum**, dedicated to displaying and explaining ornate plasterwork. The ruins of the Trinitarian Friary of **Cross Kirk**, founded in 1261, are to the west of the town, and the tower of the former **St Andrews Church** still survives just off Neidpath Road. The present **Peebles Parish Church** is an imposing Victorian building at the west end of the High Street, a short distance from the **Cuddy Bridge** over the Eddleston Water, a tributary of the Tweed.

West of the town, on the A72, is **Neidpath Castle**. It was built by the Hay family in the 14th century, and is the epitome of the Scottish castle. It sits by the banks of the Tweed, and is a tall, sturdy tower house that would surely defy anything thrown at it. The main tower originally consisted of three great vaulted halls, one above the other (though the top vault was subsequently removed and replaced by a timber roof), reached by winding stone staircases, and there is a genuine dungeon below what was the guardroom. Prisoners were lowered in by rope, and in some cases, forgotten about. Mary Stuart and James VI both visited the castle, reflecting the importance of the Hay family in the 16th century.

Kailzie Gardens are located east of Peebles, on the B7062. Extending to 14 acres, the main

Kailzie Gardens

part is contained in an old walled garden, and are open to the public.

AROUND PEEBLES

INNERLEITHEN

6 miles E of Peebles on the A72

Innerleithen is a small town which was the original for Sir Walter Scott's St Ronan's Well. It used to be a spa town, and the **St. Ronan's Well Interpretive Centre** at Well's Brae explains the history of the wells, whose waters were full of suplhur and other minerals. In the High Street is **Robert Smail's Printing Works**. This was a genuine print works which still retained many of its original features and fittings when taken over by the National Trust for Scotland in 1987. Now you can see how things were printed at the turn of the century, and even have a go yourself.

TRAQUAIR

6 miles SE of Peebles on the B709

Traquair is a small village visited mostly for the magnificent **Traquair House**. It is reputed to be the oldest continuously inhabited house in Scotland, and has its origins in a royal hunting lodge built on the banks of the Tweed in about AD950. In its time, 27 kings and queens have visited the place, including Alexander I in the 11th century, Edward I of England (known as the "Hammer of the Scots") in the 13th, and Mary Stuart in the 16th. One laird of Traquair fell with his king at Flodden, and in the 18th century the then laird supported the Jacobite cause. Charles Edward Stuart visited in 1745, and when he left, the laird closed the **Bear Gates** at the end of the long drive, vowing that they would never be opened again until a Stuart ascended the British throne once more. They have remained closed ever since. Within the house itself are secret passages and priests' holes.

In 1965 the then laird renovated the brewhouse which lies beneath the chapel, and the **Traquair House Brewery** now produces a fine range of ales.

DRUMELZIER

8 miles SW of Peebles, on the B712

Where the Drumelzier Burn joins the Tweed, just north of the village, is the place where one of King Arthur's knights is said to be buried. At one time **Drumelzier Castle** stood here, but now little remains above ground. In the graveyard of **Drumelzier Parish Church** is an old burial vault of the Tweedies.

LYNE

4 miles W of Peebles on the A72

Lyne Church, perched picturesquely on a hillside above the road, is one of the smallest churches in Scotland. It contains a pulpit and two pews reputed to be of Dutch workmanship.

STOBO

5 miles W of Peebles on the B712

Stobo Kirk, one of the oldest and most beautiful in the area, has a Norman tower, nave and chancel, with some later features and additions. **Stobo Castle** is set in some lovely grounds, and is now one of Scotland's leading health farms and spas. Two miles south, along the B712, is the **Dawyck Botanic Garden and Arboretum**, an outpost of the National Botanic Gardens of Scotland in Edinburgh. It sits on the Scrape Burn, a tributary of the Tweed, and houses a unique collection of conifers, rhododendrons and associated tree species within its 62 acres.

BROUGHTON

10 miles W of Peebles, on the A701

Broughton is forever associated with the author and Governor-General of Canada, John Buchan, whose most famous work is undoubtedly The Thirty Nine Steps. Though born in Perth, his maternal grandparents farmed nearby, and his father, a free church minister, married his mother in the village. The old free kirk is now the **John Buchan Centre**, with displays about his life and writings.

WEST LINTON

9 miles NW of Peebles, just off the A702

West Linton is a delightful village, and one of the hidden gems of Peeblesshire. The picturesque **St Andrews Parish Church** of 1781 stands in the middle of the village, and the surrounding gravestones testify to the craftsmanship of the many stone carvers who used to live in the area. The local **Whipman** ceremonies take place in June each year. They originated in 1803, when some local agricultural workers decided to form a benevolent society known as the "Whipmen of Linton". Now the week-long festivities include honouring the Whipman (meaning a carter) and his Lass. In the centre of the village stands **Lady Gifford's Well**, with a stone carving of 1666 on one of its sides.

West Linton Church

2 Dumfries and Galloway

It's no wonder the local tourist board calls Dumfries and Galloway "Scotland's best-kept secret". People scurrying north along the M74 rarely turn off at Gretna and head for a wonderful area that can match anything in Scotland for beautiful scenery, grandeur and history.

River Nith, nr Thornhill

There is over 200 miles of coastline, for instance, with small coves, neat fishing ports and wonderful sandy beaches. There are beautiful villages, old abbeys, castles and country roads that meander through soft, verdant scenery or climb up into bleak moorland landscapes that were made for walking. In the fields you are more than likely to see herds of the region's own indigenous cattle - the Belted Galloways, so called because they have a wide white band running round their black bodies.

Then there are the towns. Dumfries is the largest town in the area, and is a lovely place, full of old red sandstone buildings and great shopping. Kirkcudbright, because of its quality of light, has always had an artist's colony. Stranraer, with its ferries, is a getaway to Northern Ireland, and Lockerbie is forever associated with the Lockerbie disaster of 1988.

High Street, Kirkcudbright

The area contains three former counties, Dumfriesshire, Kirkcudbrightshire and Wigtownshire, and each one has its own particular charm. You can explore Dumfriesshire's Burns connections, for instance. Kirkcudbrightshire was the birthplace of John Paul Jones, founder of the American navy, and Wigtownshire was where Christianity was introduced to Scotland.

Priory Ruins, Whithorn

All around are the high hills and bleak moorland which cut off Dumfries and Galloway from the rest of Scotland. For this reason, the area was almost independent of the Scottish kings in medieval times, and was ruled by a succession of families, from the Lords of Galloway to the mighty Douglases. All have left their mark in stone, such as Devorgilla's Bridge in Dumfries and the mighty Threave Castle, built on an island in the River Dee.

Then there are the abbeys, for, like the Borders, this was an area much favoured by medieval monks. At New Abbey is one which gave the word "sweetheart" to the English language; at Glenluce - a word which means "valley of light" - are the wonderful ruins of Glenluce Abbey; and south of Kirkcudbright is Dundrennan, which played host to Mary Stuart. The castles are equally as impressive. Drumlanrig - Threave - Cardoness - Caerlaverock; the names trip off the tongue, and go to the very roots of Scotland's history.

Kershopefoot, nr Canonbie

This part of Scotland has a mild climate, and at one time the coastline had the nickname of the "Scottish Riviera". First time visitors are usually surprised to see palm trees flourishing in cottage gardens near the coast, or in the grand, formal gardens such as Logan Botanic Garden in Wigtownshire. But then, Dumfries and Galloway has always been full of surprises.

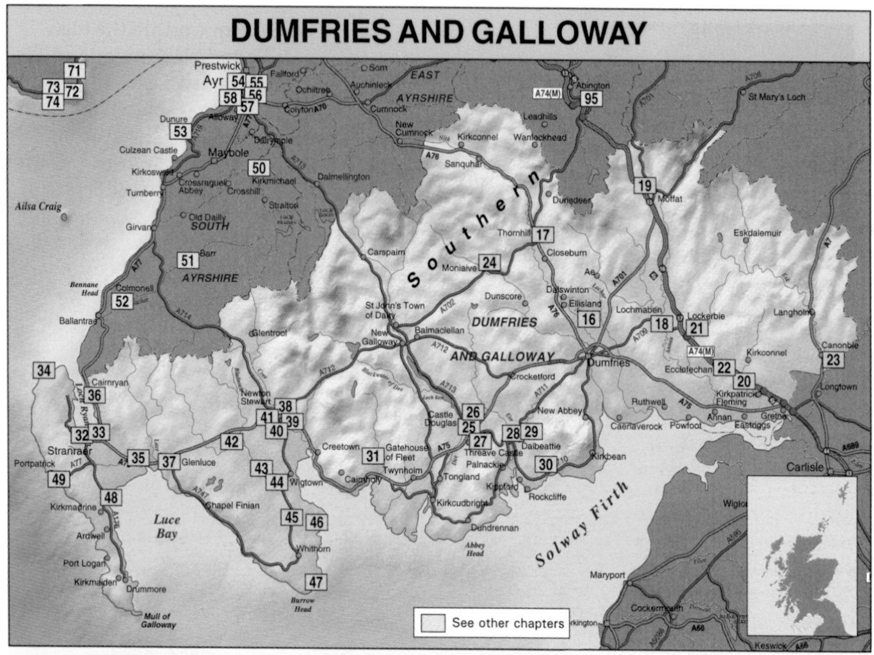

PLACES TO STAY, EAT, DRINK AND SHOP

16	Wallamhill House, Kirkton	Guest House	Page 27
17	Elmarglen Hotel, Thornhill	Hotel	Page 28
18	Ardbeg Cottage, Lochmaben	Bed and Breakfast	Page 31
19	Well View Hotel, Moffat	Hotel	Page 31
20	Village Inn, Kirtle Bridge	Pub, accommodation and food	Page 32
21	Tarras Guest House, Lockerbie	Guest House	Page 33
22	Cressfield Country House Hotel, Ecclefechan	Hotel and restaurant	Page 34
23	Cross Keys Hotel, Canonbie	Hotel and restaurant	Page 36
24	Glenluiart Holiday Cottages, Moniaive	Self catering	Page 40
25	Harmony B&B, Castle Douglas	Bed and Breakfast	Page 44
26	The Rossan, Castle Douglas	Bed and Breakfast	Page 44
27	Rose Cottage, Gelston	Self catering	Page 44
28	Belle Vue, Dalbeattie	Bed and Breakfast	Page 46
29	No 13 B&B, Dalbeattie	Bed and Breakfast	Page 46
30	St Ninian's, Sandyhills	B&B and self catering	Page 47
31	Anwoth Hotel, Gatehouse-of-Fleet	Hotel	Page 48
32	The Arches Restaurant, Stranraer	Restaurant	Page 49
33	Petrucci's Pizzeria, Stranraer	Restaurant	Page 49
34	Corsewall Lighthouse Hotel, Corsewall Point	Hotel	Page 50
35	East Challoch Farm, Dunragit	B&B and self catering	Page 50
36	Cairnryan Caravan Park, Cairnryan	Self catering	Page 50
37	Whitecairn Farm Caravan Park, Glenluce	Self catering	Page 52
38	Creebridge House Hotel, Minnigaff	Hotel and restaurant	Page 52
39	Ivy Bank Cottage, Creebridge	Bed and Breakfast	Page 53
40	Galloway Arms Hotel, Newton Stewart	Hotel	Page 53

PLACES TO STAY, EAT, DRINK AND SHOP

41	Duncree House, Newton Stewart	Bed and Breakfast	Page 54
42	Craigwelder B&B, Kirkcowan	Bed and Breakfast	Page 54
43	Clugston Farm, nr Newton Stewart	Bed and Breakfast	Page 54
44	Ford Bank Country Hotel, nr Bladnoch	Hotel and restaurant	Page 55
45	The Pheasant Inn, Sorbie	Pub, accommodation and food	Page 57
46	Harbour Inn, Garlieston	Pub, accommodation and food	Page 57
47	Queen's Arms Hotel, Isle of Whithorn	Hotel and restaurant	Page 58
48	Tigh-Na-Mara Hotel, Sandhead	Hotel and restaurant	Page 59
49	Harbour House Hotel, Portpatrick	Hotel and restaurant	Page 60

DUMFRIES

The Royal Burgh of Dumfries certainly lives up to its nickname of the "Queen of the South". It was once named as the town with the best quality of life in Britain, and has a lovely location on the banks of the Nith.

The town is forever associated with Scotland's national poet, Robert Burns. Though born in Ayrshire, he died in Dumfries in 1796, and lies in the **Burns Mausoleum** within the kirkyard that surrounds **St Michael's Parish Church**, built in the 1740s. Also buried there is his wife, Jean Armour, and five of their family. Burns had a family pew in St Michael's (marked by a plaque), and long after his death his wife was a regular attender. The mausoleum was built in 1815, in Grecian style, and in that year Burns' remains were transferred there. Also in the kirkyard are the graves of many of his friends.

Not far away is Burns Street (formerly called Mill Vennel), where **Burns' House** is situated. Here he died when he was only 37. It is open to the public, and though not a grand house, it was nonetheless a substantial building for its day, showing that by the end of his life Burns had achieved some form of financial stability. Burns at this time was an exciseman, and lived here with his family from 1793. On display are letters and manuscripts, as well as the pistol he carried with him on his rounds and the chair in which he wrote his last poems.

On the west bank of the Nith is the **Robert Burns Centre**, which tells the full story of the poet and his connections with the town. Within it are displays and exhibits, including a model of the Dumfries that Burns would have known in the late 18th century. There is also a cinema.

But the history of Dumfries doesn't start with Robert Burns. It is an ancient town, and it was here, in 1306, that Robert the Bruce murdered the Red Comyn, a rival contender for the throne of Scotland. The deed took place before the high altar of the Greyfriar's monastery, something which earned him an excommunication from the Pope. However, this didn't seem to worry the man, as he immediately had himself crowned king of Scotland at Scone in Perthshire in the presence of Scottish bishops, who continued to give him communion. Nothing now remains of the monastery, though the present **Greyfriar's Kirk**, a flamboyant Victorian building in red sandstone, is close to where it stood.

In the High Street stands the **Midsteeple**, built of red sandstone in 1707. It was formerly the town hall and jail, and on its south face

Burns's House, Dumfries

Statue of Robert Burns

has a carving of an ell, an old Scots cloth measurement of about 37 inches. There is also a table of distances from Dumfries to various important Scottish towns. One of the towns however, is in England - Huntingdon. Three successive Scottish kings in medieval times held the earldom of Huntingdon, and it was one of the places where Scottish drovers took cattle to market in the 17th and 18th centuries. Rather appropriately, in Shakespeare Street stands the famous **Theatre Royal**, one of the oldest theatres in Scotland, dating from 1792. Burns regularly attended performances there.

Dumfries proper sits on the east bank of the Nith. On the west, up until it was amalgamated into Dumfries in 1929, was **Maxwelltown**, which had been a separate burgh since 1810. Joining the two towns is **Devorgilla's Bridge**. Though the present bridge dates from 1431, the original structure was built by Devorgilla, Lady of Galloway, in the 13th century. Her husband was John Balliol, who founded Balliol College in Oxford (see also New Abbey).

At the Maxwellton end of the bridge is the **Old Bridge House**. This houses a small museum illustrating everyday life in the town. Also on the Maxwellton side of the river is **Dumfries Museum**, housed in an 18th century windmill, and with a **Camera Obscura**.

On the northern outskirts of the town are the beautiful remains of **Lincluden College**. Built originally in 1164 as a Benedictine nunnery by Uchtred, Lord of Galloway, it was suppressed in the late 14th century by **Archibald the Grim**, fourth Earl of Douglas, and replaced by a collegiate church. The present ruins date from that time. One of its main features is the elaborate canopied tomb of Princess Margaret, daughter of Robert III. Adjoining the site is the Norman **Lincluden Motte**, which was later terraced and incorporated into a garden.

To the east of the town at Heathhall is the **Dumfries and Galloway Aviation Museum**, run by a group of amateur enthusiasts. It has three floors of display area on an old RAF airfield, and holds a fascinating collection of military aircraft, both propeller and jet driven,

River Nith and Dumfries Town

as well as engines, memorabilia and photographs. The **Crichton Royal Museum** is within what was Crichton Royal Hospital, and charts the history of mental health care in Great Britain. For those interested in genealogy, the **Dumfries and Galloway Family History Research Centre** in Glasgow Street must be visited. There are archives, fiches and books about local history and families, though there is a modest fee for the use of the facilities.

The hamlet of **Holywood** sits just off the A76, two miles north of Dumfries. The present **Holywood Parish Church** of 1779 was partly built from the stones of a great medieval abbey which once stood here, of which nothing now remains. Close by is a stone circle known as the **Twelve Apostles**, though one massive stone is now missing.

One other writer is associated with Dumfries, and that is J.M. Barrie (see also Kirriemuir). Though not born here, he attended **Dumfries Academy**, a handsome building in Academy Street. While at the school, he stayed in a house in George Street, and later admitted that the games of pirates he and his friends played in the garden there, which sloped down to the Nith. gave him the idea for Peter Pan and Captain Hook.

AROUND DUMFRIES

DALSWINTON

6 miles N of Dumfries on a minor road off the A76

The hamlet of Dalswinton is no more than two rows of cottages on either side of the road. But it is an attractive place, built as an estate village. When Robert Burns was living locally at Ellisland Farm, Patrick Millar owned Dalswinton House, in the policies of which was **Dalswinton Loch**. Patrick encouraged William Symington to experiment with his steam driven boat on the waters of the loch in the late 18th century, and it is thought that Burns may have been a passenger on one of the sailings.

ELLISLAND

6 miles N of Dumfries off the A76

Robert Burns brought his family south from Mauchline to Ellisland in June 1788. He leased it from Partick Millar of Dalswinton, but found the soil to be infertile and stony. So much so that by 1791 he gave up the unequal struggle to make a living from it, and moved with his family to Dumfries. It sits in a beautiful spot beside the Nith, and it was this romantic location which had made Burns lease it in the first place. Here he wrote some of his best poetry, including Auld Lang Syne and his masterpiece of the comic/macabre, Tam o' Shanter. Burns used to recount that Tam o' Shanter was conceived as he walked the banks of the Nith, chuckling out loud as he thought up his hero's adventures with the witches. Now the place houses a lively museum dedicated to his memory. To the north is **Hermitage Cottage**, which Burns used as a place to muse and write poetry.

AE

8 miles N of Dumfries on a minor road off the A701

The small village of Ae is famous for having the shortest name of any town or village in Britain. It was founded in 1947 to house forestry workers, and is set in a great conifer forest which has some good walks and footpaths.

CLOSEBURN

11 miles N of Dumfries on the A76

Closeburn sits in one of the most beautiful parts of Dumfriesshire - Nithsdale. To the north of the village the wooded dale closes in on either side, with the River Nith tumbling through it. To the south, it gradually opens out into a wide, fertile strath, dotted with green fields and old, whitewashed farms. The **Parish Church of Closeburn** sits some distance away from the village, and is an attractive Victorian building with a slim tower. Fragments of the older church, which date from 1741, can be seen in the kirkyard. **Closeburn Castle** (not open to the public) has been continuously inhabited since the 14th century, when it was built by the Kirkparticks, who were closely associated with Robert 1

One unusual tale about Closeburn concerns a character called Elspat Buchan, commonly known as **Mother Buchan**, who founded a religious cult called the Buchanites in Irvine in Ayrshire in the 18th century. She was the daughter of a publican, and attracted a wide following, claiming she could bestow immortality on a person by breathing on them, and that she herself was immortal. The cult was eventually hounded from Irvine by its magistrates, and it headed south towards Dumfries. In a large field near Closeburn she decided to hold a religious service, and set up a large platform from which to conduct it. However, in the middle of the service the platform collapsed, throwing her and several leading followers to the ground. The sect eventually broke up when Elspat had the nerve to die a natural death (see also Irvine and Crocketford).

A small road winds up eastwards from just south of Closeburn into the moorland above the village. It makes an interesting drive, and takes you past the small but picturesque **Lock Ettrick**.

THORNHILL

13 miles N of Dumfries on the A76

This lovely village, with its wide main street and pollarded trees, has a French feel to it, and was laid out in 1714 by the Duke of Queensberry. At the crossroads in the middle of the village is a monument surmounted by a winged horse, a symbol of the Queensberry family. In a field to the west of the village, and close to the bridge over the Nith, is the 15th century **Boatford Cross**, associated with the ferry and ford that preceded the bridge.

Three miles north of the village is stately **Drumlanrig Castle**, Dumfriesshire home of the Duke of Queensberry and Buccleuch. It was built in the 1670s and 80s on the site of an earlier castle, and contains many fine paintings, including works by Gainsborough, Rembrandt and Hans Holbein. Surrounding it is a country park and gardens, and some of the outbuildings have been converted into craft workshops.

About two miles west of Thornhill is the village of **Penpont**, which is well worth a visit in the summer months to see the colourful gardens that surround some of the old picturesque cottages. And two miles south of Penpont is the hamlet of **Keir**, famous as the birthplace of **Kirkpatrick MacMillan**, inventor of the bicycle. He was born in 1813, and while his brothers all went on to become successful in careers, Kirkpatrick was content to stay at home and ply the trade of a blacksmith.

Drumlanrig Castle, nr Thornhill

Hobby horses, which relied on riders pushing themselves forward with their feet, had been on the go since the early part of the 19th century, but Kirkpatrick Macmillan's bicycle was the first to incorporate pedals. On June 6 1842 he set out on a 70 mile ride to Glasgow on his bicycle, and was greeted by milling crowd when he arrived there. However, while passing through the Gorbals, he knocked down a young girl, and even though she wasn't badly injured, he was fined five shillings by a Glasgow magistrate, the first recorded case of a cyclist being fined for a traffic offence. However, rumour has it that the magistrate offered to pay the fine out of his own pocket if Kirkpatrick would allow him to have a go on the bicycle.

TYNRON

15 miles N of Dumfries on a minor road off the A702

This small, pretty conservation village has only one building dating after 1900. The **Parish Church**, which looks as if it is far too big for such a small place, was built in 1837, and was one of the last in Scotland to be lit by oil lamps. Early in the 20th century a distillery was situated in the village which had a contract to supply the Palace of Westminster.

DURISDEER

19 miles N of Dumfries on a minor road off the A702

The tiny hamlet of Durisdeer consists of a handful of cottages and a **Parish Church**. built in 1699. The church is unusual in that it has, attached to it, the former parish school. But the church also hides a secret - the wonderful **Durisdeer Marbles**. They are, in fact, an elaborate funerary monument to the second Duke of Queensberry and his wife, who are buried in the crypt beneath. They were carved in marble by the Flemish sculptor Jan Nost, and are the best of their kind in the country.

Durisdeer Marbles

WANLOCKHEAD

25 miles N of Dumfries on the B797

People are usually surprised to discover that Scotland's highest village isn't in the Highlands, but in the Lowlands. Wanlockhead, in the Lowther Hills, is 1531 feet above sea level, and is a former lead mining village. In the middle of the village you'll find the **Museum of Lead Mining**, which explains all about the industry, and gives you the opportunity to go down a real lead mine, the **Lochnell Mine**. The **Miners' Library** is situated on the hill above the Museum, and was founded in 1756 by 35 men. At the height of its popularity it has 3000 books on its shelves. Within the village you'll also find the **Beam Engine**, which used to pump water from one of the mines.

The **Leadhills and Wanlockhead Light Railway** is Britain's highest adhesion railway,

Wanlockhead Beam Engine

reaching 1498 feet above sea level. It was originally built to take refined lead to Scotland's central belt, but finally closed in 1938. Now a length of two foot gauge track has been reopened between Wanlockhead and its twin village of Leadhills, and trips are available.

Lead is not the only metal associated with Wanlockhead. In olden days, this whole area was known as "God's Treasure House in Scotland" because of the gold found there. In fact, the Scottish regalia was made from Lowther Hills gold, and 5000 men were employed to mine it. The largest nugget of gold ever discovered in the UK was found close to Wanlockhead. It weighed all of two pounds, and was the size of a cricket ball. Gold panning is still a popular activity in the local streams, and indeed the **UK National Gold Panning Championships** are held here every year.

SANQUHAR

28 miles N of Dumfries on the A76

Sanquhar (pronounced (San-kar) is a small town in Upper Nithsdale that was created a royal burgh in 1598. The name comes from the language of the ancient Britons, and means "Old Fort". The site of this fort was on a small hill to the north of the present town, close to **St Bride's Parish Church**, built in 1824 on the site of a much older church. The handsome **Sanquhar Tolbooth** was built to the designs of William Adam in 1735 as a town hall, schoolroom and jail, and now houses a small museum. In Main Street is **Sanquhar Post Office**, dating from 1712, and the oldest continuously used post office in the world. The Southern Upland Way passes through the burgh, and the **Sanquhar Historic Walk** takes you round many of the town's attractions and historic sites.

To the south of Sanquhar are the ruins of **Sanquhar Castle**, an old Douglas stronghold. It was here that William Douglas, who wrote the original version of Bonnie Annie Laurie, was born there in 1672. It was founded in the 11th century, though what you see now dates from much later.

Further south, deep in the heart of Nithsdale, is Eliock House, birthplace in 1560 of **James Crichton**, otherwise known as the "Admirable Crichton". He was the son of the then Lord Advocate of Scotland, and was educated at St Andrews University. He travelled extensively in Europe, where he followed careers in soldiering and in lecturing at universities. Though a young man, he could speak twelve languages fluently, and was one of the best swordsmen of his day. However, this didn't prevent him being killed in Mantua in Italy in 1582 while a lecturer at the university there. The story goes that he was returning from a party one evening when he was set upon by a gang of robbers, and defeated each one in a sword fight. He then realised that one of the robberss was his pupil at the university, Vincentio di Gonzaga, son of the ruler of the city, the Duke of Mantua. Realising what he had done, he handed Vincentio his sword and asked forgiveness. Vincentio, however, was a nasty piece of work. He took the sword and stabbed the defenceless James through the heart with it, killing him outright.

In the 17th century, Sanquhar was a Covenanting stronghold. Charles II had imposed bishops on the Church of Scotland, and the Covenanters took up arms to keep the church Presbyterian. These times were known as the "Killing Times", and many people were executed for following the dictates of their conscience. One of the most militant Covenanters was **Richard Cameron**, who rode into Sanquhar in 1680 and attached what became known as the **Sanquhar Declaration** to the Market Cross. This disowned the king, and effectively declared war on him. He was subsequently killed at the Battle of Airds Moss in the same year (see also Falkland).

One of the more unusual cottage industries in Sanquhar during the 18th century was hand knitting, and the intricate patterns used soon made the garments popular throughout the country. Up until the 1950s these patterns had never been published. Now it is possible once more to buy both hand and machine knitted garments with the distinctive patterns on them.

KIRKCONNEL (UPPER NITHSDALE)

31 miles N of Dumfries on the A76

This former mining village in upper Nithsdale is not to be confused with Kirkconnell House near New Abbey or with Kirkconnel graveyard in Annandale. **St Connel's Parish Church** dates from 1729, and is a fine looking building to the north of the village.

LOCHMABEN

8 miles NE of Dumfries on the A709

Lochmaben is a small royal burgh situated in Annandale. In the vicinity are many small lochs, and in some of them is found the vendace, a rare species of fish. Near the Castle Loch stands the scant remains of **Lochmaben Castle**, which originally covered over 16 acres. An earlier castle was the headquarters of the Bruce family, Lords of Annandale, and is said to be the birthplace of Robert the Bruce (later Robert 1), though Turnberry in Ayrshire lays a similar, and perhaps more likely, claim.

About three miles to the south west is Skipmyre, where **William Paterson**, driving force behind the ill-fated Darien Scheme of 1698 to found a Scottish colony in modern day Panama, was born. He was more successful in another venture - he founded the Bank of England in 1694 (see also New Abbey).

MOFFAT

20 miles NE of Dumfries on the A 701

Sheep farming has always been important to Moffat, and this is illustrated by the ram which surmounts the **Colvin Fountain** in the middle of the wide High Street. The town is situated in a fertile bowl surrounded by low green hills, and at one time was a spa, thanks to a mineral spring discovered on its outskirts in the 17th century. By 1827 the sulphurous water was being pumped into the town, and by Victorian times it had become a fashionable place to visit and "take the waters".

Moffat was the birthplace, in 1882, of **Air Chief Marshal Lord Dowding**, architect of the Battle of Britain. A statue of him can be found in **Station Park**. Though he wasn't born in the town, **John Loudon McAdam**, the great road builder, is buried in the old graveyard. He lived at Dumcrieff House, outside the town, and died in 1836 (see also Ayr). The small **Moffat Museum** at The Neuk, Church Gate, charts the history of the town and the people associated with it.

The **Black Bull Inn** is one of the oldest in Dumfriesshire, and dates from 1568, Burns was a regular visitor, and Graham of Claverhouse used it as his headquarters while hunting Covenanters in the district. Another hostelry in Moffat that has a claim to fame, albeit a more unusual one, is **The Star Hotel** in the High Street. It is only 20 feet wide, making it the narrowest hotel in Britain. On the other side of the road is the former **Moffat House**, designed by John Adam for the Earl of Hopetoun and dating from 1750s. It too is now a hotel.

The A708 winds north east from the town, and takes you past St Mary's Loch as you head for Selkirk. About eight miles along the road is a waterfall called **The Grey Mare's Tail**, fed by the waters of tiny Loch Skeen, high in the hills. It is owned by the National Trust for Scotland, and there is a car park and visitors centre.

A few miles north of the town, close to the A701, is **Tweedswell**, the source of the River Tweed, which flows north east from here before turning east near Peebles. It seems strange that within an area of no more than a few miles, two other rivers rise - the Annan and the Clyde. The Annan flows south, and the Clyde flows north. And close by is a great hollowed out area among the hills known as the **Devil's Beeftub**. Here, in olden times, Border reivers used to hide their stolen cattle. To the east towers the 2,651 feet high **Hartfell**, supposedly the seat of **Merlin the Magician** in Arthurian days.

ESKDALEMUIR

23 miles NE of Dumfries on the B709

Eskdalemuir, high in the hills, holds one of Dumfriesshire's hidden gems. The **Samye Ling Centre**, founded in 1967 by two refugee Tibetan abbots, is the largest Tibetan Buddhist monastery in Western Europe. Not only is it a monastery, it is a place where Tibetan culture, customs and art is preserved. To see its colourful Eastern buildings, its flags flying and its prayer wheels revolving in what is a typical Scottish moorland setting, comes as a great surprise. Close by is **Eskdalemuir Observatory**, erected in 1908.

LANGHOLM

24 miles NE of Dumfries on the A7

Though within Dumfriesshire, the "muckle toon" of Langholm, in Eskdale, is more of a Borders town than a Dumfries and Galloway one. It was here, in 1892, that Christopher Grieve the poet, better known as **Hugh McDiarmid**, was born (see also Biggar). The **Armstrong Clan Museum** at Lodge Walk in Castleholm traces the history of this great Borders family. In the parish of **Westerkirk**, a few miles north west of the town, **Thomas Telford** the great civil engineer was born in 1757. Within the parish is the unique **Bentpath Library**, founded in 1792 for the

Village Inn

Kirtle Bridge, near Lockerbie, Dumfriesshire DG11 3LZ
Tel/Fax: 01461 500221

Looking for somewhere close to the M74 for a comfortable overnight stay or a dinner? Then the **Village Inn** at Kirtlebridge is for you. It boasts four tastefully decorated rooms, one en suite, and has a great reputation for its food and standards of service. Owners Alison and Les Shortreed have created a warm and friendly establishment – one that you will be sure to come back to again and again. There's also a well stocked and cosy bar, (a favourite with the locals) and the menus offer beautifully cooked dishes at remarkably low prices.

use of the antimony miners who used to work in the nearby Meggat Valley. On the last Friday in July the annual **Common Riding Ceremony** is held in Langholm.

LOCKERBIE

10 miles NE of Dumfries off the M74

This quiet market town in Annandale is remembered for one thing - the **Lockerbie Disaster** of 1988. On the evening of December 21, Pan Am flight 101 exploded in mid air, due to a terrorist bomb. Its cockpit crashed into a field at **Tundergarth** to the west, and its fuselage crashed into the town, killing all the passengers and crew, as well as 11 people in the town itself. The **Remembrance Garden** is situated within the town cemetery beyond the motorway, on the A709. It is a peaceful spot, though there is still an air of raw emotion about the place, and no one visits without developing a lump in the throat.

In 1593, the **Battle of Dryfe Sands** took place near Lockerbie. The two great families in the area - the Maxwells and the Johnstones - were forever fighting and bickering, and eventually they met in battle. The Maxwells,

Lockerbie

with 2000 men, looked the likeliest victors. However, the Johnstones, with only 400 men, won the day. Over 700 Maxwells were killed.

ANNAN

14 miles E of Dumfries, on the A75

The picturesque old Royal Burgh of Annan, even though it is a mile from the sea, was once a thriving seaport, and even had a boat building yard. Edward Irving, the founder of the Catholic Apostolic Church, which thrived on elaborate ceremony and a complicated

hierarchy of ministers and priests, was born here in 1792. Another Annan man was **Thomas Blacklock**, born in 1721. He was the first blind man to be ordained a minister in the Church of Scotland. The solid **Annan Parish Church** in the High Street, with its stumpy spire, dates from 1786. The place has associations with the Bruce family, who were Lords of Annandale. In Bank Street is the **Historic Resources Centre**, a small museum that puts on a programme of displays and exhibitions.

Haaf Net Fishing is a means of catching fish that stretches back to Viking times, and it is still carried out at the mouth of the River Annan from April to August each year. The fishermen stand chest deep in the water wielding large haaf nets, which are attached to long wooden frames. In 1538 James V granted the haaf net fishermen of Annan a royal charter. In 1992 the rights of the fishermen were challenged in court by the owners of a time share development further up the river, but the judge took the view that the charter still held good today.

South of the town, at one time, was the **Solway Viaduct**, a railway bridge that connected Dumfriesshire to Cumbria across the Solway Firth. It was opened for passenger trains in 1870, and at the time was the longest railway bridge across water in Britain. In 1881 parts of the bridge were damaged when great ice flows smashed into its stanchions. The then keeper of the bridge, John Welch, plus two colleagues, remained in their cabin on the bridge as the great icebergs, some as big as 27 yards square, careered into the bridge's supports. At 3.30 in the morning, when disaster seemed imminent, they were ordered to leave. Two lengths of the bridge, one 50 feet long, and one 300 feet long, collapsed into the firth, and 37 girders and 45 pillars were smashed beyond repair. However, unlike the Tay Bridge disaster, there was no loss of life. Finally, in 1934, the bridge was dismantled, and all that is left to see nowadays are the approaches on either shore, and a stump in the middle of the water.

ECCLEFECHAN

14 miles E of Dumfries on the B7076

This small village's rather curious name means the church of St Fechan or Fechin, an Irish saint that lived in the 7th century. Within it

CRESSFIELD COUNTRY HOUSE HOTEL

Ecclefechan, Dumfriesshire DG11 3DR
Tel: 01576 300281; Fax: 01576 300838
e-mail: thelma.jackson@talk21.com

In the peaceful village of Ecclefechan, just off the M74, you'll find an outstanding small hotel – the **Cressfield Country House Hotel**. The building, of warm red sandstone, dates from 1873, and has connections with the family of Thomas Carlyle the writer, who was born in the village. There are 10 comfortable en suite bedrooms, each one decorated to an exceptionally high standard, and the cuisine is out of this world. Thelma Jackson is mine host, and she insists that only the finest local produce is used wherever possible. The bar is cosy yet spacious, and carries a full stock of beers, wines and spirits, plus soft drinks if you're behind the wheel. This wonderful area of Scotland isn't overrun by tourists, so is quiet and friendly. And yet it has history and scenery aplenty, and the Cressfield would make the ideal base in which to explore it. The rugged charms of Dumfries and Galloway – the Burns Country – the beautiful Scottish Borders – the City of Glasgow – all are within easy reach. And with a function suite that can take up to 200 people, it's the idea place for a wedding reception or that business function you've been thinking about. Thelma extends a warm welcome to people wishing to stay, or perhaps just to turn up for a lunch or an evening meal.

you will find **Carlyle's Birthplace** (National Trust for Scotland), where Thomas Carlyle was born in 1795. The house, called The Arched House, was built in the main street by Thomas's father and uncle, who were both master masons. Within it is a collection of memorabilia about the great man.

KIRKCONNEL (KIRTLEBRIDGE)
16 mile E of Dumfries off the M74

In the kirkyard of the ruined Kirkconnel Church are said to be the graves of **Fair Helen of Kirkconnel Lee** and her lover **Adam Fleming**. Their story is a romantic one, and a famous ballad was written about it. Helen was loved by two men, Adam Fleming and a man named Bell (whose first name isn't known). Helen found herself drawn towards Adam, and Bell was consumed with jealousy. He therefore decided to kill his rival. He waylaid the couple close to the kirkyard, and pulled out a pistol. As he fired, Helen threw herself in front of her lover, and was killed. There are two versions of the story after this. One says that Adam killed Bell where he stood, and another says he pursued him to Madrid, where he killed him. Either way, he was inconsolable, and joined the army. But he could never forget Helen, and one day he returned to Kirkconnel, lay down on her tombstone, and died of a broken heart. He was buried beside her.

It's a poignant tale, but no proof has ever emerged that the events actually took place.

EASTRIGGS
18 miles E of Dumfries on the A75

A huge government works manufacturing explosives once stretched from Longtown in the east to Annan in the west, a total of 11 miles. The **Eastriggs Heritage Project** traces the history of the daily life of the 30,000 workers who manufactured what was known as "The Devil's Porridge".

KIRKPATRICK FLEMING
19 miles E of Dumfries off the M74

This pleasant little village is visited mainly to see **Robert the Bruce's Cave.** Sir William Irving is supposed to have hidden Robert the Bruce here for three months. It is also where Bruce is supposed to have seen the famous spider which made him redouble his efforts to defeat the English, though other caves in Scotland and Ireland make similar claims.

GRETNA GREEN
23 miles E of Dumfries off the M74

This small village, just across the border from England, is the "romance" capital of Britain. In the 18th century it was the first stopping place in Scotland for coaches travelling from the south, so was the ideal place for runaways from England to get married. In 1754 irregular marriages in England were made illegal, and the legal age at which people could get married without parental consent was set at 21. However, this didn't apply in Scotland, and soon a roaring trade in runaway marriages got underway in the village. The actual border between Scotland and England is the River Sark, and one of the places where marriages took place was the **Old Toll House** (now bypassed by the M74) on the Scottish side of the bridge across the river. Another place was **Gretna Hall**.

But perhaps the most famous was **The Old Blacksmith's Shop**, built in about 1712. A wedding across the anvil became the popular means of tying the knot, and the Anvil Priests, as they became known, charged anything from a dram of whisky to a guinea to conduct what was a perfectly legal ceremony. By 1856, the number of weddings had dropped, due to what was called the "Lord Brougham Act",

The Od Blacksmith's Shop, Gretna Green

which required that at least one of the parties to the marriage had to have been resident in Scotland for the previous 21 days. This act was only repealed in 1979. In 1940, a further Act of Parliament was passed which stated that all marriages had to take place either in a church or a registry office, and the Gretna marriage trade stopped.

However, couples still come from all over the world to get married across the anvil in Gretna Green, though the ceremony is no more than a confirmation of vows taken earlier in the registry office. The Old Blacksmith's Shop is still open, and houses an exhibition on the irregular marriage trade.

Gretna Green was within the Debatable Lands, so it was therefore a lawless area in the 15th and 16th centuries. About a mile to the south west is the **Lochmaben Stone**, a huge rock where representatives from the two countries met to air grievances and seek justice.

Not so long ago, Gretna Green became run down and tacky, but recent improvements have made it the second most visited tourist attraction in Scotland. Nowadays there are are many high quality shops and restaurants in the village. In the nearby village of **Gretna** is the **Gretna Gateway Outlet Village**, a complex of shops selling designer label fashions.

CANONBIE

26 miles E of Dumfries off the A7

Canonbie means the "town of the canons", because a priory once stood here. It was destroyed by the English in 1542, and some of the stones may have been used in the building of **Hollows Bridge** across the River Esk, Scotland's second fastest flowing river. This is the heart of the **Debatable Lands**, which, in the 15th and 16th centuries, were neither within Scotland or England. It was therefore a lawless place, and a safe haven for the reivers. Beyond the bridge, and marked by a stone and plaque, is the site of **Gilnockie Castle**, home of **Johnnie Armstrong**, one of the greatest reivers of them all, who was hanged in 1530 by James V. The story goes that Johnnie and his men were invited to a great gathering at Carlanrig in Teviotdale where they would meet the king, who promised them safe passage. Taking him at his word, Johnnie and a band of men set out. However, when they

Cross Keys Hotel

Canonbie, Dumfriesshire DG14 0SY
Tel: 013873 71382/71205 Fax: 013873 71878
website: www.gretnaweddings.com/crosskeys.html

The picturesque village of Canonbie sits just over the Border from England, and is run by mine hosts Barbara and Michael Kitching. At the heart of the village is a former 17th century coaching inn called the **Cross Keys Hotel**, one of the oldest inns in the area. This whitewashed hostelry riots with colour in the summer months, due to its hanging baskets and tubs of flowers, and is the ideal place for a quiet stay, a meal, a pub lunch or even just a relaxing drink. If it's the peace and quiet of the countryside coupled with friendly efficient service you're after, this is the place for you.

All of the nine well appointed rooms are en suite, and its cuisine has become a local legend! Full dinners, simple snacks or bar lunches are all beautifully cooked and presented, and of course there's an extensive wine list that has something to complement any meal. A traditional carvery is available every Friday and Saturday evening, as well as Sunday lunchtime, and this is popular with the locals. There's a cosy lounge bar and a public bar, and both ooze character and warmth. The surrounding countryside is stunning, and deserves to be explored, and marvellous facilities for golf, horse riding and horse racing are not too far away.

Parish Church, Canonbie

got there, James forgot about his promise and had them all strung up on the spot. Perhaps the most amazing aspect of this tale is that the king was no world weary warrior, but an 18 year old lad at the time. Some of the castle's stones also went into building Hollows Bridge.

Standing beside the river is **Hollows Mill**, the last commercial mill in Scotland still to be powered by water. And close by, but not open to the public, is **Hollows Tower**, which dates from the 16th century.

RUTHWELL

10 miles SE of Dumfries off the B724

Within the **Parish Church** of 1800 is the famous 18 feet high **Ruthwell Cross.** It dates from about AD800, when this part of Scotland formed part of the Anglo Saxon kingdom of Northumbria. The carvings show scenes from the Gospels, twining vines and verses from an old poem called The Dream of the Rood, at one time thought to have been written by Caedmon of Whitby.

In 1810, the world's first savings bank was founded in the village by the **Rev. Henry Duncan**, and the small **Savings Bank Museum** has displays and artefacts about the savings bank movement.

POWFOOT

13 miles SE of Dumfries on a minor road off the B724

Today Powfoot is a quiet village on the Solway coast. But in the late 19th and early 20th centuries there were plans to make it a grand holiday resort, with hotels, formal gardens, woodland walks, a promenade, a pier, golf courses and bowling greens. The whole plan eventually collapsed, though some of the attractions were actually built. Now the village is famous for its red brick housing and terraces, which look incongruous on the shores of the Solway, but wouldn't look out of place in Lancashire.

CAERLAVEROCK

7 miles S of Dumfries on the B725

Think of an old, romantic, turreted medieval castle surrounded by a water-filled moat, and you could be thinking of **Caerlaverock Castle** (Historic Scotland). It was built by the Maxwells, one of the great local families, as their chief seat in the 13th century, and was attacked by Edward I in 1300 during the Wars of Independence. It is triangular in shape, with a turret at two corners and a double

Powfoot Village

Caerlaverock Castle

turret at the other, where the entrance is located. It was attacked by Covenanters in 1640 and dismantled, though in the early 1600s the then Earl of Nithsdale had some fine courtyard buildings constructed within the walls in the Renaissance style. **Caerlaverock Wildfowl and Wetlands Trust** is about three miles west of the castle, and is situated in a 1,350 acre nature reserve. Here a wide variety of wildlife can be observed, including swans and barnacle geese. If you're lucky, you may also come across the extremely rare natterjack toad. There are three observation towers, 20 hides and a wild swan observatory linked by nature trails and screen approaches. There are also picnic areas, a gift shop, refreshments and binocular hire. Some facilities are wheelchair friendly.

The place is on the well signposted **Solway Coast Heritage Trail**, which stretches from Gretna in the east to Stranraer in the west.

NEW ABBEY

6 miles S of Dumfries on the A710

This attractive little village sits in the shadow of **The Criffel**, a 1,866 feet high hill which can be seen from miles around. Within the village you'll find the beautiful red sandstone ruins of **Sweetheart Abbey** (Historic Scotland), founded by Devorgilla, Lady of Galloway, in 1273 (see also Dumfries). Her husband had been John Balliol of Barnard Castle in County Durham, who founded Balliol College in Oxford. After his death she carried his embalmed heart around with her everywhere in a small casket, and when she herself died, she was buried along with the heart in front of the abbey's high altar, where her tomb can still be seen. The Cistercian monks gave the name "Dolce Cor" to the abbey, and thus was born the word "sweetheart". In its graveyard lies William Paterson, founder of the Bank of England.

At the other end of the village is the **New Abbey Corn Mill** (Historic Scotland), dating from the 18th century. It is in full working order, and there are regular demonstrations on how a water powered mill works. The original mill on the site is thought to have belonged to Sweetheart Abbey.

Sweetheart Abbey

Shambellie House is a large mansion on the outskirts of New Abbey which houses the **Shambellie House Museum of Costume**, part of the National Museums of Scotland. The house and its collection was given to the National Museums in 1977 by the then owner, Charles Stewart, and most of these costumes, which range from Victorian to the 1930s, are now displayed in appropriate settings.

Shambellie House Museum of Costume

KIRKBEAN

10 miles S of Dumfries, on the A710

About two miles south of the village is the estate of **Arbigland**, birthplace in 1747 of the founder of the American navy, **John Paul Jones**. The cottage on which he was born is now a small museum. **Kirkbean Parish Church** was built in 1776, and inside is a font presented by the American Navy in 1945. To continue the American theme, also born on the estate was **Dr James Craik**, Washington's personal physician.

CROCKETFORD

9 miles W of Dumfries, on the A75

It was at Crocketford that the sorry tale of Elspat Buchan, who founded a religious sect called the Buchanites, came to a macabre end. Part of the sect's beliefs was that Elspat was immortal, and that she bestow immortality on others by breathing on them. After having been driven out of Irvine, she and her followers headed south towards Dumfriesshire and settled there. Alas, Elspath disappointed her followers by dying a natural death, and the sect broke up. But one man, who lived in Crocketford, still believed in her immortality, and that she would rise from the dead. He therefore acquired her dead body, and kept it in a cupboard in his cottage in the village, where it gradually mummified. Every day he would go to the cupboard and open it to see if Elspat had come alive again, but every time he was disappointed. However, it didn't shake his belief in her, and the body remained in the cottage with him for many years (see also Closeburn and Irvine).

DUNSCORE

8 miles NW of Dumfries, on the B729

This pretty little village has a neat, whitewashed **Parish Church** dating from 1823. In the previous church that stood on the site, Burns and his family used to worship when they stayed at Ellisland farm. Within the parish of Dunscore was born the only British person to have died at Auschwitz during World War II. She was a remarkable woman called **Jane Haining**, who was born at Lochenhead Farm in 1897. She joined the Church of Scotland's Jewish Mission Service, and was eventually appointed matron of the Jewish Mission in Budapest in 1932. In 1944 she was arrested by the German Army, purportedly because she had been listening to the BBC broadcasts, but in actual fact because of her work among the Jews. She was deported to Auschwitz, and on July 17 1944 died there. Her death certificate said that the cause of death was cachexia, a wasting disease, but there is little doubt that she was gassed.

MONIAIVE

16 miles NW of Dumfries on the A 702

Moniaive, caught in a fold of the hills at the head of Glencairn, through which the Cairn Water flows to join the Nith, must surely be one of the prettiest villages in Dumfriesshire. It is actually two villages, Moniaive itself and Dunreggan, on the other side of the river. Within the village is the **James Renwick Monument**, which commemorates a Covenanting martyr who died in 1688.

In the village is a shop which claims to be the only one of its kind in the world. Opened in 1999 by Jackie Goddard, the **Poetry Shop**, as its name suggests, sells individual, original poems written to order for every occasion.

James Paterson was a painter who was a member of that group known as the "Glasgow Boys". In 1882 he settled in the village with his wife, and lived there until 1906, when he moved to Edinburgh. The **James Paterson**

Glenluiart Holiday Cottages

Moniaive, Dumfriesshire DG3 4JA
Tel: 01848 200331 Fax: 01848 200675
e-mail: sue@badpress.demon.co.uk
website: www.moniaive.com

Owned and run by Sue Grant, the **Glenluiart Holiday Cottages** offers self catering accommodation in four picturesque and comfortable stone cottages built round a shared courtyard. They date from about 1900, but have been modernised and upgraded. Two of the cottages have one double bedroom, one has a double bedroom and a twin, and one has a double, a twin and two singles. All are tastefully decorated throughout, and all are well equipped. Each has a sitting room/diner with TV, a bathroom and a kitchen that boasts a cooker, a microwave, crockery, glasses, cutlery and all cooking utensils. Two of the cottages also have washing machines.

The furniture is comfortable, and all the cottages are clean and well maintained. All bed linen and towels are included in the price, as is electricity, and high chairs and cots are available on request. The cottages sit at the entrance to a large driveway, with five acres of garden behind them. There is plenty of parking space, and the cottages are available all year round. Well behaved dogs are welcome. They make excellent bases for a quiet, relaxing holiday among some of the best scenery in Scotland, or for exploring the Solway coast or the Burns Country. Moniaive itself is full of history, and boasts two pubs, a garage, a café and a grocery store. There are some excellent walks in the surrounding hills, and leaflets are available about walks in the village itself.

Museum is within a small cottage in North Street, and has displays and exhibits on the man. It was founded by the painter's grand daughter, Anne Paterson-Wallace, herself a painter of some note.

Three miles east is the great mansion of **Maxwelton House** (not open to the public), formerly known as Glencairn Castle. It was here that Anna Laurie, of Bonnie Annie Laurie fame, was born in 1682. The song was written by William Douglas of Fingland, though he later jilted her in favour of becoming a soldier. Anna herself went on to marry Alexander Fergusson, 14th Laird of Craigdarroch.

Moniaive Village

KIRKCUDBRIGHT

Kirkcudbright (pronounced "Kirk-coo-bree") must be one of the loveliest small towns in Scotland, and one of its real "hidden places". Its name simply means the church of St Cuthbert, as the original church built here was dedicated to that saint. It was an established town by the 11th century, and has been a royal burgh since 1455. It sits close to the mouth of the Dee, and is still a working port with a small fishing fleet.

Kirkcudbright High Street

Kirkcudbright was once the county town of Kirkcudbrightshire, also known as the "Stewartry of Kirkcudbright". It is a place of brightly painted Georgian, Regency and Victorian houses, which make it a colourful and interesting place to explore. This part of Galloway has a very mild climate, thanks to the Gulf Stream washing its shores, and this, as well as the quality of light to be found here, encouraged the founding of an artist's colony in the town. On a summer's morning, the edge between light and shadow can be as sharp as a knife, whereas during the day it becomes diffused and soft, and artists have been reaching for their paints and palettes for years to try and capture these two qualities. Even today, straw-hatted artists can still be seen at the harbourside, trying to capture the scene.

It is said that St Cuthbert himself founded the first church here, which was located within the present town cemetery. In fact, down through the years, grave diggers have often turned up carved stones which belonged to it. Within the graveyard is **Billy Marshall's Grave**. Billy was known as the "King of Galloway Tinkers", and the gravestone reveals that he died in 1792 aged 120 years. The present **St Cuthbert's Parish Church** is a grand affair near the centre of the town, and dates from 1838. A much older church is to be found near the harbour. **Greyfriar's Kirk** is all that is left of a Franciscan monastery which stood here, and dates from the 16th century, though it has been much altered over the years. Within it is the grand tomb of **Sir Thomas MacLellan of Bombie** and his wife Grizzell Maxwell, which was erected in 1597. But the tomb isn't all it seems to be. The couple's son, in an effort to save money, used effigies from an earlier tomb within what is essentially a Renaissance structure. The friary is thought to have been founded in 1224 by Alan, Lord of Galloway, and father of Devorgilla, who founded Sweetheart Abbey. The kirk sits on a slight rise known as the **Moat Brae**, where Roland, Lord of Galloway in the 12th century, may have had a castle.

Nearby, in Castle Street, are the substantial ruins of **MacLellan's Castle** (Historic Scotland), built by the same Sir Thomas who lies in the Greyfriar's Kirk. It isn't really a castle, but a grand town house, and Sir Thomas, who was obviously his son's role model where thrift was concerned, used the stones from the friary as building material. Sir Thomas was a local magnate and favourite of the king who became Provost of Kirkcudbright. The castle is open to the public.

Walk up the side of the castle into Castle Bank, passing the whitewashed **Harbour**

MacLellan's Castle

Broughton House and Gardens

Cottage Gallery, and you arrive at the **High Street**. It runs parallel to Castle Street, then half way along takes a dog leg to the left. This must be one of the most charming and colourful streets in Scotland. The elegant Georgian and Regency houses - some of them quite substantial - are painted in bright, uncompromising colours, such as yellow, green and pink. **Auchingool House** is the oldest, having been built in 1617 for the McCullochs of Auchengool. **Broughton House**, dating from the 18th century, is now owned by the National Trust for Scotland, and was the home of A.E. Hornel the artist. He was one of the Glasgow Boys, and died in 1933. The house is very much as it was when he lived there. Behind the house is the marvellous **Japanese Garden**, influenced by trips that the artist made to that country.

Further along the street is **Greengates Close**, (not open to the public) which was the home of Jessie M. King, another artist. At the dog leg stands the early 17th century **Tolbooth**, which now houses a museum and art gallery telling the story of the artist's colony. It was opened by the Queen in 1993. This was the former town house and jail, and John Paul Jones, founder of the American navy, was imprisoned here once for murder. He got his revenge in later years when he returned to the town aboard an American ship and shelled the nearby **St Mary's Isle**, where the seat of the Earl of Selkirk was located, and where a medieval priory of nuns once stood. This "isle" is in fact a peninsula, and to confuse matters even further, one of the smaller bays in Kirkcudbright Bay (itself an inlet of the Solway Firth) is called **Manxman's Lake**, one of the few instances of a natural stretch of water being called a lake rather than a loch in Scotland (see also Lake of Menteith, Stenton and Ellon). A walk up St Mary's Wynd beside the Tolbooth and past the modern school takes you to **Castledykes**, where once stood a royal castle. Edward I stayed here, as did Henry VI after his defeat at the Battle of Towton in 1461, and James 1V used it as a staging post on his many pilgrimages to Whithorn. In St Mary's Street, close to where it meets with the High Street, is the **Stewartry Museum**, which is dedicated to the history and artefacts of the Stewartry of Kirkcudbright.

The town also has its literary associations. **Dorothy L. Sayers** set her Lord Peter Wimsey whodunit Five Red Herrings among the artist's colony. It's not one of her best, as it over relies on a detailed knowledge of train times between Kirkcudbrightshire and Ayrshire, and of the paints found on an artist's palette. **Ronald Searle** also knew the town, and he based his **St Trinians** innocents on St Trinian's School in Edinburgh, attended by the daughters of Kirkcudbright artist W. Miles Johnston.

AROUND KIRKCUDBRIGHT

TONGLAND

2 miles N of Kirkcudbright on the A711

The small village of Tongland was once the site of the great **Tongland Abbey**, and the scant remains - no more than a medieval archway in a piece of preserved wall - can still be seen in the kirkyard. Tours are available of

Tongland Bridge

Tongland Power Station, part of the great Galloway hydroelectric scheme of the 1930s. Close by is **Tongland Bridge**, a graceful structure across the Dee designed by Thomas Telford and built in 1805

LOCH KEN

9 miles N of Kirkcudbright between the A713 and the A762

Loch Ken is a narrow stretch of water almost nine miles long, and nowhere wider than a mile. It was created in the 1930s as the result of the great Galloway hydroelectric scheme, with the turbines being housed in the power station at Tongland, further down the Dee. Other schemes were constructed at Clatteringshaws and Loch Doon. Loch Ken is a favourite spot for bird watching and water sports such as sailing and water skiing.

NEW GALLOWAY

17 miles N of Kirkcudbright on the A762

Though New Galloway is a small village with a population of about 300, it is still a proud royal burgh, and a picturesque place. We are in that part of Kirkcudbrightshire known as the **Glenkens**, an area that combines the high drama of lonely stretches of moorland with fertile, wooded valleys. At **Kells Churchyard**, north of the town, is the grave of a Covenanter, shot in 1685.

Each year New Galloway plays host to the **Scottish Alternative Games**, where sports such as gird and cleek (hoop and stick) racing, hurlin' (throwing) the curlin' stane, flingin' the herd's bunnet (bonnet) and tossin' the sheaf are indulged in.

BALMACLELLAN

18 miles N of Kirkcudbright off the A712

This attractive little village was the home of **Robert Paterson**, a stonemason who was the model for Old Mortality in Scott's book of the same name. He travelled Scotland cleaning up the monuments and gravestones of the Covenanters, a group of men and women who fought Charles II's attempts to impose bishops on the Church of Scotland. Eventually he left home for good to concentrate on this work, leaving behind a no doubt angry wife and five children. Up to his death in 1800, he continued to travel the country, usually on an old grey pony.

In the village you will find **The Clog and Shoe Workshop**, where 18 styles of footwear are manufactured. Visitors can look round the workshop and see shoes being made.

ST JOHN'S TOWN OF DALRY

19 miles N of Kirkcudbright on the A713

St John's Town of Dalry, sometimes known simply as Dalry, is on the Southern Uplands Way, and is a picturesque Glenkens village with many old cottages. Within the village is a curious chair-shaped stone known as **St John's Stone**. Local tradition says that John the Baptist rested in it. When a reservoir was created at lonely **Lochinvar** near Dalry some time ago, the scant ruins of a tower house were submerged. This was the home of the famous Young Lochinvar, written about by Scott in his famous lines,

"O, young Lochinvar is come out of the west,
Through all the wide border his steed was the best..."

CARSPHAIRN

27 miles N of Kirkcudbright on the A713

Close to this quiet village there used to be leadmines. John Loudon MacAdam, who invented tarred roads, is credited with creating the world's first tarred road on the A713 north of the village. The **Carsphairn Heritage Centre** has displays and exhibits on the history of the village.

CASTLE DOUGLAS

9 miles NE of Kirkcudbright off the A75

Castle Douglas is a pleasant town, based round what was small village known as "Carlingwark". It was founded in the 18th century by William Douglas, a local merchant who earned his money trading with Virginia and the West Indies. He wished to create a thriving manufacturing town based on the woollen industry, and though he was only partly successful, he did lay the foundations for a charming town, where some of his original 18th century buildings can still be seen. On the edge of the town is **Carlingwark Loch**, which at one time was going to be joined to the sea by a canal as part of the overall plan.

In Market Street is the **Castle Douglas Art Gallery**, gifted to the town in 1938 by the artist Ethel Bristowe. There is a continuing programme of exhibitions of painting, sculpture and crafts. The **Sulworth Brewery** is in King Street, and here you can see the brewing process from barley to beer, and enjoy a complimentary half pint of Galloway real ale.

HARMONY B&B

33 Abercrombie Road, Castle Douglas,
Kirkcudbrightshire DG7 1BA
Tel: 01556 503103

Under the careful ownership of Lena and David Laidlaw, the **Harmony B&B** in Castle Douglas has earned an enviable reputation for the warmth of its welcome and the comfortable rooms it offers to discerning tourists. Three rooms are available, one double , one single and one en-suite twin room, with coffee making facilities in each one. A hearty Scottish breakfast is available each morning to set guests up for a day exploring an area that has much to offer by way of sports, history and stunning scenery!

THE ROSSAN

Achincairn, Castle Douglas, Kirkcudbrightshire DG7 1QR
Tel: 01556 640269 Fax: 01566 640278
e-mail: bardsley@rossan.freeserve.co.uk
website: www.the-rossan.co.uk

With three well appointed and extremely comfortable rooms, **The Rossan** (which means "little wood") is a Victorian ex church manse which prides itself on its facilities and the warmth of its Scottish welcome. Open all year round, it caters for special diets, with gluten free and vegetarian dishes available. The hearty breakfasts are all made from free range produce, and children are more than welcome if prior notice is given. Tea, coffee and cocoa making facilities are available in each room.

ROSE COTTAGE

Gelston, Castle Douglas, Kirkcudbrightshire DG7 1SH
Tel/Fax: 01556 502513

With a name like **Rose Cottage**, you would expect this self catering establishment owned by Sheila and Kerr Steele to be picturesque and cosy. And you would be right! It is in a quiet village in Dumfries and Galloway, and can sleep eight in two twin and two double bedrooms, all of which have TVs. There is a lounge (with TV and video), conservatory/dining room, well equipped kitchen and bathroom, and a large garden. Well behaved pets are welcome at this establishment, which is almost a home from home for the discerning tourist.

THREAVE CASTLE

8 miles NE of Kirkcudbright, close to the A75

Threave Castle

On an island in the River Dee stands the magnificent ruins of **Threave Castle** (Historic Scotland), reached by a small ferry that answers the call of a bell on a small jetty on the riverbank. It was built by Archibald Douglas, 4th Earl of Douglas, known as Archibald the Grim, soon after he became Lord of Galloway in 1369. On his death at Threave in 1400, he was the most powerful man in southern Scotland, and almost independent of the king, Robert III. When James II undertook a siege of the castle in 1455, it took two months before the occupants finally surrendered, and the powerful Douglas family was overthrown.

To the south west lie **Threave Gardens and Estate** (National Trust for Scotland), which surround a house built in 1872 by a Liverpool businessman. Unlike other gardens owned by the Trust, which were taken over, Threave Gardens were created from scratch. They now house the Trust's School of Practical Gardening.

Threave Gardens

KIPPFORD

10 miles NE of Kirkcudbright off the A710

The tides in the Solway Firth are among the fastest in Britain, but this hasn't prevented the picturesque village of Kippford from becoming a great yachting centre. Like its neighbour Rockcliffe, five miles away it was once a smuggling village.

PALNACKIE

10 miles NE of Kirkcudbright on the A711

This small, attractive village on the Urr Water is a mile from the sea, though at one time it was a thriving port. Each year, in summer, it hosts one of the most unusual competitions in Great Britain - the annual **World Flounder Tramping Championships**. People come from all over the world to compete, making it a truly international event. The object is to walk out onto the mud flats south of the village at low tide, feel for flounders hiding beneath the mud with your toes and collect them. The person with the largest weight of flounders wins the championship. It may seem a light hearted and eccentric competition, but it is firmly based in history, as this was a recognised way of catching fish in the area in olden times.

The **North Glen Gallery** features glassblowing and interior and exterior design, and people can visit the glassblowing workshops. It is also a good place to get advice on local walks and wildlife. A mile south west of Palnackie is **Orchardton Tower**, the only round tower house in Scotland. It dates from the middle of the 15th century, and was built by John Cairns.

DALBEATTIE

11 miles NE of Kirkcudbright on the A711

This small town and burgh stands just east of the furthermost point of navigation on the Water of Urr, and was at one time a small port. Ships of up to 60 tons could make the four mile trip upriver from the sea, pulled by teams of horses. Now the "Pool of Dalbeattie" (the name given to the port area) is derelict, and the river has silted up. Dalbeattie was a planned town, founded in the 1790s as a textile centre. Close by there were also easily

BELLE VUE

Port Road, Dalbeattie, Kirkcudbrightshire DG5 4AZ
Tel: 01556 611833 e-mail: snraajj@bellevuebandb.freeserve.co.uk
Mobile: 07931 932029 website: www.bellevuebandb.co.uk

Belle Vue is a real 'home from home' style B&B situated on the edge of the picturesque town of Dalbeattie. This no smoking establishment boasts four rooms, two on the ground floor and two on the first floor, and all have either full ensuite facilities or access to a private bathroom. They are extremely comfortable, well appointed, and spotlessly clean. The breakfasts are hearty and filling, and there are many restaurants close by where evening meals are served. Children are very welcome in this B&B, which makes an ideal base from which to explore an area rich in magnificent scenery and history.

No 13 B&B

13 Maxwell Park, Dalbeattie,
Kirkcudbrightshire DG5 4LR
Tel: 01556 610830
e-mail: kandb@tattersfield.freeserve.co.uk

The comfortable and beautifully appointed **No 13 B&B**, situated in the small market town of Dalbeattie, is open all year. It has three bedrooms - two doubles and a twin, with one of the doubles being en suite. Barbara Tattersfield, the owner, has created an immaculately clean and modern establishment where the service is excellent and the welcome warm, and for her efforts has earned four coveted stars from VisitScotland, an accolade that is not given lightly.

This no smoking establishment welcomes children, and the full Scottish breakfast that is on offer is sure to set you up for a day exploring a wonderful part of Scotland where there is so much to see and do. There is private parking available, and there are TVs and hair dryers in each room. Delicious picnic lunches can be made up, and tea and coffee are available on request. This is the ideal base - cosy and friendly - from which to explore Dumfries and Galloway, and even on into the wonderful Burns Country in Ayrshire. Barbara will give you a fine Scottish welcome, and once you've stayed here, you're sure to come back again and again!

worked deposits of granite, and these were quarried as well.

On the west bank of the Urr, about a mile from the town, is all that remains of **Buittle Castle and Bailey**, home to John Balliol, son of Devorgilla, whom Edward I placed on the throne of Scotland as a puppet king. Robert I established a burgh here in 1325, and a recent archaeological dig has revealed that the castle's large bailey may have housed it. A later tower house stands close by.

Dundrennan Abbey Ruins

On the wall of the former town hall is a the **Murdoch Memorial** to Lt William Murdoch, who was the First Officer aboard the Titanic when it sank in 1912. Through the years he has been unfairly accused of being, among other things, a coward who shot passengers attempting to leave the ship, not allowing third class passengers near the life boats and of accepting bribes from first class passengers to let them board life boats to which they were not entitled. The recent film also treated him unfairly, though the witness statements presented at the later official Board of Trade Enquiry cleared him of all these charges. In 1996 his name was finally and officially cleared of any wrongdoing.

Three miles north of Dalbeattie is the **Motte of Urr**, a 12th century motte-hill which is the largest non-industrial man-made hill in Scotland. At its summit would have been at one time a large, wooden castle, supposedly built by William de Berkeley.

ROCKCLIFFE

10 miles E of Kirkcudbright on a minor road off the A710

Rockcliffe was at one time a great smuggling centre, but is now a quiet resort. Off the coast is **Rough Island**, a National Trust for Scotland bird sanctuary. Close to the village is the great **Mote of Mark**, the site of a prehistoric fort.

DUNDRENNAN

4 miles SE of Kirkcudbright on the A711

This quiet village is now visited mainly because of the ruins of the once substantial Cistercian **Dundrennan Abbey** (Historic Scotland). It was founded in 1142 by David I and Fergus, Lord of Galloway, and was where Mary Stuart spent her last night on Scottish soil before sailing for England and her eventual execution. Little of the grand abbey church now remains, though the chapter house and some of the other buildings are well worth seeing, as are some interesting graveslabs.

CAIRNHOLY

11 miles W of Kirkcudbright off the A75

Cairnholy comprises two chambered cairns dating from between 2000 and 3000BC. The most remarkable thing about their construction is how our ancestors managed to raise such huge stones. About a mile north of the cairns are the ruins of **Carsluith Castle**, dating from the 16th century. The castle was built by the Browns of Carsluith.

CREETOWN

15 miles NW of Kirkcudbright on the A75

Set at the mouth of the River Cree, the neat village of Creetown was once a centre for the mining of granite. Now it is visited chiefly because of the **Creetown Gem Rock Museum**, housed in a former school. It was established in 1971, and since then has amassed a remarkable collection of gemstones and minerals from all over the world. There are also exhibitions on geology and on the formation of our landscapes from earliest times. It even has an "erupting volcano".

The Creetown Exhibition Centre in St John's Street has exhibits on local history and wildlife, as well as occasional exhibitions by local artists. Each year in September the **Creetown Country Weekend** takes place, featuring the best in country music.

TWYNHOLM

3 miles NW of Kirkcudbright on the A75

Twynholm is the home village of David Coulthard. The **David Coulthard Museum** in the main street has exhibits about the racing driver's life.

GATEHOUSE OF FLEET

7 miles NW of Kirkcudbright off the A75

This neat little town was the original for the "Kippletringan" of Scott's Guy Mannering. It sits on the Water of Fleet, about a mile from Fleet Bay, and was at one time a port, thanks to the canalisation of the river in 1823 by a local landowner, Alexander Murray of Cally House. The port area was known as **Port**

ANWOTH HOTEL

1 Fleet Street, Gatehouse-of-Fleet, Kirkudbrightshire DG7 2JT
Tel: 01557 814217 Fax: 01557 814030

With ten comfortable en suite rooms, there is no doubt that the **Anwoth Hotel** is the ideal base from which to explore this corner of Scotland. The food is superb, the wine is excellent, and the whisky well, over 300 single malts grace the bar. The owner, Ivan Bell, is proud of this array of liquid gold, as he is of the standards of comfort offered throughout his establishment. It even has literary associations, because, Dorothy L. Sayers' author of the whodunnit Five Red Herrings, stayed here in the 1930's and had potato scones and ginger cake daily. The service has remained high ever since!

MacAdam, though the site has now been grassed over. Within one of the former cotton mills is a museum called the **Mill on the Fleet**, which explains the history of the weaving industry in the town.

Gatehouse of Fleet was laid out in the 1760s as a cotton weaving centre by James Murray of Broughton, and today it remains more or less the way he planned it. He wished to create a great industrial town, though nowadays it is hard to imagine "dark Satanic mills" in such an idyllic setting.

It was supposedly in Gatehouse of Fleet, in the **Murray Arms**, that Burns set down the words to Scots Wha Hae. About a mile west of the town stands the substantial ruins of 15th century **Cardoness Castle** (Historic Scotland), former home of the McCullochs of Galloway. It stands on a rocky platform above the road, and is open to the public.

STRANRAER

Sitting at the head of Loch Ryan, and on the edge of the **Rhinns of Galloway**, that hammer shaped peninsula that juts out into the Irish Sea, Stranraer is a royal burgh that is now one of the main Scottish ports for Northern Ireland. It was granted its royal burgh charter in 1617, and is a town of narrow streets and old alleyways. In the centre of the town is the **Castle of St John**, a tower house which dates from the 16th century. Claverhouse used it as a base while hunting down Covenanters in the area, and it was later used as the town jail. It is now a museum. There is another museum in Stranraer. Situated in the **Old Town Hall**, it explains the history of the town and the county of Wigtownshire.

North West Castle is now a hotel, but at one time it was the home of **Sir John Ross** (1777-1856), who explored the legendary North West Passage between the Atlantic and the Pacific. He was born near Kirkcolm, son of a minister, and on one of his expeditions he discovered the Boothia Peninsula, mainland America's northernmost point.

On the sea front is the **Princess Victoria Monument**, which commemorates the sinking of the car ferry Princess Victoria in January 31 1953. It had left Stranraer bound for Larne with 127 passengers and 49 crew,

THE ARCHES RESTAURANT

77 Hanover Street, Stranraer, Wigtownshire DG9 7RX
Tel: 01776 702196

If it's good food you are after when visiting Stranraer, why not pay a visit to **The Arches Restaurant**? This spotlessly clean establishment can seat up to 60 in absolute comfort. Owed and run by June Cash, who is a great cook, it is popular with both visitors and locals alike. The varied menu is available all day, and contains many fine home made dishes using only the finest local produce where possible. The speciality of the restaurant is its roast of the day, and so popular is the place that you are advised to book in the summer months. Beers, wines and spirits are available to diners, and children are very welcome.

PETRUCCI'S PIZZERIA

2/6 George Street, Stranraer DG9 7RL
Tel: 01776 705837 Fax: 01776 706559

Set in the heart of Stranraer, **Petrucci's Pizzeria** is famous in the area for serving good food at reasonable prices. It is owned and managed by Sheila and Rafik Danelian, who take great pride in the food they serve. The pizza dough is made on the premises, as is the ice cream, and the menu is sure to contain something that will appeal to the most demanding of palates. The speciality, of course, is pizzas, and there is a fine selection to choose from. But the menu also includes soups, baked potatoes, salads, filled baguettes and an 'all day breakfast'. There is also a daily specials board and a children's menu that contains many tasty and appealing dishes.

Corsewall Lighthouse Hotel

Corsewall Point, near Stranraer,
Wigtownshire DG9 0QG
Tel: 01776 853220 Fax: 01776 854231
e-mail: lighthousehotel@btopenworld.com
website: www.lighthousehotel.co.uk

If you're looking for a place to stay with a difference, the the **Corsewall Lighthouse Hotel** is the place for you! It is set within the former living quarters of an 1815 lighthouse on a rocky headland - one that is still operational. This is Scottish hospitality at its best. Under the supervision of owner Gordon Ward, the living quarters have been refurbished to a high standard, and there are now nine sumptuous en suite rooms. The cuisine is outstanding, as you would expect in one of Scotland's newest luxury hotels one with a character all its own!

East Challoch Farm

Dunragit, near Stranraer DG9 8PY
Tel: 01581 400391

East Challoch Farm is seven miles east of Stranraer, and has panoramic views over Luce Bay. The farmhouse is homely and cosy, and offers three B&B rooms - a double, a twin/double and a single, all with en suite bathroom. All have a colour TV and tea and coffee making facilities. A comfortable and beautifully appointed self catering cottage is also available which sleeps six in three bedrooms. Hearty breakfasts are served each morning for both the B&B and self catering guests, with evening meals available by arrangement. This is an establishment which gets many repeat visitors, which is a recommendation in itself.

Cairnryan Caravan Park

Cairnryan, near Stranraer, Wigtownshire DG9 8QX
Tel: 01581 200231 Fax: 01561 200207

Cairnryan Caravan Park is family owned, and set in five acres overlooking beautiful Loch Ryan. It is the perfect place for a caravan holiday that can be as quiet or as hectic as you like. It sits close to Cairnryan village, the ferry terminal for Northern Ireland, and four miles from the large town of Stranraer. Each modern caravan is maintained to an extremely high standard, and are fully equipped with fitted kitchen, shower, wc and colour TV. The lounges are spacious, and the bedrooms are comfortable and cosy. All units have continental quilts, sheets and pillowcases for one double and two single beds, though towels and tea towels are not supplied. There is plenty of space round each van, and parking is easy.

The site itself has a fully licensed pub with pool and billiards tables, a laundrette, a swimming pool and a modernised shower and toilet block. In addition, there are many things to do and see in the area. Stranraer itself has a sports and leisure centre and many shops and supermarkets, and there are facilities for angling, both sea and fresh water. Golfers will appreciate the three challenging 18-hole courses within an easy drive of the site, and Turnberry – where the British Open is regularly held – is only 30 miles to the north. But why not own your own luxury unit on the site? There are a number of new and pre-owned caravans always for sale, and details are available on request. This part of Scotland is both picturesque and historic, and if you holiday here, you are sure to return again and again!

and on leaving the shelter of Loch Ryan encountered a horrific gale. Though lifeboats were launched, it eventually sank with the loss of 134 lives.

Three miles east of Stranraer are the magnificent **Castle Kennedy Gardens**. They cover 75 acres between two small lochs, and are laid out around the ivy-clad ruins of Castle Kennedy, destroyed by fire in 1710. The 2nd Earl of Stair began creating the gardens in 1733, and being a field marshal under the Duke of Marlborough, he used soldiers to construct some of it. Also within the gardens is the relatively modern **Lochinch Castle**, the present home of the Earl and Countess of Stair. It is not open to the public. South of the A75 is Soulseat Loch, where there is good fishing. A narrow peninsula with a few bumps and indentations on it juts out into the water - the site of **Soulseat Abbey**, of which not a stone now remains above ground. Three miles beyond Castle Kennedy on the A75 is the village of Dunragit, where you'll find **Glenwhan Gardens**, overlooking beautiful Luce Bay. They were started from scratch in 1979, and now cover 12 acres.

AROUND STRANRAER

CAIRNRYAN

5 miles N of Stranraer on the A77

Cairnryan is strung out along the coast of Loch Ryan. Between the main road and the coast is a complex of car parks, piers, jetties and offices, as this small village is the Scottish terminus of the P&O ferries to Larne, Northern Ireland. It was developed as a port during World War II, and had a breakers yard. It was here that the famous aircraft carrier **HMS Ark Royal** was scrapped.

GLENTROOL

20 miles NE of Stranraer on a minor road which leaves the A714 at Bargrennan

It was here, close to the lovely but lonely waters of Loch Trool, that Robert I defeated an English army in 1307. His soldiers had hidden themselves in the low hills above the loch, and when the English troops went past, they rolled great boulders down on them before attacking. It was a turning point in the Wars of Independence, as up until then Robert had had little success. **Bruce's Stone** above the loch commemorates the event.

GLENLUCE

10 miles E of Stranraer off the A75

The attractive little village of Glenluce has been bypassed by the A75, one of the main routes from southern Scotland and Northern England to the Irish ferries at Stranraer and Cairnryan. At one time it was the home of **Alexander Agnew**, nicknamed the "Devil of Luce", who was hanged for blasphemy in the 17th century. A mile to the north west are the ruins of **Glenluce Abbey** (Historic Scotland), founded in 1192 by Roland, Lord of Galloway. Mary Stuart once visited, as did James 1V and Robert I. **Castle of Park** is an imposing mansion built in about 1590 by Thomas Hay, son of the last abbot of Glenluce.

Immediately after the Reformation, the then Earl of Cassillis, head of the great Kennedy family, claimed the property and lands of Glenluce. He persuaded one of the monks to forge the abbot's signature on a document granting him the lands, then had the monk

River Cree, nr Newton Stewart

WHITECAIRN FARM CARAVAN PARK

Glenluce, Wigtownshire DG8 0NZ
Tel: 01581 300267 Fax: 01581 300434
e-mail: enquiries@whitecairncaravans.co.uk
website: www.whitecairncaravans.co.uk

Set in some wonderful rolling countryside one and a half miles from the historic village of Glenluce, **Whitecairn Caravan Park** has a four star VisitScotland grading for its modern amenities and hospitality. Touring caravans are more than welcome, and the toilets, washing blocks and shower rooms have the cleanliness you would expect from such a prestigious establishment. Electric hook up points, of course, come as standard, and in addition, there is a fine array of static caravans that can be hired by the week or fortnight. You can even buy one and set it up permanantly in a beautiful part of Scotland that just cries out to be explored on foot or by car!

Prices start at about £3,000 for a used model right up to £9,000. Two and three bedroom models are available. This six acre site is family run, so you know you'll be getting personal service if you bring along your tourer, or decide to rent or buy. Children are more than welcome, and the owners, the Rankin family, will go out of their way to make you more than welcome as a visitor or as a permanent guest should you decide to buy from the range of wonderful models on offer.

CREEBRIDGE HOUSE HOTEL

Minnigaff, Newton Stewart,
Dumfries and Galloway DG8 6NP
Tel: 01671 402121 e-mail: info@creebridge.co.uk
Fax: 01671 403258 website: www.creebridge.co.uk

Dumfries and Galloway is a fascinating and historic area of Scotland that is gradually being discovered and explored by discerning tourists. It sits in the south west of the country, where it is warmed by the Gulf Stream, meaning that the climate is almost always mild. The award winning **Creebridge House Hotel** sits right in the heart of the area, close to the picturesque and tranquil town of Newton Stewart on the River Cree. It is set in three acres of wonderful gardens and woodland, two minutes walk from the centre of town, and has 19 en suite rooms that are the last word in taste and comfort. Each room has a satellite TV, direct dial telephone and tea and coffee making facilities.

The cuisine is wonderful, and uses fresh local produce wherever possible to create a menu that fuses tradition with up to date ideas on cooking and presentation. There are table d'hote and à la carte menus in the main restaurant, as well as more informal meals in Bridge's Brasserie. And if it's a quiet drink you're after, then the Bridges Bar is the place for you, with its fine selection of real ales, wines and malt whiskies. For that relaxing break, you can't go far wrong with the Creebridge House Hotel!

IVY BANK COTTAGE

Creebridge, Newton Stewart, Wigtownshire DG8 6PQ
Tel: 01671 403139
e-mail: chris@ivybank.fslife.co.uk

Set on the beautiful banks of the River Cree on the outskirts of this thriving town, **Ivy Bank Cottage** is one of the best bed and breakfast establishments in the area. The two storey building itself is very picturesque, and goes back over 300 years, making it one of the oldest dwelling houses in Dumfries and Galloway. It has been tastefully refurbished while retaining many period features, but there's nothing old about the standards of service and hospitality. Chris and Diane Izod have created a real home from home, and with only two letting rooms you are assured of that personal touch. There's a TV, plus drink making facilities in both rooms, and the cottage is only five minute's stroll from the centre of town.

Dogs are allowed by prior arrangement in this non smoking establishment, and with a beautiful garden that slopes down to the river, you're sure of a place to while away those warm summer evenings you get in this part of Scotland because of the Gulf Stream. There is private parking, drying facilities, a resident's lounge and a dining room which overlooks the garden and the river. The breakfasts are the best, Chris is told, so why not try for yourself. The area itself really is Scotlands best kept secret for golf, fishing, walking, birdwatching or just relaxing and ....empty roads!

GALLOWAY ARMS HOTEL

54-58 Victoria Street, Newton Stewart DG8 6DB
Tel: 01671 402653 e-mail: gordon@gallowayarmshotel.fsnet
Fax: 01671 401202 website: www.gallowayarms.org.net

The **Galloway Arms Hotel** dates from about 1750, and is Newtown Stewart's oldest building. But it offers service, quality and comfort that is firmly rooted in the 21st century. There are 19 rooms, all en suite, and each has a TV and tea and coffee making facilities. The place was once owned by the Earl of Galloway when it was one of the best coaching inns in the south of Scotland, and the present owners, Wilma and Gordon Andrews, want to make sure that this reputation is maintained and enhanced. They are determined that the kitchens, for instance, make use of only the finest local produce wherever possible.You can have a full dinner with fine wines, a pub lunch or even just a tasty snack.

One part of the hotel, the Toll House, has been turned into a small museum that celebrates the railways of Scotland, and the way to the beer garden takes you through Invergordon Station. Not the real one of course, but a room that holds signs and other memorabilia from a railway station that once stood in the Highlands. So if it's good food, comfort and a memorable stay you're after, you're on the right track if you make for the Galloway Arms Hotel!

Duncree House

King Street, Newton Stewart, Wigtownshire DG8 6DL
Tel: 01671 402792 Fax: 01671 402088
e-mail: susan-p@duncreehouse.fslife.co.uk
website: www.duncreehouse.com

Situated on the edge of the attractive town of Newton Stewart, **Duncree House** is owned and managed by Susan Pianta-Morrish and Pietro Cardile. It is a substantial and impressive Victorian stone-built house in two and a half acres of grounds, and was formerly a shooting lodge built by the local laird. It has a number of comfortable and beautifully decorated rooms, some en suite, and is the ideal place for a B&B stopover or a longer, relaxing break. Healthy living retreat weeks are available, with fully inclusive tariffs, where you can get away from it all, rediscover your creative self, and recharge your batteries!

Craigwelder B&B

34 Main Street, Kirkcowan, Newton Stewart DG8 0HG
Tel: 01671 830205 Fax: 01671 830246
e-mail: cbb1262@aol.com

Set in the main street of this quiet and picturesque village, the **Craigwelder B&B** offers the best in accommodation for the discerning tourist. It has two huge, comfortable letting rooms which sleep up to eight people in comfort and style in a house which is nearly 400 years old. There is a TV in each room, as well as coffee and tea making facilities. In addition, there is a fridge, microwave and toaster. This quiet area of Scotland is rich in history and stunning scenery, and this is the ideal place to stay while you explore it.

Clugston Farm

near Newton Stewart,
Wigtownshire DG8 9BH
Tel: 01671 830338

Clugston Farm is a 500 acre sheep and cattle farm set in some stunning countryside a few miles outside Newton Stewart.

It has bed and breakfast accommodation in three comfortable rooms in the traditional farmhouse, plus two self catering flats in a newly converted wing. The flats each have an open plan living living//dining/cooking area which is fully equipped with all mod cons, plus a bedroom and a bathroom with en suite shower room. Each one has central heating and double glazing. The three rooms consist of a double and twin upstairs, and a double with wash hand basin downstairs. All three are well appointed and extremely comfortable.

In addition, there is a small picturesque cottage, called Ash tree Cottage, near the River Bladnoch, and it is available on a self catering basis. It can accommodate up to five people and is fully equipped to make any stay a comfortable and memorable experience. Unlike the Highlands, this area isn't crowded at any time of the year, though it has history and heritage aplenty. Janet Adams, who owns the accommodation, offers you the best of Scottish hospitality in one of the best areas of Scotland for a quiet break.

murdered. He then prosecuted the men who had done the foul deed on his behalf, and executed them in the name of justice.

NEWTON STEWART

22 miles E of Stranraer on the A75

The burgh of Newton Stewart sits on the River Cree, close to where it enters Wigtown Bay. It is a pleasant, clean town which makes the ideal centre for fishing or walking. **Newton Stewart Museum**, in York Road, has displays and exhibits about the history of the town and immediate area. In Queen Street you'll find an unusual but internationally known little museum called **Sophie's Puppetstube and Dolls House Museum**, which has 50 beautifully made doll's houses and room settings. The scale is 1:12, and all the exhibits are behind glass. There is also a collection of over 200 exquisitely dressed dolls.

Martyrs' Graves

Six miles west of Newton Stewart is the picturesque village of **Kirkcowan**, with a church dating from 1834 which has external stairs to the gallery.

WIGTOWN

23 miles E of Stranraer on the A714

This small royal burgh has achieved fame as being **Scotland's Book Town**, and has many bookshops and publishing houses. In the kirkyard of Wigtown Parish Church are the **Martyrs' Graves.** In 1685, during the time of the Covenanters, two women - one aged 18 and one aged 63 - were tied to stakes at the mouth of the River Bladnoch for adhering to the Covenant. Rather than renounce their principles, they drowned as the tide rose over their heads. The spot where the martyrdom took place is marked by a small **Martyrs Monument** on what are now salt marshes (see also Stirling). On a small hill behind the town is another **Covenanters Monument**, this time a slender column.

One mile west of the town is **Bladnoch Distillery**, Scotland's most southerly whisky distillery. There is a visitors centre, and guided tours showing the distilling process are available.

CHAPEL FINIAN

16 miles SE of Stranraer on the A747

Beside the road that runs along the western shore of **The Machars**, the name given to that great peninsula that sticks out into the Irish Sea between Luce and Wigtown Bays, you'll find the foundations of a small church called Chapel Finian. The most interesting thing about them is their great age, as they probably date from the 10th century. At a later date the chapel was probably used as a stopping off point for people making a pilgrimage to Whithorn, 12 miles to the south east. St Finian of Moville lived during the 6th century, and had founded a great monastic school in Northern Ireland where St Columba studied.

WHITHORN

27 miles SE of Stranraer on the A746

This tiny royal burgh is often called the "Cradle of Scottish Christianity". Long before Columba came to Iona, a monk called **St Ninian** had set up a monastery here. It would have been a typical Celtic monastery, with a high circular bank, or "rath", enclosing an area of monks' cells, workshops and chapels. But this monastery was different in one respect. The main church was made of stone, not the more common wood, and was painted white. For this reason it was called **Candida Casa**, or "White House", When this part of Scotland was later absorbed into the kingdom of Northumbria, the name was translated into Anglo Saxon as "Hwit Aerne", and thus the name Whithorn came about.

The place was subsequently an important ecclesiastical and trading centre. In the 12th century Fergus, Lord of Galloway, founded **Whithorn Priory** (Historic Scotland) here, and its church became the cathedral for the diocese of Galloway. All that is left of the priory church is its nave and crypt, and to the east of the crypt may be seen some scant foundations which may have belonged to Ninian's original whitewashed church. The cathedral, with its relics of St Ninian, eventually became a place of pilgrimage, and many Scottish monarchs came to pray here.

Whithorn Priory Ruins

The town's main street, George Street, is wide and spacious, with many small Georgian, Regency and Victorian houses lining it. **The Pend**, dating from about 1500, is an archway leading to the priory ruins, and above it are the royal arms of Scotland. Close to the priory is the **Priory Museum** (Historic Scotland), with a collection of stones on which are carved early Christian symbols. One of them, the **Latinus Stone**, dates from the 5th century, and may be the earliest carved Christian stone in Scotland. Some years ago, excavations were undertaken at Whithorn, and at the **Whithorn Visitors Centre** you can learn about what was found during the dig.

Three miles to the south east is the tiny fishing village of **Isle of Whithorn.** On a headland are the 13th century ruins of the tiny **St Ninian's Chapel**. It was probably built for pilgrims to Whithorn Priory who came by sea. On the shore at nearby Glasserton is **St Ninian's Cave**, which has incised crosses on its walls. A legend states that St Ninian himself came to this cave to seek solitude and pray.

Isle of Whithorn Village

THE PHEASANT INN

2 Wigtown Road, Sorbie, Wigtownshire DG8 8EL
Tel: 01988 850223 Fax: 01988 850307
e-mail: pheasant.inn@virgin.net
website: www.pheasant-hotel.co.uk

Close to Wigtown, Scotland's book town, is the peaceful village of Sorbie, where you will find picturesque **The Pheasant Inn**, which dates back to the 17th century. Owned and run by Linda Marlow and Jim Powell, it offers first class holiday or B&B accommodation in four attractive and comfortable rooms, two of which are en suite, with the other two having private facilities. All have TVs and tea/coffee making facilities. The restaurant serves excellent food, and you can also have a bar meal in the 'locals bar' or the cosy lounge. It is open all year, and makes an excellent base from which to explore an area steeped in history and legend.

HARBOUR INN

18 South Crescent, Garlieston, Wigtownshire DG8 8BQ
Tel: 01988 600688

Set in a building which dates from the 18th century, the **Harbour Inn** is a hostelry with lots of 'olde worlde' character. Owned and managed by Margaret Harrison, it offers excellent food and drink as well as three well appointed and comfortable en suite B&B rooms. The bar is popular with locals and visitors alike, as is the restaurant. In fact, you are well advised to book a table at weekends for the Saturday evening meals and the ever popular Sunday roasts Not far away is the small town of Whithorn, Scotland's 'cradle of Christianity', and it makes an excellent base from which to explore this historical and picturesque corner of Scotland.

QUEEN'S ARMS HOTEL

22 Main Street, Isle of Whithorn, Newton Stewart, Wigtownshire DG8 8LF
Tel: 01988 500369 Fax: 01988 500807
e-mail: queens.arms@virgin.net

Wigtownshire in South West Scotland is is the cradle of Christianity in Scotland, and one of the most historic areas in the country. In the picturesque fishing village of Isle of Whithorn (not really an island!), with its St Ninian associations, you will find the **Queen's Arms Hotel,** a superb family run inn that offers the best in Scottish hospitality. The whitewashed buildings date from 1689, and were formerly two old cottage and a stable which has been converted into the bottom bar. Leaseholders Ann and Peter Stafford had been coming on holiday to the Isle of Whithorn for over 33 years before taking over the hotel two years ago, and during that time they have created a real home from home atmosphere for its residents as well as a great place to eat or have a quiet drink. Their efforts were rewarded in 2001 when they were nominated for the prestigious Carlsberg Award for Customer Service.

It boasts nine no smoking rooms, seven of which are fully en suite. Some of them have beautiful sea views, and all are comfortable and beautifully appointed, with tea and coffee making facilities in each one. You can book on a B&B or room only basis, and there are special discounts for longer stays. The bar is warm and cosy in winter and cool and welcoming in summer. One of its main features is an open fire that adds to the 'olde worlde' ambience of the place. It is popular with both visitors and locals alike, and is the ideal place to relax and chat to the local people, who will make you more than welcome. There is always a locally brewed ale on offer, as well as Tetley Smooth, Calder's Cream, Carlsberg, Stella, Guinness and Strongbow cider. A fine range of wines and malt whiskies is also available plus a selection of soft drinks should you be behind the wheel.

The food at the Queen's Arms Hotel is excellent. Peter is a self taught chef who loves creating new dishes, and he has earned quite a reputation in the area for his cooking! The cuisine is based on local produce in season wherever possible, with fish, naturally enough, playing a prominent part. Peter prides himself on the freshness of his ingredients and the attention he gives to each dish. The restaurant area seats 60 in absolute comfort , and is a spacious yet welcoming place, with bright table covers, parquet floor and prints on the wall. Lunches are served between 12.00 - 14.30 and dinner between 118.30 - 21.00 throughout the year. But beware - so popular is the restaurant that you are well advised to book a table between April and October.

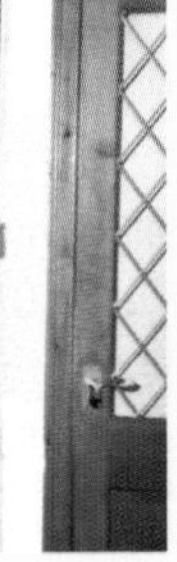

The Queen's Arms Hotel is one of those establishments that combine excellent service with good old fashioned value for money. This is why people come back to it time and again. As soon as you discover its delights, you will too!

KIRKMADRINE

8 miles S of Stranraer on a minor road off the A716

In the porch of what was the tiny medieval parish church of Toskerton are some old inscribed stones, the **Kirkmadrine Stones**, thought to be the oldest in Scotland after those at Whithorn. They were discovered when the ruins of the church were being rebuilt and converted into a burial chamber by a local family.

ARDWELL

10 miles S of Stranraer on the A716

Ardwell Gardens are grouped round the 18th century Ardwell House on the Rhinns of Galloway. They are a testimony to the mildness of the climate in these parts, and feature both a woodland and a formal garden, as well as good views out over Luce Bay.

PORT LOGAN

12 miles S of Stranraer on the B7065

Port Logan is a small fishing village situated on Port Logan Bay. Close by is the **Logan Fish Pond**, a remarkable tidal pond, famous for its tame sea fish, which can be fed by hand. It was constructed in about 1800 as a source of fresh fish for the tables of nearby Logan House.

If anywhere illustrates the mildness of the climate in this part of Scotland, it is **Logan Botanic Garden**, part of the National Botanic Gardens of Scotland. Here, growing quite freely, are exotic plants and trees such as the tree fern (which can normally only survive in glass houses in Britain), the eucalyptus, palm trees, magnolias and passion flowers. In fact, over 40 per cent of all the plants and trees at Logan come from the Southern hemisphere.

KIRKMAIDEN

15 miles S of Stranraer on the B7065

Kirkmaiden is the most southerly parish in Scotland. Four miles south of the village is the **Mull of Galloway**, Scotland's most southerly point. People are sometimes surprised to discover that it is further south than either Durham or Hartlepool in England. The lighthouse was built in 1828 to the designs of Robert Stevenson, and sits on the massive cliffs, 270 feet above the sea.

PORTPATRICK

6 miles SW of Stranraer on the A77

This lovely little seaside village is at the

The Front, Portpatrick

Harbour House Hotel

Harbour Square, Portpatrick, Wigtownshire DG9 8JW
Tel: 01776 810456 Fax: 01776 810488
e-mail: iancerexhe@aol.com
website: www.harbourhouse.co.uk

Portpatrick is a small, picturesque holiday resort and port on the beautiful Rhinns of Galloway. Within the village you will find the family-run **Harbour House Hotel**, housed in a smart, whitewashed building that dates from 1790. The interior of this hotel is full of olde-worlde atmosphere, with dark wood, log fires, luxury carpeting and a magnificent circular stone staircase. Sitting close to the sea front, it offers nine rooms to the discerning tourist, most of them en suite, and all are comfortable, well furnished and tastefully decorated. each one has a colour TV, tea and coffee making facilities, and most have splendid sea views.

The restaurant (which is open to non-residents) holds 30 in comfort, and superb food is served at lunch time and in the evenings, using only the finest and freshest local produce wherever possible. You can also eat in the cosy lounge bar, which is a favourite haunt of the locals – always the sign of a first class establishment. You can choose from a printed menu or from a daily specials board. Or why not relax over a quiet drink? The bar has a great selection of beers, lagers, real ales, wines, spirits, liqueurs and soft drinks, and there is sure to be something to please everyone. On Friday and Saturday evenings, there is usually some form of live musical entertainment. The Harbour House Hotel welcomes children, and the lounge bar holds a children's certificate. Why not organise a fishing or golf break, using the hotel as your base? You can ring for details, and special rates apply.

western end of the Southern Upland Way. At one time it was the main Scottish port for Northern Ireland, but was in such an exposed position that Stranraer eventually took over. It sits round a little harbour that is always busy, and, with its old cottages and craft shops, has become a small holiday resort. On a headland to the south of the village are the ruins of **Dunskey Castle**, built in the early 16th century by the Adair family. Within the village is the ruined **Portpatrick Parish Church**. It was built in the 17th century, and unusually, had a round tower. South of the village is **Knockinaam Lodge** (privately owned) where Churchill and Eisenhower met over several months to plan the D-Day landings.

3 Ayrshire and Arran

Ayrshire was at one time Scotland's largest Lowland county. Facing the Firth of Clyde, it is ringed by high moorland and hills which slope down to a rich agricultural patchwork of small fields, country lanes, woodland and picturesque villages. The poet Keats, when he visited it to pay his respects to the birthplace of Burns, compared it to Devon.

Bennane Head

The county was formerly divided into three parts: Carrick, Kyle and Cunninghame.

Carrick is the most southerly, and its scenery owes a lot neighbouring Galloway. It is separated from Kyle, a rich dairying area where the native Ayrshire cattle can be seen doting the fields, by the River Doon. To the north, beyond the River Irvine, is Cunninghame, which at one time was the most industrialised of the three, though it managed this without losing its rural aspect. But Kyle itself was divided by the River Ayr into Kyle Regal and Kyle Stewart, reflecting the fact that one section was owned by the king while the other was owned by high stewards of Scotland, who eventually went on to be kings in their own right.

Ayrshire and Robert Burns, known to all Scottish people as "Rabbie" (never, ever Robbie!) are inextricably linked. He was born in Alloway, which nowadays is a well-off suburb of Ayr, and spent most of his life in the county before moving south to Dumfriesshire when he was 29 years old. We know a lot about the man, and all around you will see Burns associations - places he visited, places he lived, places where he drank, places where his friends lived - and all are carefully signposted. A full week could easily be spent tootling around the main roads and narrow lanes of the county visiting such places as Tarbolton, Mauchline, Ayr, Kilmarnock, Irvine, Failford and Kirkoswald.

Isle of Arran from Ardrossan

There are three main towns in the county - Ayr, Kilmarnock and Irvine. Irvine is the largest, though it was not always thus. In the 1960s it was designated a new town, and took an overspill population from Glasgow. Industrial estates were built, factories were opened and new housing established. However, its central core is still worth exploring. Kilmarnock is traditionally the industrial centre, though it is an ancient town, and Ayr was the administrative and commercial capital before Ayrshire as a local government unit ceased to exist in the 1970s.

Carnell Countryside

Up until the 1960s, when more exotic places took over, the Ayrshire coast was Glasgow's holiday playground. Known as the "Costa Clyde", it attracted thousands of people each year who flocked to such holiday resorts as Troon, Largs, Prestwick, Girvan and Ayr itself. These halcyon days are now gone, though it is still a popular place for day trips and for people to retire to, giving it a new nickname - the "Costa Geriatrica". The coastline is also famous for another reason - golf. The first British Open Golf Championship was held at Prestwick in 1860, and both Troon and Turnberry regularly host the tournament in modern times.

Ayrshire is also a county of castles, from the spectacular Culzean (pronounced "Cull-ane") perched on a clifftops above the sea in Carrick, to Kelburn near Largs or Dean Castle in Kilmarnock, with its collection of rare musical instruments.

The Ayrshire coalfield used to employ thousands of people, though nowadays not a deep mine remains. But even at its height, the industry never did as much damage to the environment as in, say, South Yorkshire or the Welsh valleys. Now you wouldn't know that the industry ever existed, and a day just motoring round the quiet lanes is a relaxing experience in itself.

Twenty miles offshore is the island of Arran, at one time within the county of Buteshire, but now more associated with Ayrshire. It has been called "Scotland in Miniature", and is a wonderful blend of wild scenery, pastoral views and rocky coastlines. Its history stretches right back into the mists of time, as the many standing stones and ancient burial cairns testify. Also within Bute were two other islands - Great and Little Cumbrae. Little Cumbrae is largely uninhabited, apart from one or two houses, but Great Cumbrae has on it the town of Millport, a gem of a holiday resort. But within Millport is another, but lesser known, gem - Cumbrae Cathedral, the smallest cathedral in Britain. It is truly one of the hidden places of Scotland.

AYRSHIRE AND ARRAN

PLACES TO STAY, EAT, DRINK AND SHOP

50	Jock's Restaurant and Crafts, Kirkmichael	Restaurant, tearoom and shop	Page 64
51	Kings Arms Hotel, Barr	Hotel and restaurant	Page 66
52	Boars Head Hotel, Colmonell	Hotel	Page 67
53	Dunduff Farm, nr Dunure	B&B and self catering	Page 70
54	Christina's Bar, Ayr	Pub with restautant	Page 71
55	Café Med, Ayr	Café and restaurant	Page 72
56	Beechwood Guest House Hotel, Ayr	Guest House	Page 72

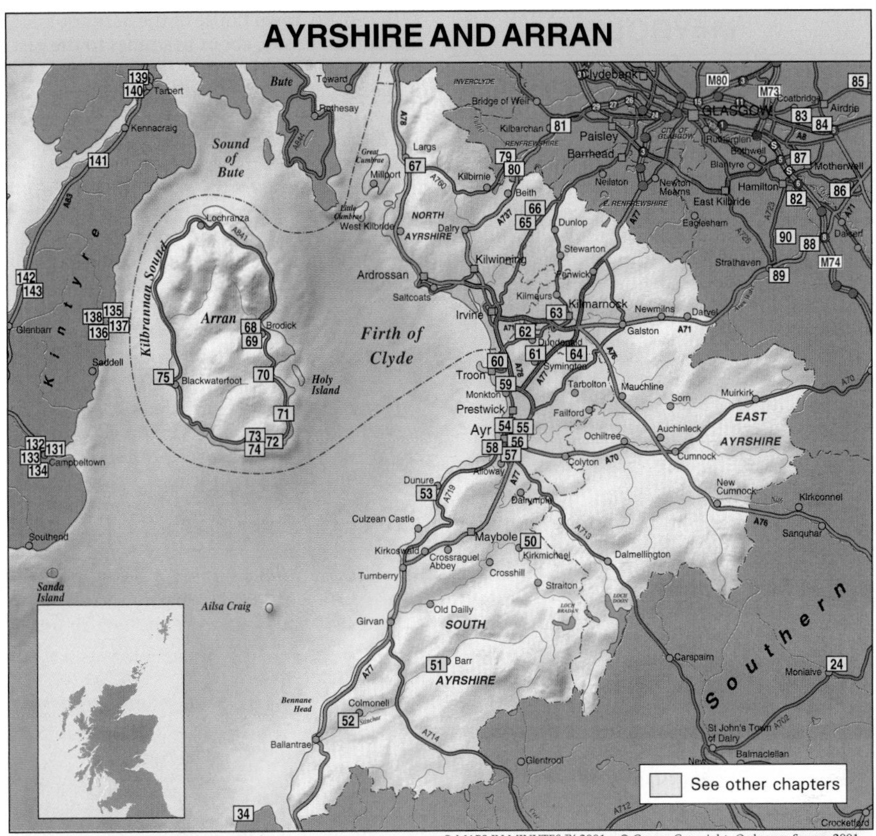

© MAPS IN MINUTES ™ 2001 © Crown Copyright, Ordnance Survey 2001

PLACES TO STAY, EAT, DRINK AND SHOP

57	Belmont Guest House, Ayr	Guest House	Page 72
58	Beaches Tearoom And Gift Shop, Ayr	Café, tearoom and gift shop	Page 72
59	The Wheatsheaf Monkton Inn, Monkton	Pub with food	Page 74
60	Fordell, Barassie	Bed and Breakfast	Page 74
61	Stable Cottage, Symington	Self catering	Page 75
62	Taste Buds, Dundonald	Café and tearoom	Page 76
63	The Coffee Club, Kilmarnock	Café, tearoom and restaurant	Page 80
64	Craigie Inn, Craigie	Pub with food	Page 80
65	Burnhouse Manor Hotel, Burnhouse	Hotel and restaurant	Page 86
66	Shotts Farm, Barrmill	Bed and Breakfast	Page 86
67	Belmont House, Largs	Bed and Breakfast	Page 88
68	Dunvegan House, Brodick	Guest House	Page 88
69	Point House and Cottages, Kings Cross	Self catering	Page 90
70	Glenisle Hotel, Lamlash	Hotel and restaurant	Page 90
71	Norwood, Whiting Bay	Self catering	Page 91
72	Drumla Farm, Kildonan	Self catering	Page 92
73	Breadalbane Hotel, Kildonan	Hotel and restaurant	Page 92
74	Kildonan Schoolhouses, Kildonan	Self catering	Page 93
75	Blackwaterfoot Lodge, Blackwaterfoot	Hotel, restaurant and self catering	Page 94

MAYBOLE

This quiet town is the capital of Carrick, and sits on a hillside about four miles inland from the coast. It was here that Burns's parents, William Burnes (he changed the name to Burns not long after) and Agnes Broun met in 1756.

In 1562, a famous meeting took place in Maybole between John Knox, the Scottish reformer, and Abbot Quentin Kennedy of nearby Crossraguel Abbey. The purpose of the meeting was to debate the significance and doctrine of the Mass, and it attracted a huge crown of people, even though it was held in the small room of a house where the provost of the town's collegiate church lived. Forty people from each side were actually allowed into the room to hear the debate, which lasted for three days. It only broke up - with no conclusion reached - when the town ran out of food to feed the thronging masses round the door. The ruins of **Maybole Collegiate Church** can still be seen.

There are two "castles" in Maybole. One, now part of the former **Town Hall**, was the 17th century town house of the lairds of Blairquhan Castle, about five miles to the east of the town. The other is still referred to as **Maybole Castle**, though it too was a town house, this time for the Earls of Cassillis. There is a curious legend attached to the building. It seems that Lady Jean Hamilton, daughter of the Earl of Haddington, was in love with Sir John Faa of Dunbar (nicknames "King of the Gypsies"), but was forced against her will to marry John, 6th Earl of Cassillis, head of the great Kennedy family. Unwillingly she went to live in Ayrshire, but never forgot her first love. One day when the Earl was away on business, Sir John came to Ayrshire with 14 gypsies, and carried away his love.

However, the earl returned unexpectedly, and set out in pursuit. He caught the gypsies and made his wife watch as he hung Sir John and his men at his main castle of Cassillis. He then incarcerated his wife in Maybole Castle, where she spent the rest of her life in one small room making tapestries. A window high in the castle is still pointed out as the room where she lived, and above it are some carvings of heads, said to be those of Sir John and his gypsies. However, the story is

Jock's Restaurant and Crafts

24 Patna Road, Kirkmichael, Ayrshire
Tel: 01655 750499

Kirkmichael is a picturesque village which nestles among the Ayrshire hills. Every year in May it hosts the Kirkmichael International Guitar Festival, and **Jock's Restaurant and Crafts** participates fully. It is an excellent place to stop for a lunch, snack or evening meal, and is situated within what were 17th century weavers cottages.

The interior is full of character and charm, and under the ownership of Rosalind McIlwraith and Bob Russell, it has an enviable reputation for its cuisine. Thanks to resident chef Bill Baird, it serves a wonderful range of lunches, afternoon teas and dinners. Vegetarian dishes are available, as well as steaks, lamb, pork, poultry and fish. And during the summer months you must try the Ayrshire potatoes that accompany some of the dishes – they are delicious! The restaurant also sells a fine range of craft goods. Bob himself works in wood, and most of the wooden pieces on offer are by him. There is superb garden furniture, small turned bowls and vases, pieces in bronze, Burns souvenirs, model ships, and a wonderful selection of greetings cards made in the village itself.

The place is named after a local man who was once the village's "Jock of all Trades". But Jock's Restaurant and Crafts specialise in only two things – great food and wonderful craftwork!

completely untrue, as letters written by both the Earl and his Countess to each other show that they were a close and loving couple.

A few miles west of Maybole, near the farm of Drumshang, is the curiously named **Electric Brae**, on the A719 road between Ayr and Turnberry. Stop your car on the convenient layby at the side of the road (people used to do this on the road itself, but it became too busy), put it out of gear, let off the brake, and be amazed as it rolls uphill. Better still, lay a football on the layby's surface, and watch it roll uphill as well. The phenomenon has nothing to do with electricity, and everything to do with an optical illusion. The surrounding land makes you think that the road ascends the side of a low hill when in fact it descends.

AROUND MAYBOLE

KIRKMICHAEL

3 miles E of Maybole on the B7045

Like its neighbour Crosshill, Kirkmichael is a former weaving village. However, its roots go deeper into Scottish history. The **Parish Church** dates from 1790, and the picturesque lych-gate from about 1700. Within the kirkyard is the grave of a Covenanter called Gilbert MacAdam, killed in 1686.

Kirkmichael is the scene, every May, of the **Kirkmichael International Guitar Festival**, which draws musicians from all over the world. It covers everything from jazz to pop and country to classical. Huge marquees are erected, and local pubs host impromptu jamming sessions and folk concerts.

DALMELLINGTON

11 miles E of Maybole on the A713

This former mining village sits on the banks of the Doon. Over the last few years, it has exploited its rich heritage, and created some visitors centres and museums that explain the village's industrial past. The **Dunaskin Open Air Museum** covers 110 acres, has many facets and each one is well worth exploring. The **Iron Works** were first opened in the 1840s, and are now the largest restored Victorian Ironworks in Europe. There are also **The Brickworks**, and at the **Scottish Industrial Railway Centre** steam trains run on a restored track. The **Cathcartson Centre** in the village is housed in weaving cottages dating from the 18th century, showing how weavers lived long ago.

A couple of miles beyond Dalmellington is a minor road that takes you to lovely **Loch Doon**, the source of the river that Burns wrote about. It was here, during World War I, that a **School of Aerial Gunnery** was going to be set up. Millions of pounds were wasted on it before the plans were finally abandoned. When a hydroelectric scheme was set up in the 1930s, the water level of the loch was raised. **Loch Doon Castle**, which had stood on an island in the loch, was dismantled stone by stone and reassembled on the shore.

CROSSHILL

3 miles SE of Maybole, on the B7023

Crosshill is a former weaving village, established in about 1808, with many small cottages where the weavers formerly lived. Most were Irish, attracted to the place by the prospect of work. There are no outstanding buildings, nor does it have much history or legend attached to it. But it is a conservation village with a quiet charm, and well worth visiting because of this alone.

STRAITON

6 miles SE of Maybole on the B741

From this lovely little village on the Water of Girvan runs a narrow road south called the **Nick o' the Balloch**. It doesn't go through the Carrick of gentle fields or verdant valleys, but over the wild hills and moorland that make the edges of this area so beautiful, and finally drops down into Glentrool.

Straiton itself is composed of picturesque little cottages facing each other across a main street, some with roses growing round the door. The local pub, The Black Bull, dates from 1766, while parts of **St Cuthbert's Parish Church** are even older, dating back to 1510. Close to the village is **Blairquhan**, a Tudor-Gothic mansion that sits on the site of an earlier tower house. It was once a Kennedy stronghold, but is now owned by the Hunter Blair family. On a hill above the village stands the **Hunter Blair Monument**, built in 1856 to commemorate James Hunter Blair, killed at the Battle of Inkerman.

OLD DAILLY

9 miles S of Maybole on the B734

The ruins of **Old Dailly Parish Church** stand beside the road. They date from the 16th century, and within the kirkyard are two hefty stones called the **Charter Stones**. They were used in local trials of strength when people tried to lift them.

Within the kirkyard is buried the pre-Raphelite artist **William Bell Scott**, who was staying at nearby **Penkill Castle** when he died. Many members of the pre-Raphelite Brotherhood visited the place, including **Dante Gabriel Rossetti**. Close by is the 17th century **Bargany House**, with its marvellous gardens. The mining village of **New Dailly**, with its T shaped **New Dailly Parish Church** of 1766 is three miles to the east.

BARR

11 miles S of Maybole on the B734

Tucked in a fold of the Carrick hills, Barr is an idyllic village which was once the site of the wonderfully named **Kirkdandie Fair**. It was the largest annual fair in Southern Scotland during the late 18th and early 19th centuries, and was held on a strip of land where once had stood Kirkdandie Church. It's main claim to fame was the fighting that took place every year. People even came over from Ireland to participate, and there would be great pitched battles.

Above Barr is the estate of Changue (pronounced "Shang"), to which an old legend is attached. The **Laird of Changue** was always penniless, so he made a pact with the Devil. If he became wealthy, Satan could claim his soul. He duly became rich, but at the appointed time of his death he refused to hand over his soul. He challenged the Devil to fight for it. Drawing a large circle on the ground, he said that the first person to be forced out of it would be the loser. After a bitter struggle, the Laird won. Up until the end of the 19th century, a great circle on some grassland was shown as the place where all this took place.

A small leaflet has been produced which describes some walks that can be taken in the surrounding hills.

KINGS ARMS HOTEL

1 Stinchar Road, Barr, near Girvan,
Ayrshire KA26 9TW
Tel: 01465 861230 Fax: 861604
e-mail: kingsarmsbarr.co.uk

The Kings Arms Hotel has been described as the "best kept secret in Ayrshire", and this is no idle boast. It is set in the conservation village of Barr, and is an old coaching inn dating back over 100 years. It is full of character, with whitewashed walls and old beams.

But not only is it a superb hotel which boasts six tastefully decorated rooms, it is also the village pub, with a bar/lounge that serves great beers, wines and spirits. This is an historic area, and the locals will regale you with tales of when the village was at the heart of the smuggling trade! The Pot Restaurant forms part of the hotel, and serves superb food. You can order from a comprehensive menu that includes steaks, fresh fish, chicken and a range of vegetarian dishes, all cooked on the premises. This isn't "pub grub", but cuisine of the highest quality at affordable prices. The speciality of the house is the "Barr Steak Pie" - like no other you've tasted, and made with large chunks of flavoursome steak topped with puff pastry.

So seek it out – such is the quality and service that the Kings Arms Hotel may not be a secret for much longer!

Boars Head Hotel

4 Main Street, Colmonell, near Girvan, Ayrshire KA26 0RY
Tel/Fax: 01465 881371

The Boars Head Hotel is a friendly hostelry that offers a great Scottish welcome. With its six ensuite rooms, it also offers the finest in hospitality. Owned by Pauline and Alasdair Ash, it makes the ideal base for exploring this unspoilt part of Ayrshire, or for fishing in the Stinchar. It also has a friendly bar, and people come from all over to sample the evening meals, which are cooked using the freshest of ingredients. To work up a hearty appetite, walk to the top of nearby Knockdolian Hill. On a clear day you can see Ireland!

COLMONELL

19 Miles S of Maybole on the B734

The River Stinchar is the southernmost of Ayrshire's rivers, and flows through a lovely valley bordered on both sides by high moorland and hills. In this valley, four miles from the mouth of the river, sits Colmonell. It's an attractive village of small cottages, with the romantic ruins of **Kirkhill Castle** close by. Knockdolian Hill, two miles west, was at one time called the "false Ailsa Craig" because of its resemblance to the volcanic island out in the Firth of Clyde.

BALLANTRAE

23 miles S of Maybole on the A77

When on a walking tour of Carrick in 1876, R.L. Stevenson spent a night in Ballantrae, a small fishing village on the coast. However, the reception he got was icy, as the villagers took exception to his avant garde clothes. He got his revenge by writing "The Master of Ballantrae", which confused everyone by having no connection with the place whatsoever.

In the churchyard is the **Bargany Aisle**, containing the ornate tomb of Gilbert Kennedy, laird of Bargany and Ardstinchar, who was killed by the Earl of Cassillis (also a Kennedy) in 1601. A bitter feud between the Cassillis and Bargany branches of the Kennedy family had been going on right through the 16th century, with no quarter given or taken. Matters came to a head when the two branches met near Ayr, and Bargany was killed. The power of the Bargany branch was broken forever, and the feud fizzled out. The ruins of **Ardstinchar Castle**, Bargany's main stronghold, can still be seen beside the river.

Carleton Castle ruins lie near **Lendalfoot**, about five miles north of Ballantrae. This was home to Sir John Carleton, who, legend states, had a nice line in earning a living. He married ladies of wealth then enticed them to **Gamesloup**, a nearby rocky eminence, where he pushed them to their deaths and inherited their wealth. Sir John went through seven or eight wives before meeting the daughter of Kennedy of Culzean. After marrying her, he took her to Gamesloup, but instead of him pushing her over, she pushed him over, and lived happily ever after on his accumulated wealth.

But if it's a gruesome tale you're after, then you should head for **Sawney Bean's Cave**, on the shoreline north of Bennane Head, and

Bennane Head

Crossraguel Abbey

easily reached by a footpath from a layby on the A77. Here, in the 16th century, lived a family of cannibals led by Sawney Bean, which waylaid strangers, robbed them, and ate their flesh. They evaded capture for many years until a troop of men sent by James VI trapped them in their cave. They were taken to Edinburgh and executed. It's a wonderful story, but no documentary proof has ever been unearthed to prove that it really happened.

CROSSRAGUEL ABBEY

2 miles SW of Maybole, on the A77

These romantic ruins (Historic Scotland) sit complacently beside the main Ayr-Stranraer road. They are very well preserved, and give a wonderful idea of the layout of a medieval abbey. Some of the medieval architecture and stone carving, such as that in the chapter house, is well worth seeking out. It was founded by 1244 by Duncan, Earl of Carrick, for Clunaic monks, though most of what you see nowadays dates from after the 13th century. To the north are the ruins of **Baltersan Castle**, an old fortified tower house.

KIRKOSWALD

4 miles SW of Maybole on the A77

It was to Kirkoswald, in 1775, that Burns came to learn surveying for one term. Though his poem Tam o' Shanter is set in Alloway, all the characters he mentions came from the parish of Kirkoswald, which was where his maternal grandparents came from.

Kirkoswald Parish Church dates from 1777, and was designed by Robert Adam at the same time as he was working on Culzean Castle. Dwight D. Eisenhower worshipped here twice, one of the occasions being when he was president of the United States. Another visitor is not so well known, but the airline he helped to found is. The late Randolph Fields, together with Richard Branson, founded Virgin Airlines. Randolph loved this part of Ayrshire, and when he died in 1997, he left some money for the restoration of the church. A year later his widow presented the church with a small table, on which is a plaque commemorating the event.

The **Old Parish Church of St Oswald** lies at the heart of the village. It is a ruin now, but in its kirkyard are the graves of many people associated with Burns, including David Graham of Shanter Farm near Maidens, the real life "Tam o' Shanter". The church also contains one interesting relic - **Robert the Bruce's Baptismal Font** . Both Lochmaben in Dumfriesshire and Turnberry Castle, within the parish of Kirkoswald, claim to have been the birthplace of Robert the Bruce. Turnberry is the more likely, as it was the ancestral home of the Countess of Carrick, Bruce's mother, and it is known that she was living there at about the time of the birth. The story goes

Kirkoswald Parish Church

that the baby was premature, and that he was rushed to Crossraguel Abbey for baptism in case he died. The abbey's font was used, and when Crossraguel was abandoned, the people of Kirkoswald rescued the font and put it in their own church.

Within the village you'll also find **Souter Johnnie's Cottage**, owned by the National Trust for Scotland. John Davidson was a cobbler, and featured in Tam o' Shanter. Now his thatched cottage has been turned into a small museum.

TURNBERRY

7 miles SW of maybole on the A719

Very little now survives of **Turnberry Castle** where Robert the Bruce is supposed to have been born. The story of how his parents met is an unusual one. The Countess of Carrick was a young widow who saw a knight passing by Turnberry Castle. She immediately became infatuated with him, and had him kidnapped and brought into her presence. He turned out to be Robert de Brus, Lord of Annandale, and she persuaded him to marry her. The result of the marriage was Robert the Bruce, who himself became Earl of Carrick on his mother's death. Because Robert ascended the throne of Scotland as Robert I, the earldom became a royal one, and the present Earl of Carrick is Prince Charles.

Built onto the scant ruins of the castle is **Turnberry Lighthouse**, surrounded by the championship golf course. The elegant **Turnberry Hotel** is situated south east of the castle, just of the main road, and is one of the premier hotels in Scotland. It even has its own small runway for aircraft. During World War II, all this area was an airfield, and the runways can still be seen.

Turnberry Golf Course

GIRVAN

10 miles SW of Maybole on the A77

This pleasant little town is the main holiday resort in Carrick. It is also a thriving fishing port, with many fishing boats in its harbour at the mouth of the Water of Girvan. Though there is a long, sandy beach and a boating pond, the town is a quiet place, overlooked by the bulk of **Byne Hill** to the south. From the top a there is a fine view of the Firth of Clyde, and on a clear day the coast of Northern Ireland can be seen. Out in the Firth of Clyde the bulk of **Ailsa Craig** rises sheer from the water. It is the plug of an ancient volcano which is now a bird sanctuary. Trips round it are available from Girvan harbour.

Ailsa Craig

Within the town, on Knockcushan Street, is a small, curious spired building which has been given the nickname of **Auld Stumpy**. It dates from the 18th century, and at one time was attached to the later McMaster Hall, which burnt down in 1939. Behind Knockcushan House, near the harbour, are **Knockcushan Gardens**, the site of a court held by Robert the Bruce in 1328. At the **McKechnie Institute** in Dalrymple Street art exhibitions are sometimes held.

CULZEAN CASTLE

4 miles W of Maybole off the A719

This castle, perched spectacularly on a cliff above the Firth of Clyde, is owned by the National Trust for Scotland, and is their foremost attraction. It was designed by Robert Adam in 1777, and built round an old keep for the 10th Earl of Cassillis. It has some wonderful features, such as the Oval Staircase and the Circular Saloon with its views out over the Firth. Surrounding the castle is a **Culzean Country Park**, with such attractions as a Walled Garden, the Swan Pond, the Deer Park and the Fountain Court.

In gratitude for his part in World War II, the National Trust for Scotland presented General Eisenhower with the life tenure of a flat in Culzean. Eisenhower accepted, and spent a few golfing holidays there. The **Eisenhower Presentation**, within the castle, explains his connections with the area, and has exhibits about D-Day.

On the shoreline are the **Gasworks**, which at one time produced coal gas to heat and light the castle.

Culzean Castle Staircase

DUNDUFF FARM

near Dunure, Ayrshire KA7 4LH
Tel: 01292 500225 Fax: 01292 500222
e-mail: gemmelldunduff@aol.com
website: www.gemmelldunduff.co.uk

Close to the picturesque fishing village of Dunure, on the Ayrshire coast, you will find **Dunduff Farm**, where a warm welcome awaits you. The main building dates partly from the 15th to 17th centuries with later additions, and is a beautiful, listed building. It is a family run farm extending to 600 acres, and its location ensures good walks among stunning scenery and sea fishing. The accommodation has been given four stars by VisitScotland, and comprises three guest rooms, two of which are fully en suite and one with private facilities. The rooms are outstanding - comfortable, well decorated and fully equipped with colour TV, tea and coffee making facilities, hair dryer and central heating. In addition there is a small farm cottage sleeping two to four people which is available to let as self catering accommodation.

The farm itself is non-smoking, and well behaved pets are allowed in the farm cottage. In charge is Mrs Agnes Gemmell, who has been providing top class B&B accommodation for 12 years. She is renowned for her hearty, Scottish breakfasts, which should set anyone up for a hard day's sightseeing in an area that is particularly rich in history and scenery. From the farm house there are magnificent views across the lower reaches of the Firth of Clyde towards Arran, Holy Island and Ailsa Craig, and the sunsets can be truly stunning. This is the perfect base from which to explore the Burns Country, and the holiday resorts of Ayr, Troon and Girvan are within easy reach. Culzean Castle, Butlins Wonderwest World and Turnberry Golf Course are only a few miles away, and on the farm itself are the ruins of Dunduff Castle and an old graveyard.

Culzean Castle

spit over a great fire. Eventually Allan signed away the lands, and was released.

But he immediately protested to the king, who ordered Kennedy to pay for the lands. But such was Kennedy's power that he ignored the order, and got away with both his crime and the lands of Crossraguel.

DUNURE

5 miles NW of Maybole off the A 719

This pretty little fishing village would not look out of place in Cornwall. Arriving by car, you drop down towards it, giving excellent views of its cottages and pub grouped round a small harbour. To the south of the village are the ruins of **Dunure Castle**, perched on the coastline. This is the original Kennedy castle, and dates mostly from the 14th century. It was here that the famous **Roasting of the Abbot** took place in 1570. The Kennedies were at the height of their powers, and Gilbert Kennedy, 4th Earl of Cassillis, owned most of the land in Carrick. However, he never owned the lands of Crossraguel Abbey, which, at the Reformation, had been placed in the hands of Allan Stewart, commendator of the abbey. In effect he was the abbot, though he wasn't a monk. Gilbert invited Allan to Dunure Castle, where he incarcerated him in the Black Vault. He then stripped him and placed him on a

AYR

Ayr is the major holiday resort on the Ayrshire coast. It stands on the south bank of the River Ayr where it meets the sea, and was formerly the county town of Ayrshire. Always an important place, it was granted its royal charter in the early 1200s, and is the old capital of the Kyle district. Its most distinctive feature is the tall, elegant steeple of its **Town Hall**, built between 1827 and 1832 to the designs of Thomas Hamilton. Seen from the north, it blends beautifully with a cluster of fine Georgian buildings beside the river. After the Battle of Bannockburn, Bruce held his first parliament here, in the ancient St John's Kirk. This kirk is gone now save for the tower, now called **St John's Tower**, which stands among some Edwardian villas near the shore. Oliver Cromwell dismantled the church and used the stone to build **Ayr Citadel**, which has now gone as well, save for a few feet of wall near the river, and an arch in a side street. In its place he built the **Auld Parish Kirk** of Ayr on the banks of the river where a friary once stood. It dates from the mid 1600s, and is a mellow old T-plan building surrounded by old

CAFÉ MED

52 Smith Street, Ayr, Ayrshire KA7 1TF
Tel: 01292 287193

Situated opposite Ayr Railway Station, the **Café Med** is one of the town's finest restaurants. Owned and run by Elizabeth and Yannis Kourkoulos, it offers wonderful food, with Greek and Italian cuisine predominating. Yannis is a superb cook, and uses only the finest and freshest of local produce wherever possible to create many imaginative dishes. You can choose from a printed menu or a daily specials board, and every dish represents amazing value for money. This is the perfect place for a light snack or a full lunch. It is open from 9.00 until 21.00 during the week, and later on Friday and Saturday evenings.

BEECHWOOD GUEST HOUSE HOTEL

39 Prestwick Road, Ayr, Ayrshire KA8 8LE
Tel: 01292 262093

The **Beechwood Guest House Hotel** is a beautifully appointed and comfortable private hotel ten minutes walk from the centre of Ayr. It is family run, and has recently been completely refurbished to offer accommodation of the highest quality. It has eleven rooms, nearly half of which are en suite, and some have views towards the lovely Isle of Arran. Children are very welcome, and there is an ironing service and a toy box service with them in mind. The full Scottish breakfasts would set anyone up for a day exploring an area that is rich in history and landscape!

BELMONT GUEST HOUSE

15 Park Circus, Ayr, Ayrshire KA7 2DJ
Tel: 01292 265588 Fax: 01292 290303
e-mail: belmontguesthouse@btinternet.com
website: www.belmontguesthouse.co.uk

Situated close to all the amenities of the popular resort of Ayr, **Belmont Guest House** is a superior establishment offering the very best in Scottish hospitality. The house was built in 1877, and has five en suite guest rooms that are fully equipped with TV, radio/alarm clock, hair dryer and tea/coffee making facilities. Hearty Scottish breakfasts are served in a spacious dining room (with vegetarian options available), and there is a comfortable lounge where guests can relax after a hard day's sightseeing!

BEACHES TEAROOM AND GIFT SHOP

10a Seafield Road, Ayr, Ayrshire KA7 4AD
Tel: 01292 284441

Ayr has always been a popular seaside holiday resort, and right on the sea front you will find the **Beaches Tearoom and Gift Shop**, where you can have a relaxing cup of tea or coffee and a tasty snack or meal. It has a printed menu and a specials board, and favourites include toasties, home made soup and a fine range of ice creams. A children's menu is available, and in the summer months you can sit out of doors and enjoy excellent views of the sea and the Heads of Ayr. There is car parking adjacent to it, and there is also a good range of gifts and souvenirs on sale. If you visit Ayr, you can't afford to miss this excellent establishment!

gravestones. Within the **Kirkyard Lychgate** can be seen a couple of mortsafes, which at one time were placed over fresh graves to prevent grave robbing.

Ayr was the starting off point for Tam o' Shanter's drunken and macabre ride home after spending the evening at an inn, as portrayed in Burns's poem of the same name. In the High Street is the thatched **Tam o' Shanter Inn**, where the ride was supposed to have started. At one time it was a small museum, but now it has thankfully reverted to its original purpose, and you can enjoy a drink within its walls once more.

Bridge over River Ayr, Ayr

Robert Burns and Ayr are inseparable. He was born in a village to the south of the town which has now become a well-heeled suburb, and his influences are everywhere. Off the High Street is the **Auld Brig o' Ayr**, which dates from the 14th century, and down river is the **New Bridge**, dating from 1878. In a poem called "The Twa Brigs" Burns accurately forecast that the Auld Brig would outlast the new one. He was right - the New Bridge of Burns's time was swept away in a flood, to be replaced by the present New Bridge, while the Auld Brig still survives.

Apart from St John's Tower, the oldest building in the town is **Loudoun Hall**, close to the New Bridge. It was built about 1513 as a fine town house for Campbells of Loudoun, hereditary sheriffs of Ayr. It was due for demolition just after the war, but was saved when its importance was realised. South of Loudoun Hall, in the Sandgate, is **Lady Cathcart's House**, a tenement building which dates from the 17th century. Within it in 1756, John Loudon McAdam, the roads engineer who invented macadamised roads, was supposed to have been born (see also Moffat).

The bridges of Ayr take you to **Newton upon Ayr** on the north bank of the river, once a separate burgh but now part of Ayr. Part of its old Tolbooth survives as **Newton Tower**, caught in an island in the middle of the street.

South of the town, perched precariously on a clifftop, and always seeming to be in imminent danger of collapsing, is **Greenan Castle**, a 17th century tower house. As a building it has no great claim to fame, but many experts now believe that it marks the real spot where King Arthur's **Camelot** once stood (see also Kelso).

Loudoun Hall

AROUND AYR

PRESTWICK

2 miles N of Ayr town centre, on the A79

Prestwick is one of the oldest towns in Scotland, having been granted its original burgh charter in the 12th century. It was one of the most popular Clyde Coast holiday resorts until foreign holidays took over, and still has a long, sandy beach. To the north is **Prestwick International Airport**, at one time the main transatlantic airport for Glasgow. It is still a busy place, being a favourite starting point for those holidays in warmer climes that eventually saw off Prestwick as a holiday resort. On March 2 1960, the airport had possibly its most famous visitor - **Elvis Presley**. Having been discharged from the American army, his plane touched down at the airport for refuelling when he was returning home from Germany. He stayed at the American air force base there (now gone) for just under an hour, and then re-boarded his flight. It was the only time that "The King" set foot in Britain. A plaque near the Graceland Bar in the airport commemorates the visit, and people still turn up from all over Europe to pay their respects. In later life, someone asked Elvis what country he would most like to visit, and he replied that he would like to go back to Scotland.

The name Prestwick means "priest's burgh", and the ruins of the ancient **Parish Church of St Nicholas** are near the coastline. At **Kingcase** was a lazar house where Robert the Bruce went to seek a cure for his leprosy. **Bruce's Well** can still be seen there.

MONKTON

4 miles N of Ayr on the A79

Traffic between Glasgow and Ayr used to thunder through Monkton, but now it is more or less bypassed. It sits on the edge of Prestwick Airport, and at one time the main road cut right across the main runway. This meant that buses and cars were held up every time an aircraft took off or landed - a magnificent site, but time consuming for people in a hurry. The ruins of 13th century **St Cuthbert's Church** sit at the heart of the village, and at one time the Rev. Thomas Burns, Robert Burns's nephew, was minister here. William Wallace, it is said, once fell asleep in the church, and had a dream in which an old man presented him with a sword and a young woman presented him with a wand. He took it to mean that he must continue his struggle for Scotland's freedom.

To the north of the village is a curious monument known as **MacRae's Monument**. It commemorates James MacRae, Governor of Madras in the early 18th century. He was born into poverty and died a rich man.

The Wheatsheaf Monkton Inn

17/19 Main Street, Monkton, Prestwick, Ayrshgire KA9 2RN
Tel: 01292 470345
e-mail: enquiries@jjinns.com website: www.jjinns.com

The delightful village of Monkton lies north of Prestwick Airport, and in it you will find **The Wheatsheaf Monkton Inn**, one of the best pubs and eating places in the area. It has recently been refurbished to offer the highest standards in good food and drink, and was formerly a coaching inn (still with many period features) dating from the 18th century. You can choose from a printed menu or a daily specials board, and everything is freshly cooked on the premises. It has a great range of drinks, from beers and lagers to wines, spirits, and, should you be driving, soft drinks. It's the ideal place for relaxing over a pub lunch as you explore the Ayrshire coast and countryside.

Fordell

43 Beach Road, Barassie, Troon, Ayrshire KA10 6SU
Tel: 01292 313224 Fax: 01292 312141
e-mail: morag@fordell-troon.co.uk
website: www.fordell-troon.co.uk

Troon is famous for its golf courses. It is a ferry port for Northern Ireland, and sits at the heart of the Burns Country, an area that is both picturesque and historic. And the ideal base from which to explore it is **Fordell**, a superior B&B establishment owned and run by Morag Mathieson. It offers two exceedingly comfortable twin rooms that have wash hand basins, TVs and tea/coffee making facilities. The Scottish breakfasts are hearty and filling (with Continental breakfasts also available), and evening meals can be cooked by arrangement. The residents' lounge has a superb view across the Firth of Clyde to the lovely island of Arran.

The estate of Ladykirk is to be found a few miles east of Monkton. It was here, in **Ladykirk Chapel**, which has all but vanished, that Robert II married Elizabeth Mure of Rowallan, mother of Robert III.

Royal Troon Golf Course

TROON

5 miles N of Ayr, on the A759

This seaside resort is synonymous with golf, and the British Open has been held here many times. It is a young town, laid out in the early 1800s by the 4th Duke of Portland, who wished to create a harbour from which to export the coal from his Ayrshire coalfields. It formed the western terminus of Scotland's earliest rail line, the **Troon/Kilmarnock Railway**, which was opened in 1812. In 1816 the Duke introduced a steam locomotive onto the line, and it started pulling passenger trains (see also Kilmarnock).

On the shoreline is the **Ballast Bank**, created over the years by ships which discharged their ballast before taking on coal for Ireland. Behind Troon a narrow road climbs up onto the **Dundonald Hills**, from where a magnificent view of the Firth of Clyde can be obtained.

SYMINGTON

6 miles N of Ayr off the A77

Symington is a pleasant village of old cottages, though a large estate of council housing on its northern edge has somewhat marred its picturesqueness. At the heart of the village is **Symington Parish Church**, Ayrshire's oldest church still in use. This Norman building was originally built in the early 12th century, and has in its east wall a trio of delightful Norman windows. On a hillside to the west of the village, at a spot called Barnweil, is the **Wallace Monument**. This marks the spot where Wallace watched the "barns o' Ayr burn weel" after he set fire to them. Next to it are the scant ruins of **Barnweil Church**, where John Knox once preached.

DUNDONALD

8 miles N of Ayr on the B730

Dundonald Castle (Historic Scotland) sits on a high crag overlooking the village. The crag has been occupied for at least 2,000 years, and has been the site of at least three medieval castles. What you see nowadays are the remains of the third castle, built in the 14th century by Robert II, grandson of Robert the Bruce and the first Stewart king of Scotland, to

Taste Buds

Olympic Business Park, Drybridge Road, Dundonald, Ayrshire KA2 9BE Tel: 01563 850047

One of the best places for a tasty snack or light meal in the Dundonald area of Ayrshire is **Taste Buds**, owned and managed by Elizabeth Turley. There is a printed menu or a daily specials board, with a wide range of dishes that are made on the premises from only the finest local produce where possible. It can seat 30 in comfort, though it is so popular at weekends that you are well advised to book. On the menu are such dishes as lasagne, roast pork and apple sauce, dressed haddock, juicy sirloins steaks and various salads. The place is always spotless, the service is excellent, and all the food represents amazing value for money!

mark his accession to the throne in 1371. It was here, in his favourite residence, that Robert died in 1390. When Boswell and Dr Johnson visited the castle in 1773 during their Scottish journey, Johnson was much amused by the humble home of "Good King Bob". Since then, the castle has been owned by many families, including the Wallaces and the Cochranes, who later became Earls of Dundonald.

TARBOLTON

7 miles NE of Ayr on the B744

When Burns stayed at nearby Lochlee Farm (not open to the public) both he and his brother Gilbert looked to Tarbolton for leisure activities. They founded a debating society which met in a thatched house in the village. This house is now the **Bachelor's Club** (National Trust for Scotland). It was here that Burns also took dancing lessons, something of which his father didn't approve. Round the fireplace in the upper room you'll see a helical pattern drawn in chalk - an old Ayrshire custom to prevent the Devil from entering the house by way of the chimney.

Tarbolton Parish Church is an elegant, imposing building of 1821 standing on a slight hill.

MAUCHLINE

10 miles NE of Ayr on the A76

When Burns's father died at Lochlee near Tarbolton, the Burns family moved to **Mossgiel Farm** near the village of Mauchline. The farm that Burns knew is no more, but its successor still stands to the north of the village. It was in Mauchline that he met Jean Armour, his future wife, and it was here that they first settled down. Their home in Castle Street (which at that time was the main street of the village) now houses the **Burns House Museum**. The red sandstone building actually had four families living in it in the 18th century, but it has now been converted so that various displays can be accommodated. Robert and Jean's apartment has been furnished in much the same way as it would have been in when they moved in in 1788. Across from it, but now a private house, was **Nance Tinnock's Inn**, Burns's favourite drinking place.

The **Parish Church** you see today is not the one that Burns knew. It was pulled down and rebuilt in 1826, though the kirkyard still has many graves connected with the poet

Burns House Museum

Poosie Nansy's Inn

(including the graves of four of his children), and a chart on the church wall explains where each one is. One to look out for is **William Fisher's Grave**. William was an elder in Mauchline Kirk, and the butt of Burns's satirical poem Holy Willie's Prayer, in which he attacks the cant and hypocrisy of the church. Willie asks God's forgiveness for his own, understandable sins, no matter how vile, while asking that He severely punishes the sins of others. Opposite the church is **Poosie Nansy's Inn**. Though not a great frequenter of this inn, the poet still drank there occasionally, and Burns enthusiasts can still drink there today.

To the north of the village is the **Burns Memorial**, built in 1897. It is a tall building in red sandstone with a small museum inside. From the top, you get good views of the rich agricultural lands of Ayrshire. Beside the memorial, and forming part of it, are some pleasant cottages for old people.

Gavin Hamilton was Burns's friend and landlord, and he stayed in the village. His house can still be seen, and attached to it is the 15th century **Abbot Hunter's Tower**. It looks like a small castle, but was in fact the monastic headquarters of the Ayrshire estates owned by Melrose Abbey.

The **Ballochmyle Viaduct**, to the south of the village, carries the Glasgow to Dumfries line across the River Ayr, and is considered to be one of the finest railway bridges in the world. Work started on it in 1843, and it is still Britain's highest stone and brick railway bridge, being 163 feet above the river. It has three smaller arches at either end, and one long, graceful arch in the middle that spans 181 feet.

FAILFORD

7 miles E of Ayr on the B743

Near this little village, in 1786, Burns took his farewell of Highland Mary, who would die soon after in Greenock (see also Greenock and Dunoon). The **Failford Monument**, on a slight rise, commemorates this event.

A mile east of Failford, in a field, are the remains of a tumulus known as **King Cole's Grave**. Legend tells us that Old King Cole of nursery rhyme fame was a real person - a British king called Coel or Coilus. In the Dark Ages, he fought a great battle in Ayrshire against the Scots under their king, Fergus. Cole's army was routed, and he fled the battlefield. Eventually he was captured and killed. His supporters later buried him with some pomp at the spot where he died (see also Coylton).

The tumulus was opened in 1837, and some cremated bones were discovered. Up until not so long ago the nearby stream was referred to locally as the "Bloody Burn", and one field beside the stream was known as "Deadmen's Holm", as that is where those killed in the battle were supposedly buried. Tales were often told of bits of human bone and armour having been turned up by men ploughing the field.

COYLTON

6 miles E of Ayr on the A70

One of the most enduring myths in Ayrshire is that the district of Kyle is named after a famous monarch - **Old King Cole**. There certainly was a Dark Ages king called Coel, or Coilus, to give him his Latin name, and tradition says that he was killed in a great battle somewhere on the banks of the Doon (see Failford). Coylton is supposed to be named after him as well (see also Failford).

OCHILTREE

11 miles E of Ayr on the A70

Ochiltree was the birthplace of yet another Ayrshire writer. **George Douglas Brown** was born here in 1869, and went on to write The House with the Green Shutters. With this book he wanted to banish the "kailyard school" of writing, which saw Scotland's countryside as being comfortable and innocent, populated with people of unquestionable worth. He set his book in the fictional town of "Barbie", which was a thinly disguised Ochiltree, and not many characters in the book have redeeming features. The cottage where he was born (not open to the public) has sprouted green shutters, and is itself known as **The House with the Green Shutters**.

AUCHINLECK

13 miles E of Ayr off the A76

Burns is not the only literary person associated with Ayrshire. Though born in Edinburgh, James Boswell's home was **Auchinleck House**, near the mining village of Auchinleck. His father, Lord Auchinleck, was a Court of Session judge who was sorely tried by his son's seemingly wayward ways. He had the house built in about 1760 as his country seat, and Boswell brought the great Dr Johnson there to meet Lord Auchinleck when the pair were doing their Scottish tour. They didn't hit it off.

Boswell himself is buried in a small mausoleum attached to **Auchinleck Kirk**, which is no longer used for worship, but instead houses a museum dedicated to the writer and biographer.

SORN

14 miles E of Ayr on the B743

Sorn is one of the most picturesque villages in the county. It sits on the River Ayr, with an ancient bridge spanning it, and has many delightful cottages. **Sorn Parish Church** dates from 1658, and the lofts, or galleries, are reached by stairs on the outside of its walls. **Sorn Castle** dates from the 14th century, with later additions. James V or VI (no one is quite sure which one) once visited Sorn Castle on horseback in the depths of winter to attend a wedding.

Alexander Peden was born at Auchincloich near Sorn in 1626. Known as **Prophet Peden**, he was a Covenanter who held conventicles - secret prayer meetings - at lonely spots all over central Ayrshire. In fact, the area abounds with places that have been named after him, such as "Peden's Pulpit" and "Peden's Table". There is even a field called "Preaching Peden".

CUMNOCK

15 miles E of Ayr off the A76

Cumnock is a small industrial town which was granted its burgh charter in 1509. In the middle of its square sits **Cumnock Old Parish Church**, built in the mid 1800s. It's a foursquare building that seems to sprout transepts, apses and porches in all directions. Two miles west of the town, at Lugar, is **Bello Mill** (not open to the public), birthplace in 1754 of William Murdoch, discoverer of gas lighting. He conducted his experiments in a cave on the banks of the Lugar Water upstream from Bello.

Dumfries House (not open to the public), west of Cumnock, was designed for the 4th Earl of Dumfries in the mid 1700s by John and Robert Adam.

MUIRKIRK

23 miles E of Ayr on the A70

This former mining town is surrounded by bleak but lovely moorland. To the west is the site of the **Battle of Airds Moss**, fought in 1680 and marked by a memorial,. A Covenanting army was heavily defeated by Government troops.

NEW CUMNOCK

19 miles SE of Ayr on the A76

It was near here that the **Knockshinnoch Mining Disaster** took place in 1950. 129 miners were trapped underground when a slurry of mud and peat filled some workings that were near the surface. 116 were eventually brought out alive, and great bravery was shown by the rescuers. A feature film was later made about the disaster. To the south of the village is **Glen Afton**, through which flows the Afton Water. A cairn marks the spot where Burns was inspired to write Flow Gently Sweet Afton.

DALRYMPLE

5 miles SE of Ayr on the B7034

In this quiet little village of weavers' cottages Burns first received an education. While staying at Mount Oliphant, he and his brother Gilbert attended the Parish School on alternate weeks. The village sits on the Doon, and has a small **Parish Church** built in 1849. Two miles south, and straight out of a fairy tale, is **Cassillis Castle** (not open to the public), the home of the present Earl of Cassillis (whose senior title is now the Marquis of Ailsa) and head of the Kennedy family. It is a wonderful concoction of turrets and towers built originally in the 14th century but added to through the years.

ALLOWAY

2 miles S of Ayr town centre on the B7024

Robert Burns was not the uneducated "ploughman poet" from the peasant classes so beloved of his more romantic admirers. His father was a tenant farmer, and although not well off, still managed to employ workmen and serving girls on his farm.

Burns himself was a highly educated man for his time, thanks to his far-sighted father. He knew his Classics, he could speak French and some Latin, he could read music, he took dancing lessons, and he could play both the fiddle and, surprisingly, the guitar. When he went to Edinburgh in later life, he was possibly better educated than some of the gentry who patronised him. Two of his sons, James Glencairn Burns and W. Nicol Burns, attained the ranks of Liet. Colonel and a Colonel respectively in the British Army.

At one time, Alloway was a small country village. Now it forms part of Ayr, and is full of large, impressive houses, which illustrate the affluence of this part of Ayrshire. It was here, in 1759, that Robert Burns was born in a cottage that his father built with his own hands. Now **Burns Cottage** is a place of pilgrimage, and people come from all over the world to pay their respects. Within the grounds of the cottage is the **Burns Museum**, containing many of his manuscript, letters and possessions.

Burns Memorial, Alloway

Alloway Kirk is where Robert's father, William Burnes, is buried, and it was the main setting for the poem Tam o' Shanter. It dates from the early 16th century, but even in Burns's day it was a ruin. Across the road, within some beautiful gardens, is the Grecian **Burns Monument**, built in the 1820s. Inside is a small museum.

Spanning the Doon is the graceful **B ' Doon**, a single arched bridge dating from at least the 15th century, possibly earlier. It was across the Brig o' Doon that Tam o' Shanter was chased by witches he disturbed in Alloway Kirk. However, he managed to gain the keystone of the bridge (as witches cannot cross running water) and escaped unharmed, even though his horse lost its tail. In Burn's day it lay on the main road south into

Burns Cottage, Alloway

THE COFFEE CLUB

30 Bank Street, Kilmarnock, Ayrshire KA1 1HA
Tel: 01563 522048 Fax: 01563 522848
e-mail: thecoffeeclub@ukonline.co.uk

Situated opposite the historic Laigh Kirk in the oldest part of Kilmarnock, **The Coffee Club** has been an institution in Ayrshire since the late 1950s. The whole area of the town in which it is situated has recently been upgraded, and is now picturesque, with the Coffee Club itself having a striking early Victorian facade that speaks of the town's heritage. Owned and managed by Frederik Overdijking since 1999, it's already fine reputation has been consolidated and enhanced, and it still remains *the* place in the town to have a relaxing cup of coffee, a snack or a full meal. The food is famous, not just in Kilmarnock, but throughout a wide area. There are actually two restaurants within The Coffee Club, both offering excellent food and great value for money. On the ground floor is a snack bar with counter service where you can order a wide range of snacks such as pastries, toasties, burgers and baked potatoes, as well as soft drinks, coffee and tea. Downstairs, in the basement, is a cosy and intimate waitress service restaurant that offers good food all day between 9.00 and 22.00 Monday to Saturday.

The menu features dishes ranging from all day breakfasts through salads, vegetarian choices, steaks and hot roast platters to the ever popular 'soup 'n' sweet' - a brimming plate of home made soup with bread, followed by a generous portion of fruit tart with lashings of fresh cream and finished off with a cup of coffee. The healthier options on the menus are highlighted by a tick, denoting a lower fat and higher fibre content, and there is a children's menu. A range of wines and beers are available, but only to diners. This is an establishment which really does have the feel of a 'club' about it, with regular patrons getting a newsletter telling them of the latest activities, such as party plans, Christmas events and jazz evenings. Visiting the Coffee Club is a unique experience, and if you do, you are sure to return the next time you're in town. So put your name down to receive the newsletter!

CRAIGIE INN

Craigie, by Kilmarnock, Ayrshire KA1 5LY
Tel: 01563 860286 website: www.craigieinn.com

High on a ridge to the south of Kilmarnock, on an unmarked road, is the tiny village of Craigie. Though it is no more than a few old cottages and a church nestling amid green fields, people seek it out for one reason - **The Craigie Inn**. This quaint, old whitewashed pub started off life many years ago as a simple alehouse, but is now one of the most picturesque country inns in Ayrshire. The inside is cosy and quaint, with lots of warm wood and comfortable carpeting, and it is popular with both locals and visitors. The bar carries a fine selection of spirits, ales, beers, wine and soft drinks, and there is sure to be something to suit everyone's taste. The same can be said for the fine cuisine served in the Craigie Inn. The produce for the many dishes is sourced locally wherever possible, and is always as fresh as can be.

You can choose from a printed menu or a daily specials board, and there is also a high tea menu that represents amazing value for money. You can choose from such dishes as home made beef olives, braised shank of lamb, juicy steaks, smoked Scottish salmon, warm salad of smoked chicken and breast of Gressingham duck, all with a selection of vegetables in season. Children are most welcome, and there is a beer garden and play area. Food is served between 12.00 - 14.30 and 17.30 -21.00 every day except Mondays in winter, and the inn has such a fine reputation that you are advised to book for Saturday and Sunday evenings. There is plenty of parking space and disabled access. Occasional Scottish banquets are held, and you should ring or see the website for details.

Carrick, but a newer, wider bridge now carries traffic south.

Across the road from Alloway Kirk is the **Tam o' Shanter Experience**, a visitors centre with two audio visual shows within its large auditorium. One illustrates Burns's life and times, and the other recreates what happened to Tam o' Shanter after he left the inn and made his fateful ride south from Ayr.

East of Alloway is **Mount Oliphant Farm** (not open to the public) to which Burns and his family moved when he was seven years old.

KILMARNOCK

Though it is largely an industrial town, Kilmarnock was granted its burgh charter in 1592, so its roots go deep into Scottish history. Legend says it grew up round a church founded by St Marnock, a Celtic saint, in the 7th century. The present **Laigh Kirk** in Bank Street, which has a 17th century steeple (the date on it says 1410, but this is incorrect), is supposed to stand on the site of this church. The town's other old church is the **Old High Kirk**, which dates from the 1730s.

Kilmarnock has many Burns associations, and the first edition of his poems was published in the town, at Star Inn Close (now gone) in 1786. Now a copy is worth thousands of pounds. A stone marking the spot can be found in the small shopping mall. Also in the mall is a stone marking the spot where Covenanting martyr **John Nesbit** was executed in 1683. His grave can be seen in the kirkyard of the Laigh Kirk.

Burns Monument, Kilmarnock

Many of the people mentioned in Burns's poems are buried in the two kirkyards, and a **Burns Statue**, recently unveiled by the Princess Royal, stands at Kilmarnock Cross. In the Kay Park stands another memorial to the poet - the **Burns Monument**. Though not now open to the public, it is an impressive red sandstone building.

It was in a shop in King Street, the town's main shopping street, that Johnnie Walker first started bottling and selling whisky in 1820. The **Johnnie Walker Bottling Plant** in Hill Street is one of the largest plants of its kind in the world.

One place not to be missed is the **Dick Institute**, the town's museum, art gallery and library. It is house in a grand classical building, and has impressive collections connected with geology, archaeology, biology and local history. The gallery is also impressive, with paintings by Corot,

Old High Kirk

Dean Castle

Constable, Turner and Kilmarnock's own painter, Robert Colquhoun. The area around the Dick Institute is particularly attractive, with a war memorial, Victorian houses, and the richly decorated facade of the old technical college. Across from the Dick Institute is the statue of Kilmarnock's own Dick Whittington - **James Shaw** (known affectionately in the town as "Jimmy Shaw") who became Lord Mayor of London in 1805.

To the north east of the town centre is the town's oldest building, **Dean Castle**. It was the home of the Boyd family, who became the Earls of Kilmarnock, and is in fact two separate castles within a curtain wall - the 14th century Keep and the later Palace. Both are open to the public, and house wonderful collections of tapestries, musical instruments and armour. Surrounding it is **Dean Castle Country Park** with many walks, and a small children's zoo..

The Boyd family rose to become the most important family in Scotland in the 1460s, when Sir Robert Boyd became Regent of Scotland. But in 1746 the last earl was beheaded in London for fighting alongside Charles Edward Stuart at Culloden, and all his lands and titles were forfeited.

During his trial in London, his young wife, the Countess of Kilmarnock, stayed at the Boyd's other residence in the town - Kilmarnock House (now gone). Daily she walked its grounds, awaiting news of his fate. These grounds are now the **Howard Park**, and it has a tree lined avenue known as **Lady's Walk**. The Countess herself died shortly after her husband, and some people say that her ghost still haunts the park (see also Falkirk).

Across from the new sheriff court building near the park is the **Old Sheriff Court**, an attractive building in neo classical style. It sits on the site of one of the termini of Scotland's first railway, the Troon/ Kilmarnock Railway, built by the Duke of Portland in 1812 (see also Troon). Two miles west of the town is the **Gatehead Viaduct**, built in 1807 to take the railway over the River Irvine. Though it no longer carries a railway line, it is still Scotland's oldest railway bridge.

Though Elderslie in Renfrewshire seems a likelier location, there are those who claim that **William Wallace** was born in at Ellerslie in **Riccarton**, a suburb of Kilmarnock (and named after Sir Richard Wallace, a relation of William). There was certainly a Wallace castle in the area, and young William is known to have had his first skirmish with English troops on the banks of the River Irvine.

And in 1862, at **Crosshouse**, a former mining village west of Kilmarnock, was born **Andrew Fisher**, who rose to become Prime Minister of Australia on three separate occasions.

AROUND KILMARNOCK

FENWICK

4 miles N of Kilmarnock off the A77

Fenwick (pronounced "Fenick") is really two villages - High Fenwick and Laigh Fenwick. They lie on the edge of the Fenwick Moors which separate the farmlands of Ayrshire from Glasgow and its suburbs, and were orgininally weaving villages. Some of the cottages still show their weaving origins, with two windows on one side of the door (to allow plenty of light to enter the room containing the loom) and one window on the other. **Fenwick Parish Church**, which dates from 1643, is an attractive whitewashed building with a Greek cross plan. On one wall hangs the original **Jougs**, where wrongdoers were chained by their necks to the wall.

Two miles south east of the village is the quaintly named, and often photographed, hamlet of **Moscow**, which actually has a burn called the Volga flowing through it. And five miles to the north, off the B764, is **Lochgoin Farm**, which has a small museum commemorating the Covenanters.

Fenwick Parish Church

STEWARTON

5 miles N of Kilmarnock on the A735

Stewarton is famous as being the home of bonnet making in Ayrshire. It was the birthplace, in 1739, of **David Dale**, the industrialist and social reformer who founded New Lanark (see also Lanark). The **Parish Church of St Columba** dates originally from 1696, though it has been much altered.

DUNLOP

7 miles N of Kilmarnock on the A735

Dunlop is a delightful village of small weavers' cottages. The **Parish Church** dates from 1835, though it has fragments from the earlier church incorporated in the north aisle. In the kirkyard is the ornate early 17th century **Hans Hamilton Tomb**, contained within a small mausoleum. Hamilton was Dunlop's first Protestant minister, and was made Viscount Clandeboyes by James VI. The small **Clandeboyes Hall**, beside the mausoleum, dates from the 17th century, and was the village's first school.

GALSTON

4 miles E of Kilmarnock on the A71

This pleasant little town in the Irvine Valley has a splendid **Parish Church** dating from 1808. Another church not to be missed is **St Sophia's RC Church**, modelled on the Hagia St Sophia in Istanbul. **Barr Castle** is a solid, 15th century tower house in which John Knox preached in 1556. An ancient game of handball used to be played against its walls by the locals.

To the north of the town are the impressive ruins of **Loudoun Castle**, ancestral home of the Campbells of Loudoun. It was burnt down in 1941, and in its time entertained so lavishly that it was called the "Windsor of Scotland". Three ghosts reputedly haunt it - a Grey Lady, a Phantom Piper and a Benevolent Monk. At one time the great sword of William Wallace was kept within the castle, but it was sold in 1930. Beside its walls is the **Auld Yew Tree**, under which the draft of the Treaty of Union between Scotland and England was prepared by Hugh, 3rd Earl of Loudoun.

Loudoun Castle was the birthplace of **Lady Flora Hastings**, who severely shook the monarchy and government in 1839. Queen Victoria was 20 years old at the time, and had been on the throne for just two years. Lady Flora was a Lady of the Bedchamber who contracted a liver disease which so swelled her stomach that she appeared pregnant. Gossip raged through the court, and she was shunned, even though medical opinion confirmed that she was ill. Neither the government nor the Queen did anything to dispel the rumours, and soon people began to sympathise with the young woman. It was the Queen's turn to be shunned, and she was shocked when people turned their back on her as she processed through London by coach. It wasn't until Lady Flora was on her deathbed that a grudging reconciliation took place, though no apology was ever given. She now lies buried in medieval **Loudoun Kirk**, whose ruins can be seen a couple of miles to the west of the castle.

Today the **Loudoun Castle Theme Park** fills the grounds of the castle.

NEWMILNS

7 miles E of Kilmarnock on the A71

Scottish Maritime Museum, Irvine

Newmilns, like Darvel, is a small lace making and weaving town in the Irvine Valley which was granted its charter in 1490, making it the oldest inland burgh in Ayrshire. The small crowstepped **Town House** dates from the 1730s, and behind the Loudoun Arms, which itself dates from the 18th century, is **Newmilns Tower**, an early 16th century tower house built by the Campbells of Loudoun.

During the American Civil War, the weavers of Newmilns sent a message of support to Abraham Lincoln, and he in turn sent back an American flag. This was subsequently lost, but in 1949 the American Embassy gave the town a replacement, which is now housed in the early 19th century **Parish Church**.

DARVEL

8 miles E of Kilmarnock, on the A71

Situated in the lovely Irvine Valley, Darvel is a small, attractive town which was laid out in the late 18th and early 19th centuries. Like its neighbour Newmilns, it is a lace making town, the skills having been brought here by the Dutch in the 17th century. It was in Lochfield, near Darvel, that **Sir Alexander Fleming**, the discoverer of penicillin, was born in 1881. To the east of the town is the immense bulk of **Loudoun Hill**, the plug of a former volcano. Both William Wallace and Robert the Bruce fought battles here against the English, in 1297 and 1307 respectively. South of the town is the quaintly named **Distinkhorn**, the highest hill in the area.

IRVINE

7 miles W of Kilmarnock on the A71

Irvine is an ancient seaport and royal burgh which, in the 1960s, was designated as Britain's first seaside new town. It is a mixture of old and new, and has many industrial estates surrounding it. Robert Burns learned flax dressing here in 1781, and lodged in a house in the cobbled **Glasgow Vennel**. A small museum has been created within both it and the heckling shop behind it.

Irvine has other, more unexpected, literary associations, however. In 1815 the American writer of macabre tales, Edgar Allan Poe, spent a couple of months in the town, and attended the local school. It is said that part of his lessons was to copy the epitaphs from the tombstones in the kirkyard of the **Parish Kirk**, which may have prepared him for some of the more morbid tales he wrote in later life. Irvine was also the birthplace of the writer **John Galt**, a relative of the man who adopted Edgar Allan Poe in the United States. **Alexander MacMillan**, who founded the great London publishing house, was also a native of the town.

In the nearby village of **Dreghorn** was born in 1840 yet another famous Ayrshireman - **John Boyd Dunlop**, who invented the pneumatic tyre. **Dreghorn Parish Church**, built in 1780, is unusual in that it is octagonal in plan.

The ruins of **Seagate Castle** date from the early 16th century, and it is said that Mary Stuart lodged here briefly in 1563. Every August the town has its **Marymass Week**, which supposedly commemorates her stay. It is more likely, however, that the celebrations have more to do with a pre-Reformation religious festival, as the parish church was formerly dedicated to St Mary.

In the 18th century, Irvine saw the birth of perhaps the most unusual religious cult ever seen in Scotland - the Buchanites. Elspet Buchan was the daughter of a publican, and claimed she could bestow immortality on a person by breathing on them, and that she herself was immortal. She attracted a wide following, including a gullible Irvine clergyman, but eventually she and her followers were hounded from the town. She eventually died a natural death, and the cult broke up (see also Closeburn and Crocketford).

Down by the harbourside is the **Magnum Leisure Centre**, one of the biggest centres of its kind in Scotland, and on the other side of the river is **The Big Idea**, which bills itself as the world's first inventor centre. It's a combination of exhibition, laboratory, discovery centre and workshop, and is devoted to invention and innovation. It cost over £14 million to build.

Near the Magnum Centre is one of the three sites of the **Scottish Maritime Museum** (see also Dumbarton and Glasgow). It houses a wide collection of ships, most of which you can board and explore. There's also the Linthouse Engine Works which houses a vast collection of maritime machinery, such as engines, winding gear and so on. In the Shipworker's Tenement Flat, a typical "room and kitchen" flat dating from the 1920s has been recreated, showing how shipyard workers lived in those days.

Irvine was the setting, in 1839, of the grand **Eglinton Tournament**, organised by the 13th Earl of Eglinton at his home of Eglinton Castle, on the outskirts of the town. It was to be a recreation of a great medieval tournament, with jousting, horse riding and other knightly pursuits, and the great and the good from all over Europe congregated to take part. Alas, the three day event was a wash out, due to colossal rainstorms. Little remains of the castle, but the grounds have been turned into **Eglinton Country Park**.

ARDROSSAN, SALTCOATS & STEVENSTON

11 miles W of Kilmarnock on the A78

These towns form a trio of holiday resorts on the Ayrshire coast. Ardrossan is the most industrialised, and is the ferry terminal for Arran. It is a planned town, and its core was laid out in the early 19th century by the 12th Earl of Eglinton. The 15th century ruins of **Ardrossan Castle**, once a stronghold of the Montgomeries, sit on a low hill overlooking the main streets. Cromwell is said to have plundered its masonry to build the citadel at Ayr. **The Obelisk** beside the ruins commemorates a local doctor. At the foot of the hill stands **St Peter in Chains**, built in 1938, and reckoned to be one of the finest modern churches in Ayrshire.

At Saltcoats the **North Ayrshire Museum**, housed in a former church, has an interesting local history collection. The town has a fine beach, and its name is a reminder of the times when salt was produced here from sea water. The small harbour dates from the late 17th century, with many alterations, and at low tide fossilised trees can be seen on the harbour floor. It was in Saltcoats, in 1793, that **Betsy Miller**, the only woman ever to have become a registered ship's captain, was born.

Stevenston is a straggling town, with a **High Church** that dates from 1832. It has a good beach, though it is some way from the centre of the town. Nearby, at Ardeer, the British Dynamite Company established a factory in 1873. It later became Nobel's Explosives Company, and in 1926 became part of ICI.

KILMAURS

2 miles NW of Kilmarnock, on the A735

Kilmaurs is a former weaving village, and though only a few fields separate it from

Kilmaurs Parish Church

Kilmarnock's suburbs, it is still a small, self-contained community with many small cottages. At its centre is the old 17th century **Tolbooth**, still with the jougs, or neckring, attached, which was placed round wrongdoers' necks as a punishment. The **Parish Church** dates from 1888, and replaced an earlier church that was collegiate in medieval times. **Glencairn Aisle**, the 16th century burial vault of the Earls of Glencairn, still stands however, and it has an ornate monument inside to the 8th Earl and his family.

John Boyd Orr, first director of the United Nations Food and Agricultural Organisation and Nobel prizewinner, was born here in 1880.

KILWINNING

9 miles NW of Kilmarnock on the A737

Though nowadays a continuation of Irvine, Kilwinning was, up until 1975, a separate burgh. The ruins of great Tironensian **Kilwinning Abbey**, built in the 12th century, still dominate the town centre, though they are not as extensive as those of Ayrshire's other great abbey, Crossraguel. The tower you see nowadays attached to the abbey ruins was built in 1815, and replaced the original medieval one which fell down the year before. It is here that a competition is held every year called the **Papingo Shoot**, where archers shoot upwards at a target (the papingo) held from a window of the tower. Tha papingo is usually a wooden pigeon, and papigno shoots were once common throughout Britain.

A few miles out of town, on the A737, is **Dalgarven Mill**, dating from about 1620. It is now a museum dedicated to country life in Ayrshire.

DALRY

11 miles NW of Kilmarnock on the A737

This small industrial town's square is dominated by the **Parish Church of St Margaret**, dating from the 1870s. The name comes from the Gaelic "Dal Righe", meaning the "King's Field", which shows that at one time it must have had a royal connection. To the south east of the town is **Blair**, a large mansion centred on what was a typical Scottish tower house. The parkland which surrounds it was laid out by William Blair in the 1760s.

BURNHOUSE MANOR HOTEL

Burnhouse, by Beith, Ayrshire KA15 1LJ
Tel: 01560 484006 e-mail: enquirer@burnhousencrol.co.uk
Fax: 01560 484114 website: burnhousemanor.co.uk

The Burnhouse Manor Hotel sits in the heart of the picturesque Ayrshire countryside. Owned by Jack and Anne Peters, it is housed in an imposing 18th century farmhouse which has been tastefully converted to offer the best in Scottish hospitality. The food is outstanding, and the menu features many imaginative dishes that use fresh local produce wherever possible. There is a lounge/bar, a 30-seat dining room, and a function suite that can take 200 guests. The whole place speaks of quality and taste, and is an ideal base for exploring Ayrshire or Glasgow.

SHOTTS FARM

Barrmill, Beith, Ayrshire KA15 1LB
Tel: 01505 502273 Mobile: 07890037766

Set amid the rolling hills of Ayrshire you'll find **Shotts Farm**, where Jane Gillon offers first class B&B accommodation within the picturesque farmhouse. There are three rooms, a family and two doubles, and all are superbly furnished and equipped, and exceedingly comfortable. This is country living at its very best, within a 200 acre dairy farm that has been farmed by the same family for three generations. Jane's B&B hasn't been established for quite as long, but so good is it that it attracts lots of repeat business! Evening meals can be cooked by prior arrangement, and the breakfasts are large and hearty.

BEITH

12 miles NW of Kilmarnock off the A737

Beith is a small attractive town in the Garnock Valley. The remains of the **Auld Kirk** date from the late 16th century, while the impressive **High Church** dates from the early 19th century. **Eglinton Street** is the most attractive part of the town, with small, neat two-storey buildings dating from the late 18th and 19th centuries.

KILBIRNIE

13 miles NW of Kilmarnock on the A760

Within this small industrial town you'll find the **Barony Parish Church**, dating from the 15th century. Inside is some wonderful woodwork from the 17th and 18th centuries, including the extravagant Crawford Loft and the Cunninghame Aisle. Standing next to the golf course are the ruins of **The Place of Kilbirnie**, a castle dating from the 15th century.

WEST KILBRIDE

16 miles NW of Kilmarnock off the A78

West Kilbride is a sedate village of Glasgow commuters, perched above its twin village of **Seamill**, on the coast. **Law Castle** is a 15th century castle built for Princess Mary on her marriage to Thomas Boyd of Kilmarnock, later to be the Earl of Arran. At the hamlet of Portencross, out on a headland beyond Seamill, are the substantial ruins of 14th century **Portencross Castle**, another Boyd stronghold. On the same headland are **Hunterston Castle** (not open to the public), and **Hunterston Nuclear Power Station**, which has a visitors centre which explains the workings of a nuclear power station.

CUMBRAES

19 miles NW of Kilmarnock, in the Firth of Clyde

These two islands - **Little Cumbrae** and **Great Cumbrae** - were once in the former county of Bute. Little Cumbrae is privately owned, but Great Cumbrae can be visited by a ferry from Largs on the mainland. Its only town is **Millport**, a small, attractive holiday resort with one unique feature - the **Cathedral of the Isles**, Britain's smallest cathedral. It is a real hidden gem of a place, and was completed in 1851 as part of a theological complex funded by the George Boyle, who later became the 6th Earl of Glasgow. It's nave is 40 feet by 20 feet, and can only seat 100 people. It was designed by William Butterfield, who also designed Keble College, Oxford. The ceiling is painted with all the wild flowers found on the island.

On the eastern shore of the island, facing the mainland, is the **University Marine Biological Station**. It is an institution of both Glasgow and London Universities, and offers students research facilities, tuition in diving, and tuition in marine biology. It houses a museum which is open to the public.

LARGS

19 miles NW of Kilmarnock on the A78

Largs is the epitome of the Ayrshire seaside town. During the last fortnight in July, hordes of Glaswegians used to descend on places like this for their annual fortnight's holiday. These days are gone, but the towns themselves have adapted, and now cater for retired people and day trippers.

Largs itself is a lively, attractive place, and is the mainland terminal for the Cumbrae ferry. It was near here, in 1263, that the **Battle of Largs** took place, when the Scots finally threw off the Viking yolk. A tall thin monument

Largs Town

BELMONT HOUSE

2 Broomfield Place, Largs KA30 8DR
Tel: 01475 676264 e-mail: belmont.house@largs.i12.com
website: www.belmont.i12.com

Commanding stunning views over the Isles of Cumbrae and the Kyles of Bute, **Belmont House** is situated on The Broomfields of Largs. It has unrestricted views to the shoreline, where one can wander south at a leisurely pace to the large marina, via the Pencil Monument. Alternatively you can meander along the North Esplanade, visiting the town centre, if desired. The town centre is small enough to be intimate and houses many individual shops that will delight the shopper. Largs was the site of the Battle of Largs in 1263, when the Scots finally defeated the Vikings, and the Pencil Monument commemorates the great victory.

Within the area there are many activities to suit the individual, from pony trekking, sailing, fishing, diving, walking and golf to sightseeing among the beautiful islands of Great Cumbrae, Arran and Bute. And Largs is a superb base from which to explore the surrounding areas of interest. Should you miss the bright lights of the city, Largs is 25 miles from Glasgow, with trains every hour from Largs Station, and fine open roads that will take you there within the hour by car. Belmont House was built in 1811, and retains many of its original features. The owners, Betty and Alan Clarke, opened their B&B at Easter 2000, and have already gained a reputation for offering a warm and friendly atmosphere to their guests. The three rooms are tastefully decorated, each with a hostess tray, hair drier and radio alarm clock. The dining room/guest lounge is on the ground floor, and has views out over the Firth. the room is unique in that it is completely oval in shape, with even the doors being curved!

DUNVEGAN HOUSE

Shore Road, Brodick, Isle of Arran KA27 8AJ
Tel/Fax: 01770 302811 website: www.dunveganhouse.arran.co.uk

Situated within the picturesque village of Brodick on Arran you will find **Dunvegan House**. It is a traditional sandstone building that has been tastefully renovated and decorated throughout to create a spacious four star licensed guest house that offers superb accommodation for the holidaymaker. Owned and managed by Helen and George McAdam, it sits right on the sea front, between the pier (Arran's main ferry terminal) and the heart of the village. From here you get magnificent views of Brodick Bay, the Ayrshire coast and Goatfell, Arran's highest mountain. The guest house has nine rooms, eight of which are fully en suite and the ninth having private facilities, and all are beautifully furnished and decorated, with a TV, radio/alarm and tea and coffee making facilities. There is a cosy and welcoming guests' lounge, where you can relax after a hard day's sightseeing or hillwalking. It even has a small cocktail bar where you can choose an aperitif and savour it slowly while studying the evening's menu.

The dining room is bright and airy, and overlooks Brodick Bay. Helen and George pride themselves on the high standards of their cuisine, and use only the freshest of local produce wherever possible. Whether it's the full Scottish breakfasts or the beautifully cooked and presented evening meals, you are sure to be amazed at the wonderful service and great value for money. The table d'hote menu includes such starters as melon and prawn salad, cream of carrot and ginger soup and crepes filled with mushroom sauce and topped with cheese . The main dishes include Kintyre grilled salmon, Scotch sirloin steak or chicken with Arran mustard. You can then choose from a selection of sweets or the cheeseboard. other menus are available on request. This is the ideal place for a relaxing holiday on one of Scotland's most beautiful islands, and if you arrive by ferry, either Helen or George will be more than pleased to pick you up from the ferry if you give prior notice.

south of the town called **The Pencil** commemorates the event. Within the town you'll find **Vikingar!** a museum and interpretation centre that explains the life and travels of the Vikings all these years ago.

Largs Museum, with its local history collection, is also worth a visit, as is the **Skelmorlie Aisle**. This sits in the old kirkyard in the centre of the town, and was a transept of the former medieval parish church. Within it is the mausoleum of Sir Robert Montgomery of Skelmorlie and his wife. A Renaissance-style tomb with wonderful stone carving, it was built in 1634. In the local cemetery is buried Sir William Burrell, shipping magnate and millionaire, who gave the Burrell Collection to the city of Glasgow in 1944 (see also Hutton).

Kelburn Castle stands to the south of the town. It is the ancestral home of the Boyles, Earls of Glasgow, and its grounds are now a country park, with woodland walks and craft workshops.

ISLE OF ARRAN

Arran (13 miles from Ardrossan by ferry) has been called "Scotland in Miniature", as it is mountainous in the north, low lying in the middle and rises again towards the south. It is 19 miles long by about ten miles wide at its widest, and within its 165 square miles it has history and spectacular scenery aplenty. This is an island of Celtic saints, standing stones, craft workshops, cairns and old castles. The northern portion can be every bit as spectacular as the Highlands, and for those with the stamina, a climb up **Goat Fell**, at 2,866 feet the island's highest peak, is a must. The ferry from Ardrossan (a 55 minute crossing) takes you to **Brodick**, a large village and resort strung round Brodick Bay, and in the summer months a smaller ferry runs from the Mull of Kintyre to **Lochranza**, on the northern coast, and this takes about 35 minutes.

Just north of Brodick is the **Arran Brewery**, which has viewing galleries where you can see the brewing process. And at Home Farm, also near Brodick, is **Arran Aromatics**, Scotland's leading producer of body care products and scented candles. Again, you can watch the manufacturing processes from a viewing gallery.

Arran was a Gaelic speaking island up until the early 19th century, though the place names owe as much to the language of the Norsemen who settled here in the 10th and 11th centuries as they do to Gaelic. Dominating Brodick is Goat Fell, with, beneath it, **Brodick Castle** (National Trust for Scotland). This former Hamilton family stronghold (the Hamiltons became the Earls of Arran after the title was forfeited by the Boyds of Kilmarnock) sits in a wonderful location, surrounded by mature gardens. There has been a castle of sorts on the site since the Dark Ages, but the present building dates from the 16th century and later. Inside there is a collection of paintings and furniture. On the northern outskirts of the village is the **Isle of Arran Heritage Museum**, which is well worth a visit, as it shows the history of the island's ordinary people. North of Brodick, on the A841 is the beautiful village of **Corrie**, with its whitewashed cottages and its gardens aflame with colour in the summer months.

The road from Corrie follows the coast north, then turn north west and goes through the bleak but extremely beautiful **Glen Chalmadale** before bringing you to **Lochranza** ("Loch of the rowan tree river"). This small village has the ruins of **Lochranza**

Brodick Bay, Isle of Arran

Point House And Cottages, Kings Cross, Isle of Arran

Glenashdale Properties, Pier Buildings, Brodick, Isle of Arran KA27 8AX
Tel: 01770 302121/700257 Fax: 01770 302123 e-mail: ukfilter@lineone.net

The Isle of Arran is often called 'Scotland in Miniature' and sits in the Firth of Clyde.With frequent ferry services, short distance to Glasgow, and excellent road links to the South, getting there is much less hassle than to the Hebrides which are much further away. Kings Cross with its Viking fort, ancient grave, and famous connection with Robert the Bruce is a beautiful spot. The current owners have been letting **Point House and Cottages** for two decades, and are continually upgrading the properties to achieve top quality accommodation. The properties are reached by private road, and with 7 acres of mixed lawns and woodlands, house guests are assured of seclusion. The grounds lead directly to the beach, with magnificent views to the Goat Fell mountain range and Holy Isle. There is ample car parking and safe play areas for children.

Point House has four bedrooms - two doubles (one downstairs), a twin and a single - comfortably furnished lounge, dining room with a small sunroom extension, bathroom, toilet, and kitchen. Heating is electric, with also an open fire in the dining room and an oil fired Rayburn stove in the kitchen. Point House Cottage has two double bedrooms (2nd by arrangement) and a bunk room, lounge, bathroom with bath and shower, and fitted kitchen with small dining room off. Heating is electric, with also a wood burning stove in the lounge. Garden Cottage has one double bedroom with en suite bathroom, one bunk room,shower room/toilet, fitted kitchen, and open plan lounge/dining room incorporating a conservatory leading to a patio. All kitchens have electric cookers, automatic washing machines, fridge/freezers and microwaves, while Garden Cottage also has a dishwasher. All lounges have colour TV. Linen is provided for continental quilts and pillows but guests are asked to bring their own sheets and towels. Pets are welcome in two of the properties.

Glenisle Hotel

Lamlash, Isle of Arran KA27 8LS
Tel: 01770 600559/600258 Fax: 01770 600966
website: www.yellcom=glenislehotelarran.com

Lamlash is Arran's main village, and sits on Lamlash Bay, facing the historic Holy Island, where, in the 6th and 7th centuries, St Molas lived a life of austerity, and where a modern Tibetan Buddhist monastery and retreat has now been established. On the sea front in the village you will find the **Glenisle Hotel**, a picturesque, whitewashed building that offers superb accommodation combined with good food and drink. It is a family run hotel, owned and managed by Fred and Liz Wood. Before buying it, Fred was the manager, so has had 14 years continuous employment there. The hotel has 13 fully en suite rooms, all well appointed and decorated, with comfortable furnishings and a 'home from home' feel. There is a bar that serves a wide range of lagers, beers, wine and spirits, and a cosy cocktail bar where you can relax over a drink or aperitif before dinner.

The centrepiece of the hotel is undoubtedly the restaurant, where some of the finest food on the island is served. It is spacious and elegant, with crisp linen on the tables, luxury carpeting and old ornaments and plates on the mantelpiece and walls. It uses fresh local produce wherever possible, and both locals and visitors alike are drawn to it by the superb cuisine on offer. On the menu there is a wide range of dishes that is sure to contain something to your liking, The dinner menu, for instance, contains such things as roast of the day with all the trimmings, rack of lamb, poached sea salmon, juicy pan-fried steaks, rainbow trout, baked supreme of farmhouse chicken and Glenisle's own peppered pork. The starters and sweets are equally delicious, and all the dishes represent amazing value for money. Vegetarian dishes are also available, and the wine list contains something that is sure to please the most demanding of palates. The Glenisle Hotel, which is closed during January and February, is the ideal base from which to explore Arran, and both Liz and Fred will extend a warm Scottish welcome should you decide to visit!

Castle (Historic Scotland) on its shore, built in the 16th century on the site of an earlier castle. At the entrance to the village is the **Isle of Arran Whisky Distillery**, which has guided tours and a visitors centre. Beyond Lochranza is the small village of **Catacol**, with a row of identical whitewashed cottages known as **The Twelve Apostles**. They were built in the 19th century to accommodate islanders cleared from Glen Catacol in favour of deer. From here you get a good view across to the Mull of Kintyre, which is only four miles away.

Sunset over Arran

Further on, and inland from Machrie Bay, is the wonderful **Auchagallon Stone Circle**, a Bronze Age burial cairn with a circle of stones surrounding it. It is one of several ancient monuments in the area, and the **Machrie Moor Stone Circle** and the **Moss Farm Road Stone Circle** are also worth exploring. The magnificent cliffs at **Drumadoon** stand high above a raised beach, and are spectacular. **The King's Cave** is close to the the coastline, and is supposed to be the cave where Robert the Bruce saw his spider, though there is no evidence to support this. From the village of

Norwood

Smiddy Brae, Whiting Bay, Isle of Arran KA27 8PR
Tel: 01770 700536 e-mail: ekmccormack@hotmail.com

Set right on the sea front in the picturesque village of Whiting Bay on Arran you will find **Norwood**, which offers superb self catering accommodation for the discerning tourist. It consists of two VisitScotland four star graded self catering cottages, 'The Smiddy' and 'Norwood Cottage', and both are owned and managed by Elizabeth McCormack. These well maintained and extremely comfortable cottages offer everything needed for a relaxing holiday, and are near local shops and beaches. On the ground floor of The Smiddy there is one double en-suite and one twin room, a bathroom with shower and wash hand basin, a separate wc and a utility room (with washing machine, tumble dryer, iron and ironing board), as well as a spare room with pull down couch. A spiral staircase leads up to an open plan living area with a wonderful sea view. It is well equipped with a TV, video and mini hi fi unit. The kitchen/dining area boasts a gas hob, oven/grill, dishwasher, fridge/freezer and microwave. There is oil fired central heating throughout, linen and towels are provided, and there is ample parking beside the house and a small enclosed garden.

Norwood Cottage is an old, traditional stone building that sleeps four people, and has two twin rooms upstairs whilst downstairs there's a well appointed bathroom, kitchen/dining area with fridge, microwave, electric cooker and washer/dryer. The spacious living room has an electric fire, an optional open fire (coal can be bought locally), TV and mini hi fi. In addition there is 'total control' electric central heating throughout. Fresh sheets, pillowcases, duvet covers and dish towels are provided each week, with ordinary towels also available on request. There is a small garden as well as private parking close by. Cots can be provided for both properties by arrangement, but Mrs MacCormack regrets that pets are not allowed.

DRUMLA FARM

Kildonan, Isle of Arran KA27 8RP
Tel: 01770 820256 e-mail: catherine.mcneil@talk21.com
Fax: 01770 820390 website: www.arransites.co.uk/drumlafarm

Drumla Farm offers a unique haven on a working sheep farm, situated in an elevated position at the south end of the island with panoramic views across the sea to Pladda Lighthouse and Ailsa Craig, and has been described as a 'wee corner of paradise'. Owned and managed by the MacNeil family, the traditional, stone built farmhouse has been converted into three apartments offering superb self catering accommodation for discerning holidaymakers. 'The Whins' is the ground floor apartment, and sleeps six in three bedrooms - a double (with en suite shower/bathroom), a twin and a bunk bedroom,bathroom with bath, w.c. and wash handbasin. A spacious lounge with open log fire, a well appointed kitchen/dining room with gas cooker, microwave, dishwasher and fridge/freezer, central heating and a large private garden.

'Willow' and 'Beech' are upper villa apartments, with 'Willow' facing south and 'Beech' facing east. Both sleep four, and have a double and twin bedroom bedrooms, bathroom with bath, wash hand basin, w.c. and bidet. In addition there are open plan lounge/kitchen/ dining rooms with sea views, fully equipped kitchen and central heating. There is a colour TV in all properties, and a payphone is available. All bed linen is provided. The farmhouse has convenient parking, children's play area, and well behaved pets are welcome by arrangement. Drumla Farm is just a ten minute walk from Kildonan's sandy beaches and shops and eating places are within a two mile radius. This is the ideal location for a quiet, 'get away from it all' holiday in all seasons.The Isle of Arran is described as Scotland in Miniature, which offers historical sites, hill walking, golf, wildlife, fishing, or taking in the arts, cultural crafts and history, or simply relaxing.

BREADALBANE HOTEL

Kildonan, Isle of Arran KA27 8SE
Tel/Fax: 01770 820284
e-mail: yvonne@breadalbanehotel.co.uk
website: breadalbanehotel.co.uk

The Breadalbane Hotel is a warm and friendly coastal inn with superb views of the islands of Pladda and Ailsa Craig. Situated on the shore road in the quiet village of Kildonan, we attract both locals and visitors alike to enjoy our excellent home cooked meals, real ales and fine whiskies. Our aim is to fulfil the tradition of the village inn, providing quality accommodation, food and drink at a reasonable price. All our rooms are en suite and finished to a high standard, with colour TV, hair dryer, tea and coffee making facilities and little extras to make your stay more comfortable.

All rooms have central heating and sea views. Our friendly lounge bar is the ideal place to unwind. With its large, open fireplace, it is warm and cosy, even in the depths of winter. As the local "watering hole" there is always a relaxed atmosphere and a varied mix of people. Meals and snacks are served from 12.00 until 21.00. Our extensive menu, with a daily changing specials board, has something to suit everyone's taste. Local produce, including lamb, pork, beef, free range eggs, potatoes and vegetables are used whenever possible. Meals may be eaten in the dining room, bar or sun lounge overlooking the sea.

Lochranza, Isle of Arran

Blackwaterfoot, south of Machrie Bay, a road called **The String** cuts cross the centre of the island towards Brodick. The village of **Shiskine**, on The String, has the lovely **St Molas Church**, with an ancient stone carving of the saint embedded in the wall. Also worth a visit is the **Balmichael Visitor Centre**, on String Road.

South of Blackwaterfoot the road continues on towards **Lagg**, and if you need convincing about the mildness of the climate hereabouts, the palm trees in the gardens of the Lagg Inn should do the trick. The **Torrylinn Creamery**, which makes traditional Dunlop cheese in the old fashioned way, has a viewing gallery and shop. Further on the tiny island of **Pladda** can be seen about a mile from the coast before the road turns north once more towards **Whiting Bay**, another small village and holiday resort. At one time it was a small fishing port, and it takes its name from the whiting that were caught in the bay. A splendid walk starts from south of the village towards **Glenashdale Falls** and the prehistoric burial cairns known as the **Giant's Graves**.

Lamlash sits on Lamlash Bay. Having the local high school, the hospital and the local government offices, it is the island's capital. In

BLACKWATERFOOT LODGE

Blackwaterfoot, Isle of Arran KA27 8EU
Tel: 01770 860202 e-mail: info@blackwaterfoot-lodge.co.uk
Fax: 01770 860570 website: blackwaterfoot-lodge.co.uk

Situated only 50 yards from Blackwaterfoot's picturesque harbour, and a five minute stroll from the sandy beach below, the **Blackwaterfoot Lodge** is the last word in comfort and hospitality. This unique hotel offers a home from home atmosphere in a friendly, family run establishment that puts friendly service, high standards and value for money first. It is owned by Ann and Ian Relf, and offers eight comfortable and tastefully decorated rooms, seven of which are fully en suite. Two family rooms are available, three doubles (one not en suite), two twins and a single, most with a colour TV and tea and coffee making facilities. Also on offer is 'Smuggler's End' a beautifully appointed two bedroom self catering cottage, which stands within the hotel's substantial grounds.

The popular Bistro Restaurant offers "a taste of Arran", with local produce predominating in its cuisine, which fuses old and new in its range of exciting and innovative dishes. The licensed bar is cosy and welcoming, and has a wide range of drinks available, including the locally brewed real ale from Arran Breweries. It is the ideal place to relax after a day's sightseeing on the wonderful and historic island of Arran. A full Scottish breakfast is included in the B&B rate, and a Continental breakfast in the room rate. Children are more than welcome, and cots and intercoms can be supplied. Well behaved pets are welcome by prior arrangement. The lodge also boasts a substantial library, where you can settle down with a good book or the newspaper.Ann and Ian take a great pride in the Blackwaterfoot Lodge, and will go out of their way to make your stay as comfortable and memorable as possible.

the bay sits the magnificent bulk of **Holy Island**, so called because the Celtic St Molas lived a life of austerity there in the 6th and 7th centuries. Nowadays it has regained its religious significance, as it is home to a Tibetan Buddhist monastery and retreat. Near Lamlash is the factory of **Arran Provisions**, the island's biggest employer. It makes a wide range of mustards, jams and preserves, and has a visitors centre and shop.

4 Glasgow and West Central Scotland

This area covers the city of Glasgow, as well as the counties of Dunbartonshire, Renfrewshire and Lanarkshire. It is the most populous area of Scotland, and is where the bulk of the country's industry and commerce is located. But it is still well worth exploring, as much of Scotland's history was played out here, and there is much to see and do.

The scenery can be outstanding, from the upper reaches of the Clyde, where lonely hills and moorland make ideal walking country, to the grandeur of the upper reaches of the Firth of Clyde and, of course, the waters of Loch Lomond. Then there's Glasgow. Once a gritty, industrial place with an image problem, it has transformed itself into a clean, cosmopolitan European city with a burgeoning café society (at least once during a visit, do what the locals do - sit at a pavement café sipping coffee while people watch you watching them). There are art galleries and museums galore, sophisticated bars, shops and shopping malls (it is reckoned to be the second best shopping centre in Britain), award winning restaurants, glitzy hotels, concert halls and night clubs. It is home to Scottish Opera, The Royal Scottish National Orchestra, Scottish Ballet, and a string of theatres where you can see everything from serious drama to variety shows. It is also one of Britain's best dressed cities, and it is reckoned that there are more Armani and Versace outfits worn here than anywhere else in Britain outside London.

Glasgow Cathedral

And it's an easy place to get out of. Within half an hour of the city centre you can be admiring the grandeur of bens, glens and lochs, taking it easy in some wonderfully bucolic pastoral scenery, or strolling along a lonely beach which has a backdrop of magnificent hills.

Loch Lomond is renowned the world over for its beauty. A train from Glasgow's Central Station can take you straight to its bonnie banks in just under an hour, and it's a journey thousands of Glaswegians make. We're on the edge of the Highlands here. Indeed, the Highland Boundary Fault, which separates the Highland from the Lowlands, passes through the loch.

The River Clyde has traditionally been a working river, and its banks once rang to the sound of shipbuilding and heavy industry. But there is another Clyde, one which isn't so well known. The upper reaches of the river, in rural Lanarkshire, present an altogether different picture. Within the verdant Clyde Valley itself you'll find quiet orchards, green fields, woodland, small attractive villages and cosy pubs. And the lonely moorland and rounded hills where the river rises has a gaunt but compelling beauty.

View from Lyle Hill, Greenock

The towns, too, have their attractions, from Helensburgh, Gourock and Dumbarton (once the capital of the Kingdom of Strathclyde) to Hamilton, Lanark, Motherwell and East Kilbride, where you'll find one of Scotland's largest indoor shopping centre. Yes, there are towns and areas where the excesses of industry blighted the landscape, but these are being cleaned up, and some places, such as Summerlee at Coatbridge, have taken this industrial heritage and turned it into a tourist attraction.

This whole area was once the powerhouse of Scotland, and is not ashamed of the fact, not should it be. Coal was mined here, steel was produced, heavy industry sent smoke pluming into the sky, ships were built, deals struck and lots of money made. And though most of it has long gone, to be replaced by electronics, banking, broadcasting and publishing, the area still takes a pride in its past.

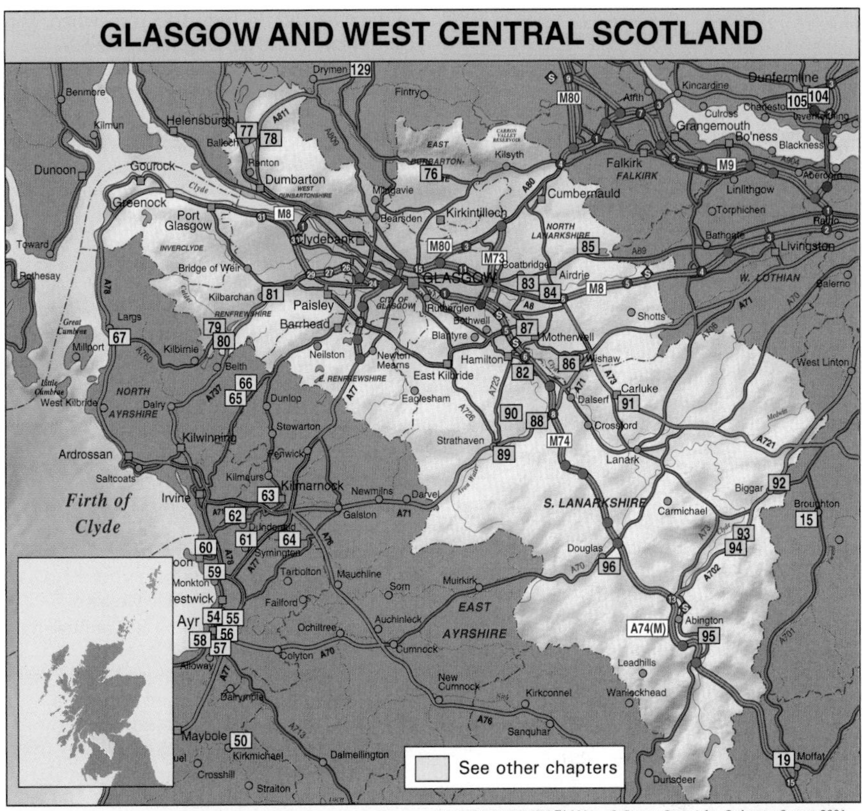

PLACES TO STAY, EAT, DRINK AND SHOP

76	Eilean, Lennoxtown	Bed and Breakfast	Page 101
77	Alvermann Guest House, Balloch	Guest House	Page 103
78	Braeburn Cottage, West Auchencarroch Farm	Bed and Breakfast	Page 104
79	Brown Bull, Lochwinnoch	Pub with food	Page 106
80	East Lochhead, Lochwinnoch	Self catering	Page 106
81	Tower House, Kilbarchan	Bed and Breakfast	Page 106
82	The Owls Restaurant, Ferniegair	Restaurant	Page 108
83	The Mint, Coatbridge	Pub with food	Page 108
84	Shawlee Cottage, Chapelhall	Bed and Breakfast	Page 108
85	The Owl and Trout Country Inn, Hillend	Pub with restautant	Page 109
86	Commercial Hotel, Wishaw	Bed and Breakfast	Page 109
87	The Bentley Hotel, Motherwell	Hotel and restaurant	Page 110
88	Shawland Hotel, nr Stonehouse	Hotel and restaurant	Page 110
89	Strathaven Gift Shop/Tea Room, Strathaven	Café, tearoom and gift shop	Page 111
90	Glassford Inn, Glassford	Pub with restautant	Page 111
91	The Chardonnay Restaurant, Carluke	Restaurant	Page 113
92	Daleside, Biggar	Bed and Breakfast	Page 114
93	Culter Mill Restaurant And Bistro, Coulter	Restaurant	Page 114
94	Murray Luxury Dumplings, Coulter	Café, tearoom and shop	Page 114
95	Heatherghyll Motel , Crawford	Hotel and restaurant	Page 116
96	Dallmartin Cottage, Douglas	Bed and Breakfast	Page 116

GLASGOW

Glasgow has worked hard on its image over the last few years. Gone are the constant references to gang fights, organised crime, drunkenness, ugly industrial townscapes and bad housing. Now people talk of trendy night spots, restaurants, pavement cafés and art galleries. But the city has changed its image more than once over the years. It started as a small religious community grouped round its cathedral. In the 17th and 18th centuries it became a city of trade, dealing with the American colonies in such commodities as tobacco and cotton, which made many people very rich indeed. In the 19th century it became a city of industry, with shipyards and heavy engineering works. Now it relies mostly on tourism, the media, service industries and the arts for employment.

The **Cathedral of St Mungo** (Historic Scotland) is where it all started. This was where St Kentigern, or Mungo, established a small church in the 6th century. The present cathedral was founded in the 12th century by David I, and the building shows work from this period onwards. In its crypt is the **Tomb of St Mungo**, while the **Blackadder Aisle** is a wonderful piece of architecture added by Bishop Blackadder in about 1500. Behind the Cathedral, on a hill, is the **Necropolis**, Glasgow's ancient burial ground, and in front of the cathedral is the modern (and looking anything but modern) **St Mungo Museum of Religious Life and Art**. Across from it is Glasgow's oldest house, **Provand's Lordship**, built in 1471 as a manse for the former St Nicholas Hospital.

"The Clyde made Glasgow, and Glasgow made the Clyde", runs an old, but true, saying. In the 17th century, the River Clyde was so shallow that people could wade across it. But in 1768, a man called John Golborne began canalising and deepening it to allow large ships to sail right up into the city. **The Tall Ship at Glasgow Harbour** at Stobcross Road tells the story of the river and the industries it spawned. The centrepiece is the tall ship itself, the **S.V. Glenlee**, built in 1896. At Braehead, on the south side of the river, is another museum which celebrates the Clyde - **Clydebuilt**. It is part of the Scottish Maritime Museum (see also Irvine and Dumbarton), and tells the river's story from the 1700s up to the present day.

Close to the Tall Ship is the **Scottish Exhibition and Conference Centre**, a mammoth complex of halls and auditoriums, including what Glaswegians now refer to as the **Armadillo**, a metallic and glass creation that owes more than a little to Sydney Opera House. And across the river from it is the city's newest attraction, the **Glasgow Science Centre**. Built on the site of the Glasgow Garden Festival, it is a combination of museum, laboratory and hands-on exhibition area that explores science and discovery, and has four floors featuring over 300 exhibits. The accompanying **Glasgow Tower** is Scotland's tallest free standing structure at 412 feet, and there's also an **IMAX Theatre**.

Glasgow has always been a city of museums and art galleries, even when it had an unsavoury reputation. Like most large citys, its **West End** is where the well-off built their mansions, as the prevailing south westerly winds carried the smells of the city away from them. Here you'll find the **Kelvingrove Art Gallery and Museum**, housed in a grand red sandstone building that froths with detail. It has internationally important collections on

River Clyde, Glasgow

archaeology, botany, zoology, geology and all the other ologies you can think of. There are Egyptian mummies, fossils, stuffed animals, dinosaur skeletons, clothing and uniforms from all over the world, weapons, and a host of other material. The art collection is stunning, and is possibly the most comprehensive civic collection in Europe.

Across the road from it is the **Glasgow Museum of Transport**, with trains, carriages, motor cars and a marvellous collection of model ships. Perhaps the most striking display is the one on Glasgow's "underground" system. The system forms a simple loop round the city centre and West End, and in the late 70s was upgraded, with orange trains taking the place of the much-loved wood and metal ones. The Glaswegians immediately dubbed it the "Clockwork Orange" and the name has stuck. More properly, it is known as the **Glasgow Subway**, rather than "underground" or "metro".

City Chambers, Glasgow

Also in the West End are the **Hunterian Museum** and the **Hunterian Art Gallery**, which form part of Glasgow University. The museum has fine collections covering geology and numismatics, while the gallery has paintings, furniture and interior design by Mackintosh and Whistler. Not far away is the **Glasgow Botanic Gardens**, with at its centre the **Kibble Palace**, a huge greenhouse with plants from all over the world.

The heart of Glasgow nowadays is **George Square**, a huge open space in front of the Victorian **City Chambers** (conducted tours available). There are statues galore, and it is a favourite place for city workers to relax in the sun. Round the corner you'll find **Hutcheson's Hall** (National Trust for Scotland), founded in 1641 as a hospice, though the building itself is 18th century. It was designed by David Hamilton, and has a small exhibition about Glasgow's **Merchant City**, that area that housed the homes and offices of the rich 17th and 18th century merchants who traded with America. Nowadays it is an area of expensive apartment blocks, smart bars, restaurants and pubs. Not far away, in Queen Street, is the **Gallery of Modern Art**, with four floors of work by modern artists such as Peter Howson, Beryl Cook and Sean Reid. In Buccleuch Street near Charing Cross, is the **Tenement House** (National Trust for Scotland). Built in the late 19th century, it recreates the genteel tenement living conditions that were common among Glasgow's lower middle classes in the early 20th century.

Glasgow is synonymous with football, and at the redeveloped Hampden Park, on the south side of the Clyde, is the **Scottish Football Museum**. It reveals the sights, sounds and stories of the world's most popular game, and tells how it almost shaped the history of Glasgow in the late 19th and 20th centuries. You can see such things as the oldest football ticket in the world, the Scottish Cup Trophy and Kenny Dalglish's 100th Scottish cap.

Charles Rennie Mackintosh is the most famous of Glasgow's architects, and was born in 1868. He designed a number of buildings in Glasgow, and there is nothing more rewarding than a tour round them. His most famous building is the **Glasgow School of Art** in Renfrew Street. It is still a working college, though tours round it are available. On the south side of the river is the **Scotland Street School**, now a museum dedicated to education. Another school is the **Martyr's Public School** in Parson Street, which is open to the public. The **Willow Tea Rooms** in Sauchiehall Street still sells teas amid Mackintosh's designs, and the **Queen's Cross Church** on Garscube Road is now the headquarters of the Charles Rennie Mackintosh Society. At Bellahouston Park, on the south side, is the **House for an Art Lover**, which interprets some of Mackintosh's incomplete designs he submitted to a competition in a German magazine. It incorporates many of his ideas. **The Lighthouse**, Scotland's centre for architecture, design and the city, is in Mitchell Lane, and has a Mackintosh interpretation centre. In the Hunterian Art Gallery there is also the **Mackintosh House**, featuring the principal rooms from Mackintosh's own house, together with a collection of designs and watercolours.

Another Glasgow architect, formerly overshadowed by Mackintosh, but now more widely known, was Alexander Thomson, known as **Greek Thomson** because of the Greek influences in his work. **St Vincent Street Church** was designed by him, as was **Holmwood House** (National Trust for Scotland) in Netherlee Road, south of the river.

Perhaps Glasgow's crowning glory is the **Burrell Collection**, housed in a purpose built complex of galleries in **Pollok Country Park**. William Burrell gifted a huge collection of art objects to the city of Glasgow, and now over 8,000 of them are on display. A whole day could be spent going round the collection. Also in the park is **Pollok House** (National Trust for Scotland), a Georgian mansion that houses the Stirling Maxwell collection of decorative arts.

Glasgow Green, a huge area of parkland, has been called Glasgow's lung, and it's here you'll find the **People's Palace**, which tells the city's own story. Close by is one of the city's most colourful buildings - **Templeton's Carpet Factory** (now a business centre). It is based on a Venetian design, with coloured bricks incorporated into the walls.

Glasgow is Britain's second largest shopping centre, with the three main shopping streets being Argyll Street, Sauchiehall Street, and Buchanan Street. There are also shopping malls. The **St Enoch Centre** is just off Argyll Street, the **Buchanan Galleries** are at the corner of Buchanan Street and Sauchiehall Street, and the **Braehead Shopping Centre** is on the city's western fringes, near Renfrew. There's also the **Forge** at Parkhead.

Within the city centre there are two exclusive retail developments. **Princes Square**, off Buchanan Street, is a mix of upmarket shops and cafés, while the **Italian Centre** is where you'll find your Armanis and Versaces.

AROUND GLASGOW

KIRKINTILLOCH

7 miles NE of Glasgow city centre on the A803

The old burgh of Kirkintilloch sits on the **Forth and Clyde Canal**, which has recently been re-opened between the Firth of Clyde and the Firth of Forth. The **Auld Kirk Museum** is housed in the former parish church, which dates from 1644. In **Peel Park** are some Roman remains from the Antonine Wall.

CUMBERNAULD

12 miles NE of Glasgow off the A80

Cumbernauld is one of Scotland's new towns, and the setting for the early 1980s film "Gregory's Girl". It sits on a hill above the A80, and has an indoor shopping centre. **Palacerigg Country Park** covers 750 acres, and is to the south east of the town. It was established in the 1970s on what was a bleak upland farm. Though it sits to the north east of Glasgow, Cumbernauld, like Kirkintilloch, was once in a detached part of Dunbartonshire.

RUTHERGLEN

2 miles SE of Glasgow city centre on the A749

This royal burgh is one of the oldest in Scotland, having been granted its royal charter

Eilean

2 Whitefield Lodge, Service Street, Lennoxtown, Glasgow G66 7JW
Tel: 01360 312123 e-mail: ian.white@eilean.freeserve.co.uk
websites: http://www.scotlandsbestbandbs.co.uk/eilean
http://stayatlochlomond.com/eilean

Eilean is a superb family run STB four star B&B in a rural village north of Glasgow. It boasts three en suite rooms - one twin and two doubles, and each one is comfortable, well decorated and fully equipped with radio/alarm, TV, hair dryer, shaver point and tea/coffee making facilities. This no smoking establishment is ideally placed to explore Loch Lomond, Glasgow, Edinburgh, Stirling and the Trossachs, and the owners, Eileen and Ian White, extend a warm welcome to their guests old and new. The breakfasts are hearty and filling, and vegetarian options are always available.

by David I in the 12th century. For a short while the burgh was incorporated into the city of Glasgow, something which was greatly resented by some of its citizens, but it now forms part of South Lanarkshire. The gable of the former **Parish Church** survives in the kirkyard of its more modern successor.

NEWTON MEARNS

7 miles S of Glasgow on the A77

Newton Mearns is a commuter town of smart bungalows and substantial houses. The four square **Parish Church** dates from 1755, and close by is **Greenbank House** (National Trust for Scotland) surrounded by gardens.

CLYDEBANK

5 miles W of Glasgow city centre on the A814

Clydebank is a former ship building town, and it was here that the Queen Mary, the Queen Elizabeth and the Queen Elizabeth II were built. The town suffered more damage than any other British town from air raids in World War II in proportion to its size. In early 1941, during the **Clydebank Blitz**, the centre of the town was flattened, other parts severely damaged. and many people were killed. The **Clydebank Museum** at the Town Hall in Dumbarton Road has exhibits devoted to the Blitz, as well as to the former Singer sewing machine factory which once stood in the town.

PAISLEY

5 miles W of Glasgow city centre on the A761

The large town of Paisley is centred on the great Abbey Church of Saints Mary the Virgin, James the Greater of Compostella, Mirin and Milburga, otherwise known as **Paisley Abbey**. It was founded in the 12th century by Walter FitzAlan, first High Steward of Scotland and progenitor of the Stewart dynasty. Within its walls are the tombs of all the non-royal High Stewards, as well as that of Princess Marjory, daughter of Robert the Bruce, who married Walter, the sixth High Steward, and Robert III. It can legitimately claim to be the birthplace of the Stewart dynasty, because Robert II, the first Stewart king, was born here in 1316. The building as you see it now dates from the 12th century onwards, though the bulk dates from the 15th century. The ruined choir was rebuilt in the early 1900s. Within the abbey is a memorial to

Paisley Abbey

Gleniffer Braes Country Park

John Witherspoon, a former minister of the abbey who signed the American Declaration of Independence (see also Gifford).

Another famous Paisley church is the Baptist **Thomas Coats Memorial Church**, sometimes known as the "Baptist Cathedral" because of its size. It was built in 1894 in memory of Thomas Coats of the Coats and Clark thread making firm. The same Thomas Coats gifted the **Coats Observatory** to the town's Philosophical Institution in 1883. It is now open to the public. Adjacent is **Paisley Museum and Art Galleries**, with displays of Paisley shawls and other memorabilia.

At the Corner of Shuttle Street and George Place are the 18th century weaving cottages known as **Sma' Shot Cottages**, housing an interpretation centre which gives an insight into the living conditions of Paisley weaving families in the past. Nearby, in New Street, is **Paisley Arts Centre**, housed in the former Laigh Kirk of 1738.

In the 18th century, the town was famed for its poets, the most famous being Robert Tannahill, who was born in **Tannahill Cottage** in Queen Street in 1774. He was a silk weaver who wrote the words to such beautiful songs as "Jessie the Flower o' Dunblane" and "The Braes o' Gleniffer". The actual braes themselves now form part of the **Gleniffer Braes Country Park**, just outside the town. One mile north of the town is the ancient burgh of **Renfrew**, which was granted its charter in 1143, making it one of the oldest in Scotland. It was here, in 1164, that the **Battle of Renfrew** took place between Somerled, Lord of the Isles, and the royal army of Malcolm IV led by Walter Fitzallan, founder of Paisley Abbey. This battle brought the Western Isles fully into the Kingdom of Scotland.

BEARSDEN AND MILNGAVIE

6 miles NW of Glasgow city centre on the A809 and A81

These two towns are firmly within Glasgow's inner commuting belt, and are full of large Victorian and Edwardian mansions, as well as the more modest bungalows of the 1930s. The **Antonine Wall** (named after Roman Emperor Antininus Pius) passes close by. It was built of turf by the Romans in the 2nd century to keep out the warring tribesmen of the north, and stretched for 37 miles between the Clyde and the Forth. In Bearsden there are the remains of a **Roman Bathhouse** (see also Falkirk).

Mugdock Country Park sits off the A81 north of Milngavie (pronounced "Mull-guy"), which is the starting point for the 95 mile long **West Highland Way**, which connects the Glasgow conurbation with Fort William.

DUMBARTON

The town is dominated by **Dumbarton Castle** (Historic Scotland), high on a volcanic plug 240 feet above the Firth of Clyde. It is one of the oldest fortified sites in Britain, and was the ancient capital of the kingdom of Strathclyde, which wasn't incorporated into Scotland until the 11th century. The name itself means the "Fort of the Britons", and though the town is called Dumbarton, the former county is Dunbartonshire, with an "n". The castle now mainly consists of modern barracks, but there is still plenty to see, including a 12th century gateway, a dungeon and a museum. From the top there is a splendid view of the Firth of Clyde. It was from Dumbarton Castle in 1548 that Mary Stuart left Scotland for France to marry the Dauphin.

The **Denny Tank Museum** in Castle Street forms part of the Scottish Maritime Museum (see also Glasgow and Irvine). It is the oldest experimental water tank in the world, and is the length of a football pitch. It was built in

River Clyde, Dumbarton

1882 as part of Denny's shipyard, and it was here that hull shapes were tested in water using carefully crafted models before the ships themselves were built. On display are many of the models built by the Denny yard.

In Church Street is an old archway called the **College Bow** from the long gone Collegiate Church of St Mary.

In **Alexandria**, north of Dumbarton, is the **Antartex Village Visitor Centre**. It incorporates a factory making sheepskin coats (with factory tours available), a mill shop and a small craft village. Close by is the **Loch Lomond Factory Outlets and Motoring Memories Museum**, housed in the quite magnificent building where one of Scotland's former makes of car, the "Argyll", were once manufactured. On the hillside above the town is the beautiful **Overtoun Estate**, with wonderful views over the Firth. **Old Kilpatrick**, to the west of the town, is supposed to be the birthplace of St Patrick (though Wales is a likelier location), who was captured by raiders and taken to Ireland in the 4th century.

AROUND DUMBARTON

BALLOCH

4 miles N of Dumbarton on the A811

This pleasant town sits at the point where the River Leven leaves **Loch Lomond** on its way to Dumbarton and the Clyde. The loch is recognised as Scotland's largest and most beautiful sheet of water, covering over 27 square miles. The **Loch Lomond and the Trossachs National Park** will be the first such park in Scotland, and the **Loch Lomond Shores** will include the National Park Gateway. It is due for completion some time in 2002.

The loch is at its widest to the south, and it gradually narrows and gets deeper as it goes north. At some points it reaches a depth of over 600 feet, making it the third deepest loch in Scotland. Many songs have been written about it, the most famous being the Bonnie, Bonnie Banks o' Loch Lomond. It was written by a Jacobite prisoner held in Carlisle Castle who was due to be executed. He is telling a fellow Jacobite whose life had been spared that he (the condemned man) will be in Scotland before him because he will take the "Low Road", i.e., the road of death, while his colleague will take the "High Road", or the road of life.

At the nearby village of **Gartocharn** is **Duncryne Hill** (nicknamed "The Dumpling" by locals), where you get a marvellous view, not just of the loch, but of the surrounding countryside. The **Highland Boundary Fault**, which separates the Lowlands of Scotland from the Highlands, passes through Loch Lomond from Glen Fruin on the western shore to Balmaha on the eastern. North of this point is the **Queen Elizabeth Forest Park**, soon to be part of Scotland's first national park (see also Aberfoyle). The **Balloch Castle Country Park**, north east of Balloch, has lochside walks, gardens and a visitors centre. South from the town you can follow the **Leven Valley Heritage Trail**, taking you down the valley of the Leven to Dumbarton, passing such small industrial towns as **Alexandria** and **Renton**.

LUSS

11 miles N of Dumbarton off the A82

This beautiful little village - one of the loveliest in Scotland - is the setting for Scottish Television's soap opera High Road, where it's called Glendarroch. It's an estate village, built by the Colquhouns of the local big house, and sits on the banks of Loch Lomond. On the opposite shore, the mighty bulk of **Ben Lomond** can be seen. It is the most southerly of Scotland's "Munros", or mountains over 3,000 feet, and is a comfortable climb for the fit and healthy. The **Parish Church of St MacKessog** is well worth a visit.

HELENSBURGH

8 miles W of Dumbarton on the A814

Like Garelochhead, this town now finds itself within Argyllshire, though it used to be in Dunbartonshire. It was created in the 18th century by Sir James Colquhoun of Luss, and named after his wife Helen. **John Logie Baird**, the inventor of television, was born in this lively holiday resort in 1888. It is one of the ports of call in July and August for the **PS Waverley**, the world's last ocean-going paddle steamer.

In Upper Colquhoun Street you'll find one of Charles Rennie Mackintosh's materpieces - **Hill House** (National Trust for Scotland). It was commissioned by Walter Blackie, the Glasgow publisher, in 1902, and contains some of Mackintosh's best work. For not only did he design the building, he also designed the interior decoration, the fittings and most of the furniture. There are also small gardens surrounding the house. **Geilston Gardens** (National Trust for Scotland) are at Cardross, to the east of the town. Also at Cardross is **St Mahew's Chapel**, dating originally from 1294.

North of Helensburgh is **Glen Fruin**, which takes you over to Loch Lomond. It was the scene of a battle in 1603 when the MacGregors defeated the Colquhouns with much loss of life.

GARELOCHHEAD

14 miles NW of Dumbarton on the A814

This old village at the head of the beautiful **Gare Loch** now finds itself in Argyllshire for administrative purposes. However, along with the picturesque **Rosneath Peninsula**, it was once part of the old county of Dunbartonshire, and it is to Dumbarton that it still looks for shopping and other services. It makes a fine centre for hillwalking and yachting. At **Cove**, on the Rosneath Peninsula, are the **Linn Botanical Gardens**.

GREENOCK

Situated on the south bank of the Firth of Clyde, at a point known as **The Tail of the Bank**, Greenock is a bustling industrial town and port. It was the birthplace, in 1736, of **James Watt**, the inventor of steam power. Hills pile up behind the town, and on the slopes at Lyle Hill is a huge **Cross of Lorraine** mounted on an anchor, which was built in 1946, and commemorates the Free French sailers who lost their lives on the Atlantic during World War II.

Customhouse Quay was the departure point for thousands of Scottish emigrants sailing away to America in the 19th and early 120th centuries. The nearby **Custom House**, built in 1810, reflects the port's importance in bygone days, and it now houses a small museum. Another museum is to be found at the **McLean Museum and Art Gallery** on Kelly Street, which features exhibits on local history and paintings by Courbin, Boudin and the Scottish Colourists.

In Greenock cemetery is the grave of Robert Burn's **Highland Mary**, whose real name was Mary Campbell (see also Failford and Dunoon). Burns had met her at a low point in his life in Mauchline, and had asked her to acompany him to the West Indies when he thought of emigrating. Unfortunately, on a trip home to Dunoon to arrange for her departure, she died. She was previously buried in the kirkyard of the former Old West Kirk, but was exhumed and reburied in 1920. When

Model Ship, McLean museum

the Old West Kirk, which dated from the late 16th century, was dismantled in 1926, some of its stones were used to build the new **Old West Kirk**, on the Esplanade. It has some wonderful stained glass and wood carving.

AROUND GREENOCK

PORT GLASGOW

3 miles E of Greenock on the A8

Before the Clyde at Glasgow was canalised and deepened, this town was Glasgow's main port. **Newark Castle** (Historic Scotland) lies close to the riverbank, and dates from the 16th and 17th centuries. Two miles west of Port Glasgow is the **Finlaystone Estate**, where the present head of the Clan Macmillan lives. It is open to the public, and features gardens and 140 acres of woodland which can be explored. Finlaystone House, at the heart of the estate, dates back to the 14th century, though it has been extended over the centuries. It can be visited by special arrangement.

Brown Bull

Main Street, Lochwinnoch, Renfrewshire PA12 4AH
Tel: 01505 843250; Fax: 01505 842448
e-mail: jim@thebrownbull.co.uk

The **Brown Bull** is a delightful, family run pub situated in the picturesque village of Lochwinnoch. It dates from 1809, when it was a coaching inn used by traders who dealt with the local mills and weavers in nearby Paisley. The bar areas are full of olde worlde character, with low ceilings and the original wooden flooring, and serve a wide array of beers, wine, spirits and soft drinks. The bar lunches are tasty, ample and always beautifully cooked, and are made from fresh local produce wherever possible. This is an establishment which offers real Scottish hospitality and wonderful value for money - don't miss it!

East Lochhead

Largs Road, Lochwinnoch, Renfrewshire PA12 4DX
Tel/Fax: 01505 842610 e-mail:eastlochhead@aol.com
website: www.eastlochhead.co.uk

East Lochhead offers four superbly comfortable self catering cottages and a flat to the holiday maker who demands that little bit more from their holiday accommodation. Owned and managed by Janet and Ross Anderson, the cottages are arranged round a central courtyard within farming country, and each one is well appointed, spacious and comfortable. The development has been awarded four coveted stars by VisitScotland, and in addition it has 'five diamonds' from the AA and another five stars from Taste of Scotland for the quality of the food that Janet prepares for guests by arrangement.

Tower House

Milliken Park Road, Kilbarchan, Renfrewshire PA10 2DB
Tel/Fax: 01505 703299 e-mail: tvanbreugel@cs.com

Tower House is situated within the historic conservation village of Kilbarchan, and offers the very best in B&B accommodation to holidaymakers. It has three en suite rooms, all of which are very comfortable and tastefully decorated, and all of which have a TV and hospitality tray. The house is steeped in history. At one time was owned by a niece of Sir Walter Scott, and it also played host to Frédéric Chopin the pianist, who gave a recital here. Owners Gladys and Tony van Breugel extend a warm welcome to visitors old and new, and assure them of a relaxing, home from home atmosphere in this most lovely of B&Bs. Dutch, German and French are all spoken.

KILBARCHAN

11 miles SE of Greenock, off the A761

This is undoubtedly the most picturesque village in Renfrewshire, and is a huddle of old 18th century weaving cottages. **The Weaver's Cottage** (National Trust for Scotland) dates from 1723, and shows what a typical weaver's cottage (complete with working loom) was like. A few miles south is **Lochwinnoch**, a former textiles village, with the **Clyde Muirshiel Regional Park** close by, where there are nature trails, moorland walks and watersports on Castle Semple Loch.

Chateleherault House and Country Park

GOUROCK

2 miles W of Greenock town centre on the A770

This little holiday resort is now more or less a suburb of Greenock, though at one time it was a separate burgh. It is on a most attractive part of the Clyde, opposite Kilcreggan, the Gareloch and the entrance to Loch Long, where the mountains tumble down towards the sea. The Firth of Clyde is a famous yachting area, and the town is the home of the **Royal Gourock Yacht Club**, near the Promenade. At Cloch Point, four miles to the south west, is the **Cloch Lighthouse** of 1797, a famous landmark for ships sailing on the Clyde. Between Castle Gardens and Kempock Street in the town is the curiously named **Granny Kempock's Stone**, which dates from prehistoric times. It is shaped like a cloaked figure, and to walk round it is said to bring good luck.

HAMILTON

Once the county town of Lanarkshire, Hamilton is now the adminstrative centre for South Lanarkshire. It became a royal burgh in 1548, though it lost its royal status in 1669. It is very much connected with one of the most important families in Scotland, the Dukes of Hamilton, Scotland's premier dukes. Up until the 1920s, when it was demolished in possibly the greatest act of vandalism in Scotland, the immense Hamilton Palace was the grandest non royal residence in Britain. Not a stone now remains of it above ground, though the Hamilton's burial place, the grandiose **Hamilton Mausoleum**, still remains. It is a curious building, with an immense dome, and is full of Masonic symbolism. It consists of a chapel above and a crypt below, and was built in the mid 19th century for Alexander, the 10th Duke, who had his ancestors removed from what was left of the old Collegiate Church of Hamilton (now gone) and reinterred in the crypt. When he himself died, he was laid to rest in the sarcophagus of an ancient Egyptian princess which reposed in the chapel. The bodies were all removed in 1921, and the place can now be visited. One thing to note is that the crypt doors lock from the inside. The reason is simple - once a month a servant was sent down to clean and polish the coffins, and to prevent ghoulish sightseers, she locked herself in.

A two mile long Grand Avenue once stretched from the palace all the way to **Chateleherault**, a hunting lodge east of the town. Most of the avenue is gone, but Chatelherault survives, having been refurbished in the 1980s. It was originally designed by William Adam, and built in the 1730s. The lodge once also housed the Duke's hunting dogs, and was therefore known as the "Dog Kennels". Now it houses a museum and interpretation centre. The lodge got its name because the Dukes of Hamilton were also the Dukes of Chatellerault near Poitou in France. The title was given to the Hamiltons in 1548 by Henry II of France in recognition of the part the family played in arranging the marriage of Mary Stuart to the Dauphin. The spelling of the name changed over the years, and Chatellerault gradually became Chatelherault. Surrounding the lodge is the **Chatelherault Country Park**, with over ten miles of woodland walks. The ruins of **Cadzow Castle**, the original home of the Hamiltons, and where Mary Stuart once stayed, can be see within the park. There are also the remains of an old **Iron Age Fort** and the **Cadzow Oaks**, which are very old. In a field in front of Chatelherault is a small but famous herd of **White Cattle**.

Within the town is **Hamilton Parish Church**, also designed by William Adam, which dates from 1734. It is in the shape of a Greek cross, with a cupola over the crossing. The pre-Norman **Netherton Cross** stands at the church entrance, and in the kirkyard is the **Heads Monument**, commemorating four Covenanters beheaded in Edinburgh after the Pentland Rising of 1666. In Almada Street you'll find the town's most prominent landmark - the **County Buildings**. They were built in the 1960s for the then Lanarkshire County Council, and bear an uncanny resemblance to the United Nations Building in New York.

Based on an old 17th century coaching inn

THE OWLS RESTAURANT

195 Carlisle Road, Ferniegair, Hamilton ML3 7TU
Tel: 01698 285937 Fax: 01698 283165

The **Owls Restaurant** is easily reached from Junction 6 or 7 of the M74, the main road north from England to Glasgow, so makes an excellent lunch or dinner-time stop. It seats 40, mostly in a non-smoking conservatory-type extension, and offers great food at amazing prices. You can choose from the printed menu or the daily specials board, and all dishes are freshly prepared on the premises. Why not try its chicken Rob Roy, which is chicken stuffed with haggis and Arran mustard, or one of the seafood dishes for which it renowned? The place is open every day 12.00-21.00 except Tuesday in winter.

THE MINT

16 Academy Street, Coatbridge ML5 3LU
Tel/Fax: 01236 44191

The Mint is something special - a well designed and beautifully furnished town centre pub that sells excellent, keenly priced food as well as a great range of drinks. It appeals to people from eighteen to eighty, with its mahogany bar, slate and wood floors and even a revolving door at its entrance! The place was a bank until the 1960s, and is now a popular venue for locals and visitors alike. There is a small beer garden and children's play area to the rear and a 'conservatory' style extension at the front, where you can enjoy a relaxing drink or a meal (such as its famous steak pie) as you watch the world go by.

SHAWLEE COTTAGE

108 Lauchope Street, Chapelhall, near Airdrie ML6 8SW
Tel: 01236 753774; Fax: 01236 749300
e-mail: cathy@csaitken.fsbusiness.co.uk
website: csaitken.fsbusiness.co.uk

Shawlee Cottage is an outstanding three star B&B in a small village just outside Airdrie in Scotland's Central Belt. It is situated just off the A73, and is handy for both the M8 and the M74 (Junction 5). It has five en suite rooms, all on the ground floor, and all warm, comfortable and beautifully decorated. You can book in on B&B or B&B and evening meal rates, and children are more than welcome. The breakfasts and evening meals are all beautifully cooked at this non smoking establishment, and the owners, Cathy and Sandy Aitken, take a great pride in the good old Scottish hospitality they offer.

once known as the Hamilton Arms is the **Low Parks Museum**, which has displays and memorabilia on local history. It also houses a large display on Lanarkshire's own regiment - **The Cameronians (Scottish Rifles)**. Raised as a Covenanting force in the 17th century, it chose to disband itself in 1968 rather than amalgamate with another regiment (see also Douglas). In the Bent Cemetery is the simple grave of one of Scotland's best known entertainers, **Sir Harry Lauder**. Nearby is the plot where the Hamiltons who were removed from the Mausoleum are now buried. A curious fact is that the 10th Duke still lies in his Egyptian sarcopagus.

Hamilton is the start of one of Scotland's ten national tourist routes, the **Clyde Valley Tourist Route**. It follows the Clyde Valley all the way south to Abington on the M74.

AROUND HAMILTON

AIRDRIE AND COATBRIDGE

8 miles N of Hamilton on the A89

The twin towns of Airdrie and Coatbridge are industrial in character. In Coatbridge, in 1889, was born **John Reith**, first general manager of what was then the British Broadcasting Company. Single-handedly he shaped the character of the organisation. The town is home to the **Summerlee Heritage Centre**, which traces the history of the area's old industries - steelmaking, coalmining and the manufacture of heavy plant. Tramlines have been laid out in it, and there is a small collection of trams from all over Europe. There is also a short section of the Summerleee branch of the **Monkland Canal** (now closed), which ran from Glasgow to the Lanarkshire coalfields. The canal was built between 1770 and 1794, and at one time was the most profitable in Scotland.

Also in the town is the **Time Capsule**, one of the largest leisure centres in the area.

MOTHERWELL AND WISHAW

3 miles E of Hamilton on the A721

The twin towns of Motherwell and Wishaw, up until 1975, were included in the one burgh. They were formerly steelmaking towns, though the steelworks at Ravenscraig have now gone. The award-winning **Motherwell Heritage Centre** on High Road has a number

THE OWL AND TROUT COUNTRY INN

39 Airdrie Road, Hillend, near Caldercruix, Airdrie ML6 8PA
Tel: 01236 843227
e-mail: ireneowl@hscali.co.uk

A couple of miles east of Airdrie you will find **The Owl and Trout Country Inn**, set in a scenic position next to both Hillend and Lily Lochs. It is owned and run by Irene and Trevor Filshie, and was once a coaching inn. Irene is an excellent cook, and there is a printed menu or a daily specials board which contains many dishes such as fish, venison and chicken stuffed with haggis. The restaurant seats 45, and the bar serves a great range of beers, wine, spirits and soft drinks. So popular is the place that you need to book at all times.

COMMERCIAL HOTEL

420 Main Street, Wishaw, Lanarkshire ML2 7NG
Tel: 01698 351367/372458

The **Commercial Hotel** is the ideal base from which to explore the Central Lowlands of Scotland, as Glasgow, Edinburgh and the Burns Country are all within an hour's drive. It boasts five comfortable rooms on a B&B basis in an establishment that offers good, old fashioned Scottish hospitality and great value for money. The full Scottish breakfasts are always beautifully cooked, with hearty portions that should set you up for a day's sightseeing. There is a comfortable bar area, and as mine host Frank McGuinness knows the area well, he can advise on places to visit and things to see.

The Bentley Hotel

19 High Road, Motherwell, Lanarkshire ML1 3HU
Tel: 01698 265588; Fax: 01698 253418
e-mail: the bentleyhotel@barbox.net

You can't miss **The Bentley Hotel** in Motherwell, as its "tower" has been a distinctive landmark for many years! The building dates from 1874, and has been transformed into a stylish three star hotel that offers 18 fully en suite rooms to discerning travellers. Each one is stylish and beautifully decorated, and boasts tea and coffee making facilities, remote control colour TV, direct dial telephone and trouser press. The food, as you would expect, is outstanding, and the elegant dining room offers a range of menus to suit all occasions lunch, pre-theatre, à la carte and dinner. The cuisine is a mixture of traditional and adventurous, with the chefs using only finest and freshest of local produce wherever possible.

Sunday lunch is served between 13.0 and 18.00, and is so popular that you are well advised to book in advance. After a day's driving, or exploring the local area, why not relax over a welcoming drink in the hotel's cosy and comfortable lounge bar? It offers a fine range of beers, wines, spirits and, should you be driving, soft drinks. The hotel is also the ideal venue for that special function, be it a birthday party, wedding reception or anniversary. The "Back o' Barns" function suite can accommodate up to 120 people depending on the layout, and is also the ideal venue for a business meeting or function. The hotel sits within walking distance of Motherwell Station, which is a stopping point on the main Glasgow Central/London Euston line. The town sits between Glasgow and Edinburgh, and it makes an excellent base for exploring both cities. Plus it has the picturesque and historic Clyde Valley on its doorstep. As it is close to the M74, it also makes a great overnight stopping place as you head north to the Highlands or south to England.

Shawland Hotel And Travel Lodge

Ayr Road, near Stonehouse, Lanarkshire ML9 2TZ
Tel: 01698 791111 Fax 01698 792001

Situated only a few yards from Junction 8 on the M74, the **Shawland Hotel and Travel Lodge** is the idea overnight stopping place when travelling north to Glasgow and the Highlands. It is close to the beautiful Clyde Valley, so also makes an ideal base for exploring an area that is particularly rich in history and landscape. The Lodge has 21 comfortable and tastefully decorated rooms, with full en suite facilities, heated towel rails, colour TVs (with Sky), direct dial telephones and tea/coffee making facilities. There are also specially adapted rooms for the disabled, and non smoking rooms are available on request. The hotel contains two well-stocked bars. The public bar has a relaxed and informal atmosphere with an open log fire, and is the ideal place for meeting people over a quiet drink. The spacious lounge bar is the ideal place for a quiet meal, and has an ambience that speaks of warmth and friendliness.

There is a great range of drinks available, from beers and lagers to wine, spirits, liqueurs and, should you be driving, soft drinks. The elegant Lewis Restaurant serves wonderful food, and comes highly recommended from all those who have used it. It seats 30 in absolute comfort, and the chef uses only the finest, freshest local produce wherever possible in the cuisine. A small room is also available for an intimate dinner with friends or family. The Shawlands is also the ideal venue for a function such as a wedding, party or business seminar. The MacMillan Function Suite offers comfort and privacy, plus there is a full wedding package available, taking some of the strain off organising one! The Shawlands Hotel and Travel lodge offers great value for money, with everything keenly priced. The welcome you will get is warm and friendly, and if you decide to stay, you will be sure to come back!

of exhibitions, and hosts varied activities with a heritage theme. To the west of Motherwell is the 1100 acres of **Strathclyde Country Park**, built on waste ground in the early 70s. Within it there is an international size rowing lake, where the rowing events of the 1986 Commonwealth Games were held. On its banks are the remains of a **Roman Bathhouse**. There are guided walks throughout the year, as well as nature trails and a camping and caravanning site.

DALSERF

6 miles SE of Hamilton town centre off the A72

Once a sizeable village with inns and a ferry across the Clyde, Dalserf has now shrunk to no more than a few cottages and a church. **Dalserf Parish Church**, with its whitewashed walls, looks more like a house than a church, and dates from 1655, though an ancient chapel dedicated to St Serf stood here before that. In the kirkyard is a pre-Norman "hogs back" graveslab, which was dug up in 1897, and also a memorial to the **Rev. John Macmillan**, sometimes called "the last of the Covenanters". He died in 1753.

STRATHAVEN

7 miles S of Hamilton on the A726

Strathaven (pronounced "Stray-ven") is a real gem of a small town that sits at the heart of Avondale. The ruins of **Strathaven Castle** are all that is left of a once large and powerful 14th century stronghold. It was built by the Douglas family, passed to the Stewarts, and landed up in the hands of the Hamitons. A legend says that before the Reformation, a wife of one of the owners was walled up alive in the castle, and when parts of a wall fell down in the 19th century, human bones were found among the masonry. On the edge of the **John Hastie Park** is the **John Hastie Museum**, which has local history collections.

To the west of the town, at Drumclog, was fought the **Battle of Drumclog**, where an army of Covanenters overcame government troops in 1679. A memorial on a minor road off the A71 commemorates the event.

EAST KILBRIDE

5 miles W of Hamilton town centre on the A726

East Kilbride is the largest and undoubtedly the most successful of Scotland's post war new towns. Work started on laying it out in 1947 round an old village, and now it has a population of about 70,000. It is renowned for its shopping facilites, and has three shopping malls, **Princes Mall**, **The Plaza** and the **Olympia Centre**, which together make one of the largest undercover shopping areas in Scotland. A new mall being built should extend it even further.

In the Calderwood area of the town is **Hunter House**, birthplace in the 18th century of the Hunter Brothers, pioneering surgeons who worked both in Glasgow and London. The Hunterian Museum in Glasgow is one of their legacies. The house now has a small display and museum about the two men and their lives.

On the outskirts of the town is **Calderglen Country Park**, based on Torrance House (not open to the public). It has play areas, nature trails and a children's zoo. To the north of the town is the **James Hamilton Heritage Park**, with a 16 acre boating loch. Behind it is the restored 15th century **Mains Castle** (not open to the public). Close by is the town's newest attraction, the **Scottish Museum of Country Life**, based around Wester Kittochside Farm, which had been home to the Reid family since the 16th century. In 1992, the last of the family, Margaret Reid, gifted it to the National Trust for Scotland. Run jointly by the National Museums of Scotland and the National Trust, it explains rural life in Scotland throughout the ages, and has a huge collection of farm implements and machinery. The elegant farmhouse of Wester Kittochside, which dates from 1783, is also open to the public.

EAGLESHAM

9 miles W of Hamilton on the B764

The conservation village of Eaglesham was planned and built by the Earl of Egltinton in the mid 1700s. It is shaped like a huge "A", with the point facing the moorland behind the village. Between the two arms of the "A" is a large village green area known as the "Orry", on which once stood a cotton mill. The lovely period cottages and houses in the village make a perfect picture of Scottish rural life, though the village has largely been colonised by commuters from Glasgow. The **Parish Church**, which dates from 1788, has the look of an Alpine church about it, and it is reckoned that the 10th Earl was influenced by villages he had admired in northern Italy when planning Eaglesham.

It was in a field near Eaglesham in 1941 that **Rudolph Hess**, Hitler's deputy, landed when he parachuted (while the plane was upside down) from an ME 110. He was found by a local farmer called David McLean, who took him home and treated him firmly but politely. Hess gave his name as Alfred Horn, but it was soon established that he was Hitler's deputy. He said he was on a secret mission to speak to the Duke of Hamilton, and a map he possessed showed that had been trying to reach Dungavel House, the Duke's Lanarkshire home near Strathaven.

He was then taken to Maryhill Barracks in Glasgow, where he was sometimes in the custody of Corporal William Ross, who went on to become the Secretary of State for Scotland in the Wilson government. Hess was later moved to Buchanan Castle near Drymen in Stirlingshire, where he was interrogated (see also Drymen).

BOTHWELL

2 miles NW of Hamilton town centre off the M74

In the centre of this small town is **St Bride's Parish Church**, with a chancel dating from 1398. It was built as part of a collegiate church by Archibald the Grim, 3rd Earl of Douglas, and has a roof made entirely of stone. Outside the west end of the Victorian nave is a monument to **Joanna Baillie**, a playwrite and poetess born at Bothwell manse in 1762. She was praised by Scott as being one of the finest writers of the 18th century.

On the banks of the Clyde, some distance from the town, are the massive and impressive remains of **Bothwell Castle** (Historic Scotland). Historians have rated it one of the most important secular medieval buildings in Scotland. It was most likely built in the 13th century by Walter de Moravia. Upstream is Bothwell Bridge, scene, in 1679, of the **Battle of Bothwell Bridge** between the Royalist forces of the Duke of Monmouth and a Covenanting army. The Covenanters were heavily defeated, with over 500 being killed and 1,200 taken prisoner. The bridge you see today is basically the same bridge, though much altered and widened. A memorial commemorates the event.

BLANTYRE

3 miles NW of Hamilton town centre, on the A724

Blantyre is a former mining town which nowadays is visited because of the **David Livingstone Centre** (National Trust for Scotland). Here, at Shuttle Row, was born the African explorer and missionary David Livingstone in 1813. A great cotton mill stood here at one time, and Shuttle Row was a tenement block that housed some of the workers. The great man was born in a one-room flat, though the whole tenement has now been given over to housing displays and mementos about his life and work.

New Lanark

LANARK

Set above the Clyde Valley near the upper reaches of the Clyde, the ancient royal burgh of Lanark is an historic town that has its roots deep in the heart of Scotland's history. Every year, in June, the town celebrates **Lanimer Day**, which originated as a ceremony of riding the bounds of the burgh.

High on a wall of the 18th century **St Nicholas's Church** is a statue of William Wallace the Scottish freedom fighter. It recalls an event which took place when the town's castle (now gone) was garrisoned by English troops. Wallace was taken prisoner in the castle, but his "lenman" (girlfriend) helped him escape. For this, she was executed by the English sheriff. Wallace later returned and killed the sheriff in revenge. In the Westport you'll find the **Royal Burgh of Lanark Museum**, which explains the incident, as well as the town's history. Near the centre of the town are the ruins of the original place of worship, **St Kentigern's Church**. In its kirkyard is buried **William Smellie** (pronounced Smillie), the father of modern midwifery, who died in 1763.

On the banks of the Clyde lies the village of **New Lanark**, nominated as a World Heritage Site. It was here, in 1785, that David Dale (see also Stewarton) founded a new cotton mill village of 2,500 people that was to become a model for social reform. Under his son-in-law **Robert Owen**, who was manager, there were good working conditions, decent homes, fair wages, schools and health care.

The mills were still in production up to 1968, but now the village has been turned into one great museum and interpretation centre. Under the care of the New Lanark Conservation Trust, it has become one of the most popular tourist destinations in Scotland, even though people still live in some of the original tenements and cottages to this day.

Attractions include a **Visitors Centre** (including the New Millennium Ride and a Textile Machinery Exhibition), the

DALESIDE

165 High Street, Biggar, Lanarkshire ML12 6DL
Tel/Fax: 01899 220097

For over ten years, Margaret and Peter Brotherstone have owned and managed **Daleside**, a superior B&B establishment in the small, picturesque town of Biggar. It has three beautifully decorated and comfortable bedrooms, a double and two twins, with a wash hand basin in each. The full Scottish breakfasts are filling and hearty, and packed lunches can be made up on request. Both Margaret and Peter are very knowledgeable about the area, and can suggest places to visit. The building itself is over 250 years old, though the standards of hospitality and value for money are completely up to date!

CULTER MILL RESTAURANT AND BISTRO

Coulter Village, by Biggar, Lanarkshire ML12 6PZ
Tel/Fax: 01899 220950 website: www.eatinscotland.com
e-mail: johnstirratlimited@cultermill.fsbusiness.co.uk

The village may be 'Coulter', but its mill is'Culter', and it's within the old mill building that you'll find the **Culter Mill Restaurant and Bistro**, one of the best eating places in South Lanarkshire. A mill has stood on the site since at least the 12th century, though the present building dates from around 1820. It even has its own ghost - one Robert Forest, the resident miller, who died alone in the top room of the mill in 1923. The restaurant and bistro was opened in 1990, and has been owned and managed by John Stirrat since 2001. He has continued its tradition of serving fine food to discerning diners, and the place has a fine reputation for its high standards of cuisine.

Downstairs is a small bistro seating 35, where you can relax over a cup of coffee or alcoholic drink and enjoy one of the beautifully cooked light meals or snacks on offer. The place is intimate and cosy, with a low beamed ceiling and wall lighting that adds to the atmosphere. Upstairs is the Waterwheel Restaurant, which seats 45 people in absolute comfort. With its dark walls, old wood and crisp table linen, it is the ideal spot for a that intimate dinner with good food and fine wines. Head chef Donald Bryson has put together a menu that only uses the finest of local produce in season wherever possible.

Starters include soup of the day, chicken liver pate studded with pistachio nuts, honeydew melon and feta cheese salad. Main course dishes include fillet of Scottish salmon, braised beef cooked in its own juices, fillet of Scotch beef and the Waterwheel's 'signature dish' - wild boar marinated in oriental spices, stir fried with crispy vegetables and served with saffron rice. So proud of this dish is the Culter Mill staff that the recipe is even printed on the menu! There is also a great choice of puddings and cheeses, including the locally made Lanark Blue. Just watch out for the ghost of Robert Forest!

MURRAY LUXURY DUMPLINGS & FACTORY KITCHEN

Coulter Park Farm, Coulter, near Biggar,
Lanarkshire ML12 6HN
Tel: 01899 221363 Fax: 01899 221672

Set amid the lovely scenery of South Lanarkshire, the **Murray Luxury Dumplings & Factory Kitchen** is the ideal place to enjoy a cup of tea, a snack or a light lunch in delightful, olde worlde surroundings. You can even sample that great Scottish delicacy, the 'clootie dumpling'(a rich and delicious fruit pudding boiled or steamed within a cloth or 'clootie') as it is made in the adjacent kitchens from a secret recipe and sent all over Scotland. There is also a small craft centre, making this an essential stop in any tour of Scotland.

Millworker's House, the **Village Store Exhibition** and **Robert Owen's House**. Other buildings have been converted into craft workshops, and there is also a hotel housed in a former mill. A 3-D show called **Annie Mcleod's Story** is shown in **Robert Owen's School**, and uses the latest in 3-D technology. Also in the village is a **Scottish Wildlife Trust Visitors Centre**.

The mills were at one time poweerd by the waters of the Clyde, and close by are the **Falls of Clyde** waterfalls, the most famous being Cora Linn and Bonnington. Unfortunately, a hydro-electric scheme now harnesses the power of the water, and the falls are only seen at their most spectacular at certain times of the year.

A few miles north of the town is **Carluke**, which stands above the Clyde Valley. which is noted for its orchards, introduced in medieval times by the monks of Lesmahagow Priory. The bell tower of the former parish church, built in 1715, still stands.

AROUND LANARK

BIGGAR

10 miles SE of Lanark on the A702

Biggar must have more museums per head of population than any other place in Britain. **The Biggar Gas Works Museum**, housed in the town's former gas works, explains how gas was produced from coal in former times, and the **Moat Park Heritage Centre** has exhibits and displays about the area round the town from when it was formed millions of years ago right up until the present day. **Greenhill Covenanter's House** used to stand at Wiston, 10 miles away, but was transported to Biggar stone by stone, and is now dedicated to the Covenanters. These were the people who, in the 17th century, resisted Charles II's attempts to impose bishops on the Church of Scotland, and sometimes payed with their lives for doing so. The **Gladstone Court Museum** has recreated a Victorian street, with dressmakers, bootmakers and even a schoolroom.

The Albion Building houses the **Albion Motors Archives**, which are the records of the Albion Motor Company, started up locally in 1899. It soon grew to be the largest manufacturer of commercial vehicles in the British Empire, and is now part of Leyland DAF. At Brownsbank Cottage, a mile and a half from the town, lived the Scottish poet Christopher Grieve, better known as **Hugh McDiarmid** (see also Langholm). He died in 1978, and his wife Valda continued to live there until her death in 1989. Now it has been restored to exactly how it looked when MacDairmid lived there, and it is home to a writer-in-residence. It can be visited by appointment only.

Biggar is the home of the professionally run **Biggar Puppet Theatre**, which has a Victorian-style theatre which can seat up to 100 people, plus a museum. It is Scotland's largest puppet company, and regularly presents shows all over Britain.

St Mary's Church was founded in 1546 by Lord Fleming, Chancellor of Scotland. It is a graceful, cruciform church, and was the last one to be built in Scotland before the Reformation.

To the west of the town, just off the M74, are the twin settlements of **Abington** and **Crawford**, which have a number of services, and make ideal stopping off places when heading north.

CARMICHAEL

4 miles S of Lanark on a minor road west of the A73

The small **Carmichael Parish Church** dates from 1750, and has an interesting laird's loft. One of the past lairds, the Earl of Hyndford, left a sum of money called the Hyndford Mortification to provide the local schoolmasters with a yearly pair of trousers and a supply of whisky. The **Discover Carmichael Visitor Centre** is situated on the Carmichael Estate, and has a display of waxwork models (of Madame Tussaud's standard) that depict famous characters and events in Scotland's history, such as the execution of Mary Stuart. There is also a small display about wind energy.

LEADHILLS

18 miles S of Lanark on the B797

Like its neighbour Wanlockhead (which is in Dumfriesshire), Leadhills is a former leadmining village. It has the highest golf course in Scotland, and is full of old 18th and 19th century lead miners' cottage. It forms one terminus for the Leadhills and Wanlockhead Light Railway (see also Wanlockhead). The **Allan Ramsay Library** is the oldest subscription Library in Scotland, and is named after the famous poet born here in 1684 (see also Penicuik). In the graveyard is the grave of **John Taylor**, a lead miner who lived to be 137 years old. Next to the cemetery is a monument to **William Symington**, who was born in the village in 1764. He worked as an engineer in the mines, and was a pioneer of steam propulsion in ships. His paddle-boat the Charlotte Dundas was launched at Grangemouth in 1802.

DOUGLAS

8 miles SW of Lanark on the A70

It was in Douglas, in 1968, that the Cameronians (Scottish Rifles), a proud Scottish regiment, disbanded itself in 1968. The ceremony took place in the grounds of **Castle Dangerous**, ancestral home of the Douglases, of which only a tower now survives. It was here, in 1689, that the regiment was raised by **James, Earl of Angus**. His statue now stands in the village.

The centre of Douglas is a conservation area, with many old cottages and and houses. **The Sun Inn** of 1621 was once the village's Tolbooth, where justice was meted out. **Old St Bride's** is the choir of the former parish church, which dated from the 14th century. Within it are memorials to members of the Douglas family, including Archibald, the 5th Earl of Angus. He was killed at Flodden in 1513, and had the curious nickname of "**Bell the Cat**". There is also a memorial to "the Good Sir James of Douglas", killed by the Moors in Spain while taking Robert the Bruce's heart to the Holy Land for burial. The clock in the clock tower was gifted to the church by Mary Stuart in 1565, and is the oldest working public clock in Scotland.

CROSSFORD

4 miles NW of Lanark on the A72

This lovely little village sits in the heart of the Clyde Valley, on the banks of the river. Above it you'll find the substantial ruins of **Craignethan Castle** (Historic Scotland), where Mary Stuart once stayed. It was built about 1530 by Sir James Hamilton of Finnart, and Sir Walter Scott used it as a model for his "Tillietudlem Castle" in Old Mortality.

5 Edinburgh and The Lothians

This area, The Lothians, consists of three former counties - East Lothian, Midlothian and West Lothian. It is generally low lying, with areas of industry - especially in the west - and areas of good arable farmland to the east. This is the heartland of Scottish history, full of castles, grand houses and churches. It is also a place of quiet, pastoral villages and marvellous scenery. The only towns that could possibly be said to be industrial are Dalkeith and Bathgate, and even here industry never intruded too much.

Dominating it all is the city of Edinburgh, which probably has more history attached to it that any other comparable city in the world. But it's a compact place, and its tentacles haven't yet spread out too much into the surround-ing countryside. Behind the city are the Pentland Hills, a lonely area of high moorland streching south west towards the Lanarkshire boundary, and to the south and south east are the Moorfoot and Lammer-muir Hills respectively, which thrust down into the Borders.

Linlithgow Palace, Linlithgow

East Lothian (formerly "Hadding-tonshire") is a farming county, and is a patchwork of fields, with small, neat villages dotted all over it. The quiet country lanes cry out to be explored by car, and though there is none of the grandeur of the Highlands here - indeed, the scenery has an almost rural English feel to it - it is still a beautiful area. The county rises to the south, where it meets the Lammermuir Hills, and here the landscape changes, though it never loses it gentle aspect. Haddington is the county town, and is full of old buildings. The railway bypassed the place, so it was never developed as a place of industry or as a dormitory town for Edinburgh (though the advent of the car has now changed this). The tower of the cathedralesque St Mary's Church is sometimes called the "Lamp of the Lothians". A succession of small resorts ring the coast of the Firth of Forth, though none have been commercialised to any great extent.

Mid Lothian was at one time called "Edinburghshire". Towards the south it meets the Moorfoot Hills, and has a string of small towns to the north, which sit like satellites round Edinburgh itself. Coalmining was once important here, though all vestiges of it have now gone. It is home to such places as Dalkeith and Bonnyrigg, which have never been overwhelmed by industry, and the world famous Rosslyn Chapel, which, people claim, conceals a mystery that goes to the heart of Christianity.

The county town of West Lothian used to be Linlithgow. It is an ancient burgh with a royal palace, and is the birthplace of Mary Stuart. West Lothian is more industrial in character that the other two Lothians, and at one time mined both coal and shale, which was used to produce oil. Both industries have gone, though the occasional shale spoil heap (called a "bing" hereabouts) can still be seen.

But there are still plenty of tranquil places that can be visited, such as Torphichen, with its preceptory of St John, and South Queensferry, in the shadow of the two Forth bridges. A full day could be taken up exploring Linlithgow itself, with its royal palace, medieval church, canal basin and old, stone buildings. Then there are the county's grand houses, such as Hopetoun and The Binns, which deserve to be visited and explored.

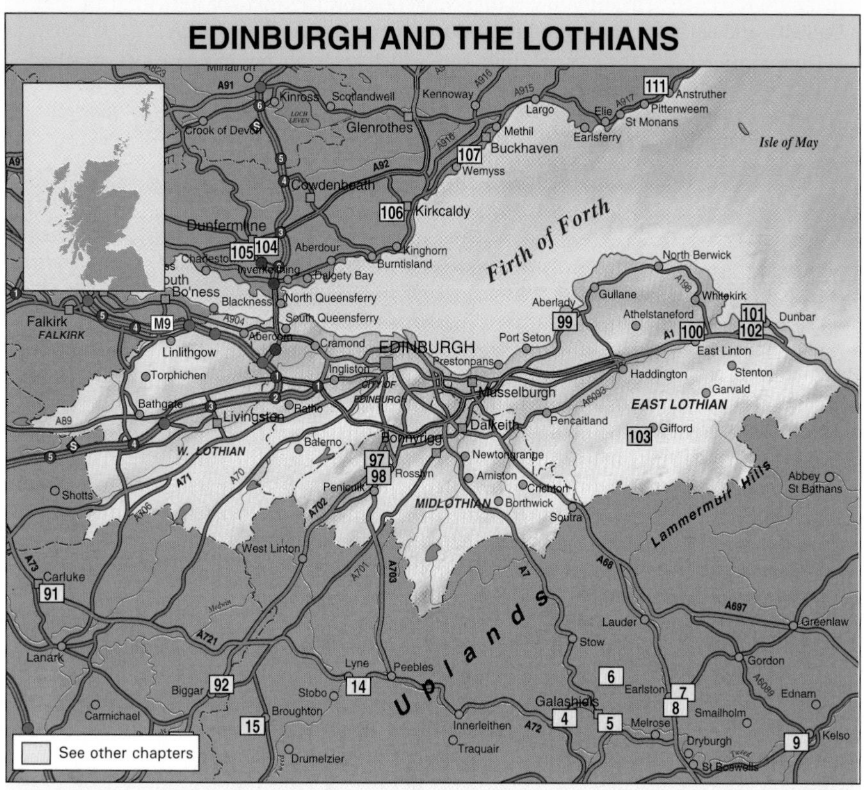

PLACES TO STAY, EAT, DRINK AND SHOP

97	Roslin Glen Hotel, Roslin	Hotel and restaurant	Page 124
98	The Original Roslin Inn, Roslin	Pub, accommodation and restaurant	Page 124
99	The Old Aberlady Inn, Aberlady	Pub, accommodation and restaurant	Page 128
100	Kippielaw Farmhouse, East Linton	Bed and Breakfast	Page 130
101	Cuckoo Wrasse, Cromwell Harbour	Restaurant	Page 130
102	Muirfield, Dunbar	Bed and Breakfast	Page 131
103	Goblin Ha' Hotel, Gifford	Hotel and restaurant	Page 132

EDINBURGH

Edinburgh, the cultural and administrative capital of Scotland, is one of the great cities of the world. It used to be called the "Athens of the North", and a full week would not be enough to see everything it has to offer the tourist. Whereas Glasgow has had to work hard at building a new image, Edinburgh has never needed to do so, though this has led to a certain amount of complacency on occasions.

With the advent of the Scottish Parliament, the world has rediscovered Edinburgh, and it now has all the feel and buzz of a great capital city once more. It is one of the most important financial capitals in Europe, and both the Church of Scotland and the Scottish law courts have their headquarters here.

The name has two possible origins. It either comes from the old Brithonic "eiden burgh", meaning "fortress on the hill slope", or "Edwin's Burgh", from an 7th century Anglo Saxon king of Northumbria who originally built a fort where the castle now stands. Whatever the explanation, there's no denying that **Edinburgh Castle** (Historic Scotland) is where it all began. It sits on a volcanic plug, with a narrow ridge flowing east from it, where sits the old town. It is deservedly the second most visited historical attraction in Britain after the Tower of London. The first stone castle on the site was probably built by Malcom III in the 11th century, though the castle as you see it now dates from all periods. The oldest part is **St Margaret's Chapel**, which dates form the 12th century. St Margaret was the wife of Malcolm III who placed the Scottish Church under the jurisdiction of Rome, and swept away the last vestiges of Celtic monasticism. The chapel may have been built by her son David I in her memory. Every year in August the **Castle Esplanade** hosts the **Edinburgh Military Tattoo**, an extravaganza of military uniforms, marching, music and spectacle that is known the world over.

Overlooking the Esplanade and the entrance is the **Half Moon Battery**, built by Regent Morton in the 16th century, and behind it is the **National War Memorial**. The **King's Lodging** opposite originally dates from the 15th century, and it was here that the monarch had his personal apartments. One of the rooms, **Queen Mary's Room**, is where Mary Stuart gave birth to her son James, who later became James VI of Scotland and I of England. There is a curious story about this birth. Some people claimed that Mary's baby was stillborn, and that another baby was substituted in its place. At a later date, when the room was being refurbished, workmen are supposed to have found an infant's bones within the walls of the room.

In the **Crown Chamber** can be seen the Scottish crown jewels, known as the **Honours of Scotland**, and the **Stone of Destiny** (see also Dunadd and Scone), supposed to be the pillow on which Jacob slept, and on which in later years the ancient kings of Ireland and Scotland were crowned. It was taken from Scone near Perth by Edward I in 1297, and lay in Westminster Abbey for 700 years. Some people claim, however, that it is merely a copy, and that the monks of Scone gave Edward a worthless drain cover and hid the real one. Others claim that, when the Stone was "liberated" from Westminster Abbey in 1953 by Scottish Nationalists, the perpetrators substituted another stone in its place when it

Edinburgh Castle

was returned. Whatever is the truth of the matter, there is no doubt that it is a potent symbol of Scottish nationhood. The **National War Museum of Scotland** is also within the castle, and explores military service over the last 400 years.

Leading from Edinburgh Castle down to the **Palace of Holyroodhouse** is the **Royal Mile**, one of the most famous streets in the world. It follows the crest of a ridge that slopes down from the castle, and was the heart of the old Edinburgh. It is actually four streets - Castlehill, Lawnmarket, the High Street and the Canongate, and each one had tall tenements on either side. The city was surprisingly egalitarian in olden days, and the gentry and the poor lived in the same tenement blocks, the rich at the top, the professional classes in the middle, and the poor at the bottom.

The **Scotch Whisky Heritage Centre** on Castlehill tells the story of Scotch, and brings three hundred years of its history to life. You'll learn about how it's made, and every Sunday afternoon there is a tasting session.

Between July and September, Edinburgh plays host to many festivals, the most important being the **Edinburgh International Festival** (with its attendant **Fringe)** in August. **The Royal Mile** then becomes a colourful open air theatre, when Fringe performers and buskers take over every inch of pavement to present drama, juggling, classical music, magicians, jazz, folk music and what have you.

Edinburgh has often been called the "medieval Manhatten", as the 16th and 17th century tenement blocks on the Royal Mile went as high as six or seven storeys, due to a lack of building land within the old city. **Gladstone's Land** (National Trust for Scotland), in the Lawnmarket, belonged to Thomas Gledstone, a rich merchant. It was built about 1620, has painted ceilings, and is furnished in the way it would have been in the 17th century. In Lady Stair's House, off the Lawnmarket, you'll find the **Writer's Museum**, with displays on Scotland's trio of great writers, Burns, Scott and Stevenson. The house is named after Lady Stair, who owned the house in the 18th century.

The glory of the Royal Mile is **St Gile's Cathedral**. Originally the High Kirk of Edinburgh, it was only a cathedral for a short

St Giles Cathedral

while in the 17th century when the Church of Scotland embraced bishops. It is now the spiritual home of Presbyterianism in Scotland. The first church in Edinburgh was built in the 9th century by monks from Lindisfarne, and St Giles is its direct descendant. It dates mainly from the 15th century, with a magnificent crown steeple which is, along with the castle, one of Edinburgh's icons. At one time, in the Preston Aisle, an armbone of St Giles was kept as a holy relic. Attached to the cathedral is the ornate **Thistle Chapel**, designed by Sir Robert Lorimer and built in 1911. It is the home of the **Most Ancient and Noble Order of the Thistle**, founded by James III. One of the delights of the wood carving is an angel playing the bagpipes. Behind the cathedral is **Parliament House**, where Scotland's parliament met up until the Treaty of Union in 1707. The building itself dates from the late 17th century, though the facade was added in 1829.

Across from the cathedral are the **Edinburgh City Chambers**, home to the city council. Under the Chambers is **Mary King's**

Close, a narrow Edinburgh street which was closed off and built over after the bubonic plague visited the city in 1645. Conducted tours of this most moving of places are available through Mercat Tours, though participants are advise to seek out a pub afterwards, as the place is suppose to be haunted!

Royal Highland Games, Edinburgh

Further down the Royal Mile is the **Museum of Childhood**, a nostalgic trip down memory lane for most adults. It features toys, games and books, and even medicines such as castor oil. **John Knox's House** is almost opposite. It dates from the 15th century, and is thought to be where John Knox lived, though there is no real proof. We're in the **Canongate** now, so called because it is the "gate" or street, of the canons of Holyrood Abbey. At one time Canongate wasn't part of Edinburgh, and the **Canongate Tolbooth** of 1591, which held the courtroom and jail for the burgh, is a curious building with a clock that projects out over the pavement. **The Museum of Edinburgh** gives an insight into the history of the city itself, and is packed with exhibits from its colourful past.

Canongate Church of 1688 has Dutch influences, and in the kirkyard is buried **Adam Smith**, the famous economist, **Agnes McLehose**, for whom Burns wrote Ae Fond Kiss, and **Robert Fergusson** the poet. He was Burns's hero, and died aged 24 in a madhouse. Burns himself actually paid for the tombstone over his grave. **White Horse Close**, beyond the church, is the most picturesque of Edinburgh's closes, and it was from the White Horse Inn that the London and York coaches left before the days of steam.

The **Palace of Holyroodhouse** is the Queen's official residence in Scotland. It grew out of the Abbey of Holyrood, of which only the ruined nave remains. Legend says that while out hunting, David I had been injured by a stag, and while he grappled with it he found himself grasping, not the stag's antlers, but a holy cross or "rood". As an act of thanksgiving he founded the abbey in 1128 for Augustinian canons. It became a favourite residence for Scottish kings, being much less draughty than the castle up the hill. It was here that Mary Stuart set up court on her return from France in the 16th century, and it was here that the murder of Rizzio, her Italian secretary took place (see also Seton). The picture gallery contains portraits of over 100 Scottish kings. Close to Holyrood is the site of the new **Scottish Parliament Building**, designed by the late Catalan architect Enric Miralles. It is due to open at the end of the year 2002.

Princes Street in Winter

In Holyrood Road is **Our Dynamic Earth**, an exhibition and visitors centre that takes you on a journey through the history of the universe, from the beginning of time and on into the future. It features dinosaurs, earthquakes, lava flows and tropical rainstorms.

To the south of the Royal Mile, in Chambers Street behind the old college of Edinburgh University, is the **National Museum of Scotland** and the new **Museum of Scotland**. They house internationally important collections relating to natural history, science, the arts and history. One of Edinburgh's hidden gems can be found in the Cowgate - the **Magdalen Chapel** of 1547. Built by the Guild of Hammermen, it contains pre-Reformation stained glass and the tomb of the founder. Another famous church south of the Royal Mile is **Greyfriars**. Built in 1612, it was here that the National Covenant rejecting bishops in the Church of Scotand was signed in 1638. From this, the adherents of Presbyterianism in the 17th century got the name "Covenanters". In nearby Candlemaker Row is the famous **Greyfriar's Bobby** statue. It commemorates a terrier who faithfuly kept guard over his former master's grave for 14 years.

North of the Royal Mile is Edinburgh's **New Town**. In the late 18th and early 19th centuries the medieval city was overcrowded and unhealthy, so the New Town was laid out in a series of elegant streets and squares. **Princes Street** was one of these streets, and is now the city's main shopping area. It faces **Princes Street Gardens**, created from the drained bed of the old Nor' Loch. Within the new town's Charlotte Square you'll find the **Georgian House** (National Trust for Scotland), which recreates the interiors found in the New Town when it was being built. At **No 28 Charlotte Square** is the National Trust for Scotland's headquarters and art gallery. And within the Square gardens each August is held the **Edinburgh Book Festival**. At the west end of the New Town is one of Edinburgh's most spectaular churches - **St Mary's Cathedral**. It was built in Victorian times as the cathedral for the Epsicopalian diocese of Edinburgh, and is as large and grand as a medieval cathedral, with three soaring spires that have become Edinburgh landmarks.

The **National Gallery of Scotland** on the Mound, the **Scottish National Portrait Gallery** in Queen Street, the **Dean Gallery** and the **Scottish National Gallery of Modern Art** in Belford Road are all within, or close to, the New Town. A bus service runs between all four. At the east end of Princes Street you'll find **Register House**, where the National Archives of Scotland are stored. It was designed by Robert Adam, with the foundation stone being laid in 1774. Also in Princes Street is the Gothic **Scott Monument**, which soars to over 200 feet, and offers a marvellous view from the top.

Further north, off Inverleith Row, are the **Royal Botanic Gardens**, 70 acres of greenery and colour surrounded by the bustle of the city. They were founded in 1670 as a "physic garden" at Holyrood, but were transferred here in 1823. And at Leith, up until the 1920s a separate burgh, you'll find the **Royal Yacht Britannia** moored at the new **Ocean Terminal**, a leisure and entertainment complex. It is open to the public, and is now one of the city's main tourist attractions. In Pier Place in Newhaven, to the west of Leith, is the **Newhaven Heritage Museum**. which explains the history of Newhaven, which used

Craigmillar Castle

to be a small, separate fishing village. Further to the west, at Corstorphine, are the **Edinburgh Zoological Gardens**, set in 80 acres. The zoo is famous for its penguins, and the daily "penguin parade" is not to be missed.

Craigmillar Castle (Historic Scotland) is on the south east outskirts of the city. The extensive ruins date from the 14th century, with many later additions. Mary Stuart stayed here after her Italian secretay Rizzio was murdered. **Lauriston Castle**, near Davidson's Mains, is also worth visiting. It is set in 30 acres of parkland. One of its owners was the father of **John Napier**, who invented logarithims. It now has a collection of furniture and decorative arts. **The Royal Observatory** sits on Blackford Hill, south of the city centre, and has displays and exhibits relating to astronomy.

AROUND EDINBURGH

MUSSELBURGH
6 miles E of Edinburgh city centre on the A199

At the mouth of the River Esk used to be beds of mussels, which gave this town its name. Now it is a dormitory town for Edinburgh. The **Tolbooth** dates from the 1590s, and was built of stones from the former Chapel of Our Lady of Loretto. **Inveresk Lodge Gardens** (National Trust for Scotland), with their terraces and walled garden, shows methods and plants that can be used in a home garden. The **Battle of Pinkie**, the last battle fought between Scottish and English national armies, took place near Musselburgh in 1547.

PRESTONPANS
7 miles E of Edinburgh city centre on the B1348

At the **Battle of Prestonpans** in 1745 the Jacobite army of Charles Edward Stuart defeated a Hanovarian army under Sir John Cope. The whole battle only took 15 minutes, with many of the Hanovarian troops being trapped against a high wall (which can still be seen) surrounding **Prestongrange House**. Contemporary accounts tell of terrified Hanovarian troops trying to scale the wall and drop into the comparative safety of the house's grounds. Ever since, Sir John Cope has been a figure of fun for his handling of the battle, though in truth he wasn't wholly to blame.

PORT SETON
9 miles E of Edinburgh city centre on the B1348

Seton Collegiate Church (Historic Scotland) was built, but never completed, in the 14th century as a collegiate church. It is dedicated to St Mary and the Holy Cross, and has some tombs of the Seton family, as well as fine vaulting. In 1544 it was looted and stripped by the Earl of Hertford and his English army. **Seton Castle** dates from 1790, and was designed by Robert Adam. It replaces the former Seton Palace, one of the grandest Scottish buildings of its time. Mary Stuart visited the Palace after the murder of Rizzio by her husband, Lord Darnley (see also Edinburgh).

DALKEITH
7 miles SE of Edinburgh city centre, on the A68

This pleasant town is nowadays a dormitory for Edinbugh, but at one time was an important market town on the A68, the main road south from Edinburgh and on into England. **Dalkeith Palace** was built around Dalkeith Castle for Anne, Duchess of Monmouth and Buccleuch in the early 18th century. It became known as "grandest of all classical houses in Scotland", and its grounds are now a country park. The **St Nicholas Parish Church** is a large building with, attached to it, the ruins of an old apse in which lie buried the remains of Anne, Duchess of Monmouth and Buccleuch. Her husband, James Scott, Duke of Monmouth, was an illegitimate son of Charles II. He plotted to murder his father, had himself declared king at Taunton, and was eventually executed in the Tower of London in 1685.

NEWTONGRANGE
8 miles SE of Edinburgh city centre on the A7

Coal mining in the Lothians was started by the monks of Newbattle Abbey in the 13th century. The Lady Victoria Colliery houses the **Scottish Mining Museum**, which tells the story of coal mining in Scotland from those days right up until the present. There is a recreated coalface, as well as the original winding engines and a visitor's centre.

ARNISTON

10 miles SE of Edinburgh off the A7

Arniston House has been the home of the Dundas family for over 400 years. Both William and John Adam worked on the designs, and it was built between 1726 and the 1750s on the site of an old tower house. The interior detail is wonderful, and there is also a fine collection of paintings by artists such as Raeburn and Ramsay. In the 17th century the Dundas family was one of the most powerful in Scotland, and held many important posts in the Scottish legal system.

BORTHWICK

11 miles SE of Edinburgh city centre off the A7

Borthwick Castle is a massive ruin which dates from about 1430. It was to this castle that Mary Stuart and Bothwell came after their marriage in 1566. It was a marriage which displeased the Scottish nobility, and 1000 Scottish nobles cornered them there. They demanded Bothwell's head for his part in the murder of Lord Darnley, Mary's first husband, and also demanded that Mary give him up. Bothwell escaped, leaving his wife to the mercy of the nobles, and fled to Dunbar. On

ROSLIN GLEN HOTEL

2 Penicuik Road, Roslin, Midlothian EH25 9LH
Tel: 0131 440 2029 e-mail: roslinglen@aol.com
Fax: 0131 440 2229 website: roslinglenhotel.co.uk

The **Roslin Glen Hotel** is nestled at the foot of the Pentland Hills in the quiet conservation village of Roslin, famous for the Rosslyn Chapel and links to the Knights Templar and Freemasonary. Pleasant rooms, all en-suite, are well equipped with telephone, tea/coffee making facilities and television to ensure an enjoyable stay. The restaurant and lounge provide an imaginative menu using fresh local ingredients. The Roslin Glen Hotel is the ideal base for those who enjoy the tranquility of the countryside, yet require easy access to the many major attractions in Scotland's Capital city.

THE ORIGINAL ROSLIN INN

Main Street, Roslin, Midlothian EH25 9LE
Tel: 0131 440 2384 Fax: 0131 440 2514

The Original Roslin Inn is an old coaching inn that dates back to at least 1700. At one time it was a temperance hotel, until, in 1827, the landlord of the nearby Roslin Inn moved in, bringing his licence with him. and its appearance has changed little over the years. However, its standards of service have changed, and it now offers the very best in Scottish hospitality. It is family run, and the owners, Maureen and Grahame Harris, have retained many period features both indoors and out, making it full of olde worlde character and ambience. It boasts six bedrooms, all fully en suite, and all with colour TV, trouser press and tea and coffee making facilities. Each one is tastefully decorated and furnished, and two of them are available as honeymoon suites with four poster beds. The menu is excellent, and all the food is prepared on the premises from only the finest and freshest of local produce wherever possible.

Whether it is an intimate candlelit dinner you are after, or a formal dinner party, the inn can meet your needs exactly. And the recently refurbished Rosabell Suite is the ideal place to host weddings, parties, dinner dances or business seminars. It can seat up to 160 people in absolute comfort. If it's a quiet drink you are after, then the inn has no less than four bars. The attractive lounge bar serves good food as well as drink, and the lively public bar - a popular place with locals, which is always a good sign - serves light snacks as well as a great selection of drinks both alcoholic and non alcoholic. There is also a cocktail bar attached to the dining room, and the Rosabell Suite also boasts a bar of its own. The Original Roslin Inn is an establishment that prides itself on the warmth of its welcome and great value for money. It is a great base from which to explore nearby Edinburgh or the historic attractions of the Lothians.

hearing of his escape, the nobles immediately retired from the Queen's presence, thinking that she had seen through his treachery. However, no sooner had they left her than she tore off her fine gowns and put on breeches and a pageboy's shirt, and made her escape so that she could rejoin her husband.

The modern **Borthwick Parish Church** has a 15th century aisle with effigies of the first Lord and Lady Borthwick.

CRICHTON

11 miles SE of Edinburgh city centre on the B6367

The substantial ruins of **Crichton Castle** (Historic Scotland) dates from the 14th century with later additions. The north wing has a lovely Renaissance Italianate facade, with protruding boses. The **Collegiate Church** was built in 1449. **Vogrie Country Park** lies to the north of Crichton, and is centred on Vogrie House. It has woodland walks, picnic areas and a golf course.

SOUTRA

16 miles SE of Edinburgh off the A68

From Soutra, it is reckoned that you get the best view in Central Scotland. On a clear day you can see the full sweep of the Firth of Forth with Fife beyond, and at least 60 Highland peaks. **Soutra Aisle** is all that remains of a medieval hospital. It was dedicated to the Holy Trinity, and it was here that Augustinian monks looked after travellers, pilgrims and the sick and wounded. A recent archaeological dig uncovered evidence of surgery and the treatment of patients by herbal remedies. Even some pieces of bandage with human tissue still attached to them were recovered.

ROSSLYN

7 miles S of Edinburgh city centre on the B7006

Rosslyn (also known as Roslin), according to some people, is the most important place in Christendom. It's all due to **Rosslyn Church**, an extravaganza of a building on which work began in 1446. It's founder was Sir William St Clair, third and last Prince of Orkney, who lived at nearby **Rosslyn Castle**. It is the choir of this unfinished church (still in use) that has both Masonic and Knights Templar associations

The stone carving in the interior is spectacular, and shows plants that only grow in the New World, even though Columbus hadn't yet sailed across the Atlantic when it was built. There are also pagan carvings of "The Green Man", as well as the famous **Apprentice Pillar**. This was said to have been carved by the apprentice to the master mason working on the building. When he saw the workmanship, the mason is supposed to have murdered the apprentice in a fit of jealousy.

Legends abound about the church, and much has been written about it lately. One theory says that the writings of Christ lie in its unopened vaults. Another says that the bodies of Knights Templar lie in the vaults, dressed in armour. A third says that the **Holy Grail** is embedded in one of the pillars. And yet another says it is a recreation of **Solomon's Temple** in Jerusalem.

There's even a theory that the body of Christ himself lies in the vaults. If this were true, it would being down Christendom, as the Resurrection never took place. Whatever the truth of the matter, and the theories seem to get wilder and wilder as time goes by, there's no denying that it is one of the most beautiful buildings in Britain. There is certainly an aura about the place that can almost be felt (see also Kilmartin).

Nearby is the **Roslin Glen Country Park**, with woodland walks which go past an old gunpowder works.

PENICUIK

9 miles S of Edinburgh city centre on the A701

To the west of Penicuik rise the Pentland Hills, with **Scald Law** being the highest peak at 1,898 feet. In the grounds of Penicuik House stands the **Allan Ramsay Obelisk**, dedicated to the memory of Allan Ramsay, known as the "Pentland Poet" (see also Leadhills). **St Mungo's Parish Church** dates from 1771, and has a 12th century detached belfry. The **Edinburgh Crystal Visitor Centre** at Eastfield has displays and exhibits about the history of crystal and glass making in Scotland, plus factory tours.

CRAMOND

5 miles W of Edinburgh city centre on a minor road off the A90

Cramond is a charming village of old

Malleny Garden, Balerno

whitewashed cottages on the banks of the River Almond where it enters the Firth of Forth. The **Parish Church** of 1656, with its medieval tower, sits within the ruins of a **Roman Fort**. The Rev. Robert Walker, who was painted by Raeburn skating on Duddingston Loch in thbe 18th century was minister here. At one time, the village was famous for the quality of the nails it manufactured.

INGLISTON

7 miles W of Edinburgh off the A8

Amost in the shadow of Edinburgh International Airport at Turnhouse is the **Royal Showground**, home each year of the Royal Highland Show, Scotland's premier country and farming fair.

BALERNO

7 miles SW of Edinburgh city centre off the A70

Malleny Garden (National Trust for Scotland) is a walled garden extending to three acres and dominated by 400 year old yew trees. There are herbaceous borders, a fine collection of roses, and it houses the National Bonsai Collection for Scotland.

RATHO

8 miles W of Edinburgh city centre on a minor road off the A8

Ratho sits on the Union Canal, and from the **Edinburgh Canal Centre** canal cruises are available. **Ratho Parish Church** dates from the 12th century, though it has been much restored over the years.

SOUTH QUEENSFERRY

9 miles W of Edinburgh city centre off the A90

South Queensferry is named after St Margaret, husband of Malcolm III, who founded a ferry here in the 11th century to carry pilgims across the Forth bound for Dumfermline Abbey and St Andrew's Cathedral. Now the ferry has been replaced by the **Forth Rail Bridge** and the **Forth Road Bridge**, two mammoth pieces of civil engineering. The Rail Bridge was built between 1883 and 1890 to link Edinburgh and Aberdeen, and the road Bridge was completed in 1964. In the shadow of the Rail Bridge is the historic **Hawes Inn** of 1683, which features in R.L. Stevenson's Kidnapped. Opposite is the slipway from which the former ferry sailed.

The town has a glorious mix of cottages and houses dating from the 16th century onwards. **Plewlands House** (National Trust for Scotland) dates from 1643, and has been converted into private flats. The **Queensferry Museum**, in the High Street, has exhibits and displays on local history. The church of the former **Carmelite Friary** in Rose Lane dates from the 15th century, and is now an Episcopalian church.

Forth Bridge

Dalmany House, to the east of the town, overlooks the Firth of Forth. It is the home of the Earls of Roseberry, and was built in the 1820s. There is an excellent collection of tapestries and furniture. **Dalmeny Church** is one of the best preserved Norman churches in Britain. The south doorway is richly carved, as is the chancel and apse.

HADDINGTON

The royal burgh of Haddington received its royal charter in the 12th century from David I, and is thought to be the birthplace of John Knox in 1505. At one time it was the fourth largest town in Scotland, and it was here that the Scottish parliament met to sanction Mary Stuart's marriage to the Dauphin of France. It is a quiet town of old buildings, including the quite superb cathedralesque **Parish Church of St Mary**. It was formerly collegiate, and dates mainly from the 15th century. Its ruined choir was restored in the early part of the 20th century, and such is its size and beauty (it is the longest parish church n Scotland) that some people erroneously refer to it as the church of a former abbey. In the choir is the burial place of **Jane Welsh** (Thomas Carlyle's wife), who was born in the town. The **Lauderdale Aisle** is unique in that it is a small Episcopalian chapel within a Presbyterian Church. This ecumenicalism continues every year in May with the **Haddington to Whitekirk Pilgrimage**, featuring people of all the main Christian religions (see also Whitekirk). St Mary's is one of the few Church of Scotland churches to have a full peel of bells, which were installed in 1999. Nearby are the ruins of the small **St Martin's Church**, dating from the 12th century. The 16th century **Nungate Bridge** over the Tyne is behind St Mary's, and is named after a nunnery that used to stand close to it.

Also born in Haddington in 1812 was **Samuel Smiles**. Though he wrote many books, he is best known for Self Help. Alexander II and William the Lion may also have been born here, in a royal castle that has long gone. The **Town House**, with its graceful spire, was designed by William Adam and built in the late 1740s, though the spire was added in 1831. Close to Haddington is **Lennoxlove**, home to the Dukes of Hamilton since 1946. It houses the death mask of Mary Stuart, which shows her to have been, as many contemporaries observed, an extremely beautiful woman. The origins of the house go back to at least the 13th century, when it was called Lethington Hall, and the home of the Maitland family.

About four miles east of Haddington is **Traprain Law**, from the top of which there are superb views. The summit was occupied from Neolithic times right up until the Dark Ages, and the outline of a fort can clearly be seen. It was the capital of a tribe the Romans called the Votadini, which roughly translated means "the farmers". More Roman finds have been made here than anywhere else in Scotland, including a horde of Roman silver.

AROUND HADDINGTON

GULLANE

6 miles N of Haddington on the A198

This village sits inland from the Firth of Forth, but has fine views north towards Fife. Nowadays it is a small golfing resort and the British Open course at **Muirfield** is home to Honourbale Company of Edinburgh Golfers. The **Heritage of Golf** exhibition on the West Links Road traces the golfing history of the area.

DIRLETON

6 miles N of Haddington off the A198

The impressive ruins of **Dirleton Castle** (Historic Scotland) dominate this pleasant village. They date back to the end of the 13th century, though there have been extensive additions and alterations over the years. During the Wars of Independence it was taken by Edward I of England in 1298, but was back in Scottish hands by 1311. It was originally built by the Norman family of de Vaux., though it has also been owned by the Halyburton family and the Ruthvens. The third Lord Ruthven was implicated in the murder of Mary Stuart's Italian secretary Rizzio. To the west of the castle are some formal terraced gardens.

THE OLD ABERLADY INN

Main Street, Aberlady, East Lothian EH32 0RF
Tel: 01875 870503 Fax: 01875 870209

Situated in the heart of the village of Aberlady, the **Old Aberlady Inn** is a picturesque family run hostelry that has been in existence for hundreds of years. It offers a number of comfortable and well equipped bedrooms to the holidaymaker, each one having TV, telephone and tea/coffee making facilities. It has earned a marvellous reputation for the quality of its cuisine, with meals being served in the restaurant or one of the cosy, attractive bars. The place is popular with locals and visitors alike, and makes a marvellous base for exploring the area, or for a relaxing golfing holiday, as this part of Scotland is renowned for its championship courses.

ABERLADY

6 miles N of Haddington on the A198

This pleasant small village sits on the shores of the Firth of Forth. It was formerly the port for Haddington, but the bay has now silted up. The **Aberlady Bay Nature Reserve** covers 1439 acres of foreshore and dunes, and is popular with bird watchers. The village was the home of one of Scotland's most popular historical novelists, **Nigel Tranter**, who died in the year 2000. There is a small cairn to his memory close to Quarry House, where he used to live.

Myreton Motor Museum contains displays of motor cars, cycles and military vehicles. **Aberlady Parish Church** was remodelled in the 19th century, though an interesting 16th century tower is still attached. To the east of the village is **Luffness Castle**, once the ancestral home of the Hepburns. It is now an hotel.

ATHELSTANEFORD

2 miles NE of Haddington on the B1343

Athelstaneford has a special place in Scottish history. It was here that the Scottish flag, the **Saltire**, or St Andrew's Cross, was adopted. Athelstane was a king of Northumbria who fought a combined army of Picts and Scots at Athelstanford in AD832. The Pictish leader, Angus mac Fergus, on the day before the battle, saw a huge white cross made of clouds in the sky, and took it as an omen. Athelstane was duly defeated, and the Saltire was adopted as the flag of Scotland, making it the oldest national flag in Europe.

This is why the Saltire on its own should be a white cross on an azure background, whereas when it is incorporated into the Union Jack the blue darkens. The **National Flag Centre** in Athelstanford explains the story of Scotland's national flag.

NORTH BERWICK

7 miles NE of Haddington on the A198

North Berwick is one of Scotland's best known holiday and golfing resorts. It is a clean, attractive town which was granted a royal charter by Robert II in 1373. **North Berwick Law**, a volcanic plug, rises to a height of 613 feet behind the town, and makes a wonderful viewpoint. Two miles off the coast lies the **Bass Rock**, another volcanic plug that broods over the waters of the Firth of Forth. Over 150,000 sea birds nest each year on the 350 feet high Bass Rock and other, smaller islands such as Fidra and Craigleith. From the **Scottish Seabird Centre** on a promontory near North Berwick Harbour you can use remote controlled cameras to study them without disturbing the colonies. There are also powerful telescopes on a viewing deck, a film about Scotland's sea birds, and a café restaurant.

In the 8th century the Bass Rock was home to the hermit St Baldred, who evangelised this part of Scotland. In later times it also served as a prison for both Jacobites and Covenanters, and there are traces of old fortifications on it.

Also on the promontary are the scant ruins of the **Auld Kirk**, which date from the 12th century onwards. The kirk was finally abandoned in the 17th century due to coastal erosion. When the Seabird Centre was being built, over 30 well-preserved skeletons from the old graveyard were uncovered, the earliest one dating back to the 7th century. In School Road is the **North Berwick Museum**, housed in a former school, which has displays and memorabilia about local history, natural history and golf.

In the 16th century the town was supposed to have been the home of a notorious **Witches Coven**, and a well publicised trial took place in 1595. One of the accusations made was that the witches had caused a terrible storm which beset James VI's ship as he returned from Denmark with his new bride. It all started when a poor serving girl called Gelie Duncan was found to have remarkable healing powers, which aroused suspicion. Her master, Chamberlain David Seaton, tried to extract a confession of witchcraft from her using thumbscrews, and when this failed he had her body examined for the "marks of the devil". These were duly found on her throat, and she confessed and was thrown in jail.

On being tortured further, Gellie claimed to be one of 200 witches and warlocks in the town who, at the behest of the Earl of Bothwell, David Seaton's sworn enemy, were trying to harm the king. At Hallowe'en in 1590, Gelie told them, the witches convened at the Auld Kirk, where Satan appeared to them and preached a sermon from the pulpit. King James had all the women identified by Gelie put to death, including one Agnes Sampson and a schoolmaster from Prestonpans called John Fian. Gelie herself was burnt on the Castle Esplanade in Edinburgh.

Tantallon Castle

Though some people have subsequently claimed that the Earl of Bothwell dressed up as Satan to take part in the Hallowe'en coven in the kirk, there's little doubt that Gelie made up the stories to save herself from further torture, and many innocent people were executed because of this. It was indeed a dark time for Scottish justice.

East of North Berwick is **Tantallon Castle** (Historic Scotland). Its substantial and romantic ruins stand on a clifftop above the Firth of Forth, almost across from the Bass Rock. It was a Douglas stronghold, built in the 14th century by William, 1st Earl of Douglas. Cromwell ordered General Monk to take the castle, and in 1651, after a 12 day siege, he destroyed it.

WHITEKIRK

7 miles NE of Haddington off the A198

St Mary's Parish Church dates from the 15th century, and is the eastern end of the annual Haddington Pilgrimage (see also Haddington). But Whitekirk had been a place of pilgrimage long before this. In pre Reformation times, people used to come to the village to seek cures at the Well of Our Lady which used to be located nearby. An account of 1413 relates that over 15,000 people of all nationalities visited.

The place's most famous pilgrim - but one who didn't come seeking a cure - was a young Italian nobleman called **Aeneas Sylvius Piccolomini**. He had set out from Rome in 1435 as an envoy to the court of James I, and during the sea crossing he had been blown off course by a raging gale and blizzard. Aeneas vowed that it he made it to dry land he would offer thanksgiving at the nearest church dedicated to Our Lady. The boat was eventually shipwrecked between North Berwick and Dunbar, and Aeneas survived. He therefore set out on a ten mile pilgrimage in a snow storm to Whitekirk, where he duly offered prayers of thanks. Twenty years later, Aeneas became Pope Pious II.

EAST LINTON

6 miles E of Haddington off the A1

Anyone travelling along the A1 is well advised to make a small detour to view this picturesque village. To the east of the village is the mansion of **Phantassie**, where **John Rennie** the civil engineer was born. He it was who designed Waterloo, London and Southwark bridges in London.

Preston Mill (National Trust for Scotland) is an old, quaint water mill that has been restored. It sits in an idyllic rural spot, and dates from the 18th century, though a mill has stood on the spot for much longer. With its conical roof and red pantiles, it is a favourite subject for painters and photographers. Close by is **Phantassie Doocot** (National Trust for Scotland), which belonged to Phantassie House, and which could hold 500 birds.

Prestonkirk is an attractive small church which is close by. It was built in 1770, though the 13th century chancel still stands, now used as a mausoleum. The ruins of **Hailes Castle** lie to the west of East Linton. Its

KIPPIELAW FARMHOUSE

East Linton, East Lothian, EH41 4PY
Tel/Fax: 01620 860368
e-mail: info@kippielawfarmhouse.co.uk
website: www.kippielawfarmhouse.co.uk

If you're looking for the perfect B&B in the lovely county of East Lothian, then **Kippielaw Farmhouse** near East Linton is for you. Built in the 18th century, it boasts one twin en suite room and a double room with adjacent bathroom. Owned and run by Liz and Bill Campbell, it is friendly and comfortable, and makes the ideal base for exploring an area that is rich in history and scenery. Liz's many years experience with cooking means that a candle-lit dinner at Kippielaw is an experience that will be fondly remembered in the future!

CUCKOO WRASSE

1 Shore Street, Cromwell Harbour, Dunbar,
East Lothian EH42 1HL
Tel: 01368 865384

Named after a fish that must be one of the most colourful in British waters, the **Cuckoo Wrasse** is a delightful restaurant in the quaint and picturesque port of Dunbar. The building is very old, with crow-stepped gables, and it was here that Oliver Cromwell stayed when he arrived in Scotland by boat. Another famous visitor, it is said, was John Paul Jones, the Scottish-born founder of the American navy. Owned and managed by chef Peter McQuade, it offers superb food in an 'olde worlde' atmosphere that is both relaxing and quiet. Pride of place, of course, goes to fresh, beautifully cooked seafood, most of which is sourced in Scotland.

The Shetland mussels are a popular with visitors and locals alike, as are the seafood platters, the local smoked salmon and the paella for two. But you can also order juicy steak with all the trimmings, supreme of chicken, pasta, warm duck salad and so on. There is a daily specials board, and children can either have smaller portions or choose from their own menu. Everything is cooked on the premises, and Peter uses only the freshest of local produce wherever possible. It is open every day between 12.00 and 14.30 and 18.30 until late (except in winter, when it closes on Sunday evening). The restaurant also maintains a small but choice selection of wines, and there is sure to be something that will complement your meal. Peter believes that Scottish produce is the best in the world, and he is committed to cooking and serving it with inspiration but without pretensions, at a price that is reasonable and affordable to everyone.

earliest masonry dates from the 13th century, though it was much altered in later years by the Hepburns, who acquired the castle in the 14th century. It was to Hailes Castle that James Hepburn, Earl of Bothwell, brought Mary Stuart after seizing her at Fountainbridge in 1567. He was later to become her third husband.

The **Scottish Museum of Flight** is situated at East Fortune, to the north east of the village. Formerly a World War II airfield, it now houses a collection of aircraft, rockets, models and memorabilia. One of the exhibits is a Prestwick Pioneer, the only aircraft ever to have been wholly designed and built in Scotland. Also on display is a Soviet MIG, a Blue Streak rocket and a Lightning.

STENTON

7 miles E of Haddington on the A6370

This small, conservation village still retains its old **Tron**, on which wool brought to the Stenton Fair by local sheep farmers was weighed. To the south of the village is **Presmennan Lake**, one of the few lakes, as opposed to lochs, in Scotland (see also Lake of Menteith, Ellon and Kirkcudbright). This one, however, is artificial, created in the early 19th century by the local landowner. The **Pressmennan Forest Trail** runs along its southern shore, and from the highest point you can see Arthur's seat in Edinburgh and the Bass Rock in the Firth of Forth.

DUNBAR

11 miles E of Haddington on the A1087

The Royal Burgh of Dunbar received its royal charter in 1445. It is a former fishing and whaling port, though its main industries now are brewing and tourism. It was near here, in 1650, that the **Battle of Dunbar** took place between the troops of Cromwell and a Covenanting army under General Leslie. A stone commemorates the event. The ruins of **Dunbar Castle** date back to the 12th century. It was originally built for the Cospatrick family, which later changed its name to Dunbar. It was to Dunbar Castle that Edward II fled after his defeat at Bannockburn. He then boarded a boat for Berwick-upon-Tweed. In 1338 the Countess of Dunbar, known as "Black Agnes", held the castle for five months against an English army before being relieved by a small contingent of Scots. On the orders of the Scottish Parliament, the castle was dismantled after Mary Stuart abdicated.

The old **Town House** dates from about 1620, and houses a small museum on local history and archaeology, though a much newer "attraction" is situated south of the town, near the shore. **Torness Nuclear Power Station** was built in the early 80s, and has a visitors centre that explains how electricity is produced from nuclear power.

Dunbar was the birthplace, in 1838, of **John Muir**, founder of the American national parks system. His birthplace, in the High Street, is now the **John Muir Centre**. On the ground floor of the building his father ran a grain business.

The **John Muir Country Park** is to the north west of the town. Opened in the late 70s, this was the first park of its kind in Scotland, and covers 1760 acres.

GARVALD

6 miles SE of Haddington off the B6370

This tiny village lies on the northern slopes of the Lammermuir Hills. **Garvald Parish**

Church dates partly from the 12th century, and has a sun dial dated 1633. South east of the village is the mansion of **Nunraw**, in whose grounds Cistercian monks, who arrived here in 1946, began building the Abbey of Sancta Maria in 1952. It was the first Cistercian monastery in Scotland since the Reformation, and was colonised by monks form Tipperary in Ireland. A Cistercian nunnery, founded by nuns from Haddington, had previously been founded here in about 1158. The manison is now the abbey's guesthouse.

GIFFORD

4 miles S of Haddington on the B6369

Gifford was laid out in the 18th century, and is a pretty village with views of the Lammermuir Hills to the south. The whitewashed **Yester Parish Church**, which has Dutch influences, was built in 1708, and has a medieval bell. It was in Gifford that John Witherspoon, the only clergyman to sign the American Declaration of Independence, was born in 1723 (see also Paisley).

South east of the village is **Yester House**, designed by Adam and dating from 1745. Beyond it are the ruins of **Yester Castle**, where there is an underground chamber known as **Goblin Ha'** which dates from the 13th century. The narrow road from Gifford up into the Lammermuir Hills is a fine drive, and takes you past Whiteadder reservoir and down into Berwickshire.

PENCAITLAND

6 miles SW of Haddington on the A6093

The oldest part of **Pencaitland Parish Church** is the Winton Aisle, which dates from the 13th century. Close to the village is the 500 year old **Winton House**. It was built for the Seton family by the king's master mason, and is famous for its "twisted chimneys". It overlooks the Tyne, and has lovely terraced gardens. **Glenkinchie Distillery**, to the south of the village, has a small exhibition and offers tours showing how whisky is distilled.

LINLITHGOW

This ancient royal burgh has played a central role in Scotland's history. It is a lovely place, with many historic buildings, but none is more historic than **Linlithgow Palace** (Historic Scotland), situated on the banks of **Linlithgow Loch**. It dates from the reign of James I in the early 15th century, and replaced an older castle which stood here, where Edward I once stayed when he invaded Scotland in support of John Balliol's claim to the Scottish throne.

It was a favourite of many Scottish kings and queens, and it was here, in 1512, that James V was born. It was also the birthplace, in 1542, of his daughter, the tragic Mary Stuart. The birth room was most probably that of her father, the **Queen's Bedchamber** in the north west tower. But her association with Linlithgow Palace lasted only seven months, as she was then taken by her mother, Mary of Guise, to the more secure Stirling Castle. When Mary Stuart returned from France in 1561 after the death of her husband, the Dauphin, she only stayed briefly at the castle, and it was allowed to decay.

Cromwell stayed here briefly in 1650 when he invaded Scotland after it had declared

Linlithgow Palace

Charles II king. Then, in 1745, Charles Edward Stuart himself stayed in the Palace. A year later the troops of the Duke of Cumberland moved in, and when they moved out they left their straw bedding too close to the fires. It caught fire, and soon the whole building was ablaze, leaving it roofless and unihabitable.

The **Outer Gateway** to the palace still stands, and on it are the coats of arms of the four orders of chivalry to which James V belonged - the Garter of England, the Thistle of Scotland, the Golden Fleece of Burgundy and St Michael of France.

Opposite the Palace is **St Michael's Parish Church**, one of the most important medieval churches in Scotland. It dates from the 15th century, though a church had stood here long before that. Within the church took place one of the most unusual incidents in Scottish history. The church was especially dear to James IV, who worshipped there regularly. In 1514, he had decided to take a large army into England in support of France, which had been invaded by Henry VIII's troops. Most of the Scottish court was against the idea, as was Jame's wife Margaret, sister of Henry VIII.

But James held firm, and a few days before he and his army set out, he was at mass in St Michael's Church with his courtiers. A strange man with long, fair hair suddenly appeared in the church dressed in a blue gown tied with a white band and carrying a pikestaff. Pushing aside the courtiers, he approached James and spoke to him. He had been sent "by his mother", he said, to tell James that no good would come of the invasion of England. Furthermore, he was not to meddle with other women.

Some of the courtiers tried to grab him, but before they could the man disappeared into thin air. Confusion reigned, and people immediately took the man to be a ghost. The reference to his mother, they said, meant that he had been sent by Our Lady (of whom James was especially fond). James took no heed, and marched into England. He, and all the flower of Scottish manhood, were wiped out on the field at Flodden. The "ghost's" prophesy came true.

People nowadays discount the ghost theory, and say that the whole thing had been orchestrated by James's wife with the help of some of the court. The reference to the king's meddling with other woman was the Queen's own contribution to the event.

One of the courtiers was Sir David Lyndsay, Lord Lyon and playwright, who knew all the tricks of the stage, and he may have been involved as well. There is a theory that says that Margaret had been put up to it by her

Union Canal, nr Linlithgow

brother Henry VIII, who was totally unprepared for a Scottish invasion. though this is now discounted. All she wanted to do was protect him from his own folly.

It was in Linlithgow that the Earl of Moray, Regent of Scotland, was assasinated in the street, and a plaque on the old **County Buildings** commemorates the event. In Annet House in the High Street is the **Linlithgow Story**, with displays and exhibits explaining the history of the town. At the **Linlithgow Canal Centre** in Manse Road is a small museum dedicated to the Union Canal, which links the Forth and Clyde Canal at Falkirk with Edinburgh. Trips along the canal are also available. **Beecraigs Country Park** is to the south of the town, and is set in 913 acres of land near the Bathgate Hills. It has a loch where you can fish.

To the north of the town is the **House of the Binns** (National Trust for Scotland), ancestral home of the Dalyell family, the best known member of which is Tam Dalyell the MP, who still lives there. In 1601 the Edinburgh butter merchant Thomas Dalyell had married Janet, daughter of the first Baron Kinloss, and in 1630 he bought the lands of Binns, and set about enlarging the house. What you see now is largely that house.

His son was also Thomas, though he earned an usavoury reputation as "Bluidie Tam Dalyel", scourge of the Covenanters. He was every inch a king's man, and when Charles I was executed in 1649, he vowed never to cut his hair until there was a king on the throne once more. And indeed, Bloody Tam's portrait in The Binns shows a man with hair flowing down past his shoulders. Tam also helped the Tzar of Russia reorganise the Russian army, and was made a nobleman of Russia. For that reason he also had another nickname - "The Bluidie Muscovite".

Another stately home near Linlithgow is **Hopetoun House**, possibly the grandest "big house" in Scotland. It sits almost on the banks of the Forth, and is home to the Marquis of Linlithgow. It was started in 1699 by the 1st Earl of Hopetoun, ancestor of the present Marquis, and designed by Sir William Bruce with enlargements by William Adam, who introduced the sweeping curves. The inside is spectacular and opulent, with ornate plasterwork, tapestries, furnishings and paintings. Surrounding the house is magnificent parkland extending to 100 acres, with a deer park and spring garden. the main appraoch to the house is by the Royal Drive, which can only be used by royalty. George IV used it when he visited Scotland in 1822, and Elizabeth II also used it in 1988.

AROUND LINLITHGOW

BO'NESS

3 miles N of Linlithgow on the A904

The town's real name is Borrowstoneness, though it is always referred to nowadays by its shortened name. It is an industrial town, and was formerly one of Scotland's leading whaling ports. It was near here that the eastern end of the Antonine Wall terminated. Near the town is the Kinneil Estate, with, at its centre, **Kinneil House**. It was built by the Hamilton family in the 16th and 17th centuries. It isn't open to the public, though it can be viewed from the outside. However, within the house's 17th century stable block is the **Kinneil Museum**, which tells the story of Bo'ness over the last 2000 years. There is also an exhibition called "Rome's Northern Frontier".

The town's main attraction is the **Bo'ness and Kinneil Railway**, which has been developed since 1979 by the Scottish Railway Preservation Society. There is a Scottish railway exhibition at Bo'ness, as well as workshops and a working station. Trips on the steam trains which run between Bo'ness and Birkhill Station are popular with the public. At Birkhill are the caverns of the **Birkhill Fireclay Mine**, which can be explored.

BLACKNESS

4 miles NE of Linlithgow on the B903

Blackness Castle (Historic Scotland) must be the most unusually shaped castle in Scotland. It sits on a promontary jutting out into the Firth of Forth, and from the air looks like a ship. It was a Crichton stronghold, and the first castle on the site was built in about 1449 by Sir George Chrichton, Sheriff of Linlithgow and Admiral of Scotland. However, there is an intriguing but untrue story about how the castle eventually came to look like a ship. By the early 16th century the castle had passed to the Douglases. James V appointed Archibald

Douglas as Lord High Admiral of the Scottish fleet, but soon discovered that he had made a mistake, as every time Archibald went to sea he could not assume command because of sea sickness.

The young James was enraged, and threatened to dismiss him. Archibald, who was making a fortune out of selling commissions in the navy, wanted to retain his position. So he promised his king that if he wasn't dismissed, he would build him a ship that the English couldn't sink and on which he would never be sick. Mollified, the king agreed, and Douglas built Blackness Castle. However, a more mundane explanation of its shape is the restricted shape of the site on which it was built.

TORPHICHEN

3 miles S of Linlithgow on the B792

The Knights of the Order of St John of Jerusalem, or the Knights Hospitallers as they wer more commonly called, was a monastic order of soldier monks which had been formed in the 11th century to look after St John's Hospital in Jersusalem, and to offer hospitality and protection to pilgrims travelling to the Holy Land.

At Torphichan, in about 1124, was founded the only Knights Hospitallers monastery in Scotland, which later came to be known as **Torphichen Preceptory** (Historic Scotland). It was called a preceptory because its head was called the "Preceptor".

The only parts left standing nowadays if the original preceptory are the transepts and crossing of the monastic church. Above the crossing is a tower, which, no doubt because of the Knights' military role, looks more like a castle than a church tower. Within a small room is a display about the modern Order of St John, which was refounded in 1947 as a separate order in Scotland by George VI. Nowadays it runs old folks homes, mountain rescue units and hospitals in Scotland. Where the nave once stood is now **Torphichan Parish Church**, which dates from 1756, though masonry from the earlier building is incorporated into it.

LIVINGSTON

6 miles S of Linlithgow off the M8

Livingston is one of Scotland's new towns, built round a historic village which has the **Livingston Parish Church** of 1732. At the **Almond Valley Heritage Centre** in Millfield the visitor can find out about local history and the environment, including the Scottish shale industry which once thrived in West Lothian. There is also an 18th century water mill. The **Almondell and Calderwod Country Park** is three miles west of the town centre, and has woodland and riverside walks. Almondell was originally a private estate which belonged to the Erskine family, and many items from Kirkhill House, with which it was associated, have been relocated within the park, such as the entrance gates and the astonomical pillar. Calderwood was also a private estate, and belonged to the barons of Torphichen. This area has been deliberately left undeveloped to encourage wildlife. The Oakbank shale bings are a reminder of the shale industry, and have been landscaped. A good view of the surrounding countryside, and even up into Fife, is available from the top.

At nearby **Mid Calder** is the **Kirk of Calder**, the apse of which dates from the 16th century. While staying at **Calder House** (not open to the public) John Knox first administered holy communion using the new reformed liturgy. In 1848 the Polish pianist Chopin also stayed here.

BATHGATE

6 miles S of Linlithgow on the A89

Bathgate is a substantial industrial town, and was formerly a centre for the shale oil industry. **Sir James Simpson**, who introduced chloroform into midwifery, was born here in 1811, as was **James "Paraffin" Young**, who opened the world's first oil refinery in 1850, extracting paraffin from the local shale. **Cairnpapple Hill** (Historic Scotland), to the north of the town, is 1017 feet high, and was the site of a temple built about 2000 - 25000 BC. Fragments of bone and pottery have been found. The view from the top is maginificent, and on a clear day both the Bass Rock in the Firth of Forth and the mountains of Arran in the Firth of Clyde can be seen. In Mansefield Street is the **Bennie Museum**, which contains collections relating to local history. **Polkemmet Country Park** is four miles west of the town, and has a golf course, a driving range, bowling green and picnic areas.

6 Fife and Kinross

The county of Fife consists of a long peninsula that stretches out eastwards between the Firths of Forth to the south and Tay to the north. It is steeped in history, and for that reason is always referred to as the "Kingdom of Fife". James II once called it a "fringe of gold on a beggar's mantle", referring to the fact that, in his day, it had a barren interior with many prosperous towns along its coastline.

Here, at Dunfermline, was Scotland's capital before it moved to Edinburgh, and here the south eastern coastline was crammed with small prosperous seaports which traded with Europe. And you can still see the European influence today. Some of the older buildings have a distinctly European feel to them, and the rooves of the older houses have red pantiles - brought in as ballast form the Low Countries - instead of slates. The ports, with names such as Crail, Pittenweem and Anst-ruther, are still there, though now they rely on tourism rather than trade.

Elie Beach, Fife

Of all the towns on the county's east coast the most famous is surely St Andrews. Seen from a distance, it shimmers with spires and church towers, and was formerly a place of pilgrimage because of its great cathedral, the impressive ruins of which overlook the shoreline. It still attracts pilgrims, but now they come in the name of sport, for this is the recognised world home of golf. It is also a university town, and even today students can be seen dressed in the traditional red gown as they scurry to lectures during term time. The town is crammed with old buildings and historical associations, and it would take at least a week to do justice to them all.

The county's largest town is Kirkcaldy, famous for the manufacture of linoleum. So much so that people used to say that you could always tell when you were approaching the town by its "queer-like smell". But this royal burgh is so much more that a manufacturing centre, and has many historical associations. At one time it was known as the "Lang Toun", because it appeared to consist of one long street, though it has now spread inland as well. And it can lay fair claim to being the birthplace of economics, because, in 1728, Adam Smith was born here.

To the west of the county another industry held sway - coal mining. The Fife coal fields used to employ thousands of men, but now it has all but gone, leaving in its wake many small mining villages that are proud and fiercely independent. Dunfermline is the largest town in this area - another Fife royal burgh whose roots go deep into Scotland's history. It's abbey, like the cathedral at St Andrews, was once a place of pilgrimage, and is now the resting place of one of Scotland's great heroes, Robert the Bruce. And, like Kirkcaldy, it too has its famous sons. Charles I was born here in 1600, as was his sister Princess Elizabeth, and Andrew Carnegie the millionaire philanthropist in 1835.

Mining has given way to electronics as an employer, and this part of Fife is well and truly part of "silicon glen". But the area hasn't lost its attractiveness, and one of the places that must be visited is Culross, surely one of the loveliest of small Scottish towns.

Pittenweem Harbour

Kinross-shire sits to the west of Fife. Before local government reorgan-isation, it was Scotland's second smallest county, and it sits in a great saucer shaped depression with, at its heart, Loch Leven. It's main industry is farming, and the gentle countryside, ringed by hills, is well worth exploring if only for the sense of "getting away from it all" that this gives. But even here there is history. Mary Stuart was held captive in a castle on an island in Loch Leven, and made a daring escape from it. At Crook of Devon a coven was discovered in 1662, with the witches being put on trial and subsequently executed. And at Scotlandwell we have yet another place of pilgrimage. A friary once stood here, along with a holy well, and people came from all over Scotland seeking cures for their illnesses. The well is still there, and the waters may still be drunk.

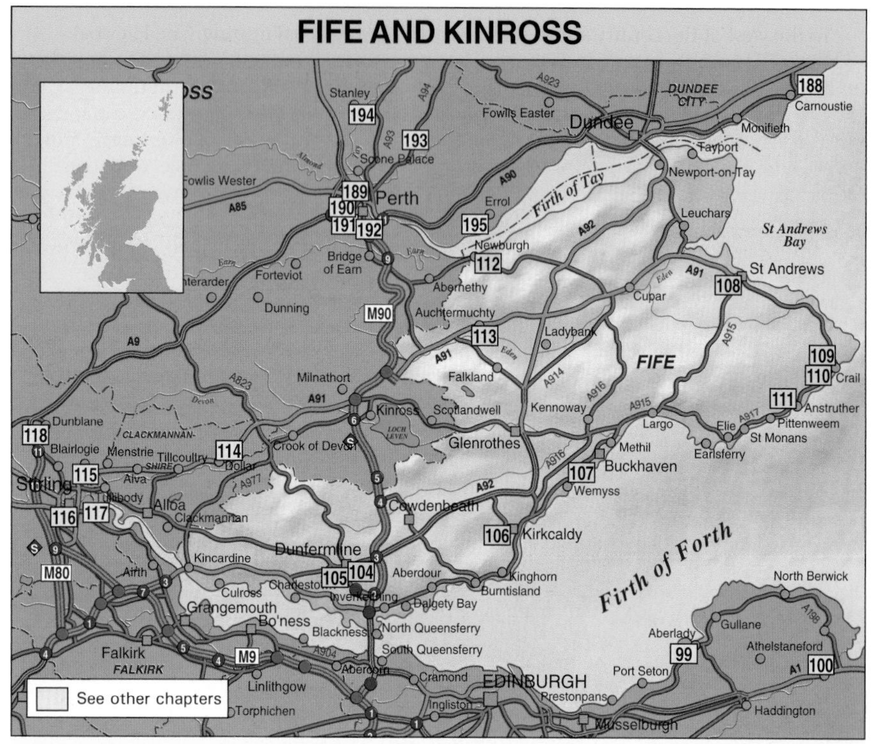

PLACES TO STAY, EAT, DRINK AND SHOP

104	Jokers, Dunfermline	Pub with food	Page 139
105	The Commercial Inn, Dunfermline	Pub with food	Page 140
106	Nicols, Kirkcaldy	Pub with food	Page 147
107	Wemyss Central Hotel, East Wemyss	Pub, accommodation and food	Page 149
108	Kingask Country Cottages, St Andrews	Self catering	Page 152
109	Denburn House, Crail	B&B and self catering	Page 154
110	East Neuk Hotel, Crail	Hotel and restaurant	Page 155
111	The Smuggler's Inn, Anstruther	Pub, accommodation and restaurant	Page 156
112	The Ship Hotel, Newburgh	Hotel and restaurant	Page 158
113	Tannochbrae Tearoom, Auchtermuchty	Café and tearoom	Page 158

DUNFERMLINE

Now an important industrial town, Dunfermline was at one time the capital of Scotland, and still has many reminders of its glory days. It was here that Malcolm III (known as "Malcolm Canmore") and his queen, later to become **St Margaret of Scotland**, held court in the 11th century. Malcolm and Margaret's reign was a turning point in Scotland's history. Margaret was the daughter of Edgar Aetheling, heir-apparent to the English throne, and was half Saxon and half Hungarian. When she came to the Scottish court, she was shocked at what she found, and, with her husband's consent, set about changing things. The Scottish church, though nominally subservient to Rome, was still observing the old Celtic rites, which she found abhorrant. So the church was the first thing she set about overhauling. A Culdee (from the Irish céli dé, meaning "servants of God") monastery manned by Celtic-Irish priests had previously been established in Dunfermline, and she banished these priests and founded a Benedictine priory (later to become Dunfermline Abbey) in its place, inviting monks from Durham to serve in it.

Scotland in the 11th century was a small kingdom, perched precariously on the edge of the known world. It was Margaret who introduced refinement into the court, and made the country think of itself as an integral part of Europe. Under her, trade with the continent flourished. She didn't do it on her own, of course. Her husband Malcolm was a driving force. Though he could neither read nor write, he hankered after refinement and culture, and had only a few years before moved Scotland's capital from Perthshire to Dunfermline to be nearer the Fife ports that traded with Europe. Under Margaret, the centre of power shifted once more - this time to Edinburgh, which later became the nation's capital.

One other innovation is attributed to St Margaret - buttons on the sleeves of men's jackets. She had been disgusted to see that Scottish courtiers - in common with courtiers throughout Europe - wiped their noses on their sleeves, so set about making this habit as uncomfortable as possible!

She died soon after her husband and son were killed in Northumberland in 1093, and was buried in the abbey she had founded. Soon a cult grew up round her, and her burial spot became a place of pilgrimage. In 1250 she was canonised, and even today she is looked upon with reverence in Scotland. The remains of her shrine, destroyed during the Reformation, can still be seen.

Dunfermline Abbey as we see it today is a mixture of dates. The heavily buttressed nave is Norman, and is reminscent of Durham Cathedral. Beneath it lie the remains of the original church. The choir was rebuilt in the early 19th century as the parish church, and it was during its construction that workmen came across the skeleton of a man. It was lying within a stone coffin, and wrapped in lead and gold cloth. It was immediately recognised as that of Robert the Bruce, King of Scots, as the breastbone and ribs had been sawn away. After he died, Bruce's heart had been removed from his body so that it heart might be taken to the Holy Land (see also Melrose). It was re-interred with due reverence, and now a brass plate beneath the pulpit marks the spot. Around the battlements of the abbey tower are the words "King Robert the Bruce".

Jokers

68 Hospital Street, Dunfermline KY11 3AT
Tel: 01383 735075

Dunfermline is the ancient capital of Scotland, and it is here that you will find **Jokers**, which is only five minutes walk from the town centre. It serves a great range of fine beers, lagers, wines, spirits and, should you be driving, soft drinks. Good, honest pub food at affordable prices is available every day except Sunday, with all the dishes being cooked on the premises from fresh Scottish produce wherever possible. You can eat throughout the establishment, and choose off a menu or specials board. The inside is spacious yet cosy, and makes a lovely stopping off point as you explore a town that at once was at the heart of Scottish history, and still has many reminders of that time.

Dunfermline Abbey

The **Abbot House Heritage Centre** is housed in a 14th - 16th century house to the north of the abbey in Maygate. It was formerly the Abbot's Lodgings for the great Benedictine monastery, as well as its administrative centre. Poets, kings and bishops visited, and it played its part in some of the great events in Scottish history.

St Margaret's Shrine has been reconstructed with its wall, showing just how rich the interior of the abbey was when it was at the height of its powers. In all, over 1000 years of history can be seen, from the Picts right up until the present day.

The **Dunfermline Abbey and Palace Visitors Centre** (Historic Scotland) tells of the history of the abbey and of the later palace that was built on the site of the monastic buildings. A magnificent 200 foot long buttressed wall is all that now remains of the palace.

To the west of the abbey is a great mound known as **Malcolm's Tower**, all that remains of Malcolm's fortifications. It sits within **Pittencrieff Park** (famous for its peacocks), which was gifted to the town by Andrew Carnegie in 1908. The park had always fascinated him as a boy, though being privately owned at the time, access was always denied him. So when he had the money, he bought it and threw it open to the people of the town. Also in the park is **Pittencrieff House Museum**, based in a 17th century mansion, which has an art gallery and displays on local history.

Near Chalmers Street Car Park, about a quaster of a mile north of Abbot House, can be found **St Margaret's Cave**, where the pious queen prayed in solitude. A legend has it that Malcolm became suspicious of his wife's unexplained absences from court, and fearing that she had a lover, he followed her one day to the cave, and found her kneeling in prayer.

Andrew Carnegie was, in the 19th century, the richest man in the world. He was born in Dunfermline in 1835, and had emigrated with his parents to the United States in 1848. By the 1880s, he had amassed a fortune through iron and steel making, and retired from business in 1901 to distribute his wealth. His humble birthplace in Moodie Street, a former weaver's cottage, is now the central feature of the **Andrew Carnegie Birthplace Museum**. It tells the story of the great man from his humble origins to his death in 1919. In

Pittencrief Park, close to the **Louise Carnegie Gates** (named after his wife) is a statue of the man.

It is not only New York that has a **Carnegie Hall** - Dunfermline has one as well, housing a theatre and concert hall. It can be found in East Port, near the **Dunfermline Museum** inViewfield. Here the history of the town is explained, including its time as a centre of manufacture for linen and silk, which continued right up until the 20th century.

To the north of the town, at Lathalmond, is the **Scottish Vintage Bus Museum**, housed in a former Royal Navy Stores depot. It is possibly the largest collection of vintage buses in Britain, and has been open since 1995.

AROUND DUNFERMLINE

COWDENBEATH

5 miles NE of Dunfermline, off the A909

This small town was at the centre of the Fife coalfields, and though the mines have long gone, it still has the feel of a mining community about it. It's football team has perhaps the most unusual nickname of any senior team in Scotland - the "Blue Brazils". **Cowdenbeath Racewall** has stock car racing every Saturday evening from March to November.

LOCHGELLY

7 miles NE of Dunfermline on the B981

Lochgelly is a small mining town, famous throughout Scotland at one time for the manufacture of the "Lochgelly", the leather strap used to punish children in school. Near the town is the **Lochore Meadows Country Park**, set in 919 acres of reclaimed industrial land. The last pits closed here in 1966, and now the area is a haven for wildlife. Loch Ore, created as a result of mining subsidence, is stocked with brown trout.

ABERDOUR

6 miles E of Dunfermline on the A921

Aberdour is a small coastal burgh that received its charter in 1500. The restored **St Fillan's Parish Church** is partly Norman, and has what is known as a "leper window". The town has two beaches, one of which has won a Europan blue flag for its cleanliness. The ruins of **Aberdour Castle** (Historic Scotland), close to the church, date from the 14th century, later additions being made in the 16th and 17th century.

DALGETY BAY

4 miles SE of Dunfermline off the A921

The ruins of **St Bridget's Church** date from the 12th century. It was near Dalgety Bay that the murder of James Stewart, the **2nd Earl of Moray**, took place, remembered in one of the best known of Scottish songs, The Bonnie Earl o' Moray (see also Doune). He was the grandson of Regent Morton, regent of Scotland when Mary Stuart abdicated in favour of her infant son, later to be James VI. He was a popular nobleman, dashing and handsome. But he was always feuding with the Earls of Huntly, one of the great Catholic families of the time, and was implicated in a coup to overthrow James VI, though he probably had no involvement.

But Huntly saw his chance, and armed with a king's warrant, set out to seize Moray. He eventually found him at his mother's castle at Donibristle, in what is now Dalgety Bay. Huntly demanded that he give himself up, but Moray refused, so Huntly set fire to the building. Some men ran out from the front while Moray ran out the back way, hoping to hide near the shore. Unfortunately, unknown to Moray, his bonnet had caught fire, and this gave him away. He was hacked to death, with Huntly, it is said, striking the fatal blow. When James VI discovered that Moray had been killed, he feigned outrage, though when the crowds later discovered that Huntly had been armed with a king's warrant, James had to flee to Glasgow to escape the wrath of the crowd.

It was a death that touched the pulse of the common people of Scotland at a time when the country was in turmoil, not knowing if the Reformation would take hold or whether Roman Catholicism would make a return. Huntly spent a few weeks in Blackness Castle as a punishment, and was then released.

INCHCOLM

6 miles SE of Dunfermline, in the Firth of Forth

This small island was at one time known as

the "Iona of the East". On it are the substantial ruins of **Inchcolm Abbey** (Historic Scotland), which was dedicated to St Columba. The story goes that Alexander I, son of Malcolm III and Queen Margaret, was crossing the Forth in 1123 when a storm blew up, and the royal party had to seek refuge on the island, which had, for many years, supported a succession of hermits. The hermit inhabiting the island at the time shared his meagre provisions with his guests for three days until the storm subsided, and Alexander could continue on his journey to Fife. When he reached dry land he vowed to build a monastery dedicated to St Columba on the island in thanksgiving for his safe passage, but before he could put his plans into effect he died. His younger brother David I ascended the throne, and he founded a priory which eventually became the Abbey of Inchcolm.

A small stone building to the west of the abbey may have been the monks' cell, though it has been much restored over the years. The abbey buildings as we see them now date mainly from the 15th century, and represent the most complete medieval abbey in Scotland, with most of the buildings remaining intact.

In the late 18th century, a military hospital was set up on the island to look after wounded sailors from the Russian fleet, which was using the Firth of Forth as a base. In the 20th century it was fortified as part of the United Kingdom's sea defences, and some of these can still be seen. Over 500 troops were stationed on the island, and the first air raid of World War II took place not far away, when German bombers, in 1939, dropped bombs not far from the Forth Rail Bridge.

INVERKEITHING

3 miles S of Dunfermline off the A90

Inverkeithing is an old royal burgh which received its royal charter in about 1193. It sits close to the Forth Road and Rail Bridges, and has many old buildings. The **Mercat Cross** is 16th century, and the **Old Town Hall** opposite, with its outside staircase, dates from 1770. Of the 15th century **St Peter's Church**, only the tower remains, as the rest was built in 1826. **Inverkeithing Museum**, house in the hospitum of an old friary, tells the story of Inverkeithing and of **Admiral Sir Samuel Greig**, a local man born in 1735 who largely created the modern the Russian navy, manning it initially with Scottish officers.

Near the town, in 1651, was fought the **Battle of Inverkeithing** between a Royalist force under Sir Hector MacLean of Duart and the Parliamentarian forces of Cromwell. The result was a victory for the Parliamentarians, and the death of Sir Hector MacLean. The immediate result of the battle was the plundering of Inverkeithing and Dumfermline, and the long term result was the ascendancy of Cromwell in Scotland. A small cairn by the roadside opposite Pitreavy Castle, erected by the Clan MacLean, commemorates the event.

NORTH QUEENSFERRY

4 miles S of Dunfermline off the A90

This small town was the northern terminus for the ferry that plied across the Forth from South Queensfery in West Lothian. It sits on a small peninsula which juts out into the Forth, making this the river's narrowest point before the Kincardine Bridge.

The **Forth Bridges Visitors Centre** is housed within the Queensferry Lodge Hotel, and tells the story of the two bridges spanning the Forth. There is a magnificent scale model of the Firth of Forth, as well as photographs, documents and arrtifacts. **Deep Sea World** is billed as Scotland's aquarium, and takes you

Forth Bridge

on a walk along the "ocean floor", thanks to a long underwater tunnel, which is made of specially toughened glass. Fish swim above and beside you as you stand within it, and you can see piranha fish, stingrays and electric eels, as well as touch a real shark.

North Queensferry is the start of the **Fife Coastal Path**, a 78 mile long pathway which will eventually take you through most of the small picturesque towns and villages on the Fife coast, ending at the Tay Bridge.

Culross Palace and Gardens

CHARLESTOWN

3 miles SW of Dunfermline on a minor road

This small village was established in 1756 by Charles Bruce, 5th Earl of Elgin, to exploit the large deposits of limestone in the area. There were 14 kilns here producing lime for building, agriculture and the making of iron and glass. It was a self sufficient community, with its own harbour, shops and school, and the houses were arranged in the shape of the founder's initials - E.

The works only closed in 1956, having produced in their 200 years of existence over 11 million tons of quicklime. Now guided walks round the complex are available in the summer months thanks to the Charlestown Lime Heritage Trust. Nearby is the village of **Limekilns**, which was once the port for the monks of Dunfermline Abbey.

CULROSS

7 miles W of Dunfermline on a minor road off the A985

If you wish to see what a Scottish burgh looked like in the 16th, 17th and 18th centuries, then Culross is the place to do it. Though having a population of no more than a few hundred, it is in fact a proud royal burgh, and up until local government reorganisation in 1975 had its own town council and provost.

It is undoubtedly the loveliest of Fife's old burghs - a situation which owes more to the town's relative poverty in the 19th and early 20th century than any wish to preserve the past. The council, over the years, didn't have the money to make "improvements" or rebuild the huddle of old houses that form the town's central area. And to cap it all, the town once had an abbey, the church of which is the present day parish church. Now it is a town caught in time, and largely owned by the National Trust for Scotland.

It is, however, a thriving and lively community with most of the quaint crow-step gabled houses occupied. The streets are cobbled, and those around the old **Mercat Cross** (dating from 1588) have a feature known as the "crown o' the causie", a raised portion in the middle where only the wealthy were allowed to walk, while the rest of the townsfolk had to walk on the edges, where water and dirt congregated.

The town's main industries were coalmining, salt panning and the making of baking girdles. Coal mining had been introduced by the monks of the abbey, at a time when coal was little known about, and wondrous tales spread round Scotland about the "stones that could burn". After the Reformation, the mines were taken over by a man called Sir George Bruce, a descendant of Robert the Bruce. Between 1575 and his death 50 years later he had revolutionised the industry. He even had a tunnel dug under the waters of the Firth of Forth, which was a marvel in its time. It stopped one mile from the coast, where it came up to sea level surrounded by a stone wall to keep the water out. James VI was fascinated by Culross's industry, and paid a visit. Sir George took him on a tour of the mine, and led the unsuspecting king along the tunnel. When he emerged and found himself surrounded on all four sides by water, he panicked, shouting "treason!".

As an off shoot of the mining industry, salt panning soon became another major industry in the town. It is reckoned that at one time there were 50 salt pans along the coast, all using inferior coal to heat salt water from the sea. Another industry was the making of iron girdles for cooking. Culross blacksmiths are said to have invented these round, flat implements for frying and cooking after Robert the Bruce, in the 14th century, ordered that each one of his troops be given a cooking utensil to cook oatcakes.

Nothing now remains of Sir George's mining ventures. However, his home, now called **Culross Palace**, still stands, and is open to the public. Work started on it in 1597, and is a typical residence of its time for someone of Sir George's standing in society. It has splendid kitchen gardens. Along from it is the **Town House**, gifted to the National Trust for Scotland in 1975 when Culross Town Council was wound up. It was built in 1625 with later additions, and at one time the ground floor was a debtors' prison, while the attic was used as a prison for witches. It now houses the local tourist information centre.

Beside the Mercat Cross is the the building known as **The Study**. It was built about 1610, and after the Palace, is Culross's grandest house. When the Church of Scotland was Episcopalian, the town formed part of the diocese of Dunblane, and it was here that Bishop Robert Leighton stayed on his visits. The quaint Outlook Tower housed his study, hence the name of the house. If you continue past The Study, along Tanhouse Brae and into Kirk Street, you will eventually reach **Culross Abbey**. The choir of the church (restored in 1633) still stands, and is used as the parish church, though the other buildings have either disappeared or are in ruins. It was founded in 1217 by Malcolm, Earl of Fife, and housed a Cistercian order of monks. Off the north transept is the Bruce Vault, where there is an impressive monument to Sir George Bruce, his wife and their eight children.

Culross was the birthplace, in AD514, of St Kentigern, patron saint of Glasgow. In 1503 Archbishop Blackadder of Glasgow erected a small chapel on the spot where the birth is supposed to have taken place, and its ruins can still be seen to the east of the village. The story goes that he was the son of Thenew (also known as Enoch), a princess of the kingdom of the Lothians. When her father Loth (after which the kingdom was named) discovered that she was pregnant, he banished her from his lands, and she set sail in a boat across the Firth of Forth. She landed at Culross, and here she gave birth to her son, who was taken into care by St Serf, who had established a monastic school here. There may be some truth in the story, though it is now known that St Serf lived in the century following Kentigern's birth.

But Culross's attractions aren't all historical. Close to the town is **Longannet Power Station**, one of Scotland's largest. There are organised tours (which have to be prebooked), and you can see the huge turbine hall from a viewing platform, as well as tour the visitor's centre, which shows how coal produces electricity.

Stretching from Longannet past Culross to Combie Point on the shores of the Firth of Forth is the **Torry Bay Local Nature Reserve**, where you can see many species of birds, such as shelduck, greenshank and great crested grebe.

KINCARDINE ON FORTH

10 miles W of Dunfermline, on the A985

This small burgh, which received its charter in 1663, sits at the north end of the **Kincardine Bridge**. Up until the Forth Road Bridge opened in 1964, this was the only road crossing of the Forth before Stirling. It dates from 1936, and the middle section used to swivel open to allow ships to pass up the river.

The town is full of small, old fashioned cottages with red pantiled rooves, and there are the ruins of the 17th century **Tulliallan Church**. The burgh's **Mercat Cross** dates from the 17th century, and it was in the town, in 1842, that Sir James Dewar, inventor of the vacuum flask was born. To the west of the town is **Tulliallan Castle**, now the main police training college in Scotland.

KINROSS

Once the county town of Kinross-shire, this small burgh now sits quietly on the shores of

Loch Leven. The opening of the M90 motorway has put it within half an hour of Edinburgh, and over the last fifteen years it has expanded to become a peaceful haven for commuters. The town's **Tolbooth** dates from the 17th century, and on the **Mercat Cross** are the "Jougs", an iron collar placed round the neck of wrongdoers. **Kinross House** dates from the late 17th century, and was built for Sir William Bruce, Charles II's surveyor and master of works, who was responsible for the fabric of the Palace of Holyrood in Edinburgh. It is an elegant Palladian mansion with wonderful formal gardens that are sometimes open to the public. The story goes that it was intended as a home for the ill-fated James VII, then Duke of York, in anticipation of the fact that he might not succeed to the throne.

Loch Leven is one of Scotland's most famous lochs, not because of its size (it covers no more than 3,250 acres) or its spectacular beauty, but because of the wonderful trout fishing that was found there. Though this has gone into decline in recent years, the trout are still highly prized for their delicate pink flesh, caused by the small fresh water shellfish on which they feed. The whole loch is a National Nature reserve, and on the south shore of the loch, close to the B9097, is the **Vane Farm Nature Reserve**, adminstered by the Royal Society for the Protection of Birds. It hosts a programme of events throughout the year, and was the first educational nature reserve in Europe.

The loch has two islands. On **St Serf's Island** are the remains of a small priory and chapel, and on the other are the ruins of **Lochleven Castle** (Historic Scotland). From June 1567 until May 1568 Mary Stuart was held prisoner here, having been seized in Edinburgh for her supposed part in the murder of her husband Lord Darley. She was 25 years old at the time, and married to Bothwell, who was also implicated in Darnley's murder. While kept prisoner in the castle, she was constantly being asked to abdicate and divorce Bothwell, but this she refused to do, as she was already pregnant by him. Shortly after she arrived on the island, she gave birth to stillborn twins, and eventually signed the deeds. But it was not her stay on the island that made the castle famous, rather it was the way she escaped.

The castle was owned by the Dowager Lady Douglas, mother of Mary's half brother the Earl of Moray, who became regent when Mary abdicated. Both she and her other sons Sir William and George Douglas looked after Mary during her imprisonment. But George gradually fell under Mary's spell, and hatched various plans for her to escape. All failed, and he was eventually banished from the island. But someone else had fallen under Mary's spell - 16 year old Willie Douglas, who was thought to be the illegitimate son of Sir William, and who was kept as a page.

After the various attempts at escape, Mary was being held in the third storey of the main tower, above the Great Hall where the Douglas family dined. One evening young Willie "accidentally" dropped a napkin over the castle keys, which his father had placed on the table while dining. On picking up the napkin, he picked up the keys as well.

As the meal progressed, Mary and one of her attendants crept out of her room and made for the main doorway, where they were met by Willie. He unlocked the door, and the both slipped out. He then locked the door behind him and threw the keys into the water (where they were recovered in the 19th century) before rowing the two women ashore. There they were met by George Douglas, Lord

Birdwatching, Vane Farm, Loch Leven

Seton and a troop of loyal soldiers, and taken to the safety of Niddrie Castle.

Nowadays, trips to the island on a small ferry leave from the pier at Kinross. People are sometimes surprised to see how far the castle is from the shore of the loch, and wonder why sentries on the castle walls never saw her running towards the shoreline. But in those days the level of the water was at least four feet higher than it is now, so it must only have been a few steps from the door to the boat.

Within the town are the premises of Todd and Duncan, where a small exhibition called **Cashmere at Lochleven** traces the history of this luxury cloth. And at Portmoak there's the **Scottish Gliding Centre**, where the adventurous can try an "air experience flight". Close to Kinross every year in July is held Scotland's biggest outdoor rock festival, **T in the Park**.

AROUND KINROSS

MILNATHORT

2 miles N of Kinross off the M90

Milnathort is a small, former wool manufacturing town. To the east are the impressive ruins of **Burleigh Castle**, built of warm red stone, which was a stronghold of the Balfour family.

SCOTLANDWELL

5 miles E of Kinross, on the A911

Scotlandwell takes its name from the springs which bubble up to the surface in this part of the county, on the western slopes of the Lomond Hills. In the early 13th century the Bishop of St Andrews set up a hospice here, and his successor gave it to the "Red Friars", or "Trinitarians", a monastic order which had originally been founded to raise money for the release of captives in the Holy Land during the Crusades. They exploited the springs, and established a **Holy Well**. Soon it became a place of pilgrimage, bringing huge revenue to the monks.

The local landowners, the Arnots of **Arnot Tower**, the ruins of which can still be seen, gazed enviously at the wealth of the Trinitarians, and decided to "muscle in" on the venture. They placed younger sons of the family within the order as fifth columnists, and when enough of them were in place, they occupied the friary and ejected those friars who weren't Arnots. They established Archibald Arnot, the Laird of Arnot's second son, as minister (the name given to the head of the friary), and began creaming off the vast wealth. At the Reformation, the lands and income of the friary were given to them, and the takeover was complete.

Today, the holy well still exists. In 1858 the Laird of Arnot commissioned David Bryce to turn it into a memorial to his wife Henrietta, and this is what can be seen today. The friary has compelety disappeared, though a small plaque in the graveyard marks the spot where it once stood.

CROOK OF DEVON

5 miles W of Kinross on the A977

This small village seems quiet enough now, but in the 17th century it achieved notoriety as a centre of witchcraft. A coven of witches had been "discovered" in the area, and in 1662 three women were tried and sentenced to be strangled to death and their bodies burnt at a "place called Lamblaires". A few weeks later four women and one man were executed in the same manner, and not long after two women were tried, one of whom excaped death because of her age. The other was burnt at the stake.

By this time the other members of the "coven" had fled from the area. But in July two further women were put on trial, one of whom was executed and the other, called Christian Grieve, acquitted. But the acquittal was looked upon as an affront by the local people - especially the clergy - and she was retried and eventually executed.

There is no doubt that the trials were a travesty, and that many old scores were settled by naming people - especially old women - as witches. It was also not unknown in Scotland at that time for the accused, who knew their fate was sealed, to get their own back on their accusers by naming them as witches and warlocks as well. Thus Scotland seemed to be awash with devil worship, when in fact true Satanism was almost non-existent.

Today Lamblaires is a small grassy knoll in a field adjoining the village. It looks peaceful enough, and nothing reminds you of the horrible stranglings and burnings that took place there.

KIRKCALDY

Kirkcaldy is the largest town in Fife, and is famous for the manufacture of linoleum. At one time it was known as the "Lang Toun", due to the fact that it appeared to stretch out along one main street. It was created a royal burgh in 1644, and one of the famous events held here every year in April is the **Links Market**, reckoned to be the longest street fair in Europe. The town's Esplanade is cordoned off from traffic, and taken over by swings, roundabouts, dodgems, carousels, hoopla stalls and all the other attractions of a modern funfair.

Within **Kirkcaldy Museum and Art Gallery** is an exhibition devoted to **Wemyss Ware**, a form of earthenware pottery that produced in the town by Robert Heron and Son between 1882 and 1930. It is now much collected, and is possibly the most sought after pottery ever to have been made in Scotland. Its most distinctive feature was its decoration, which was bold, simple and direct. Because of the methods of firing used, there was a lot of waste, which meant that the pottery was always expensive. The museum also houses a local history collection, plus an extensive collection of Scottish paintings.

The extensive ruins of **Ravenscraig Castle** sit on a promentary adjacent to a public park. It was built in the 15th century by James II for his queen, Mary of Gueldres. In 1470 it passed to Lord Sinclair, Earl of Orkney, who gave up his earldom to acquire it. Overlooking the town harbour is **Sailor's Walk**, the town's oldest house. The **Old Parish Church** sits at the top of Kirk Wynd, and dates from 1808. However, its tower is medieval, making it the oldest building in the town.

Ravenscraig Castle

Beyond Ravenscraig Castle is **Dysart**, which, up until 1930, was a separate burgh. Around its harbour area it is very picturesque, with whitewashed cottages and houses dating from the 16th, 17th and 18th centuries. At one time this was a salt panning area, and **Pan Ha'** (meaning "Pan Haugh") is a group of

NICOLS

10 Nicol Street, Kirkcaldy, Fife KY1 1RP
Tel: 01592 264364

Nicols is a friendly and welcoming lounge bar close to the town centre and sea front. It is beautifully decorated and spotlessly clean, offering a menu that contains a wide selection of pub lunches and snacks, from steak pie and roast chicken to all day breakfasts and three course lunches. The bar carries a wide selection of beers, wine, spirits and soft drinks, making this the ideal place for a relaxing drink as well as a meal when visiting the historic town of Kirkcaldy. There are also OAP reduced rate special meals every day from 11.00 to 18.00, which are great value for money.

Dysart, Fife

particularly fine buildings of the 17th century with red pantiled rooves. **St Serf's Tower** is the tower of the former parish church, and dates from the 15th century. It looks more like a castle than a tower, and reflects the troubled times this area once knew, when English ships attacked it. In Rectory Lane is the **John McDouall Stuart Museum**, dedicated to the life of a locally born exploer who, in 1861-62, made the first return journey across the Australian continent.

Adam Smith, the founder of the science of economics, was born in Kirkcaldy in 1723. He went on to occupy the chair of moral philosophy at Glasgow University, and his famous book, The Wealth of Nations was partly written in his mother's house (now gone) in the town's High Street. Also born in the town was **William Adam** the architect, and his son, **Robert Adam**.

In the town's Abbotshall Kirkyard stands a statue in memory of another person born in Kirkcaldy, **Marjory Fleming**, the child writer, known as "Pet Margory". She died in 1811, and yet her writings have intrigued and delighted people down through the ages. She kept a journal, in which she jotted down thoughts, poems and biographical scraps. She was, by all accounts, a "handful", and when her mother gave birth to another girl in 1809, Margory she was sent to live with her aunt in Edinburgh. This is where her writing began, encouraged by her cousin Isa, and she eventually filled three notebooks. Nobody knows what she might have achieved in adulthood, because, one month short of her ninth birthday, and after she had returned to Kirkcaldy, she tragically died of meningitis. Her last piece of writing was a touching poem addressed to her beloved cousin. Her writings were subsequently published, and found great favour with the Victorians, though some frowned on her absolute honesty when it came to describing her tantrums and innermost thoughts.

AROUND KIRKCALDY

GLENROTHES

6 miles N of Kirkcaldy on the A92

Glenrothes was one of the new towns established in Scotland in the late 1940s. In **Balbirnie Park**, which extends to 416 acres, is a late Neolithic site dating from about 2900BC.

FALKLAND

10 miles N of Kirkcaldy on the A912

This little royal burgh sits in the shadow of the **Lomond Hills**. There are two distinct peaks - East Lomond, at 1,471 feet, and West Lomond at 1,713 feet, the highest point in Fife. It has quaint old cobbled streets lined with 17th and 18th century cottages, and at one time was a favourite place of the Scottish kings. **Falkland Palace** (National Trust for Scotland) was built in the 15th century on the site of an earlier castle built by the Earls of Fife, and in the 16th century James V employed stonemasons to turn it into a magnificent Renaissance palace. It was never an important castle like Edinburgh or Holyrood. Rather it was a country retreat for Stuart kings to hunt deer and boar, and get away from the affairs of state. James V died in Falkland Palace in 1542, and his daughter Mary Stuart, it is said, spent the best years of her tragic life at Falkland.

Mary was born a few days before James V

Falkland Palace and Gardens

died, and the story is told that when he was on his deathbed, and told about the birth of a daughter, he exclaimed: "It cam' wi' a lass, and it'll gang wi' a lass!", meaning that the House of Stuart had started with Margorie, daughter of Robert the Bruce, and it would die out with his daughter. In this prediction, he was both right and wrong. It did die out "wi' a lass", but not Mary Stuart. The last Stuart monarch was Queen Ann, who died in 1715. The Palace is still nominally the property of the monarch, and its chapel, housed in what was the banqueting hall in the South Range, is the only Roman Catholic church in the country within royal property.

Both Charles I and Charles II visited Falkland, and it was in the Palace, in 1650, that Charles 11 founded the Scots Guards. His father Charles I had founded a regiment in 1642 called "Argyll's Regiment" to act as his personal bodyguard in Ireland, and this had later merged with nine small regiments to fom the Irish Companies. Charles II renamed this regiment The King's Lyfeguard of Foot while at Falkland, and proclaimed it to be his bodyguard. It was later renamed the Scots Guards.

In the East Range can be seen the King's Bedchamber and the Queen's Room, and within the Gatehouse are the Keeper's Apartments. The gardens were laid out in the mid 20th century, and have mangificent herbaceous borders. Within the gardens is the **Royal Tennis Court**, which dates from the early 16th century, and the oldest in the country still in use. Here "real tennis" is played, with the rooves of the "lean tos" on either side of the court playing an integral part in the game. Tennis is still played here today, and there is a thriving club.

The burgh's **Town Hall**, which dates from 1805, houses an exhibition about the town. Close to it, in the square, is a house with a plaque which commemorates Richard Cameron, a local schoolmaster and Covenanter, who was killed at the Battle of Airds Moss in Ayrshire in 1680 (see also Sanquhar).

WEMYSS

4 miles NE of Kirkcaldy on the A955

Below the substantial ruins of **MacDuff Castle**, near the shore line, are some caves which have old carvings. The date mainly from Pictish times, and it has been claimed that there are more carvings within these caves than in all the other caves in Britain put together. However, due to erosion and subsidence, most of the caves can no longer be entered, though they may be views from the shore.

BUCKHAVEN AND METHIL

7 miles NE of Kirkcaldy on the B931

Buckhaven and Methil constituted one burgh, which was created in 1891. It's motto was Carbone Carbasoque, which means " By Coal and by Sail ", reflecting the fact that it used to export coal. As with other Fife seaports, it also had saltpans, and by 1677 three pans were in operation, fuelled by coal. The Methil docks were opened in 1887. In Lower Methil's High Street is the **Methil Heritage Centre**, a lively community museum which explains the history of the area.

Buckhaven, to the west, was never as industrialised as Methil. It was once a fishing port and ferry terminal, and has some old, quaint cottages. In College Street there is the **Buckhaven Museum**, which has displays about the town's industries, including fishing.

LARGO

11 miles NE of Kirkcaldy on the A915

There are two Largos - Lower Largo on the shores of the Forth and Upper Largo about half a mile inland, where the **Parish Church**, some parts of which date from the early 17th century, stands. It was here that Scotland's greatest seafarer, and Admiral of its Fleet, **Sir Andrew Wood**, had his home. He died in 1515, and was buried in the kirkyard. He commanded the largest and most magnificent fighting ship of its day, the **Great Michael**, flagship of the Scottish fleet. Nothing now remains of Wood's castle but a tower.

Another seafaring man was born in Lower Largo. **Alexander Selkirk** was born in 1676, the son of a shoemaker. While sailing on a ship called the Cinque Ports in 1704, he quarrelled with the captain, who put him ashore on the unihabited island of Juan Fernandez in the Pacific Ocean. He remained there until 1709, when he was rescued. Daniel Defoe, though he never met Selkirk, based his novel Robinson Crusoe on his adventures. A statue of Selkirk can be found near the harbour.

On the eastern edge of Upper Largo can be found **Scotland's Larder**, a shop, restaurant and visitor's centre which promotes Scottish food in all its diversity.

KINGHORN

4 miles SW of Kirkcaldy on the A921

This quiet little royal burgh saw one of the most decisive events in Scottish history. At the **Pettycur Crags** to the west of the town, in 1286, Alexander III was killed, throwing Scotland into turmoil. He was the last of Scotland's Celtic kings, and had previously married Princess Margaret, daughter of Henry III of England, and she had given him two sons. But Margaret and the sons died; so, at the age of 45, he married again, this time to Yolande, daughter of the Count of Dreux in France, in the hope of continuing the direct royal line.

After a meeting of his nobles at Edinburgh, Alexander was anxious to return to Queen Yolande, who was residing at Kinghorn. The weather was stormy, and some of his men tried to dissuade him from crossing the Forth. However, he was adamant, and was taken across to Fife. But while riding along the Pettycur Crags, almost in sight of the castle where his wife was staying, his horse stumbled, sending him over the cliffs to his death.

The heir to the Scottish throne was now three year old Margaret, known as the "Maid of Norway". She was the daughter of Alexander's own daughter, who had married Eric II of Norway. But while crossing from Norway to Scotland, Margaret died also, leaving no heir to the throne. In the resultant vacuum, noblemen jockeyed for position, putting forward many claimants to the throne. Edward I of England was asked to intercede, and he saw his chance. He tried to incorporate Scotland into his own kingdom by installing a puppet king, and thus began the Wars of Independence.

A tall monument at the side of the road, erected in 1886, marks the spot where Alexander was killed.

BURNTISLAND

6 miles SW of Kirkcaldy on the A921

This small royal burgh, called Potus Gratiae, or "Port of Grace" by the Romans, is overlooked by a 632 feet high hill called **The Binn**. It was formerly a port for exporting coal from the Fife coalfields, though its history goes well back beyond this. **St Columba's Parish Church** is a four square building dating from 1592, and is possibly based on a Dutch design. It was the first church built in Scotland after the Reformation, and has a wealth of detail inside, including elaborate lofts and pews. The Holy Table sits at the centre of the church, with the pews facing it on four sides, emphasising the "equality of all believers". It is the birthplace of the **Authorised Version of the Bible**, as James VI attended a General Assembly of the Church of Scotland here in 1601, and put forward the proposal for a translation of the Bible into English. The suggestion was enthusiastically received, but it was not until James had assumed the throne of Great Britain that work began.

The **Burntisland Edwardian Fair Museum** is in the High Street, and features displays about Edwardian fairgrounds and local history Off the coast of the town, in 1633, Charles I lost most of his treasure when his baggage ship, the Blessing of Burntisland, foundered and sank. Since then treasure hunters have been trying to trace the wreckage on the sea bed.

ST ANDREWS

St Andrews is one of the most important and historic towns in Britain. Perhaps one should call it a city, as it was, in pre Reformation times, Scotland's ecclesiastical capital on account of its huge cathedral - Scotland's largest building in medieval times. It is also a university town, and the home of golf.

St Andrews Cathedral (Historic Scotland) was begun by Bishop Arnold in 1160, though the maginificent ruins you see nowadays date from many periods. The choir was the first part to be built, and shows both Norman and Gothic details. The nave was completed in the late 13th century, though the great west front was blown down in a gale and had to be rebuilt. The whole building was finally consecrated in July 1318 in the presence of Robert the Bruce.

Swilken Burn, Old Course St Andrews

But this wasn't the first cathedral on the site. In about 1127 a more modest church was built, a remnant of which still remains. This remnant is **St Rule's Tower**, to the south of the ruins, and its attached chancel. From its top, there's a magnificent view of the town. Legend tells us that St Rule (or Regulus) came from Patras in Greece in the 4th century, carrying with him the bones of St Andrew. He set up a shrine for them on the Fife coast, at what was then called Kilrimont - present day St Andrews. A more likely story is that the bones of St Andrew (if indeed they were his bones) were brought here by Bishop Acca of Hexham in 732. The relics were eventually transferred to the later building, housed in a shrine behind the high altar. St Andrews soon became a place of pilgrimage, with people coming from all over Europe to pray at the shrine.

To the east of the cathedral and outside its precincts are the scant ruins of another church, **St Mary on the Rock**. It seems that when the catherdral was being built, there were still Culdee monks of the old Celtic church at St Andrews, and they refused to join the catherdal priory. In the 13th century they built this church for themselves, which became the first collegiate church in Scotland. However, the monks gradually adopted the rites of the Catholic church, and its priests were soon allowed a place in the cathedral chapter.

St Andrews Castle was the archbishop's residence. It too sits on the coast, and its ruins are sturdy yet picturesque. It was here, in 1546, that **Cardinal David Beaton,**

Kingask Country Cottages

Kingask House, St Andrews,
Fife KY16 8PN
Tel: 01334 472011
Fax: 01334 470900
e-mail: info@kingask-cottages.co.uk
website: www.kingask-cottages.co.uk

Fife is never referred to as a county in Scotland - it is always referred to as the 'Kingdom of Fife', reflecting its long history and royal associations.

Set in and around St Andrews and Crail (surely two of the loveliest places in the county) you will find **Kingask Country Cottages**, which offers a splendid range of self catering accommodation to the discerning tourist.

There are twelve luxury holiday cottages in beautiful rural locations between the two towns, many with sea views. they have private gardens, children's play areas, and excellent opportunities for walking right on the doorstep. They make ideal bases for exploring the area's many attractions, or just relaxing in an atmosphere of homely comfort.

In addition, there is a country house just 12 minutes walk from Crail that sleeps 12, with excellent views across the Firth of Forth to the Isle of May. There is a large, secure private garden and a play area for kids.

For that feeling of real luxury, there is also a beautiful Georgian town house that sleeps 14 in seven bedrooms, and is situated in one of the most desirable areas in this historic town, close to the Old Course, beach, restaurants and shops. There is a private garden and free on-street parking.

Please contact us at the above address or via our e-mail and website for further information.

Archbishop of St Andrews, was murdered. In March of that year, George Wishart the Protestant reformer had been burnt at the stake in front of the castle on Beatons' authority, which made him many enemies. In May a group of Fife lairds broke into the castle and murdered him in his bedroom in revenge, and hung the corpse from the window. There then followed a long siege of the castle, during which time sappers working for the Earl of Arran dug a tunnel beneath the fortifications to gain entry. These tunnels can still be seen today.

But Beaton was not the only archbishop to have been murdered. The other one was **Archbishop James Sharp**, the Protestant archbishop when the Church of Scotland was Episcopalian. He had embarked upon a savage and bloody persecution of Covenanters, those people who wished the church to remain Presbyterian, and so was a hated man. In May 1679 he was returning to St Andrews from Edinburgh in a coach with his daughter. At Magus Muir, near the city, his coach was waylaid by Covenanters. Not averse to acts of unspeakable cruelty themselves when it suited them, they stabbed the archbishop to death in front of his daughter.

Nor was Wishart the only Protestant to have gone to the stake in the town. There were others, including **Partick Hamilton**, who was burnt at the stake in 1528. The spot is marked by his initials incorporated into the cobbles outside **St Salvator's Church** in North Street. This old church forms part of **St Salvator's College**, part of the university, founded by Bishop Kennedy in 1450.

It was at the beginning of the 15th century that Pope Benedict XIII issued a papal bull which founded the university. In the 16th century two other colleges were founded, **St Leonard's College** and **St Mary's College**. St Leonards was eventually incorporated into St Salvator's, and a girl's school now stands on the site. **St Leonard's Chapel** still exists, however, and the earliest parts date from the 12th century, showing it had been built long before the college was founded.

St Mary's College must be the loveliest of today's colleges. Step through the arch from South Street and you are in a grassed quadrangle surrounded by old, mellow buildings from the 16th century and onwards. At the foot of the Stair Tower is **Queen Mary's Thorn**, said to have been planted by Mary Stuart in 1565. Mary Stuart visited the town five times, and possibly lodged at what is now known as **Queen Mary's House**, in South Street. It dates from about 1525, and was built by one of the cathedral's canons. Charles II also stayed in it in 1650.

Further along South Street, in front of **Madras College**, one of the town's schools, is all that remains of the **Dominican Friary**. This is the 16th century north transept of the friary church, with some wonderful tracery in its wondows. The friary was orginally founded in the 13th century by Bishop William Wishart.

Almost across from it is **Holy Trinity Parish Church**. It was founded in the 15th century, though the building as we see it today dates largely from a rebuilding early in the 20th century. The only surviving parts of the medieval building are to be found in the west wall, some pillars and the tower. It contains a memorial to Archbishop Sharp, slain in 1679, though his body no longer rests under it. No doubt it had been removed and disposed of as soon as the Scottish church reverted to Presbyterianism.

At the west end of South Street can be found the **West Port**, one of the original gates into the town. It was built about 1589 on the site of an earlier port. In North Street can be found the **St Andrews Preservation Trust Museum and Garden**, housed in a charming building dating from the 16th century.It has displays and artifacts illustrating the town's history. The **St Andrews Museum** at Kinburn Park also celebrates the town's heritage.

At the Scores, down near the shore, you'll find the **St Andrews Aquarium**, which not only lets you see lots of fish and animals from sea horses to seals and shrimps to sharks, but lets you touch some as well. Also on the Scores is the **Martyr's Monument**, which commemorates the Protestant martyrs who were executed in St Andrews. It is a tall, needle-like monument, erected in 1842. Close by is the **British Golf Museum**, which illustrates the history of a game that Scotland gave to the world, with a particular focus on St Andrews. It has an array of exhibits from over 500 years of golfing history, and gives an insight into "surprising facts and striking feats".

St Andrews and golf are inseparable. The

town is still a place of pilgrimage, only today the pilgrims come weighed down by golf bags and wearing Pringle sweaters. **The Royal and Ancient Golf Club** is the world's ruling body on the game, with the exception of the United States, and formulates its rules as well as organising the yearly British Open Championship. The most famous of the courses is the **Old Course**, and it is here, in the clubhouse, that the Royal and Ancient has its headquarters.

Two of the greatest names in golf were born in St Andrews - **Tom Morris** and his son, also called Tom. Old Tom was made greenkeeper at the Old Course in 1865, and was one of the best golfers of his day. His son, however, was even better, and won the Open Championship three times in a row while still a teenager. He eventually died in 1875, aged only 24, some say of a broken heart after his wife died in childbirth. Memorials to both men can be seen in the cathedral graveyard.

At Troywood near St Andrews, off the B9131, is perhaps the most unusual visitor attraction in the area. The **Secret Bunker** was Scotland's secret underground command centre, an amazing labyrinth going as far as 100 feet underground, and encased in 15 feet thick concrete walls. It was from here that the country was to have been run in the event of a nuclear strike from the Soviet Union. It is entered by an innocent looking farmhouse, and is guarded by three tons of blast proof doors. As well as operations rooms and living quarters, it also contains two cinemas and a café. Several similar bunkers were built aroud the country, and this is one of the largest. It came off the Official Secrets list in 1993 as a result of the end of the Cold War.

AROUND ST ANDREWS

CRAIL

8 miles SE of St Andrews on the A917

Crail is one of the oldest ports in this area of Fife, which is known as the East Neuk. It is also possibly the most picturesque, and the small harbour has featured on countless

Crail Harbour

EAST NEUK HOTEL

67 High Street, Crail, Fife KY10 3RA
Tel: 012333 450225 Fax: 01333 450760
e-mail: eastneukhotel@aol.com website: www.simplyreserve.co.uk

Crail is one of the most picturesque small fishing ports in Fife. **The East Neuk Hotel** sits in the heart of the village, and boasts five comfortable and beautifully decorated en suite rooms, making it the ideal base from which to explore the area. The hotel is housed in a building which is over 200 years old, and the interiors are warm and cosy to reflect this age. There is a wide range of drinks available, and good food is served in the bar, lounge bar and restaurant, with everything being cooked on the premises. Food is available 12.00-15.00 and 17.00-21.00 in winter, and 12.00-22.00 in summer. So good is it that you are advised to book at all times in season.

calendars and post cards. Artists also flock to the place because of the light and the quaint buildings. The **Tolbooth** dates from the early 16th century, and has Dutch influences. In the Marketgate is the **Crail Museum and Heritage Centre**, which traces the history of the town and its industries.

ANSTRUTHER

9 miles S of St Andrews off the A917

Anstruther (sometimes pronounced "(Ainster") is a former herring fishing port. It comprises two ancient royal burghs, Anstruther Easter and Anstruther Wester, and is a picturesque place with many old white washed cottages with red pantiles and crow stepped gables.

There is a story that, after the Spanish Armada was defeated by the English in 1588, one of the ships of the Spanish fleet put in at Anstruther and was civilly received by the people of the town. The ship's commander was one Jan Gomez de Midini, and he and his crew were offered hospitality (this at a time when Scotland and England were still independent countries). A few years later the Spaniard repayed the people of the town when he discovered fishermen from Ansthuther marooned in a foreign port after their boat had been wrecked. He re-equipped them and sent them homewards once more.

Located in 16th century St Ayles House, once a lodging house for the monks from Balmerino Abbey, is the **Scottish Fisheries Museum**. Here you can follow the fleet with the "herring lassies", explore a typical fishing family's cottage and see skilled craftsmen at work. Also on display are the two boats - the Zulu, based on an original African design, and the Reaper, a herring boat. The museum also incorporates the poignant Memorial to Scottish Fishermen Lost at Sea.

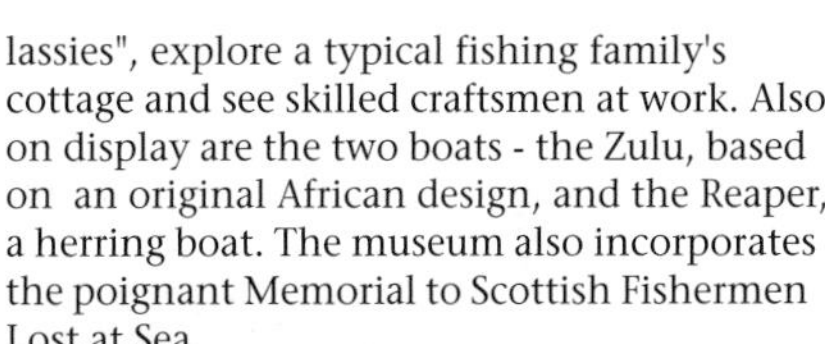

Six miles SE of Anstruther, in the Firth of Forth, is the **Isle of May**. There are ruins of an old priory, and the whole place is now a nature reserve. It was on this island that Scotland's first lighthouse was built in 1635. It was no more than a small stone tower with a brazier atop it which burnt coal. Trips to the island are available from the pier at Anstruther.

PITTENWEEM

9 miles S of St Andrews on the A917

The older houses in this small royal burgh crowd round the picturesque fishing harbour. Like most of the houses in the East Neuk, they

Pittenweem Harbour

The Smuggler's Inn

High Street East, Anstruther, Fife KY10 3DQ
Tel: 01333 310506 Fax: 01333 312706
e-mail: smuggs106@aol.com

The Smuggler's Inn is situated in the main street of Anstruther (pronounced 'Anster'), a famous fishing village noted for its picturesque harbour and old, quaint buildings. The Inn itself is housed in a lovely building that dates partly from the year 1300, and is cosy and full of character, with many lovely period features. The whitewashed walls add an ambience to the place, and the interiors have exposed beams, warm wood, bare walls and open fireplaces. In the days of Queen Anne it was a noted tavern, and when the Old Pretender was proclaimed king by the Earl of Strathmore at Anster Cross during the 1715 Jacobite Uprising, he was staying at The Smugglers. History records that he never paid for the pistols used or the wine consumed!

But though it may be steeped in history, the place offers the very best in modern, up-to-date service and outstanding value for money. It has nine extremely comfortable bedrooms which are available on a B&B basis or as longer lets (with rates for special breaks available), and all are fully en suite. They each have a colour TV, telephone, central heating and tea and coffee making facilities, making the inn the ideal base from which to explore an area rich in history and landscape. Even Glasgow, Edinburgh, Perth and Dundee are within easy reach.

The food is outstanding, and is served seven days a week between 12.00-14.00 and 18.30-21.00, with traditional Scottish high teas being served from 16.00-18.00 on Sundays. All the produce used is sourced locally wherever possible, and is fresh and wholesome. The supper menu contains many fine seafood dishes, as you would expect, as well as juicy steaks with all the trimmings, lamb chops, supreme of chicken, pizza, pork, salads and so on. There are two restaurants - one on the ground floor and one upstairs, and they are extremely popular with residents, visitors and locals. The spacious downstairs restaurant holds 40 in absolute comfort, and it is recommended that you book for evening meals, as people come from near and far to dine here and sample the fine wines on the wine list.

The decor in the bars and lounges reflects the history of the inn, and also adds a touch of modern comfort and convenience. There is a resident's lounge, and the cocktail lounge features open fires to add to the ambience. Great use has been made of old, warm wood and exposed walls, and the carpeting is soft and welcoming underfoot. There is a great array of drinks in the public bars, from beers, lagers and cider to wines, spirits, liqueurs and soft drinks, and an enjoyable and relaxing evening could be spent talking and gossiping with the locals, who are friendly and open.

The inn has no smoking areas, and children are most welcome. Well behaved pets are also welcome by arrangement. For the very best in accommodation, food and drink, the Smuggler's Inn is the ideal place!

are whitewashed, with red pantiled rooves and crow steppped gables. An Augustinian Priory was founded here in 1141, of which very little now remains. The **Parish Church** has a substantial tower (which looks more like a small castle than a piece of ecclesiastical architecture) dating from the 16th century, while the rest is Victorian.

St Monans Parish Church

St Fillan's Cave is supposed to be where St Fillan, an 8th century missionary to the Picts, used to go for private prayer (see also Tyndrum and St Fillans). It was renovated and re-dedicated in 1935. **Kellie Castle** (National Trust for Scotland) dates from the 14th century, and is one of the best examples in the Lowlands of the domestic architecture of the time. It contains superb plaster ceilings, murals, painted panelling and furniture designed by Sir Robert Lorimer, who refurbished the place in the late 19th century. There are fine gardens with old roses and hebaceous borders.

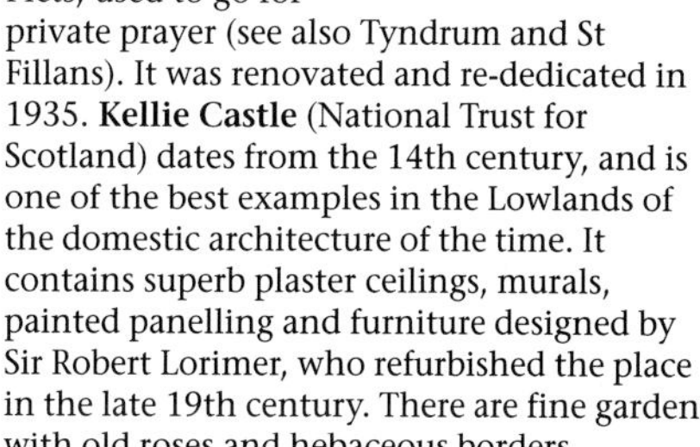

ST MONANS

10 miles S of St Andrews on the A917

This little fishing port's motto is Mare Vivimus, meaning "From the Sea we Have Life" It is famous for the **Parish Church of St Monans**. It stands almost on the shoreline, and was built by David II, son of Robert the Bruce, in thanksgiving after he survived a shipwreck on the Forth. It is a substantial building consisting of a nave, transepts and stumpy spire atop a tower. The chancel was never built.

Salt panning was once an important industry in the town, and the 18th century **St Monans Windmill** at one time formed part of a small industrial complex which produced salt from sea water.

EARLSFERRY AND ELIE

10 miles S of St Andrews off the A917

These two villages are small holiday resorts surounding a sandy bay. The older of the two is Earlsferry, which is a royal burgh. It was once the northern terminal for ferries which plied between it and ports on the south banks of the Forth. The "earl" in its name comes from an incident concerning Macduff, who was a thane of the Earl of Fife. He escaped from King Macbeth, and took refuge in a cave at Kincraig Point near the town, and was then ferried across the Forth to Dunbar. **Gillespie House**, in Elie, dates from the 17th century, has a fine carved doorway.

At one time an old road called the "Cadgers Road" led from Earlsferry to Falkland, and it was along this that supplies of fresh fish were taken to feed the royal party staying there.

CUPAR

8 miles W of St Andrews on the A91

This small country town, sitting on the River Eden, was once the capital of Fife. It is a pleasant place, and well worth strolling round just to see and appreciate its many old buildings. The **Mercat Cross**, topped with a unicorn, was moved from Tarvit Hill to its present location in 1897 to commemorate

Queen Victoria's Diamond Jubilee. In Duffus Park is the **Douglas Bader Garden**, designed with the disabled in mind. The **Old Parish Church** dates from 1785, though the tower is medieval.

Hill of Tarvit Mansionhouse (National Trust for Scotland) is a fine Edwardian mansion that lies two miles south of the town, and was designed by Sir Robert Lorimer in 1906. It has French, Scottish and Chippendale furniture, a collection of paintings, an Edwardian laundry and fine gardens. Close by is **Scotstarvit Tower** (Historic Scotland). It was built by the Inglis family around 1487, when they were granted the lands of Tarvit. In 1612 it was bought by Sir John Scott.

Three miles south of Cupar is the lovely village of **Ceres**, with a village green and the hump-backed medieval **Bishop's Bridge**. The memorial by the bridge commemorates the men of the village who followed Bruce to Bannockburn. The **Parish Church** contains some medieval tombs of the Earls of Crawford, and in the **Fife Folk Museum** you can find out about what everyday life was like in Fife in bygone days.

A few miles west of Cupar, at Rankeilor Park, is the **Scottish Deer Centre** and **Raptor World**. At the Deer Centre you can see - and even feed - both species of deer native to Scotland, plus other species from around the world. At the Raptor Centre there are exhibitions about birds of prey such as owls, hawks and falcons, plus there are spectacular flying demonstrations. There is also a small shopping court, an indoor adventure play area and picnic areas.

NEWBURGH

16 miles W of St Andrews on the A913

This small royal burgh stands on the banks of the Tay. Close to it are the ruins of **Lindores Abbey**, founded in 1178 for Tironenisan monks. It was the first abbey in Scotland to be sacked by Protestant sympathisers, 17 years before Scotland officially became a Protestant country. The **Laing Museum** in the High

The Ship Hotel

78 High Street, Newburgh, Cupar, Fife KY14 6AQ
Tel/Fax: 01337 840566
e-mail: john@theship.freeserve.co.uk
website: http://mysite.freeserve.com/TheShipHotel

The Ship Hotel sits on the A913 in the heart of Newburgh, and has unrivalled views across the Firth of Tay. It is a short drive from the M90, and is makes a first class overnight stop or a base from which to explore the area. There are four comfortable and impeccably clean guest rooms, and the bar carries a fine range of beers, lagers, spirits and wines. Hot bar snacks are available at all times. The adjacent lounge is open at weekends from 12.00-14.00 and in the evenings by prior arrangement. The food is mostly home-made and served in generous portions. Children are very welcome, and a large function room overlooking the Tay is ideal for weddings, parties and other functions of up to 120 people.

Tannochbrae Tearoom

44 High Street, Auchtermuchty, Fife KY14 7DD
Tel: 01337 827447
e-mail: neal.robertson@virgin.net

Auchtermuchty doubled as Tannochbrae, the town in which the second series of Dr Finlay's Casebook was set. The splendid **Tannochbrae Tearoom** was named in its honour, and serves a wonderful range of lunches, snacks and dinners. This no smoking establishment open six days a week (closed Tuesday) between 10.00 and 18.00 and 12.00-18.00 on Sunday. Evening meals are by booking only. This is the place to enjoy good, wholesome Scottish food at its best. Everything is beautifully cooked, and the prices represent amazing value for money. You can choose from a printed menu or a specials board, and all the dishes are tasty and filling. Children are most welcome.

Street concentrates on Newburgh's history from medieval burgh to industrial town.

AUCHTERMUCHTY

16 miles W of St Andrews on the A91

Auchtermuchty is a typical inland Fife town. It is small and compact, and sits in a fertile area known as the Howe o' Fife. The **Tolbooth** dates from 1728, and it was here that the TV series Dr Finlay was filmed, its town centre being turned into a typical townscape of the 1930s.

LEUCHARS

4 miles NW of St Andrews, on the A919

Every September, the Royal Air Force puts on on the **Leuchars Air Show**, held in one of Scotland's biggest RAF bases. The village is also famous for it's **Parish Church of St Athernase**, one of the finest Norman churches in the country. The best parts are the finely carved chancel and apse. A bell tower was added to the apse in he 17th century.

Earlshall Castle (not open to the public) was started in 1546 by Sir William Bruce, and completed by his descendant of the same name in 1617. It subsequently fell into disrepair, but was rebuilt in 1891 under the direction of Sir Robert Lorimer.

NEWPORT-ON-TAY

9 miles NW of St Andrews on the A92

This little town sits at the southern end of the Tay Road Bridge, and at **Wormit**, about a mile to the west, is the start of the Tay Rail Bridge. The ruins of **Balmerino Abbey** (National Trust for Scotland) sits five miles to the west. It was founded in 1229, and colonised by monks from Melrose. The ruins are not open to the public, but can be viewed from nearby.

7 Stirling and Clackmannan

That area of Scotland between the Firths of Clyde and Forth has always been of great strategic importance. It is often referred to as Scotland's "waist", and before the Kincardine Bridge was built in 1936, the bridge at Stirling was the lowest crossing point of the River Forth. To the west of the town are the Campsie and Kilsyth Hills, which form another natural barrier, so the bridge at Stirling became the gateway to Perthshire and the Highlands.

That's why so many battles have been fought in and around Stirling and Falkirk, including Scotland's most important, the Battle of Bannockburn, which secured Scotland's future as an independent nation. It is also the reason why Stirling Castle was built. It sits sentinel on a great rocky outcrop, with the town of Stirling laid out below it to the west. From its top, an approaching army could be seen even if it was miles away.

Loch Dochart

This is an area which has witnessed great changes over the years due to local government reorganisations. Dunblane, for instance, to the north of Stirling, was at one time in Perthshire, as was Callander and Port of Menteith. For a while, Clackmannanshire ceased to exist (though it remained alive in the hearts of all people born within its boundaries). Now it has come back , and still proudly proclaims itself to be Scotland's smallest county, with an area of only 55 square miles. It sits in the shelter of the Ochils to the north, which rise to well over 2,000 feet in places, and was a centre for woollens and textiles. The string of "hillfoot villages" at the foot of the Ochils are all picturesque, and well worth visiting for this alone.

Around Falkirk and Grangemouth, Stirlingshire is unashamedly industrial. It is an area of petro-chemical plants, with great refineries on the shores of the Forth. It was also at one time a coal mining area, though the mines have long gone. But travel north west from Stirling, and you enter one of the most beautiful areas of Scotland - the Trossachs.

Loch Katrine

Though its hills aren't as high as those of the Grampians or Cairngorms, and don't have that brooding majesty we tend to associate with Highland scenery, it is still Highland in character. The hills slip down to the wooded banks of lochs such as Loch Katrine, Loch Venachan and the wonderfully named Loch Drunkie, which are among the most picturesque in Scotland, and the skies seem endless and sweeping.

The town of Stirling is one of the most historic in Scotland, and has played a leading role in shaping the country's destiny. The castle has been fought over countless times by the Scottish and the English, and eventually became a favourite royal residence. Mary Queen of Scots stayed there, and her son, who became James VI, had his coronation in the town's Church of the Holy Rood. Falkirk, though more industrial in character, is also an ancient town, and has witnessed two important battles as Scotland's history was played out. Alloa, Clackmannanshire's largest town, is also industrial in character, though it too has history aplenty. At one time this was Scotland's brewing capital, though only one brewery now remains.

For those interested in architecture, the place has some memorable buildings to offer. There are many old, historical buildings in Stirling, including Stirling Castle itself, given a Renaissance makeover by James IV, as well as Dunblane Cathedral, Alloa Tower, the ruins of Camubuskenneth Priory, the Wallace Monument, and both Doune Castle and Castles Campbell

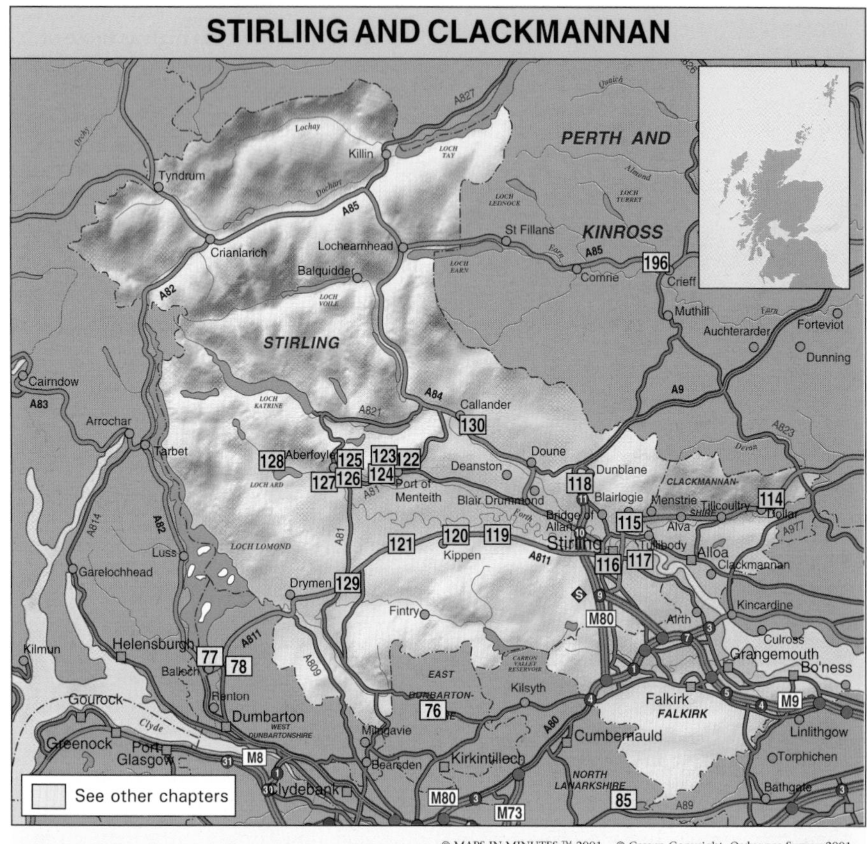

© MAPS IN MINUTES ™ 2001 © Crown Copyright, Ordnance Survey 2001

PLACES TO STAY, EAT, DRINK AND SHOP

114	Strathallen House, Dollar	Hotel and restaurant	Page 163
115	Watergate, Blairlogie	Self catering	Page 165
116	Hannibals Restaurant, Stirling	Restaurant	Page 168
117	Carseview, Cambuskenneth	Guest House	Page 170
118	Rokeby House, Dunblane	Guest House	Page 172
119	Glenfoyle Cottage, Gargunnock	Self catering	Page 172
120	Fordhead Cottage, Fordhead	Self catering	Page 173
121	Thorntree, Arnprior	Self catering	Page 174
122	The Lake Hotel, Port of Menteith	Hotel and restaurant	Page 174
123	Cardross Holiday Homes, Port of Menteith	Self catering	Page 175
124	Glenny Cottages, Port of Menteith	Self catering	Page 176
125	Forth Inn, Aberfoyle	Pub, accommodation and restaurant	Page 176
126	Town House Hotel, Aberfoyle	Hotel and restaurant	Page 177
127	Forth House, Aberfoyle	B&B and self catering	Page 177
128	Creag-Ard House, by Aberfoyle	Café, tearoom and shop	Page 178
129	The Aizle, Balat Crossroads	Café, tearoom and shop	Page 179
130	Poppies Hotel, Callander	Hotel and restaurant	Page 180

CLACKMANNAN

This small town was granted its burgh charter in 1550. In the centre of the town is the belfry of the old **Tolbooth**, built by William Menteith in the late 16th century. He was the sheriff of the town, and objected strongly with having to hold felons in his own home, so he built the Tolbooth to hold them instead. Beside it stands the **Mannau Stone**. Legend states that when St Serf came to this part of Scotland in the 6th century to convert it to Christianity, he found the locals worshipping the sea god Mannau, or Mannan, in the form of the stone (known as the "clach mannau"). From this, the town supposedly got its name. Another legend states that the name derives from an incident in the life of Robert the Bruce. It seems that he once rested close to the stone, and on remounting his horse, left his glove lying on it. He ordered one of his servants to return to the "clach" (stone) and retrieve his "mannan" (glove).

Clackmannan Tower, built on a hill where once stood a royal hunting lodge, dates from the 14th century, with later alterations, and was once owned by Robert the Bruce. Though in the care of Historic Scotland, it can only be viewed from the outside at present. Robert Burns visited the area in the 1787, and was "knighted" by a direct descendant of Robert the Bruce, a Mrs Bruce, who lived in a mansion house (now gone) near the castle. She was in her nineties at the time, and a woman of "hospitality and urbanity". She still possesed her ancestor's helmet and two handed sword, and she used the sword to carry out the ceremony, declaring that she had a better right to confer knighthoods than "some people" (meaning the Hanovarian kings who were on the throne).

Clackmannan's **Parish Church** dates from 1815, though the original church may have been founded by St Serf in the 6th century. Inside is the beautiful Coronation Window, gifted to the church by its congregation to mark the coronation of Elizabeth II in 1953. The Queen visited the church specially to view it in 1997, so it seems that the loyalty of at least some of the people of Clackmannan is not in doubt any more.

Two miles north of the town is the **Gartmorn Dam Country Park**. It is centred on the 170 acre Gartmorn Dam, the oldest man made reservoir in Scotland. It was constructed by John Erskine, 6th Earl of Mar, to power the pumps which pumped water out of his coal mines around nearby Sauchie. Now a nature reserve, the park is popular with walkers and nature lovers, and the reservoir itself is stocked with brown trout.

AROUND CLACKMANNAN

TILLICOULTRY

4 miles N of Clackmannan on the A91

Tillicoultry is one of the "hillfoot villages" which relied on water tumbling down from the Ochils to power the mills in which most people were employed. It became a town in 1871, and behind it is the picturesque **Tillicoultry Glen**, whose waters once powered eight mills in the town using a system of laids and channels.

DOLLAR

5 miles NE of Clackmannan on the A91

Dollar is another "hillfoot village", famous as the home of **Dollar Academy**. This private school (the equivalent of an English public school) was founded in the early 19th centrury thanks to a bequest by John McNabb, a local herd boy born in 1732 who amassed a fortune before his death in 1802. He would no doubt be puzzled, and maybe a little angered, by the school's status today, for he had intended it to be a school for the children of the poor in Dollar parish. The elegant, colonnaded building was designed by the eminent architect William Playfair, and was opened in 1819.

Within Dollar is the small **Dollar Museum**, which has displays on the history of the village and on the Devon Valley railway.

Castle Campbell

Above the town, and reached through the wooded **Dollar Glen** (National Trust for Scotland), is **Castle Campbell** (National Trust for Scotland). It was one of Clan Campbell's Lowland homes, and was formerly known as "Castle Gloom". Close by are two burns called Care and Sorrow, and even the name Dollar itself is said to derive from "dolour", meaning sadness. It seems strange that such a beautiful spot should have such depressing names. The castle dates essentially from the 15th century, with some later additions.

Dollar Academy, Dollar

ALVA

3 miles NW of Clackmannan on the A91

Alva sits at the foot of the Ochils, and is one of the "hillfoot villages" where weaving and spinning were the main industries. To the north east is the Ochil range's highest peak, the 2,363 feet **Ben Cleuch**. At the **Mill Trail Visitor Centre** there are displays and exhibits that explain what life was like in mill factories over the last 150 years. There is also a shop and a café. **The Mill Trail** itself is a signposted route taking you to many mills with retail outlets. **The Ochil Hills Woodland Park** has attractive walks and a visitors centre.

Alva Glen, also called the "Silver Glen", is very picturesque. Silver was once mined here in the 18th century, and **St Serf's Parish Church**, which dates from 1815, has some communion vessels made from local silver. It was the Erskine family that mined the silver, and it was a hit or miss affair. A story is told of one member of the family, Sir John Erskine, showing two of the mines to a friend. "Out of that hole there I earned £50,000," he told him. "And in that hole there I lost it all again."

MENSTRIE

4 miles NW of Clackmannan on the A91

In **Menstrie Castle**, in 1567, was born **Sir William Alexander**, 1st Earl of Stirling, founder of Nova Scotia, Scotland's only real colony in the North America (see also Stirling). The only part of the castle open to the public is the Nova Scotia Commemoration Room, which has displays about the colony. There are also the armorial bearings of the the 109 Nova Scotia baronetcies created in Scotland, which went on sale at 3,000 Scots merks each.

Sir Ralph Abercromby, who commanded the British troops at the Battle of Alexandria in 1801, was born in Menstrie in 1734. He died at Alexandria of wounds he received during the battle.

BLAIRLOGIE

6 miles NW of Clackmannan on the A91

Blairlogie is possibly the most beautiful of the "hillfoot villages", and was the first conservation village in Scotland. It sits in the shadow of **Dumyat**, which has the remains of a hilltop fort on its summit. The name derives from Dun Maetae, meaning the fort of the Maetae, a Pictish tribe.

ALLOA

2 miles W of Clackmannan on the A907

With a population of about 15,000, Alloa is the largest town in Scotland's smallest county. The name is supposed to mean "the way to the sea", and indeed the town sits on the banks of the River Forth where it is still tidal. It was traditionally an engineering, brewing and glass making town, though today these industries are less important than they once were.

St Mungo's Parish Church dates from 1817, though it incorporates the 17th century tower of an earlier church. **Alloa Tower** (NTS) is all that is left of the ancestral home of the Erskines, one of the most important families in Scotland. They eventually became the Earls of Mar, and as such were (and still are as the Earls of Mar and Kellie) Hereditary Keepers of Stirling Castle. The tower was built for Alexander Erskine, the 3rd Lord Erskine, in the late 15th century, and later remodelled by the 6th Earl of Mar in the 18th century. It has the original oak roof beams, medieval vaulting and a dungeon.

The Erskines were custodians of Mary Stuart during her infancy, and she lived in the tower for a time. James VI, while still a boy, also stayed here. The 6th Earl was an ardent Jacobite, and after the 1715 Uprising he was sent into exile. The story of the Erskines is told within the tower, and the present Earl has loaned a superb collection of paintings to it, including works by Raeburn and Kneller.

Alloa Museum and Gallery, in the Speirs Centre in Primrose Street, has exhibits tracing the history of the town.

TULLIBODY

4 miles W of Clackmannan on the B9140

Legend says that Tullibody was founded by King Kenneth McAlpine, the first king of Scots, who united the kingdoms of Dalriada and the Picts in AD843. He called it "Tirlbothy", meaning the "oath of the crofts", as he and his followers made an oath there that they would not lay down their arms until their enemies or themselves were killed. A stone once stood at the point where the oath was made.

Tullibody Auld Brig, which spans the River Devon, was built about 1535 by James Spittal, tailor to the royal family (see also Doune). In 1559 the eastern most arch of the bridge was dismantled to impede a French army which was in Scotland in support of Mary of Guise, mother of Mary Stuart and widow of James V. However, the French army dismantled the roof of **St Serf's Church** and made a new bridge.

Robert Dick, the eminent, but self taught, botanist was born in Tullibody in 1811.

FALKIRK

Falkirk is Stirlingshire's largest town, and received its burgh charter in 1600. It sits at an important point on the road from Edinburgh to Stirling, and at nearby **Stenhousemuir** was once the meeting place of various drove roads coming down from the Highlands. Here great herds of cattle were kept before being sold and taken further south to the markets of Northern England. It has been estimated that over 24,000 head of cattle were sold annually at the three trysts held each year.

The name of the town literally means the "kirk of mottled stone", a reference to its first stone built medieval church. The present **Old Parish Church** dates from1810, and incorporates fragments of an earlier church. It's tower dates from 1734. The church was the burial place for many prominent local families, and buried in the churchyard is Sir John de Graeme, who was killed at the Battle of Falkirk fighting in William Wallace's army.

The **Town Steeple** was built in 1814, and was designed by the famous architect David Hamilton. It replaced an earlier building which dated from the 17th century, and has traditionally been a meeting place for the people of the town. In 1927 the upper portion of the steeple was struck by lightning and had to be rebuilt.

Near Falkirk the two great Lowland canals - the Forth and Clyde and the Union Canal - meet. Thanks to the Millennium Link Project, they have recently been restored, and the magnificent new 120 foot high **Antonine Wheel** (also called the Falkirk Wheel) will carry boats between one canal and the other, which are on different levels.

Centred on the village of Bonnybridge, two miles west of Falkirk, is the **Bonnybridge Triangle**, so called because there have been more sightings of UFOs and unexplained phenomena in this area than anywhere else in the UK. It all started in 1992 when a cross shaped cluster of lights was seen hovering above a road, and it has continued up until the present day, with mysterious football-sized lights, delta shaped craft and even spaceships with opening doors being seen as well.

Two great battles have been fought in or near Falkirk. In 1298 the Scottish army of William Wallace was defeated by the English after his initial victory at Stirling Bridge the previous year. The superior horsemen and archers of the English won the day, and Wallace became a fugitive, finally being captured in 1305. And in 1746, after its retreat form Derby, the Jacobite forces of Charles Edward Stuart defeated a Hanoverian army.

The town sits on the line of the Antonine Wall, a massive turf wall on a stone base built on the orders of the Roman emperor Antonius Pius just after AD138. It stretched the 38 miles from the Firth of Clyde at Bowling to the Firth of Forth west of Bo'ness. **Rough Castle** (National Trust for Scotland) five miles from the town, is one of the best preserved of the wall's fortifications. Parts of the wall can be seen in the town's **Callendar Park**, in which you will also find **Callendar House**. This magnificent building, modelled on a French chateau, has played a major role in Scotland's history. In 1293 Alexander II granted land to one Malcolm de Kalynter, and he may have built a wooden castle. A descendant of Malcolm became involved in plots againt David II in 1345, and the estates were forfeited and given to Sir William Livingstone, whose descendants lived there until the 18th century.

The Livingstones were close to Mary Stuart, and the queen visited the estate many times. In 1600 James VI rewarded the family by making them Earls of Linlithgow. But with the rise of Jacobitism, the family's fortunes went into decline. The 5th Earl was forced into exile for siding with the Old Pretender in 1715, and his daughter, Lady Anne married the ill-fated Earl of Kilmarnock, who was beheaded in London for his part in the 1745 Uprising (see also Kilmarnock). A story is told that on the evening before the Battle of Falkirk, the commander of the Hanovarian troops, General Hawley, dined at Callendar House with Lady Anne. He so enjoyed her company that he ignored requests to leave early to be appraised of the Jacobite movements. His troops were soundly beaten the following day.

In 1783 the house and estate was bought by the businessman William Forbes, whose descendants lived there for almost 200 years. It has now been restored by the local council as a heritage centre and museum, with a working Georgian kitchen, printer's and clockmaker's workrooms and a general store. In the Victorian library is an extensive archive of books, documents and photographs on the history of the area, and the Major William Forbes Falkirk exhibition traces the history of the town. The **Park Gallery**, which runs a series of art exhibitions and workshop activities, is also located in Callendar Park.

AROUND FALKIRK

AIRTH

5 miles N of Falkirk on the A905

It is hard to imagine that a huge royal dockyard was once situated in this small village in the 15th and 16th centuries. Now it is visited because of one of the most unusual buildings in Scotland - **The Pineapple** (National Trust for Scotland) in Dunmore Park. It is a summer house, built in 1761, and on top of it is a huge, 45 feet high pineapple made of stone. It can be rented as a holiday home. Also at Dunmore are 16 acres of gardens.

Parts of the nearby **Airth Castle** (now a hotel) date from the 14th century. An earlier castle stood on the site, and it was here that an uncle of William Wallace was held by the English before Wallace freed him.

GRANGEMOUTH

3 miles E of Falkirk on the A904

Grangemouth is a modern town, and the centre of Scotland's petrochemical industry. It was one of Scotland's first planned towns, having been established by Sir Laurence Dundas at the same time as the Forth and Clyde Canal was being dug in the late 18th century. His son Thomas continued the work.

On Bo'ness Road is the **Grangemouth Museum**, which traces the history of the town. The **Jupiter Urban Wildlife Garden** is off Wood Street, and was established in 1990 on a piece of land that was once a railway marshalling yard by Zeneca (formerly ICI) and the Scottish Wildlife Trust. Surrounded by industrial buildings and smokestacks, this oasis of green shows how derelict industrial land can be cleaned up and reclaimed for nature. It has four ponds, an area of scrub birch known as The Wilderness, a wildlife plant nursery, a formal wildlife garden, as well as meadows, marshland and reed beds that attract lots of wildlife.

STIRLING

Stirling is one of the most historic and strategically placed towns in Scotland. It sits astride the main route north from the Lowlands, and whoever was in possession of its castle virtually controlled the whole of the central belt.

It was this importance which gave it its history. On a craggy volcanic hill a castle was built, which in medieval times became a royal residence, and a settlement was eventually established on the eastern slope of the hill to cater for its needs. The old town is a mixture of buildings from all periods from the 15th century onwards, and a day could be spent walking about and admiring them.

Stirling Castle (Historic Scotland) is a mixture of styles and dates. Because of the strategic importance of the rock upon which it stands, some form of fortification has no doubt stood there since before the Dark Ages. It enters recorded history in the early 12th century, when Alexander I dedicated a chapel there. We next hear of it in 1174, when William the Lion was compelled to hand over various Scottish castles to the English, Stirling included.

During the Wars of Indepencence in the 13th and 14th centuries, Stirling Castle played a leading role. By this time it was back in Scottish hands, and Edward I was outraged by the fact that it was the last Lowland castle to hold out against his conquest of the country, and a barrier to further conquest in the north. So, in 1304, he set out to besiege it, and it eventually fell. For the next ten years it was garrisoned by the English. In 1313 Edward Bruce, brother of Robert I, laid siege to it, and its commander, Sir Philip Mowbray, agreed to surrender if the castle wasn't relieved by June 24 1314.

By this time Edward I was dead, and his son Edward II was on the throne. He didn't want to lose Stirling, so sent a great army north to relieve the castle. The Scots met this army at Bannockburn, and secured a great victory - one that sealed Scotland's independence.

All traces of the castle as it was at the time of Bannockburn have long gone. Most now dates from the 15th century and later. James III was the first of the Scottish kings to take an interest in its architecture, and built the Great Hall as a meeting place of the Scottish parliament and for great ceremonial occasions. James IV then began building a new palace building in the Renaissance style, with his son James V finishing the work. In 1594 James VI had the Chapel Royal built, and these three building represent the most important architectural elements in the castle.

A curious tale is told of Stirling Castle. It concerns James IV and John Damien, the Abbot of Tongland in Kirkcudbrightshire, who earned the nickname of the **Frenzied Friar of**

Tongland. He was an Italian, and a learned man, who spent a lot of time at court. In 1507 he convinced James IV that man could fly, and to prove it, he told him that he would jump from the walls of Stirling Castle and soar as free as a bird.

Stirling Castle

A date was set for the flight to take place, and a bemused James IV and his court assembled on the battlements. Meanwhile, Abbot Damien had told his servants to amass a large collection of feathers from birds which could fly and construct a large pair of wings from them. However, his servants couldn't collect enough feathers of the right kind in time, so incorporated some chicken feathers as well. The Abbot duly presented himself on the battlements of the castle with the wings strapped to his back and wrists. No mention is made in contempoarary accounts of how the king and the court viewed this unusual sight, but there must have been a few suppressed sniggers.

Damien stood on the battlements, made a short speech, and began flapping his wings. He then jumped - and fell like a stone, landing in the castle midden, on which more than the kitchen scraps were heaped. His fall couldn't have been that far, as all he succeeded in doing was breaking his leg. When he later discovered that his servants had incorporated chicken feathers in the wings, he blamed this for the failure of his flight. The court poet William Dunbar was present at this attempt at the world's first manned flight, and wrote some verses about it.

The **Church of the Holy Rude** on St John Street is Stirling's parish church. It dates from the 15th century, and was built on the site of an earlier place of worship at the command of James IV, who, tradition says, worked alongside the masons. It is one of the finest medieval churches in Scotland, and has its original oak roof. It was here, in 1543, that Mary Stuart was crowned Queen of Scots. In 1567, the infant James VI, her son, had his coronation here as well. It has the largest organ of any church in Scotland.

The kirkyard was once the castle's tiliting ground, where great tournaments of jousting and horsemanship were held. One of the monuments in the kirkyard is the **Martyr's Monument**, commemorating two women who were drowned for their religious beliefs at Wigtown in 1685 (see also Wigtown). **Lady's Rock** sits next to the kirkyard, and was where the ladies of the court sat and watched staged events take place on the fields below. Close by is **Cowane's Hospital**, on which work started in 1639. It is named after John Cowane, who bequeathed funds to establish an almshouse for the unsuccessful merchants, or "decayed guildsmen" of the town. It was later used as a school and an epidemic hospital, and is now a venue for ceilidhs and concerts.

The King's Knot sits beneath the castle and church, on their south side, and is all that is left of a formal garden, originally planted in the 1490s. It is in the shape of an octagonal mound, now grassed over. Near it used to be the **King's Park** (where houses and the modern King's Park now stand), once a favourite hunting ground for the Scottish kings.

The **Old Town Jail** was opened in 1847 to take the prisoners that were formerly held in the town's Tolbooth. Now it has been reopened as a tourist attraction, and shows what life was like for prisoners and wardens in the 19th century. You'll also meet a character called Jock Rankin, who was the town's hangman. If, during your visit, a prisoner should try to escape, you should remain calm and follow the advice of the warden!

The intriguingly named **Mar's Wark** is close to the parish church. It was the "wark" (meaning work, or building) of the Earl of Mar, Regent of Scotland and guardian of the young James VI. In 1570 he began building a new palace that would reflect his status and power, and Mar's Wark was the result. In the 18th century it became a military hospital, but soon after fell into disrepair. Now all that is left of the Renaissance building is a facade along the street front.

On the opposite side of the street is **Argyll's Lodging** (Historic Scotland), a Renaissance mansion built about 1630 by Sir William Alexander, the founder of Nova Scotia (see also Menstrie). It was further enlarged by the 9th Earl of Argyll in the 1670s, and is possibly the best example of a 17th century town house in Scotland. Most of the rooms have been restored, showing what life would have been like when the Earl lived there.

Stirling is one of the few Scottish towns with parts of its **Town Wall** still standing. It was built in the 1540s as a defence against the English armies of Henry VIII when he was trying to force a marriage between his son Edward and Mary Stuart. The remaining parts stretch along the south side of the town, from near the Old Town Jail to Dumbarton Road. Incorporated into the Thistle Shopping Mall is the16th century **Bastion**, one of the wall's defensive towers. It contains a vaulted guardroom above an underground chamber, and has a small display about the history of the town. There was no wall to the north of the town, as attacks never came from that quarter, though people who lived there were supposed to build thick, high walls at the backs of their gardens as a defence, and keep them in good repair.

One bloody association with Scotland's past is to be found at the **Beheading Stone**, well to the north of the castle. It was here, in 1425, that James I took his revenge on the Duke of Albany, his two sons and the Earl of Lennox by having them beheaded. The Duke had controlled Scotland for 18 years while James was held captive by the English, and he and his cronies had brought the country to its knees by their greed and cruelty.

The **Tolbooth** sits at the heart of the old town. It was built in 1704 by Sir William Bruce, and was where the town council met and looked after the affairs of the burgh. A courthouse and jail were added in 1809. It is now used as a venue for concerts and rehearsals. The **Mercat Cross**, close to the Tolbooth, has the figure of a unicorn on top, and this is known locally as the "puggy".

Two famous battles have been fought near Stirling. The **Battle of Stirling Bridge** took place in 1297, when William Wallace defeated an English army under John de Warenne, Earl of Surrey, and Hugh de Cressingham. Wallace, who was a guerrilla fighter and a master tactician, used the bridge to divide the English forces - leaving one contingent on each bank - before launching his attack. It was a major set back for Edward I, and he more or less had to start his conquest of the country all over again. The bridge in those days was a wooden one, and the present **Old Stirling Bridge**, which stands at the same spot, was built in the late 15th century. Up until 1831, when **Stirling New Bridge** was built downstream, this was the lowest crossing point of the Forth, which made it one of the most important bridges in Scotland.

The other famous battle was the **Battle of Bannockburn**, fought to the south of the town in 1314. The actual site of the battle still arouses much debate, but there is no doubt that it was a defining moment in Scotland's history. Edward I had died by this time, and it was his son Edward II who was in charge of the English army, which was trying to reach Stirling Castle to relieve it. Robert the Bruce, one of Scotland's great heroes, achieved a stunning victory - one which secured the country's status as an independent nation. **The Bannockburn Heritage Centre** (National Trust for Scotland), on the A872 two miles south of the town, commemorates this victory. There are exhibitions, an audio visual display and a huge statue of Bruce on his war horse.

Scotland's other national hero, of course, is William Wallace, and on Abbey Craig, to the east of the town and across the river, is the **National Wallace Monument**. This spectacular tower is 220 feet high, with 246 steps, and from the top you get a panoramic view that takes in the Forth Bridges to the east and Ben Lomond to the west. Here you can learn about the Battle of Stirling Bridge, plus see a recreation of Wallace's travesty of a trial at Westminster. You can even gaze on his great two-handed broadsword.

The scant ruins of **Cambuskenneth Abbey** (Historic Scotland) also lie on the eastern banks of the Forth. It was founded in 1140 by David I as an abbey for Augustinian monks, and in 1326 Robert the Bruce held an important parliament here. The detached bell tower of the abbey is more or less complete, though only the foundations of the rest of the buildings survive. James III and his queen are buried before the high altar, and a monument marks the spot.

The **Smith Art Gallery and Museum** in Albert Place chronicles Stirling's long history through displays, exhibitons and artifacts. It has a fine collection of paintings, including ones by Naysmith and Sir George Harvey, who painted great works depicting Scottish history. One of the more unusual exhibits in the museum is the world's oldest football.

AROUND STIRLING

BRIDGE OF ALLAN

2 miles N of Stirling off the M9

Bridge of Allan, which is almost a suburb of Stirling nowadays, was once a small spa town and watering place with a pump room and baths. Now it is chiefly known for being the home of Stirling University, based in the grounds of the **Airthrie Estate**, with its picturesque lake. In 1617, James VI wanted to establish a college or university at Stirling, but it was not until 1967 that his wish came true, when the first 180 students enrolled. Now it has over 3,500 students, and is one of the premier universities in Scotland.

Airthrie was owned by Sir Robert Abercrombie, who was instrumental in setting up the village as a spa, having had the waters of a local spring analysed. In 1844 the estate was bought by a Major Henderson, who developed the town even further. The **Fountain of Ninevah** on Fountain Road was built by him in 1851 to commemorate the archaeological excavations going on at Nineveh at the time. Though healing waters are no longer drunk in the town, other, equally interesting, liquids are. **The Bridge of Allan Brewery Company**, a micro brewery in Queens Lane, has tours showing how beer is produced.

Holy Trinity Church was built in 1860, and inside it are some furnishings designed by the Glasgow architect Charles Rennie Mackintosh.

DUNBLANE

5 miles N of Stirling off the M9

Before local government reorganisation, Dunblane (and most of the area north and north west of Stirling) used to be in Perthshire. This small town, or more properly city, is famous for two things. The first is the horrific shooting that took place here in 1996 when 16 schoolchildren and their teacher were killed in a local school. The second is the mangificent **Cathedral Church of St Blane and St Lawrence** (Historic Scotland). It dates mainly from the 13th century, and was built by Bishop Clement, who was elected in 1233. He decided that the only part of the Norman church which would be left standing was the tower, though two extra storeys were added to it in the 15th century.

Christianity first came to Dunblane in the 7th century, thanks to a Celtic monk called Blane (or Blaan), who was born on Bute in AD602. It was a place of some inportance, and no doubt a great monastery stood on the site of the present cathedral, looked after by a Celtic abbot and bishop. In about 1150 a stone cathedral was built, and a Roman Catholic bishopric established. However, the diocese was a poor one, and the Pope eventually authorised the bishops of Dunkeld and Glasgow to give a fourth of their income to help establish it properly. With this income, Clement managed to build most of the cathedral before his death in 1258.

In the 16th century, with the arrival of Protestantism, only the choir was used for worship, and the nave fell into decay. So too did the city, and it became a small weaving centre. But in 1898 the whole building as restored, and the nave reroofed. In 1914 Sir Robert Lorimer did further work on the choir, and the present choir stalls - one of the glories of the cathedral - were designed by him.

With the coming of the railways, Dunblane became a popular place in which to holiday, and it regained some of its former prosperity. **Dunblane Hydro** was built in 1875 to cash in on the tourist boom, and it is still a luxury hotel to this day.

Within the **Dean's House**, built in 1624 and lived in by Dean James Pearson, is a small museum which explains the history of the city

ROKEBY HOUSE

Doune Road, Dunblane, near Stirling FK15 9AT
Tel: 01786 824447 Fax: 01786 821399
e-mail: rokeby.house@btconnect.com
website: www.aboutscotland.com/stirling/rokeby.html

Within the quiet town of Dunblane, with its lovely cathedral, you'll find **Rokeby House**, a magnificent Edwardian mansion. Owned by Richard Beatts, it has been turned into a luxuriously appointed guest house that offers the best in Scottish hospitality. It has three double bedrooms, and one twin bedroom, all luxuriously appointed and furnished to the highest standards. In addition, one of the double rooms and the twin room, along with a bathroom, can be used as a family suite.

In July and August a self catering cottage is also available in the gardens, which sleeps 2 people. The guest house is a member of "Taste of Scotland". which guarantees the high standards of its food and wine. Richard offers a full Scottish breakfast, and superb evening meals are available by arrangement. His wines are mainly French, and have been hand picked to complement the cuisine. Small conference facilities are also available. Such is the style and facilities offered by Rokeby House it has been given 5 stars by the Scottish Tourist Board and 5 diamonds by the AA.

GLENFOYLE COTTAGE

Village Square, Gargunnock, Stirlingshire
Tel: 01786 860668

Located in the picturesque village of Gargunnock, **Glenfoyle Cottage** is a stone-built self catering terraced cottage dating from the late 18th century. It comprises two upstairs bedrooms - a double (which is en suite) and a twin - as well as a comfortable downstairs lounge with open fire, off which is a dining room/conservatory. There is a fully equipped kitchen and a bathroom with shower, as well as off street parking for one car. This cottage makes the ideal base for exploring the nearby town of Stirling and the surrounding countryside.

and its cathedral, and **Bishop Leighton's Library**, housed in a building that dates from 1681, contains over 4,000 books, some rare and priceless.

About three miles north east of the town is the site of the **Battle of Sheriffmuir** (see also Callander), one of the deciding battles in the 1715 Jacobite Uprising. It was an unusual battle, in that the outcome was a stalemate. The Jacobite forces were led by John Erskine, 11th Earl of Mar, and the Government forces by John Campbell, 2nd Duke of Argyll.

FINTRY

12 miles SW of Stirling on the B818

This charming village sits on the nothern slopes of the **Campsies**, that great range of hills that forms a northern backdrop for the city of Glasgow. There are some fine walks on the hills, which are popular at weekends and holidays with Glaswegians. The village regularly wins awards in the "Best Kept Small Village in Britain" and the"Britain in Bloom" competitions. The **Loup of Fintry**, east of the village, is a fine cascade and waterfall caused by the Endrick Water tumbling down a 94 foot high slope.

Culcreuch Castle (now a country house hotel) is a 700 year old tower house within a large estate that was once owned by the Galbraiths. The last Galbraith chieftain to live there was Robert Galbraith, who fled to Ireland in 1630 after killing a guest in his home. **Carron Valley Reservoir**, to the east of the village, was built in the 19th century to supply Falkirk and Grangemouth with a water supply. It now offers trout fishing (permit required).

KIPPEN

9 miles W of Stirling on the B822

This attractive little village sits to the south of that expanse of flat land called **Flanders Moss**. It has, in **Kippen Parish Church**, built in 1825, one of the finest post Reformation churches in Scotland. The ruins of the old church, built in 1691, still survive, surrounded by an old graveyard.

In 1891, a man called Duncan Buchanan planted a vineyard in Kippen within a glasshouse, and one of the vines, later to be called the **Kippen Vine**, grew to be the largest in the world. When fully grown, it had an annual crop of over 2000 bunches of table grapes, and in 1958 created a record by producing 2956 bunches. By this time it was enormous, covering an area of 5000 square feet and stretching for 300 feet within four large greenhouses. It became a tourist attraction, and people came from all over Scotland and abroad to gaze at it.

But alas, the vinery closed down in 1964 (when it could also boast the second and third largest vines in the world) and the Kippen Vine was unceremoniously chopped down. The land was later used for housing.

At nearby **Arnprior** there lived, in the early 16th century, a man called John Buchanan, who had styled himself the **King of Kippen**. One day a party of hunters was returning to Stirling Castle with some venison for James V's court, and passed John's castle. John captured them and confiscated the venison. The hunters told him that the meat was for the king, but John merely replied that if James was King of Scotland, then he was King of Kippen.

The king was duly informed of this, and

THORNTREE

Arnprior, Stirlingshire FK8 3EY
Tel/Fax: 01786 01786 870
e-mail: info@thorntreebarn.co.uk
website: www.aboutscotland.com/central/thorntree

If its peace and quiet of the countryside and stunning views you're after (including one of Ben Lomond!), then **Thorntree** is for you. Part of this attractive farmhouse has been converted into spacious and well appointed self-catering accommodation (with central heating) that can sleep six to seven people. There are three twin bedrooms (most with antique furniture), a living room with kitchen, dining room, a patio and lawns. It is the ideal base from which to explore central Scotland, and all linen and towels are provided.

THE LAKE HOTEL

Port of Menteith, Perthshire FK8 3RA
Tel: 01877 385258 Fax: 01877 385671
e-mail: enquiries@Lake-of-Monteith-Hotel.com

Situated right on the banks of the Lake of Menteith, the **Lake Hotel** must have one of the loveliest locations of any hotel in Scotland. It's lawns go right down to the water's edge, and many of its 16 en suite rooms have great views over the loch towards the Isle of Inchmahome and the hills beyond. Under owners Graeme and Ros McConnachie, it has become the top hotel in the area, gaining a coveted four stars from the Scottish Tourist Board. Its standards of comfort and hospitality are truly outstanding, and its choice of foods and wines are sure to satisfy the most demanding of tastes.

However, it has still retains all the friendliness and warmth of a family run establishment, and a relaxing stay here is an experience to be savoured. Fishing is available on the lake, using the hotel's own boat, and it makes the ideal base to explore the Trossachs, one of the loveliest areas in Scotland. Visitors to the hotel invariably check out at the end of their stay vowing that, one day, they'll be back!

instead of being angry, found the incident amusing. He and some courtiers rode out from Stirling one day to pay the King of Kippen a visit. He approached John's castle, and demanded that he be allowed to enter. His demand was refused by a guard, who told the king that John Buchanan was at dinner, and could not be disturbed.

James V had a habit of dressing up in peasant's clothes and slipping out of his palaces alone to meet and speak to his subjects and gauge their opinions of their king and country. When he did this, he assumed the guise of the "Guidman of Ballengeich", Ballengeich being the name of a pathway he always took down from Stirling Castle when in disguise.

He therefore told the guard to tell Buchanan that the Guidman of Ballengeich was at his door, and he humbly requested an audience with the King of Kippen. When informed, John Buchanan knew who his visitor was, and rushed out in trepidation. But James greeted him cordially, and laughed at the escapade of the venison. Buchanan invited the king into his home to dine, and the king agreed. Soon the company was merry, and the king told Buchanan that he could take as much venison as he liked from the royal hunters that passed his door. He also invited the King of Kippen to visit his brother monarch at Stirling any time he liked.

To the east of Kippen, and off the A811, is the village of **Gargunnock**, with a picturesque parish church built in 1774.

PORT OF MENTEITH

14 miles W of Stirling on the B8034

This little village sits on the shore of the **Lake of Menteith**, sometimes erroneously called the only lake (as opposed to loch) in Scotland. However, there are several bodies of water in Scotland - some natural, some man made - which are lakes (see also Kirkcudbright, Stenton and Ellon).

But there is no doubting that it is one of Scotland's most beautiful stretches of water. It is only a mile wide by a mile and a half long, with low hills sloping down towards it northern shores. Its name is probably a corruption of Laigh (meaning a flat piece of land) of Menteith, as the land to the south of the lake, Flanders Moss, is flat.

On the island of Inchmahome are the beautiful ruins of **Inchmahome Priory** (Historic Scotland), within which Mary Stuart was kept after the Battle of Pinkie in 1547. Within the reroofed chapter house are many carved effigies and tombstones. The priory was founded in 1238 by Walter Comyn, Earl of Menteith, for Augustinian canons. On the nearby **Inchtulla** the Menteiths had their castle, and on **Dog Island** the Earl kept his hunting dogs.

The priory can be reached by a small ferry from the jetty at Port of Menteith.

ABERFOYLE

17 miles W of Stirling on the A821

Aberfoyle has been called the Gateway to the **Trossachs** (see also Callander), and sits on the River Forth after it emerges from beautiful Loch Ard. The **Duke's Road** (named after a Duke of Montrose) goes north from the village to the Trossachs proper, and has some good views over Lochs Drunkie and Vennacher.

The **Scottish Wool Centre** is situated within the village, and tells the story of Scottish wool. You can visit the Spinner's Cottage, and have a go at spinning wool into yarn. There are also occasional visits from local shepherds, who put on sheepdog demonstations. There is also a shop where woollen items - from coats to blankets - can be bought.

The **Queen Elizabeth Forest Park**, whose visitors centre is close to Aberfoyle, covers 75,000 acres, and is administered by the Forestry Commission (see also Balloch). It takes in the eastern shores of Loch Lomond, as well as Lochs Ard, Lubnaig and Achray, and has walks and trails. This whole area, however, will soon come within Scotland's first national park, and it will include all of the Trossachs as well as Loch Lomond (see also Balloch).

It was in Aberfoyle that the famous and mysterious disappearance of the **Rev. Robert Kirk**, minister at Aberfoyle Parish Church, took place. He was born in 1644, and had an abiding interest in fairies, even writing a book called The Secret Commonwealth of Elves, Fauns and Faires.

Legend states that the fairies were none to pleased that Robert had revealed their secrets. One day in 1692, while walking on Doon Hill, well known in the area as one of the entrances to the fairy realm, Robert disappeared. People

GLENNY COTTAGES

Port of Menteith, near Aberfoyle and Trossachs,
Stirlingshire FK8 3RD
Tel: 01877 385229

Commanding superb views over the Lake of Menteith, **Glenny Cottages** make the ideal location for a relaxing holiday. Buzzard Cottage has two well appointed ensuite bedrooms, one with a double bed and the other with two singles and a third pull out single, along with two childrens' beds. Kestrel Cottage has one comfortable bedroom and a studio folding couch in the lounge. The cottages are the epitome of comfortable country living, with central heating, wood burning or gas stoves, fully equipped kitchens and well appointed lounges with TVs.

FORTH INN

Main Street, Aberfoyle, Stirlingshire FK8 3UQ
Tel/Fax: 01877 382372
e-mail: phil@forthinn.com website: www.forthinn.com

The Forth Inn is located in the lovely village of Aberfoyle, and offers a real "home from home" experience to the discerning traveller. Owned since 1998 by Phil and Tristan Crowder, it has been refurbished to an exceptionally high standard, and now offers six en suite rooms, all beautifully appointed and decorated. The inn still retains a friendly and homely feel, and its food is gaining quite a reputation in the area. And a drink in its bar may turn into a toe-tapping occasion, as it is the haunt of local folk musicians!

Queen Elizabeth Forest Park

claimed that he has been taken to the fairy kingdom, and that one day he would come back, looking no older than he did when he disappeared. To this day, he has not returned. Another legend states that Robert's wife was given the chance of getting her husband back. He would appear, she was told, during Sunday service in the kirk, and she had to throw a knife at him which should penetrate his flesh. Robert did appear during the service, but his wife couldn't throw the knife, so he disappeared once more.

Robert Kirk was indeed a minister in Aberfoyle kirk in the 17th century, and he did indeed disappear one day while out walking. Was he taken by the fairies? Or was he the victim of a more earthly crime? No one will ever know - unless he turns up again.

South of Aberfoyle, near the conservation village of **Gartmore**, is the **Cunninghame Graham Memorial** (National Trust for Scotland). Robert Cunninghame Graham of Ardoch was a Scottish author and politician who died in 1936. The memorial once stood at Castlehill in Dumbarton, but was moved here in 1980.

DRYMEN

20 miles W of Stirling off the A811

During World War II, **Buchanan Castle** was a military hospital. Its most famous patient was Rudolph Hess, Hitler's deputy, who was kept here after he parachuted into Scotland on a secret mission to see the Duke of Hamilton (see also Eaglesham). The castle itself dates from 1855, and was built by the 4th Duke of Montrose after the former castle was destroyed by fire three years previously. It is now partly ruinous, but can be viewed from the outside.

Drymen is on the West Highland Way, the footpath that stretches from Milngavie on the outskirts of Glasgow to Fort William. It is also the gateway to the eastern, and less busy, shores of Loch Lomond, which lie three miles away. The small village of **Balmaha** (also on the West Highland Way) sits on the shore of the loch, and should be visited for the wonderful views it gives of Britain's largest sheet of water. **Balfron**, four miles east of Drymen, is an attractive village with a parish church that dates from 1832. Alexander "Greek" Thomson, the noted architect, was a native of Balfron.

BLAIR DRUMMOND

5 miles NW of Stirling on the A84

Blair Drummond Safari and Adventure Park is one of the most visited tourist attarctions in Scotland. You can tour the park by car or coach, and see such animals as elephants, lions, zebras, giraffes, white rhino and ostriches in conditons that allow them plenty of freedom. You can take a boat trip round Chimp Island, watch the sea lion show or glide above the lake on the "Flying Fox".

DOUNE

7 miles NW of Stirling on the A820

The bridge across the River Teith in this picturesque village was built by James Spittal,

Creag-Ard House

by Aberfoyle, Stirlingshire FK8 3TQ
Tel/Fax: 01877 382297
e-mail: cara@creag-ardhouse.co.uk
website: www.creag-ardhouse.co.uk

Loch Ard must be one of the most beautiful lochs in Scotland. Right on its shores stands **Creag-Ard House**, owned by Cara and David Wilson. It is the last word in comfort and character, and has six bedrooms, all en suite, with four looking onto beautiful gardens and two enjoying views over the loch and hills. The furnishings have been carefully chosen to reflect the overall ambience of the place, and each room been tastefully decorated in country house style.

A traditional Scottish breakfast awaits you each morning in the beautifully appointed dining room, and you can choose from the traditional full Scottish breakfast, or a fillet of smoked haddock, or, for a real taste of Scotland, scrambled eggs with smoked salmon.

By special arrangement, Cara will also cook dinner and David will enlighten you with his knowledge and vast list of the finest Scottish whiskies. To complete a marvellous stay, why not hire a boat for trout fishing on the loch?

tailor to James IV (see also Tullibody). Legend has it that he arrived at the ferry that once operated where the bridge now stands without any money, and the ferryman refused to take him across. So, out of spite, he had the bridge built to deprive the ferryman of a livelihood.

Doune Castle (Historic Scotland) is one of the best preserved 14th century castles in Scotland, and was the seat of the Earls of Moray (see also Dalgety). It stands above the River Teith, and was originally built for the Duke of Albany, Regent of Scotland during the minority of James I. Later James had the Duke executed for plotting against his brother, and the castle passed to him. It has two main towers connected by a Great Hall with a high wooden ceiling. In 1883 the castle was restored by the 14th Earl of Moray.

The village itself gained its burgh charter in 1611, and originally stood close to the castle. In the early 1700s, however, the village was moved to its present position, and its 17th century **Mercat Cross** was moved there also. The village was, at one time, famous as a centre of pistol making. The industry was started in about 1646 by a man called Thomas Cadell, and so accurate and well made were his guns that they soon became prized items. By the18th century Cadell's descendants were all involved in making guns, and began exporting them to the Continent. It is said that the first pistol fired in the American War of Independence was made in Doune.

DEANSTON

8 miles NW of Stirling on the B8032

Deanston is a village on the banks of the River Teith, built round a cotton mill founded in 1785 by four brothers, one of whom was associated with Sir Richard Arkwright. It passd through several hands before finally closing in 1965. Now the mill houses the **Deanston Distillery**, which makes a range of whiskies, using the same water that once powered the weaving machines.

CALLANDER

13 miles NW of Stirling on the A84

This pleasant holiday town stands to the east of the Trossachs, and has some wonderful walking country on its doorstep. It is home to the **Rob Roy and Trossachs Visitor Centre**. It is housed in a former church in Ancaster

The Aizle

Balat Crossroads, near Balfron,
Stirlingshire G63 0SE
Tel: 01360 440456 Fax: 01360 440826

Situated on the A81 at the gateway to Scotland's first National Park, you will find **The Aizle**, a coffee shop that serves some of the best and tastiest food in the area. The name literally means 'burning ember', and it is a friendly, family run establishment that is popular with both locals and visitors alike. The Aizle has a reputation for good service, value for money and a warm welcome. It seats 80 people in comfort, and the staff offers a 'one-to-one' service, so that customers can feel relaxed. Everything is cooked on the premises, and all the produce used in the kitchen is locally sourced wherever possible, making sure it is as fresh as possible.

The dishes are all reasonably priced, with the menu including such favourites as home made soup, sandwiches, toasties, baked potatoes with a range of fillings, filled baguettes, baked beans on toast, lasagne, paté and oatcakes, croissants, macaroni and cheese and salads galore. It sits right on the A81, 30 minutes drive from both Glasgow and Stirling, so is the ideal stopping place if you are heading north on holiday. But the Aizle is so much more than just a restaurant. Beside it you will find shops selling glass ornaments, vases, ceramics, gift items and biscuits etc, as well as ones selling ladies' and children's fashions. There is also a gallery where you can buy original works of art and prints - just right for that souvenir to take back home. And from March to October a garden shop sells a wide range of plants, flowers and bushes. With so much going for it, The Aizle is a place you will want to return to again and again!

Square, and, as the name suggests, tells the story of both the Trossachs and its most famous son, Rob Roy MacGregor (see also Balquhidder). His real name was Robert MacGregor (1671-1734) and even today people still cannot agree on whether he was a minor crook, an out and out brigand, a freedom fighter or the Scottish Robin Hood. His lands were confiscated by the Duke of Montrose in 1712, and he was imprisoned by the English in the 1720s. He was made famous by Daniel Defoe's book Highland Rogue, by Sir Walter Scott's novel Rob Roy, and by the recent film.

However, there's no denying that the man was an outstanding leader who could read and write in both English and Gaelic, and possesed a large library. It was Sir Walter Scott who made him behave dishonourably at the Battle of Sheriffmuir (see Dunblane), when in fact he acquitted himself with courage and honour fighting for the Jacobites. At his funeral on New Year's Day 1735 people came from all over Scotland to pay their respects.

Also in Callander is the **Hamilton Toy Museum**, five rooms of model cars, planes, dolls, teddy bears and such TV collectables as Thunderbird, Star Trek and Star Wars figures.

LOCH KATRINE

23 miles NW of Stirling close to the A821

There is no doubt that Loch Katrine is one of the most beautiful lochs in Scotland. It is surrounded by high. craggy hills, which in autumn blaze with orange and gold. But the loch as you see it today has more to do with man than with nature. In the mid 19th century, the loch became one huge reservoir for the city of Glasgow, and the depth of the water was increased considerably. In 1859 Queen Victoria opened the new reservoir, and 90 million gallons of water a day flowed towards Glasgow, over 30 miles away.

The engineering that made this happen was well ahead of its time, and consisted of tunnels and aqueducts that relied purely on gravity to carry the water towards the city. The engineering surrounding the loch was equally as spectacular. The water from **Loch Arklet**, high in the hills between Lochs Katrine and Lomond, used to flow west into Loch Lomond. By the use of dams, this was changed so that it

Loch Katrine

flowed east into Loch Katrine. The whole scheme was the largest of its kind in the world for many years, and even today, Glasgow still gets its water from Loch Katrine.

The loch was made famous by Sir Walter Scott, who set his poem The Lady of the Lake here. And at **Glengyle**, at the western end of the loch, Rob Roy MacGregor was born, though it cannot be reached by car.

The steamer **Sir Walter Scott** has been sailing the waters of the loch from the beginning of the 20th century, and it still does so today. It takes you from the pier at the east end of the loch towards **Stronachlachar**, some six miles away. The small islet at Stronachlachan is known as the **Factor's Island**, and recalls one of Rob Roy's exploits. He captured the Duke of Montrose's factor, who was collecting rents in the area, and imprisoned him on the island. He then sent a ransom note to the Duke, but none came. So Rob Roy calmy relieved the man of the £3000 he was carrying and sent him on his way.

This is the heart of the Trossachs (the name translates as "bristly" or "prickly"), and there are other equally as attractive lochs nearby. **Loch Lubnaig**, to the east, is the largest. **Loch Venachar**, **Loch Achray** and **Loch Drunkie** (which can only be reached by a footpath through the forest) are well worth visiting. At the southern end of Loch Lubnaig are the **Falls of Leny**.

BALQUIDDER

24 miles NW of Stirling on a minor road off the A84

This small village sits to the east of the picturesque **Loch Voil**. It lies in that area of Scotland known as **Breadalbane** ("uplands of Alban", as Alban is the ancient name for Scotland), and in the heart of Clan MacGregor country. In the kirkyard of the roofless kirk is **Rob Roy MacGregor's Grave** (see also Callander), plus those of some of his family. Rob Roy MacGregor was a famous freebooter whom Sir Walter Scott imortalised in his novel of the same name.

KILLIN

30 miles NW of Stirling on the A827

Killin sits close to the western end of **Loch Tay**, which stretches for 15 miles eastwards into Perthshire. The best views of the loch are from the wooded south shore road, though the northern road is wider and straighter.

The **Falls of Dochart**, a series of cascades on the River Dochart, are within the village, and next to them is the **Breadalbane Folklore**

Falls of Dochart

Centre, which gives an insight into life and legends of the area. Three miles north on a minor road are the **Falls of Lochay** on the River Lochay, though care should be taken when approaching them. The **Moirlanich Longhouse** (National Trust for Scotland) on the Glen Lochay road dates from the 19th century, and is a rare surviving example of a Scottish longhouse, where a family and their livestock lived under the one roof. In an adjacent shed is a display of working clothes found in the longhouse, along with displays which explain the building's history and restoration. The ruins of **Finlarig Castle**, which date from the 16th century, are to the north of the village. Within its grounds are the remains of a beheading pit.

CRIANLARICH

32 miles NW of Stirling on the A82

Surrounding this village, which is on the souther edge of Breadalbane, is some marvellous walking and climbing country. The West Highland Way passes close to the village, The twin peaks of **Ben More** (3,843 feet) and **Stobinian** (3,821 feet) are to the south east, while the picturesque **Falls of Falloch** (with a small car park close by) lie four miles to the south west on the A82.

TYNDRUM

40 miles NW of Stirling on the A82

This little village has a population of no more than 100 people, and yet it has two railway stations. One on the line from Glasgow to Oban, and the other on the line from Glasgow to Fort William. It is at the head of **Strath Fillan**, which snakes south towards Crianlarich, and through which is the West Highland Way. At **Dalrigh**, in 1306, Robert the Bruce was defeated in battle, and nearby was the site of **Strathfillan Priory**, founded by Bruce in 1318. St Fillan was an Irish monk who lived during the 8th century, and who founded a monastery in the vicinity (ses also Pittenweem and St Fillans). It is said that while building the monastery, a wolf attacked and killed one of the oxen used to bring materials to the site. St Fillan then prayed, and a miracle occurred - the wolf took the place of the ox.

8 Argyllshire and the Inner Hebrides

Argyllshire is one of the most diverse and beautiful counties in Scotland. It sits on the western seaboard, where long sea lochs penetrate deep into its interior and mountains tumble down towards fertile glens. Most of the Inner Hebridean islands, such as Mull, Jura and Islay (pronounced Eye-lah) belong to it, and ferries criss-cross the waters between them and the mainland. "Argyll" itself comes from the Gaelic Earraghaidheal, meaning the "coastline of the Gaels".

It can truly claim to be the cradle of Scotland, for this was, at one time, the kingdom of Dalriada, founded by the "Scotti" (who originally came from Ireland) in the 6th century. Here, at the fortress of Dunadd, they established their capital. From Dunadd, in 843, Kenneth MacAlpin, king of Dalriada, set off towards Scone in Perthshire (taking the Stone of Destiny with him) to claim the throne of the Picts , thus uniting the two great northern kingdoms and creating an embyonic Scotland. In the 11th century the kingdoms of the Angles, called Lothian (centred on Edinburgh) and Strathclyde (centred on Dumbarton) were absorbed, and Scotland as we know it today was formed.

The other great Dalriadan centre was at what is now Dunstaffnage, north of Oban. The sight is now occupied by Dunstaffnage Castle, one of the most spectacular fortifications on Scotland's western seaboard. The 12th century Castle Sween, on the

Glencoe in Winter

shores of Loch Sween, is reckoned to be the oldest stone built castle on the Scottish mainland.

Though it has attractive towns such as Oban, Lochgilphead, Tobermory, Inveraray and Campbeltown, Argyllshire is an open, sparsely populated place. There are no clogged up roads here (though Oban can get very busy in the summer months), and driving is a pleasure. New vistas are constantly being opened up as you drive along roads such as the one from Lochgilphead to Oban, and even on overcast days (which are not unknown in this part of Scotland) they are a constant source of wonder and delight. The climate is mild, thanks to the Gulf Stream, and the place has many fine gardens to explore, such as Ardkinglas, Crarae and Arduaine, some with palm trees and other species you wouldn't expect to thrive so far north

Loch Leven

Man has lived in Argyllshire for centuries, and around Kilmartin there are cairns and standing stones built long before the Pyramids were thought of. Iona, off the western tip of Mull, is one of the most sacred places, not just in Scotland, but in Christendom. Here St Columba established his great monastery, and from here missionaries set out to convert the northern lands.

St Columba wasn't the first man to bring Christianity to Scotland - that honour goes to St Ninian - but he was the most influential, and we know a lot about his life. And what we know of him paints a picture of an all too human person - vengeful yet forgiving, impetuous yet thoughtful, arrogant yet unassuming and boastful yet modest. Today Iona is still a place of pilgrimage, though most people now come as tourists to see and admire the later abbey buildings, and experience the feeling of calm the island seems to give anyone who visits.

Argyllshire is also a place of intriguing legends. When that great order of monastic soldiers called the Knights Templar was suppressed by Pope Clement V in 1307, it was to this part of Scotland, we are told, that they fled. Robert the Bruce, the Scots king, had been excommunicated by the Pope, so Papal authority didn't extend to this part of Europe at the time, and here the warrior monks could settle in peace. Their legacy, some people claim, is to be found in wonderfully carved tombstones with Templar carvings on them in such places as Kilmichael Glassary and Kilmartin. Legend also says that a troup of Knights Templar from this area helped Robert the Bruce defeat the English at Bannockburn.

Rothesay Castle, Isle of Bute

The Argyllshire coastline is rugged and rocky, as are most of the islands which belong to the county. The largest are Mull, Jura and Islay, but there are other hidden gems to be discovered, such as Lismore, Colonsay, Coll, Tiree and Bute. The last mentioned, along with Arran and the Cumbraes, used to form the county of Buteshire, but local government reorganisation in the 70s shared it out between Argyll and Ayrshire. Local government reorganisation also took Morven, Sunart and the Ardnamurchan peninsula, north of Mull, from Argyllshire, and today they form part of the Highlands local government area. But at the same time parts of what were formerly Dunbartonshire, such as the town of Helensburgh and the Rosneath Peninsula, are now within Argyll, although they are dealt with in another section of this book.

That great peninsula known as the Mull of Kintyre, which hangs down into the Atlantic like an arm, is also in Argyllshire. This is a remote part of Scotland - part of the mainland yet as isolated as any island. Though Glasgow is only 60 miles from Campbeltown as the crow flies, it takes the average driver three or four hours over twisting, loch-girt roads to reach it. This is the area made famous by Sir Paul MacCartney's song, where he sings of "mists rolling in from the sea".

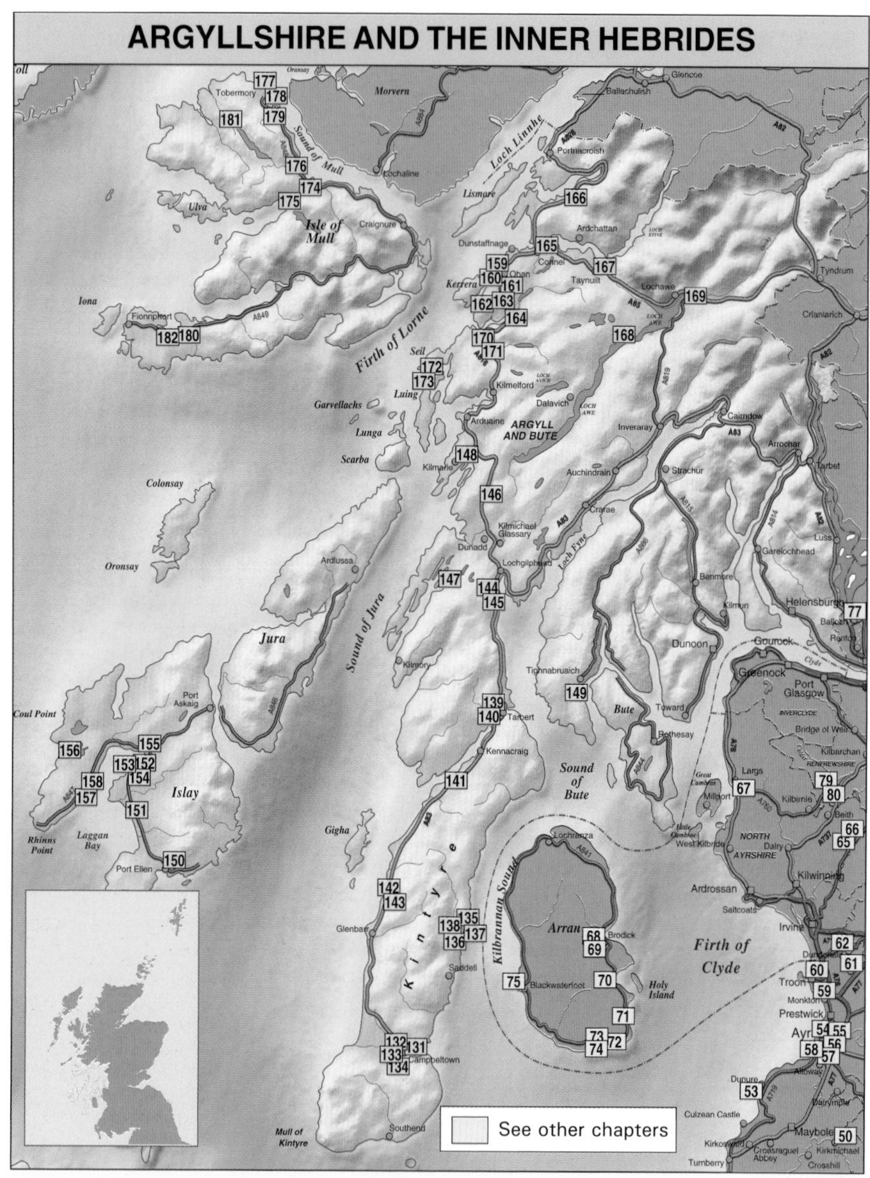
ARGYLLSHIRE AND THE INNER HEBRIDES
Morvern
Tobermory
Sound of Mull
Lochaline
Loch Linnhe
Ballachulish
Glencoe
Portnacroish
Lismore
Ulva
Isle of Mull
Craignure
Dunstaffnage
Ardchattan
Connel
Oban
Kerrera
Taynuilt
Lochawe
Tyndrum
Crianlarich
Iona
Fionnphort
Firth of Lorne
Seil
Luing
Garvellachs
Lunga
Scarba
Kilmelford
Dalavich
Arduaine
ARGYLL AND BUTE
Inveraray
Cairndow
Arrochar
Tarbet
Kilmartin
Auchindrain
Strachur
Colonsay
Oronsay
Crarae
Kilmichael Glassary
Dunadd
Lochgilphead
Loch Fyne
Luss
Garelochhead
Ardlussa
Benmore
Kilmun
Helensburgh
Sound of Jura
Jura
Kilmory
Dunoon
Gourock
Greenock
Port Glasgow
Tighnabruaich
Bute
Toward
Rothesay
Port Askaig
Coul Point
Tarbert
Kennacraig
Sound of Bute
Bridge of Weir
Kilbarchan
Largs
Kilbirnie
Beith
Islay
Great Cumbrae
Millport
Rhinns Point
Laggan Bay
Gigha
Lochranza
West Kilbride
NORTH AYRSHIRE
Dalry
Port Ellen
Kilwinning
Kilbrannan Sound
Ardrossan
Saltcoats
Irvine
Glenbarr
Kintyre
Arran
Brodick
Firth of Clyde
Saddell
Blackwaterfoot
Holy Island
Troon
Monkton
Prestwick
Ayr
Campbeltown
Alloway
Dunure
Culzean Castle
Southend
Mull of Kintyre
Maybole
Dalrymple
Kirkoswald
Crossraguel Abbey
Kirkmichael
Crosshill
Turnberry
See other chapters
177 178 179 181 176 174 175 166 165 167 159 160 161 162 163 164 169 170 171 168 182 180 172 173 148 146 147 144 145 77 149 139 140 155 156 153 152 154 158 157 151 141 67 79 80 66 65 150 142 143 138 135 137 136 68 69 62 61 60 75 70 59 71 73 72 74 54 55 56 58 57 132 131 133 134 53 50

PLACES TO STAY, EAT, DRINK AND SHOP

131	Ardshiel House, Campbeltown	Hotel and restaurant	Page 190
132	Craigard House, Low Askomil	Hotel and restaurant	Page 190
133	Homeston Farm , Campbeltown	B&B and riding	Page 190
134	Rosemount Guest House , Low Askomil	Bed and Breakfast	Page 190
135	Mains Cottages, Carradale	Self catering	Page 192
136	Torrisdale Castle, Torrisdale Castle	Self catering	Page 192
137	Dunvalanree, Port Righ	Hotel and restaurant	Page 192
138	Carradale Hotel, Carradale	Hotel	Page 192
139	Columba Hotel, Tarbert	Hotel and restaurant	Page 193
140	West Loch and Brenfield , Tarbert	Self catering	Page 193
141	Balinakill Country House Hotel, Clachan	Hotel and restaurant	Page 194
142	North Beachmore, Muasdale	Restaurant	Page 194
143	Muasdale Holiday Park, Muasdale	Self catering	Page 195
144	Allt-Na-Craig, Ardrishaig	Guest house and self catering	Page 196
145	Bridge House Hotel, Ardrishaig	Hotel and restaurant	Page 196
146	Dunchraigaig House, Kilmartin	Bed and Breakfast	Page 197
147	Seafield Farm Cottages, Achnamara	Self catering	Page 198
148	Galley of Lorne Inn, Ardfern	Pub, accommodation and restaurant	Page 198
149	Kames Hotel, Kames	Hotel and restaurant	Page 202
150	Ballivicar Farm, Port Ellen	Self catering	Page 202
151	Glenegedale House , Glenegedale	Pub, accommodation and food	Page 203
152	The Bowmore Hotel, Bowmore	Hotel and restaurant	Page 204
153	The Islay Whisky Club, Bowmore	Whisky club and shop	Page 204
154	Cnoc Ard Taighean Gorm, Bowmore	Self catering	Page 205
155	Coullabus Keeper's Cottage, Bridgend	Self catering	Page 206
156	Kilchoman House Cottages, Kilchoman	Self catering	Page 206
157	Octomore Cottage, Port Charlotte	Self catering	Page 207
158	Lorgba Holiday Cottages, Port Charlotte	Self catering	Page 208
159	Aulay's Bar, Oban	Pub with food	Page 209
160	Avoriaz , Oban	Bed and Breakfast	Page 210
161	Markie Dans, Oban	Pub with food	Page 210
162	Gallanach, by Oban	Self catering	Page 210
163	Lerags House, by Oban	Guest House	Page 211
164	Yacht Corryvreckan, Kilmore	Yacht cruises	Page 211
165	Wide Mouthed Frog, Connel	Pub with food	Page 212
166	Barcaldine House Hotel, Barcaldine	Hotel and self catering	Page 213
167	Polfearn Hotel, Taynuilt	Hotel	Page 214
168	Roineabhal Country House , Kilchrenan	Guest House	Page 214
169	Blarghour Farm Cottages, Blarghour Farm	Self catering	Page 215
170	Eleraig Highland Lodges, Kilninver	Self catering	Page 216
171	Bragleenbeg, Kilninver	Self catering	Page 217
172	Balvicar Farm, Isle of Seil	Self catering	Page 218
173	Inshaig Park Hotel, Easdale	Hotel	Page 218
174	Rock Cottage, Salen	Self catering	Page 219
175	Torlochan, Gruline	Self catering	Page 220
176	Island Encounter Wildlife , Aros	Wildlife safaris	Page 220
177	Isle of Mull Silver & Goldsmiths, Tobermory	Silver and Goldsmiths	Page 221
178	Tobermory Hotel, Tobermory	Hotel and restaurant	Page 222
179	Mull Pottery, Tobermory	Pottery, café and tearoom	Page 223
180	Tigh Na Lochan Guest House, Bunessan	Guest House	Page 224
181	Achnadrish House, by Tobermory	Guest House	Page 225
182	Argyll Restaurant, Bunessan	Restaurant	Page 226

BUTE

The island of Bute used to be part of the small county of Buteshire, which also took in Arran and the Cumbraes. Though it now comes under Argyllshire, the Highland Boundary Fault passes right through **Loch Fad**, in the heart of the island, which means that the northern part is in the Highlands while the southern part is in the Lowlands. The scenery reflects this, with the north being rugged and relatively uninhabited, while the south is pastoral, with many small farms and settlements.

There are two ferries connecting Bute with the mainland. The main one is from Wemyss bay in Renfrewshire to Rothesay, while another, smaller one, travels the short distance between Ardentraive on the Cowal penisula and Rhubodach.

The main town is **Rothesay**, an ancient royal burgh which was given its charter in 1401. It is one of the most famous holiday resorts on the Firth of Clyde, and at one time attracted thousands of Glasgow tourists during the "Glasgow Fair", which is always the last two weeks in July. Fine Victorian mansions line the front, built to take Glasgow merchants who would descend on the town, complete with family and servants, for weeks at a time. There were also more modest establishments that took in the working classes for what was their one and only holiday of the year. It eventually earned the nickname of "Scotland's Madeira", not just because it was on an island, but because palm trees flourish here due to the influence of the Gulf Stream.

The gentleness of the climate can best be appreciated at **Ardencraig Gardens** in Ardencraig Lane, which were bought by the town council of Rothesay in 1968. Every summer it shimmers with colour, and is a popular spot with holidaymakers. Another popular spot is **Canada Hill**, to the south of the town, where there are spectacular views of the Firth of Clyde. From here, people used to watch ships sailing down the Firth taking Scottish emigrants to North America, hence its name.

Rothesay Castle (Historic Scotland) is a royal castle, and one of the oldest in Scotland. It dates at least from about the 13th century, when history tells us that it was besieged by the Vikings. King Haakon of Norway took it in 1263, but afterwards was defeated at the Battle of Largs. It was a favourite residence of the first Stuart king, Robert II, and his son, Robert III, who may have died there. It was Robert III who created the dukedom of Rothesay, and conferred it on his eldest son. Ever since, all royal heirs have been given the title, and prince Charles is the present duke. The whole building was in a ruinous state until 1816, when it was partly rebuilt by the 2nd Marquis of Bute.

In Stuart Street, close to the castle, is the **Bute Museum**, which has displays and artifacts about Rothesay, the Firth of Clyde and the island of Bute itself. The ruined **Church of St Mary**, on the southern outskirts of the town, is close to the present High Kirk. It dates mainly from the 13th and 14th century, and has two canopied tombs. One contains the effigy of a woman and child, and the other of a man, possibly Walter, High Steward of Scotland (and ancestor of the Stuart dynasty), who died in about 1326.

The **Isle of Bute Discovery Centre** is housed in the town's Winter Garden, on the front. It houses an exhibition highlighting life on the island through interactive displays and plasma screens, as well as a cinema/theatre. Scotland's first "anibod", a robot lookalike of popular Scottish comedian Johnny Beattie, forms part of the exhibits. He performed many

Isle of Bute Pier

times in the Winter Garden before it was refurbished.

But Rothesay has more unusual attractions as well, and one of the most unusual is the **Victorian Toilets** at the end of the pier, which date from 1899. They are fully functional, and full of ornate design. They were recently voted the second best place in the world to spend a penny. If you want the best place, you'll have to go to Hong Kong if you can hang on that long.

To the south of Rothesay, near Kilchattan, is **St Blane's Chapel**. The ruins of this Norman structure sit within what was a Celtic monastery, founded by St Blane in the sixth century. The whole area shows how such a monastery would have been laid out. The cashel, a low wall surrounding the site, can still be seen, as can the foundations of various beehive cells in which the monks lived. There are two old graveyards - one for men, and one for women.

There are lots of other religious sites on Bute, some dating right back to the Dark Ages. At **Straad** (a name which tells you that the island once belonged to the Vikings) there are the scant remains of **St Ninian's Chapel**, and at **Kilmichael** there are the ruins of the old **St Macaille Chapel**.

Mount Stuart House, near the lovely village of **Kerrycroy**, is the ancestral home of the Marquesses of Bute. In 1877 a fire destroyed most of the old house, and the third Marquess employed Robert Rowand Anderson to design the present Victorian Gothic one. It is an immense house, full or treasures, and reflects the history and importance of the family who owned it. When built, it was full of technological wonders. It was the first house in Scotland to be lit by electricity, and the first private house to have a heated indoor swimming pool. Surrounding the house are 300 acres of delightful gardens.

Near **Port Bannatyne**, north of Rothesay, is **Kames Castle**, dating from the 14th century. Neither it nor its beautiful gardens are open to the public, but they can be viewed from the road. One place which can be visited, however, is **Ascog Hall Fernery and Garden**, three miles south of Rothesay. It was built about 1870, and has a sunken fern house which houses over 80 sub-tropical fern species. It was awarded the first ever Scottish prize by the Historic Gardens Foundation, which promotes historic gardens and parks throughout the world.

DUNOON

Dunoon is one of the best known Clyde Coast holiday resorts, and at one time was a favourite with Glasgow holiday makers. It sits opposite the Renfrewshire coast, and an all year ferry connects it to Gourock. Each year in August the town hosts the **Cowal Highland Gathering**, one of the largest in Scotland, where competitors indulge in tossing the caber, throwing the hammer and other Scottish events.

The **Castle House Museum** is in the Castle Gardens, and has a permanent exhibition entitled "Dunoon and Cowal Past and Present". There are models, artifacts and photographs which bring the Dunoon of yesteryear to life. There are also furnished Victorian rooms and a shop. The statue of **Highland Mary** is close by (see also Failford and Greenock). She was a native of Dunoon,

Highland Games, Dunoon

Ardshiel Hotel

Kilkerran Road, Campbeltown, Argyllshire PA28 6JL
Tel: 01586 552133 e-mail: ardshiel@aol.com
Fax: 01586 551422 website: www.ardshiel.freeserve.co.uk

The **Ardshiel Hotel** is one of Campbeltown's finest family run establishments, and has nine attractive rooms, seven of which are en suite, with TVs, tea/coffee making facilities and direct dial phones. There is a comfortable lounge with an extensive range of fine malt whiskies and a spacious restaurant selling excellent Scottish food, with the emphasis on seafood and game, using local produce wherever possible. A children's menu is available. This is a hotel that caters for the discerning tourist, and makes an excellent base from which to explore the Mull of Kintyre.

Craigard House

Low Askomil, Campbeltown, Argyllshire PA28 6EP
Tel: 01586 554242; Fax: 01586 551137
e-mail: info@craigard-house.co.uk
website: www.craigard-house.co.uk

In Campbeltown, on the beautiful Mull of Kintyre, you will find **Craigard House**, one of the best hotels in the area. It has 11 comfortable and beautifully appointed rooms, all en-suite, and each one with TV, tea/coffee making facilities, hair dryer and phone. It sits on an elevated site overlooking Campbeltown Loch, and was built in 1882. It has a elegant residents' lounge, and a spacious dining room where good food and fine wines are served. It is the ideal base from which to explore an area rich in wildlife and heritage, or to play golf at the famous Macrihanish course.

Homeston Farm

Campbeltown, Argyllshire PA28 6RL
Tel: 01586 552437
e-mail: lorna@ridescotland.com website: www.relaxscotland.com

Owned and managed by Lorna and Malcolm McArthur, **Homeston** offers a wonderful, relaxing base from which to explore this glorious, unspoilt part of Scotland. You can stay B&B only or have four course dinner also, chosen from the daily changing menu. The food is superb with everything home-made, even the oatcakes for cheese. The en suite rooms are very comfortable with fresh fruit, sweets and tea and coffee making facilities. Fresh home baking is provided for your afternoon tea each day. The farm is also the base for all inclusive trail riding holidays where you cover 120 miles in a week, riding excellent horses through moorland, forests and over long, sandy beaches.

Rosemount Guest House

Low Askomil, Campbeltown, Argyllshire PA28 6EP
Tel: 01586 553552

Rosemount is an award winning guest house about ten minutes walk from the centre of Campbeltown that offers the very best in holiday accommodation to the discerning tourist. It has lovely views over Campbeltown Loch, and boasts five en suite rooms that are both comfortable and extremely cosy. Breakfasts are filling and hearty, and use only the finest local produce wherever possible. There are no evening meals, but the owners, Janet and Trevor Scott-Dodd, can recommend may good local establishments that serve wonderful food. Rosemount has a real home-from-home feel to it, and visitors are always given a good Scottish welcome!

and worked as a nursemaid near Mauchline in Ayrshire. Burns met her there, and asked her to accompany him to the West Indies when he was thinking of emigrating. She agreed, but on a trip home to Dunoon to make arrangements, she died and was buried in Greenock. In Hamilton Street is the factory of **Dunoon Ceramics**, which makes mugs and other items. There is a shop, and guided tours of the factory are available see how the mugs are made and fired.

To the north of Dunoon is the **Holy Loch**, at one time an American nuclear submarine base. It was chosen as a base not just because of the deep water, but because this part of Argyllshire has a cloud covering for the majority of the year, thwarting satellite and aerial photography. The Americans left in 1992, taking with them their large American cars and their accents, which were once familiar things in the streets of Dunoon.

AROUND DUNOON

KILMUN

3 miles N of Dunoon on the A880

Kilmun Church was a collegiate church founded in 1442 by Sir Duncan Campbell of Lochawe, ancestor of the present Dukes of Argyll. All that remains is the tower, now roofless. In 1794 a Campbell mausoleum was built close to the present church of St Munn, and in the kirkyard is the grave of **Elizabeth Blackwell**, who, in 1849, was the first woman in modern times to graduate in medicine. Close by is the grave of the **Rev. Alexander Robinson**, a former minister who was deposed after being accused of heresy.

On a hillside is the **Kilmun Arboretum**, extending to 180 acres. First planted in 1930, it has a wide range of trees from all over the world, and is maintained by the Forestry Commisssion, which does research work here.

BENMORE

6 miles N of Dunoon off the A815

The **Younger Botanic Garden** is a specialist sector of the Royal Botanic Garden in Edinburgh, and in its 140 acres you can see a wide collection of trees and shrubs from all over the world. There are 250 species of rhododendron, an avenue of giant redwoods from America and a formal garden. Within the Glen Massan Arboretum are some of the tallest trees in Scotland, including a Douglas fir over 178 feet high. From the top of Benmore Hill within the gardens there is a magnificent view across the Holy Loch to the Firth of Clyde and the Renfrewshire coast.

TOWARD

6 miles S of Dunoon on the A815

The ruins of **Toward Castle** date from the 15th century. It was a stronghold of the Lamonts, who supported Charles II in his attempts to impose bishops on the Church of Scotland, while the Campbells were Covenanters, and bitterly opposed to episcopacy. An episode in 1646 shows just how the Scottish clans took matters into their own hands when dispensing justice. The Campbells laid siege to the castle, and after trying unsuccessfully to blow it up offered safe passage as far as Dunoon to the Lamonts sheltering within.

The Lamonts duly left the castle, and were immediately rounded up and taken to Tom-a-Moid ("Hill of Justice") in Dunoon, where 36 clansmen were hung. It wasn't just the political differences that had prompted this massacre. Previous to this, the Lamonts themselves had slaughtered Campbells at Strachur and attacked and slaughtered the villagers of Kilmun, who had hid in the church.

CAMPBELTOWN

Campbeltown has the reputation of being the most isolated town on the British mainland. It sits on the Mull of Kintyre, that great peninsula that hangs down from the main body of Argyllshire. It received its royal charter in 1700, making it the second youngest royal burgh in Scotland. Though 140 miles from Glasgow by road, it is only 12 miles from Nothern Ireland. It also has the distinction of being the most southerly town in the Scottish Highlands, and is 25 miles further south than Berwick-upon-Tweed.

At one time the main industries were fishing and distilling, but the fishing fleet has gone now, and only three distilleries remain of

Mains Cottages

The Steading, Carradale, Argyll PA28 6QG
Tel/Fax: 01583 431683 e-mail: cottages@wallishunter.co.uk
website: www.wallishunter.co.uk

With three superb self catering units, **Mains Cottages**, north of Saddell, make the ideal base from which to explore the Mull of Kintyre. They form part of the original home farm of Carradale House, with No 2 The Mains boasting two bedrooms, a spacious living room, a fully equipped kitchen and a bathroom. No 3 East and No 3 west are two studio cottages suitable for couples or singles, with a comfortable and cosy bed/sitting room each, an integral kitchen and a bathroom. The cottages are owned by Trish and Mike Hurst, who own a successful jewellery manufacturing studio next to them.

Torrisdale Castle

Torrisdale Castle, Carradale, Argyllshire PA28 6QT
Tel/Fax: 01583 431233
e-mail: machall@torrisdalecastle.com
website: www.torrisdalecastle.com

Torrisdale Castle, north of Saddell, is the ancestral home of the Macalister Hall family, and offers some of the best self catering holiday accommodation in Kintyre. Within the castle itself are three extremely comfortable and well appointed holiday flats, sleeping four, five and six. In the grounds there are also five cottages, which sleep between two and ten. All the cottages are well furnished and decorated, and have open fires. All the accommodation on the estate is cosy yet spacious, and all have a quiet charm that is sure to add to the enjoyment of a holiday among some of Scotland's most beautiful scenery.

Dunvalanree

Port Righ, Carradale, Kintyre, Argyllshire PA28 6SE
Tel: 01583 431226 e-mail: hps@dunvalanreee.com
Fax: 01583 431339 website: www.dunvalanreee.com

Dunvalanree in Carradale is a family run hotel that offers the very best in Scottish hospitality. This hotel whose advertising grab line is 'at the waters edge', is owned and managed by Alyson and Alan Milstead, and offers a variety of comfortable and attractive en-suite rooms, equipped to a high standard. There is a spacious dining room serving superb food and a guest lounge with wonderful sea views. Port Righ Cottage, behind the hotel, also offers superior self catering accommodation for two. Dunvalanree makes the ideal 'get away from it all' base from which you can explore the heritage and wildlife of this particularly attractive but little known part of Scotland.

Carradale Hotel

Carradale, Argyllshire PA28 6RY
Tel/Fax: 01583 431223
e mail: carradaleh@aol.com website: www.carradalehotel.com

Situated 12 miles north of Campbeltown within the small village of Carradale, the family run **Carradale Hotel** is a superb base from which to explore the Mull of Kintyre. It boasts twelve fully en suite rooms that are the last word in comfort and amenity, and the cuisine is out of this world. Come on a dinner, bed and breakfast rate or a bed and breakfast rate, and enjoy the very best of Scottish hospitality in an establishment that prides itself on the warmth of its welcome! The food is superb; the drink is wonderful in the relaxed atmosphere of the Carradale Hotel!

the 30 or so that once produced over two million gallons of whisky a year.

It sits on Campbeltown Loch, which is guarded by the small island of **Davaar**. Within a cave on the island is a famous painting of the Cruxifiction painted by local artist David MacKinnon in1887. The island can be reached on foot at low tide by a long shingle beach known as The Doirlinn. **Campbeltown Cross**, erected near the harbour, dates from the 14th century. It was used as the mercat cross after the town became a royal burgh. **Campbeltown Museum** has exhibits and artifacts dealing with the history of the area.

AROUND CAMPBELTOWN

SOUTHEND

8 miles S of Campbeltown on the B842

This is the most southerly village in Argyllshire. It was near here, at **Keil**, that St Columba is supposed to have first set foot on Scottish soil before sailing north towards Iona. In the ancient churchyard at Keil are footprints which are said to mark the spot. It was near here also that a massacre of 300 MacDonald clansmen took place in 1647.

SADDELL

8 miles N of Campbeltown on the B842

It was here, in 1148, that **Saddell Abbey** (Historic Scotland) was founded by Somerled, Lord of the Isles, and completed by his son Reginald, who also founded Iona Abbey and Nunnery. Only scant remains can now be seen, most notably the presbytery and the north transept. As at other places in Argyllshire, stone carving once flourished here, and no fewer than 11 beautiful graveslabs, each one showing a knight in full armour or a monk, can be seen. **Saddell Castle** (not open to the public) was built in 1508 for the Bishop of Argyll.

TARBERT

31 miles N of Campbeltown on the A83

This small fishing port sits at a point where Kintyre is no more than a mile wide. To the east is East Loch Tarbert, and to the west is

West Loch Tarbert, where, at **Kennacraig**, the ferries leave for Islay and Jura. In 1093 King Magnus Barelegs of Norway is said to have been dragged in his galley across the narrow ithsmus. **An Tairbeart**, to the south of the village, is a heritage centre that tells of the place's history and people.

North of the village is Stonefield Castle, now a hotel. Attached is **Stonefield Castle Garden**, which is open to the public. As with so many gardens in the area, it is famous for its rhododendrons. There are also plants from Chile and New Zealand, and conifers such as the sierra redwood.

Balinakill Country House Hotel

Clachan, near Tarbert,
Argyllshire PA29 6XL
Tel: 01880 740206 Fax: 01880 740298
e-mail: info@balinakill.com
website: www.balinakill.com

Balinakill Country House Hotel is a beautiful Victorian mansion dating from the 1890s. It is set in six acres of lush parkland on the Kintyre Peninsula, and has views across some of the most majestic and romantic scenery in Scotland towards Jura and Islay. Under the careful ownership of Susan and Angus Macdiarmid, it is now one of the best hotels in Argyllshire, and is furnished with beautiful antiques throughout. It has eleven extremely comfortable fully en suite rooms (with two on the ground floor), and every one has a character of its own. Some even have log fires! History is attached to the hotel as well. If you stay in Room 4, you'll be sleeping in the room where the late King Leopold Belgium once slept! All the rooms have central heating, colour TV, hair dryer, clock radio and tea and coffee making facilities.

The food, as you would expect, is excellent, with the kitchens using only the finest of local, free range and organic produce wherever possible. And to complement your meal, the hotel's wine list boasts many fine wines, all of which are competitively priced. The residents' sitting room is within the Oak Room, which has an enormous fireplace and comfy armchairs. Within the magnificent Drawing Room (which is non smoking) is a wide range of books, and there is also a Games Room with a variety of board games available. Kintyre is an area of great natural beauty which as yet has not been discovered by tourists, and is the ideal place for a relaxing yet invigorating holiday.

North Beachmore

Muasdale, near Tarbert, Argyllshire PA29 6XD
Tel: 01583 421328

North Beachmore is a restaurant which not only offers some of the best food in Argyllshire, it also offers great panoramic views. The kitchen is open plan, so you can also view the food being prepared! The dishes on the menu range from fresh salmon salad and marinated herrings to juicy steaks and roast turkey, and all are prepared by the owner Eileen McInnes from only the finest and freshest local produce wherever possible. Food is served from 12.00 to 21.00 daily, though so popular is the place that you should book for weekend dinners.

MUASDALE HOLIDAY PARK

Muasdale, Tarbert, Argyll PA29 6XD
Tel: 01583 421207 Fax: 01583 421137
e-mail: enquiries@muasdaleholidays.com
website: www.muasdaleholidays.com

Muasdale Holiday Park is on the west coast of the Kintyre peninsula, and has a superb view over the Atlantic Ocean. It offers quality holiday accommodation in 7 one, two and three bedroomed caravans, all of which are very comfortable and equipped to an extremely high standard. There is also a park for tourers, motor homes and tents, with electric hook ups, a washing up area and a toilet/shower block with continuous hot water. Also on offer is a self catering first floor apartment in an old stone built house, which has three bedrooms, lounge/diner, kitchen and bathroom.

Seven miles south of Tarbert is **Skipness Castle** (Historic Scotland), which dates originally from the 13th century. The first historical mention of it is in 1261 when it was owned by the McSweens, though it later came into the possession of Walter Stewart, Earl of Mentieth. It finally came into the possession of the Campbells, and was abandoned in the late 17th century, when a newer, more comfortable house was built close by. The ruins of **Kilbrannan Chapel**, near the foreshore, dates from the 13th century, and were dedicated to St Brendan. Five medieval graveslabs are to be found inside the chapel walls and in the kirkyard.

GLENBARR

10 miles NW of Campbeltown on the A83

At the **Clan Macalister Centre** in Glenbarr Abbey (not an abbey but a mansion house) are exhibits tracing the history of Clan Macalister as far back as Somerled, Lord of the Isles, nearly 900 years ago.

GIGHA

17 miles NW of Campbeltown off the west coast of Kintyre

This small island, no more than six miles long by two miles wide at its widest is reached by ferry from Tayinloan, and in 2001 was bought by its inhabitants. The name Gigha means "God's island", and it lives up to the name. More than one person has said that it seems to have a climate of its own, and while the rest of Argyllshire is enveloped in cloud, Gigha is bathed in sunshine. The Gulf Stream washes its shores, and it can easily be explored by bicycle. The 50 acre **Achamore Gardens**, near the ferry port at Ardminish, are open to the public. They were founded by Sir James Horlick, of bedtime drink fame, after he bought the island in 1944. They are famous for their rhododendrons and camellias.

LOCHGILPHEAD

Lochgilphead, as the name suggests, stands at the head of Loch Gilp, a small inlet of Loch Fyne. It is the main shopping centre for a wide area known as Knapdale, that portion of Argyllshire from which the long "arm" known as the Mull of Kintyre descends. It is an area steeped in history, and though it now seems to be on the edge of things, at one time it was at the crossroads of a great commucations network. Ireland was to the south west, the Hebrides were to the north, and the bulk of Scotland itself was to the east, and all could be easily reached by boat.

Kilmory Woodland Park, off the A83, surrounds Kimory Castle, which has been turned into offices for the local authority. The park contains many rare trees, plus a garden and woodland walks.

The **Crinan Canal** (known as "Scotland's most beautiful shortcut") starts at **Ardishaig**, a couple of miles south of Lochgiplhead, and skirts the town as it heads across the peninsula towards the village of Crinan on the west coast. In 1795 an act of Parliament had allowed the building of a canal between Lochs Gilp and Crinan, and work started in 1794. But the work was beset with problems, and it finally opened, albeit in an incomplete form, in 1801. By 1804 it still wasn't complete, and had debts of £140,000. Then, in 1805, some of the canal banks collapsed and had to be rebuilt. It was finally opened in 1809, though in 1815 Thomas Telford the civil engineer inspected it, and declared that even more work needed doing. In 1817 it reopened, this time to everyone's satisfaction. It is nine miles long, and has, in this short length, fifteen locks. In 1847 it got the royal seal of approval when Queen Victoria sailed its length as she was making a tour of the Highlands. Perhaps the most unusual craft to have used it were midget submarines during World War II.

AROUND LOCHGILPHEAD

DUNADD

4 miles N of Lochgilphead off the A816

Dunadd (Historic Scotland) is one of the most important historical sites in Scotland. This great rock rises from a flat area of land called Crinan Moss, and is where the ancient kingdom of **Dalriada** had its royal fort and capital. From here, its kings ruled a kingdom that took in all of modern day Argyllshire. It was founded by immigrants from Antrim in present day Northern Ireland in the 5th century, and gradually grew in importance. With them from Ireland they brought that great icon of Scottish nationhood, the Stone of Destiny (see also Scone and Edinburgh).

A climb to the top of Dunadd (which is quite difficult in parts) gives a wonderful view over the surrounding countryside, which is the reason the fort was established here in the first place. Parts of the fort's ramparts can still be seen, and near the top, on a flat outcrop of rock, are some carvings that may have been to do with the inauguration of the Dalriadan kings. There is the carving of a boar, a footprint, a bowl and some ogham writing.

The kings of Dalriada were special. In those days, kings were looked upon more as great tribal leaders and warriors than as men set apart to rule a kingdom. But one man changed all that - St Columba. His monastery on Iona was within Dalriada, and on that island he conducted what is recognised to be the first Christian coronation in Britain. No crowning ceremony took place - the kings were anointed instead. In AD574 he anointed Aidan king of the Dalriadans in a ceremony that relied on

Biblical precedents. It also contained an element that is still used in today's coronations, when the assembled crowds shouted out "God Save the King!" in unison. There is no doubt that Aidan sat on the Stone of Destiny during the ceremony.

Though it may now look austere and lonely, Dunadd, in its heyday, would have been a busy place, as excavations have shown that it traded with England and the Continent. The River Add, no more than a couple of feet deep, winds its way round the base of the rock before entering the sea at Loch Crinan. In olden days, before parts of Crinan Moss were drained for agriculture, it would have been navigable right up to the rock itself. Boats would have been tied up at the banks, with Dunadd itself bristling with stone and wood buildings. Soldiers guarded its entrance, and colourful pennants flew from the ramparts, especially if the king was in residence. At its base there would have been workshops for crafting jewellery, weapons and so on, plus a small township to house the king's retainers.

The other great kingdom north of the Rivers Forth and Clyde was the kingdom of the Picts, and for years it and Dalriada had traded, fought, mingled and intermarried. Eventually, in 843, because of this intermariage, Kenneth MacAlpin, king of Dalriada, inherited the throne of the Picts also. By this time the centres of power had moved to the west, so Kenneth MacAlpin set off towards Scone in Perthshire (taking the Stone of Destiny with him) and established his capital there. Thus was born the kingdom of Scotland, though it would be another 200 years before the kingdoms of the Lowlands - the Angles of the Lothians and the British of Strathclyde - were absorbed as well.

KILMICHAEL GLASSARY

4 miles N of Lochgilphead on a minor road off the A816

In common with many other kirkyards in this part of Argyllshire, the kirkyard of the 19th century **Parish Church** has a fine collection of carved medieval and later graveslabs.

KILMARTIN

8 miles N of Lochgilphead on the A816

The whole area surrounding the village of Kilmartin is said to be Scotland's richest prehistoric landscape. Within a six mile radius of the village over 150 prehistoric and 200 later monuments are to be found. The whole place is awash with standing stones, stone circles, cairns, henges, burial mounds, forts, crannogs, cup and ring carved stones, castles, carved graveslabs and crosses.

A church has stood in the village for centuries, though the present **Parish Church** was only built in 1835. Within it is a decorated cross that dates from about the 9th century, and within the kirkyard are three further crosses, dating also from the 9th century.

Also in the kirkyard is the finest collection of carved medieval graveslabs in Western Scotland. Most date from the 14th or 15th century, though there are some which might be older. They show knights in armour, swords, crosses and coats of arms.

But it is the prehistoric monuments that make Kilmartin so special. In a field behind the church is the **Glebe Cairn**, a round pile of stones that dates from about 1500-2000BC. It is the most northerly of five surviving cairns known as the linear cemetery, which stretches for a mile along the floor of Kilmartin Glen. The others are **Nether Largie North Cairn**, **Nether Largie Mid Cairn**, **Nether Largie South Cairn** and **Ri Cruin Cairn**. All are accessable by foot. In addition, there is the **Dunchraigaig Cairn**, just off the A816, which doesn't form part of the linear cemetery.

The **Temple Wood Circles**, south of Kilmartin, date from about 3500BC. There are two of them, with the northern one possibly being used as a solar observatory when agriculture was introduced into the area. Burials were introduced at a later date.

The **Nether Largie Standing Stones** are close to the Temple Wood Circle, and the **Ballymeanoch Standing Stones** are to the south of them. Of the seven stones, only six now survive in their original positions.

To the north of Kilmartin are the substantial ruins of **Carnassarie Castle** (Historic Scotland), dating from the 16th century. It was built for John Carswell, Bishop of the Isles, the man who translated Knox's Book of Common Order into Gaelic. It was the first book ever to be printed in the language.

If you find all these stone circles, cairns,

SEAFIELD FARM COTTAGES

Achnamara, near Lochgilphead, Argyllshire PA31 8PS
Tel/Fax: 01546 850274
e-mail: seafield3@aol.com
website: www.scotland2000.com/seafield

Seafield Farm Cottages are three warm and comfortable self catering holiday homes set around the shores of Loch Sween, with its glorious scenery and abundant wildlife. They sleep a maximum of four (plus cot) in two bedrooms and are very well equipped. The Byre and the Stable, VisitScotland four star cottages, have been converted from the stonebuilt farm steading. Each has a spacious lounge/dining room, a kitchen and a bathroom. Kirkland, three star chalet, has an enclosed garden and loch views. It has a lounge with woodburner, kitchen/diner and a shower room.All accommodation is non smoking and no dogs please. Home baking and willow basketmaking available.

GALLEY OF LORNE INN

Ardfern, Argyllshire PA31 8QN
Tel: 01852 500284
e-mail: galleyoflorne@aol.com

The **Galley of Lorne Inn** is a whitewashed, olde worlde inn situated overlooking picturesque Loch Craignish, a favourite haven for yachts and small boats. It was originally an early 18th century drover's inn, but is now a comfortable hostelry which brims with character and atmosphere. It's Galley Bar is a favourite haunt of yachtsmen and locals, and has low beams and plenty of old wood that speaks of history and continuity. In the winter months, a roaring log fire welcomes you, making it the ideal place to enjoy a quiet drink or a beautifully prepared bar lunch. A wide selection of beers, lagers, wines, soft drinks and spirits is available, with a range of single malt whiskies being ever popular. The restaurant is spacious and comfortable, and occupies the former stable yard, with glass doors opening on to a terrace above the waters of the loch.

Outstanding food is served in the restaurant area throughout the spring, summer and autumn, with local sea food featuring prominently in season. Only the best local produce is used in the kitchen wherever possible, with the vegetables being grown within a polytunnel in the gardens of the inn. The Galley of Lorne also offers seven comfortable and beautifully furnished rooms to discerning tourists, all on the ground floor and all fully en suite. It recently won a coveted Egon Ronay 'atmospheric pub' award - one which was richly deserved, as this is one of the best hostelries in an area of Argyllshire that is famed for its rugged scenery, history and its warm,welcoming people.

castles, carvings and burial mounds too much to take in, then you should visit the award winning **Kilmartin House Museum** next to the church in the village. Using maps, photographs, displays and artifacts it explains the whole chronology of the area, from about 7000BC right up until 1100AD.

Not explained, however, are the intriguing theories now being put forward that this part of Argyllshire was where the remnants of the **Knights Templar** settled when that monastic order of knights was brutally suppressed in 1307 by Pope Clement V and Philip IV of France. The many sites in the area which have 14th and 15th century graveslabs may be associated with them, and some of the carvings on them certainly show what seems to be Templar and Masonic symbolism (see also Kilmarie, Kilmichael Glassary and Kilmory). It is known that the Templars had accummulated a great amount of wealth, and it may have been that Pope Clement and Philip suppressed the order to lay their hands on it. But they never did. On the same day as the suppression, 18 galleys from the Templar's navy, based at La Rochelle, disappeared into oblivion.

Did they head for Argyllshire, knowing that the Scottish king, Robert the Bruce, had been excommunicated by the Pope, and that therefore Scotland was beyond the Pope's jurisdiction? Did they take the Templar treasure with them? Some respected people certainly think so. It is known that Edward I of England was constantly complaining that the Scots seemed to have money enough to fund the defence of their country - money that could not be accounted for. Did it come from the Templars? An even more intriguing theory has been put forward that the treasure was in the form of a great secret regarding Jesus, who either survived the cruxifiction or who had married Mary Magdalene, who had borne him children.

Whatever the truth, many books have been written linking this part of Argyllshire - and other parts of Scotland - with the Knights Templar (see also Rosslyn).

KILMORY

13 miles SW of Lochgiulphead on a minor road off the B8025

North of Kilmory, on the shores of Loch Sween, stands the bulky ruins of **Castle Sween**, mainland Scotland's oldest stone castle. It was started by one Suibhne, ancestor of the MacSweens, over 800 years ago, and in later years became a centre of craftsmanship and artistry. This is shown by the **Kilmory Scultpured Stones**, at the 700 year old Kilmory Knap chapel. There was a thriving settlement here in medieval times, and within the ruins of the chapel is a remarkable collection of carved stones collected from the kirkyard, some going back at least 1000 years. The symbols on them include men in armour, blacksmith's and woodworker's tools, swords and crosses. They probably all marked the graves of craftsmen and warriors associated with Castle Sween over the years.

The most spectacular stone is **MacMillan's Cross**, which dates from the 15th century. On one side it shows the Crucifixion, and on the other is a hunting scene. There is a Latin inscription which translates as "This is the cross of Alexander MacMillan". Across Loch Sween, on a small peninsula, is **Keils Chapel**, which has another fine collection of graveslabs.

KILMARIE

On the B8002 10 miles NW of Lochgilphead

If you take the B8002 a few miles north of Kilmartin, you will find youself on the Craignish Peninsula. Beyond the attractive village of **Ardfern**, a popular haven for yachtsmen, is **Kilmarie Old Parish Church**. This roofless ruin, dedicated to St Maelrubha, dates from the 13th century, and contains a wonderful collection of carved graveslabs dating from the 14th and 15th centuries.

INVERARAY

Standing on the western shores of Loch Fyne, Inveraray is a perfect example of a planned 18th century Scottish town. It was built in the mid 18th century when the 3rd Duke of Argyll decided to pull down his decaying castle and replace it with a new, more comfortable one which would reflect his importance in society. The original township stood between this old castle and the loch, so the duke decided to demolish it and built a new town to the immediate south. The result is an elegant royal burgh with wide streets and well proportioned, whitewashed houses. It is actually no bigger than a village, but so well planned is it that it has all the feel of a busy metropolis, and indeed in the summer months tourists flock to it, making it an extremely busy place.

Inveraray Castle

Inveraray Castle sits to the north, and is an elegant, four square stately home. With its four turreted towers - one at each corner of the building - it looks more like a grand French chateau than a typical Highland castle, but this was the intention. It was designed to tell the world that the Campbells, Dukes of Argyll, belonged to one of the most poweful families in the land. It was designed by Roger Morris and Robert Mylne, and contains a famous armoury, French tapestries, Scottish and European furniture, and a genealogy room that traces the history of Clan Campbell.

There are two churches within the town - the **Parish Church**, which dates from 1794, and the Episcopalian **Church of All Saints**. The Parish Church was designed by Robert Mylne, and is divided so that services can be held in both English and Gaelic, though this is seldom done nowadays. All Saints Church, which dates from 1886 has a bell tower with the second heaviest ring of ten bells in the world. Each bell is named after a saint, and has the name inscribed on it. Ringers can sometimes be watched in action, and visiting bellringers can have a go by appointment.

Being the main town for a large area, Inveraray was the place where justice was meted out. **Inveraray Jail** takes you on a trip through Scotland's penal system in the 1800s, and you can see what the living conditions were like in the cells that housed murderers, madmen and thieves. There are two prison blocks, one built in 1820, and one in 1848, which had more "enlightened" conditions. You can also see the branding irons, thumb screws and whips that passed for justice before the 18th century, and see what life is like in prison today. There is also a courtroom and tableau, complete with sound, which shows how a trial was conducted before a High Court judge.

Within the Arctic Penguin, a three masted schooner built in 1911, is the **Inveraray Maritime Museum**. Here the maritime history of Scotland's western seaboard is vividly brought to life. There's an on board cinema with an archive of old film, and people can see what conditions were like aboard a ship taking them to a new life in America. Two miles south of the town is the 60 acre **Argyll Wildlife Park**. Here you can walk along woodland paths and try to see such animals as fallow deer, badgers, foxes, wild goats and wallabies.

Inveraray

One of the area's most famous sons was **Neil Munro**, the writer and journalist who wrote the ever popular Para Handy books. On the A819 through Glen Aray towards Loch Awe is monument which commemorates him. It stands close to his birthplace at Carnus.

AROUND INVERARAY

CAIRNDOW

6 miles NE of Inveraray across the loch on the A83

This small village stands at the western end of Glen Kinglas, on the shores of Loch Fyne. Within the Arkinglas Estate is the 25 acre **Arkinglas Woodland Garden**. High annual rainfall, a mild climate and light, sandy soil have created the right conditions for coniferous species. The Callander family established the collection in about 1875, and it has seven champion trees that are either the tallest or widest in Britain. There is also one of the best collection of rhododendrons in the country.

At Clachan Farm, near Arkinglass, you'll find the **Clachan Farm Woodland Walks**, which allow you to see many species of native tree, such as oak, hazel and birch. The walks vary from a few hundred yards in length to one of two and a half miles.

ARROCHAR

13 miles E of Inveraray on the A83

Arrochar sits at the head of Loch Long. Two miles to the west is the small village of **Tarbet**, which sits on the shores of Loch Lomond, and it surprises people who don't know the area that Britain's largest sheet of fresh water is so close to the sea. From the jetty at Tarbet small ships offer cruises on the loch.

Some of Argyllshire's finest mountains are to be found close by, such as **Ben Narnain** (3,036 feet) and **Ben Ime** (3,318 feet). This area could fairly claim to be the homeland of Scottish mountaineering, as the first mountaineering club in the country, the Cobbler Club, was established here in 1865. The road westwards towards Inveraray climbs up past the 2,891 feet Ben Arthur, better known as **The Cobbler**, and over the wonderfully named **Rest and Be Thankful** above Glen Croe until it drops down again through Glen Kinglas to the shores of Loch Fyne. It is a wonderful drive, with the floor of Glen Croe being several hundred feet below the road at some points.

Near the Jubileee Well in Arrochar you can gain access to the **Cruach Tairbeirt Walks**. These footpaths (totalling just over a mile and a half in length) give some wonderful views over Loch Lomond and Loch Long. Though well surfaced, in some places the paths are quite steep.

AUCHINDRAIN

5 miles S of Inveraray on the A83

Auchindrain Township is an original West Highland village which has been brought back to life as an outdoor museum and interpretation centre. Once common throughout the Highlands, many of these settlements were abandoned at the time of the Clearances, while others were abandoned as people headed for the cities to find work. Queen Victoria visited Auchindrain when it was inhabited, and now you can see what she saw. Most of the cottages and other buildings have been restored and furnished to explain the living conditions of the Highlanders in past centuries. The visitor centre also has displays on West Highland life, showing many of the farming and household implements.

STRACHUR

4 miles S of Inveraray across the loch on the A815

Strachur sits on the shores of Long Fyne, on the opposite bank from Inveraray. **Strachur Smithy** has now been restored as a small museum and and craft shop, and has some original tools and implements used by blacksmiths and farriers. **Lachlan Castle**, ancestral home of the MacLachlans, lies six miles south of Strachur, on the B8000. You are now on the Cowal Peninsula, and if you continue along the B8000, you will eventually arrive at a turn off to the right for **Portavadie**, where the Portavadie-Tarbert ferry will take you onto the Mull of Kintyre (summer only). Turn left at the same junction and head north again, passing through **Tighnabruaich** on the Kyles of Bute, and you will arrive at **Glendaruael**. The road hugs the shoreline most of the way, and gives some wonderful views of sea and hill.

CRARAE

10 miles S of Inveraray on the A83

Crarae Garden is one of the finest woodland gardens in Scotland. Rare trees and exotic shrubs thrive in the mild climate, and over 400 species of rhododendron and azeleas

Kames Hotel

Kames, by Tighnabruaich,
Argyllshire PA21 2AF
Tel: 01700 811489 Fax: 01700 811283
e-mail: Kameshotel@aol.com
website: www.Kames-hotel.com

By the beautiful shores of the Kyles of Bute you'll find one of the best family run hotels in Argyllshire, the **Kames Hotel**. With 10 en suite rooms, it offers the very best in Scottish hospitality and comfort. Owned and run by Margo and Tom Andrew and their son Colin, it is the perfect spot for relaxed, carefree holidays or participating in sports such as golf, fishing, walking, sailing, windsurfing and seasonal rough and game bird shooting. Traditional fare is served in the cosy bars or in the elegant dining room which is open to residents and non residents alike. Seafood and venison are local specialities and Kames Hotel prides itself in the quality of its fish and game menu selections

Tom is proud of his fine selection of malts and real ales, and an evening in one of the friendly bars over a dram and listening to live music – both planned and impromptu – makes the perfect ending to a day among the wonderful scenery of the West Highlands!

Ballivicar Farm

Port Ellen, Isle of Islay PA42 7AW
Tel/Fax: 01496 302251
e-mail: ballivicar@tinyworld.co.uk
website: www.ileach.co.uk/ballivicar

Ballivicar Farm is a traditional working farm with cattle, sheep and horses on the beautiful island of Islay, and sits at the heart of 250 acres of land. It is within a few miles of the island's airstrip, and within one mile of the Port Ellen Ferry Terminal which links with Kennacriag near Tarbert on the mainland. It offers three spacious and extremely comfortable self catering apartments that are sure to please the discerning tourist. There is one large apartment ("The Chougherie") which can sleep four to six people in two bedrooms, plus two smaller one bedroomed apartments ("The Bothy" and "The Hayloft") that sleep two to four.

All have fully equipped kitchens, with hob, oven and microwave, as well as bathrooms and living areas with colour TVs. Extra beds can be hired, and a charge for electricity is not included in the price. The apartments are open all year round, and winter rates are available on request. All three apartments have a two star rating from VisitScotland, and have full central heating throughout. At Port Ellen you will find grocery shops and a post office, and most of the island's famous distilleries are easily reached by car, which can easily be hired. The farm also offers pony trekking, and both beginners and experienced riders are welcome. You can ride among the hills or on the wide, sandy beaches on the sturdy Highland ponies, and experienced riders can enjoy longer rides with a possible stop over at a suitable hostelry. Jumping practice and games on horseback can also be arranged.

Crarae Gardens

provide a colourful display in spring and summer, with the fine collection of deciduous trees adding colour and fire to autumn. There are sheltered woodland walks and a spectacular gorge. The Scottish Clan Garden features a selection of plants associated with various Argyllshire clans.

ISLAY

33 miles W of Dunoon in the Atlantic Ocean

Clan Donald made Islay the centre of their vast Lordship of the Isles, which at one time was almost a separate kingdom, beyond the reach of Scottish monarchs. It is a truly beautiful island, with a range of hills to the east, which reach 1500 feet in height, and low, fertile farmland. It is famous for its distilleries, with over four million gallons of whisky being produced each year. Most of the distilleries have tours explaining the distilling process, and offer a dram at the end of it. An Islay malt has a taste all of its own, as it has a peaty flavour, due to the grain being dried over peat fires.

On islands in **Loch Finlaggan**, west of **Port Askaig** (where there is a ferry to both Feolin

THE BOWMORE HOTEL

Jamieson Street, Bowmore, Isle of Islay PA43 7HL
Tel: 01496 810416 Fax: 01496 810110
e-mail: reception@bowmorehotel.co.uk
www. bowmorehotel.co.uk

If it's comfortable and spacious accommodation, friendly service and good food and drink you are after on the beautiful island of Islay, then the family-run **Bowmore Hotel** is for you. It has nine guest rooms, four of which are en suite, and all have colour TVs and tea and coffee making facilities. Owned and managed by Linda and Peter MacLellan and their son, it comes highly recommended by those who have stayed there in the past. The friendly, cosy bar offers a wide range of drinks, including lager, beer, cider, wine, liqueurs and a good range of single malt whiskies. Soft drinks are also available should you be driving. This is the ideal place to relax and unwind after exploring an island that is rich in wonderful scenery, wildlife and history.

The food is outstanding, and makes good use of fresh, local produce wherever possible. In fact, so good is it that you are well advised to book a table beforehand. The Bowmore's own traditional steak pie is a firm favourite with visitors and locals alike. The hotel has a great reputation for its seafood and curries, and Linda makes all the pasta and lasagna that is on offer. You can choose from a menu that contains many fine dishes such as Loch Fyne mussels in garlic, juicy steaks with all the trimmings, shellfish cream and brandy stew, salmon steak with ginger prawns, and many more. You can also choose from a daily specials board. The wine list is comprehensive, and is sure to contain something that will complement your meal perfectly. Dinners are served up until 21.00, though later times can be arranged, and the full Scottish breakfasts, which are hearty and filling, are served between 7.30 and 10.00. Lunches are not generally served, though soup, toasties and sandwiches are always available.

THE ISLAY WHISKY CLUB

Shore Street, Bowmore, Isle of Islay PA 43 7LB
Tel: 01496 810324 Fax: 01496 810764
e-mail: info@islaywhiskyclub.com
website: www.islaywhiskyclub.com

The **Islay Whisky Club** can be found in an elegant Victorian clubhouse in the heart of Bowmore - the centre of Islay. Built in the late 1800's, the building retains its original Victorian features and has been completely refurbished to a high standard offering visiting club members a relaxing and intimate ambience to enjoy the company of fellow Islay Single Malt Whisky lovers. The Bar Lounge offers an extensive range of Islay Single Malt Whisky as well as draught beer and a selection of special cigars to have with your whisky. Light refreshments are also available during the day for members. The lounge and non-smoking lounge are tastefully furnished to a high standard offering members a relaxing and comfortable area to enjoy the benefits of this club. Day membership is available (at the discretion of the President).

The Boutique is open to non club members and children are welcome. It carries a vast range of whisky related gifts, souvenirs, games, toys, clothing and Single Malts. Islay's distilleries will have a selection of their branded merchandise on display. Perhaps you would like a kilt made for you in the Islay Whisky Club Tartan? This unique tartan has been specially designed for the club and can be purchased in lengths or we can arrange for the cloth to be made into a kilt (subject to availablility). More information can be found on the website. Major credit cards are accepted.

Spacious bedrooms with en-suite facilities are available to full members on an overnight B&B basis. A warm welcome awaits you at The Islay Whisky Club.

Ferry on Jura and Tarbert on the Mull of Kintyre) you will find the ruins of the medieval centre of the Lordship of the Isles, with a visitor centre close by. There are ancient burial slabs here as well, thought to mark the graves of women and children, as the chiefs would have been buried on Iona. At Port Askaig itself are the **Bunnahabhain** and the **Caol Ila** distilleries.

Bowmore Round Church

To the east of **Port Ellen** (which also has a ferry to Tarbert) you can visit the distilleries of **Lagavulin** and **Ardbeg**. Near Lagavulin, are the ruins of **Dunyveg Castle**, a MacDonald stronghold. At one time it was owned by a man called Coll Ciotach, or "left handed Coll". While he was away on business, the castle was captured by his enemies, and his men taken prisoner. They then waited for Coll to return so that they could overpower him. But one of the prisoners was Coll's personal piper, and he alerted his master by playing a warning tune. Coll escaped, but the piper had his right hand cut off, and never again could he play the pipes.

At Ardbeg is the **Kildalton Cross and Chapel**. The incised cross dates from the 9th century, and is one of the finest in Scotland. Keeping on a religious theme, **Bowmore**, on the A874 beside the shores of Loch Indaal, has one of only two round churches in Scotland. It was built in 1767 by Daniel Campbell, and,

Coullabus Keeper's Cottage

Newton House, Bridgend,
Isle of Islay PA44 7PO
Tel and Fax: 01496 810293
e-mail: newtonhouse@isle-of-islay.com
website: www.isle-of-islay.com

Coullabus Keeper's Cottage is a completely modernised and refurbished cottage that sleeps six people in three bedrooms – one double and two twins. It has been tastefully decorated and furnished throughout, and offers the ideal accommodation for a self catering holiday on the beautiful island of Islay that can be as relaxing or as energetic as you wish. As well as the three bedrooms, there is a large entrance hall, a spacious sitting room with colour TV, a dining room, a bathroom and separate shower room and a fully equipped kitchen. This comes complete with electric cooker, fridge, washing machine and dish washer. All crockery, cutlery, glasses and cooking utensils are also supplied. The place is centrally heated throughout, so is the ideal location for a winter break, and there is an immersion heater.

As an added attraction there is an open fire in the sitting room where local peat or coal can be burned in the evenings. All bed linen and towels are supplied, and a cot is available if required. Pets are very welcome. The cottage lies only five minutes walk from the Loch Gruinart Reserve, where barnacle and white fronted geese can be observed between October and April. Islay is also home to a great array of wildlife, including eagles, choughs, otters and deer. It is an island steeped in history, and a short ferry crossing takes you to the lovely island of Jura to the north. There's no doubting that Coullabus Keeper's Cottage offers the very best in self catering accommodation on an island that just cries out to be explored!

Kilchoman House Cottages

Kilchoman, by Bruichladdich, Isle of Islay PA49 7UY
Tel: 01496 850382 Fax: 01496 850277
e-mail: ian@kilchoman.demon.co.uk website: www.kilchomancottages.co.uk

Kilchoman House Cottages are situated at one of the most beautiful locations on the beautiful island of Islay. They are on the Atlantic side of the island, surrounded by grassy areas where children can run about to their heart's content in absolute safety. Close by is Kilchoman Beach, plus secluded bays, dramatic cliffs and wonderful walking country. This is an area where fulmar, chough and wild goats are to be found, and where golden eagles are regular visitors. There are six cottages in all – Choughshiew, Glebe, Crags Lea, Byresend, Fieldgate and Shepherd's Cottage, with the first four having two bedrooms and the other two having three. Each one has a four star rating from VisitScotland, and is comfortable and beautifully decorated, with a homely, relaxing atmosphere.

There is central heating throughout, and double glazing has been installed. Downstairs there is a spacious open plan dining/living area and a well equipped kitchen (gas hob, electric oven, microwave and fridge with small freezer), with bedrooms and bathroom upstairs. The living areas all have colour TVs, and the cost of electricity is included in the overall charge. Although the cottages have been designed for four to six people, fold down beds are sometimes available for a nominal fee of £10. All bed linen, tea towels, kitchen towels and bath mats are supplied, and personal towels are available on request, though they must not be used for sea bathing. As the cottages are surrounded by fields where sheep and cattle graze, the number of dogs on the site is restricted, and there is a £15 charge for each animal.

OCTOMORE COTTAGE

Port Charlotte, Isle of Islay PA48 7UA
Tel: 01496 850235

Octomore Cottage is a renovated, traditional cottage close to Port Charlotte on the beautiful island of Islay. It overlooks Loch Indaal, and has some wonderful sweeping views of sea and low hills. The cottage is a picturesque, whitewashed building set sturdily on a low hillside above the village, and is extremely comfortable and cosy, with off peak central heating throughout. There are three bedrooms – two spacious twin rooms and a bunk bedroom, and all are tastefully decorated and furnished to an extremely high standard. There is also a large, carpeted lounge/ dining area with an open fireplace, and it comes complete with colour TV and comfortable furniture – just right for relaxing in after a hard day's sightseeing! The fully equipped kitchen has a fridge, washing machine, cooker, crockery, glasses, cutlery and cooking utensils. The shower room also has a wash hand basin and a wc. Lettings in this quality self catering cottage run from 15.00 on Saturday afternoon to 10.00 on the following Saturday morning, and all linen is included in the cost, though visitors must bring their own towels. The cottage comes complete with garden chairs, a barbecue and plenty of parking space. The summer evenings are long, still and clear on Islay, and there is nothing finer than sitting outside and watching the world go by!

Port Charlotte itself is a short walk away, and boasts two hotels with friendly bars and the Croft Kitchen, which all provide meals should you wish to eat out. There is also a Spar shop for groceries, an award winning museum and the Islay Field Centre. Bicycles are available for hire, and with these you can get "off the beaten track" and explore the surrounding countryside, which is truly beautiful. Further afield there is the village of Bowmore, with its round church and a sports centre with swimming pool, gym and sauna. The village also has one of the island's working distilleries, and, like the others, conducted tours are available, with a small refreshment laid on at the end of it.

The island is famous for its wildlife, and the RSPB reserve at Gruinart is the place to see barnacle and Greenland white fronted geese, which visit the island in great numbers every year. Other activities include walking, scuba diving (the waters around Islay are clean and clear) pony trekking and fishing, and at Machrie, near the airport, a golf course has been laid out. The island is connected to Jura by a modern ferry, so that lovely island can be explored as well.

Octomore Cottage is the perfect base for a holiday which can be as relaxing or as hectic as you like. Its owners, Sheila and James Brown, take a great pride in the amenities it offers to the discerning tourist, and will offer you a warm Scottish welcome should you decide to stay there!

LORGBA HOLIDAY COTTAGES

Port Charlotte, Isle of Islay, PA48 7UD
Tel/Fax: 01496 850208

For that special holiday you've always promised yourself, there is nowhere better than the beautiful Isle of Islay. And on the island you will discover **Lorgba Holiday Cottages**, which offers some of the best self catering accommodation around. They close to a beautiful sandy bay no more than five minutes from the village of Port Charlotte, where you will find a general store, post office, hotel and garage. It is truly an idyllic spot, enhanced by the quality of the accommodation on offer. There are five cottages, each one comfortable, spacious and spotlessly clean. The Creag sleeps two people, and comprises a sitting room with two divans, a kitchen/dining room and a bathroom. A patio door leads from the sitting room onto a lawn above the beach.

Mara and Cladach sleep up to four people each, and have a sitting room with divans, a twin bedroom, a kitchen/dining room and a bathroom. Carraig cottages are set apart from the other cottages, and have a sweeping lawn in front with uninterrupted views of the sea. Each one has two bedrooms (a double and a twin) a sitting room, a kitchen/diner and a bathroom. All the cottages are extremely well appointed, and have ample parking. There are open fires in the sitting room – just right for relaxing in front of after a hard day's sightseeing, with perhaps a glass of Islay malt in your hand! For those who appreciate the freedom of an island holiday and the simple pleasures of beachcombing, bird watching or fishing, or more hectic activities such as wind surfing, pony trekking or cycling, then the Lorgba Holiday Cottages are for you!

having no corners, the devil could not hide anywhere within it. **Bowmore Distillery** - one of the most famous on the island - can be visited, and on the opposite shore of the loch is the **Bruichladdich Distillery**, which recently went back into production.

Port Charlotte, also on Loch Indaal, is home to the **Islay Natural History Trust**. It has a wildlife information centre, and provides information on the natural history and wildlife of Islay. Also in the village is the **Museum of Islay Life**, which tells of everyday life on the island through the ages. Continue past Port Charlotte on the A874 and you will come to **Portnahaven**. About four miles from the village, on moorland, is the **Cultoon Stone Circle**. Not all the stones have survived, but three are still standing and twelve have fallen over at the point where they once stood.

JURA

34 miles W of Dunoon in the Atlantic Ocean

Jura is an island of peat bog, mists and and mountains, notably the **Paps of Jura**, to the south. The highest mountain in the range is **Ben an Oir**, at over 2,500 feet, though **Ben Shaintaidh** and **Ben a' Chaolais** aren't far behind.

The island's only road takes you from **Feolin Ferry**, where there is a ferry to Islay, north along the east coast, where all of the island's population lives. You will pass **Jura House Garden**, with its collection of Australian and New Zealand plants. They thrive in this mild and virtually frost and snow free environment. **Craighouse**, with its distillery, is the island's capital. Behind the Parish Church is a room with some old photographs of life on Jura through the ages. A mile or so north of the village is the ruined **Chapel of St Earnadail**. St Earnadail was a disciple of St Columba, and the story goes that he wanted to be buried on Jura when he died. When asked where on the island, he is reputed to have said that a cloud of mist would guide the mourners to the right spot.

The road then takes you north to **Ardlussa**, where it peters out. Within the old burial ground is the tombstone of **Mary MacCrain**, who dies in 1856 aged 128. They were long lived in Jura, for the stone goes on to say that she was a descendant of Gillouir MacCrain, *"who kept one hundred and eighty Christmases in*

Craighouse, Jura

his own house, and died during the reign of Charles 1".

Off the north coast of the island, between it and Scarba, is the notorious **Corrvrekkan** whirlpool. The name comes from the Gaelic Coire Bhreacain, meaning "speckled cauldron", and it is best viewed from the safety of the cliff tops on Jura - even though you have to walk about three miles to get there - as it has sent many boats to the bottom in its time. It is caused by a tidal race, and the best time to see it is when a spring tide is running westward against a west wind. The sound of it can sometimes be heard at Ardfern on the mainland, over seven miles away.

The whirlpool's name, according to legend, has a different derivation. A Norwegian prince called Breachkan visited the Scottish islands, and fell in love with a princess, a daughter of the Lord of the Isles. Her father disapproved, but allowed the two of them to marry, providing Breachkan could moor his galley in the whirlpool for three days.

The Prince agreed to the challenge, and had three cables made, one of hemp, one of wool and and one from the hair of innocent women. He then sailed to Corryvrekkan, and while there was a slack tide, moored his boat in the whirlpool. The tides changed, and the whirlpool became a raging monster. The hemp cable snapped on the first day and the wool one snapped on the second. But Breachkan wasn't worried, for he knew that the one made from the hair of innocent women would keep him safe.

But on the third day it too snapped, sending the prince to his death. It seems that some of the hair had come from a woman who wasn't innocent, and it was her strands that snapped first.

OBAN

Seeing Oban nowadays, it is hard to imagine that in the18th century it was no more than village, with a handful of cottages built round a small bay. It got its burgh charter in 1820, but even then it was an unimportant place. With the coming of the railway in 1880, the town blossomed as people discovered its charms. Great Victorian and Edwardian villas were built by prosperous Glasgow merchants, and local people began to cater for holidaymakers.

Now it is the capital of the Western Highlands, and is known as the "Gateway to the Western Isles". It has two cathedrals, the

AVORIAZ

Duncraggan Road, Oban, Argyllshire PA34 5DU
Tel: 01631 562054
e-mail: janetavoriaz@hotmail.com
website: www.obanbandb.co.uk

With superb views out over Oban and its harbour to the islands beyond, **Avoriaz** is one of the best B&B establishments in this lovely and historic town. Owned and managed by Janet Orr, it offers a real home from home feel, and has three fully en suite bedrooms that are both comfortable and spacious. There is a lovely guests' lounge that is cosy and inviting, and an outside deck/balcony where you can relax after a hard day's sight seeing! The full Scottish breakfasts are beautifully cooked, filling and hearty, and Janet can direct you to many fine eating places that serve tasty lunches and dinners.

MARKIE DANS

Victoria Crescent, Corran Esplanade, Oban, Argyllshire PA34 5PN
Tel: 01631 564448 Fax: 01631 566854
e-mail: markiedan@aol.com
website: www.corranhouse.co.uk

Situated on the edge of Oban's town centre, **Markie Dans** is a superior old pub that dates back at least 120 years. Under the careful ownership of Susan and Roddy Scott, it has been tastefully refurbished in traditional style, so that it offers a comfortable and cosy place to enjoy a quiet drink or good, honest pub grub that is always beautifully cooked and presented. There is also a good selection of real ales, plus a fine range of beers, lagers, wines and spirits. Food is served daily from 11.00 - 21.00 in the high season, and from 17.00-20.30 out of season.

GALLANACH

by Oban, Argyllshire PA34 4QL
Tel/Fax: 01631 571041
e-mail: gallanach@aol.com
website: www.obanholdings.co.uk

Gallanach is a family run Highland estate owned by the MacDougalls of Gallanach for over 300 years.

Now the house offers excellent and comfortable self catering holiday accommodation within what was the staff quarters. It consists of a sitting/dining room (with TV, video and CD player), one double and three twin bedrooms, a wc, a fully equipped kitchen and a bath-room. The place is beautifully decorated and furnished, and linen is provided.

This the ideal spot for a relaxing holiday among some of the most spectacular scenery in Scotland, while still being close to all the amenities of Oban, the 'Gateway to the Islands'.

Roman Catholic **Cathedral of St Columba**, a 20th century granite building, and the Episopalian **Cathedral Church of St John the Divine**, built in the 19th century. Dominating the town is **McCaig's Folly**, a vast colosseum of a building that was begun in 1897. To call it a folly is a misnomer, because the man who built it, Oban banker John Stuart McCaig, wanted to establish a museum and art gallery inside it, but he died before it was completed. As the town had a lot of unemployed people at the time, he also wanted to create work for them. In his will he left money for a series of large statues of himself and his family around the parapet, but these were never built.

Oban Harbour

The oldest building in Oban is **Dunollie Castle**, the ruins of which can be seen on the northern outskirts of the town beyond the Corran Esplanade. It was built on a site that has been fortified since the Dark Ages, and was a MacDougall stronghold. The pier at Oban is where most of the ferries leave for the Western Isles. You can go from here to Lismore, Mull, Coll, Tiree, Colonsay, Barra and South Uist, and some time just watching the large, graceful ferries come and go is time well spent.

Near the old pier is the award winning **A World in Miniature** exhibition, which has sixty minute tableaux filled with miniature objects of furniture and furnishings, all hand

WIDE MOUTHED FROG

Dunstaffnage Marina, Connel, near Oban, Argyllshire PA37 1PX
Tel: 01631 567055 Fax: 01631 571047
website: www.widemouthedfrog.co.uk

Situated on the shores of the marina at Dunstaffnage, the **Wide Mouthed Frog** is a warm and welcoming inn that offers the very best in Scottish hospitality. It is full of genuine character and charm, and is owned and managed by Linda and Stuart Byron, who like to refer to the inn as a 'restaurant with rooms'. This is a fair description of the hostelry. It has seven lovely rooms, one family, three twin and three double, and all are smart, spotlessly clean, comfortable and fully en suite, with TVs and tea and coffee making facilities. The cosy and inviting bar serves a full range of beers, lagers, spirits, wines, and should you be driving, soft drinks. In the summer months there is nothing better than sitting outside, glass in hand, admiring the view or watching the boats and yachts in the marina. Both Linda and Stuart share a passion for good quality seafood, and this is reflected in the establishment's cuisine.

The menus change weekly, and are well balanced, with all the dishes combining exceptionally high standards of cooking and amazing value for money. The fish and shellfish used in the dishes are as fresh as possible, and were more than likely caught that very day! But you can also order dishes based on game or beef, and again only the finest local produce is used wherever possible. The cuisine has definite Mediterranean influences, and this, combined with the Scottish produce, ensures that the dishes are always beautifully cooked and extremely tasty. Dunstaffnage is an idyllic spot, with an old, romantic castle nearby that saw many stirring episodes in Scottish history. Linda and Stuart have great plans for the Wide Mouthed Frog, and this, combined with its stunning setting, should make it even more popular as a base from which to explore this part of Argyllshire, or as a place to have a meal or a quiet drink.

made by craftsmen. There are even miniatures of well known paintings, all faithfully copied and hanging on the walls.

The **Oban Distillery** in Stafford Street produces a whisky that is one of the six "classic malts" of Scotland, and has tours showing the distillery at work. The whisky is a lightly peated malt, and the tour includes a free dram. **Armaddy Castle Garden** is another of the local gardens that benefit from the area's mild climate. It lies eight miles south of Oban, off the B844 road for Seil Island.

Sheltering Oban Bay is the small rocky island of **Kerrera**, which can be reached by passenger ferry from a point about two miles south of Oban. At the south end of the island are the ruins of **Gylen Castle**, another former MacDougall stronghold.

The **Connel Bridge** straddles the entrance to Loch Etive, about four miles north east of Oban, and at one time was a railway bridge. The entrance to this sea loch is very shallow, so watch out for the **Falls of Lora** beneath the bridge, especially as the tide is ebbing. The water pours over a cataract out of Loch Etive and back into the Firth of Lorne. Just south of Barcaldine, a few miles north of the bridge, is the **Oban Seal and Marine Centre**. It is Scotland's leading marine animal rescue centre, and it looks after dozens of seal pups that have been injured or orphaned before returning them back into the wild.

AROUND OBAN

DUNSTAFFNAGE

3 miles N of Oban off the A85

On a promentary sticking out into Ardmuchnish Bay, on the Firth of Lorne, is the substantial **Dunnstaffnage Castle** (Historic Scotland). Seen from the east, it has a glorious setting, with the island of Lismore behind it, and beyond that the hills of Morvern. It was originally built in the 13th century by Ewan MacDougall on the site of an important Dalriadan fort and settlement, though the castle as seen today dates from all periods up to the 19th century.

In 1309 the castle fell into the hands of Robert the Bruce, and he gave it to the Stewarts. In 1470 Colin Campbell, the first Earl of Argyll, was created hereditary Captain, or keeper of Dunstaffnage. In 1363 a dark deed was carried out here. The then Stewart owner was set upon outside the castle and murdered by a band of MacDougalls, who still considered the castle theirs. The band then attacked the castle, and it fell into their hands once more. A few months later a force of men sent by David II retook it.

The castle's resident ghost is called the **Ell Maid**, and sometimes on stormy nights she can be heard wandering through the ruins, her footsteps clanging off the stone as if she were wearing armour. If she is heard laughing, it means that there will be good news for the castle. If she shrieks and sobs, it means exactly the opposite.

Dunstaffnage Chapel sits outside the castle, and also dates from the 13th century. It is unusual in that chapels were usually within the defensive walls of a castle. A small burial aisle for the Campbells of Dunstaffnage forms an eastern extension.

KINLOCHLAICH GARDENS

11 miles N of Oban on the A828

This old walled garden was created in 1790 by

John Campbell. It sits on the shores of Loch Linnhe, in an area known as Appin, and it has one of Scotland's largest plant and nursery centres.

ARDCHATTAN

8 miles NE of Oban on a minor road on the north shore of Loch Etive

Archchattan Priory (Historic Scotland) was built in the 13th century by Duncan McDougall for the Valliscauliain order of monks. The ruins of the priory church can still be seen, though the rest of the monastic buildings was incorporated into Ardchattan House in the 17th century by John Campbell, who took over the priory at the Reformation. **Ardchattan Priory Garden** is open to the public, and has herbaceous borders, roses, a rockery and a wild flower meadow.

TAYNUILT

9 miles E of Oban on the A85

Taynuilt lies close to Ben Cruachan. Nearby, close to Inverawe, is the **Bonawe Furnace**, which dates from 1753. Ironworking was carried out here for over 100 years, and the furnace made many of the cannonballs used by Nelson. In 1805 the workers erected a statue to Nelson, the first in Britain, and it can still be seen today near Muchairn Church.

At Barguillean Farm you will find **Barguillean's Angus Garden**, established in 1957. It extends to nine acres, and is on the shores of Loch Angus. It was created in memory of Angus Macdonald, a journalist who was killed in Cyprus in 1956.

LOCH AWE

16 miles E of Oban on the A85

If you take the road east from Dunstaffnage Castle, passing near the shores of Loch Etive and going through the Pass of Brander, you will come to Scotland's longest loch, Loch Awe. This is its northern shore, and it snakes south west for a distance of nearly twenty five and a half miles until it almost reaches Kilmartin. Near the village of Lochawe are the impressive ruins of **Kilchurn Castle** (Historic Scotland), right on the shores of the loch. It was home to a cadet branch of the Campbells who eventually became the Earls of Breadalbane, and was originally built in the

15th century, though what you see now dates from later periods as well.

St Conan's Kirk, also on the banks of the loch, is reckoned to be one of the most beautiful churches in Scotland, though it dates only from the 1880s, with later additions. It was built by Walter Douglas Campbell, brother to the Earl of Breadalbane, who had built a mansion house nearby. Not only did he commission it, he designed it and did some of the woodwork as well. But this original church was small, so in 1907 Walter began extending it, though he died in 1914, before it was finished. World War I interrupted its completion, and it was finally finished in its present state in 1930. It has a superb chancel, an ambulatory, a nave with a south aisle, various chapels, and, curiously for a small church, cloisters.

The waters of Loch Cruachan, high on Ben Cruachan above Loch Awe have been harnessed for one of the most ambitious hydro electric schemes in Scotland. Not only does the **Cruachan Power Station** produce electricy from the waters of Loch Cruachan as they fall through pipes towards its turbines and then into Loch Awe; it can actually pump 120 tons of water a second back up the pipes towards Loch Cruachan by putting its turbines into reverse. This it does during the night, using the excess electricity produced by conventional power stations. In this way, power is stored so that it can be released when demand is high, and it was the first station in the world to use the technology. Now it is used all over the world.

The turbine halls are in huge artificial caves beneath the mountain, and tours are available taking you round one of the wonders of civil engineering in Scotland - one that can produce enough electricity to supply a city the size of Edinburgh.

KILMELFORD

11 miles S of Oban on the A816

To the west of this little village, near the shores of Loch Melfort, there was once a gunpowder mill, one of the many small industries which at one time dotted Argyllshire. In the kirkyard of the small **Parish Church** of 1785 are some gravestones marking the burial spots of people killed while making the "black porridge".

ELERAIG HIGHLAND LODGES

Kilninver, by Oban, Argyllshire PA34 4UX
Tel/Fax: 01852 200225
e-mail: robingrey@eleraig.co.uk
website:www.scotland2000.com/eleraig

Eleraig Highland Lodges are situated in a private glen in Argyllshire, close to lovely Loch Tralaig and some of the most magnificent scenery in Scotland. Warmed by the Gulf Stream, which ensures that palm trees flourish in some areas of Argyllshire, they are ideal for a holiday which can be as relaxing or adventurous as you wish. All the chalets, no matter the size, are extremely comfortable, and designed and built to exacting Scandinavian standards, with double glazing and insulation to ensure year round warmth. There are seven models to choose from, sleeping from four to eight people, depending on the model.

Cruachan overlooks Loch Tralaig, and sleeps six in three bedrooms - one double and two with bunk beds. It has a living room, a dining/kitchen area and a bathroom. Etive sits at the foot of a wooded slope, and offers the same layout. Feochan sleeps up to six in two bedrooms - one twin bedded and the other one with bunks. The living/dining room has a double sofa bed, and there is an open plan kitchen. Tralaig faces a wooded hill, and sleeps up to six in three bedrooms, one of which has a double bed, with the other two having bunk beds. There is an open plan kitchen and a living/dining area. Lorne, next to Tralaig, sleeps four in two bedrooms - one with a double bed and the other with bunk beds. It also has a living/dining area and an open plan kitchen. Clotteraig, sitting in a meadow, sleeps eight. It has three bedrooms (one with twin beds and two with bunk beds), plus an open plan kitchen and a living room/dining area with an additional double sofa bed. Oude looks down to the river Oude, and sleeps six in three bedrooms - one with a double bed and two with bunk beds. There is also a living/dining area and a kitchen.

All the lodges are carpeted throughout, and have integral bathrooms, with a full sized bath, a shower, wash basin, wc and shaver point. The kitchens are exceedingly well appointed, with cooker, fridge with freezer compartment, microwave, toaster, kettle and all cutlery, crockery, glassware and cooking utensils. The bunk beds are full-sized and comfortable, and all linen (duvets, covers, pillows, bed-linen, blankets, tea towel and oven cloth) is included in the cost. Towels can be hired, and additional Z-beds are available at no extra cost. The living areas in each lodge are spacious yet cosy, with colour TVs. Videos are also available on request. Well behaved dogs are more than welcome,though they must be kept under control at all times, as the lodges are situated within a working farm.

An Eleraig lodge is the perfect base from which to explore a beautiful and historic area of Scotland. It is easily reached from Glasgow, Edinburgh and the south, and Oban - with its many shops, restaurants and supermarkets - is only 20 minutes away. Loch Tralaig has brown trout, and two rowing boats are available at no charge should you wish to fish on its waters.

BRAGLEENBEG

Kilninver, by Oban PA34 4UU
Tel: 01852 316283 e-mail: jackie.handley@lineone.net
website: www.bragleenbeg.co.uk

Standing at the head of lovely Loch Scammadale, **Bragleenbeg** is a substantial stone-built house, parts of which have been converted into two self contained, spacious and extremely comfortable holiday apartments. The Feochan apartment sleeps six, and has a sitting room, a well appointed kitchen/dining room, a bathroom and a separate toilet. Fineglen sleeps nine in three bedrooms, and boasts a sitting/ dining room, a fully fitted kitchen and a bathroom with toilet. Both sitting rooms have gas-fired stoves. All gas and electricity used is free of charge, and bed linen and towels are supplied. There is a small laundry room, and both flats have electrical heating, a TV and a radio/CD player.

ARDUAINE

13 miles S of Oban on the A816

The 50 acre **Arduaine Gardens** are situated on a south facing slope overlooking Asknish Bay, and are in the care of the National Trust for Scotland. It is another testimony to the mildness of the climate on Argyllshire's coast, and has a wonderful collection of rhododendrons. There are also great trees, herbaceous borders and a diversity of plants from all over the world.

DALAVICH

13 miles SE of Oban on a minor road on the banks of Loch Awe

If you follow the B845 south from Taynuilt, then turn onto a minor road near Kilchrenan, you will eventually reach the **Dalavich Oakwood Trail**. It is a two mile long walk laid out by the Forestry Commission, with not only oaks to see, but alder, hazel, downy birch and juniper as well. There are also small sites where 18th and 19th century charcoal burners produced charcoal for the Bonawe Iron Furnace near Taynuilt.

Arduaine Gardens

SEIL ISLAND AND LUING

9 miles S of Oban on the B844

These two islands are known as the "slate isles", because of the amount of slate that was quarried here at one time. Seil is a genuine island, but is connected to the mainland by the **Bridge Across the Atlantic**, designed by Thomas Telford and built in 1792. It is more properly called the Clachan Bridge, with the water below being no more than a few yards wide. It got its nickname because at one time it was the only bridge in Scotland to connect an island with the mainland. Now it is dwarfed by the more recent Skye Bridge. On the island side of the bridge is a late 17th century inn called the Tigh na Truish, or "House of Trousers". This recalls the aftermath of the Jacobite Uprising, when the wearing of the kilt was forbidden. The islanders, before crossing onto the mainland by the ferry which preceded the bridge, would change out of their kilts here and into trousers.

On the west coast of the island is the village of **Ellenabeich**, with, facing it, the small island of **Easdale**. Ellenabeich was itself an island at one time, but the narrow channel separating it from the mainland was gradually filled up with waste from the local slate quarries. One of the biggest quarries was right on the shoreline, with the floor of the quarry well below the water line. During a great storm, the sea wall was breached, and the quarry filled with water. Now it is used as a harbour for small craft.

An Cala Garden dates from the 1930s, and is behind a row of cottages that was turned into one home. There are meandering streams, terracing built from the local slate, and wide lawns. A 15 feet high wall of grey brick protects the garden from the worst of the gales that occasionally blow in from the Atlantic. One of the cottages in the village has been tuned into a **Heritage Centre** with a number of displays connected with the slate industry. Offshore lies the small island of **Easdale,** connected to Ellenabeich by a small pasenger ferry. This too was a centre of slate quarrying, and one of the small cottages has been turned into the **Easdale Island Folk Museum**.

On Seil's southern tip is the small ferry port of **Cuan**, where a ferry plies backwards and forwards to Luing, to the south. This is a larger island than Seil, though is more sparsely populated. Here too slate quarrying was the main industry.

LISMORE

7 miles N of Oban, in Loch Linnhe

Lismore is a small island, no more than a mile and a half wide at its widest and nine miles long. It's name means "great garden", and it is a low lying, fertile island which is connected to Oban by a daily ferry. The main village and ferry terminal is **Achnacroish**, though a smaller pedestrian ferry plies between Port Appin on the mainland and the north of the island in summer. The highest point in the island, at a mere 412 feet, is **Barr M-rr**, but from the top there is a wonderful panoramic view in all directions.

Lismore, before the Reformation, was the centre of the diocese of Argyll. **Lismore Cathedral** stood at **Kilmoluaig**, near the small village of Clachan. It was destroyed just after the Reformation, but the choir walls were later lowered and incorporated into the present church in 1749. The site had been a Christian one for centuries, and was where St Moluag set up a small monastery in AD564.

Balvicar Farm

Isle of Seil, Argyllshire PA34 4TE
Tel: 01852 300355

Drive across the 'bridge across the Atlantic' and you will be in the beautiful island of Seil, where you will find **Balvicar Farm**. It offers a large, self catering caravan to the discerning holidaymaker, which boasts two smart and comfortable bedrooms, a well equipped kitchen, a spacious lounge and a wc and shower unit. This is the perfect place for a quiet, 'get away from it all' holiday, while still being within half an hour by car of all the modern amenities of Oban. The views are lovely, and those hiring the caravan can also pitch a tent beside it if required.

Inshaig Park Hotel

Easdale, by Oban, Argyllshire PA34 4RF
Tel: 01852 300256

Take a trip over the "Bridge over the Atlantic" to beautiful Seil Island, where, at Easdale, you'll find the **Inshaig Park Hotel**. This Victorian house boasts all the comforts and conveniences of a first class hotel, and has seven en suite rooms that are both stylish and welcoming. It is owned and managed by Graham Dale, and both the cuisine and the views across to the Scottish islands are outstanding. This is the ideal base from which to explore beautiful Argyllshire.

Lismore was a prized island even then, and it seems that St Moluag and another Celtic saint, St Mulhac, had a quarrel about who should found a monastery there. They finally agreed to a race across from the mainland in separate boats, with the first one touching the soil of Lismore being allowed to found his monastery. Just as the boats were approaching the Lismore shore, Moluag realised that he was going to lose, so he took a dagger, cut off one of his fingers and threw it onto the beach. This was supposed to have taken place at Tirefour, where there are the remains of a broch now called **Tirefour Castle**.

On the west coast of the island, facing the tiny Bernera Island, are the ruins of **Achadun Castle**, where the Bishops of Argyll once lived, and further up the coast are the ruins of **Coeffin Castle**, built by the MacDougalls in the 13th century.

MULL

8 miles W of Oban, in the Atlantic Ocean

The island of Mull is one of the largest and most beautiful of the Inner Hebrides. It also has the added advantage of being easy to reach, as a car ferry plies all day between the pier at **Craignure** on the island and Oban.

Its name comes from the Gaelic Meall, meaning a rounded hill. It is steeped in history, and was known even to the Romans and Greeks, as Ptolemy wrote about it, calling it Maleus. The highest peak, at 3,140 feet, is **Ben More**, the only Munro (a mountain above 3,000 feet) in any of the Scottish islands.

Close to Craignure is **Torosay Castle**, with its fine gardens. The **Mull and West Higland Railway**, a one and a quarter mile long narrow gauge line, connects the castle with the pier. Also in the vicinity is **Duart Castle**, perched on the cliffs above Duart Point. It is the ancestral home of the MacLeans, and still houses the clan chief. It was confiscated after Culloden, but in 1911 the 26th Maclean chief, Sir Fitzroy MacLean, bought it back and had it restored.

Some MacLean chieftains were unsavoury characters. The 11th chief for instance, so detested his wife, a sister of the Earl of Argyll, that he had her tied up and marooned on a rocky island near the castle that flooded at each high tide. She was eventually drowned and washed away, and the "distraught"

TORLOCHAN

Gruline, Isle of Mull, Argyllshire PA71 6HR
Tel: 01680 300380 Fax: 01680 300664
e-mail: diana@torlochan.sol.co.uk
website: www.holidaymull.org/members/torlochan.html

At Gruline, right in the heart of the wonderful island of Mull, is **Torlochan**, a small working croft with 40 acres of land and a large variety of animals. The holiday accommodation is within two cottages and two log cabins, all with lovely views over moorland and mountain, and all supremely comfortable and cosy, with electric heating throughout. There is also B&B accommodation in Tor Beg, a mini log cabin. Dairidh Cottage sleeps four in two double bedrooms, while Claghaig Cottage sleeps two in one double bedroom, and both have three coveted stars from VisitScotland. In each cottage there is a well appointed open plan kitchen/dining area, as well as a lounge and a bathroom with shower.

Both log cabins sleep four in double and twin rooms, and they have all the conveniences you find in the cottages. Tor Beg sleeps two, and there is TV and tea and coffee making facilities. Hearty Scottish breakfasts are served in the dining room. Children are welcome at this year-round establishment, as well as behaved dogs. Parking space is ample, and there is a small children's play area. Mull is rich in wildlife, and Torlochan is the ideal base from which to explore and get to know it.

ISLAND ENCOUNTER WILDLIFE AND BIRDWATCHERS SAFARIS

Arla Beag, Aros, Isle of Mull, Argyllshire PA72 6JS
Tel: 01680 300441 e-mail: islandencounter@easicom.com
website: www.mullwildlife.plus.com

Mull is a paradise for those interested in wildlife, and if you want to see it at its best, then **Island Encounter Wildlife and Birdwatchers Safaris** are for you. Golden eagles soaring in silent glens - white tailed sea eagles hunting in coastal bays - black, red and great northern divers in their summer plumage - hen harriers and owls gliding over scrub and marshes - merlin and peregrine falcons stooping to catch their prey - otters and seals in seaweed bays - perhaps porpoises slicing the offshore waters - all these creatures and more are regularly seen on the safaris. Guided by a local expert, you will spend a memorable day among wonderful and sometimes spectacular scenery. A little easy walking is done, but the Island Encounter's own eight seat vehicle transports you in comfort between locations where you will see the wildlife of the island at its best.

Pickups can be arranged from all ferry terminals (with setting down times which fit in with sailings back to the mainland), and for those staying on the island, there are also pickups at Tobermory, Salen and Craignure. Lunch snacks are provided, as are binoculars. There are special rates for those under 14, though it is felt that the safaris might not be suitable for very young children. For every pound received from the clients, Island Encounter donates one penny to the Scottish Wildlife Trust.

husband reported her sad death to the Earl.

The Earl immediately invited him to his castle in Inveraray, and when the chief got there, he discovered his wife alive and well. She had been rescued by a fisherman, though nothing was said during the chief's visit. They eventually went home together, and still nothing was said. By this time the chief was terrified, as he knew that retribution would come eventually. But before it did the wife died naturally, and the chief heaved a sigh of relief. He married again, and she too died. When he was married to his third wife 30 years later, and she bore him a son. He eventually had to go to Edinburgh on business. While there, he was murdered in mysterious circumstances, and for no apparent reason. Retribution had come at last.

Duart Castle, Isle of Mull

Further along the coast from Craignure, on the A849, is **Fishnish Pier**, where a ferry connects the island to Lochaline on the mainland, across the Sound of Mull. At **Salen** the road becomes the A848. Here you can visit **Macquarrie's Mausoleum**, where lies Major General Macquarrie, Governor General of New South Wales and sometimes called the "Father of Australia". Eight miles further along this road you'll come to **Tobermory**, the island's capital. Its name means "Mary's Well", and it

Tobermory Hotel

Tobermory, Isle of Mull, Argyllshire PA75 6NT
Tel: 01688 302091 Fax: 01688 302254
e-mail: tobhotel@tinyworld.co.uk
website: www.thetobermoryhotel.com

Set right on the sea front overlooking picturesque Tobermory Bay, the **Tobermory Hotel** must be one of the most delightfully situated hotels in Argyllshire. The place is renowned for its warm welcome and high standards, and is a unique combination of elegance, informality and that home from home feeling. Originally three substantial fishing cottages in a waterfront street that must be the most colourful in Scotland, it has been tastefully converted into a great base from which to explore the beautiful island of Mull. Owned and managed by Ian and Andi Stevens, it has 16 rooms, 15 of which are en suite, and all display a comfort and attention to detail that is hard to match. In each room there is a colour TV, tea and coffee making facilities and a hairdryer. And there is one ground floor room which is wheelchair friendly. The hotel prides itself on its staff, who are recruited locally, and are friendly and always willing to help. They also know the area, and can suggest places to visit and things to see!

The lounges are all spacious and comfortable, and the ideal place to relax after a hectic day's sightseeing. Children are more than welcome, and both cots and toys are available. Needless to say, the food is wonderful, and served in the stylish and cosy Water's Edge Restaurant, with views over Tobermory Bay. Under the careful eye of award winning chef Stephen Boswell, the hotel has put together a menu that combines the best of old and new, with that added flair that can only come from experience and using the best and freshest of local produce wherever possible. Why not indulge your taste buds with Angus beef casserole with crusty bread and cheese trencher? Or omelette with smoked haddock, salmon and Mull cheddar? Some other dishes reveal subtle influences from around the world, such as the crab salad with tropical fruit, or the pannecotta with strawberry compote. And vegetarian dishes are available as well. But remember - so popular is the restaurant that you are well advised to book in advance!

Great care has gone into selecting the wine list, which features wines from the Old and New Worlds, and which complement the food wonderfully. And, of course, there is a grand selection of beers, wines and spirits, including fine Scottish malts and soft drinks served in the lounges.

The Tobermory Hotel is a family-based establishment that is determined to give its guests a taste of Scottish hospitality at its very best. It's a place you will remember for all the right reasons.

is an attractive small burgh with many brightly painted houses and buildings fronting Tobermory Bay. **Mull Museum** is situated in Glengorm Road, and has displays explaining the history of the island.

Tobermory Harbour

At the bottom of the bay lies the famous wreck of the **San Juan de Sicilia**, part of the Spanish Armada fleet. Fleeing in 1588 from the English ships, she weighed anchor in the bay to take on provisions. A mysterious explosion blew her up, and she sank. Stories started circulating that she had 30 million ducats aboard her, and though some items were recovered, successive dives to locate the ducats failed. She now lies completely covered in silt, and it is unlikely that anything will ever be recovered from her again.

The narrow B8073 rises up from Tobermory and passes through **Dervaig** before reaching **Calgary**, on Calgary Bay. Dervaig is home to the 38 seat **Little Mull Theatre**. Though it is tiny, it is a proper professional theatre that puts on a season of plays every year. In 1883 a member of the Royal Canadian Mounted Police visited Calgary, and was so impressed by the scenery that he named a city in Canada after it.

The road continues along the shores of **Loch Tuath**, giving views across to the island of **Ulva**, visited by Boswell and Johnson in

Mull Pottery

Baliscate Estate, Salen Road, Tobermory,
Isle of Mull, Argyllshire PA75 6QA
Tel/Fax: 01688 302347
e-mail: info@mullpottery.fsnet.co.uk
website: www.mullpottery.com

The **Mull Pottery and Café** enjoy a tranquil setting on the outskirts of Tobermorey, where sheep wander the hills and outdoor seating offers a panorama over the Sound of Mull. Both locals and tourists alike escape the busy Main Street to visit the pottery - just a ten minute walk from the village centre. Established 25 years ago, Peter Walker's ceramic designs have been strongly influenced by Mull's beautiful coastal waters, inspiring well-known table and giftware ranges, as well as individual pieces. These items, sought after by local and international collectors, are for sale in the Gallery, the Main Street Shop and through mail order.

This all-weather facility provides something for everyone, year round. View skilled potters at their craft in the studio or browse through the Gallery where pottery is complemented by a large selection of Scottish and locally made items including ceramics, turned wood, glass, original paintings and prints of local and Scottish landscapes.

The mezzanine-level Café overlooks the Gallery, where freshly prepared fare drawing on Mull's best produce and the well known Costa brand of coffee are served on pottery tableware. This setting provides an airy, yet homey atmosphere with plenty for the eye to discover. Such a place will remind you of Mull for many years to come!

TIGH NA LOCHAN GUEST HOUSE

Assapol, Bunessan, Isle of Mull,
Argyllshire PA67 6DW
Tel/Fax: 01681 700247

Mull is one of the most beautiful of the Inner Hebrides, and in Bunessan, on the road to the atmospheric and wonderful island of Iona, is the **Tigh na Lochan Guest House**. The name means the "house by the small loch", and this is no idle boast. It is in a peaceful and secluded setting overlooking Loch Assapol, with a large garden and wonderful views. The house, a long, low bungalow that seems to fit in with the spectacular scenery, was built in 1994, and is owned and run by Libby and Frank Rothwell. Together they have created a comfortable guest house that offers the very best in Scottish hospitality, one that seems to go just that wee bit further in the warmth of its welcome! It is also easy to find. Just follow the A849 east from Craignure (where the Oban ferry docks) for 34 miles and take the well signposted turning 500 yards past the primary school. The house boasts four well appointed rooms - two doubles and two twins, all ensuite. The doubles and twins have tea and coffee making facilities, clock radios and hair dryer, and all have colour TV sets. The place is spotlessly clean, and the breakfasts, either traditional Scottish or Continental (depending on your wishes), are hearty, and always beautifully cooked. They are served in the conservatory overlooking the loch, so there is more than just the food to savour - there is the view as well!

For that extra touch, why not have a candlelit evening dinner within the conservatory? Libby takes a pride in the guest house's cuisine, and her food is always beautifully and imaginatively cooked from fresh local produce wherever possible. And if you prefer to eat vegetarian, Libby can provide this as well. The residents' lounge, off which the conservatory is situated, has all the amenities that make Tign na Lochan a real home from home - a wide screen TV, video machine, email facilities, an open log fire, piano and CD player. Dogs (up to a maximum of two) are welcome if arranged in advance.

This guest house is the perfect spot from which to explore an island that is rich in wildlife, history and heritage. Fionnphort, the Mull terminal for the Iona ferry, is only five miles away, and there are splendid opportunites for fishing (both sea and fresh water), bird watching, walking and other outdoor activities. And if you like, the guest house offers tasty packed lunches which you can take with you. But even if you just wish to have a relaxing time away from the hustle and bustle of modern life, then Tigh na Lochan Guest House is the place for you. Libby and Frank will give you a real Scottish welcome, and promise to make your stay a memorable one - for all the right reasons, of course!

1773. It then joins the B8035, which, if you turn right, takes you along the beautiful **Loch na Keal** to the A849 once more.

At **Bunessan** is the **Ross of Mull Historical Centre**, which explains the local history of the area. At the end of the A849 is **Fionnphort**, the ferry point for **Iona**. Before crossing, a visit to the **Columba Centre** should prepare you for what you'll find on the island. No cars are allowed on Iona, though it is so small (no more than three miles long by a mile and a half wide) that everything on it can easily be visited on foot. It is one of the most sacred spots in Europe (and unfortunately, during the summer months, one of the busiest), and was where **St Columba** set up his monastery in AD563. From here, he evangelised the Highlands, converting the Picts to Christianity by a mixture of saintliness, anger, arrogance and perseverance.

Coast of the Isle of Iona

Columba's monastery would have been built of wood and wattle, and little now survives of it apart from some of the cashel, or surrounding wall. The present **Iona Abbey**, on the site of the original monastery, was founded in 1203 by Reginald, son of Somerled, Lord of the Isles, though the present building is early 16th century. It was a Benedictine foundation, and later became a cathedral. By the 18th century it was roofless,

Argyll Restaurant

Bunessan, Isle of Mull, Argyllshire PA67 6DG
Tel: 01681 700291

If you are looking for somewhere great to eat when you are in Bunessan on the Isle of Mull, then the **Argyll Restaurant** is the place for you. Situated in a picturesque whitewashed house on the main street, it offers the very best in food and drink. Only the finest Scottish produce is used wherever possible, and you can chose from a menu that includes everything from a sirloin steak with all the trimmings to salads, chilli, jacket potatoes and toasted sandwiches. This cosy restaurant is crammed with antiques and prints, most of which are for sale.

and the cloister and other buildings were in ruin. In the 20th century they were restored by the Rev George MacLeod, a Church of Scotland minister who went on to found the **Iona Community**.

Isle of Staffa

Beside the cathedral is the **Reilig Odhrain**, or St Oran's Cemetery. Within the cemetery is the **Ridge of the Chiefs**, which is supposed to contain the bodies of many West Highland chiefs who chose to be buried here in medieval times. Close by is the **Ridge of the Kings**, where, it is said, no less than 48 Scottish, eight Norwegian and four Irish kings lie buried, including Macbeth. However, modern historians now doubt if any kings are buried there at all. One man who does lie within the cemetery is **John Smith** the politician, who was buried here in 1994.

St Oran's Chapel was built as a funeral chapel in the 12th century by one of the Lords of the Isles. The ruins of **St Mary's Nunnery** are near the jetty, and date from the 13th century. It was founded by the same Reginald who founded the abbey, and he placed his sister Beatrice in charge as prioress. A small museum has been established in the **Chapel of St Ronan** close to the ruins.

Entrance to Fingal's Cave

Of the many crosses on the island, the best are the 10th century **St Martin's Cross**, outside the main abbey door, and the 16th century **MacLean's Cross**. The **Road of the Dead**, part of a cobbled roadway which led to St Oran's Cemetery, goes past the front of the abbey church. Just west of the cathedral is the **Tor Ab**, a low mound on which St Columba's cell may have been situated.

In the former parish church manse (designed by Telford) is

the **Iona Heritage Centre**, which traces the history of the people who have lived on the island throughout the years.

Six miles north of Iona is the island of **Staffa** (National Trust for Scotland), which can be reached by excursion boats from Oban. The most remarkable feature on this small uninhabited island is **Fingal's Cave**, which was visited by the composer Felix Mendelssohn and inspired his musical work of the same name. The cliffs are formed from hexagonal columns of basalt that look like wooden staves, some over 50 feet high. The Vikings therefore named the island Stav ¯y (Stave Island) from which it got its modern name.

COLL AND TIREE

50 miles W of Oban in the Atlantic Ocean

These two islands, lying beyond Mull, can be reached by ferry from Oban. They are generally low lying, and can be explored by car in a few hours. Robert the Bruce granted Coll to Angus Og of Islay, and it was Angus who was responsible for building the now ruined **Breachacha Castle**, to the south of the island.

It was in Coll that an incident later called the **Great Exodus** took place. In 1856 the southern part of the island, which was the most fertile, was sold to one John Lorne Stewart. In spite of protests from the crofters who farmed there, he raised their rents to a level they could not afford. So the tenants took matters into their own hands. Overnight, they all left their crofts and moved north to the less hospitable lands owned by the Campbells, where the rents were reasonable. Thus Lorne Stewart was left with no rent income whatsoever, and there was nothing he could do about it.

Tiree means the "land of corn", as it is one of the most fertile of the Inner Hebridean islands. It is sometimes called Tir fo Thuinn, meaning the "land beneath the waves", because of its relative flatness. Its highest peaks are **Ben Hynish** (460 feet) and **Ben Hough** (387 feet).

Tiree has the reputation of being the sunniest place in Britain, though this is tempered by the fact that it is also officially the windiest. The ferry terminal is at **Scarnish**, and not far away is the tiny airport serving the island. Near Vaul to the north east of the island is a curious marked stone called the **Ringing Stone**, which, when struck, makes a clanging noise. Legend says if it is ever broken the island will disappear beneath the Atlantic. At Sandaig is the tiny **Sandaig Museum**, housed in a restored thatched cottage.

COLONSAY AND ORONSAY

40 miles SW of Oban in the Atlantic Ocean

The twin islands of Colonsay and Oronsay are separated by an expanse of sand called **The Strand**, which at high tide is completely covered with water. Colonsay is the bigger of the two, and has a ferry service connecting it to Oban. It is a beautiful island, full of rocky or sandy coves and areas of fertile ground. Perhaps the most beautiful part is **Kiloran Valley**, which is sheltered and warm, and where **Colonsay House**, built in 1722 (not open to the public), stands. It is said that the builder, Malcolm MacNeil, used stones from an old chapel which stood close by.

Oronsay is famous for the substantial ruins of **Oronsay Priory**, perhaps the most important monastic ruins in the west of Scotland after Iona. Tradition gives us two founders for the abbey. The first is St Oran, companion to St Columba, who founded it in 563. The second is St Columba himself. When he left Ireland, the story goes, he alighted first on Colonsay, then crossed over to Oronsay, where he established the small abbey. But he had made a vow that he would never settle where he could still see the coastline of Ireland. He could from Oronsay, so eventually moved on to Iona.

John, Lord of the Isles, founded the present priory in the early 14th century, inviting Augustinian canons from Holyrood Abbey in Edinburgh to live within it. The church is 15th century, and the well preserved cloisters date from the 16th century. A series of large carved graveslabs can be seen within the Prior's House, and in the graveyard is the early 16th century **Oronsay Cross**, intricately carved, and carrying the words Colinus, son of Christinus MacDuffie. Another cross can be found east of the Prior's Chapel, with a carving of St John the Evangelist carved at its head.

9 Perthshire and Angus

The two counties of Perthshire and Angus straddle the Highland Boundary Fault, which separates the Highlands from the Lowlands. So there is a wide variety of scenery within them, from mountains, glens and lochs to quiet, intensely cultivated fields and picturesque villages. The glens of Angus, such as Glen Prosen, Glen Clova and Glen Doll, are particularly beautiful as the wind their way into the foothills of the Cairngorms. The A9 north from Perth towards the Drumochter Pass passes through deeply wooded glens, and skirts such historic towns and villages as Dunkeld, Pitlochry and Blair Atholl. In fact, Perthshire likes to call itself the "Big Tree County", as it has some of the most remarkable woodlands anywhere in Europe.

Loch Rannoch

Perthshire is a wholly inland county, a place of agriculture, high hills and Highland lochs. It is the county of Loch Rannoch and Loch Tummel, and of possibly the loneliest railway station in Britain, Rannoch station, where the road peters out into a bleak expanse of moorland called Rannoch Moor. It is also the county of the Gleneagles Hotel, one of Britain's most luxurious, and of rich farmland surrounding Perth itself. Angus has a coastline that takes in high cliffs and sandy beaches. Blairgowrie is the centre of Scotland's fruit growing industry - fruit that fed the Dundee jam makers. The coastal towns are famous. Carnoustie, where the British Open is sometimes held; Montrose and its almost land-locked basin where wildfowl can be seen; and of course Arbroath, with the ruins of an abbey where one of the momentous documents in Scottish history was signed - the Declaration of Arbroath.

Perth is a city, and before local government reorgansiation in the 70s, had a lord provost, one of only six places in Scotland that could claim that distinction, the others being Edinburgh, Glasgow, Dundee, Aberdeen and Elgin. No legal document has ever specifically taken that honour away from it, so it remains a city still. It is often referred to as the "Fair City of Perth", and this is no idle description. It may be in the Lowlands, but it has never been scarred by the industrial developments of the 19th century. It remains a confident, attractive place with many fine buildings and a good quality of life.

Dundee, on the other hand, is a city of industry. It sits on the north bank of the Firth of Tay, and was one of the powerhouses of Scotland, relying on its three traditional industries of jute, jam and journalism. But it is an old place as well, and its roots go deep into Scottish history. One of Scotland's famous historical characters, John Graham of Claverhouse, adopted its name when he became1st Viscount Dundee. He was a man who was loved and loathed at the same time in 17th century Scotland. To the Covenanters, he was Bloody Clavers, a ruthless and cruel persecutor of those opposed to Charles II and the introduction of bishops to the Church of Scotland. To the Jacobites he was Bonnie Dundee, a dashing and gallant supporter of the Stuarts.

The Hermitage, Dunkeld

Everywhere in Perthshire and Angus there is history. There are medieval cathedrals at Dunkeld and Brechin, and the impressive ruins of an abbey at Arbroath. In AD685, at Nechtansmere, the Northumbrians were defeated by a Pictish army under King Nechtan. The Battle of Killiecrankie in 1689 was the first of the Jacobite battles in Scotland, and though the Jacobites under Bonnie Dundee won, Dundee himself was killed. At Scone, outside Perth, was where Scottish kings were crowned as they sat on the Stone of Destiny; at Blair Atholl the Duke of Atholl keeps the only private army in Britain; and Glamis Castle is the childhood home of Queen Elizabeth the Queen Mother.

There are literary associations as well. J.M. Barry was born at Kirriemuir, and Violet Jacob was born near Montrose. The Dundee publisher D.C. Thomson has given us a host of characters that have delighted children (and adults) for ages, such as Desperate Dan, Beryl the Peril, Denis the Menace, Lord Snooty, The Bash Street Kids and Oor Wullie.

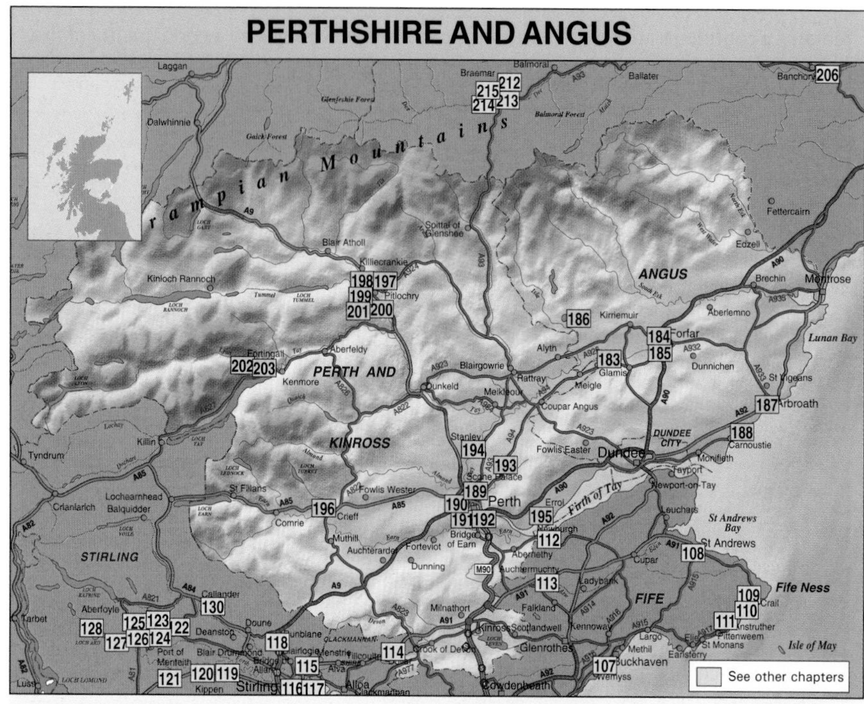

PLACES TO STAY, EAT, DRINK AND SHOP

183	Castleton House Hotel, by Glamis	Hotel and restaurant	Page 233
184	Chapelbank House Hotel, Forfar	Hotel and restaurant	Page 234
185	Wemyss Farm, Forfar	Bed and Breakfast	Page 234
186	Lochside Lodge, Bridgend of Lintrathen	Hotel and restaurant	Page 235
187	Hotel Seaforth, Arbroath	Hotel and restaurant	Page 236
188	The Old Manor, Carnoustie	B&B and self catering	Page 239
189	Huntingtower House, Perth	Bed and Breakfast	Page 240
190	Cherrybank Inn, Perth	Pub, accommodation and food	Page 240
191	Brambles Coffee Shop & Restaurant, Perth	Café, tearoom and restaurant	Page 240
192	Achnacarry Guest House, Perth	Guest House	Page 241
193	MacDonald Arms Hotel, Balbeggie	Pub, accommodation and food	Page 242
194	Glensanda House, Stanley	Bed and Breakfast	Page 243
195	The Old Smiddy, Errol	Pub with food	Page 244
196	Glenearn House, Crieff	Guest House	Page 245
197	Acarsaid Hotel, Pitlochry	Hotel and restaurant	Page 246
198	Dalshian Chalets, Pitlochry	Self catering	Page 246
199	Pooltiel, Pitlochry	Bed and Breakfast	Page 246
200	Craigvrack Hotel, Pitlochry	Hotel and restaurant	Page 247
201	Gardener's Cottage, Faskally	Bed and Breakfast	Page 248
202	Fortingall Hotel, Fortingall	Hotel	Page 251
203	Kinnighallen Farm B&B, Fortingall	Bed and Breakfast	Page 251

DUNDEE

Dundee is Scotland's fourth largest city, and sits on the banks of the Firth of Tay. Although it is a manufacturing town, at one time famous for the "three Js" of jam, jute and journalism, it is a city brimming with history and heritage. It was granted royal burgh status in the 12th century, when it was one of the largest and wealthiest towns in the country.

It is joined to Fife across the Tay by two bridges, the **Tay Road Bridge**, opened in 1966, and the **Tay Rail Bridge**, opened in 1887. The road bridge opened up a huge area of north Fife to commuters wishing to work in Dundee, and making it the main shopping centre for the area as well. The rail bridge, as everyone knows, replaced an earlier bridge, built in 1878. On the evening of December 28 1879, during a violent westerly gale, this bridge collapsed while a train was crossing it. The 75 passengers on the train perished.

One of Dundee's best known sons, **William Topaz McGonagall**, later wrote a poem to the disaster which has became almost as famous as the disaster itself:

Beautiful Railway Bridge of the Silv'ry Tay!
Alas! I am very sorry to say
That ninety lives have been taken away
On the last Sabbath day of 1879,
Which will be remember'd for a very long time.

It has been called, rather unfairly perhaps, "the worst poem ever written", but McGonagall - a simple hand loom weaver whose formal education stopped when he was seven years old - was trying to put into words the horror he felt at the tragedy.

He had been born in Edinburgh in 1830 the son of Irish immigrants, and came to Dundee with his parents after having lived in both Paisley and Glasgow. In 1877, he took to writing poetry, having felt "a strange kind of feeling stealing over me", and he wrote until he died in September 1902.

The **Old Steeple** of St Mary's Church, in the heart of the city, dates from the 15th century, and is reckoned to be one of the finest in the country. The rest of the church dates from the 18th and 19th centuries, and was once divided into four separate churches. Until the 1980s, when they finally amalgamated, there were still three churches within the building - the Steeple Church, Old St Paul's and St David's. You can climb the steeple and see the peel of eight bells and, below it, the ringing chamber. There is also a great view over the city from the parapet, and in an antiquities room you can see a collection of carved stones from Dundee buildings that have been demolished over the years.

Another reminder of Dundee's past is the **Wishart Arch** in the Cowgate. It is one of the city's old gateways, and from its top, George Wishart preached during the plague of 1544.

RSS Discovery, the ship of Captain Scott the Antarctic explorer, was built in Dundee and launched in 1901. It now forms the centrepiece of **Discovery Point & RSS Discovery**, at Discovery Quay. It was one of the last wooden three-masted ships to be built in Britain, and the first to be built solely for scientific research. You can explore the ship, "travel" to Antarctica in the Polarama Gallery and find out about one of the greatest stories of exploration and courage ever told, as well as Dundee's maritime heritage. At City Quay you'll find **HM Frigate Unicorn**, the oldest British-built ship still afloat. It was built at Chatham in 1824 for the Royal Navy, and carried 46 guns. The conditions on board a wooden sailing ship during the time of Nelson have been recreated, with officers' quarters, cannons, and the cramped condititons within which the crew lived.

Maritime Centre, Dundee

In 1999, **The Verdant Works**, in West Henderson's Wynd, was voted Europe's top industrial museum. Jute was once a staple industry in Dundee, employing over 40,000 people in its heyday. Here, in a former jute mill, you are taken on a tour of the trade, from its beginnings in India to the end product in all its forms. You will see the processes involved in jute manufacture, you'll see the original machinery, and you'll see the living conditions of people both rich and poor who earned their living from the trade. There are interactive displays, film shows, and a guided tour.

Another factory to visit is **Shaw's Dundee Sweet Factory**, especially if you have a sweet tooth. Situated within the old Keiller factory (where Keiller's famous marmalade was once made) on Mains Loan, it explains the processes used in the manufacture of sweets. The machinery used dates from the 1930s to the 1950s, and the recipes date back as far as 1879.

Sensation is Dundee's science centre. Located in the Greenmarket, it is a place where "science is brought to life" using specially designed interactive exhibits. Here you can find out how a dog sees the world, and how to use your senses to discover where you are, and why things taste good or bad. Also dealing with matters scientific is the **Mills Observatory**, Britain's only full time public observatory. Situated in Balgay Park, a mile west of the city centre, and accessed from Glamis Road, it houses a 25mm Cooke telescope, and has a small planetarium and display area.

The **McManus Galleries** are housed within a Gothic building in Albert Square, and contain many 18th and 19th century Scottish paintings as well as a museum of more than local interest, with a particularly fine collection of artifacts from Ancient Egypt. To the east of the city is the suburb of **Broughty Ferry**, once called the "richest square mile in Europe", because of the many fine mansions built there by the jute barons. The **Broughty Ferry Museum** is at Castle Green, and housed within a 15th century castle. It has displays on local history, and tells the story of Dundee's former whaling fleet, at one time Britain's largest. If you visit Broughty Ferry at New Year, you can see the annual **N'erday Dook**, held on January 1, when swimmers attempt to cross the Firth of Tay towards Tayport in Fife. **Dudhope Castle**, at Dudhope Park in Dundee, dates from the 13th century, and was once the home of the Hereditary Constables of Dundee. In its time it has also been a woollen mill and a barracks. It is not open to the public, though it can be viewed from the outside.

Dundee Law (571 feet) looms over the city, and from its summit there is a superb view south towards the Tay Bridges and the Fife coast, and the **Carse of Gowrie**, one of the most fertile parts of Scotland, to the west. And on the Coupar Angus Road is the **Camperdown Wildlife Centre**, with a fine collection of Scottish and European wildlife, including brown bears, Scottish wildcats, wolves and bats.

Four miles north of the city centre, near Balgray, is the **Tealing Souterrain**, an underground dwelling dating from about AD100. It was accidentally discovered in 1871, and consists of a curved passage about 78 feet long long and seven feet wide with a stone floor.

AROUND DUNDEE

FOWLIS EASTER

6 miles W of Dundee city centre on a minor road off the A923

This small village has one of the finest small churches in Scotland. The **Parish Church of St Marnan** dates from about 1453, and still has part of its rood screen, as well as medieval paintings and a sacrament house that is reckoned to be the finest in Scotland.

GLAMIS

10 miles N of Dundee city centre on the A94

Glamis Castle is famous as being the childhood home of Queen Elizabeth the Queen Mother and the birthplace of Princess Margaret. The lands of Glamis (pronounced "Glams") was given to Sir John Lyon in 1372 by Robert II, and still belongs to the family, as the Earls of Strathmore and Kinghorne are their direct descendants. In 1376 Sir John married Robert's daughter, Princess Joanna, and the castle has had royal connections ever since. The present castle was built in the 17th century to resemble a French chateau, though

Glamis Castle

fragments of an earlier 14th century castle still survive in the tower.

It is the setting for Shakespeare's Macbeth, and Duncan's Hall, the oldest part of the castle, is said to have been built on the spot where Macbeth murdered Duncan, though history tells us that Duncan most probably died in battle near Elgin. It may even be that Shakespeare visited Glamis, as he and his troup of actors were sent to Aberdeen by Elizabeth I to perform before James VI.

Tragedy seems to stalk Glamis Castle. In 1540 Lady Glamis was burnt as a witch in Edinburgh and for plotting to murder James V, and the lands siezed by the crown. She was later found to have been innocent of all the charges, and the lands were restored to her son. It has the reputation of being one of the most haunted castles in Scotland. There is a Grey Lady who haunts the chapel, a Black Page, and a window which looks out from a room which has no door on the inside. Legend has it that in the room, which might be within the thickness of the walls of the Crypt, one of the Lords of Glamis and the Earl of Crawford played cards with the devil, and were sealed up because of this. This Crypt is actually the lower hall of the castle, and was where the servants would have eaten and slept.

Within the village of Glamis, at Kirkwynd, is the **Angus Folk Museum** (National Trust for Scotland), housed in a row of 18th century stone cottages. It contains one of the finest folk collections in Scotland, including a restored 19th century hearse, and shows how the people of rural Angus lived in times past.

FORFAR

13 miles N of Dundee city centre on the A932

Once the county town of Angus, Forfar is now a small royal burgh and market town. It gives its name to one of Scotland's culinary delights - the **Forfar Bridie**. It has meat and vegetables contained within a pastry crust, and used to be popular with the farm workers of Angus, as it was a self-contained and easily portable meal.

To get an insight into the town's history and industries, you should visit the **Meffan Museum and Art Gallery** in West High Street. During the Dark Ages this part of Scotland was inhabited by the Picts, who, as far as we know, had no alphabet. However, they were expert carvers, and in the museum is a superb display of their carved stones. You can walk down an old cobbled street and peer into shops and workshops. There is also a display about witchcraft in Angus.

Chapelbank House Hotel & Restaurant

69 East High Street, Forfar, Angus DD8 2EP
Tel: 01307 463151 Fax: 01307 461922

With four beautifully appointed en suite rooms, the **Chapelbank House Hotel and Restaurant** is the perfect place to have an overnight stay when heading north towards Aberdeenshire and Royal Deeside. It is also the perfect base from which to explore the lovely Angus countryside and glens.

Under owners Adrian and Catherine Gunn, this hotel, rated four star by VisitScotland, has earned an enviable reputation as one of the best places to eat in Forfar. Adrian is a first class chef, and has put together a menu that combines the best of Scottish produce with the best of French cuisine. Chapelbank was originally a large Victorian house, and here traditional hospitality are the watchwords, with everything being done to make the visitor's stay as comfortable as possible.

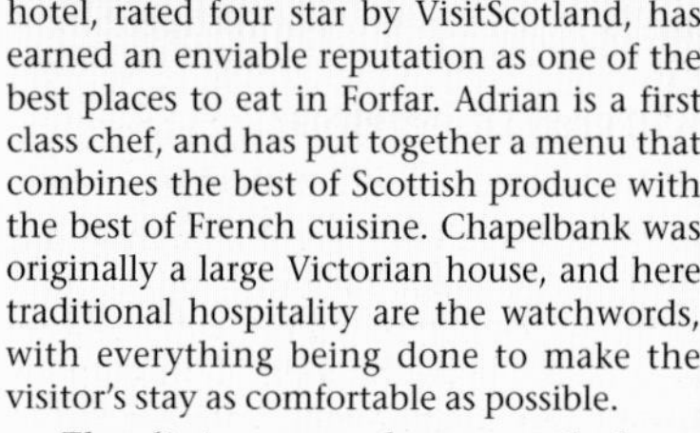

The dining room has recently been refurbished to an extremely high standard, and there is no better way to relax than having an aperitif or a cup of coffee in the smart coffee lounge. A stay at Chapelbank is a truly memorable experience!

Wemyss Farm

Montrose Road, Forfar, Angus DD8 2TB
Tel/Fax: 01307 462887
e-mail: wemyssfarm@hotmail.com

Wemyss Farm is a family run farm of 190 acres set amid the lovely countryside of Angus which also offers B&B accommodation of the highest standard. There are two beautifully appointed rooms available, plus two bathrooms – one with shower and one with bath. Owned and run by Deanna and William Lindsay, it prides itself on offering the best in Scottish hospitality, plus a warm and friendly welcome. Evening meals are available, and the place has a well deserved three-star rating from VisitScotland.

Five miles east of Forfar is **Balgavies Loch**, a Scottish Wildlife Trust reserve, where you can see goldeneye, great crested grebe, cormorant and other birds. Keys to the hide are available from the ranger at the Montrose Basin Wildlife Centre. The ruins of **Restenneth Priory** (Historic Scotland) sits about a mile and a half from the town, on the B9113. It was founded by David I for Augustinian canons on the site of a much earlier church, and its tower has some of the earliest Norman work in Scotland. It was sacked by Edward I, but under the patronage of Robert the Bruce it soon regained its importance. Prince Robert, one of Bruce's sons. is buried here.

KIRRIEMUIR

15 miles N of Dundee city centre on the A926

At 9 Brechin Road is **JM Barrie's Birthplace** (National Trust for Scotland). The creator of Peter Pan (first performed in 1904) was born here in 1860, the son of a handloom weaver, and the outside wash house was his first theatre. He was a bright child, and attended both Glasgow Academy and Dumfries Academy (see also Dumfries) before going on to Edinburgh University. He also wrote many stories and novels, setting them in a small town called "Thrums", which is a thinly disguised Kirriemuir.

In 1930 Barrie donated a **Camera Obscura** (National Trust for Scotland) to the town, one of only three such cameras left in the country. It is situated within the cricket pavilion on top of Kirriemuir Hill, and is open to the public. The **Kirriemuir Aviation Museum** has a private collection of World War II memorabilia, and is situated at Bellies Brae.

Kirriemuir is the gateway to many of the beautiful Angus glens, and in the **Gateway to the Glens Museum** in the High Street you can find out about life in the glens and in Kirriemuir itself before setting out to explore them. The B955 takes you into **Glen Clova**. At the head of the glen it forms a long loop, so you can travel along one side of the glen and return along the other. A minor road at the Clova Hotel takes you up onto lonely **Glen Doll** before it peters out among the high peaks of the Cairgorms. At Dykehead you can turn off the B955 onto a minor road for **Glen Prosen** and follow it as it winds deep into the glen. A cairn close to Dykehead commemorates the Antarctic explorers Robert Scott and Edward Adrian Wilson. Wilson lived in Glen Prosen, and it was here that some of the Antarctic expedition was planned.

Glen Isla is the southernmost of the Angus glens, and you can follow it for all of its length along the B951, which eventually takes you onto the A93 and up to Braemar if you wish. You will pass the **Loch of Lintrathan**, which is noted for its birdlife. A couple of miles further up the glen a minor road takes you to lonely **Backwater Reservoir** and its dam.

DUNNICHEN

13 miles NE of Dundee on minor road off the B9128

Close to the village was fought, in AD685, the **Battle of Nechtansmere** between the Picts and the Northumbrians. It was a turning point in early Scottish history, as the Northumbians were agressively trying to extend the boundaries of their kingdom, and they had already taken the Lothians and Fife. The Northumbrians, under King Ecgfrith, were roundly beaten, and Ecgfrith himself was killed. At the crossroads in Dunnichen village is a cairn which commemorates the battle. The picturesque village of **Letham**, which is close by, was founded in 1788 by George Dempster, the local landowner, as a place for farm workers who had been forced to leave the land because of farming reforms. It became a centre of weaving and spinning, though the introduction of power looms to mills in nearby towns killed it off.

ARBROATH

16 miles NE of Dundee city centre on the A92

The ancient town of Arbroath is special to all Scots. It was here, in 1320 , that the nobles of Scotland declared their independence from England in the **Declaration of Arbroath**. It was sent to the Pope in Rome, and in it, they claimed that they weren't fighting for glory, riches or honour, but for freedom. They also, in no uncertain terms, declared that they would remain loyal to their king, Robert the Bruce, only as long as he defended Scotland against the English. It was a momentous thing to declare in those far off days, when unswerving loyalty to a sovereign, no matter what, was expected at all times.

The Declaration was drawn up in **Arbroath Abbey** (Historic Scotland), the ruins of which still stand within the town, and sometimes a re-enactment of the signing is held within its walls. A Visitor Centre tells the story of the abbey and the Declaration. The ruins date from the 12th century and later, and are of warm red sandstone. It was founded in 1176 by William the Lion for the Tironensian order of monks, and dedicated to St Thomas of Canterbury. Portions of the great abbey church remain, including the south transept, with its great rose window. In 1951 the abbey was the temporary home of the Stone of Destiny after it was removed from Westminster Abbey by students with Nationalist sympathies.

The award winning **Arbroath Museum**, at Ladyloan, is housed in the elegant signal tower for the Bellrock Lighthouse, and brings Arbroath's maritime and social history alive through a series of models, sounds and even smells.

Arbroath has had a harbour at the "Fit o' the Toon" (Foot of the Town) since at least the 14th century, and it supported a great fishing fleet. The town gave its name to that delicacy called the **Arbroath Smokie** (a smoked

Hotel Seaforth

Dundee Road, Arbroath,
Angus DD11 1QF
Tel: 01241 872232
Fax: 01241 877473

Arbroath, with the ruins of an abbey that is at the heart of Scotland's history, is a seaside resort that has always been a popular place for a holiday or short break. And the **Hotel Seaforth** is *the* place to stay while in the town. It sits on the sea front within its own ample grounds, where there is plenty of space for car parking. Bill and Sandra Rennie are mine hosts, and they have created a sophisticated yet homely establishment with 19 en suite rooms that are the last word in comfort and convenience. Most overlook the sea, and there are colour TVs and tea and coffee making facilities in each one. The hotel has recently been completely redecorated and upgraded, offering some of the best hospitality on the Angus coast. The hearty Scottish breakfasts are legendary, and the lunchtime and evening cuisine (vegetarian dishes are available) is superb, with a large wine list and menus that use only the finest local produce. The hotel's own leisure centre has a swimming pool, sauna, spa bath, fitness room and steam room. So after a hectic workout, why not head for the bar, where you can relax over a quiet drink, or sit out in the beer garden that overlooks the sea? There are over two dozen wonderful malts from which to choose, as well as a wide range of beers and spirits to suit everyone's taste.

haddock) though the supposed origins of the smokie are to be found not in the town, but in **Auchmithie**, a fishing village four miles to the north. The story goes that long ago it was the practice to store fish in the lofts of the fishermen's cottages. One day, a cottage burned down, and the resultant smoked fish was found to be delicious. Not only that - it preserved them.

The **Cliffs Nature Trail** winds for one and a half miles along the red sandstone cliffs towards Carlinheugh Bay. There is plenty of birdlife to see, as well as fascinating rock formations. The town is also a holiday resort, and at West Link Parks is **Kerr's Miniature Railway**, always a favourite with holidaymakers. It is open during the summer months, and is Scotland's oldest miniature railway. It runs for over 400 yards alongside the main Aberdeen to Edinburgh line.

ST VIGEANS

18 miles NE of Dundee on minor road off the A92

When the 11th century **Parish Church of St Vigeans** was being rebuilt in the 19th century, 32 sculptured Pictish stones were discovered. They are now housed in the **St Vigeans Museum**, a cottage close to the small knoll where the church stands.

ABERLEMNO

18 miles NE of Dundee city centre off the B9134

Within the village are the Pictish **Aberlemno Sculptured Stones** (Historic Scotland). One is situated in the kirkyard of the parish church, and the others are within a stone enclosure near the roadside north of the church. The one in the kirkyard shows a fine cross on one side surrounded by intertwining serpents, and a typical Pictish hunting scene on the other. The other two have crosses, angels, and battle or hunting scenes.

BRECHIN

22 miles NE of Dundee city centre off the A90

If the possession of a cathedral makes a town a city, then Brechin is indeed a city, even though it has a population of only 6,000. **Brechin Cathedral** dates from the 12th century, though most of what we see today is 13th century and later. It was the successor to a Celtic church which stood on the site, and which had originally been endowed by the queen of Kenneth II, king of Scots between 971 and 995. It soon became the premier church for Angus, though by the 11th century Roman Catholic clergy had succeeded the Celtic priests.

In 1806 the nave, aisles and west front were remodelled, though between 1901 and 1902 the church was restored to its original design. Adjacent to the cathedral, and now forming part of its fabric, is an 11th century **Round Tower**. These towers are common in Ireland, though this is the only one of two to have survived in Scotland (see also Abernethy). It was used as a place of refuge for the priests of the church during troubled times. The scant ruins of the **Maison Dieu Chapel** are all that is left of an almshouse founded in 1267 by Lord William de Brechin.

In St Ninian's Square is **Brechin Museum**, which has exhibits and displays about the cathedral, the ancient city crafts, and local archaeology. **Brechin Castle** (not open to the public) is the seat of the Earls of Dalhousie, and within the **Brechin Castle Centre** is a garden centre, walks and a model farm. There is also **Pictavia**, an exhibition which explains about the enigmatic Picts, who occupied this part of Scotland for centuries. Their name means the "painted people", and they fought the Romans, the Vikings and the Anglo Saxons, and eventually formed themselves into a powerful kingdom which united with the kingdom of the Scots of Dalriada in 843. At Menmuir, near Brechin, are the White and Brown **Caterthuns**, on which are the well preserved remains of Iron Age forts. The hills also give good views across the surrounding countryside.

The **Caledonian Railway** runs on Sundays during the summer, when passengers can travel between the Victorian Brechin Station on Park Road and the nearby Bridge of Dun. The railway has seven steam engines and eight diesel, and is run by the Brechin Railway Preservation Society.

To the north west of Brechin is **Glen Lethnot**, one of the beautiful Angus glens. Flowing through it is the West Water, and near the head of the glen is an old trail that takes you over the Clash of Wirren into Glen Esk. This was used as a route by illicit distillers in days gone by, who hid their casks in the corries among the hills. For this reason it became known as the **Whisky Trail**.

MONTROSE

25 miles NE of Dundee city centre on the A92

Montrose is an ancient royal burgh which received its charter in the middle of the 12th century. It sits on a small spit of land between the North Sea and a shallow tidal basin called the Montrose Basin, which is famous for its bird life. The **Montrose Basin Wildlife Centre** is visited by thousands of bird watchers every year who come to see the many migrant and resident birds.

At the old Montrose Air Station, where some of the Battle of Britain pilots trained, is the **Montrose Air Station Museum**. In 1912, the government planned 12 such air stations, to be operated by the Royal Flying Corps, later called the Royal Air Force. Montrose was the first, and became operational in 1913. Now it houses a small collection of aircraft, plus mementoes, documents and photographs related to flying.

To the west of the town, beyond the Basin, is the **House of Dun** (National Trust for Scotland). It was designed by William Adam in 1730 for David Erskine, Lord Dun, and contains good plasterwork, sumptious furnishings and a collection of embroidery carried out by Lady Augusta Kennedy-Erskine, natural daughter of William IV and his mistress Mrs Jordan.

Montrose was adopted as the title of the Graham family when it was ennobled, and the most famous member was James Graham, 5th Earl and 1st Marquess of Montrose. He was born in 1612, and succeeded to the earldom in 1625. At first he was a Covenanter, then changed sides. He was made Lieutenant-General of Scotland by the king, and unsuccessfully tried to invade Scotland with an army. He later went to the Highlands in disguise to raise a Royalist army. During a succession of skirmishes, he defeated the Covenanting army due to his brilliant leadership and almost reckless courage. Charles's defeat at Naseby, however, left him powerless, and his forces were eventually soundly beaten at Philiphaugh in 1645. Afterwards he fled to the Continent but returned in 1650 in support of Charles II. Charles, however, disowned him and he was hanged.

Montrose Nature Reserve

EDZELL

27 miles NE of Dundee city centre on the B966

The ruins of **Edzell Castle** (Historic Scotland) dates from the 15th century. It was a seat of the Lindsays, and once the finest castle in Angus. It illustrates the fact that life in a Scottish castle was not the cold, draughty existence that people imagine from seeing bare, ruined walls. They could be places of refinement and comfort, and at Edzell we have evidence of this. The gardens especially were tasteful and elegant, and were laid out in 1604 by Sir David Lindsay, though he died in 1610 before they could be completed. The walled garden has been described as an "Italian Renaissance garden in Scotland", and featured heraldic imagery and an array of carved panels representing the liberal arts, deities and the cardinal virtues.

In 1715 the Jacobite Lindsays sold the castle to the Earl of Panmure, also Jacobite sympathisers, so that they could raise a Jacobite regiment. After the rebellion the castle and lands were forfeited to the crown, and sold to an English company which went bankrupt in 1732. The castle gradually became ruinous, and in the 1930's the gardens were restored to their former glory. The summer house contains surviving examples of the carved panelling that was in the castle in its heyday.

One of the delights of Edzell village is the **Dalhousie Arch**, erected in 1887 over a road into the village as a memorial to 13th Earl of Dalhousie and his wife, who died within a few hours of each other.

Edzell is the gateway to **Glen Esk**. It is the longest and most northerly of the glens, and you can drive the 19 miles to Invermark Lodge, close to Loch Lee, where the road peters out. Along the way you can stop at the **Glen Esk Folk Museum**, which traces the life of the people of the glen from about 1800 to the present day.

MONIFIETH

6 miles E of Dundee city centre on the A930

This little holiday resort sits at the entrance to the Firth of Tay, and has some good sandy beaches. It's golf courses were used in the qualifying rounds of the British Open. At one time it was an important Pictish settlement, and at **St Rule's Church** some carved stones were discovered that are now in The National Museum of Scotland in Edinburgh.

CARNOUSTIE

11 miles E of Dundee city centre on the A930

There is no doubt that golf is king in Carnoustie. This small holiday resort on the North Sea coast hosted the Open Golf Chamionships in 1931 and 1999, and is a favourite destination for golfing holidays.

But it has other attractions. **Barry Mill** (National Trust for Scotland) is a 19th century working corn mill. You can see the large mill wheel turning, and also find out how corn is ground. There is an exhibition explaining the historical role of the mill, as well as a walkway along the mill lade. Three miles north west of the town are the **Carlungie and Ardestie Souterrains** (Historic Scotland), underground earth houses dating from the 1st century AD.

PERTH

The "Fair City" of Perth sits on the Tay, and in medieval times was the meeting place of Scottish kings and parliaments. Though a large place by Scottish standards, having a population of about 45,000, it's location away

Huntingtower House

Crieff Road, Perth PH1 3JJ
Tel: 01738 624681 Fax: 01738 639770
e-mail: huntingtowerhouse@btinternet.com

If it's comfort and convenience you're after, then **Huntingtower House** is for you. Linzee and Hendry Lindsay have run this well appointed and popular guest house for eleven years now, and know what makes the perfect home from home. There are two superb bedrooms with large private bathrooms. In addition there is a self catering cottage based in what was an old coachman's cottage dating from the 1830s. The cottage has one twin room, one double room, a kitchen, bathroom and lovely lounge. Within the B&B establishment there is a TV lounge, and the whole thing is ringed by large gardens where you can relax in the sun during the summer months.

In the winter, you can take brisk walks in an area that is full of history and heritage before settling down before an open log fire in the lounge. The whole house is tastefully furnished with some antique pieces, giving it a cosy air. Huntingtower, a fascinating old castle which is open to the public, is close by, as is the lovely city of Perth itself, where there is much to do and see. And an hour and a half up the A9, at Aviemore, is one of Scotland's main skiing areas. Children over 10 years are welcome in this non- smoking establishment, where you are sure of a warm welcome at all times.

Cherrybank Inn

210 Glasgow Road, Perth, Perthshire PH2 0NA
Tel: 01738 624349 Fax: 01738 444962
e-mail: jackfindlay@kenscottsagehost.co.uk
website: www.cherrybankinn.co.uk

The **Cherrybank Inn** is something special - an old drovers inn dating from 1751 that served great drink, fine food and has comfortable, reasonably priced B&B accommodation. There are six twin rooms and one double, and all have ensuite facilities as well as TVs and tea/coffee making facilities. One room has been specially adapted for the disabled. The cosy bar sells a wide range of drinks, including three real ales (one of which is locally brewed), and the cuisine is excellent. Everything from bar meals to full dinners are available, and so popular is the place that you are advised to book at all times.

Brambles Coffee Shop And Restaurant

11 Princes Street, Perth, Perthshire PH2 8NG
Tel: 01738 639091 e-mail: tinderbox20@hotmail.com
website: www.bramblescoffeeshop-perth.co.uk

If you're looking for good food and excellent teas and coffees in the 'Fair City of Perth' then the **Brambles Coffee Shop and Restaurant** is for you. It is owned and run by Anne and Syd Dodds, who take a great pride in the quality of their food and high standards of service. The dishes include everything from pasta, black eyed bean cakes, rib eye steaks, chicken and ham pie to interesting salads, open sandwiches, freshly baked potatoes and grannies facourite, clootie dumpling. An extensive range of alocoholic and non-alcoholic drinks are also available, with traditional home-baking to complete the choice. The interior is spacious and interesting, and everything is keenly priced, making it one of the best establishments in the city.

from the Central Belt ensured that it never succumbed to the intense industrialisation that many other towns experienced. But it did succumb to the ravages of modernisation, and many of the ancient buildings that played a part in Scotland's story were swept away.

The city centre lies between two large open spaces, the **North Inch** and the **South Inch**, and is filled with elegant 18th and 19th century buildings. Up until the local government reorganisations of the mid 70s, it had a lord provost, and was truly a city. However, the city status was never taken away from it, and though it no longer has a lord provost, it remains a city to this day. It even has **St Ninian's Cathedral**, which dates from the 19th century. Perth has played a large part in the history of Scotland. James I chose it as his capital, and if he hadn't been murdered in the city in 1437, it might have been Scotland's capital to this day. The story of James's murder has been embellished over the years, but the facts are simple. He was an unpopular monarch, and when he was staying in the city's Dominican Friary (now gone), he was attacked by a group of nobles under the Earl of Atholl, who hoped to claim the crown. James tried to make his escape through the sewer which ran beneath his room, but was caught and stabbed to death. An embellishment to the story is that one of his Queen's ladies-in-waiting stuck her arm through the bolt holes of the door as a bar to prevent the entry of the assassins. However, it is probably a later invention.

In the centre of the city is **St John's Kirk**, one of the finest medieval kirks in Scotland. From this church, the city took its earlier name of St Johnstoune, which is remembered in the name of the local football team. It was consecrated in 1243, though most of what you see nowadays dates from the 15th century. It has some Renaissance glass, and it was here that John Knox first preached after his exile on Europe. His sermon more or less launched the Reformation in Scotland.

Perth

In Balhousie Castle in Hay Street you'll find the **Black Watch Regimental Museum.** Raised in 1725 to patrol or "watch" the Highlands after the first Jacobite Uprising, it is now the senior Highland regiment (see also Aberfeldy). The **Perth Museum and Art Gallery** is in George Street, and is one of the oldest in Britain. It houses material whose scope goes beyond the city and its immediate area, as well as a collection of fine paintings and sculpture. The **Fergusson Gallery** in Marshall Place is dedicated to the painter JD Fergusson (1874-1961), who, along with Peploe, Cadell and Hunter formed a group called the Scottish Colourists. The gallery opened in 1992 in a former waterworks built in 1832.

In 1928 Sir Walter Scott's novel *The Fair Maid of Perth* was published, the heroine of which was Catherine Glover, daughter of Simon Glover, who lived in Curfew Row. It was set in the 14th century, and tells of how Catherine, a woman noted for her piety and beauty, was sought after by all the young men of the city. The Duke of Rothesay, son of Robert III, also admired her, though his intentions were not honourable. He was thwarted by Hal Gow, who came upon the Duke and his men trying to enter Catherine's house in the dead of night. The ensuing skirmish resulted in one of the Duke's retainers having his hand hacked off by Hal before they fled in disarray. Through it all, Catherine slept, though Hal wakened her father and showed him the severed hand. The story ends happily when Hal subsequently marries Catherine. The present **Fair Maid's House** (not open to the public) doesn't go back as far as the 14th century. However, it is over 300 years old, and incorporates some medieval walls which may have belonged to the original house that stood on the site. In 1867 Bizet wrote his opera *The Fair Maid of Perth*, based on Scott's book, and the story became even more popular.

Two miles north west of Perth is **Huntingtower** (Historic Scotland), a restored 15th century tower house once owned by the Ruthvens, Earls of Gowrie. In 1582 the famous "Raid of Ruthven" took place here, when the Earl and his friend the Earl of Mar tried to kidnap the young King James VI. **Elcho Castle** (Historic Scotland) lies three and a half miles south east of Perth, and was the ancient seat of the Earls of Wemyss. It is a fine example of a fortified 16th century mansion.

Bell's Cherrybank Centre is an 18-acre garden adjacent to the headquarters of Bell's whisky distilling company on the western edge of the city. It incorporates the Bell's National Heather Collection, which has over 900 varieties of heather. **Kinnoull Hill**, to the east of Perth, rises to a height of 729 feet above the Tay. If you are reasonably fit, you can walk to the summit, where there is a folly, and get some wonderful views across the Tay and down over the Carse of Gowrie.

AROUND PERTH

SCONE PALACE

2 miles N of Perth off the A93

Historically and culturally, Scone (pronounced "Scoon") is one of the most important places in Scotland. It was the site of **Scone Abbey**, (now gone) outside of which, on the **Moot Hill** (which can still be seen) the Scottish kings were crowned sitting on the Stone of Destiny (see also Dunadd and Edinburgh). A replica of the stone is to be found at the summit. The last king to be crowned at Scone was Charles II in 1651. This stone is also called Jacob's Pillow, and is supposed to have been the pillow on which the Biblical Jacob slept. Scone Palace itself is the home of the Earls of Mansfield, and dates from the early 19th century. It has collections of fine furniture, porcelain and needlework.

Scone Palace

STANLEY

6 miles N of Perth on the B9099

The picturesque small village of Stanley sits on the River Tay, and is a former mill village. Sir Richard Arkwright had an interest in the mills here, the first of which was founded in 1786. Three large mills were built in the 1820s, powered by seven waterwheels. Four miles away are the ruins of 13th century **Kinclaven Castle**, once a favourite residence of Alexander II.

MEIKLEOUR

10 miles N of Perth city centre on A984

The **Meikleour Hedge**, just outside the village on the A93, is the world's largest. It borders the road for over 600 yards, and is now over 100 feet high. It is of pure beech, and was supposed to have been planted in 1746 as a memorial to those who fell at Culloden.

BLAIRGOWRIE

14 miles N of Perth city centre on the A93

This trim village, along with its sister village of **Rattray**, is noted as the centre of a raspberry and strawberry growing area. It sits on the Ericht, a tributary of the Tay, and the riverside is very attractive. **Cargill's Visitor Centre**, housed in former corn mill, sits on its banks, and at **Keithbank Mill**, which has Scotland's largest water wheel, there is a small heraldic museum.

The **Cateran Trail** is named after medieval brigands from beyond Braemar who used to descend on Perthshire to wreak havoc and steal cattle. It is a 60-mile long circular route centred on Blairgowrie, and uses existing footpaths and minor roads to take you on a tour of the area. It has been designed to take about five or six days to complete, with stops every 12 or 13 miles, and takes in parts of Angus as well as Perthshire.

COUPAR ANGUS

12 miles NE of Perth city centre on the A94

Situated in Strathmore, Coupar Angus is a small burgh which was given its burgh charter in 1607. The scant ruins of **Coupar Angus Abbey**, founded for the Cistercians, stand in the kirkyard.

The Old Smiddy

The Cross, Errol, Carse of Gowrie, Perthshire PH2 7QW
Tel: 01821 642888

The Old Smiddy, as the name suggests, is housed in a former blacksmith's cottage in this quaint old village. Owned and managed by Howard McCabe (who is a chef to trade, and oversees all the cooking), it has a fine reputation for its food, especially its seafood and Angus steaks. It also serves a good selection of beers, wines and spirits, including at least one real ale. The interior is cosy and traditional, with bare stone, warm, rich wood and open fires, and it is ideal place for a quiet drink or a beautifully cooked meal. Though open seven days a week, no food is served on Monday or Tuesday.

ERROL

9 miles E of Perth city centre on a minor road off the A90

Set in the **Carse of Gowrie**, a narrow stretch of fertile land bordering the northern shore of the Firth of Tay, Errol is a peaceful village with a large **Parish Church** of 1831 which is sometimes called the "cathedral of the Carse". It gives its name to an earldom, which means that there is an "Earl of Errol" (see Slains Castle). A leaflet is available which gives details of most of the old kirkyards and kirks in the Carse.

ABERNETHY

6 miles SE of Perth city centre on the A913

The **Abernethy Round Tower** (Historic Scotland), is one of only two round towers in Scotland (see also Brechin). It dates from the end of the 11th century, and was used as a place of refuge for priests during times of trouble.

FORTEVIOT

6 miles SW of Perth city centre on the B935

This little village was at one time the capital of a Pictish kingdom. In a field to the north of the River Earn stood the **Dupplin Cross**, erected, it is though, in the 9th century by Kenneth I. It was taken to the National Museum of Scotland in 1998 for restoration, after which it will be housed in St Serf's Church in Dunning.

DUNNING

8 miles SW of Perth city centre on the B934

This quiet village is mainly visited because of **St Serf's Parish Church**, with its fine 12th century tower. A couple of miles outside the village, near the road, is a monument topped with a cross which marks the spot where **Maggie Wall**, a witch, was burned in 1657.

AUCHTERARDER

12 miles SW of Perth city centre on the A824

Situated a couple of miles north of the Gleneagles Hotel, Auchterarder is a small royal burgh with a long main street. It has been bypassed by the busy A9, and retains a quiet charm. At **Auchterarder Heritage**, within the local tourist office, there are displays about local history.

About three miles west of the town is the cruciform **Tullibardine Chapel** (Historic Scotland), one of the few finished collegiate chapels in Scotland that have remained unaltered over the years. It was founded by Sir David Murray of Dumbarton, ancestor of the Dukes of Atholl, in 1446.

MUTHILL

15 miles SW of Perth city centre on the A822

Within the village are the ruins of the former **Muthill Parish Church** (Historic Scotland), which date mainly from the early 15th century. The tower however, which was once free standing, is Norman. A Culdee settlement of Celtic priests existed here before the church was built.

Three miles east of Muthill, at Innerpeffray, is **Innerpeffray Library**, one of the oldest libraries in Scotland. It was founded in 1691 by David Drummond, and is housed in a building specially built for it in 1750. It contans some rare books, such as a copy of the Treacle Bible and the Ship of Fools dating from 1508. Before moving to its present building it was housed in **Innerpeffray Chapel**, (Historic Scotland), built in 1508 by Sir John Drummond of Innerpeffray as a collegiate church.

To the west of the village you'll find **Drummond Castle Gardens**, one of Perthshire's hidden jewels. They were first laid out in the 17th century, improved and terraced in the 19th, and replanted in the middle of the 20th. In 1842, Queen Victoria visited, and planted some copper beech trees which can still be seen.

To the east of the village are the sites of two Roman signal stations - the **Ardunie Signal Station** and the **Muir O'Fauld Signal Station**. They were two of a series of such stations running between Ardoch and the Tay, and date to the 1st century AD.

FOWLIS WESTER

12 miles W of Perth on a minor road off the A85

The **Parish Church of St Bean** sits on a spot where a church has stood since at least the eighth century. The present one dates from the 15th century. A ten foot high cross slab with Pictish carvings stands within the church, as does a smaller one as well. A replica of the larger one stands on the village green. Also in the church is a fragment of the McBean tartan, taken to the moon by American astronaut Alan Bean.

CRIEFF

14 miles W of Perth on the A85

This inland holiday resort is the "capital" of that area of Scotland known as Strathearn. It sits at the beginning of Glen Turret, within which are the picturesque **Falls Of Turret**.

At the **Crieff Visitor Centre** on Muthill Road you can see paperweights, pottery and miniature animal sculptures.

The **Glenturret Distillery** at the Hosh is Scotland's oldest, and tours (with a dram at the end) are available, where you can see the distilling process in action.

COMRIE

21 miles W of Perth city centre on the A85

This village is often called the "earthquake capital of Scotland", as it sits right on the Highland Boundary Fault. The first recorded

ACARSAID HOTEL

8 Atholl Road, Pitlochry, Perthshire PH16 5BX
Tel: 01796 472389

The Acarsaid Hotel is situated in Pitlochry, surrounded by some of the best scenery in Scotland. It is privately run, and offers great hospitality in a house that is the epitome of Victorian comfort coupled with modern conveniences. There are 20 well appointed rooms (all en suite), as well as two lounges where you can enjoy a quiet malt or two, and a restaurant that serves what is acknowledged to be the best food in the area. Staying in the Acarsaid Hotel is an experience not to be missed!

DALSHIAN CHALETS

Old Perth Road, Pitlochry, Perthshire PH16 5TD
Tel/Fax: 01796 473080
e-mail: info@dalshian-chalets.co.uk

Nestling in a secluded woodland garden one and a half miles south of Pitlochry, these three chalets represent the best in self catering accommodation. Furnished and equipped to a very high standard, with full electric heating and double glazing, the chalets provide year round warmth and comfort. The large three bedroomed chalet has a master bedroom with en-suite shower room, and one of the two bedroomed chalets incorporates specially designed facilities for a disabled guest. If you enjoy peace and quiet, **Dalshian Chalets** are the perfect base for exploring the many attractions of Highland Perthshire.

POOLTIEL

Lettoch Road, Pitlochry, Perthshire PH16 5AZ
Tel/Fax: 01796 472184
e-mail: ajs@pooltiel.freeserve.co.uk
website: www.pooltiel.freeserve.co.uk

Overlooking the picturesque town of Pitlochry, **Pooltiel** has a stunning view of the Tummel Valley and the hills beyond. The town itself, with its professional theatre, its restaurants and its compact shopping area, is well worth exploring, and surrounding it is good walking country, as well as some of the best fishing in Scotland.

Under its owners, John and Kathleen Sandison, Pooltiel is a friendly, three star bed and breakfast establishment, offering all that is best in Scottish hospitality. Accommodation consists of one double room, one twin room and a family room, each one beautifully appointed, with colour TVs, hair driers and tea and coffee making facilities. For out of season visitors, the place is centrally heated.

A full Scottish breakfast is included in the overnight cost (with vegetarians and vegans catered for), and there is plenty of parking. Children are welcome, and baby changing facilities, a cot and a high chair are available. There are clothes drying and ironing facilities, and pets are accepted by prior arrangement.

tremor here took place over 200 years ago, and in 1839 a major one took place. **The Earthquake House**, built in 1869, houses an array of instruments to measure the tremors. North of the village, in Glen Lednock, is the **De'ils Cauldron Waterfall**, overlooked by a monument to Henry Dundas, 1st Viscount Melville (1742-1811). The village was the "Best Large Village" in the 2001 Britain in Bloom contest.

ST FILLANS

26 miles W of Perth city centre on the A85

St Fillans stands at the eastern end of Loch Earn, where the River Earn exits on its way to join the Firth of Tay, and is a gateway to the new Loch Lomond and Trossachs National Park. It is named after the Irish missionary St Fillan (see also Pittenweem and Tyndrum). Two relics of the saint - his bell and his pastoral staff - are now housed within the National Museum of Scotland. The Abbot of Inchaffray carried relics of St Fillan into battle at Bannockburn, and the Scots partly attributed their victory to this. At the top of **Dunfillan Hill** (600 feet) is a rock known as **St Fillan's Chair**. To the south west, overlooking Loch Earn, is **Ben Vorlich** (3,224 feet).

PITLOCHRY

This well known Scottish town is one of the best touring bases in Scotland. It is famous as being at the geographical heart of the country, and as such, it is as far from the sea as it is possible to be in Scotland. It was the 2001 winner as the "best small country town" in the Britain in Bloom contest.

Railway Station, Pitlochry

Though not a large town, it is full of hotels and guest houses, and makes a good stopping off point for those travelling further north. But it has its own attractions, not least of which is the marvellous scenery surrounding it. The B8019 west towards Loch Tummel, whose waters have been harnessed for the production of electricity, is particularly beautiful, and passes the **Forestry Commission Visitor Centre** which interprets the wildlife of the area. From the **Queen's View** there is a magnificent view west towards Loch Tummel and beyond. Queen Victoria stopped at this point during her Highland tour in 1866 and praised the view, though it is said that it was Mary Stuart who originally gave the place its name when she visited in 1564.

CRAIGVRACK HOTEL

West Moulin Road, Pitlochry, Perthshire PH16 5EQ
Tel: 01796 472399 Fax: 01796 473990
e-mail: irene@criagvrack-hotel.demon.co.uk
website: www.craigvrack-hotel.demon.co.uk

With sixteen en suite rooms, two of which are family rooms and one with disabled facilities, the **Craigvrack Hotel** represents Scottish hospitality at its best. All rooms have a TV, dial telephones, drinks facilities and hair dryers, and there is central heating throughout. The cuisine is outstanding, with vegetarian dishes always available, and the comfortable cocktail bar serves keenly priced bar lunches. There is also a quiet, cosy lounge where you can have a relaxing drink, and pets are welcome by prior arrangement. The Craigvrack makes the perfect stopping off point as you head north, or you can use it as a base to explore the wonderful countryside that surrounds Pitlochry.

Loch Faskally is a man-made loch, but is still a lovely stretch of water. It forms part of the Tummel hydro electric scheme, and at the **Pitlochry Visitor Centre**, near the dam which holds back its waters, there is the famous **Salmon Ladder** which allows salmon to enter the loch from the River Tummel below. There is a vewing gallery which allows you to watch the salmon, and displays about how electricity is produced from flowing water. Beside the loch is a picnic area, with an archway called the **Clunie Arch**. It is the exact dimensions of the tunnel that brings the waters from Loch Tummel to the Clunie Power Station.

The **Edradour Distillery**, situated among the hills to the east of Pitlochry, is Scotland's smallest, and possibly its most picturesque distillery. It was established in 1825 and produces a hand-crafted malt using only local barley. Conducted tours, finished off with a tasting, are available. Another place not to be missed is the **Pitlochry Festival Theatre**, housed in a purpose-built theatre beside the river. It presents a varied programme of professional plays every summer, and is one of Scotland's most popular venues.

The A924 going east from Pitlochry takes you up into some marvellous scenery. It reaches a height of 1,260 feet before dropping down into Kirkmichael and then on to Bridge of Cally. On the way, at Enochdhu, you will pass **Kindrogan**, a Victorian country house where the Scottish Field Studies Association offer residential courses on Scotland's natural history.

There are many fine guided walks in the area, some organised by such bodies as Scottish Natural Heritage, the Scottish Wildlife Trust and the Forestry Comission. A small booklet is available which lists them.

AROUND PITLOCHRY

SPITTAL OF GLENSHEE

13 miles NE of Pitlochry on the A93

As the name suggests, a small medieval hostelry once stood close to the village, which lies in the heart of the Grampian Mountains at a height of 1,125 feet. It sits on the main

Gardener's Cottage

Faskally, near Pitlochry,
Perthshire PH16 5LA
Tel: 01796 472450

Nestling in the hills near Loch Faskally at Pitlochry, but still close to the A9, **Gardener's Cottage** is a superb B&B establishment that offers the very best in Scottish hospitality. Boasting three tastefully decorated bedrooms with TV and coffee making facilities, it dates from 1860, and has wonderful views across to Loch Faskally and the Clunie Hills.

Under the ownership of Margaret Viner, it is a quiet retreat from the hustle and bustle of modern life which doesn't sacrifice those modern amenities we take for granted. As the name implies, it was originally a gardener's cottage, and has retained some marvellous period features, such as the fireplaces and the pine doors. A full Scottish breakfast is served in the comfortable breakfast room each morning, and as you feast on your bacon and eggs you can also feast your eyes on some more wonderful views of hill, woodland and water.

There's ample parking, and dogs are welcome. This is a beautiful part of Scotland, and Margaret will go out of her way to make your visit one to remember!

road north from Perth to Braemar, and surrounding it is some marvellous scenery. The Glenshee skiing area (Britain's largest) lies six miles north of the village, and is dealt with in the Aberdeen, Kincardineshire, Banffshire and Moray section of this guidebook. The **Devil's Elbow** on the A93 lies about five miles north. A combinaton of steep inclines and double bends made it a notorious place for accidents in days gone by, though it has been much improved. At **Cairnwell** the road reaches a height of 2,199 feet, making it the highest public road in Britain. During the winter months the road can be blocked by snow for weeks on end.

DUNKELD

11 miles S of Pitlochry off the A9

Though it has all the appearance of a small attractive town, Dunkeld is in fact a cathedral city. **Dunkeld Cathadral** sits on the banks of the Tay, and consists of a ruined nave and a restored chancel which is now used as the parish church.

For a short period Dunkeld was the ecclesiastical capital of Scotland. Kenneth 1, when he ascended the throne as the first king of Scots in 843, established his capital at Scone, near Perth, and brought relics of St Columba with him. He placed them in the church of a Celtic monastery set up at Dunkeld, no doubt because Iona was too vulnerable to Viking attack. In 865, records show that the abbot of Dunkeld was the chief Scottish bishop, though St Andrews gradually took over in the middle of the 10th century.

The cathedral as we see it nowadays dates from many periods. The eastern limb (the present parish church) was built mainly in the early 14th century, while the nave was built in the early 15th century. Within the church is the tomb of Alexander Stewart, son of Robert II, known as the **Wolf of Badenoch**, the man who sacked Elgin Cathedral in the 14th century (see also Elgin and Fortrose).

In 1689 the town was the scene of the **Battle of Dunkeld**, when Jacobite forces were defeated by a force of Cameronians under **William Cleland**. This was an unusual battle, as the fighting and gunfire took place in the streets and buildings of the town, and not on a field of battle. William Cleland was fatally wounded during the encounter, and now lies in the ruined nave of the cathedral.

That is why most of the "little houses" in Dunkeld date from the early 18th century - they were built to replace those that had been destoyed in the fighting. Now the National Trust for Scotland looks after most of them. On the wall of one house in the square called the **Ell Shop** is portrayed an old Scottish length of measurement called the "ell", which corresponds to 37 inches. Also in the square is the Atholl Memorial Fountain, erected in 1866 in memory of the 6th Duke of Atholl.

Another, but not so famous, man lies in the nave of the cathedral. Curiously enough he lies beside William Cleland, and yet he was the grandson of the greatest Jacobite of them all, Charles Edward Stuart. The Prince's illegitimate daughter Charlotte had an affair with the Archbishop of Rouen, the result being **Count Rohenstart** (a name made up from "Rouen" and "Stuart"). On a trip to Scotland in 1854 he was killed in a carriage accident.

Within and around the Birnam Institute is the **Beatrix Potter Exhibition and Gardens**, which tells the story of the young Beatrix. She used to holiday in the area, and gained some of her inspiration from the surrounding countryside.

ABERFELDY

8 miles SW of Pitlochry on the A827

In 1787 Robert Burns wrote a song called The Birks of Aberfeldy, and made famous the small

Ben Lawers over the River Tay

town and its surrounding area. "Birks" are simply birch trees, but it is by no means certain that the song is about about this particular spot. Some scholars say that Burns was writing about Abergeldie near Crathie in Aberdeenshire.

The village sits on the River Tay, and crossing it is **General Wade's Bridge**, built in 1733 as part of a network of roads so that the Highlands could be properly policed during the Jacobite unrest. At about the same time, six independent regiments were raised to "watch" the Highlands for signs of this unrest. These six regiments later amalgamated to form the 43rd Highland Regiment of Foot under the Earl of Crawford, and it paraded for the first time at Aberfeldy in May 1740. The regiment later became the Black Watch, and the **Black Watch Memorial**, built in 1739, near the bridge commemorates the event.

Wade's Bridge, Aberfeldy

Right on the A827 is **Dewar's World of Whisky**. Here you will find out about one of Scotland's most famous whisky firms, located in the distillery where Aberfeldy Single Malt is made. And in Mill Street is the **Aberfeldy Water Mill**. It was built in 1825 and restored in 1987. Visitors can see stone ground oatmeal being made, and there is a film showing the history of milling in Scotland.

A mile or so north of the village near Weem is **Castle Menzies**, home to Clan Menzies (pronounced Ming -iz in Scotland). It was built in the 16th century by James Menzies of Menzies, son-in-law of the then Earl of Atholl. The last member of the main line died in 1910, and it is now owned by the Menzies Charitable Trust. Parts of it are open to the public, and it houses a Clan Menzies museum. Charles Edward Stuart spent two night within its walls in 1746.

KENMORE

13 miles SW of Pitlochry on the A827

Kenmore sits at the western end of **Loch Tay**, and is a planned village founded by the Earl of Breadalbane. The loch is the source of the River Tay, and is one of the most picturesque in Scotland. It is fourteen and a half miles long, less than a mile wide, and plunges to a maximum depth of over 500 feet. Overlooking it, on the northern shore, is **Ben Lawers** (4,033 feet), with the **Ben Lawers Mountain Visitor Centre** on a minor road off the A827.

The Scottish Crannog Centre, run by the Scottish Trust for Underwater Archaeology, explains how people in the past lived in crannogs, which were dwelling houses situated in the shallow waters of a loch that offered defence against attack. They were either built on artificial islands or raised on stilts above the water, and were in use from about 2500BC right up until the 17th century. Off the north shore of the loch is **Eilean nan Bannoamh** ("Isle of the Holy Women") where once stood a small nunnery founded in the 13th century.

FORTINGALL

15 miles SW of Pitlochry on a minor road off the B846

This little village has one unique claim to fame. It is said to be the birthplace of **Pontius Pilate**, the governor of Judea at the time of Christ's execution. It is said that his father, a Roman officer, was sent here by Augustus Caesar as the commander of a unit which kept the local Pictish clans in check. Whether Pontius was born of a union between Pontius and a local woman, or whether Pontius had brought a wife with him, isn't recorded. There is no proof whatsover that the story is true, but there was certainly a Roman camp nearby.

Fortingall was laid out as a model village in

the 19th century by Sir Donald Currie, and it has some picturesque thatched cottages that wouldn't look out of place in a South of England village. In the kirkyard of the parish church is the **Fortingall Yew**, said to be the oldest living thing in Europe. The tree looks rather the worse for wear nowadays, but it may be as much as 3,000 years old, so perhaps this isn't surprising.

The village sits at the entrance to **Glen Lyon**, at 25 miles long, Scotland's longest, and perhaps loveliest, glen. Tumblng through it is the River Lyon, which rises at Loch Lyon, part of a massive hydro electric scheme. At Bridge of Balgie a minor road strikes south, rising into some wild scenery and passing **Meall Luaidhe** (2,535 feet) before dropping down towards the Ben Lawers Mountain Visitor Centre (see Kenmore) and the shores of Loch Tay. Bridge of Balgie is also home to a gallery that houses prints and orginal paintings by renowned artist Alan Hayman.

On the B846 four miles north of Fortingall is the **Glengoulandie Deer Park**, with its herd of red deer, Highland cattle, goats and rare breeds of sheep.

KINLOCH RANNOCH

17 miles W of Pitlochry on the B846

This small village, laid out in the 18th century by James Small, a government factor, sits at the eastern end of **Loch Rannoch**, which has roads on both the northern and southern sides. It is overlooked by the conically shaped **Schiehallion** (3,547 feet), from the summit of which there is a wonderful view as far south as the Lowlands.

An obelish in the centre of the village commemorates **D'ghall Bochanan**, who died here in 1786. He was one of the Highland's greatest religious poets, and was buried at Balquidder.

The B846 carries on westward past Kinloch Rannoch, and skirts the northern shores of Loch Rannoch. It eventually comes to an end at **Rannoch Station**. This station, on the Glasgow/Fort William line, is the loneliest railway station in Britain. Beyond it is **Rannoch Moor**, said to be the most desolate spot in Scotland, and "Europe's last great wilderness". In the summer months it can be a hauntingly beautiful place, but in the winter, when snow covers it, it is treacherous, and no one should venture out onto it unless they're experienced.

But the moor's landscape isn't a natural one. Even here, man has made his mark. The whole of the moor was once covered in the trees of the old Caledonian Forest, but man has gradually cleared them to use as fuel and for building. The whole of the moor is littered with large boulders, debris carried by the glaciers that once covered this area.

Soldiers Leap, Killiecrankie

KILLIECRANKIE

3 miles N of Pitlochry off the A9

It was here, in 1689, that the **Battle of Killiecrankie** took place. The Pass of Killiecrankie is a narrow defile, and as government troops under General Mackay passed gingerly through it regiment by regiment, they were attacked from above by Jacobite forces under Bonnie Dundee (see also Blair Atholl). It ended in a victory for the Jacobites, but Bonnie Dundee himself was killed. The **Killiecrankie Visitors Centre** (National Trust for Scotland) has displays explaining the battle.

At the north end of the pass is a spot known as the **Soldier's Leap**, high above the River Garry. It is said that, after the battle, a government trooper called Donald McBean leapt across the 18 foot wide gap to escape from some Jacobites who were chasing him.

Blair Atholl Castle

BLAIR ATHOLL

6 miles NW of Pitlochry off the A9

Blair Castle is one of the most famous castles in Scotland. It sits above the village, and with its whitewashed walls looks more like a great fortified mansion house than a castle. It is the ancestral home of the Murrays, Dukes of Atholl, and originally dates from 1269, though what you see nowadays is from18th and 19th century refurbishments. About 30 furnished rooms are open to the public, with fine furniture, paintings, china and armour on display. The Duke of Atholl is the only person in Britain who is allowed to have a private army, the **Atholl Highlanders**, and a small museum has displays of uniforms, weapons and musical instruments.

In the kirkyard of **St Bride's Kirk** in Old Blair is the grave of John Graham, 1st Viscount Dundee, known as "Bonnie Dundee", who was killed at the Battle of Killiecrankie in 1689 (see also Killiecrankie). At Bruar, four miles north of Blair Atholl, is the **Clan Donnachaidh Museum.** Though the name translates into English as Donnachie, it traces the history of the Clan Robertson, and shows their place in local and Scottish history. **The Falls of Bruar** are close by, and fall through a picturesque ravine, with footbridges over them. The **House of Bruar** advertises itself as the "ultimate shopping experience in Highland Perthshire".

10 Aberdeenshire, Kincardine-shire, Banffshire and Moray

The North East of Scotland is rich in scenery of all kinds. High mountains, wooded glens, cityscapes, beaches, rich farmland, towering cliffs, moorland - it's got the lot. And yet it is relatively unknown by those outside Scotland, apart from some areas in the Grampians and along Deeside. The beaches are quiet and uncrowded, the country lanes are a joy to drive in, and there is history and heritage aplenty.

Heather Moor, The Grampians

And always, in the background are the Grampians, which form a chain diagonally across Scotland, reaching their highest peaks here. Queen Victoria popularised Deeside, a glen which goes deep into the heart of the mountains, and it has remained firmly on the tourist trail ever since. But who has taken the time to explore the rest of the Grampians? Who has explored the farmlands of Buchan, with their rich soil, which, even though they are above the Highland line, have more of a Lowland feel about them? How many people stop in Kincardineshire, with its fishing villages and its literary connections? It was here that Robert Burns's father was born. It was here that Lewis Grassic Gibbon, a local man, set his dark novels of country life, ones that had little to do with the couthy images of simple, happy people that had prevailed up until then. And who, except those in the know, visit Elgin, a charming small city with the ruins of what was one of the largest and grandest cathedrals in Scotland?

Brig O'Dee, nr Braemar

As with many parts of Scotland, the tourist traps such as Deeside and Aberdeen swarm with people, while other places, equally as interesting and picturesque, are bypassed. To go off the beaten track in the North East is to be rewarded with some wonderful discoveries. The local tourist board, for instance, has organised a "castles trail", for nowhere else in Europe is there such a concentration of castles - around 1,000 at the last count. And then there are the Speyside distilleries, for which a Whisky Trail has also been laid out. The industry is centred mainly on Morayshire, where the streams are swift flowing and the water is pure. It's amazing that two distilleries a mile apart can make whiskies that are totally different in character.

The inland villages are quiet and peaceful, and the market towns, such as Inverurie, Forres and Huntly, are packed with history and charm. The coastline is as dramatic as anywhere in Britain. Yet another trail, the Coastal Trail, takes you on a tour of it, from St Cyus in the south to Findhorn in the west. The ruins of Dunnotter castle are perched dramatically above the sea, while the Ythan Estuary is a Site of Scientific Interest, rich is aquatic and bird life as well as having archaelogical sites dating back to Neolithic times. Slains Castle, south of Peterhead, was one of the inspirations for Bram Stoker's Dracula, and the fishing port of Fraserburgh was, for a very short time, a university town.

For all its crowds, especially in late summer when the Queen is visiting, Deeside cannot be missed. This long glen, following the Dee, winds up into the heart of the Grampians at Braemar, officially Britain's coldest place, and yet is green and wooded for most of its length. Balmoral - Crathie - Aboyne - the names are familiar to us all through news programmes, and yet the reality of seeing them makes you realise why Queen Victoria, and subsequent monarchs, fell in love with Royal Deeside in the first place.

Aberdeen Harbour

Aberdeen is Scotland's third largest city, and Europe's oil capital. The name, which means "at the mouth of the Dee and the Don", sums up its location exactly, as the two rivers enter the North Sea here. The oil industry has brought money to the city, and it has also brought a cosmopolitan lifestyle of smart restaurants, boutiques, nightclubs and stylish pubs which are much frequented by the oil workers, who come from all over the world. But even here history is never far away. It was granted a charter as a royal burgh by King William the Lion in 1175, and Old Aberdeen, which used to be a proud separate burgh, was granted its charter in 1489.

The other city in the region is Elgin, at one time one of the most important places in Scotland. It has lost some of that importance now, but hasn't lost any of its charm. It is still a busy place, the shopping and adminstrative centre for a large fertile area called the Laigh of Moray. Here too there are quiet country lanes and small villages to explore, while at Findhorn there is the Findhorn Foundation, where the emphasis is on spiritual living and alternative lifestyles.

ABERDEENSHIRE, KINCARDINESHIRE, BANFFSHIRE AND MORAY

PLACES TO STAY, EAT, DRINK AND SHOP

204	Marine Hotel, Stonehaven	Pub, accommodation and food	Page 258
205	The Crown Hotel, Inverbervie	Pub, accommodation and food	Page 259
206	Toll Bridge Lodge, Bridge of Feugh	Self catering	Page 260
207	Gordon Arms Hotel, Kincardine O'Neil	Pub, accommodation and restaurant	Page 261
208	Strachan Cottage, Tarland	Self catering	Page 262
209	Struan Hall, Aboyne	Bed and Breakfast	Page 262
210	Arisaig Cottage, Ballater	Self catering	Page 262

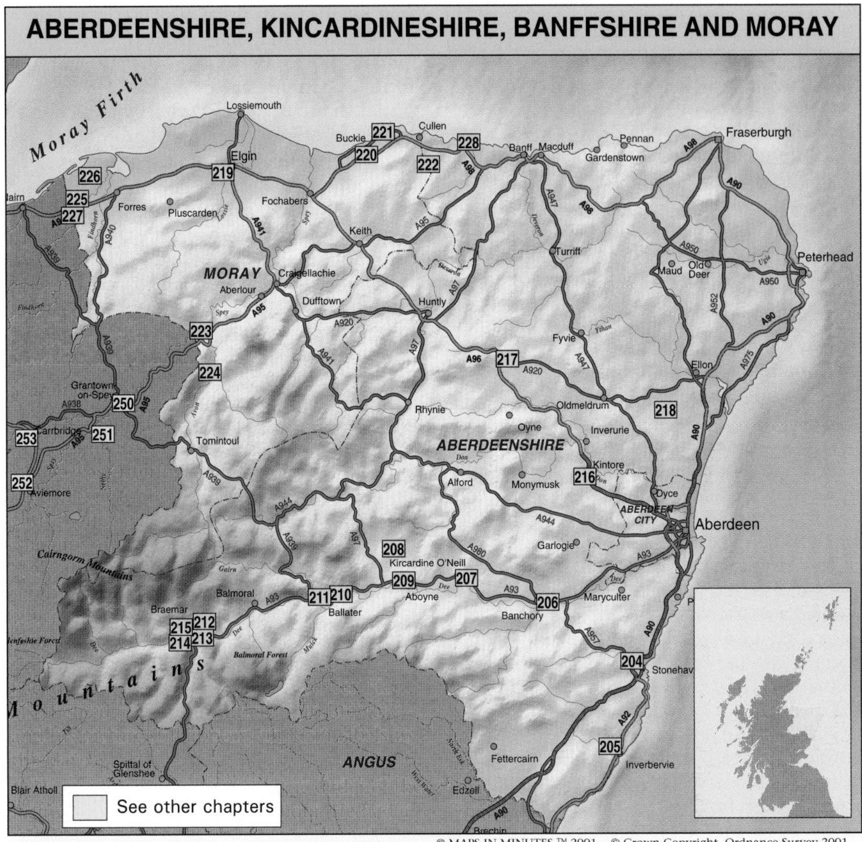

PLACES TO STAY, EAT, DRINK AND SHOP

211	Glenaden Hotel, Ballater	Pub, accommodation and food	Page 263
212	Callater Lodge, Braemar	Hotel and self catering	Page 264
213	Birchwood Cottage, Chapelbrae	Self catering	Page 264
214	Moorfield House Hotel, Chapelbrae	Hotel and restaurant	Page 265
215	Cranford Guest House, Braemar	Guest House	Page 266
216	Kingsfield House, Kintore	Self catering	Page 266
217	Morgan McVeigh's, Colpy	Restaurant and craft shop	Page 268
218	Coulliehare Farm, Udny	Bed and Breakfast	Page 269
219	Flanagan's Bar and Tapas Restaurant, Elgin	Bar and restaurant	Page 270
220	Old Monastery Restaurant, Drybridge	Restaurant	Page 272
221	Admirals Inn, Findochty	Pub with food	Page 272
222	Fordyce Castle, Fordyce	Self catering	Page 273
223	Delnasaugh Inn, Ballindalloch	Pub, accommodation and restaurant	Page 274
224	Glenlivet House, By Ballindalloch	Hotel and self catering	Page 274
225	Wellhill Farm Cottage No 1, Dyke	Self catering	Page 275
226	Wellside Farmhouse, Forres	Self catering	Page 276
227	Invercairn House, Brodie	Bed and Breakfast	Page 276
228	The Shore Inn, Portsoy	Pub with food	Page 279

ABERDEEN

With a population of about 220,000 people, Aberdeen is Scotland's third largest city. It's nickname is the "Granite City" because this is its predominant building material, one which has helped to create a stylish and attractive place that seems to glitter in the sun. It prides itself on being Scotland's most prosperous city, due to the vast oil fields that lie beneath the North Sea. For this reason it is also known as the Oil Capital of Europe, and the docks and harbours, which were once full of fishing boats, now pulse with supply ships ferrying men and machines out to the oil rigs.

It is a centre of learning, administration, shopping, business and industry. But it has never been scarred by industry in the way that some Central Belt towns have. It has managed to remain above such things, while still benefiting from their financial advantages, and its quality of life is among the best in Britain. And for all its bustle and modern office blocks, it is an ancient city, having been granted a charter as a royal burgh in 1175. Even then it was an important and busy port, trading with the Baltic states as well as the Netherlands and France. During the Wars of Independence it was sacked three times by the English, and finally razed to the ground by Edward III in 1337. One unexpected early visitor to Aberdeen was William Shakespeare, who, with his troup of actors, was sent by Elizabeth I to appear before James VI.

There are two Aberdeens - the original one, and Old Aberdeen, which was at one time a separate burgh. Perversely Old Aberdeen was only granted its charter in 1489, and is a captivating area of old, elegant buildings and quiet cobbled streets. The buildings you see throughout the city nowadays however, are mainly Georgian, Victorian and later, with some older buildings among them to add historical depth.

But Aberdeen has yet two more nicknames - Scotland's Garden City and the Flower of Scotland. Both derive from the many gardens and colourful open spaces that can be visited. It has won awards for its floral displays (including many "Britain in Bloom" awards), with **Johnston Gardens, Hazelhead Park, Union Terrace Gardens, Duthie Park** and the **Cruickshank Botanic Gardens** offering particularly fine examples.

The **Cathedral Church of St Machar's** in Old Aberdeen was founded in about 1131 in what is now Old Aberdeen. It is dedicated to a saint who was a companion of St Columba. Legend states that he was told by God to build a church at a point where a river bends in the shape of a bishop's crozier before it enters the sea. As the Don bends in this way, he established his church here. St Machar's as we see it today dates from the 14th century and later. Perhaps its most famous bishop was **William Elphinstone**, Chancellor of Scotland, and producer of the first book of liturgy in Scotland, called the Aberdeen Brevary.

Though the building is substantial, it is only the nave and the two west towers that stand today. It's Heraldic Ceiling is magnificent, the work of Bishop Gavin Dunbar, who succeeded Elphinstone in 1518. Dunbar also erected the two west towers.

The **Brig o' Balgownie** over the Don, near the cathedral, dates from the 14th century, and is a fine single arch structure. Aberdeen's other old bridge, to the south of the city, is the **Bridge of Dee**, again built by Bishop Dunbar in the early 1500s.

At Bridge of Don is **Glover House**, the family home of Thomas Blake Glover, the Scotsman who, it is said, inspired Puccini's

River Dee Suspension Bridge, Aberdeen

Seaton Park, Aberdeen

opera Madame Butterfly. Born in Fraserburgh in 1838, he first went to Japan when he was 21. He was entering a feudal society that had been closed to the west for over 300 years, but within one year he was selling Scottish-built warships and arms to Japanese rebels during the country's civil war. At the same time he sent young Japanese men to Britain to be educated. He was called the "Scottish Samurai", and helped found the Mitsubishi shipyards, the first step Japan took to becoming a great manufacturing power. He also helped found the famous Kirin Brewery, and his picture still appears on Kirin labels to this day.

He was later presented with the Order of the Rising Sun, Japan's greatest honour. He had a relationship with a Japanese woman, and when Puccini came across a short story and subsequent play based on this relationship, it sowed the seeds of Madame Butterfly.

The **Church of St Nicholas** stands in St Nicholas Street. At the Reformation it was divided into two churches, the East and the West. These were later united once more when the church was largely rebuilt in the 18th and 19th centuries. Of the original church only the transepts and the crypt survive. It's carrillon of 48 bells is the largest of any church in Britain.

Union Street, Aberdeen's main thoroughfare, runs close by. It is over a mile long, and is thronged with shops. It was laid out in the early 1800s to celebrate the union of Britain and Ireland. At one end, in Castle Street, is the city's 17th century **Mercat Cross**, standing close to where Aberdeen's long gone medieval castle stood.

Provost Skene's House, off St Nicholas Street, dates from the 16th century, and is named after a former provost of the city. It has wonderful painted ceilings and period furniture, as well as displays on modern history. **Provost Ross's House** is in Shiprow, said to be Aberdeen's oldest street still in use. The house was built in 1593, but is named after its most famous owner, John Ross, provost of Aberdeen in the 18th century. It now houses the **Aberdeen Maritime Museum**, with exhibits and displays on Aberdeen's maritime history, plus a recreated "helicopter ride" out to an offshore oil rig.

Aberdeen University was founded by Bishop Elphinstone in 1494. **King's College** stands in Old Aberdeen, and its chapel, built in 1505, forms one side of a quadrangle in the middle of which is a monument to Bishop Elphinstone. The chapel's crown steeple was erected in honour of James VI in the early 17th century. When it was blown down in a great storm in 1633 there were dark rumblings from the people of Old Aberdeen that witchcraft was involved. The **King's College Centre** explains the college's history. **Marischal College**, another university, was founded 99 years after King's College, which meant that the city had two universities - exactly the same number as the whole of England at the same time, as locals still point out. It was founded by George Keith, Earl Marischal of Scotland, and the present imposing granite buildings in Broad Street date from the 19th century. In 1860 the two universities united to form Aberdeen University. The Marischal College Museum houses a collection of classical and Egyptian objects, as well as local collections.

The **Aberdeen Art Gallery and Museums** are at Schoolhill, near Robert Gordon's College. Apart from a fine collection of paintings and sculpture by such astists as Degas, Reynolds, and Epstein, it houses displays on Aberdeen's history, including finds made at various archaeological digs throughout the city. **James Dun's House**, dating from the 18th century, forms part of the museum. The **Planetarium** at Aberdeen College in the Gallowgate Centre is a star dome which shows the planets and stars as they "move" through the heavens. And the

Gordon Highlanders Museum on Viewfield Road tells the story of what Sir Winston Churchill called "the finest regiment in the world".

At one time there were well over 100 quarries in the city mining granite. **Rubislaw Quarry**, near the Gordon Highlanders Museum, was one of the biggest. It was still being worked right up until 1971, when it was about 480 feet deep and 900 feet across. Now it has partially filled with water and fenced off. However, it can still partially be seen from Queen's Road.

Stonehaven Harbour

At Blairs, on the outskirts of Aberdeen on the B9077, there was a catholic seminary which closed in 1986. The **Blairs Museum** now holds the Scottish Catholic Heritage Collection, and is open to the public. There are objects connected with the Stuart line (including Mary Stuart and Charles Edward Stuart) on display, as well as a collection of rich vestments, church plate and paintings.

On the north bank of the Dee, where it enters the North Sea, is an area called **Footdee**, or, as it is known by Aberdonians, "Fittie". This is where Aberdeen's original fishing community lived, in rows of cottages that have now been renovated and smartened up.

AROUND ABERDEEN

STONEHAVEN

15 miles S of Aberdeen city centre off the A90

Stonehaven was once the county town of Kincardineshire. It is a fishing community, though the industry has gone into decline. Near the harbour stands the 18th century **Mercat Cross**, and the **Steeple**, from where James VII was proclaimed king in 1715. The Tolbooth is the town's oldest building, dating from the 16th century. It stands beside the harbour, and was formerly a storehouse belonging to the Earl Marischal of Scotland. Now it is the **Tolbooth Museum**, with displays and exhibits about the town's history.

Two miles south of the town is **Dunnotter Castle**. It stands on a promontory guarded on three sides by the North Sea and on the fourth by St Ninian's Den, a steep ravine. It dates from the 13th century and later, and has seen some gruesome episodes in Scotland's history. In 1297 William Wallace torched it, burning to death every English soldier within its walls. In 1652 Cromwell's troops laid siege to it to capture Scotland's Crown Jewels. However, they were foiled by the wife of the minister of Kinneff Church, who smuggled them out (see also Inverbervie) under the very noses of the troops.

Each year at Hogmanay the traditional

MARINE HOTEL

9/10 Shorehead, Stonehaven AB39 2JY
Tel: 01569 762155 Fax: 01569 766691
e-mail: marinehotel@hotmail.com

Under the ownership of Phil Duncan, the award winning **Marine Hotel** is one of the best establishments for comfort and service in the quaint old seaside burgh of Stonehaven. It has seven beautifully appointed rooms, and, no doubt because Stonehaven was once a busy fishing port, a reputation for fine cuisine based on the freshest of local fish. Children are welcome, and vegetarians are catered for. Pub lunches are available, as are snacks throughout the day. The bar offers a wide range of drinks, and the hotel even has its own specially brewed ale – Dunnottar Ale, named after a local castle.

Dunnotter Castle

Fireball Festival is held in Stonehaven. It takes place in the "Auld Toon" area of the town, where men walk along at midnight swinging on the end of stout wires huge fireballs made from wire mesh crammed with oily rags, wood and coal. The origins are rooted in paganism, when the light from the balls were supposed to attract the sun, ensuring its return after the dark days of winter.

INVERBERVIE

22 miles S of Aberdeen city centre on the A92

Though no bigger than a village, Inverbervie is in fact a royal burgh, having been granted its charter in 1341 by David II, who was supposed to have been shipwrecked there and "kindly received" by the people of the village. John Coutts, whose son **Thomas Coutts** founded the famous bank, was born here in 1699.

Three miles north, at Kinneff, is **Kinneff Church**. In 1651 the Scottish Crown Jewels were used at the coronation of Charles II at Scone, then hidden in Dunnotter Castle (see Stonehaven) so that Parliamentarian troops could not find them. But when the secret became known, they were then smuggled out by the wife of Kinneff's minister, the Rev James Grainger, and placed within the church. There they lay for ten years, beneath the floor. Every three months the minister and his wife dug them up and aired them before a fire. With the Restoration of Charles II in 1660, they were taken to Edinburgh Castle. Though no longer used for worship, the church is still open to the public and under the care of the

The Crown Hotel

10 King Street, Inverbervie, Kincardineshire DD10 0RG
Tel: 01561 361213 Fax: 01561 360050
e-mail: thecrownbervie@freeuk.com website: www.thecrownbervie.co.uk

Inverbervie is a splendid little royal burgh that sits on the marvellous Kincardineshire coastline, in an area that is rich in history. The **Crown Hotel** reflects this sense of tradition and heritage, and boasts one of the best collections of single malts in the area, with over 100 examples to choose from in the bar. There is also a fine selection of ales, wines and liqueurs, along with the usual soft drinks should you be driving. The hotel has five comfortable rooms, three of them en suite, and all have TVs and tea and coffee making facilities.

The food is wonderful, and all home-cooked on the premises under the supervision of the owners, Diane and David Wills. Local produce is used wherever possible, and the dining room, which is used for both lunches and dinners, can seat 40 in absolute comfort. One of the most popular dishes is the all day breakfast, which has become famous in the area! Pets and children are more than welcome, and high chairs are available. There is a cosy yet spacious bar – just right for that relaxing drink after a strenuous day exploring the sites – and a palatial function suite that can hold over 100 people. This is the kind of establishment where you will be given a good old fashioned Scottish welcome!

Kinneff Old Church Preservation Trust.

The village of **Arbuthnott** lies three miles inland from Inverbervie, at what is called The Mearns. **Arbuthnott Collegiate Church** dates from the 13th century onwards, and it was here that the **Arburthnott Missal** was written by James Sibbald, priest of Arbuthnott, in 1491. It lays out the form of service to be used at masses celebrated within the church. It can now be seen in Paisley Museum. The ashes of James Leslie Mitchell the author, otherwise known as **Lewis Grassic Gibbon**, lie with the kirkyard, and there is a memorial to him.

He was born in the Mearns, and, when he had settled in Welwyn Garden City near London, wrote dark brooding novels about Mearns farm life, far removed from the couthy stories about simple Scottish country folk that had gone before. **The Lewis Grassic Gibbon Centre** traces the life and works of a man who became one of the most important British writers of the 20th century.

The area has other literary associations, however. Robert Burn's father was born here before setting up home in Ayrshire, and in the kirkyard of the church at **Glenbervie** four miles to the north west is the grave of Burns's great grandfather, James Burnes (the "e" in the name was dropped when Burns's father moved to Ayrshire).

MARYCULTER

7 miles SW of Aberdeen city centre on the B9077

The land surrounding Maryculter was once owned by the Knights Templar, who established a church and preceptory, and dedicated it to St Mary. The order was suppressed in 1312 by Pope Clement V, and at trials held at Edinburgh in 1319 the last Preceptor of the house at Maryculter was given as William de Middleton of the "tempill house of Culther". On the opposite bank of the Dee a church had been established and dedicated to St Peter, and this parish became known as Peterculter.

Four miles west of the village is **Drum Castle** (National Trust for Scotland). Its keep is one of the earliest in Scotland, and was built in the late 12th century by the wonderfully named Richard Cementarius, the first provost of Aberdeen and the king's master mason. It was later owned by the Irvine family, who kept it in their possession for the next 653 years. It was enlarged in 1619 by the creation of a grand Jacobean mansion.

FETTERCAIRN

27 miles SW of Aberdeen city centre on the B974

On the edge of the fertile Howe of the Mearns, Fettercairn is an attractive village with, at its heart, the shaft of the **Kincardine Cross**. This once stood at the centre of the fomer township of Kincardine. In 1861 Queen Victoria and Prince Albert visited the village, and the **Fettercairn Arch** commemorates the event. The B974 north to Strachar and Banchory on Royal Deeside has many fine views. Close to the road, about a mile north of the town, is **Fasque**, home of William Gladstone, prime minister in the late 19th century. It has a deer park, and is open during the summer months, and at other times by arrangement.

GARLOGIE

10 miles W of Aberdeen city centre on the B9119

The **Garlogie Mill Power House** has a rare beam engine - the only one to have survived intact in its location - which used to power this woollen mill. The mill is open to the public, and there are displays about its history and machinery.

BANCHORY

17 miles W of Aberdeen city centre on the A93

This little 19th century burgh stands at the point where the River Freugh enters the Dee, and is often called the "Gateway to Royal Deeside". In Bridge Street is the **Banchory Museum**, which has collections explaining about tartans, royal commemorative china and the natural history of the area. The Scottish musician and composer **J. Scott Skinner**, "the Strathspey King", was born in the town in 1843, and a further display in the museum is dedicated to his life.

Three miles east of the town is **Crathes Castle** (National Trust for Scotland). It dates from the 16th century, with some of the rooms retaining their original painted ceilings. It was built by the Burnetts of Ley, who were granted the lands of Ley by Robert the Bruce in 1323. The ancient **Horn of Ley** hangs in the Great Hall. It was presented to the Burnetts by Bruce at the time of the land grant.

Six nature trails are laid out within the grounds, and there is also a walled garden with herbaceous borders and examples of topiary dating from 1702.

KINCARDINE O'NEILL

23 miles W of Aberdeen city centre on the A93

This little village claims to be the oldest village on Deeside. It is in fact a small burgh which was granted its charter in 1511. It was here, in 1220, that the first bridge was constructed across the Dee beyond Aberdeen, so it became an important place. The ruins of the **Kirk of St Mary** date from the 14th century. It may have been the chapel for a hospital that stood here before the Reformation. It was thatched up until 1733, when someone shot at a pigeon perched in its roof and it caught fire. The **Old Smiddy Centre** explains the history of the area, and about the workings of a smithy.

ALFORD

23 miles W of Aberdeen city centre on the A944

Alford is a pleasant village within a fertile area known as the Howe of Alford. The **Alford**

Strachan Cottage

9 Strachan Cottages, Tarland, Aboyne,
Aberdeenshire AB34 5PQ
Tel: 013398 81401

In the charming village of Tarland, four miles north west of Aboyne, you will find **Strachan Cottage**, a stone built cottage that offers the very best in self catering accommodation. It sleeps six in three bedrooms, and has a spacious and comfortable lounge, a well equipped kitchen and a bathroom. It is the ideal place for those wishing a quiet holiday close to Royal Deeside, or for the more energetic, such as anglers, golfers or ramblers. It is owned and run by Evelyn Smith, who keeps it spotlessly clean so that visitors can have a memorable holiday.

Struan Hall

Ballater Road, Aboyne, Aberdeenshire AB34 5HY
Tel/Fax: 01339 887241
e-mail: struanhall@zetnet.co.uk
website: www.struanhall.co.uk

Struan Hall is a superior establishment set in two acres of mature grounds about half a mile from the village centre. This charming old Victorian house, with its lovely granite stonework, bay windows and picturesque turret, has a welcoming and friendly aspect that is echoed in its spacious yet cosy interiors. It has three fully en suite rooms that are tastefully furnished, and all are extremely comfortable and decorated to an extremely high standard, with TVs, hair driers and tea/coffee making facilities. Struan Hall is the much loved home of Phyllis and Mike Ingham, who invite you to share its unique ambience on a B&B basis. They have paid great attention to detail, and it is one of the few establishments to have been awarded five stars by VisitScotland.

There is a choice of breakfasts, which are all beautifully cooked and presented, using local produce wherever possible, and they are hearty and filling - just the thing to set you up for exploring Royal Deeside, an area of Scotland that is full of history and beauty! And it makes a great base for exploring further afield. Aberdeen, Perth and Inverness are within easy reach, as is the Speyside Whisky Trail and the Moray Firth coast, with its quaint fishing villages and sandy beaches. Struan Hall is open between January 3 and October 31 each year, and though dinners are not served, both Phyllis and Micheal can recommend many local eating places, from smart restaurants to cosy pubs and tearooms. You might arrive as strangers but you are sure to leave as friends!

Arisaig Cottage - Royal Deeside

Victoria Road, Ballater, Aberdeenshire AB35 5QX
Tel: 013397 55177 Fax: 013397 55149
e-mail: angusdavidsonca@compuserve.com

Arisaig Cottage- Royal Deeside, is a modern yet picturesque bungalow which offers first class self catering accommodation. This double glazed property boasts two comfortable and tastefully decorated bedrooms (one double and one twin), a spacious yet cosy lounge, a well appointed kitchen/diner and a bathroom with instant heat shower. It is exceedingly well furnished, with TV, automatic washing machine, microwave, electric cooker and fridge/freezer. Pillows, duvets, linen and towels are provided. The cottage is adjacent to the first tee at Ballater Golf Course and a short walk from the centre of the village.

Valley Railway and Railroad Museum at Haughton House is a two mile long narrow gauge passenger railway with steam and diesel locomotives that runs between April and September. Close to the golf course you'll finds the **Grampian Transport Museum**, where there are dislpays and working exhibits about transport in the Grampian. area. You can even clamber aboard some of the exhibits.

Four miles south of Alford, on the A980, is one of Aberdeenshire's finest castles, **Craigievar Castle**. With its many turrets and small windows, it looks like something from a fairy tale. It was built by William Forbes in 1626, and has a fine collection of 17th and 18th century furniture, as well as family portraits. William Forbes was also known as "Danzig Willie", and was a rich Aberdeen merchant who traded with the Baltic countries.

Craigievar Castle

ABOYNE

27 miles W of Aberdeen city centre off the A93

This small Royal Deeside town is famous for the **Aboyne Highland Games**, held in late summer. The village prospered with the coming of the railway in the 19th century, and now it is a quiet settlement, popular with tourists. There is a lovely, but in places difficult, walk up **Glen Tanar** two miles west of Aboyne.

Five miles north of Aboyne, and two miles north east of Tarland is the **Culsh Earth House**, which is over 2000 years old. It is a long, dog-legged underground tunnel which was probably not used as a house, but as a store for foodstuffs. A torch is needed to explore it.

BALLATER

34 miles W of Aberdeen city centre off the A93

Set among the scenery of Royal Deeside, Ballater is surrounded by wooded hills of birch and pine, and makes an exellent base for exploring an area of outstanding beauty. It is a comparatively modern settlement, and, like Aboyne, owes its growth to the coming of the railways in the 19th century. In fact, this was as far as the Deeside line came, as Prince Albert stopped a proposed extension as far as Braemar.

There is plenty of good walking country around the village, and **Glen Muick**, to the south of Ballater, has a narrow road that takes you up towards Loch Muick (which can only be reached by foot), in the shadow of **Lochnagar**, which, notwithstanding its name,

CALLATER LODGE

9 Glenshee Road, Braemar, Aberdeenshire AB35 5YQ
Tel: 01339 741275 Fax: 01339 741345
e-mail: maria@hotel-braemar,co.uk
website: www.hotel-braemar.co.uk

Royal Deeside, with its royal connections and its stunning scenery, is an area not to be missed by anyone touring Scotland. And one of the best places to stay is the **Callater Lodge**, a friendly, family run hotel which has self catering accommodation in the grounds. The lodge itself was built in 1861 of local granite, and sits close to the heart of Braemar village, where the famous games are held each year. There are seven rooms, six of which are ensuite, and all have fine views over the surrounding countryside. There is also a comfortable guest lounge with open fire and central heating, where you can relax over coffee or a drink or two.

The self catering accommodation consists of a converted coachman's cottage in the grounds and a modern chalet. The cottage has one family and one twin bedroom, a well appointed kitchen, a living room and a bathroom. The chalet is substantial and roomy, with a bedroom (twin or double), lounge, dining room, kitchen and bathroom. Patio doors open onto a fine view of Morrone, one of the areas most beautiful mountains. The owners, Maria and Michael Franklin, would like to welcome you to their establishment, where you are assured of fine cuisine, wonderful wines and scenery that will take your breath away.

BIRCHWOOD COTTAGE

Birchwood, Chapel Brae, Braemar,
Aberdeenshire AB35 5YT
Tel: 013397 41599
e-mail: anderson.birchwood@tesco.net

Lying half a mile from the centre of the historic village of Braemar, with its royal associations, the three star **Birchwood Cottage** is a self catering cottage with a large garden that gives views over the River Dee towards the magnificent Cairngorms. It is a traditionally built, two storey building , and has two comfortable bedrooms – one double and one twin – as well as a well equipped kitchen, spacious dining room, comfortable living room and bathroom. It is owned by Sheila and Andy Anderson, who have created a wonderfully relaxing home from home for those who appreciate great scenery, fascinating history and a sense of tradition. All bed linen and towels are supplied, and there is plenty of off road parking space. Well behaved dogs are more than welcome by arrangement.

This is a cottage that can be appreciated both in summer and winter, with plenty of splendid walking country round about, as well as fishing, climbing and scenic drives that take the breath away. Balmoral is close by, and the Glenshee ski slopes are a few miles south along the A93. A warm Scottish welcome awaits those who decide to explore this area of Scotland, one that is at the heart of the country's history and tradition.

Balmoral Castle

is a mountain rising to a height of 3,786 feet. It gave its name to Prince Charles's book, The Old Man of Lochnagar. The drive is a particularly fine one, and takes you past **Birkhill** (not open to the public) which was bought by the Edward VII before he became king.

BALMORAL

42 miles W of Aberdeen city centre on the A93

The Queen's private home in Scotland was purchased by Prince Albert in 1852. Four years previously, Queen Victoria had visited and fallen in love with the area. Though the castle as you see it today, in Scottish baronial style, only dates from that time, a castle has stood here for centuries. The first recorded reference we have is in 1484, when it was called "Bouchmorale". The grounds are open all year, apart from when the Royal Family is in residence.

A quarter of a mile east of the castle is the small **Crathie Church**, where the Royal Family worships when it stays at Balmoral. It dates from 1855, and overlooks the remains of the 14th century kirk it replaced. **John Brown**, the Queen's ghillie, lies in the adjoining cemetery. The **Royal Lochnagar Distillery** is near the kirk, and has a visitors centre. It was given a Royal Warrant by Queen Victoria in 1864.

A **Victorian Heritage Trail** has been laid out which traces the footsteps of Queen Victoria not just on Deeside, but throughout the area, and a leaflet is available from most local tourism offices.

BRAEMAR

50 miles W of Aberdeen city centre on the A93

This little village high in the Cairgorms is officially Britain's coldest place. Between 1941 and 1970 its average temperature was only 6.4 degrees Celsius. On two occasions, in 1895 and 1982, it experienced the lowest

Braemar Gathering

MOORFIELD HOUSE HOTEL

Chapelbrae, Braemar, Aberdeenshire AB35 5YT
Tel: 01339 741244

Overlooking the site of the famous Royal Braemar Highland Games, the **Moorfield House Hotel** is a family run establishment that offers the very best in hospitality. It has six comfortable rooms, two of which are partially en suite. All are beautifully decorated, and offer tea and coffee making facilities. It is owned and run by Susan and Michael Ford, and serves delicious meals in either the cosy, welcoming bar or the elegant Park Restaurant. The resident's lounge boasts a colour TV, and the bar carries a great selection of drinks, from choice wines to beers and single malts. The place has a real "home from home" atmosphere, and is close to Glenshee, famous for its skiing.

River Dee, Braemar

It sits at an altitude of 1,100 feet, and is famous for the **Braemar Highland Games**, held every September, and visited by the Royal Family. **Braemar Castle** is the seat of the Farquharsons of Invercauld, and was built in 1628 by the Earl of Mar on the site of an older castle. It was used as a base by Hanovarian troops during the 1745 Rebellion. In the drawing room can be seen the world's largest Cairngorm (a semi-precious stone) which weights 52 pounds.

The 72,598 acre **Mar Lodge Estate** (National Trust for Scotland) lies five miles west of Braemar on a minor road. It has been described as the most important nature conservation landscape in Britain, and contains four out of its five highest mountains. The estate is open daily, and the Lodge itself has special open days which are well advertised. To the

temperature ever officially recorded in Britain - minus 28.2 degrees Celsius.

Cranford Guest House

15 Glenshee Road, Braemar, Aberdeenshire AB35 5YQ
Tel: 01339 741675 Fax: 01339 741209

Set in the picturesque village of Braemar, the **Cranford Guest House** has six beautifully furnished and decorated rooms, five of which are en suite and the other having private facilities. Owned and run by Pam and Jim Campbell, it offers a real "home from home" atmosphere for mature tourists, without compromising on quality or value for money. There is a large garden surrounding the house, and there is plenty of parking space. Cranford is open from the beginning of February until the end of November, and offers a warm welcome to everyone who stays there.

Kingsfield House

84 Kingsfield Road, Kintore, Aberdeenshire AB51 0UD
Tel: 01467 632366 Fax: 01467 632399

Kingsfield House is built on land given to the Hill family in the 14th century by Robert the Bruce. The steading is now a superior self catering cottage with two lovely double bedrooms, lounge, dining room, modern kitchen and bathroom. Owned and run by Jess and Pete Lumsden, the whole place is exceedingly well appointed, and there is lots of tourist information, games and a small library of books. The private garden is south facing, and ideal for barbecues. Children are welcome, and cots are available for infants and babies.

south of Braemar, on the A93, is one of Scotland's most popular winter sports areas, Glen Shee. The snowfields stretch over three valleys and four Munros, with about 25 miles of marked pistes as well as off-piste skiing.

KINTORE

10 miles NW of Aberdeen city centre off the A96

Kintore is a small picturesque royal burgh four miles south east of Inverurie. **Kintore Tolbooth** dates from 1740, and **Kintore Parish Church** was built in 1819. Incorporated in the west staircase is a piece of the sacrament house of the pre-Reformation Kirk of Kinkell.

INVERURIE

14 miles NW of Aberdeen city centre off the A96

The royal burgh of Inverurie sits where the River Urie meets the Don. A legend tells of how a Roman soldier, when the Romans came to this area, exclaimed "urbi in rure!" (a city in the countryside) when he first saw the settlement. The town adopted the words as its motto, and it is on the coat of arms of the burgh. Mary Stuart visited the town in 1562, and stayed in the royal castle which once stood where the mound known as the **Bass** now stands. The **Battle of Harlaw** was fought near the town in 1411, and a monument now marks the spot. A Lowland army fought a Highland army under Donald, Lord of the Isles, and while the result was an honourable draw, it did secure the supremacy of the Lowlands over the Highlands at that time.

In 1805, the **Aberdeenshire Canal** was opened which linked Inverurie with Aberdeen. It was never a great success, and in 1845 it was sold to the Great North of Scotland Railway Company, who drained it and used part of its route to carry their railway lines. **Port Elphinstone**, to the south east, recalls the canal, and a part of it can still be seen there. It was the only canal in Britain to be closed down every winter in case of ice and snow. Within the **Carnegie Inverurie Museum** in the Square is a small display dedicated to the canal, as well as displays on local history.

To the west of the town is the area's best known hill, **Bennachie**. Though not particularly high (1,600 feet) it has a distinctive conical shape, and is sometimes called "Aberdeenshire's Mount Fuji". Near the Chapel of Garrioch is the **Bennachie Visitors Centre**, where the natural and social history of the hill is explained.

Six miles south of Inverurie is **Castle Fraser** (National Trust for Scotland). Work started on it in 1575 by Michael Fraser, the sixth laird, and was finished in 1636. The castle contains many Fraser portraits, and fine carpets, linen and curtains.

MONYMUSK

17 miles NW of Aberdeen city centre off the B993

The **Parish Church of St Mary** dates from the early years of the 12th century. In 1929 it was restored to its orginal conditon, and it is now one of the finest parish churches in Scotland. The **Monymusk Reliquary**, which is associated with St Columba, was paraded before Bruce's troops at the Battle of Bannockburn. It is now in the National Museum of Scotland.

OYNE

21 miles NW of Aberdeen city centre on the B9002

Over 7000 ancient sites have been identified in Aberdeenshire, from Pictish carvings to stone circles, and these form the basis for the **Archaeolink Prehistory Park**, which bridges the gap between ancient history and modern times by way of exhibits and hands-on

Fyvie Castle, Fyvie

Morgan McVeigh's

Culsalmond, Colpy, Aberdeenshire AB52 6UY
Tel: 01464 841399 Fax: 01464 841390

In the shadow of Bennachie, and only a short drive from Aberdeen, is an establishment that offers some of the best shopping in Scotland – **Morgan McVeigh's**. It is open from 9.00-17.00 seven days a week, and is set in five acres of woodland, with stunning views across the Aberdeenshire countryside. An award winning Country Shopping and Restaurant complex, it is only the second tourist shop in Scotland to be awarded the coveted "five stars". It sells a wonderful mix of classic country fashions and accessories for both men and women, as well as Scottish pottery, jewellery, perfumes, glass, leather and books. In fact, this is the ideal place to buy quality souvenirs of Scotland. There is also a food hall selling such delights as hand made chocolates, whiskies and liqueurs, Scottish country wines, cheeses and cakes, many produced by small independent Scottish companies.

The food in the café/restaurant is outstanding, and represents great value for money. If it's a meal you're after, a light snack, or even just a cup of coffee, then you can relax in the main area or in the outdoor terrace. Food is served from 9.00 until late afternoon. If you're in this part of Scotland. you can't afford to miss Morgan McVeigh's, which is more that just a shopping experience – it's a good day out as well!

displays, both indoor and out. It has some of the finest collections of ancient remains in Europe.

FYVIE

23 miles NW of Aberdeen city centre off the A947

The oldest part of **Fyvie Castle** (National Trust for Scotland) dates from the 13th century, and was once a royal stronghold. There are 17th century panelling and plaster ceilings, as well as a portrait collection that includes works by Raeburn, Romney and Gainsborough. One of the legends attached to the castle is that the castle's five towers were built by the five great families in the north east - the Gordons, the Leiths, the Meldrums, the Prestons and the Setons

HUNTLY

33 miles NW of Aberdeen city centre on the A96

Huntly is an old burgh which received its charter in 1488. It sits in an area called Strathbogie, and is famous for the ruins of **Huntly Castle** (Historic Scotland). It was a Gordon stronghold, and originally built in the 12th century by the Earl of Fife. The Gordons were a powerful Border family who came north in the14th century and settled in the area. In the 1550s the castle was rebuilt by George, 4th Earl of Huntly. James VI had the castle demolished, though it was rebuilt by the sixth Earl, who subsequently became a marquis. During the turbulent Covenanting times, the castle changed hands many times until it finally fell into the hands of the Covenanters in the early 17th century.

From about the early 18th century the castle fell into decay. But even today you can see just how stately and comfortable the place must have been in its heyday. It entertained many famous people, including Mary of Guise, mother of Mary Stuart, and Perkin Warbeck, pretender to Henry VII of England's throne.

The Brander Museum in the Square has collections dealing with local history, as well as arms and armour and local author **George MacDonald**, who died in 1905. His most popular works were ones of fantasy and fairies, with a strong religious message. In the pleasant village of **Rhynie**, eight miles south of Huntly, is the **Anderson Bey Museum**, with mementos of Major George Anderson of the Seaforth Highlandrers, who went on to became a colonel in the Egyptian army.

Six miles south of Huntly, on the B9002 near **Kennethmont**, is **Leith Hall** (National Trust for Scotland). It was the home of the Leith (later Leith-Hay) family from1650 onwards, and contains many of their possessions. The family had a tradition of military service, and the most famous laird of them all, Andrew Hay, fought for Charles Edward Stuart. After Culloden he became a fugitive, which was difficult for a man who was over seven feet tall. In an exhibition called "For King and Country: the Military Lairds of Leith Hall" you can see his hose, which measure over three feet from the knee to the heel.

Leith Hall, nr Huntly

ELLON

15 miles N of Aberdeen city centre on the A948

Situated within an area known as the Formartine, Ellon is a small burgh of barony which was granted its charter in 1707. It sits on the River Ythan, with a **Parish Church** that dates from 1777. It's hard to imagine nowadays that this little town, five miles from the coast, was once a port with a small steamer that took goods up and down the river.

It is one of the stops on the **Formartine Buchan Way**, based on disused railway tracks from Dyce, just outside of Aberdeen, to Fraserburgh.

Five miles west of the town, on the A920 is the **Pitmedden Garden** (National Trust for Scotland). The centrepiece is the Great Garden, first laid out by Sir Alexander Seton, 1st Baronet of Pitmedden, in 1675. In the 1950s the garden was recreated using elaborate floral designs. Four parterres were created, three of them being inspired by designs possibly used at Holyroodhouse, and the fourth based on Sir Alexander's coat-of-arms. There is also a visitors centre and a **Museum of Farming Life**, which has a collection of old farming implements once used in this largely farming area.

Near the gardens are the substantial ruins of **Tolquhon Castle**, built by William Forbes, 7th Lord of Tolquhon in the 1580s. In 1589 James VI visited the house, and his coat of arms, together with those of Forbes, were carved over the doorway. William Forbes and his wife were buried in an elaborately carved tomb in the south aisle of the parish church at Tarves. The church has since been demolished, but the **Forbes Tomb** survives to this day.

Haddo House (National Trust for Scotland), one of the grandest stately homes in Aberdeenshire, lies 6 miles NW of Ellon. It was designed by William Adam for the 2nd Earl of Aberdeen in 1732, and restored in the 1880s. It is noted for its furniture, paintings and objets d'arts. It also has a terraced garden with rosebeds and a fountain. In the grounds is **Kelly Lake**, one of the few natural (as opposed to man made) sheets of water called "lake" rather than "loch" in Scotland (see Lake of Menteith, Kirkcudbright and Stenton).

ELGIN

Situated in the fertile Laigh of Moray, Elgin is a charming city with the ruins of what was one of the finest cathedrals in Scotland. Before the local government reforms in the mid 70s, there were only six towns in Scotland that were allowed to have lord provosts, and Elgin was one of them.

The city's layout is still essentially that of the medieval burgh, with a main street that goes from where the royal castle once stood to the cathedral in the east. It widens in the middle into a market place, where now stands **St Giles Church**. It is in Neoclassical style, and was built in 1828 to replace a medieval building.

Three 17th century arcaded merchants' houses are at the east end of the street, one of which at one time housed the bank of William Duff, a member of the family which went on to become substantial landowners in the area. The award winning **Elgin Museum** is in the High Street, and has many important collections, including natural history, archaeology and the social history of the area. Another museum worth visiting is the **Moray Motor Museum** in Bridge Street, with its collection of cars and motor cycles.

Work was started on **Elgin Cathedral**, or to give it its proper name, the Cathedral of the Holy Trinity, in about 1224. It was one of Scotland's grandest churches, and could compare to the great cathedrals of Europe. There had been three cathedrals in the dioceses before this one, at Birnie, Spynie and Kinneder, but the locations had all been unsuitable. By the end of the 13th century, building work was complete, though in 1390 the Wolf of Badenoch (see also Dunkeld and Fortrose), set fire to it after a violent quarrel with the Bishop of Moray. He did a lot of damage, and work on repairing it continued right up until the Reformation in 1560. After

the Reformation, the cathedral became a quarry for the people of the town. In 1807 a keeper of the ruins was appointed, and from then on what was left was cared for and preserved. The east gate to the cathedral precincts, known as the **Panns Port**, still stands. The **Old Mills** is the last remaining meal mill on the River Lossie. It's history goes back to the 13th century, when it was owned by Pluscarden Abbey.

North of the city are the impressive ruins of **Spynie Palace** (Historic Scotland) , the home of the bishops of Moray. The palace sits on the shores of tiny Loch Spynie, and dates from the 14th century and later. David's Tower, the main part of the building dates from the 16th century. Spynie Church, which stood nearby until 1736, was at one time the catherdal of the diocese.

The ruins of the **Church of St Peter** (Historic Scotland) stand near the village of Duffus, north west of Elgin. Though mainly 18th century, it incorporates work that is much older. Opposite the porch is the old **Parish Cross**. Close by are the ruins of **Duffus Castle**, the original seat of the de Moravia family, ancestors of the Murrays, and the people who gave the area its name of Moray. The castle dates from the 13th century onwards, and has the finest motte and bailey of any castle in the north of Scotland. **Gordonstoun**, attended by both Prince Philip and Prince Charles is close to Duffus, housed in an 18th century mansion.

AROUND ELGIN

LOSSIEMOUTH

5 miles N of Elgin on the A941

This holiday resort sits at the mouth of the River Lossie, and was established as a small port for the city of Elgin in the 18th century. There are fine sandy beaches, and the **Lossiemouth Fisheries and Community Museum** traces the history of the town and its fishing industry. There is also a reconstruction of the study used by **James Ramsay Macdonald**, Britain's first Labout prime minister, who was born in a small cottage in the town in 1866.

FOCHABERS

8 miles E of Elgin on the A96

Fochabers dates from the 18th century, when the then Duke of Gordon decided that he didn't like the huddle of cottages within his parkland that was old Fochabers. He therefore built a new village with a large spacious square, and the present day Fochabers was the result. Within the former Pringle Church is the **Fochabers Folk Museum**, and in the square is the elegant, porticoed **Bellie Church**. The imposing **Milne's High School** dates from 1844, and was built using money gifted by a native of the town who made his fortune in New Orleans.

West of the village centre is **Baxter's Highland Village**, home to one of the best known food firms in Scotland. It all started in 1868, when George Baxter, who worked for the Duke of Gordon, opened a small grocery shop in Fochabers. This is one of the most fertile areas in Britain, famed for its fruit, vegetables and cattle, and soon George's wife was making jams and conserves in the back shop. Now the factory and associated shops, restaurants and kids' play areas are tourist attractions in their own right.

BUCKIE

13 miles E of Elgin on the A990

Buckie is a major fishing port, and in the **Buckie Drifter** on Freuchnie Road there are displays that tell the story of the fishing industry on the Morayshire coast. The small fishing communities round about, such as **Findochty** and **Portnockie** are very attractive. The **Peter Anson Gallery** is within the town's

Fishing Boats, Buckie

OLD MONASTERY RESTAURANT

Drybridge, Buckie, Moray AB56 5JB
Tel: 01542 832660 Fax: 01542 839437
e-mail: val or calum@oldmonastery.com
website: www.oldmonastery.com

Set in what was a retreat for the monks of Fort Augustus, the **Old Monastery Restaurant** is now one of the most famous eating places in Scotland. It sits on a hillside above the fishing port of Buckie, and over the years, Val and Calum Buchanan have created a relaxed and friendly ambience in which to enjoy good food and wine. They have retained many of the original features of the building, and these are enhanced by the wonderful views across the Moray Firth towards Ben Wyvis in Ross and Cromarty. The restaurant is a member of "Taste of Scotland" and the International Slow Food Movement, and has a Michelin listing as well as two AA Rosettes. The produce is sourced locally wherever possible, and the restaurant takes a pride in presenting the food in a pleasing yet not overpowering manner, while retaining natural, honest flavours.

Dining out, Val and Calum believe, should be pleasurable for all the family, and not dry or formal, and for this reason children are welcome at lunchtime, though there is no separate children's menu. The wine list has been chosen with care so that they are affordable without compromising quality or taste. This is the perfect place for a lunch or dinner in summer or winter, as each season adds a certain something to the overall dining experience. It is warm and snug in winter, when heated by cosy wood stoves, and light and airy in summer.

ADMIRALS INN

6/7 Jubilee Terrace, Findochty,
Morayshire AB56 4QA
Tel: 01542 832735

The **Admirals Inn** is a traditional, well run pub overlooking the harbour in the historic fishing village of Findochty. It is owned by Fiona and David Roberts, who have created a warm and welcoming establishment that is popular with locals and visitors alike. There is a well stocked bar (as well as soft drinks, of course, if you're driving), and excellent food is served at lunchtime, between 12.00 and 14.00, and between 18.00 and 20.00 in the evening. The menu has been carefully prepared so that there is sure to be a dish that will suit your taste. Being set in a fishing village, seafood features heavily, with the most popular dish being the "Admiral's Catch", which is scallops, plaice, haddock and scampi. Everything is well presented, the portions are hearty and filling and the service friendly and efficient.

There are also sandwiches and lighter meal options and as children are more than welcome until 8.00p.m., a children's menu is also available. In the summer months the beer garden provides excellent views over the Moray Firth where you can sit and "dolphin watch". There is also a pool table and darts in the bar and occasional live entertainment throughout the year. It is an excellent stopping place if you are exploring the coastal or malt whisky trails.

library, and has a collection of paintings from all over Scotland by the maritime artist Peter Anson.

Four miles west of the town is the mouth of the River Spey. It is half a mile wide, though no great port sits here. The village of **Kingston** dates from 1784, and was founded by Ralph Dodworth and William Osbourne. They came from Kingston-upon-Hull in Yorkshire, and named their village after it. It was near here that Charles II alighted after a trip from Holland on 23 June 1650. His ship grounded in shallow water, and he had to be taken ashore "piggyback" style on the back of a villager.

Five miles south west of the town are the ruins of **Deskford Church**, within the village of the same name. It is noted for its ornately carved sacrament house. The 16th century **St Mary's Church** sits in the the small fishing village of **Cullen**, to the north of Deskford, and was formerly collegiate. In the village of **Fordyce**, south east of Cullen, is the **Fordyce Joiner's Workshop and Visitor Centre**, dedicated to the skills and tools of carpentry in north east Scotland.

CRAIGELLACHIE

12 miles S of Elgin on the A95

The **Craigellachie Bridge** dates from 1814, and is Scotland's oldest iron bridge. It was designed by Thomas Telford, and has one single graceful arch which spans the Spey. The village sits in the heart of the **Malt Whisky Trail**, and most of the distilleries organise tours round the premises, with a tasting at the end. The **Speyside Cooperage** has a visitors centre where you can learn about the skills involved in making and repairing casks and barrels. Just north of the village is the **Glen Grant Distillery**, and near **Dufftown**, four miles to the south, is the **Glenfiddich Distillery**. Overlooking it are the ruins of 13th century and later **Balvenie Castle** (Historic Scotland), once home to the Comyns. The **Glenfarclas Distillery** is seven miles south west, near **Ballindalloch Castle.** The castle dates from the 16th century, and is the home of the Macpherson-Grant family, who have lived here continuously since it was built. It is open to the public during the summer months. About four miles south of

FORDYCE CASTLE

Fordyce, Banffshire AB45 2SN
Tel: 01261 843722 Fax: 01261 843733
e-mail: info@fordycecastle.co.uk
website: www.fordycecastle.co.uk

If you've ever wanted to stay in an historic castle, then the west wing of **Fordyce Castle** is for you. It stands in the centre of the small village of Fordyce, and offers excellent and comfortable self catering accommodation on two floors for four people. There is a twin and a double bedroom with a four poster bed, a sitting room, a well appointed kitchen/dining room, a bathroom and a small garden courtyard for the exclusive use of guests. There is also private parking. The wing has been tastefully renovated by the castle's owners, Robert and Fiona McVeigh Crabbe (Baron and Lady Fordyce), and while retaining original features, now has all the modern comforts that would make a stay here a memorable experience.

The castle is a typical Scottish laird's house, built in 1592 for Thomas Menzies of Durn, a former provost and merchant of Aberdeen. There are many architectural features of interest, such as "shot holes" (one of which is in the double bedroom) and the unusual corbelling which supports the stair turret. Fordyce Castle would make an ideal but unusual base from which to explore the surrounding area – one that is rich in fauna and flora, as well as history and heritage.

Delnasaugh Inn

Ballindalloch, Banffshire AB37 9AS
Tel: 01807 500255
Fax: 01807 500389

Overlooking the River Avon, the **Delnashaugh Inn** sits right in the heart of Speyside, famous for its distilleries and wonderful scenery. It is a former drover's inn, and under the personal supervision of Dorothy and Neil Meldrum, it has become one of the best hotels in an area that is renowned for good hotels. The nine bedrooms have been decorated and furnished to an extremely high standard, and all are en suite, with colour TVs, hair dryers, electric blankets, central heating and tea and coffee making facilities. The surrounding area is peaceful and quiet, yet full of interest. Historical attractions abound, and of course the inn is firmly on the Speyside Whisky Trail (open April to October each year), which takes in many of the famous distilleries to be found in this part of Scotland. Being on the Ballindalloch Estate, shooting and fishing can be organised locally.

The comfortable lounge and lounge bar serve bar lunches every day, and the restaurant, which is open for dinner each evening, is a comfortable and relaxing place to enjoy food that is always beautifully cooked and presented. Dorothy and Neil take a pride in the fact that only local produce is used wherever possible, and that the wine list is second to none. This the kind of place where you'll experience the best in Scottish hospitality, and Dorothy and Neil will ensure you get a real Highland welcome!

Glenlivet House

By Ballindalloch, Banffshire AB37 9DJ
Tel: 01807 590376 e-mail: staylor@glenlivet.u-net.com
Fax: 01807 590363 website: www.glenlivethouse.co.uk

Glenlivet House stands in three and a half acres of land, and is a picturesque, typically Scottish country house dating from late Victorian times. Owned by Amalia and Simon Taylor, it has been tastefully modernised to reflect today's needs, and is now a superb base from which to take part in all the activities – sporting or otherwise – this wonderful part of Scotland has to offer. It is let to parties of people, one party at a time, on a weekly basis, and this can be full board or self catering. Shorter of longer bookings are also available. Whichever you choose, you are sure to appreciate the many facilities the house has to offer.

It is furnished throughout with Amalia and Simon's treasured possessions, making it a warm and welcoming place, one where you can relax and enjoy a truly Scottish lifestyle. There are ten double or twin rooms and two singles, with ten of the rooms having en suite facilities and the other two having private bathrooms. For the benefit of self catering parties, there is a well appointed kitchen, and excellent cooks are employed for full board parties. There is a well stocked bar, with parties running it themselves on a sale or return basis. Cleaning staff look after the domestic side of things, and the house is centrally heated throughout.

Ballindalloch is the **Glenlivit Distillery**, which again has organised tours.

TOMINTOUL

27 miles S of Elgin on the A939

Tomintoul, situated at a height of 1,160 feet, is the highest village in the Highlands (but not in Scotland). The A939 south west to Cockbridge is called **The Lecht**, and is notorious for being blocked by snow in winter. The ski area of the same name lies six miles from Tomintoul. The small **Tomintoul Museum** has displays on local history.

The Grampians, Tomintoul

PLUSCARDEN

6 miles SW of Elgin on a minor road

Pluscarden Priory was founded in 1230 and settled firstly by the Valliscaulian and then the Benedictine monks. In the 19th century the Bute family acquired the ruined buildings, and in 1948 presented it to the monks of Prinknash in England. At first it was a priory, but became an abbey in its own right in 1974. Since then the monks have been restoring the buildings so that nowadays it is the only medieval abbey in Britain with monks still living and worshipping in it. It is open to the public, and has a small gift shop.

FORRES

12 miles W of Elgin on the A96

This small royal burgh, which was granted its charter in the 13th century, was once one of the most important places in Scotland, and is mentioned in Shakespeare's Macbeth. The ground plan of the medieval settlement still forms the basis of the town today, though it is much more open and green than it was then, thanks to some large areas of parkland.

The 20 foot high **Sueno's Stone** (Historic Scotland) dates from the 9th century, and is the largest known stone with Pictish carvings. One side shows a cross, while the other shows scenes of battle. **The Falconer Museum** in Tolbooth Street was founded in 1871, and highlights the history and heritage of the town and its surroundings. Dominating the town is the **Nelson Tower**, built in 1812 to commemorate Nelson's victory at Trafalgar. If you're fit enough to climb its 96 steps, you'll get spectacular views over the surrounding countryside and the Moray Firth.

WELLSIDE FARMHOUSE

Kincorth Estate, Forres,
Morayshire IV36 2SP
Tel/Fax: 01309 674132

Lying between the picturesque River Findhorn and the Moray Firth, **Wellside Farmhouse** is an attractive, stone building with great views over open farmland towards the Culbin Forest. This area is famous for its sandy beaches, its historic towns and its wildlife, and Wellside makes an ideal base from which to explore it. Upstairs, the house has one double bedroom, a double/twin bedroom and two further twin bedrooms (one decorated for children), so can sleep eight in absolute comfort. There is also a roomy bathroom with separate corner shower. On the ground floor there is a cosy sitting room, a dining room, a well appointed breakfast kitchen, a utility room and a WC.

The whole place is centrally heated, and bed linen, towels, electricity and logs for the open fire are included in the rent. The kitchen is beautifully appointed with oven and hob, microwave, dishwasher and fridge/freezer. There is a telephone as well as a TV and video in the sitting room and a further TV in the childrens' bedroom. Owners Connie and Malcolm Middletow have created the perfect location for a quiet, "get away from it all" holiday for all the family in a lovely part of Scotland – one noted for its friendliness and hospitality.

INVERCAIRN HOUSE

Brodie, by Forres, Moray IV36 2TD
Tel/Fax: 01309 641261

Set in the delightful village of Brodie, close to the entrance to Brodie Castle, **Invercairn House** is the ideal B&B establishment from which to explore an area that is rich in history, heritage and wildlife. Owners Elish and Nick Malim have created a real home from home atmosphere in their substantial yet picturesque house, which dates from 1856 and was once the castle station. In fact, so good is the hospitality it offers that it has been awarded a coveted three stars from VisitScotland. Both French and German are spoken in this establishment, which has one double family room, a twin family room, a twin room and a single, and all are beautifully appointed. Each one has a colour TV, wash hand basin, hairdryer and tea and coffee making facilities. There's a drying room for wet clothes, private parking, and a shed for motor bikes and bicycles.

Breakfasts can be either Continental or traditional Scottish (which always means a hearty plateful!) and evening meals are available on request, with the food being beautifully cooked from local produce wherever possible. The house sits in half an acre of lovely gardens, where you can spend a relaxing evening just watching the world go by. Elish and Nick will extend a warm welcome should you choose to stay in their lovely home!

Brodie Castle (National Trust for Scotland) lies four miles to the west of the town. It is a 16th century tower house with later additions which give it the look of a comfortable mansion. It dates back at least to the time of Malcolm, Thane of Brodie, who died in 1285, and possibly earlier. It contains major collections of paintings, furniture and ceramics, and sits in 175 acres of ground. A couple of miles north east of Forres is **Kinloss**, with an RAF base and the scant remains of an old abbey.

On the coast north of Forres is perhaps Scotland's most unusual landscape, the **Culbin Sands**. In 1694 a storm blew great drifts of sand - some as high as 100 feet - over an area that had once been green and fertile, causing people to flee their homes. They covered cottages and fields, and eventually created eight square miles of what became known as "Scotland's Sahara". Occasionally, further storms would uncover the foundations of old cottages, which were then covered back up again by succeeding storms. The sands continued to shift and expand until the 1920s, when trees were planted to stabilise the area.

At **Findhorn**, on the Moray Firth coast, is the **Findhorn Foundation**, one of the most successful centres in Britain for exploring alternative lifestyles and spiritual living. It was founded by Dorothy Maclean and Peter and Eileen Caddy in 1962 in a caravan park. The **Findhorn Heritage Centre and Museum** has displays on the history and heritage of the village. **Dallas Dhu Distillery** (Historic Scotland) sits to the south of Forres, and explains the making of whisky.

FRASERBURGH

Fraserburgh is in that area of the north east known as Buchan. It is one of the main fishing ports in north east Scotland, and was founded in the 16th century by Alexander Fraser, eighth laird of Philorth. In 1546 he built the first harbour, used by the seamen of Broadsea, an old settlement that stood near Kinnaird Head. The **Old Kirk** in Saltoun Square isn't as old as its name would suggest. It was built in 1803 to replace the original church built by Alexander between1570 and 1571. Beside it is the Fraser Burial Aisle.

400 year Celebrations, Fraserburgh

One of Alexander's grander schemes was the founding of a university in the town, and he even went so far as to obtain James VI's permission to do so. The Scots Parliament gave it a grant, and the Rev Charles Ferme became its first principal. Unfortunately, the Rev Ferme was later arrested for attending a general assembly of the Church of Scotland in defiance of the king. The embryonic university subsequently collapsed, though one street in Fraserburgh, College Bounds, still commemorates the scheme.

Kinnaird Lighthouse (Historic Scotland) must be the most unusual lighthouse in Scotland, as it is built onto a 16th century castle built by Alexander Fraser as his main residence after founding the town. It is now a museum dedicated to Scotland's lighthouses. The most unusual building in Fraserburgh is the **Wine Tower**, next to the lighthouse. It too was built by Alexander Fraser, possibly as a chapel. It has three floors, but no connecting stairways. At Sandhead, to the west of the town, is the **Sandhead Meal Mill**, dating from the 19th century. Guided tours and models show how oatmeal used to be ground in Scotland. At Memsie, three miles south of Fraserburgh, is the **Memsie Burial Cairn**, dating from about 1500BC.

AROUND FRASERBURGH

PETERHEAD

15 miles SE of Fraserburgh on the A982

Peterhead is the second largest town in Aberdeenshire, and one of the chief fishing ports in the north east. It was founded by George Keith, the 5th Earl Marischal of Scotland in 1593, and is Scotland's most easterly burgh. Now that fishing has declined, it benefits from being one of the ports that services the offshore gas industry. The **Arbuthnott Museum** in St Peter Street tells the story of the town and its industries, and has a large collection of Inuit, or Eskimo, artifacts. Set by the harbour of refuge to the south of the town, in a purpose-built building, is **Peterhead Maritime Heritage**. This tells of the town's connections with the sea over the years, from its fishing fleet (which went as far as the Arctic in search of fish) to the modern offshore gas and oil industries.

A few miles south of the town, at Cruden Bay, are the ruins of **Slains Castle**, built by the Earl of Errol in the 16th century to replace an earlier castle. It has been rebuilt and refurbished several times since then, and the ruins you see now date from the early 19th century. It has literary associations of an an unusual kind. While staying at the nearby village of Cruden Bay in 1895, **Bram Stoker** began writing Dracula, and an early draft of the novel has the Count coming ashore at Slains rather than Whitby.

OLD DEER

12 miles S of Fraserburgh on the B9030

In a beautiful position on the banks of the River South Ugie are the ruins of **Deer Abbey** (Historic Scotland), founded in 1219 by William Comyn, Earl of Buchan for the Cistercian order of monks. Little remains of the abbey church, but some of the walls of the other buildings are fairly well preserved.

Close by is the village of **Mintlaw**, where you'll find the **Aden Farming Museum**, which sits within a country park. It traces the history of farming in this rich area of Aberdeenshire through three separate themes - the Aden Estate Story, the Weel Vrocht Grun ("well worked ground") and the country park itself.

MAUD

12 miles S of Fraserburgh on the B9029

Maud grew up around the railway line that once connected Aberdeen to Fraserburgh, and in the **Maud Railway Museum**, in the village's former station, you can relive the days of the Great North of Scotland Railway through exhibits, photographs, artifacts and displays.

TURRIFF

20 miles SW of Fraserburgh on the A947

Set in the heart of the Buchan farmlands, Turriff is an ancient burgh that was given its charter in 1512. The Knights Templar once owned land in the area, and a Templar chapel once stood here. **Turriff Parish Church** was built in 1794, though there are some good carvings on its belfry and walls from the previous kirk that stood on the site. Seven miles south west of Turriff on the B9001 is the **Glendronach Distillery**, situated on the banks of the Dronach Burn. Tours are available, and there is a visitors centre and shop.

Turriff was the scene of a famous incident concerning the **Turra Coo** ("Turriff Cow") which received widespread publicity throughout Britain. New National Insurance Acts were passed in 1911 and 1913 which required employers to pay 3d per week for each of their employees. The farmers of Aberdeenshire, in common with others all over Britain, didn't want to pay, as they reckoned that farmworkers had a healthy lifestyle, and wouldn't need much medical treatment. Curiously enough, the farm workers themselves supported the farmers on this issue.

One Turriff farmer in particular, Robert Paterson, refused to pay, so one of his cows was taken to be sold at auction to pay off his arrears. However the auction, held in Turriff, turned into a fiasco, as the cow, which had slogans painted all over its body, took fright and bolted through the streets of the town. Meanwhile, the auctioneer was pelted with raw eggs and bags of soot. Three days later the cow was taken to Aberdeen, where it was sold for £7.00. It was a hollow victory for the authorities, who had spent nearly £12 in recovering the sum. And they were further annoyed to hear that Paterson's neighbours had clubbed together and bought the cow so that it could be returned to Paterson. So, while the authorities were out of pocket over the whole affair, it hadn't cost Paterson a penny.

PENNAN

9 miles W of Fraserburgh on the B9031

Pennan is possibly the most spectacular of the little fishing villages on this coastline. It is strung out along the base of a high cliff, with the cottages having their gable ends to the sea. It is a conservation village, and is famous as being the setting for the film Local Hero.

BANFF

20 miles W of Fraserburgh on the A98

Banff was once the county town of Banffshire, and is a small fishing port close to the mouth of the River Deveron. It is an ancient royal burgh, having been granted its charter in 1163 by Malcolm IV. The **Banff Museum** in the High Street is one of Scotland's oldest, having been founded in 1828. It has a nationally important collection of Banff silver.

Duff House (Historic Scotland) was designed by William Adam and built between 1735 and 1737 for William Duff of Braco, who later became Earl Fife. After a bitter wrangle with Adam, William Duff abandoned it, and it was left to James, the 2nd Earl Fife, to complete the grand plan, including the grounds. It is now a satellite of the National Gallery of Scotland, with fine collections of paintings by such artists as Raeburn and El Greco, as well as furniture and tapestries.

The small town of **Macduff** sits on the opposite shores of the small bay where the Deveron enters the Moray Firth. It was founded by the 2nd Earl Fife in 1783, and contains the **Macduff Marine Aquarium**, which is essentially a central tank surrounded by viewing areas so that you get a good view of fish and marine mammals from all angles. The aquarium has a wave making machine which adds to the experience of seeing underwater life in its true condition. Six miles west of Banff, on the A98, is the attractive little fishing port of **Portsoy**, which is well worth visiting if only to soak in the atmosphere.

THE SHORE INN

The Old Harbour, Church Street,
Portsoy, Banffshire AB45 2QR
Tel: 01261 842831
Fax: 01261 842833

In the old fishing village of Portsoy is **The Shore Inn**, set in a 300 year old building that was once a wine merchant's house. It is as old as Portsoy's harbour itself, and there are ancient legends of smuggling and other dark deeds going on in the house before it became a respectable inn in 1864. The owners, Sandra and Kerr Hill, have created a welcoming atmosphere, and, having once owned and run a small brewery, are fastidious about the ales on offer, which are second to none. The cellar is said to be haunted, which has never done the many real ales any harm at all. Perhaps the ghost prefers spirits! In summer, the inn is cool and inviting, and in winter, when there are real open fires, it is snug and cosy, with lots of old ornaments and prints adding to the ambience.

Good food is available, and especially popular are the huge breakfasts served between 10.00 and 12.30 in the summer and at weekends out of season. There are two menus – one for lunchtime and one for evenings. The evening meals in particular are popular with locals and visitors alike, and feature good, fresh, local produce wherever possible. They are served right up until 21.00. Children are welcome, and in the summer months you can relax in the small beer garden. If you enjoy music, why not pay a visit on Thursday evenings, when there is folk music or jazz?

11 The Highlands

When people talk of Scottish scenery, they inevitably mean the scenery of the Highlands - mountains, deep glens and dark, brooding lochs. And though other areas also have these features, this is the one that has them in abundance. It also has no set boundaries, and some places described in earlier chapters, such as Aberdeen & Grampian, Argyllshire and parts of Perthshire, can lay claim to being in the Highlands as well. But the area described in this chapter can legitimately be called the heart of the Highlands. It stretches from the northernmost coast of the mainland down to Perthshire, and from the borders of Aberdeenshire and Moray to the west coast, taking in one or two of the Inner Hebridean islands as well.

It is mostly wild country, with few roads compared to other parts of Scotland, and some areas are totally inaccessible unless you go by foot over some difficult terrain. And if you do decide to do this, remember that Highland weather can be unpredictable, even in summer. Always leave word with someone about your intended route, and your estimated times of arrival at various stages.

Loch Linnhe

The capital of the Highlands is Inverness. It is a thriving city, and reckoned to be the place with the most rapid growth in Britain (if not Europe), with an enviable quality of life. Seen from the A9 as you had towards the Kessock Bridge, it has all the appearance of a large metropolis, with suburbs that sprawl along the Moray and Beauly Firths. But in fact its population is no more that 45,000, though this is growing almost daily. And some of the countryside surrounding it looks more like the Lowlands than the Highlands, though this notion is soon dispelled if you head south west along the A82 towards Loch Ness.

Within the Highlands you'll find Scotland's most famous features. Ben Nevis, Scotland's highest mountain, is here, as is Loch Morar, the country's deepest loch. Loch Ness, the most famous stretch of water in Europe, is a few miles from Inverness, and the last full battle on British soil was fought at Culloden. Here too is Glencoe, scene of the famous massacre, as well as John O' Groats, Aviemore, Skye, Fort William, Cape Wrath and Plockton, the setting for "Hamish Macbeth".

The west coast is rugged, with sea lochs that penetrate deep into the mountainous terrain. Settlements are few and far between, and most of them are to be found on the coast. Perhaps the one thing that amazes visitors to the coastline of the West Highlands are the sub tropical plants, such as palm trees, that seem to thrive here. It's all down the the Gulf Stream, which warms the shores and makes sure that snow is not as common as you would imagine. However, what the area lacks in snow it more than makes up for in rain.

The east coast, from Nairn to Inverness then north to John O' Groats, is gentler, with many more settlements. Dornoch, though small has a medieval cathedral, so is more of a city than a town, and at Fortrose there are the scant remains of another medieval cathedral. Strathpeffer was once a thriving spa town, with regular trains connecting it to Edinburgh and London.

Eilean Donan Castle

And in the middle are the mountains and lochs. The scenery is austere and gaunt, but never anything less than beautiful. No Gulf Stream here, and it is not unknown for snow to fall well into May and even June. Glencoe and Aviemore take advantage of this by being skiing centres.

In Caithness and Sutherland - Scotland's two northernmost counties - is the Flow Country, mile upon mile of low peaks, high moorland and small lochans. This isn't the dramatic scenery of the West Highlands where mountain seems to pile on mountain, but it has a ruggedness and grandeur of its own.

The Highlands is an area that amazes at every turn. The grandeur of the scenery takes the breath away, though there are areas that are as intensely cultivated as the Lowlands. There are lonely places, where another human being is likely to be miles away, and there is Inverness, which is busy and cosmopolitan. Palm trees survive on the west coast, while up in the mountains, a relatively short distance away, temperatures can barely rise above freezing for weeks on end, and snow can lie until May. All these qualities make sure that the Highlands is one of the most rewarding places in Britain to visit.

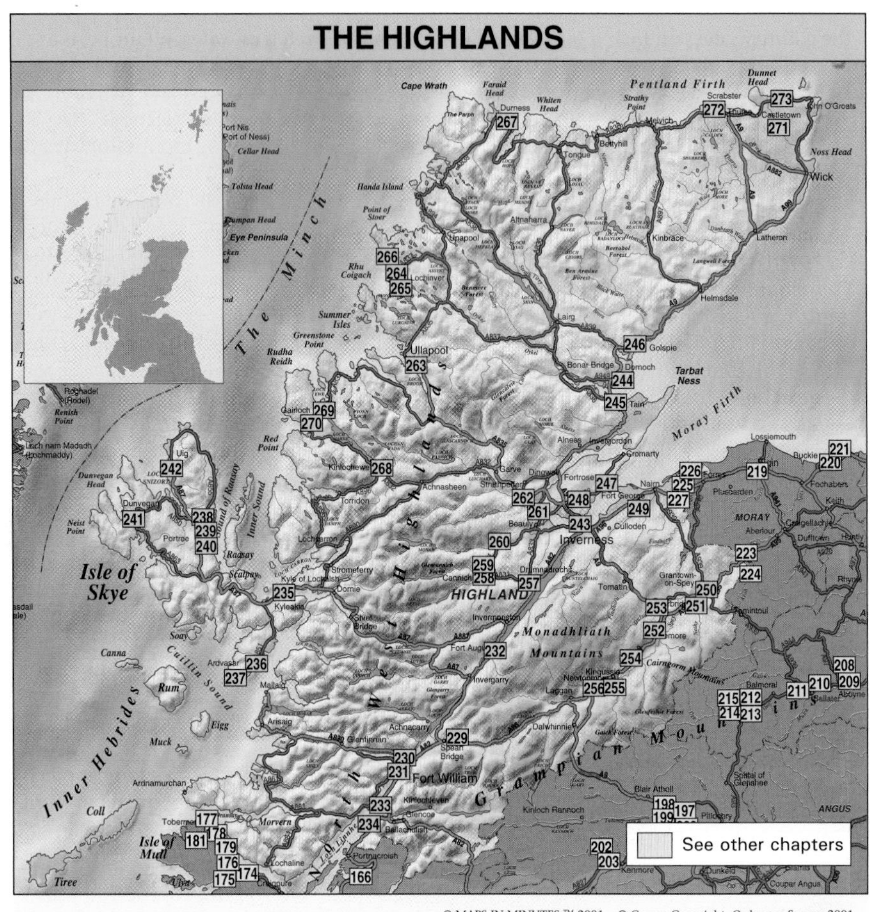

PLACES TO STAY, EAT, DRINK AND SHOP

229	Riverside Lodges, Invergloy	Self catering	Page 284
230	Crannog Seafood Restaurant, Fort William	Restaurant	Page 284
231	Torlinnhe, Fort William	Guest House	Page 285
232	The Moorings Restaurant, Fort Augustus	Bar and restaurant	Page 286
233	Allt-Nan-Ros Hotel, Onich	Hotel and restaurant	Page 287
234	Ardsheal House, Kentallan of Appin	Bed and Breakfast	Page 288
235	White Heather Hotel, Kyleakin	Hotel	Page 291
236	Sleat Holiday Homes, Ardvasar	Self catering	Page 292
237	Duisdale Country House Hotel, Sleat	Hotel and restaurant	Page 292
238	Number 25, Portree	Bed and Breakfast	Page 293
239	Urquhart Caledonian Hotel, Portree	Hotel and restaurant	Page 293
240	The Old Crofthouse, by Portree	Self catering	Page 294
241	Atholl House hotel, Dunvegan	Hotel and restaurant	Page 294
242	Uig Hotel, Uig	Hotel and restaurant	Page 295
243	Pine Guest House, Inverness	Guest House	Page 296

PLACES TO STAY, EAT, DRINK AND SHOP

244	The Trentham Hotel, Dornoch	Hotel and restaurant	Page 298
245	Dornoch Bridge Inn, Meikleferry	Pub, accommodation and restaurant	Page 298
246	Granite Villa Guest House, Golspie	Guest House	Page 299
247	Crofters Cafe Bar, Rosemarkie	Café and bar	Page 300
248	Munlochy Hotel, Munlochy	Hotel and restaurant	Page 300
249	Cawdor Tavern, Cawdor	Pub with restautant	Page 302
250	Ravenscourt Hotel, Grantown-on-Spey	Hotel	Page 302
251	Birchfield Cottages, Nethybridge	Self catering	Page 303
252	Speyside Leisure Park, Aviemore	Self catering	Page 304
253	Cairn Hotel, Carrbridge	Pub, accommodation and food	Page 305
254	Loch Insh Watersports, Kincraig	Self catering and water sports	Page 306
255	Eagle View Guest House, Newtonmore	Guest House	Page 307
256	Balavil Sport Hotel, Newtonmore	Hotel and restaurant	Page 307
257	Loch Ness Backpackers Lodge, East Lewiston	Bed and Breakfast	Page 308
258	Glen Affric Chalet Park, Cannich	Self catering	Page 308
259	Kerrow House, Cannich	B&B and self catering	Page 309
260	Culligran Cottages, Struy	Self catering	Page 309
261	The Moorings Hotel, Muir or Ord	Hotel and restaurant	Page 310
262	Balloan House Hotel, Marybank	Hotel and restaurant	Page 310
263	The Seaforth, Ullapool	Pub with restautant	Page 312
264	Hillcrest B&B, Badnaban	Bed and Breakfast	Page 312
265	Achins Bookshop/Coffee Shop, Inverkirkaig	Café, tearooms and bookshop	Page 313
266	Caberfeidh Restaurant, Lochinver	Restaurant	Page 313
267	The Smoo Cave Hotel, Sutherland	Pub, accommodation and restaurant	Page 314
268	Kinlochewe Hotel, Kinlochewe	Hotel and restaurant	Page 314
269	Am Bothan And The Gille Dubh, Poolewe	Self catering	Page 316
270	The Old Inn, Flowerdale Glen	Pub, accommodation and food	Page 317
271	The Bower Inn, Bowermadden	Pub with restautant	Page 317
272	Seaview Farm House, Hill of Forss	Bed and Breakfast	Page 318
273	Castle Arms Hotel, Mey	Hotel and restaurant	Page 319

FORT WILLIAM

The small town of Fort William lies at the western end of Glen More, in an area known as Lochaber. It is the northern "terminus" of the 95 mile long West Highland Way, which snakes its way through Western Scotland from Milngavie on the outskirts of Glasgow. The fort referred to in the town's name was first built by General Monk in the 1650s, and rebuilt during the reign of William III to house a garrison of 600 troops that would keep the Highland clans in order. It was called Maryburgh, after William's queen. Only parts of the wall survive, as the rest was dismantled in the 19th century to make way for the West Highland Railway.

It was the coming of the railway that established Fort William as one of the main centres for tourism in the Highlands, and it

Fort William and Ben Nevis

RIVERSIDE LODGES

Riverside, Invergloy, Spean Bridge, Inverness-shire PH34 4DY
Tel: 01397 712684 e-mail: enquiries@riversidelodge.org.uk
website: www.riversidelodge.org.uk

The three star **Riverside Lodges** are owned and managed by the husband and wife team of Marilyn and Steve Dennis. They have created a 12 acre site of beautiful chalet-style lodges that represent some of the best holiday accommodation in this part of Scotland. The lodges blend gracefully into their setting of sloping woodland and wild garden and are extremely spacious yet warm and cosy. Upstairs they have one double bedroom plus a twin, and on the ground floor there is a twin/bunk room, all exceedingly comfortable and with dimmer switches on the bed head lights. The ground floor lounge/dining room has sliding glass doors that open onto a verandah that is just right for those long summer evenings and has a colour TV, radio/cassette and selection of games. The kitchen is equipped with cooker, cooking utensils, cutlery and crockery, microwave and fridge/freezer. Other equipment includes washing machine, tumble dryer, iron and ironing board, clothes airer, and hair drier. These well appointed lodges also boast central heating, a fire guard to keep kiddies away from the lounge heater, a high chair, baby bath and cots. Linen may be hired, and well behaved pets are more than welcome.

Invergloy at one time was famous for its gardens, and throughout the year there is always something interesting to see. It is situated where the River Gloy enters beautiful Loch Lochy through a rocky gorge. There is a superb beach for relaxing or launching boats onto Loch Lochy and a private stocked trout pond for the angler. If it's spectacular Scottish scenery plus the warmest of Scottish welcomes you are after, then the Riverside Lodges fits the bill nicely!

CRANNOG SEAFOOD RESTAURANT

Town Pier, Fort William PH33 7PT
Tel: 01397 705589 e-mail: finlayfin@btinternet.com
Fax: 01397 705026 website: www.crannog.net

Scotland's west coast is famous for its clear, clean waters. For this reason, fishing has been an important industry here for many years, with the quality of the fish caught being famous. **The Crannog Seafood Restaurant** is also famous locally for the quality of its fine seafood. It sits at the end of Fort William's Town Pier, and offers superb cuisine using only the finest and freshest of local produce wherever possible. It is owned by Finlay Finlayson, himself a fisherman, and it is housed in his former bait store, which has been converted into a comfortable and stylish eating house. It got its name from a "crannog" an ancient fortified, self sufficient island (either natural or man-made) on which people lived in the shallow waters of a loch. The cuisine is, of course, superb, and each dish represents amazing value for money. It has won many awards, but Finlay's greatest satisfaction came when it won the Booker prize for Excellence as the Best UK Caterer.

You can choose from a printed menu or from a daily changing specials board. Whether it's crab, lobster, mussels, langoustines, trout, monkfish, scallops, lemon sole or salmon, you are sure to be delighted by the taste and presentation. Why not try, for instance, the Crannog's famous cullen skink, a delicious smoked haddock soup? Or whole trout marinated in Drambuie, with oregano, spring onions and yoghurt? The restaurant also serves wonderful Aberdeen Angus steaks and pan fried local lamb, as well as vegetarian dishes. And its cheeses are all local varieties, such as Gigha goat's cheese, Scottish Stilton, Howgate brie and caboc. In addition, you can buy produce such as oak smoked salmon, hand sliced gravadlax and smoked oysters from the Crannog Smokehouse, or order it by post or via the Crannog website. Crannog Cruises are also available from the Town pier, and take you cruising on Loch Linnhe, where you can see wildlife and get wonderful views of the town and Ben Nevis.

has remained so to this day. A few miles east of the town is **Ben Nevis**, at 4,406 feet, Britain's highest mountain. The five mile climb to the top, along a well trodden path, is fairly easy if you're fit. It is reached by way of **Glen Nevis**, often called Scotland's most beautiful glen, though there are other contenders for the title. If you do decide to climb Ben Nevis, let people know, and dress appropriately. While it may be warm and sunny at sea level, the weather on the mountain's slopes can be changeable. The rewards for the climb are immense. The Cairngorms can be seen, as can the Cuillin range on Skye and the peaks of Argyllshire. On an exceptionally clear day even the coast of Northern Ireland can be glimpsed through binoculars. At the **Glen Nevis Visitors Centre** there are exhibits about local heritage and wildlife, and, importantly, information about the weather on the mountain.

At 4,006 feet high, **Aonach Mor** is Ben Nevis's little brother, lying a mile to the east. In the winter this is a skiing area, but it is equally popular in the summer. Britain's only mountain gondola takes you half way up the mountain to a restaurant and bar, and there are several walks to enjoy when you reach them.

Within the town, in Cameron Square, is the **West Highland Museum**, with exhibits and displays about the area. The most famous exhibit is the 18th century "Secret Portrait of Prince Charles Edward Stuart". It is a meaningless swirl of colours which, when reflected onto a polished cylinder, gives a likeness of the Prince. There's also a separate display about the Queen's Own Cameron Highlanders, a regiment that merged with the Seaforth Highlanders in 1961 to form the Queen's Own Highlanders. At Corpach, north west of the town, is the award winning **Treasures of the Earth**, one of Europe's finest collections of crystals and gemstones.

The impressive ruins of 13th century **Inverlochy Castle** (Historic Scotland) sit one and a half miles north east of Fort William. It was here that Montrose had an important victory over the Campbells, who were Covenanters, in 1645. The ruins are not open to the public, though they may be viewed from the outside. Not far away, on the A82, is **Ben Nevis Distillery and Whisky Centre** which has conducted tours. One of its

TORLINNHE

products is a blend of whiskies called The Dew of Ben Nevis.

Being at the southern end of the Great Glen, Fort William is where the **Caledonian Canal** begins (see also Inverness). It is not one uninterrupted canal, but a series of canals connecting Loch Lochy, Loch Oich and Loch Ness (see Drumnadrochit for details of Loch Ness). **Neptune's Staircase** at Banavie, near Fort William, was designed and built by Thomas Telford in the early 1800s, and takes the canal through a series of eight locks while raising it over 60 feet.

Spean Bridge sits eight miles north east of Fort William. It was around here that commandos trained during World War II, and they are remembered by the **Commando Memorial**. It was designed by the sculptor Scott Sutherland, and depicts three commando soldiers. It was unveiled by Queen Elizabeth (later the Queen Mother) in 1952. **The Spean Bridge Mill**, which is nearby, has demonstrations of tartan weaving as well as a clan tartan centre.

In the summer months, the **Jacobite Steam Train** travels the famous Fort William to Mallaig line. It passes along the northern shores of Loch Eil - a continuation of Loch Linnhe after it turns westward - on a 45 mile journey that has some of the most beautiful scenery in Britain.

AROUND FORT WILLIAM

ACHNACARRY

9 miles NE of Fort William on a minor road off the B8005

Achnacarry Castle was the home of Cameron of Locheil, known as "Gentle Locheil", and one of Charles Edward Stuart's most ardent supporters. After 1745 it was burned down by Hanoverian troops. A building close to where it once stood now houses the **Cameron Museum**, which has displays, charts and exhibits relating to the history of the clan. A minor road takes you past the museum and along the lovely banks of **Loch Arcaig**, finally petering out near its western end.

THE MOORINGS RESTAURANT AND THISTLE DUBH B&B

Oich Road, Fort Augustus, Inverness-shire PH32 4DJ
Tel: (Restaurant) 01320 366484 (B&B) 01320 366380
e-mail: thistledubh@supanet.com

Set in a secluded woodland setting within a huge landscaped garden, the **Thistle Dubh B&B** is owned and run by Margaret and Gordon MacLennan. It boasts three fully en suite rooms - two double and one twin - which all have tea and coffee making facilities. This no smoking establishment is open all year, and offers the very best in Highland hospitality. From 6.30 onwards a full, traditional Scottish breakfast is served - one that is sure to satisfy the heartiest of appetites, though the times are flexible. The B&B offers fantastic views, and has ample private parking for cars. Cyclists and walkers are more than welcome, as are children, though this is a "no pets" establishment. A shed is available for both cycles and sports equipment. Travel cots and high chairs can be provided, and the establishment is less than ten minutes from the centre of Fort Augustus.

The Moorings Restaurant is situated between the Caledonian Canal and the River Oich, and serves beautifully cooked lunches, snacks and meals, which feature such favourites as haggis and neeps, breaded haddock and chips, filled rolls, chicken, salads, sandwiches, and filled potatoes. It seats 52 people in comfort, and is open from March to January from 10:00 to 20:00. Kids are more than welcome at this family run restaurant, and a children's menu is available. Margaret and Gordon take a great pride in the fact that most of the produce used is sourced locally and is as fresh as possible. There is also an extensive carry out menu which features many of the dishes on the main menu, and these are as competitively priced as the restaurant meals, and just as tasty and filling.

FORT AUGUSTUS

28 miles NE of Fort William on the A82

Fort Augustus Abbey, on the shores of Loch Ness, was founded in 1876 for Benedictine monks. It was built on the site of a fort built on the orders of General Wade between 1729 and 1742 to keep Jacobite sympathisers in check. However, this it failed to do, and was actually taken by the Jacobite army in 1745. The abbey eventually closed in 1998, due to a decline in the number of monks. Many of the valuable books and manuscripts that were in the abbey library are now owned by the National Library of Scotland.

The **Caledonian Canal Heritage Centre** is located in a converted lock keeper's cottage and explains the history and uses of the canal.

KINLOCHLEVEN

9 miles SE of Fort William on the B863

This little town sits at the head of Loch Leven, and is on the West Highland Way. **The Aluminium Story Visitor Centre** tells how hydro electric power from the Blackwater Reservoir, high on the hills behind the town, was harnessed by the great aluminium smelting works that stood here up until the year 2000.

Loch Leven

BALLACHULISH

10 miles S of Fort William on the A82

Ballachulish straggles along the southern shore of Loch Leven. To the west of the village a cairn marks the spot where Jacobite sympathiser **James of the Glen** was hanged for a crime he did not commit. He was found guilty of the murder of **Colin Campbell**, known as the "Red Fox", a government agent, by a Campbell judge and jury. Another cairn marks the site of the murder. The **Information and Interpretation Centre** in the village has displays on local history and wildlife.

To the east of the village, on the A82, is one of the most evocative places in Scotland - Glencoe. It was here, in 1691, that the infamous Massacre of Glencoe took place. Because of bad weather, Mclan of Clan MacDonald had failed to take the oath of allegiance to William III in time, and a party of Campbell troops were sent to Glencoe to massacre his people. They pretended at first to come in peace, and were offered hospitality. But in the early hours of February 13 they set about systematically killing every member of Mclan's people - men, women and children - with few escaping. A monument in the shape of a tall Celtic cross commemorates the event.

Glencoe is a wild, beautiful place, though it does get crowded in summer months. On the north side is **Aonach Eagach**, a long ridge, and on the south side three peaks of Beinn Fhada, Gearr Aonach and Aonach Dhu, known as the **Three Sisters**. About 14,000 acres within Glencoe are now owned by the National Trust for Scotland, and it has set up the **Glencoe Visitors Centre**, which tells the story of the massacre. In **Glencoe** village itself is the **Glencoe Folk Museum**, which has exhibits about the history of the area and its people.

Further along the A82 is the Glencoe skiing area with a chair lift that is open in the summer months, and gives wonderful views over Glencoe and Rannoch Moor.

ARDSHEAL HOUSE

Kentallan of Appin, Argyllshire PA38 4BX
Tel: 01631 740227 Fax: 01631 740342
e-mail: info@ardsheal.co.uk
website: www.ardsheal.co.uk

Ardsheal House sits within the magnificent Ardsheal Estate, which includes one of the oldest natural woodlands in Scotland. From it, there are magnificent views across Loch Linnhe to the mountains of Sunart. The house itself dates from the 18th century and later, though an earlier mansion, built in the 16th century, was burnt down as a result of the 1745 Uprising. It is the home of Philippa and Neil Sutherland, and has an inviting country house ambience, with a sitting room panelled in warm oak, and three delightful bedrooms furnished with antiques and pictures. All have private bathrooms, and represent the last word in tasteful elegance and comfort. Philippa serves a wonderful breakfast within the dining room or the garden fronted conservatory.

Why not relax in the sitting room, and enjoy afternoon tea as you chat with new found friends or curl up with a good book? As one titled guest, Lord Wilson of Tillyorn, remarked, it was 'memorable and wonderful to find such accomplished hosts, delicious food and courteous attention'. The Ardsheal Estate extends to 800 acres, with the immediate policies covering 11 acres, with lawns, woodlands, Victorian rockery and flower and kitchen gardens waiting to be explored. Being close to Fort William, Oban, Glencoe and Loch Ness, this is the perfect base for exploring an area of Scotland that not only has magnificent and rugged scenery, but history and heritage in abundance.

Restaurants within a twenty minute drive offer a choice from fine dining to casual suppers.

Glencoe

ARDNAMURCHAN

30 miles W of Fort William

The B8007 leaves the A861 at **Salen** (where a small inlet is usually crowded with picturesque yachts) and takes you westwards onto the Ardnamurchan Peninsula. It heads for Ardnamurchan Point and its lighthouse, the most westerly point of the British mainland, and in doing so passes some wonderful scenery. At Glenborrodale you can glimpse the late Victorian **Glenborrodale Castle**, once the home of Jesse Boot, founder of the chain of chemists. At Kilchoan there are the ruins of **Mingary Castle**, once a stronghold of the MacIan clan. It was visited by James IV in the 1490s, but later passed to the Campbells.

A few miles North of Salen, on the edge of the area known as Moidart, are the ruins of **Castle Tioram** (pronounced "Chirrum"). The castle was originally built in about 1353 by Lady Anne MacRuari, whose son Ranald gave his name to Clan Ranald. At the head of Loch Moidart is a line of five beech trees. Originally there were seven, and were known as the **Seven Men of Moidart**. They commemorate the seven men who landed with Charles Edward Stuart and sailed with him up Loch Shiel (see Glenfinnan).

STRONTIAN

20 miles SW of Fort William on the A861

Strontian (pronounced "Stron - teeh - an") sits in an area known as Sunart, which lies to the south of Loch Shiel. The village gave its name to the metal strontium, which was discovered in 1791 in the local lead mines. A few years later Sir Humphrey Davie gave it its name.

MORVERN

24 miles SW of Fort William

Morvern is that area of the mainland that sits immediately north of the island of Mull. The A884 leaves the A861 east of Strontian and travels down through it as far as Lochaline, on the Sound of Mull. **Kinlochaline Castle** sits at the head of Loch Aline, and was once the ancestral home of Clan MacInnes. The clan takes a special pride in being one of the few clans in Scotland without a chief. The last one, with all his family, was butchered by John, Lord of the Isles, in 1354.

GLENFINNAN

14 miles W of Fort William on the A830

It was here, at the northern tip of **Loch Shiel**, that Charles Edward Stuart raised his standard in 1745. He had been rowed a short distance up the loch from the house of MacDonald of Glenaladale on the western shores. The **Charles Edward Stuart Monument** (National Trust for Scotland) was erected in 1815 to commemorate the event, and a small visitors centre nearby tells the story.

ARISAIG

29 miles W of Fort William on the A830

The tiny village of Arisaig has wonderful views across to the islands of Rum and Eigg. South east of the village is **Loch nan Uamh**, where, on July 25 1745, Charles Edward Stuart first set foot on the Scottish mainland. After his campaign to restore the Stuart dynasty failed, he left for France from the same shore. A cairn now marks the spot.

MALLAIG

31 miles NW of Fort William on the A830

Mallaig is one of Britain's main herring ports,

Ben Nevis from Mallaig

and a ferry port for both Skye, South Uist and some of the smaller islands. It is also the western terminus for the Jacobite Steam Train (see Fort William). The **Mallaig Heritage Centre** on Station Road has displays and exhibits that tell the story of the districts of Morar, Knoydart and Arisaig. The **Mallaig Marine World Aquarium and Fishing Exhibition** is close to the harbour, and tells the story of Mallaig's fishing industry and the marine life found in the waters of Western Scotland.

South east of the town is water of another sort - **Loch Morar**, which has the distinction of being Britain's deepest fresh water loch. It plunges to a depth of 1,077 feet, and if you were to stand the Eiffel Tower on the bottom of the loch, its top would still be 90 feet below the surface. A minor road near Morar village, south of Mallaig, takes you to its shores.

KYLE OF LOCHALSH

40 miles NW of Fort William on the A87

Kyle of Lochalsh was once the mainland terminus of a ferry that made a short crossing across Loch Alsh to Skye. Now the ferry has been superseded by the graceful **Skye Bridge**. Three miles east of the village on the A87 is the **Lochalsh Woodland** (National Trust for Scotland), with sheltered walks beside the shores of Loch Alsh, as well as mature woodlands and a variety of shrubs, such as rhododendrons, bamboo, ferns, fuchsias and hydrangeas. Six miles east of the village is one of the most photographed castles in Scotland, **Eilean Donan Castle**, which sits on a small island connected to the mainland by a bridge. Parts of it date back to 1220, when it was built by Alexander II. It is now the ancestral home of Clan MacRae, and has a small clan museum. If you continue eastwards along the A87 you will eventually arrive at **Shiel Bridge**, at the head of Loch Duich. To the south east is Glen Shiel, where the **Five Sisters of Kintail** overlook the picturesque glen. These five mountains are on land owned by the National Trust for Scotland. Close by is the site of the battle of Glen Shiel, fought in 1719, and there is a **Countryside Centre** at Morvich Farm, off the A87.

North east of Kyle of Lochalsh is the village of **Plockton**, with its palm trees and idyllic location. This was the Lochdhub of Hamish Macbeth fame, as it was here that the TV series was filmed. It sits on Loch Carron, and on the opposite bank, off a minor road , are the ruins of **Strome Castle** (National Trust for Scotland). It was a stronghold of the Lordship of the Isles, and later belonged to the MacDonnells of Glengarry.

Kyle of Lochalsh is the western terminus for the famous Dingwall - Kyle of Lochalsh railway line (see Dingwall).

CANNA

57 miles NW of Fort William

Canna means the "porpoise island", and is now owned by the National Trust for Scotland. It is about five miles long by just over a mile wide at its widest, and is usually sunny and mild. It is reached by ferry from Mallaig.

EIGG

40 miles W of Fort William

In 1997 the island of Eigg was bought on behalf of its inhabitants by the Isle of Eigg Heritage Trust. Its most famous feature is the 1,277 feet high **An Sgurr**, which slopes gently up to a peak on one side, and dramatically plunges on the other.

South west of the main pier is the **Massacre Cave**. It got its name from a gruesome event in 1577, when nearly 400 MacDonalds took refuge there when pursued by a force of MacLeods. The MacLeods lit fires at the entrance, and every one of the MacDonalds was suffocated to death. A nearby cave is known as the **Cathedral Cave**, as it was used for secret Catholic church services following 1745.

Isle of Eigg

MUCK

46 miles W of Fort William

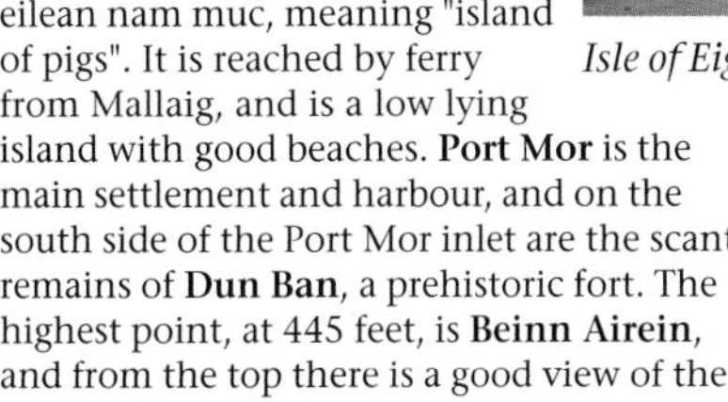

The tiny island of Muck's improbable name comes from eilean nam muc, meaning "island of pigs". It is reached by ferry from Mallaig, and is a low lying island with good beaches. **Port Mor** is the main settlement and harbour, and on the south side of the Port Mor inlet are the scant remains of **Dun Ban**, a prehistoric fort. The highest point, at 445 feet, is **Beinn Airein**, and from the top there is a good view of the whole of the island.

RUM

47 miles W of Fort William

When Sir George Bullough bought the island of Rum in 1888 he immediately changed its name to "Rhum", as he didn't like the associations it had with strong drink. However, when the Nature Conservancy Council took over the island in 1957 they changed the name back to the more correct "Rum", and it has been that ever since. Nowadays it is a Special Site of Scientific Interest and a Specially Protected Area, as its plant life has remained almost unchanged since the Ice Age.

The main settlement is Kinloch, on the east coast, and **Kinloch Castle** was built by Sir George as his main home on the island. The **Bulloch Mausoleum** in Glen Harris, to the south of the island, was built to take the bodies of Sir George, his wife Monica and Sir George's father John.

SKYE

40 miles NW of Fort William

The new **Skye Road Bridge**, opened in 1995, has robbed Skye of its island status. However, it still remains one of the most beautiful and haunting of the Inner Hebrides, and the place has beauty and history aplenty. Perhaps the most famous features on the island are the **Cuillins** (or more properly, Cuillin), a range of mountains in the south east of the island. Though not the highest, they are perhaps the most spectacular mountains in Scotland, and present a challenge to any climber. The highest peak is **Sghurr Alasdair**, at 3,309 feet.

The A87 leaves the Skye Bridge and heads west along the northern shore of the island, passing through **Broadford**, one of its main settlements. It then passes through Sconser, the southern terminus of a ferry linking Skye to the smaller island of **Raasay** (once visited by Boswell and Johnson), before reaching the island's main settlement of **Portree**. The town is the gateway to the Trotternish Peninsula, which juts out for 20 miles into the Minch, that sea channel separating the Outer Hebrides from the mainland. A road from Portree follows its coastline right round until it arrives back at the town.

Fifteen miles west of Portree along the A850 is Dunvegan, famous for **Dunvegan Castle**, perched above the waters of Loch Dunvegan. It is the home of Clan MacLeod, and though much of it is Victorian, parts date back to the 13th century. In the drawing room is the famous Fairy Flag, revered by members of Clan MacLeod, which was supposed to bring success in battle. Across the loch, and reached by the B884, is the **Colbost Croft Museum**,

SLEAT HOLIDAY HOMES

4 Calligarry, Ardvasar, Isle of Skye,
Inverness-shire IV45 8RU
Tel: 01471 844278 Fax: 01471 844471
e-mail: shonebusiness@tinyworld.co.uk

Sleat has often been called the 'garden of Skye', and this is no idle boast. It is a pleasant and fertile part of the island, easily reached by the ferry from Mallaig. **Sleat Holiday Homes** in Ardvasar, not far from the ferry terminal, offers the very best in self catering accommodation for those who appreciate comfort and convenience. The Eoin Mara, close to shops and a hotel, is a cottage that sleeps four adults in two bedrooms, a double and a twin. It is extremely well appointed, and makes a wonderful base from which to explore an island that is so rich in history and legend. Heating, lighting and cooking are all supplied through a £1-in-the-slot meter, and of peak is supplied at no cost.

There is a spacious open plan sitting room/kitchen with patio doors that look out over the Sound of Sleat to Knoydart on the mainland. It boasts a colour TV, and in the well appointed kitchen there is a cooker, microwave, washer/dryer, fridge, dishwasher, kettle and toaster, plus the usual cutlery and crockery. A 'welcome' food pack awaits you as you arrive at what is undoubtedly one of the best self catering establishments on the island. All linen is provided, and a cot and high chair is available on request. There is a small fenced garden, ample parking space, and a well behaved dog can be brought at no extra cost.

DUISDALE COUNTRY HOUSE HOTEL

Sleat, Isle of Skye IV43 8QW
Tel: 01471 833202; Fax: 01471 833404
email: marie@duisdale.com
website: www.duisdale.com

Set in an old hunting lodge built in 1867, the **Duisdale Country House Hotel** has 17 well appointed en suite rooms. Under the ownership of Marie Campbell, who trained in Paris at the Ritz Escoffier, it has earned a fine reputation for its cuisine, which relies on local. fresh produce wherever possible. The hotel's public rooms are spacious and beautifully furnished, and the whole place speaks of elegance and comfort. This is a relaxing and charming place to spend that special holiday away form the hurry and bustle of modern life.

NUMBER 25

25 Urquhart Place, Portree, Isle of Skye IV51 9HJ
Tel: 01478 612374
e-mail: elizabethmacdonald@talk21.com

A mere ten minute's walk from the centre of Portree is **Number 25**, owned and run by Elizabeth MacDonald. This superior B&B establishment is noted for its warm welcome and good old fashioned Highland hospitality, and has two excellent rooms. There is an en suite double with trouser press and a twin/triple with shared bathroom, both with colour TVs, hair dryers, plenty of books and magazines, and tea/coffee making facilities. The residents' lounge is cosy and comfortable, and boasts a TV and video. A full Scottish breakfast is served between 8 - 8.30 am (though other times can be arranged in advance), which includes coffee, tea, a selection of fruit teas, cereal or porridge, grapefruit, eggs, bacon, sausages, haggis and smoked salmon. The food is beautifully cooked, and both Continental and vegetarian options are also available. Mrs MacDonald will be pleased to make up packed lunches should you wish them. Number 15 is open all the year round, with special rates for out of season visitors. Private parking is available, and there is a shed for cycles or motor bikes. Drying out clothes is no problem should the weather be wet, as this can be arranged. This establishment makes an ideal base from which to explore the mystical island of Skye, and people come back year after year to sample Mrs MacDonald's hospitality. You may arrive here as a stranger, but you will leave as a friend!

URQUHART CALEDONIAN HOTEL

Wentworth Street, Portree, Isle of Skye IV51 9EJ
Tel: 01478 612641 Fax: 01478 613718

With eight en suite bedrooms, the **Urquhart Caledonian Hotel** is the ideal base from which to explore the romantic and picturesque island of Skye. All the rooms (four double, two family and two twin) are spacious and well appointed, with colour TV (all with Sky), coffee/tea making facilities, hair dryer and telephone. Some even have a superb view out to sea. This is a cosy and spotlessly clean family run hotel in the centre of Portree run by the Urquhart family, and they take great pride in the warmth of their welcome and the hospitality they offer. The restaurant, which seats 25 people in absolute comfort, is open to both residents and non residents, with the cuisine being based on local fresh produce wherever possible. Beautifully cooked bar lunches are also available, and the bar has a wide range of beers, wines, spirits and soft drinks to suit all tastes.

The hotel is open all year, and there is ample private parking, and on most weekends live music features in the lounge bar. There is even the opportunity of taking a boat trip on the Sound of Raasay, as a member of the Urquhart family runs a boat, and there are special discounts if you are staying at the hotel. All major credit cards are accepted, and dogs are welcome by prior arrangement. The bar has a children's licence until 8 pm. This is the ideal hotel for that relaxing holiday you have always promised yourself - one that combines comfort and high standards with an area rich in historical associations and wildlife.

THE OLD CROFTHOUSE

5 Penifiler, by Portree, Isle of Skye IV51 9NF
Tel: 01478 612476
e-mail: stay@theoldcrofthouse.co.uk
website: www.theoldcrofthouse.co.uk

If you're looking for superior self catering accommodation on Skye for that special holiday, then look no further than **The Old Crofthouse** near the island's capital of Portree. This picturesque, whitewashed cottage with a traditional slate roof is centrally heated, and is surrounded by its own garden, with lovely views west across Portree Bay. The sunsets have to be seen to be believed! And from the back windows there are spectacular views of Ben Tianavaig. Within the garden there is a rotary dryer, picnic table and facilities for a barbecue. The house boasts two airy and spacious bedrooms, one double with en suite and shower, and one double and single, with en suite bathroom.

A cot is also available if you bring along a very young guest! There is a comfortably furnished sitting room with TV, hi-fi, books and games, plus a dining room and kitchen. The kitchen is especially well appointed, with microwave, double oven, dishwasher and washing machine. This non smoking establishment is open all year, and both heating and electricity is included in the price, as is all bed linen and towels. Owners Clare and Richard Smith take a special pride in the facilities The Old Crofthouse offers discerning tourists, and have created what is the ideal base from which to explore the magical island of Skye. If you stay at The Old Crofthouse, you are sure to leave with happy memories of a magical island!

ATHOLL HOUSE HOTEL

Dunvegan, Isle of Skye IV55 8WA
Tel: 01470 521219 e-mail: reservations@athollhotel.demon.co.uk
Fax: 01470 521481 website: www.athollhotel.demon.co.uk

The **Atholl House Hotel** is situated at Dunvegan, on the mystical island of Skye, and is based in what was the manse of the local minster. It has been tastefully converted into one of the best hotels on the island, and offers superb, comfortable accommodation within nine fully en suite rooms. There are three standard doubles, two twin rooms, one family room and a single. In addition, there is something special - two four poster rooms that recall the days of gracious living. All have TV, tea/coffee making facilities and hair dryers. It is an establishment of character and charm, and commands magnificent views out across the Minch to the Western Isles, with some truly lovely sunsets.

Owner Christine Oliver and manager John Whittaker are justly proud of the high standards they have set and maintained, and are confident that any stay in their hotel will result in happy memories. A candle lit dinner at the Atholl House Hotel is something to remember. The food is carefully prepared and presented, and the chef uses only the finest local produce wherever possible to create dishes that are sure to please the most demanding of palates.

UIG HOTEL

Uig, Isle of Skye IV51 9YE
Tel: 01470 542205 Fax: 01470 542308
e-mail: manager-uighotel@hotmail.com
website: www.uighotel.co.uk

Owned and run by the MacEwan family, the **Uig Hotel** is one of the most popular hotels on the magical island of Skye. Here you can relax in complete comfort and sample wonderful Scottish hospitality, with some of the best scenery in Scotland on the doorstep. Uig sits above Uig Bay on the Trotternish Peninsula, and has ferry connections with both Tarbert on Harris and Lochmaddy on North Uist. It is therefore the ideal touring base, not just for exploring Skye itself, but for most of Scotland's western islands. A day trip to Harris is something not to be missed. The Uig Hotel is an old coaching inn, with Sobhraig House, a former steading above the hotel, having been converted into superior accommodation as well. The family took over the hotel in the year 2000, and under the overall management of Ann MacEwan, they have managed to create something special - a hotel that combines all the old fashioned values such as a warm welcome and great service with the modern ones of value for money and efficiency.

It boasts 16 fully en suite rooms, six of them being in the converted steading. So great are the views from the steading that returning guests invariably request to stay there! All 16 rooms are well appointed, with TVs, hair dryer, tea/coffee making facilities and phones, and have been decorated and furnished to an amazingly high standard. The hotel's lounges (including a sun lounge that gives wonderful views over Uig Bay) are cosy yet spacious - the ideal places to relax over a drink after a hard day's sightseeing. In the winter months, coal and wood fires add a cheeriness to their ambience. The bars serve a full range of drinks, including some wonderful single malts, and there are also soft drinks if you're behind the wheel.

The cuisine, as you would expect from such a hotel, is excellent, using only the finest and freshest local produce wherever possible. Why not try the hotel's succulent roast half chicken or rib-eye steak? They come with all the trimmings, and represent great value. Or you could try one of their superb fish dishes, such as sole fresh from Mallaig, fresh haddock cooked to suit your own taste or monkfish tails in the hotel's own special green sauce. But one word of warning - so good a reputation does the hotel's cuisine have that you are well advised to book in advance!

The Uig Hotel is open all day, and also serves morning coffee, light lunches and afternoon tea. There is ample parking, and all around there are opportunities for sightseeing, watching wildlife, sport, or just taking it easy in a corner of Scotland where life seems to move at an easier pace!

based on a "black house" (a small traditional cottage of turf or stone, topped with a thatched roof). It shows the living conditions of islanders in the past.

To the south east of the island, on the Sleat Peninsula at Armadale, is the **Armadale Castle Gardens and Museum of the Isles**. It sits within a 20,000 acre Highland estate, once owned by the MacDonalds of Sleat, and was purchased by the Clan Donald Land Trust in 1971.

INVERNESS

Inverness is the capital of the Highlands, and Scotland's newest city. It is said to be the most rapidly expanding place in Britain, and though it only has a population of about 45,000, its hinterland supports a further 20,000. But for all its size, it still has all the feel and bustle of a much larger place, and its shopping - especially in the pedestrianised High Street, where the Eastgate Shopping Centre is located - is superb.

The city sits at the north eastern end of the Great Glen, at a point where the River Ness enters a short channel connecting the Beauly and Moray Firths. It was once the capital of the Northern Picts, and it was to Inverness that St Columba came in the 6th century to confront King Brude MacMaelcon and convert him and his kingdom to Christianity. The doors of Brude's stronghold were firmly closed, but Columba marked them with the sign of the cross and they flew open of their own accord.

No one knows where this stronghold stood, though some people have suggested Craig Phadraig, two miles west of the mouth of the Ness, and others have suggested Torvean, just outside the town. The present **Inverness Castle** dates from the early 19th century, and houses the local court house. Castles have stood on the site since at least the 12th century. However, Macbeth's castle, where Shakespeare set the murder of Duncan, stood some distance away. General Wade enlarged Inverness Castle after the uprising of 1715, and its garrison surrendered to Charles Edward Stuart when he occupied the town in 1745. He then ordered the castle to be blown up. Close to the castle is a statue of **Flora**

PINE GUEST HOUSE

60 Telford Street, Inverness IV3 5LE
Tel: 01463 233032 Fax: 01463 233032

With seven spacious rooms, the **Pine Guest House** offers unrivalled accommodation within the city of Inverness. It is a large, well proportioned sandstone villa on the old road north from Inverness, and is close to the city's town centre, where there is a good mix of shops, pubs, clubs and restaurants. It is also only five or ten minute's walk from the railway station. There are three family rooms, all fully en suite, and four singles, two of which are fully en suite. Each is spacious and beautifully appointed, with colour TVs, tea and coffee making facilities. All the rooms are non smoking, though guests are allowed to smoke in the comfortable residents' lounge, where you will find a hi fi and a further television set.

The Pine Guest House is owned and run by Mrs Mackay, who takes a great pride in the establishment's 'home from home' feeling, and who offers a warm Scottish welcome to everyone who crosses the threshold. The full Scottish breakfasts are filling and hearty, and will set you up nicely for a day exploring one of Scotland's most historic cities. They are served between 8.00 and 9.00, though Mrs Mackay is flexible about these times. Continental breakfasts are also available, as well as vegetarian breakfasts by arrangement. Inverness is also the ideal base from which to explore the Highlands, and within an hour's drive of the city you can easily visit Culloden battlefield, Loch Ness, Nairn, Aviemore, Strathpeffer and Dingwall. And if you are just passing through the city on your way north, the guest house is the ideal overnight stopping place. Well behaved pets are welcome by prior arrangement. The Pine Guest House is one of those places that still sets great store by the old fashioned virtues of friendly service, comfortable accommodation and great value for money.

MacDonald, who helped Charles Edward Stuart evade capture.

Near the castle, in Bridge Street, is the **Town House**, which was completed in 1882. It was here, in 1921, that the only cabinet meeting ever held outside London took place when Lloyd George was prime minister. Across from it is the **Tolbooth Steeple**, dating from the late 18th century. It was once part of a complex of buildings that contained a court house and jail. In Castle Wynd is **Inverness Museum and Art Gallery**, which has a large collection relating to the history of the Highlands and the town in particular.

St Andrews Cathedral, Inverness

The oldest secular building in the city is **Abertaff House** in Church Street (National Trust for Scotland), which dates from 1593. It was built as a town house for the Frasers of Lovat. It isn't open to the public. **Dunbar's Hospital** is also on Church Street, and dates from 1668. It was founded by Provost Alexander Dunbar as a hospital for the poor. It has now been divided into flats. **Balnain House** (National Trust for Scotland), on Huntly Street on the opposite bank of the River Ness, was built in 1726 and is now the Trust's regional HQ. It is not open to the public. Also on the opposite bank is **Inverness Cathedral,** a gem of a building designed by Alexander Ross and built between 1866 and 1869. It was supposed to have had two large spires, but these were never built.

Inverness is one of the few Scottish towns to have retained its traditional market, and the indoor **Victorian Market** in Academy Street building dates from 1890, when it was rebuilt after a disastrous fire. **The Old High Church** in Church Street, dedicated to St Mary, is Inverness's parish church and was built in 1770, though parts of the tower may date from medieval times. After the battle of Culloden, the church was used as a jail for Jacobite soldiers, some of whom were executed in the kirkyard. The **Old Gaelic Church** was originally built in 1649, though the present building dates from a rebuilding of 1792.

The magnificent **Kessock Bridge** carries the A9 over the narrows between the Moray and Beauly Firths and connects Inverness to the Black Isle. At North Kessock is the **Dolphins and Seals of the Moray Firth Visitor and Research Centre**. The Moray Firth is famous for its blue nose dolphins, and boats leave from many small ports so that you can observe them. This visitor centre gives you one of the best opportunities in Europe to learn about the creatures, and to listen to them through underwater microphones.

River Ness, Inverness

The Trentham Hotel

The Poles, Dornoch IV25 3HZ
Tel: 01862 810551 Fax: 01862 811426
website: www.thetrenthamhotel.co.uk

The Trentham Hotel, which is two miles from the centre of Dornoch, is based on an old 17th century coaching inn used by those people who were travelling north towards the ferries for Orkney. Nowadays it is still an inn, and people heading for the islands still use it as an overnight stop. However, it is a lot more comfortable nowadays! In fact, it is one of the most comfortable and well appointed hotels in the area, and has a great reputation for its warm welcome, its great food and fine range of drinks. It is a family run hotel, owned and managed by Muriel and John Mackintosh, and has six fully ensuite rooms on offer - one family, one double, one single and three twins. All are beautifully appointed, with TV and tea/coffee making facilities.

The restaurant offers the best in Scottish and international cuisine, all home cooked from fresh local produce wherever possible. If it's a juicy, sizzling steak you're after, Cajan char grilled chicken, haggis with an onion and white wine sauce or grilled local trout, then this is the place for you. There is also a great sweet menu, and a choice selection of wines to accompany your meal. Vegetarian food is also available, as is a children's menu. The restaurant has, on many occasions, been nominated by local newspapers as restaurant of the month. The public bar is cosy and friendly, with an open fire. It is popular with tourists and locals alike, and has a fine range of drinks, including some single malts that are too good to miss! The resident's lounge, on the other hand, is a quiet retreat where you can relax in comfort and unwind after a hectic day's driving or seeing the sights. Muriel and John invite you to step over their threshold and sample some good, old fashioned Scottish hospitality!

Dornoch Bridge Inn And Restaurant

Meikleferry, Tain, Ross-shire IV19 1JX
Tel: 01862 893535 Fax: 01862 893545

Situated on the shores of the Dornoch Firth, the **Dornoch Bridge Inn and Restaurant** is housed within an old railway station that has been converted into a stylish and comfortable establishment. Owned and run by Mairi and Donnie MacPhee, it is open all year, and has an enviable reputation for its standards of hospitality and the great home-made food it serves. Within the Highland retreat next to the inn there are eight rooms available, consisting of two doubles, four twins and two singles. All rooms are comfortable and have tea and coffee making facilities and a colour TV.

The Sidings Lounge Bar is cosy and friendly, with, in the winter months, a roaring log fire and Rocky the hotel's dog will come down and meet you at night when the meals are finished! It is popular with locals and visitors alike, and serves a great range of drinks, including lager, beer, wines, spirits and soft drinks. The wood panelled dining room seats 30 people in comfort, and serves wonderful food, with all the produce being sourced locally wherever possible. Donnie has come 4th, 3rd and 2nd in the Highland Young Chef of the Year competitions, and this should tell you how good it is. The menu ranges from traditional fish and chips,to Highland Lamb, Casserole of Venison, steaks and chicken to name but a few. Vegetarian dishes are also available, and there are half portions for senior citizens and a children's menu. Special dietary requirements can be catered for with prior notification (gluten free, vegan etc).The Sunday carvery is particularly popular. The Rob Roy Room can hold up to 100 people, so is perfect for that party, conference or cosy Highland Wedding you've always wanted. A warm Highland welcome awaits you.

AROUND INVERNESS

TAIN

23 miles N of Inverness on the A9

In medieval times, Tain was a great place of pilgrimage, drawing pilgrims from all over Europe to the the shrine of St Duthac within **St Duthus Collegiate Church**. Now an exhibition and visitors centre called **Tain Through Time** explains about St Duthac himself, the pilgrimage, and the people who made it, including James IV. The museum, which is part of the centre, also has displays about Clan Ross.

DORNOCH

30 miles N of Inverness on the A949

If a cathedral confers city status on a place, then the small royal burgh of Dornoch is a city, due to **Dornoch Cathedral**, which dates originally from the early 13th century. However, the church as we see it today is largely a rebuilding of the early 19th century, though there are some old features still to be seen, mostly in the chancel and crossing. Sixteen Earls of Sutherland are said to be buried in the cathedral.

Dornoch was the scene, in 1722, of Scotland's last execution of witchcraft, when an old woman called Janet Horne was burned for supposedly turning her daughter into a pony. The judge at the trial was later reprimanded for his handling of the case. A stone on the links commemorates the events.

GOLSPIE

40 miles NE of Inverness on the A9

A steep hill path takes you to the summit of **Bienn a'Bhragaidh**, on which there is a statute by Chantry of the first Duke of Sutherland, who died in 1833. It was erected in 1834 by a "a mourning and grateful tenantry to a judicious, kind and liberal landlord". The words ring hollow, however, as the Duke was one of the instigators of the hated Clearances of the early 19th century, and there have been continued calls to have the statue removed, and in some cases blown up. Others have argued that the statue should stay as a reminder of those terrible times.

Crofters Cafe Bar

11 Marine Terrace, Rosemarkie,
Fortrose IV10 8UL
Tel: 01381 620844
Fax: 01381 620419

If it's good food and drink you're after in the pleasant village of Rosemarkie, then the **Crofters Cafe Bar** is for you. Situated on the lovely Black Isle north east of Inverness, it has been owned and run by Yvonne and Alastair Kerr and Edith Grigor since 1997, and is one of the most popular places in the area. It sits right on the waterfront, with wonderful views of the Moray Firth and across to Fort George, and has an area for smokers. The restaurant holds 40 people in absolute comfort, and the food is plentiful, beautifully cooked and tasty. Everything is prepared on the premises from fresh local produce wherever possible, and the owners are justly proud of the cuisine, which represents great value for money. From the snack menu you can choose such things as filled rolls, chips, cheeseburgers and baked potatoes.

On the main menu there are such tempting dishes as fish and chips with vegetable and side salad, juicy sirloin steaks in brandy cream and peppercorn sauce with all the trimmings, home make steak and ale pie and pasta of the day. Plus there is a daily specials board. The sweet menu is comprehensive, and is sure to contain something to your liking. All the baking is home make, and a carry out service is available. There is a small wine list to choose from, plus a fine range of beers, spirits, and, of course, soft drinks at the bar if you're driving. Children are welcome in this cosy establishment, and there are high chairs plus a special menu. This is a very popular place (open seven days a week) which gets extremely busy in the summer months, so you are well advised to book a table in advance.

Munlochy Hotel

55 Millbank Road, Munlochy, Ross and Cromarty IV8 8NL
Tel: 01463 811494 Fax: 01463 811881

At Munlochy, a few miles west of Fortrose, is the **Munlochy Hotel**. Owned and managed by Kay and Dennis Howell, it has become one of the best hotels on the Black Isle, and is popular with both tourists and locals alike. It was Kay and Dennis's "local" up until 1999 when they bought it, and they now take a great pride in the warmth of its welcome and the high standards of hospitality it has set. There are six beautifully appointed and comfortable rooms on offer - one family, three double, one twin and a single - three of which are fully en suite. All have TVs as well as tea and coffee making facilities, which makes it the ideal base from which to explore the Black Isle, an area which is steeped in history and heritage. Pickups from local stations and airports can be arranged, as can fishing and shooting parties. The bar is cosy and welcoming, and has a wide range of beers, wines, spirits and soft drinks to suit all tastes. It features live music once a month, as well as family entertainment.

The food is excellent, with two menus on offer - one for lunch and one for dinner. The dishes on the lunch menu are competitively priced, with hearty portions. They include such things as soup, smoked haddock, salmon, steak and ale pie, baguettes and chicken curry. The dinner menu is sure to satisfy the most demanding of palates, and features haggis quenelles, lemon sole, steak garni, lamb cutlets and the hotel's own "chicken Munlochy" - breast of chicken stuffed with pork and apricot, served with a whole grain mustard sauce. Delicious! Vegetarians are also catered for, and children are more than welcome. This is the kind of place where you can relax and take it easy after a hard day's sightseeing, and Kay and Dennis will go out of their way to make your stay as enjoyable and trouble free as possible!

Dunrobin Castle, the seat of the Dukes of Sutherland, is the most northerly of Scotland's stately homes and one of the largest in the Highlands. Though the core is 14th century, it resembles a huge French chateau, thanks to a remodelling in 1840 by Sir Charles Barry, designer of the Houses of Parliament. Some of the castle's 189 rooms are open to the public, and there is a museum in the summer house.

LAIRG

40 miles N of Inverness on the A836

Lairg is an old town that sits at the south eastern tip of Loch Shin, which has been harnessed for hydroelectricity. The town became important because it sits at the meeting point of various Highland roads that head off in all directions. Five miles south are the picturesque **Falls of Shin**, which has a visitors centre. **Ord Hill**, west of the town, has an archeological trail which takes you round a landscape rich in ancient sites.

FORTROSE

8 miles NE of Inverness on the A832

Fortrose Cathedral (Historic Scotland) was founded by David I as the mother church of the diocese of Ross. Building began in the 1200s, though the scant remains you see nowadays date from the 14th century. One of the fine canopied tombs is of Euphemia Ross, wife of the Wolf of Badenoch (see also Dunkeld and Elgin).

In nearby **Rosemarkie** is the **Groam House Museum**, with exhibits and displays that explain the culture of the Picts, those people who inhabited this part of Scotland in the Dark Ages.

FORT GEORGE

9 miles NE of Inverness on the B9006

Fort George (Historic Scotland) was named after George II, and sits on a headland that guards the inner waters of the Moray Firth. Work started on building it in 1748 as a direct result of the Jacobite Uprising of 1745, and it was subsequently manned by Government troops. The walls are a mile in length, and the whole thing cost over £1bn to build at today' prices. It has been called the finest 18th century fortification in Europe, and has survived almost intact from that time. The **Queen's Own Highlanders Museum** is within the fort.

NAIRN

15 miles NE of Inverness on the A96

Nairn is a small, picturesque holiday and golfing resort on the Moray Firth. Local people there will tell you that the name is a shortened version of "no rain", and indeed this area is one of the driest in Britain. It has a fine, clean beach and a large caravan park. The town is supposed to mark the boundary between the English speaking areas to the east and the Gaelic speaking areas to the west. At Auldearn, two miles east of the town, is the **Boath Doocot** (National Trust for Scotland), which sits within what was a small medieval castle. A battle was fought here in 1645.

Cawdor Castle sits a few miles south west of the town off an unmarked road. It was made famous by Shakespeare in his Macbeth, though the present castle is much later than the 11th century. With its fairy tale looks and its turrets, it is said to be one of the most romantic castles in Scotland.

CROMARTY

16 miles NE of Inverness on the A832

This picturesque small royal burgh, which received its charter in the 13th century, sits on a small headland at the start of the Cromarty Firth. It is probably the best preserved eighteenth century town in Scotland, and was where many Highlanders embarked for Canada during the Clearances of the early 19th century. It was the birthplace, in 1802, of Hugh Miller, writer and the father of geology. **Hugh Miller's Cottage** (National Trust for Scotland), where he was born, is open to the public. It has a collection of fossils and rock specimens, as well as some of his personal possessions such as his geological hammer and microscope.

The **Cromarty Courthouse Museum**, as its name suggests, is housed within the old courthouse. There is a reconstruction of an 18th century trial in the courtroom itself, plus you can see the old cells, childrens' costumes, a video presentation giving 800 years of Cromarty history and an audio tape tour of the old part of the town.

Dolphin Ecosse in Victoria Place runs boat trips to see the Moray Firth dolphins.

CAWDOR TAVERN

Cawdor, Nairnshire IV12 5XP
Tel/Fax: 01667 404777
e-mail: cawdortavern@btopenworld.com
website: www.cawdortavern.com

If you're looking for the perfect country pub and restaurant in the Cawdor area, then the **Cawdor Tavern** is for you. It is set within what used to be the joiner's workshop for the Cawdor Estate, and under the ownership of Christine and Norman Sinclair, it has become a comfortable hostelry with a great reputation among locals and visitors alike. The bars are cosy and warm, with logs fires in the winter, and, to add that authentic touch, one of them has old oak panelling that originally came from Cawdor Castle itself.

There is a great range of drinks, including over 100 single malts and a range of local real ales. Also an interesting range of soft drinks are available. The restaurant seats 60 in comfort, and serves marvellous food which is prepared from only the freshest of Scottish produce, whether it is fresh fish, local game or prime meats. Vegetarian options are also available. There are two menus – one for lunches (which can be eaten in the bars) and one for dinners, though booking is advisable as the place is so popular. The prices are remarkably reasonable and the quality is always superb. A fine range of wines is also available, sold by the bottle or the glass. 2001 Scottish & National finalists for catering pub of the year.

RAVENSCOURT HOUSE PRIVATE HOTEL

Seafield Avenue, Grantown-on-Spey,
Morayshire PH26 3JG
Tel: 01479 872286 Fax: 01479 873260
e-mail: ravenscourt@totalise.co.uk

Formerly the manse of a church minister, **Ravencourt House** is now a comfortable and well appointed private hotel run by Margo and Alan Lockey. The 19th century building has been tastefully refurbished to create the perfect ambiance for a relaxing and enjoyable stay in a wonderful part of Scotland. All of the bedrooms are elegant and spacious, with full en suite facilities (and showers with gold plated fittings!) as well as tea and coffee equipment, electric blankets and colour TVs. Breakfasts can be either Continental of full Scottish, with hearty platefuls.

There are luxurious residents' lounges where you can relax with a drink at the end of the day (the establishment has a residents' licence), and the restaurant has a cosy, intimate atmosphere that helps you enjoy the good food and fine wines. Dinners are by arrangement, and are prepared from only the finest Scottish produce wherever possible. Ravenscourt House prides itself on its warmth, its style and on its traditional hospitality. It makes an ideal base for exploring Speyside and beyond. Any guest will find that Margo and Alan will go out of their way to make a stay as comfortable and memorable as possible.

CULLODEN

5 miles E of Inverness on the B9006

The Battle of Culloden was fought in 1746, and was the last major battle to take place on British soil. The hopes of the Jacobites to return a Stuart king to the British throne were dashed on that cold, April day and the clan system was smashed forever. The battlefield is on Drumossie Moor, which, in the 18th century, was a lonely, wild place. Now it has been drained and cultivated, though the battlefield itself has been returned to the way it was. You can still see the stones that mark the graves of various clans, and there is a huge memorial cairn at the centre of the battlefield. **Leonach Cottage**, which survived the battle, has been restored, and the **Culloden Visitors Centre** (National Trust for Scotland) has displays and exhibits which explain the battle.

Leonach Cottage, Culloden

Not far from the battlefield are the **Clava Cairns** (Historic Scotland), a fascinating group of burial cairns of the early Bronze Age.

TOMATIN

14 miles SE of Inverness off the A9

Tomatin sits on the River Findhorn, just off the A9. The **Tomatin Distillery**, north of the village, is one of the highest in Scotland, and was founded in 1897. It has 23 stills, and draws its water from the Alt-na-Frithe burn. It has tours, a visitors centre and tastings.

GRANTOWN-ON-SPEY

27 miles SE of Inverness off the A939

This beautiful and elegant tourist centre is situated in the heart of Strathspey, and sits at a height of 700 feet above sea level. It was built by James Grant of Grant Castle in the

SPEYSIDE LEISURE PARK

Dalfaber Road, Aviemore, Inverness-shire PH22 1PX
Tel: 01479 810236 Fax: 01479 811688
e-mail: tp_enquiries@speysideleisure.com
website: www.speysideleisure.com

If you're looking for a superior leisure park close to Aviemore, look no further than the **Speyside Leisure Park**! Situated on the banks of the River Spey, it offers accommodation based on caravans, cabins and chalets, and has superb views out towards the Cairngorm Mountains. It makes the ideal base from which to explore an area that is rich in history and beauty and its range of accommodation is sure to suit all tastes and budgets. The chalets are two and three star graded, and sleep from two to nine in absolute comfort depending on the model. All chalets have at least one double bedroom, with the second and/or third bedroom having two full sized single bunk beds, though some models have a second bedroom with twin beds. In addition, eight and nine berth units have a double bed settee in the lounge. All the bedrooms have electric heaters, and the kitchen is well appointed with fridge gas hob, oven and microwave. The lounge/dining area has a colour TV, log effect gas fire, extremely comfortable furniture and, in some cases, a video.

The caravans come in three grades - luxury, standard and budget. The luxury units (which are all under six years old) have double insulation and heaters in all rooms and the hallway, and one has been built with disabled access in mind (though it isn't suitable for self propelled wheelchairs). All the luxury caravans, with the exception of the disabled one, are strictly non smoking. They feature a spacious lounge, dining area, kitchen, shower room and either two or three bedrooms. The lounges have colour TVs and gas fires, and the kitchens are equipped with ovens, hobs, fridges and microwaves. There is plenty of room for a cot. The standard caravans have the same basic facilities and a good level of heating, while the budget models are the oldest models on the site. They offer remarkable value for money, but are not recommended for young children in the winter months. There are four cabins on the site. One is two-bedroomed and sleeps up to four, one is three-bedroomed and sleeps up to six, while the fourth is three-bedroomed and sleeps up to eight. Central heating or gas and electric heating (depending on the cabin) guarantees cosy accommodation throughout the year. The three bedroomed models have a superb location overlooking the Spey, while the other two are set back from the river with superb views.

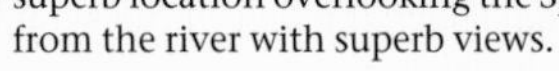

The site boasts some excellent amenities that are sure to add to the enjoyment of your holiday. There is a heated indoor pool, a sauna and a weights gym, and all are free to guests during office hours. In addition there is an outdoor children's play area, a laundry that is available 24 hours a day and an on-site telephone box. One of the site's best assets is the River Spey itself, and fishing permits (for brown trout) are available from reception.

The Leisure Park is ideally situated for numerous activities including the steam railway, the reindeer herd, the wildlife park, highland folk museum and the whisky trail. Discount tickets are available for some attractions from reception.

CAIRN HOTEL

Main Road, Carrbridge, Inverness-shire PH23 3AS
Tel: 01479 841212 Fax: 01479 841362
e-mail: cairn.carrbridge@lineone.net

With seven rooms, four of which are en suite, the **Cairn Hotel** is the ideal base from which to explore beautiful Strathspey and even beyond. It dates from 1873, and has been lovingly and tastefully added to over the years to form a hostelry that offers the very best in Scottish hospitality. The food is excellent and affordable using local produce wherever possible. There is a cosy and inviting bar with a huge open log fire – the perfect place to unwind over a single malt or a pint of real ale. Being just off the A9, it is also the perfect overnight stop as you head north to Inverness and beyond.

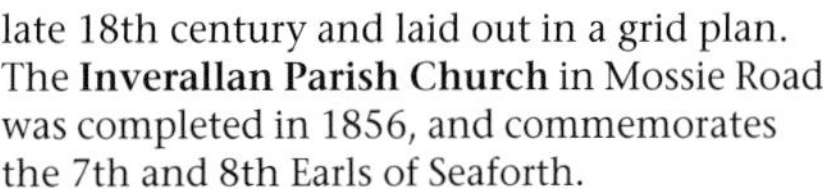

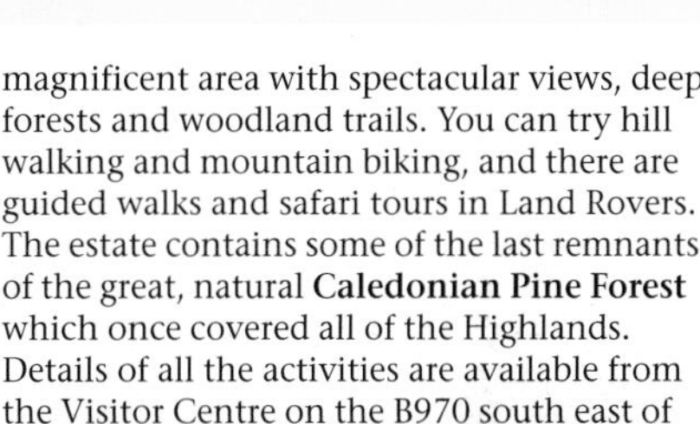

late 18th century and laid out in a grid plan. The **Inverallan Parish Church** in Mossie Road was completed in 1856, and commemorates the 7th and 8th Earls of Seaforth.

The **Revack Country Estate** is to the south of the town. It has gardens, woodland trails and an adventure playground. Revack House was built as a shooting lodge in 1860.

CARRBRIDGE

21 miles SE of Inverness on the A938

The arch of the original bridge still stands, and dates from the early 18th century. South of the village is the **Landmark Forest Heritage Park.** It is carved out of woodland, and has such attractions as a Red Squirrel Trail, Microworld (where you can explore the world of tiny insects) and the Fire Tower, the tallest timber tower in the country. It gives amazing views over the surrounding countryside. At Dulnain Bridge, six miles east of the village, is the **Speyside Heather Centre**, which explains all about a plant which has become synonymous with Scotland.

AVIEMORE

24 miles SE of Inverness off the A9

Once a quiet Inverness-shire village, Aviemore has now expanded into one of the main winter sports centres in the Highlands. The skiing area and chair lifts lie about seven miles east of the village, high in the Cairngorms. This is also the starting point of **Cairngorm Funicular Railway**, opened in late 2001, which carries passengers during winter and summer. On the road to the skiing area is the **Cairngorm Reindeer Centre**, where Britain's only permanent herd of reindeer can be seen.

The **Rothiemurchus Highland Estate** is a magnificent area with spectacular views, deep forests and woodland trails. You can try hill walking and mountain biking, and there are guided walks and safari tours in Land Rovers. The estate contains some of the last remnants of the great, natural **Caledonian Pine Forest** which once covered all of the Highlands. Details of all the activities are available from the Visitor Centre on the B970 south east of the village.

Aviemore is one of the termini of the **Strathspey Steam Railway**, which runs to **Boat of Garten**, five miles away. It was once part of the Aviemore to Forres line which was closed in the early 1960s.

KINGUSSIE

28 miles S of Inverness off the A9

Kingussie (pronounced "King - yoosy") sits in Strathspey, with good views of the Cairngorms to the east, while to the west lie the **Monadhliath Mountains**, rising to over 3,000 feet. In Duke Street sits the **Highland Folk Museum**, which gives an insight into the history and lifestyle of the ordinary people of the Highlands throughout the years.

At **Newtonmore**, four miles south of the village, is another **Highland Folk Museum**, where there is a reconstruction of an 18th century Highland township. The ruins of **Ruthven Barracks** (Historic Scotland) lie to the west of Kingussie, on the other side of the A9. They were built in 1719 to check Jacobite sympathies in the area. Charles Edward Stuart's army captured them in 1746 and burnt them. Four miles north of Kingussie is the **Highland Wildlife Park**, which has an array of Scottish wildlife, plus some animals that used to roam the Highlands but have now died out.

LOCH INSH WATERSPORTS

Kincraig, Inverness shire, PH21 1NU
Tel: 01540 651272
Fax: 01540 651208
e-mail: office@lochinsh.com
website: www.lochinsh.com

Loch Insh Log Chalets

Superb self catering pine log chalets overlooking scenic Loch Insh and the mountains, nestled in the foothills of the Cairngorms, just 7 miles south of Aviemore. Scottish Tourist Board 2/3 Star. Ideal family 4, 5, 6, 7 and 8 berths with open plan lounge, high open log ceiling, fully equipped modem kitchen, veranda and private parking. Access to sauna, mini-gym, table tennis and laundry. The 7 and 8 berth chalets have been specially adapted for wheelchair users with adapted canoes and catamaran sailing boat available at the beach. All chalets are supplied with linen and towels, garden chairs, BBQ equipment free.

Insh Hall Lodge

Just 150m from the beach offering en suite B&B for individuals, couples and families.

The Boathouse Restaurant Bar & Gift Shop

"One of the finest views in the valley" standing on the beach overlooking the activities on beautiful Loch Insh. Part of the Loch Insh Watersports Scottish Tourist Board 4 Star Visitor Attraction. Our friendly staff serve hearty Scottish Fayre, coffees, home baking, home made soups, snacks, bar meals and children's menu. The restaurant offers a tasty selection of a la carte meals during the evenings with fabulous views and pleasant ambience. The large, open balcony is the place to be on sunny days or warm evenings watching the sunset, or perhaps you may like to choose the comfortable Quarterdeck Bar with relaxing lighting and views over the loch and dry ski slope. The Bosun's Locker Gift Shop is very popular for unusual gifts, novelties, jewellery, prints, cards, children's toys and wooden craft items.

Loch Insh Watersports

Voted "Best on the Water" and "Best Small Business in the Highlands 2000". A high quality 4 Star Scottish Tourist Board Visitor Attraction covering 14 acres. Summer ~ canoeing, sailing, windsurfing, family river trips, salmon & trout fishing, dry ski slope skiing, rowing, archery and mountain bikes. Hire/instruction, children's classes, "taster" sessions, multi activities and courses. Experienced, qualified instructors. RYA/SCA recognised. Children's adventure area plus 3km lochside/forest interpretation trail. Picnic and BBQ areas. Winter ~ Downhill and Snowboarding hire/instruction and courses on Cairngorm with on site 60m dry ski slope

FREE watersports equipment hire 8.30 - 10:00 am & 4.00 - 5.30 pm daily
For all guests staying 2 or more nights

Eagle View Guest House

Perth Road, Newtonmore, Inverness-shire PH20 1AP
Tel/Fax: 01540 673675
e-mail: eagview@aol.com

The **Eagle View Guest House** is an extremely comfortable and well appointed guest house that boasts five superior rooms, most of which are en suite. The owners, Geoff and Nicola Drucquer, take a great pride in the place, and have made sure that the house is welcoming and cosy. They pride themselves in the high quality 'Taste of Scotland' cooking using fresh local produce and home baking. Dinners are available and popular but must be booked in advance. Newtonmore is just off the A9, on the road to Inverness, so the Eagle View makes a wonderful stopping off place – one where you will experience Scottish hospitality at its best.

Balavil Sport Hotel

Main Street, Newtonmore, Inverness-shire PH20 1DL
Tel: 01540 673220; Fax: 01540 673773
e-mail: balavilhotel@btinternet.com website: www.balavilhotel.co.uk

The **Balavil Sport Hotel** is a substantial, family run establishment that sits in the heart of the picturesque village of Newtonmore, just off the A9. It has 50 extremely comfortable rooms, all en suite, and all with TV, radio, Teasmade and telephone. It is the perfect base from which to explore Speyside, or a great stopping off point as you head north to Inverness. The warmth of its welcome is only matched by the quality of its cuisine, which is superb. The lounge bar is cosy and relaxing, and the ideal place to enjoy a quiet drink. The place is owned and managed by Helen and Jim Coyle, who pride themselves on the standards of service and great value for money that they offer.

A few miles south west of Kingussie, along the A86, is **Laggan**, where the BBC series Monarch of the Glen was filmed.

DRUMNADROCHIT

14 miles SW of Inverness on the A82

Drumnadrochit sits on the shores of **Loch Ness**, at Drumnadrochit Bay. The loch is famous as the home of the Loch Ness Monster, commonly called "Nessie". Whether a monster actually exists or not has never been proved, but the crowds still flock here in the hope of seeing something. The loch measures just under 23 miles long by a mile wide, and contains more water than any other loch in Britain.

The first mention we have of a monster occurs in Adamnan's Life of St Columba, written in the 7th century. In the year AD565 St Columba was heading up the Great Glen towards Inverness, when he encountered a monster attacking a man in the River Ness at the point where it enters the loch. He drove it back by praying, and the man's companions fell on their knees and were converted to Christianity.

Nowadays the monster is a bit more timid. Most sightings have been made at **Urquhart Castle** (Historic Scotland), about a mile from Drumnadrochit, and curiously enough, this is where the loch is at its deepest at 754 feet. The castle is one of the largest in Scotland, and sits on a promontory that juts out into the loch. A fortification has stood here for centuries, but the present ruins date from the 16th century, when the Grants occupied it. After the Jacobite Uprising of 1689 it was blown up and never rebuilt. A visitor centre contains a model of the castle which shows what it was like in its heyday.

Two exhibitions in the village, **Loch Ness 2000** and the **Original Loch Ness Exhibition** have displays about the Loch Ness Monster.

BEAULY

9 miles W of Inverness city centre on the A862

Within this picturesque village are the ruins of **Beauly Priory** (Historic Scotland), founded in 1230 for monks of the Valliscaulian order. What can be seen nowadays dates from between the 14th and 16th centuries. The north transept is the burial place of the

Loch Ness Backpackers Lodge

Coiltie Farmhouse, East Lewiston, Drumnadrochit,
Inverness-shire IV63 6UJ
Tel: 01456 450807 e-mail: lindsay@lochness-backpackers.com
website: www.lochness-backpackers.com

The **Loch Ness Backpackers Lodge** is situated within the village of Lewiston, close to Drumnadrochit, on the shores of beautiful Loch Ness. It is owned and managed by Lindsay Miller, and was once an 18th century farm cottage with adjacent barns. The cottage has been extended so that it is now the hostel's main area, and offers lounges, an airy dining room, self catering kitchen, toilets/showers on the ground floor, and two comfortable dormitories and a double room upstairs. The barn has been converted into four dormitories, toilets/showers and a well appointed self catering kitchen/dining area. In all there are 40 beds available in this modern and extremely well planned hostel - 16 in the main house and 24 in the bunkhouse, contained within the double room and six dormitories in all. This makes it the ideal set up for large groups of up to 40, or for smaller groups and individuals.

The sitting room has a real log fire which makes it cosy and warm in the winter months, and there is a TV video room where you can put your feet up and relax after a hard day exploring this wonderful area of Scotland. All linen is included in the reasonable nightly rates, and a buffet style Continental breakfast is available at a small cost. There is ample parking space for cars, a garden and a barbecue area for those long summer evenings. The lodge is non smoking, and is close to all the amenities of both Lewiston and Drumnadrochit. These include pubs, restaurants, a fish and chip shop, supermarket, post office and bank and gift shops. Boat trips on the loch can be booked through the hostel, and these also offer the chance to try your hand at fishing, which might mean that fresh trout is on your dinner menu!

Glen Affric Chalet Park

Cannich, Beauly, Inverness-shire IV4 7LT
Tel: 01456 415369 e-mail: info@glenaffricchaletpark.com
Fax: 01456 415429 website: www.glenaffricchaletpark.com

Glen Affric Chalet Park is situated at the southern end of the village of Cannich, at the entrance to one of the most beautiful glens in Scotland - Glen Affric. It is owned and run by Mr and Mrs MacDonald, who have created a superior chalet park which offers some of the best accommodation in the area. Though set amid peaceful Highland scenery, the vibrant city of Inverness is only half an hour away, and Drumnadrochit on the shores of Loch Ness is less than twenty minutes away by car. The wooden chalets can accommodate up to six people, and are spacious yet cosy, with three bedrooms - a double, a twin and a twin/bunk. Each bed has a duvet, and linen is provided free of charge. The large lounge/dining area has comfortable furnishings and a colour TV, and the kitchens are modern and well appointed. Each one has an electric cooker, microwave, fridge/freezer and plenty of cupboard space as standard. Within the bathroom you will find an over-bath electric shower, hand basin, w.c. and shaver point. Beside each chalet is ample parking for a car.

The park itself extends to five acres on the banks of the River Glass, and has a games room (with pay phone), a children's play area (with large climbing frame, swings and slides) and a laundry room with coin operated washing machines and tumble dryers. The site also boasts a barbecue area for those long summer evenings, plus a picnic site by the river. All the chalets face a central "green" or the picturesque riverbank. Cannich village, which has a store/post office and a hotel and restaurant, is within easy walking distance. Cots, high chairs and mountain bike hire are available, and short breaks can be arranged throughout the year except for the high season. Mid week and weekend bookings are allowed.

KERROW HOUSE

Cannich, by Beauly, Inverness-shire IV4 7NA
Tel: 01456 415243 e-mail: stephen@kerrow-house.demon.co.uk
Fax: 01456 415425 website: www.kerrow-house.demon.co.uk

Kerrow House is a bed and breakfast and self catering establishment close to the village of Cannich that offers wonderful value for money and good old fashioned Scottish hospitality. It sits in the hearty of some wonderful Highland scenery, and yet is only twenty minutes from Loch Ness and half an hour from all the amenities of Inverness. Owned and run by Gill Kirkpatrick and Stephen Bassett, it has three coveted stars from VisitScotland. The house was at one time the home of famous Scottish novelist Neil Gunn, and offers four comfortable rooms, one of which has a traditional four poster bed. All have private facilities, with either showers or bathrooms, and each has a TV and tea and coffee making facilities. The self catering accommodation is outstanding. Riverside Cottage has a spacious living room/kitchen, double and twin rooms, and a bathroom.

Fisherman's Cottage is charming, and has one bedroom, bathroom, living room and integral kitchen. Birchwood and Rowan are classic A-frame chalets, warm and cosy, with two upstairs bedrooms, sitting/dining room (with sliding doors to a raised verandah), kitchen and bathroom. The Stalker's Wing sleeps eight, and is part of Kerrow House, but is completely self contained. It has four bedrooms (two doubles, a twin and a twin/bunk), a sitting room, shower room, separate w.c. and "farmhouse" style kitchen. All the accommodation has central heating augmented by wood burning stoves, and the kitchens are well appointed with modern equipment. All the properties have recently been refurbished to an extremely high standard, making Kerrow House one of the most attractive spots from which to explore this beautiful area of the Highlands.

CULLIGRAN COTTAGES

Glen Strathfarrar,Struy, near Beauly, Inverness-shire IV4 7JX
Tel/Fax: 01463 761285
e-mail: juliet@culligran.demon.co.uk

Set amid some of the most majestic scenery in Scotland, **Culligran Cottages** offers all that is best in self catering accommodation. They are located west of Beauly at Struy, where beautiful Glen Strathfarrar strikes off westwards from the equally beautiful Strathglass. Owned and managed by Juliet and Frank Spencer-Nairn, the cottages sit snugly amid some stunning scenery protected under a National Nature Reserve agreement close to the waters of the River Farrar and within the Culligran Estate. The accommodation comprises a traditional stone built cottage and four Norwegian style chalets within a naturally wooded area, and all are comfortable and extremely well appointed. The cottage sleeps up to seven people, and has three double bedrooms, a spacious sitting room, large kitchen, bathroom and shower room.

The chalets boast an open plan living room with kitchen/dining area, a bathroom and either two or three bedrooms. A sofa bed in the living area means that they can sleep either five or seven depending on size. All are furnished to an extremely high standard, and all have double glazing, electric heaters, cooker, and fridge. Frank offers regular guided tours by Landrover of Culligran Deer Farm, where you can watch and even feed the deer. A daily permit allows you to fly fish on the Rivers Farrar and Glass. If you prefer something more energetic, you can hire a Culligran bicycle and explore the 15 miles of private road in the glen. The cottages are open between mid March and mid November each year, and are keenly priced. This area of Scotland is renowned for its sport, wild life and history, and the cottages make an ideal base from which to explore it.

THE MOORINGS HOTEL

Muir or Ord, Ross-shire IV6 7SX
Tel: 01463 870145

The Moorings Hotel is a restaurant/bar within the small picturesque village of Muir of Ord, a few miles west of Inverness. It is a cosy yet spacious and comfortable place that serves great food at reasonable prices. Run and owned by Isobel, Joe and Paul Brennan, who take a great pride in the standard of service they have set, it is a favourite spot for both visitors and locals alike. The dining area holds 48 in absolute comfort, and on the menu are such favourites as garlic mushrooms, juicy steaks with all the trimmings, chicken, giant Yorkshire puddings, a selection of tasty curries and baltis, and jacket potatoes. Food is served between 11.00 and 21.00, so this is the ideal place to have a lunch or dinner. The food is prepared on the premises from the finest local produce wherever possible, and represents outstanding value for money. The Moorings Hotel has a children's licence, so a children's menu, plus high chairs, is always available. The bar is particularly cosy, with a coal fire in the winter months.

Behind the bar there is a great range of beers, both draught and bottled, wines and spirits. As this is Scotland, there is a particularly fine selection of single malts. And, of course, if you're driving, soft drinks are also available. The bar also features a range of games, such as pool (two tables), a dart board and a juke box. Live bands and karaoke nights feature regularly, plus there is a weekly disco in the summer months and a fortnightly one in winter. This is the ideal place to stop for a bar lunch or an evening meal while exploring the area. It is warm and friendly, and will give you a great Scottish welcome should you visit.

BALLOAN HOUSE HOTEL

Marybank, Ross-shire IV6 7UW
Tel: 01997 433272 Fax: 01997 433502
e-mail: balloanhousehotel.co.uk
website: www.balloanhousehotel@tinyworld.com

Owned and managed by Rhona and Stuart Beattie, the **Balloan House Hotel** is a comfortable family run hotel in the small village of Marybank, three miles south of Strathpeffer. It is set within an old stone house, and boasts five en suite rooms - two doubles and three twins - that are beautifully decorated and well appointed. Each one has a TV, video, tea and coffee making facilities and a hair dryer. Rhona and Stuart set great store by their cuisine, as Stuart is a fully qualified chef. All the produce used in the kitchen is fresh and sourced locally wherever possible. Even the trout, when it's on the menu, comes from the trout farm which is just down the road!

Dishes on the evening menu include such things as sirloin steaks with all the trimmings, supreme of chicken Kiev, breaded Scottish scampi, and the Balloan's own mixed grill. There is also a popular Sunday menu, which includes roast beef and Yorkshire pudding, fried fillet of haddock, a seafood platter and so much more. The restaurant seats 20 in comfort, and there are high chairs for children. Vegetarians are also catered for. The bar is cosy and friendly, and serves a great range of drinks, including beers, lagers, wines and spirits. Once a month some musicians descend on the bar and have a jazz session, which is popular with locals and visitors alike. And while you're in the bar, have a look at the clock, which comes from America. We won't give the game away here by describing it, but it has to be seen to be believed!

MacKenzies of Kintail. To the south west is **Strathglass**, one of the most beautiful glens in the area. The **Wardlaw Mausoleum**, to the east of the village, is one of the burial places of the Fraser Clan. Two miles south of the village is Moniack Castle, home of the **Moniack Winery**, which makes country wines from locally grown fruits.

DINGWALL

11 miles NW of Inverness on the A862

Dingwall's name derives from the Norse thing vollr, meaning "the place of the parliament", which shows that even in ancient times it was an important settlement. It is a royal burgh, and received its charter from Alexander II in 1227. It was the birthplace of both Macbeth and **Sir Hector MacDonald**, a soldier who rose through the ranks in Victorian times to become a general and national hero. However, he eventually committed suicide in 1903 after accusations of homosexuality. A monument to him, known as the **Mitchell Tower**, stands on a hill to the south of the town.

Within the old Tolbooth of 1730 is the **Dingwall Museum**, where the town's history is explained by way of displays and exhibits. Dingwall is the eastern terminus for the famous Dingwall - Kyle of Lochalsh railway line, which runs through some of the most beautiful scenery in Scotland as it crosses the country. The **Dingwall Canal** (now closed) is Britain's most northerly canal, and was designed by Thomas Telford in 1817.

STRATHPEFFER

14 miles NW of Inverness on the A834

This small village was once one of the most famous spa resorts in Britain, and trains used to leave London on a regular basis specifically for the place. For this reason, it is full of hotels, B&Bs and genteel guest houses. So fashionable was it that the local paper used to publish a weekly list of the crowned heads and aristocratic families who were "in town". The spa days are over now, though the **Spa Pump Room** has been refurbished and recreates the halcyon days of the village when the cream of society flocked here to "take the waters". You can even sample the curative waters yourself. The adjacent Victorian gardens, where Victorian society used to promenade and play croquet, have also been restored.

Within the disused railway station is the **Highland Museum of Childhood**, with dolls, photographs, toys, games and videos. On the outskirts of the village is the **Eagle Stone**, with Pictish symbols.

ULLAPOOL

46 miles NW of Inverness on the A835

This fishing port and ferry terminal on Loch Broom was founded by the British Fisheries Society in 1788 and laid out in a grid plan. By 1792 much of the work on the port buildings and some houses was complete, settlers having been given a plot of land, free stone to build a home, and land for a garden. Over the years the fortunes of the village fluctuated as the fishing industry prospered or failed, though it managed to hang on grimly.

Now the town is the mainland terminus for the Stornoway ferry, and it has reinvented itself as a centre for tourism. The award winning **Ullapool Museum and Visitor Centre** is housed in a former church designed by Thomas Telford - one of the so-called "parliamentary churches". In 1773, before the town was established, the very first settlers bound for Nova Scotia left Loch Broom in the Hector, and there is a scale model of the ship within the museum.

One of the undiscovered jewels close to Ullapool are the **Leckmelm Gardens**, planted in about 1870. By 1985 they had become overgrown, and in that year work began in reestablishing them and revealing the beauty that had been lost for so long. At Achiltibuie, eleven miles north west of Ullapool, is the **Hydroponicum**, a "garden" where plants grow without soil. It calls itself the "garden of the future" and kits are available so that you can start growing plants without soil as well.

AROUND ULLAPOOL

LOCHINVER

17 miles N of Ullapool on the A837

This small fishing port sits on Loch Inver, at the end of the A837. A few miles west is Loch Assynt, on whose shores you will find the

THE SEAFORTH

Quay Street, Ullapool, Ross-shire IV26 2UE
Tel: 01854 612122 e-mail: drink@theseaforth.com
Fax: 01854 613133 website: www.theseaforth.com

Ullapool is the mainland port for the Stornoway Ferry which takes you to the Western Isles. And in the town, in one of its oldest buildings, is **The Seaforth**, which calls itself 'the pub by the pier'. It looks out over the harbour, and was originally a fisherman's store and smithy dating from the 18th century. The bar sells a great range of lagers, beers, wines and spirits, as well as soft drinks if you are behind the wheel. The range of malt whiskies is exceptional, covering everything from ten year old Ardbeg to Lagavulin and Laphroig. The Seaforth has twice been a runner up in the 'music pub of the year' contest, and features all types of live music from local bands to nationally known groups. But it is so much more than a pub - it is also one of Western Scotland's finest seafood restaurants. The proprietor, Harry MacRae, was once a full time fisherman, and still has an interest in a local boat which is used to supply the Seaforth with prawns, lobsters and crabs, so that his establishment is kept fully supplied with fish that is as fresh as possible. It even smokes its own salmon and haddock! Everything from a light lunch or snack to a full gourmet meal is available, and the menus feature such dishes as soup, baked potatoes, fresh oysters, dressed crab, salmon salad and traditional fish 'n' chips made in the good old fashioned way. But meat is also on the menu, and home made steak pie and haggis and neeps are real favourites! The evening menu offers many dishes that are beautifully cooked and presented, and one of the favourites is the Seaforth's own 'seafood platter', an array of fresh mussels, herrings, whole prawns, winkles, fresh and smoked salmon, dressed crab and so on. It is served with fresh salad, Marie Rose sauce and a basket of fresh bread. And if you can't finish this veritable feast, then the Seaforth will quite happily give you a doggie bag!

HILLCREST B&B

Badnaban, Lochinver, Sutherland IV27 4LR
Tel: 01571 844391

Hillcrest B&B is a large, modern yet picturesque bungalow set near the village of Lochinver. This is a particularly beautiful part of Scotland, and the house is set on a hillside that gives great views over Loch Inver. It is owned and run by Anne and Sandy Johnston, a couple who have created one of the best B&B establishments in the area. It boasts three spacious and well decorated bedrooms with separate bathroom and shower room - two double and one twin, and each one is well appointed with tea and coffee making facilities, wash basins, hair dryers and reading material. This real home from home feeling is continued in the residents' lounge, which is comfortable, cool and welcoming in the summer months. There is a colour TV with Sky, a video, music and many books, and all this creates a relaxing atmosphere which is sure to make you forget the hustle and bustle of modern life.

The establishment is open seven days a week between May and September, and there is ample parking for cars. The full Scottish breakfasts (which include smoked fish and kippers) are beautifully cooked, and served at 8:30, though other times can be arranged beforehand. Packed lunches can also be made up by prior arrangement. The Hillcrest is the perfect base from which to explore an area that is rich in history and wildlife, and Sandy is a dedicated trout fisherman and walker who knows the area well. He can advise on the best places to fish - or just to visit to admire the stunning views - and knows all the tourist attractions in the area. Dogs are more than welcome.

ACHINS BOOKSHOP AND COFFEE SHOP

Inverkirkaig, Lochinver IV27 4LR
Tel/Fax: 01571 844262 e-mail: abx@scotbooks.freeuk.com
website: www.scotbooks.freeuk.com

Looking for the perfect stopping off place for the cup that cheers in Assynt? Then the **Achins Bookshop and Coffee Shop** is for you. It sits three miles south of Lochinver, right below the spectacular (especially after rain!) Kirkaig Falls, and serves wonderful tea and coffee as well as light lunches, snacks, home made soup and a selection of baking such as fruit or cheese loaves and traditional scones. It is owned and run by Agnes and Alex Dickson, who have created the perfect ambience in which to relax after being behind the wheel for a while. There are flowers on the table, works of art by local artists on the walls and soft, lilting Gaelic music in the background. It could even be Agnes you're listening too, as she is an accomplished singer, and her tape *Ceol Mo Chridhe* (Music of My Heart) is in constant demand! But, as the name suggests, the establishment is so much more than just a coffee shop.

There is also a splendid bookshop that sells a wide variety of books and publications on Scotland as a whole and on the local area, which is one of the most spectacular in Scotland. There are also woollen goods, crafts, framed prints, children's books, Scottish music, giftware, pottery, films, postcards and a host of other things that make the shop an Aladdin's cave which is crying out to be explored. In fact, this is the perfect place to solve all your souvenir problems! The place is open during the season from 10.00 to 17.00. Both Agnes and Alex invite you to sample the fine food and refreshing drinks in their coffee shop, and browse through the wonderful and vast selection of books and other items which are on sale in their shop.

CABERFEIDH RESTAURANT

Lochinver, Sutherland IV27 4JY
Tel: 01571 844428 Fax: 01571 844066

Set within the Assynt village of Lochinver, the **Caberfeidh Restaurant** is a charming restaurant and lounge bar that combines good old fashioned service with value for money. It is owned and run by Lynne and Jacques Demay, who take a great pride in the high standards they have set. Their place is disabled friendly, and children are welcome (with high chairs available). The dining area seats 30 in absolute comfort, though you can also eat in the comfortable lounge bar. The food is beautifully cooked, with good portions, and the restaurant is renowned for its seafood (this being the Western Highlands)! The dishes on the menu include deep fried haddock, scallops, poached halibut in a Mornay sauce, juicy steaks with all the trimmings, lamb chops with rosemary, chicken Kiev, haggis with Drambuie cream and a whole lot more! For dessert, why not try the Scottish delicacy of clootie dumpling, which is a delicious fruit pudding boiled within a 'cloot', or cloth.

There is also an under twelve's menu, and vegetarian dishes are available. If it is a relaxing drink you are after, then the cosy lounge bar serves a fine range of beers, wines and spirits. This being Scotland, the malt whiskies must be sampled! If you're behind the wheel, there is also a good selection of soft drinks. The restaurant is non smoking, and in the winter there are pub games and occasional live music. The restaurant has a beer garden that overlooks the River Inver (and which affords marvellous views!), and there is plenty of parking space.

THE SMOO CAVE HOTEL

Sutherland IV27 4QB
Tel/Fax: 01971 511227
e-mail: smoo.hotel@virgin.net
website: www.index.co.uk

Situated in the small village of Durness in Sutherland, the **Smoo Cave Hotel** is named after a famous three chambered cave to the west of the village. The hotel is owned and managed by Karen and Len Campbell, who have created a small hotel which is both comfortable and full of character. It has three rooms, a double, a twin/family and a spacious en suite room. All are well appointed, with tea and coffee making facilities, heating and colour TV. The hotel is the social centre of the village, and popular with locals and visitors alike. The well stocked bar has a wide range of beers and wines, and is especially noted for its malt whiskies. Of course, if you're driving, there is also a great range of soft drinks. The bar, with its cosy stove, also offers bar games to while away those very occasional times when the Scottish weather is less than kind!

The food is outstanding, with a varied menu that is sure to satisfy the most fastidious of palates. Why not try the traditionally Scottish haggis, neeps and tatties (haggis, swede and mashed potato), or the roast of the day, which comes with all the trimmings? Vegetarians are also catered for, with the mushroom and nut fettucini being especially popular. The hotel also has a function suite which can seat up to 60 people, so is the ideal location for parties, anniversaries or small weddings. The full Scottish breakfasts, served between 8.30 and 9.30, or by arrangement, are hearty and delicious. This is the kind of family run hotel where you are guaranteed a warm welcome whatever the weather, and where good old fashioned service and value for money is still to the fore!

KINLOCHEWE HOTEL

Kinlochewe, by Achnasheen, Wester Ross IV22 2PA
Tel: 01445 760253
e-mail: kinlochewehotel@tinyworld.co.uk

Set on the edge of Europe's last great wilderness, amidst the towering peaks of theTorridon Mountains, and close to the famously scenic Loch Maree, **Kinlochewe Hotel** is ideally situated for walkers and climbers or as a base for touring the Western Highlands. For climbers there are over 20 Munros within 20 miles of the hotel. For those touring the Western Highlands, the Inverewe National Trust Gardens, the spectacular Appleross Peninsular and the Isle of Skye are all within easy reach, while the Beinn Eighe National Nature Reserve, the first of its kind in Britain is on the doorstep. The hotel has an excellent reputation for its home cooked food and varied menu, including vegetarian dishes, using local fresh fish, venison and other produce wherever possible and a well stocked bar that includes three dozen malt whiskies to sample.

The hotel, parts of which are thought to date back two hundred years, is in the centre of the tiny village of Kinlochewe. There are ten bedrooms: two singles, four doubles (one family room) and four twin rooms. Five are en-suite and all have wash hand basins. All rooms have tea and coffee making facilities and there is a residents' TV lounge. The area is abundant in flora and fauna of all descriptions. Over two hundred varieties of alpine plants grow on the surrounding mountains, and Red Deer, Golden Eagles, Sea Eagles, Pine Martens and Otters are regularly sighted. The area is well known for its collection of birds, and for the specialists, the large variety of dragon flies and beetles. Packed lunches are available daily, and for those taking to the hills and mountains who feel the need, we are able to arrange guides who can cater for all levels, from complete novices to experienced ice and snow climbers and mountaineers. It is essential that these guides are booked in advance. Fishing is also available locally for both Brown and Sea Trout, and sea fishing and boat trips are available from Gairloch

ruins of **Ardvreck Castle**, built in the 1490s by the MacLeods. It was here, in 1650, that Montrose was kept prisoner before being taken to Edinburgh to be executed. The **Assynt Visitor Centre** has small displays and exhibits about local history.

DURNESS

50 miles N of Ullapool on the A838

Durness is one of the most northerly villages in Scotland, and sits close to **Cape Wrath** - one of only two "capes" in Great Britain. To reach it, you have to cross the Kyle of Durness from Durness itself on a small ferry and walk or take a minibus to the cape itself, ten miles away. The peculiarly named **Smoo Cave** is in the cliffs a mile and a half west of the village. It consists of three chambers, and goes underneath the coast road. The name may come from the old Norse smjugga, meaning "rock".

GAIRLOCH

22 miles SW of Ullapool on the A832

This little village, on the shores of Loch Gairloch, has one of the loveliest settings in Scotland. The **Gairloch Heritage Museum** has an "illicit" still, village shop, lighthouse interior and other displays that explain how life was lived in North West Scotland in times past. Five miles north east, on the banks of Loch Ewe are the famous **Inverewe Gardens** (National Trust for Scotland). It has plant collections from all over the world, which thrive in these northern latitudes due to the Gulf Stream.

Gairloch Sands

Sixteen miles south east of Gairloch, and beyond beautiful Loch Maree, is the quiet village of **Kinlochewe**. It is in the heart of what is recognised to be some of the finest mountain scenery in Scotland.

WICK

Wick is a an ancient royal burgh on the North Sea coast with a charter dating to 1589. It was once the leading herring port in Europe, but these times have long gone. The name comes from the old Norse word vik meaning "bay", and this whole area owes more to Viking and Norse culture than it does to the culture of the Gaels on the west coast. **Parliament Square** near the Market place recalls the fact that James V held a parliament at Wick as he made a royal progress through the kingdom in 1540.

The **Old Parish Kirk** dates from 1830, though a church has stood here since medieval times. In the kirkyard is the **Sinclair Aisle**, burial place of the old Earls of Caithness.

An old story of George Sinclair, the 4th Earl, explains just how bloodthirsty times were in the 16th century. He was suspected of murdering the Earl and Countess of Sutherland so that he could marry off his daughter to their heir, and thus claim the Sutherland lands. However, in 1576, the heir left the country, and Sinclair's plans were thwarted. In revenge, he ordered his son John to lay waste to the Sutherland lands, but when he refused Sinclair had him thrown into a dungeon.

With the help of his gaoler, John hatched a plot to escape. John's brother William found out about this and told his father, who executed the jailer. When William went down to the dungeon to goad his brother, John killed him with his chains. For this, his father punished him by denying him food for five days, then feeding him salt beef without giving him anything to drink. John died in agony, his tongue swollen through lack of water. His father had him buried in the predecessor to the present church, and years later, just before he too died, full of

AM BOTHAN AND THE GILLE DUBH

8 Naast, Poolewe, Ross-shire IV22 2LL
Tel: 01445 781360(Am Bothan) 01445 781740 (Gille Dubh) Fax: 01445 781360
e-mail: nicola.taylor@virgin.net
website: www.highland-dreams.co.uk

Set amid some lovely scenery three miles from Poolewe, east of Gairloch, **Am Bothan** is a superior cottage that features the best in self catering accommodation for up to five people. It comprises a lounge, hallway, bathroom/wc, spacious kitchen/dining room, three bedrooms (double, twin and single) and porches at the front and back. The lounge is especially well appointed, with storage heater, electric fire, colour TV, video, radio cassette and Sega games console. The kitchen has a cooker, microwave, toaster, food processor, iron and ironing board and spin dryer. There is also access to a washing machine and tumble dryer, and an immersion heater provides hot water. The place is well stocked with all the utensils necessary for a comfortable and relaxing stay, and all bed linen and towels are included in the price. In addition to five adults, the cottage can also accommodate one baby, and a high chair, cot and linen are available on request. The owner of the cottage, Nicola Taylor, will be happy to babysit by arrangement if you want to go out for the evening. The cottage is within the large garden of Nicola's bungalow, and looks out over Loch Ewe.

The **Gille Dubh** bills itself as 'more than a bookshop, more than a restaurant', and this is an apt description. It stands at Inverasdale, on the shores of Loch Ewe, in a converted cotter's cottage owned by Nicola. It is a browser's paradise, and as well as good food, it sells a wide range of original art, local music, bric a brac and new and second hand books. The kitchen is managed by experienced chef Audrey Scullin, and meals are served between 12:00 and 17:00 and 19:00 until late. It is the ideal place to have a cup of coffee from the wide range of coffees available, or a pot of tea with home baking. Lunches are also available, and in the evening there is a set menu containing at least one main dish. Past dishes have included such things as beef casserole with mustard and herb dumplings, roast loin of pork or oatmeal crusted salmon with a whisky dressing. The starters range from home made soup through smoked mackerel pate to three cheese ravioli or potato and chicken liver terrine. Each evening there is also a vegetarian alternative on offer, and you are invited to bring your own wine, as there is no corkage charge.

The name Gille Dubh means 'Black Lad', and refers to a legend about a black haired fairy who looked after young girls in the area. In the early 19th century, a MacKenzie chieftain set out to capture and shoot the creature, and since then he has rarely been seen. But some people have, it is said, seen him running through the woods dressed in clothes made of twigs and leaves. If you manage to get a good photograph, the Gille Dubh will reward you with free refreshment!

Am Bothan is the ideal base from which to explore an area that is rich in legend and history, and the Gille Dubh is the perfect place to have a lunch, a refreshing cup of coffee or a beautifully cooked evening meal.

THE OLD INN

Flowerdale Glen, Gairloch, Ross-shire IV21 2BD
Tel: 01445 712006 e-mail: nomadscot@lineone.net
Fax: 01445 712445 website: www.theoldinn.co.uk

The Old Inn dates from around 1780, and is one of the most picturesque old coaching inns in the Western Highlands. Nestling at the foot of the Flowerdale Glen, with an old stone footbridge close by, it has 14 en suite rooms (three of them family rooms) that are both comfortable and well appointed, plus the separate Slioch Lodge for walkers, which sleeps 20 within six rooms, each having an en suite shower. It is owned and managed by Ute and Alastair Pearson, who have provided a relaxing and friendly family-run inn that offers a relaxing and welcoming atmosphere among some of the most spectacular scenery in Scotland. It is an ideal stopping off point for people from the Continent who are exploring Scotland, as both fluent French and German are spoken. The lounge and public bars feature cosy, crackling log fires in the winter months, and have a large range of single malt whiskies and a fine selection of real ales that have warranted the inn's inclusion in the good beer guide. The cuisine is outstanding and reasonably priced, and is based on good, fresh local produce in season wherever possible. Being so close to the Western coastline, fresh seafood is one of the inn's specialities. There is an all day menu that features old favourites such as cullen skink (a traditional Scottish fish soup), beef and ale pie, fish pie, sizzling steaks, tasty fish 'n' chips made with a real-ale batter, venison and lemon chicken. A three course set meal is also available, as are a choice of vegetarian dishes. Daily blackboard specials in the past have included such things as moules marinieres, seared scallops, local cod, lobster and hake fillets in a herb and garlic butter. The Old Inn sits at the heart of a district that offers so many activities to the visitor, such as walking, fishing, pony-trekking, golf and bird watching. But if it's just a relaxing break 'away from it all' you are after, with the most strenuous activity being the lifting of a glass of single malt, then the inn is for you as well. Ute and Alastair will offer you a warm welcome!

THE BOWER INN

Bowermadden, by Wick, Caithness
Tel: 01955 661292; Fax: 01955 661377
e-mail: roy@thebower.fsnet.co.uk

The Bower Inn is one of the most picturesque hostelries in an area that is renowned for its scenery, wildlife and history. Owned and managed by Ann and Roy Smith, it offers good food, great drink and a cosy ambience that is hard to beat. The place is famous for its food, and it has a bright, spacious dining area that can seat up to 40 people in comfort. The menu includes such classic dishes as chicken liver and brandy paté, rainbow trout, gammon steaks, prime fillet steaks with all the trimmings, supreme of chicken, and a whole lot more that is sure to satisfy the most demanding of palates.

Ann and Roy take a keen interest in the quality of their cuisine, and insist on only the finest and freshest of local produce being used wherever possible. Vegetarian dishes are also available, as is a children's menu which includes such favourites as macaroni cheese, haddock fingers and "kilted pork sausages" - pork sausages wrapped in bacon! Everything is competitively priced, and the portions are, of course, generous. There is also a menu for bar lunches, which changes on a daily basis.

The bar itself is cool in summer and cosy in winter, and welcoming all year round. It carried a full range of beers, lagers, wines, spirits and - this being Scotland - malt whiskies, as well as soft drinks should you be behind the wheel. There is live entertainment on a regular basis, as well as monthly quiz nights and karaoke.

Wick Youth Hostel

remorse for what he had done, he asked that his heart be buried beside his son.

On a hill to the south of Wick bay is a memorial to the engineer **James Bremner**, who was born in Wick and who died in 1856. He collaborated with Brunel, and salvaged the SS Great Britain when it ran aground off Ireland. The **Northlands Viking Centre** tells the story of the Vikings and Norsemen in the area, as well recounting the life of John Nicolson, a local artist and mason.

North of Wick, the two castles of **Girnigoe** and **Sinclair** stand above Sinclair Bay. They were strongholds of the Earls of Caithness. Girnigoe is the older of the two, dating from the end of the 15th century, and it was in its dungeons that George Sinclair had his son incarcerated. Sinclair Castle dates from about 1606.

AROUND WICK

LATHERON

15 miles SW of Wick on the A9

Within the old church of Latheron, which dates from 1735, is the **Clan Gunn Heritage Centre**. It traces the history of the clan from its Norse origins right through to the present day. At Dunbeath, six miles south of Lybster, is the **Lhaidhay Caithness Croft Museum**, which shows a typical Highland house, with living quarters, byre and stable all under the one roof. And in the old schoolhouse at Dunbeath is the **Dunbeath Heritage Centre**.

HELMSDALE

30 miles SW of Wick on the A9

Timespan, within this little fishing port, is a visitor centre that tells the story of Helmsdale and its surrounding communities. There are exhibits about the Clearances, Picts, Norse raids, witches and so much more.

The **Strath of Kildonan**, through which flows the River Helmsdale, was the scene of a famous gold rush in 1868. In that year a local man called Robert Gilchrist, who had been a prospector in Australia, began searching for gold in the river. He eventually found some, and once his secret was out, the Duke of Sutherland began parcelling off small plots of land to speculators. At its height, over 500 men were prospecting in the area, and a shanty town soon sprung up. But in 1870, when sportsmen complained that the prospectors were interfering with their fishing and hunting, the Duke put a stop to it all, and the gold rush was over. There is still gold there today, and it is a favourite spot for amateur gold panners.

TONGUE

50 miles W of Wick off the A838

Tongue is a small village situated near the shallow Kyle of Tongue. In 1972 a causeway was built across it to take the A838 westwards towards Loch Eribol and Durness. On a promontory to the west of the village are the ruins of **Castle Bharraich**, which once belonged to Clan Mackay. Nine miles NE of the village, within the old St Columba's Church at Farr, is the **Strathnaver Museum**, with exhibits about local history, most notably the Clearances. Strathnaver was probably the most notorious area in the Highlands for the eviction of tenants so that they could be replaced with the more profitable sheep.

ALTNAHARRA

51 miles W of Wick on the A836

Sitting close to the western tip of **Loch Naver**,

Altnaharra is a small village famous as a centre for game fishing. Loch Naver is the source of the River Naver, one of the best salmon rivers in Sutherland, which flows northwards through Strathnaver to the sea (see also Tongue).

THURSO

19 miles NW of Wick on the A9

Thurso is a fishing port on Caithness's northern coast. The ruins of **St Peter's Church** sit in the old part of the town, and date from medieval times. It was once the private chapel of the Bishop of Caithness, whose summer retreat was **Scrabster Castle**, now in ruins. The **Thurso Heritage Museum** is located within an old cottage, and has displays and mementos relating to the town's past.

JOHN O'GROATS

13 miles N of Wick on the A99

John O' Groats is 873 miles by road from Land's End in Cornwall, and 280 miles from Kirkmaiden in Wigtownshire, Scotland's most southerly parish. It is supposed to be named after a Dutchman called Jan de Groot, who, to settle an argument about precedence within his family, built an eight sided house with eight doors which gave onto an eight-sided table. This house has now gone, though its site is marked by a mound. To the west is **Dunnet Head**, the most northerly point on the British mainland. Between the two is the **Castle of Mey**, the Queen Mother's Scottish home. It is an ancient castle of the Earls of Caithness, and was built in the 16th century.

Duncansby, nr John O'Groats

12 The Western Isles

The Western Isles, lying off Scotland's west coast, look like a huge kite with a long tail streaming out behind it. The kite itself is the island of Lewis and Harris, and the tail consists mainly of the smaller islands of North Uist, Benbecula, South Uist and Barra. The whole length between Barra in the south and the Butt of Lewis in the north is about 130 miles, and they are separated from the mainland by a stretch of water called The Minch. These islands are the last bastion of true Gaeldom in Scotland, and in some places English, though spoken and understood perfectly, is still a second language. Some are also bastions of Free Presbyterianism, where the Sabbath is strictly observed, and work (and in some cases pleasure) of any kind on a Sunday is frowned upon. This has given it the reputation of being a dour and strict place that frowns on fun, but nothing could be further from the truth.

Isle of North Uist

But there are paradoxes in the Western Isles. There are just as many Norse influences here as Celtic, and most of the place names (especially in the north) have Norse origins. Up until the Treaty of Perth in 1266 the Western Isles were ruled by Norway, but in that year Magnus IV surrendered all of his Scottish possessions, with the exception of Orkney and Shetland, to Alexander III of Scotland. And though Free Presbyterianism dominates Lewis and Harris, some of the other islands are largely Roman Catholic, not through Irish immigration, but because the Reformation never fully penetrated this far.

The weather in the Western Isles, especially in winter, can be harsh. Snow is rare because of the Gulf Stream, but there are between 45 and 50 inches of rain a year, and the winds blowing the rain in from the Atlantic are invariably strong. But the compensations are enormous. The long summer evenings can be still and warm, and at midnight it is still possible in the north of Lewis to read a newspaper out of doors.

The main island is divided into two parts, Lewis and Harris, an ancient arrangement which is thought to go back as far as the 13th century. Though joined geographically, they are usually considered to be two separate islands, and indeed the differences between them are marked. Lewis is the northern, and larger part, and up until the mid 70s was within the county of Ross and Cromarty. Harris (and the smaller islands) came under Inverness-shire. A natural boundary of mountains and high moorland ran between Loch Resort on the west and Loch Seaforth on the east. Now they all form one administrative area, with the capital being at Stornoway.

The underlying rock of Lewis is gneiss, one of the oldest in the world. It is largely impermeable, so doesn't absorb water. For this reason the interior of the island is a large, empty peat moorland dotted with shallow lochs, while most of the settlements are on the coast. Harris is more mountainous, and has peaks reaching 2,500 feet. It is also an area where the underlying rocks break through to the surface like bones, giving an essentially bleak but strangely attractive landscape. It too is divided into two parts, North and South Harris, with the narrow ithsmus between West Loch Tarbert and East Loch Tarbert being the boundary.

Of the main southern islands, Berneray, North Uist, Benbecula, South Uist and Eriskay are joined by causeways. North Uist connects to Harris by a ferry between An t-Obbe and Berneray, and Barra has a ferry connection with Eriskay. Each island in the chain has its own flavour, and all are noted for their quality of light, especially in summer, when the weather can sometimes be surprisingly mild.

Drinishader, Isle of Harris

The Western Isles sit on the farthest edge of Europe, with North America being the next stop. But for all their seeming isolation, they have a long history. The standing stones at Callanish - the second largest stone circle in Britain - are over 4,000 years old, and were built for pagan ritual and possibly to record the passing of the seasons so that crops could be sown and harvested. And there are individual stones, duns, brochs and old forts dotted all over the landscape. The local people are proud of their history, and on your travels, look out for small, village-based museums which seem to be everywhere.

Norse invasions began in earnest in the 8th century, and by about AD850 Norsemen ruled all of the Outer Hebrides. But by 1266 the islands were Scottish, even though the local leaders acted independently of the crown, and there was much friction between the Scottish kings and the Lords of the Isles. But the kings gradually imposed their authority, and the islands accepted this and became fully integrated into Scotland. Some historians claim, however, that the Norse language only died out in the late 16th century. Various attempts have been made over the years to encourage industry, most notably when Lord Leverhulme bought both Lewis and Harris in 1918 and tried to promote fishing.

Today the islands rely on fishing, crofting and tourism, with the weaving of Harris Tweed being an important industry on Lewis and Harris. The weaving is usually a cottage industry, with the weavers working on their own at home or in sheds at the back of the house. Some weavers will welcome you into their weaving rooms and explain the processes involved in turning wool into fine cloth. Ferries for Stornoway leave from Ullapool, and there is also a ferry connection between Oban, South Uist and Barra, as well as one from Uig on Skye to Lochmaddy and Tarbert.

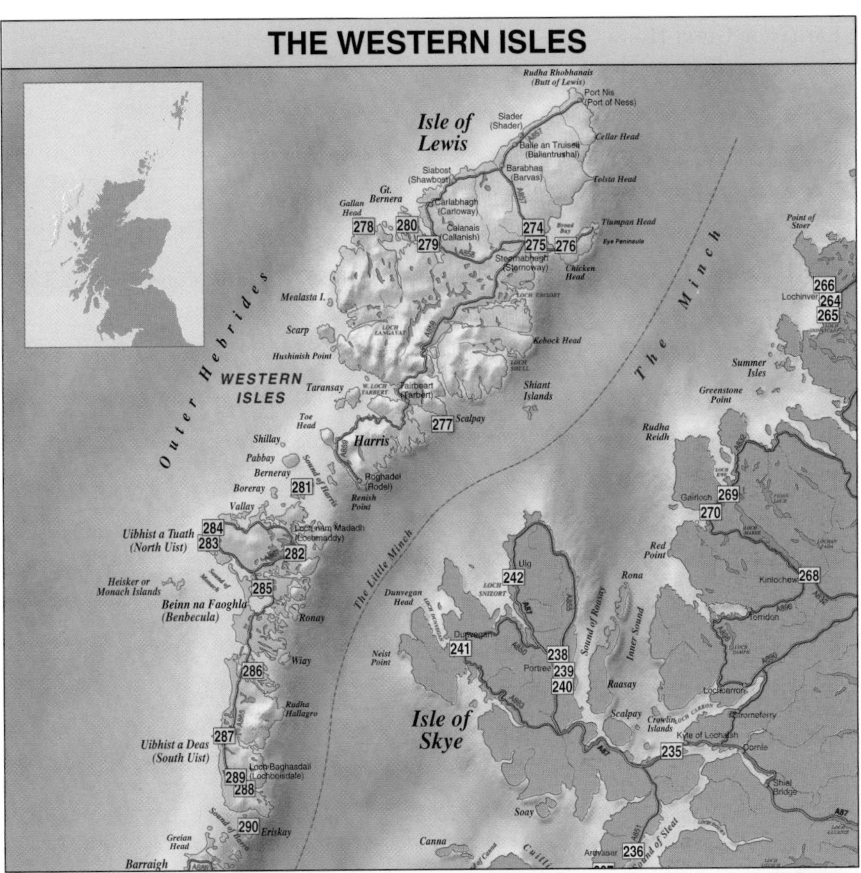

© MAPS IN MINUTES ™ 2001 © Crown Copyright, Ordnance Survey 2001

PLACES TO STAY, EAT, DRINK AND SHOP

274	Lathamor Guest House, Newmarket	Guest House	Page 324
275	22 Braighe Road, Stornoway	Self catering	Page 324
276	Ceol-Na-Mara, Point	Bed and Breakfast	Page 325
277	Bridgeside B&B/Self Catering, Bayhead	B&B and self catering	Page 326
278	Scaliscro Lodge, Uig	Self catering	Page 328
279	Creagan Cottage, Creagan	Self catering	Page 328
280	5 Hacklete, Great Bernera	Self catering	Page 329
281	Seaview Holiday House, Morven	Self catering	Page 330
282	The Old Courthouse, Lochmaddy	Bed and Breakfast	Page 330
283	Sgeir Ruadh, Hougharry	Bed and Breakfast	Page 331
284	Baleloch House, Tigharry	Self catering	Page 332
285	Knockqueen, Carinish	Self catering	Page 332
286	Orasay Inn, Lochcarnan	Pub, accommodation and restaurant	Page 333
287	Island Croft Holidays, Bornish	Self catering	Page 334
288	Lochside Cottage, Lochboisdale	Bed and Breakfast	Page 334
289	Morrison's B&B/Caravans, Lochboisdale	B&B and self catering	Page 335
290	2 Village, Eriskay	Self catering	Page 336

Lathamor Guest House

Bakers Road, Newmarket, Stornoway,
Isle of Lewis HS2 0EA
Tel/Fax: 01851 706093

Two and a half miles from Stornoway town centre, on Bakers Road off the A857, is **Lathamor Guest House**, which offers superior accommodation for discerning tourists to the Western Isles. It is a modern building, well-run and comfortable, and is owned by Helen Ferguson, who has created a home from home for her guests. Two rooms are available, a triple family and a double/twin, and each has tea and coffee making facilities, hairdryer and central heating. The shared bathroom is fully equipped, and has a corner bath/spa. Helen is an accomplished cook, and her full Scottish breakfasts are sure to set you up for a day exploring an island that is rich in wildlife and history.

If you would like an early breakfast, say before 7 am, then this can be arranged. She also serves delicious evening meals between 5 pm and 8 pm, though these times are flexible. Helen uses local produce wherever possible, and vegetarians and those with special diets can be catered for. If you like, you can bring your own wine or beer to enjoy with your meal. The house has panoramic views over Stornoway, and at the rear is a large area of moorland where guests can have an invigorating walk before or after a meal. There is ample parking and access for the disabled at the front, and a large garden with adjoining play area for children.

22 Braighe Road

22 Braighe Road, Stornoway, Isle of Lewis, HS2 0BQ
Tel: 01851 702304 e-mail:margareteng@aol.com
Fax: 01851 702305 website: www.visithebrides.co.uk

Two and a half miles from Stornoway, the Western Isles' largest town, is the self catering cottage owned by Margaret Engebretson. It is located at **22 Braighe Road**, on the Eye Peninsula to the east of the town, and is the perfect location from which to explore the island. It is a modern, whitewashed bungalow set in a small area of ground next to the owner's croft, and has fine views all around. It has all the conveniences and comforts of modern life while still offering a "get away from it all" type holiday atmosphere. The cost of hiring the cottage includes all electricity, linen and towels, and a cot is available free of charge. It has two twin rooms upstairs, and a bathroom with bath and shower. Downstairs there is one twin room and a toilet with wash hand basin.

Though the whole house has central heating, there is an open fire in the spacious and comfortable lounge, as well as a colour TV. The kitchen/dining room is fully equipped with all the modern conveniences, such as cooker, microwave, fridge, freezer and dishwasher.In addition, a small utility area has an automatic washing machine. There is ample parking adjacent to the cottage, and the local bus service to Stornoway stops by request just outside the front door. The pace of life on the Western Isles seems peaceful and unhurried, and this wonderfully appointed cottage reflects this by having a restful and relaxing atmosphere - one that is sure to add to the enjoyment of your holiday in the Western Isles.

STORNOWAY

With a population of about 6,000, Stornoway (from the Old Norse stjorna, meaning "anchor bay") is the only town of any size in the Western Isles. It is their administrative, educational and shopping centre, and is a surprisingly cosmopolitan place, with a sizable Asian immigrant population.

Stornoway Harbour

It was founded in the middle ages round an old MacLeod castle, and has a fine natural harbour and an airport. On Lewis Street is **The Parish Church of St Columba**, dating from 1794, and in **St Peter's Episcopal Church** (1839) is an old font from the Flannan Isles and David Livingstone's Bible. It's bell, which was made in 1631, was once the town bell that summoned townspeople to important meetings. The **Free Church** in Kenneth Street has the distinction of being the best attended church in all of Britain, with the Sunday evening congregation regularly exceeding 1,500.

Lews Castle, now a college surrounded by public gardens, was built in the 1840s and 50s by James Matheson, a businessman who earned a fortune in the Far East trading in tea and opium. In 1843 he bought Lewis, and began a series of improvements in what was then a backward island. He built new roads, improved the housing and brought running water and gas to the town. One of his projects was a plant to extract oil from the peat that blanketed the island, and in 1861 the Lewis Chemical Works began production. But problems had beset the setting up of the plant, and it had actually blown up, putting the citizens of of Stornoway into a state of fear and alarm. The venture finally folded in 1874.

The **Museum nan Eilean** on Francis Street has artifacts and exhibits highlighting the history of both the island of Lewis and Stornoway itself, as well as good displays about archaeology on the islands. It makes a good starting point if you want to explore the area. At the **An Lanntair Arts Centre** in the town hall there are always contemporary and traditional exhibitions, as well as varied programmes of music and drama highlighting the Gaelic culture. One of Stornoway's most famous sons was the explorer Sir Alexander MacKenzie, who gave his name to the Mackenzie river. In Francis Street, on the site of his house, is **Martins Memorial**, built in 1885.

The Western Isles are synonymous with Harris Tweed, and at the **Loom Centre** you can find out about its history and about how it is woven. To attain the "orb" symbol of genuine Harris Tweed, the cloth needs to woven from "virgin wool produced in Scotland", then spun, dyed and hand woven in the Outer Hebrides..

West of Stornoway, on the Eye Peninsula, are the ruins of **St Columba's Church**, built in the 14th century. It is said that nineteen MacLeod chiefs are buried there within carved tombs.

AROUND STORNOWAY

TARBERT

33 miles S of Stornoway on the A859

The small village of Tarbert has a ferry connection with Uig on Skye. This is the starting point of South Harris, and an ithsmus, no more that half a mile wide, separates East Loch Tarbert, which is an arm of the Minch, from West Loch Tarbert, which is an arm of the Atlantic. **Amhuinnsuidhe Castle** (not open to the public) was built in 1868 by the Earl of Dunsmore, who owned

Harris. It was the Earl's wife who introduced the weaving of Harris Tweed to the island. It was here that J.M. Barrie wrote his play Mary Rose.

The Church, Rodel

RODEL

48 miles S of Stornoway on the A859

Rodel sits near the southern tip of Harris, and is famous for **St Clement's Church**, built in 1500 by Alasdair Crotach McLeod, who lived in the church's tower from 1540 to his death in 1547. He is still within the church, in a magnificent tomb. By 1787 the church was ruinous, but in that year it was restored by Alexander MacLeod, a captain with the East India Company.

SCALPAY

33 miles SW of Stornoway

The tiny island of Scalpay, off Harris's east coast, is connected to the mainland by the £7m **Scalpay Bridge**, the biggest civil engineering project ever undertaken in the area. It was opened in 1998 by Tony Blair, the first serving prime minister ever to visit the Western Isles. The visit is also remembered because of the biting criticism he received from one of the island's more militant inhabitants - *culiciodes impunctatus*, more commonly known as the midge.

SHAWBOST

16 miles W of Stornoway on the A858

Housed within a former school, the **Shawbost School Museum** has artifacts and objects collected by school pupils as part of a project that illustrate the way people used to live in Lewis. Near it is a reconstruction of a Norse water mill.

CALLANISH

16 miles W of Stornoway on the A858

Dating back at least 4,000 years, the **Callanish Stone Circle** (Historic Scotland) is second only to Stonehenge in importance in Britain. It is more than just a mere circle of upright stones, however. Four great arms made up of monoliths radiate from it to the north, south east and west, with the northern arm (which veers slightly to the east) having a double row of stones as if enclosing an approachway.

Callanish Stone Circle

It is a mysterious place, and has attracted many stories and myths over the ages. One story tells of a race of giants who met to discuss how to defeat the new religion of Christianity that was spreading throughout the islands. This so incensed St Kieran that he performed the miracle of turning them all to stone. Another says that the stones were brought to Lewis by

SCALISCRO LODGE

Uig, Isle of Lewis HS2 9EL
Tel: 01851 672325 Fax: 01851 672393
website: www.scaliscro.co.uk

If it's peace and tranquillity you're after, then **Scaliscro Lodge** is the place for you. Set down a two mile private road off the B8011, it sits overlooking Little Loch Roag, in one of the most idyllic locations in the Western Isles. It is a family run establishment, under the personal supervision of Cree MacKenzie. The self catering lodge can accommodate twenty people in nine double/twin rooms, and two single rooms served by seven bathrooms. Its facilities include two sitting rooms with open fires, dining room, pool room with cocktail bar, drying room/laundry, kitchen and a table tennis room. There is also a large west facing sunroom where you can enjoy breathtaking sunsets over the hills of Uig and Harris.

Not far from the lodge is a well equipped self catering cottage with sea loch views. It can accommodate eight people in one double bedroom, two twins and two singles served by one bathroom and one shower room with WC. The cottage has its own garden with picnic table, sand pit and outside tap. There is a sitting room with open fire and Sky TV, an open plan kitchen/dining room, and a utility room. Scaliscro makes a wonderful base for exploring the islands of Lewis and Harris, all parts of which are in easy reach by car. Guests are also free to ramble over the 10,000 acre Scaliscro estate which has an organic salmon farm and hill farm with rare breeds including Highland cattle and Hebridean sheep. A wide range of outdoor activities can be arranged for chldren and adults of all ages, including free trout fishing on hill lochs.

CREAGAN COTTAGE

Creagan, Callanish, Isle of Lewis H52 9DY
Tel: 01851 621200
e-mail: as@creagans50.freeserve.co.uk

Ann and Angus Smith would like to welcome you to their cosy and comfortable self catering cottage on the Isle of Lewis close to the historic Callanish Standing Stones, which date back thousands of years. **Creagan Cottage** is a modern yet picturesque bungalow with great views of the Stones themselves, the sea and surrounding moorland, and boasts three spacious bedrooms. There is a double, a twin and a single, so the place sleeps five in absolute comfort, though a cot can be provided for that extra, smaller guest! There is a living room with TV, electric fire, a host of games, books and magazines, and a substantial garden where you can sit out in the long summer evenings for which the Western Isles are so famous.

The well appointed kitchen is fully fitted, with washing machine, tumble drier, fridge freezer, cooker, microwave and kettle, and the whole place is centrally heated through storage heaters. For a small extra charge, bed linen can be supplied, and all electricity is supplied through a £1 coin meter. The bathroom boasts a shower, toilet, and toilet. There is excellent fishing in the local lochs, as well as moors that just cry out to be explored on foot. Creagan Cottage makes an excellent base for that special Western Isles holiday, and Ann and Angus will like to extend a warm Scottish welcome to their visitors!

a great priest king who employed "black men" to erect them. Those men who died building the circle were buried within it. Plus there are the more modern, and unfortunately predictable, theories that the stones were erected by mysterious beings from outer space as a means of guiding their spacecraft, though why people with such technology should need such guidance seems equally as mysterious.

A visitors centre next to the stones tries to uncover the truth behind them, which may have something to do with primitive ritual and predicting the seasons for agricultural purposes.

CARLOWAY

17 miles W of Stornoway on the A858

The 1,500 year old **Dun Carloway Broch,** overlooking Loch Carloway, is one of the best preserved brochs in Scotland. It is over 48 feet in diameter, and its walls are 33 feet high in places. Some of the galleries and internal stairways are still intact.

GREAT BERNERA

18 miles W of Stornoway off the B8059

The small island of Great Bernera is connected to the mainland by the **Great Bernera Bridge**, which was the first bridge in the country made from pre-stressed concrete girders. The **Community Centre and Museum** has displays about the island, and also sells tea, coffee and cakes. On the lovely beach at **Bostadh** an Iron Age village has been excavated, and a reconstruction of an Iron Age house built.

BARVAS

13 miles NW of Stornoway on the A858

At one time, most of the population of Lewis lived in small cottages known as blackhouses. On the west coast at Arnol, the **Arnol Blackhouse** (Historic Scotland) shows what life was like in one of them. It has tiny windows because of the seasonal gales and rain (plus the fact that glass was very expensive) and its thick, drystone walls (with

SEAVIEW HOLIDAY HOUSE

Morven, Berneray, North Uist HS6 5BJ
Tel: 01876 540230 Fax: 01876 540230
e-mail:damacaskill@tinyworld.co.uk

Berneray lies just off the northern tip of North Uist, joined to the main island by a causeway. And on this beautiful, small island, with its white, sandy beaches and its lovely sunsets, you will find **Seaview Holiday House**. This well equipped and spacious self catering house sleeps nine people in comfort, and is owned and managed by Chrissie MacAskill. It is the ideal base from which to explore an area of the Western Isles that is rich in history, heritage and wildlife. On the ground floor there is one bedroom with a double and single bed, a well equipped kitchen/diner with freezer, fridge, dishwasher, washing machine, tumble dryer and microwave.

There is also a spacious yet cosy living room (with sun porch) and a shower room. Upstairs there is one double bedroom, a single bedroom and a room with a double and a single bed, and a bathroom. Well behaved pets are welcome if they are kept on the leash while out of doors, and a high chair and cot form part of the house's furnishings. There is ample parking for several cars, and the island boasts two shops. Berneray is a favourite holiday spot of HRM Prince Charles, who enjoys the peace and seclusion this lovely island offers. It is the ideal location for a quiet, restful holiday, free from the hurly burly of modern life without being too far away from modern day amenities. The machair - the wide grassland that fringes the coastline - is particular rich in wild flowers and birds, and is a mecca for those interested in ornithology and botany.

THE OLD COURTHOUSE

Lochmaddy, North Uist HS6 5AE
Tel: 01876 500358 Fax: 01876 500358
e-mail: mjohnson@oldcourthouse.fsnet.co.uk

Close to the ferry terminal at Lochmaddy on North Uist is **The Old Courthouse**, a superior B&B establishment owned and run by Margaret Johnson. This historic old building has four large, extremely comfortable and beautifully decorated rooms on offer to the discerning tourist - a twin, a double and two singles. All are completely en suite, and are well equipped with colour TV, hair dryer and tea and coffee making facilities. Each one has great views of the sea from the window. Margaret's full Scottish breakfasts are generous and hearty, with a breakfast menu that allows you to choose from such things as kippers, eggs and bacon or a Continental breakfast should you require it. They are served between 8.00 and 9.00, though earlier times can be arranged.

Evening meals can also be served by arrangement, and Margaret uses only the finest and freshest local produce when cooking them. If you require packed lunches, these can also be made up if you notify Margaret in plenty of time. Well behaved pets are more than welcome, and there is a shed where you can store sports equipment such as bicycles and fishing tackle. The Old Courthouse is the ideal base from which to explore this picturesque yet rugged island, or take part in many of the activities it offers, from bird watching and fishing to water sports and cycling. Margaret prides herself on the warmth of her welcome and great value for money, and will do everything she can to make your stay a happy and enjoyable one.

a central core of clay and earth) keep it cool in summer and warm in winter. The floor is of clay, and the fire is centrally placed, with no chimney. The houses got their name in the mid 19th century to distinguish them from the more modern whitehouses, which has mortar binding the stones.

BALLANTRUSHAL

15 miles NW of Stornoway on the B857

The **Clach an Trushal**, at 18 feet high, is the tallest standing stone in Scotland, and is said to mark the site of an ancient battle, though this is unlikely.

SHADER

16 miles NW of Stornoway on the A857

The **Steinacleit Stone Circle and Standing Stones** sit on a low hill, and date from between 2000 and 3000 BC. The stones are more in the shape of an oval than a circle. A burial cairn can be seen as well.

OTHER WESTERN ISLES

NORTH UIST

59 miles SW of Stornoway

Like most of the Western Isles, North Uist is low lying, with more water than land making up its total area of 74,884 acres. **Loch Scadavay** is the biggest of the lochs, and though it only has an area of eight square miles, it has a coastline measuring 51 miles in length. The highest point on the island, at 1,127 feet, is Eaval, near the south east corner. The island has a ferry service to An t-Obbe in Harris from Berneray, and one to Skye from **Lochmaddy**, the island's capital, and where most of the hotels and B&Bs are to be found.

Teampall na Triobad ("Trinity Temple"), on the south west shore, was once a great place of learning in the Western Isles. Indeed some people claim that it was actually Scotland's first university, with scholars and students

SGEIR RUADH

Hougharry, Longmaddy, North Uist HS6 5DL
Tel: 01876 510312
e-mail: sgeirruarh@aol.com
website: www.sgeirruadh@aol.com

Think of a three star B&B situated above a sweep of deserted, sandy beach, with panoramic views across the bay towards St Kilda. Think of a small, traditional crofting community that gives an insight into rural island life - and you could be thinking of **Sgeir Ruadh** and its setting on North Uist. This superb B&B establishment is one of the best on the island, and boasts two extremely comfortable double bedded rooms and a twin, all en suite and all with tea and coffee making facilities. In addition, there is a cosy guests' lounge with colour TV, where you can relax after a hard day sight seeing. The B&B is owned and run by Kathy Simpson, who takes a great pride in it.

The breakfasts are always filling, hearty, and beautifully cooked, and evening meals are available by arrangement, as are packed lunches. Kathy uses only the finest, freshest local produce in her cuisine, and people come back time and time again to sample her hospitality and the tranquil pace of life to be found here. Children and well behaved pets are most welcome, and vegetarians and those with special diets can be catered for. The B&B is beautifully located for beach walks, rambling over rocky headlands or exploring the rare flowers that abound on the machair. It is also the ideal base for bird watching on the nearby Balranald Bird Reserve, where corncrakes can be found in spring and summer, and for fishing for brown trout in many of the island's picturesque lochs.

making their way here from all over the country. It was founded in the early 13th century by one Beathag, a prioress from the priory on Iona. By the end of the 15th century, however, its influence began to fade, and during the Reformation it was attacked. Valuable books, manuscripts and works of art were tossed in the sea, and so much of the island's heritage was lost. The other building on the site is **Teampull MacBhiocair**, (MacVicar's Temple), where the teachers were buried.

It was in this area, in 1601, that the **Battle of Carinish** took place, the last battle on British soil not to have involved firearms. A troop of MacLeods from Harris were raiding the island, and took shelter in the Trinity Temple buildings when attacked by the MacDonalds. But the MacDonalds ignored the status of the temple, and slaughtered every MacLeod clansman except two, who escaped.

On the island's west coast, off the A865, is the **Balranald Nature Reserve**, where you can see waders and seabirds on various habitats.

BALELOCH HOUSE

Post Office House, Tigharry,
Lochmaddy, North Uist HS6 5DG
Tel: 01876 510247

Baleloch House is a traditional, stone-built dwelling on the west side of the island of North Uist. It is approximately 18 miles from Lochmaddy along the A867 road - a ½ mile long car track leads off this road up to the house which is located in its grounds of over one acre and is enclosed by a walled garden. It is an idyllic setting, nestling in a quiet, private location in an area of outstanding natural beauty. There are views of hills, of open moorlands and of the beautiful Machair pasturelands, famous for their flowers, butterflies and birds.

The silvery, sandy beaches of Hosta are only ¾ mile away and Loch Hosta, excellent for brown trout fishing, stretches out below the grounds. The house is well maintained, spacious and warm, and provides comfortable accommodation. Bed linen and towels are provided. Downstairs is a spacious lounge with open fire, dining room with open fire, large family kitchen with dining table and shower room with toilet. Upstairs there are three double bedrooms, a single bedroom and bathroom. There is an additional single bed in one of the double rooms. Fridge, chest freezer, automatic washing machine with tumble drier, microwave and payphone. Cooking and hot water is by electricity, and heating is by electricity and open peat or coal fires.

KNOCKQUEEN

8 Knockqueen, Carinish, North Uist HS6 5HW
Tel: 01876 580635

At **Knockqueen** on North Uist you will find a comfortable self catering caravan that sleeps four to six people in absolute comfort. It boasts two bedrooms, a spacious lounge, a shower room with wc and a fully equipped kitchen. It is the perfect base for a holiday that takes in cycling, walking, fishing or birdwatching, or you can just come here and relax completely and get away from it all. The caravan sits close to the sea, and has some stunning views that will make your stay on this lovely island a truly memorable one. Children are welcome, and early booking is advised.

BENBECULA

80 miles SW of Stornoway

Benbecula is sandwiched between North and South Uist. Its name in Gaelic is Beinn bheag a' bh-faodhla, meaning mountain of the fords.ÊIts landscape is low and flat, and dotted with shallow lochans, though **Rueval**, it's highest peak, soars to all of 403 feet. The island marks the boundary between the Protestant islands to the north and the solidly Roman Catholic islands to the south. There is no ferry terminal on the island, as it is connected to South Uist and North Uist by causeways.

The main settlement is **Balivanich**, on the west coast, and beside it is the small airstrip. To the south of the village, on the B892, are the ruins of **Nunton Chapel**, supposed to have been a nunnery built in the 14th century. It was Lady Clanranald from nearby Nunton House who gave Charles Edward Stuart his disguise as a serving girl when he escaped from Benbecula to Skye in 1746.

Borve Castle, about three miles south of Balivanich, was owned by Ranald, son of John of Islay, in the 14th century. The ruins show a typical tower house of the period.

SOUTH UIST

87 miles SW of Stornoway

Running down the east side of South Uist is a range of low mountains, with **Beinn Mhor** being the highest at 2,034 feet. The west side of the island is gentler, with fine white sandy beaches. Lochboisdale, in the south east corner, is the largest village on the island, and has a ferry connection to Mallaig, Oban and Castlebay on Barra.

The island is predominantly Roman Catholic, and to the north west of the island is the famous statute of **Our Lady of the Isles** which stands 30 feet high and was sculpted by Hew Lorimer. It was erected in 1957. At the **Loch Druidibeag Nature Reserve**, which is close by, many types of wildfowl can be observed.

It was in South UIst, near **Milton** on Loch Kildonan that Flora MacDonald was born in 1722. Her house is now completely ruinous, though the ruins can still be seen. She was no

ORASAY INN

Lochcarnan, South Uist HS8 5PD
Tel: 01870 610298 Fax: 01870 610390
e-mail: orasayinn@btinternet.com website: www.witb.co.uk/links/orasayinn.htrm

Some of the finest food in the Western Isles is served at the **Orasay Inn** at Lochcarnan on South Uist. This small country house hotel is owned and run by Isobel and Alan Graham, who use only the finest and freshest Hebridean and Highland produce, including locally caught fish, in their kitchens. Isobel is a 'Natural Cook of Scotland' trainer (who was one of the team chosen to prepare the gala dinner for the opening of the Scottish Parliament), and oversees a menu that contains such exceptional dishes as fresh Uist scallops, sirloin steak, Highland lamb steak, grilled duck breast in Drambuie sauce, and chicken heather cream.

The assistant chef is also a qualified baker, and produces fresh bread, scones and rolls. In addition there is a specials board that changes daily, and a bar menu that features everything from deep fried squid to Thai red curry, all at quite exceptional prices considering the quality. All meals are served in a dining room that has fine views of sea and mountain, which adds to the culinary experience. There is also a selection of fine wines to accompany your meal, and in the cosy lounge bar you can choose from a wide range of lagers, beers, spirits, liqueurs and soft drinks should you be driving. The inn boasts nine comfortable and well appointed en suite rooms, all with colour TV, tea and coffee making facilities, central heating, hair dryer and telephone.

Island Croft Holidays

5a Gearraidh Bhailteas, Bornish, South Uist HS8 5RY
Tel: 01878 710371

Owned and run by Isobel and Angus MacKenzie, **Island Croft Holidays** offers two self catering cottages on a typical Western Isles croft. Sheabhal is a detached modern house that sleeps up to eight in two double bedrooms and two twins, while Treanabhal is a traditional cottage that sleeps six. It was the original croft house, and has two double and one twin room. Both cottages are beautifully appointed, with a shower room that has a wc and basin in each, and a fully equipped kitchen that has an automatic washing machine, tumble dryer, and microwave. Though both cottages have full central heating, each spacious lounge also boasts an open fire and colour TV. There is ample car parking, with a fence area around Sheabhal.

The modern croft house, in which Isobel and Angus live, also has comfortable and cosy rooms to let on a B&B basis. There are two double rooms, a single and a twin (suitable for the disabled). All have en suite shower rooms, and Isobel's traditional Scottish breakfasts, which are hearty and beautifully cooked, are sure to set you up for a day exploring the lovely and historic island of South Uist. The cheery residents' lounge/dining room has a TV as well as a traditional peat fire - just right for relaxing in the evening. There's no problem with wet clothing (just in case it rains!) as drying facilities are available, as well as secure storage of sports equipment such as fishing tackle or bicycles.

Isobel and Angus's native tongue is Gaelic, but the warmth of their welcome and the extent of their hospitality speaks volumes in any language!

Lochside Cottage

Lochboisdale, South Uist HS8 5TH
Tel/Fax: 01878 700472

Lochside Cottage is a superior three star establishment that offers three comfortable and beautifully decorated rooms on a B&B basis to discerning tourists. There is a family room, a double and a twin, and each one has a colour TV, tea and coffee making facilities, shoe polish and hair dryer. There is also a spacious yet cosy residents' lounge with a satellite and terrestrial channel TV. This is B&B accommodation at its best, and it makes an ideal base from which to explore an island that is rich in history and wildlife. You can view otters at play, go bird watching, play golf on the nearby golf course or fish for brown trout in the nearby loch. The cottage has a shed where bicycles and other sporting equipment can be stored, and packed lunches and evening meals are available on request.

The owners, Mrs and Mrs Simpson, are more than willing to pick you up from the island's ferry terminals and bring you to the cottage. The full Scottish breakfasts are filling and hearty, and both the breakfasts and evening meals use only the finest and freshest local produce wherever possible. Also available for hire close to the cottage are two large, self catering caravans. One sleeps four, and the other six, and both are exceedingly well equipped, with cooker and microwave in the kitchen, a colour TV and a shower. As with the cottage, they make the ideal spot from which to view otters, as they look out onto the loch. The island of South Uist has long, lingering evenings during the summer months, with wonderful sunsets. The Lochside Cottage B&B and caravans are the ideal spot from which to view them.

MORRISON'S B&B AND CARAVANS

8 West Kilbride, Lochboisdale, South Uist HS8 5TT
Tel: 01878 700 351

Set on a working farm with some fantastic views, **Morrison's B&B and Caravans** offers some of the best holiday accommodation on this beautiful island. There are four lovely rooms on offer - three double and a single - with each one having tea/coffee making facilities. The full Scottish breakfasts can be timed to suite your plans, and packed lunches can also be arranged. In addition, three 6-berth caravans are available, all beautifully appointed and extremely comfortable. The views are fantastic, kids are welcome, and there is ample parking.

simple Gaelic lass, but the daughter of a prosperous farmer. The tiny **Kildonan Museum** has displays and exhibits on local history, as well as a tea room. Further north along the A865 are the ruins of **Ormiclate Castle**, built between 1701 and 1708 as a sumptuous residence for the chief of Clanranald. Alas, the chief's stay there was short lived, as it burnt down in 1715 after a rowdy Jacobite party.

Off the south coast of South Uist is the small island of **Eriskay**, which is joined to South Uist by a causeway. It is noted for one of the most beautiful of Gaelic songs, the Eriskay Love Lilt. It was here, in 1745, that Charles Edward Stuart first set foot on Scottish soil when he stepped off a French ship to reclaim the throne for the Stuarts. Legend says that he first planted the sea convolvolus which now thrives here today.

It was in February 1941 that another event took place which was to make Eriskay famous. **The SS. Politician** was heading towards the United States with a cargo of 260,000 bottles of whisky when it was wrecked on the Sound of Eriskay. Legend has it that as soon as the seamen were safe, work began on "removing" the cargo, and this lasted for a few weeks. Eventually Customs and Excise men appeared on the island, but by this time the bottles had been spirited away into peat bogs and other hidey-holes. Eventually only 19 people were charged with illegal possession. Sir Compton Mackenzie used the incident as the basis for his novel *Whisky Galore*.

The wreckage can still sometimes be seen at exceptionally low tide. In the late 1980s an attempt was made to get at the rest of the cargo, but this proved unsuccessful.

South Uist

BARRA

105 miles S of Stornoway

Barra is the southernmost of the Western Isles, separated from South Uist by the Sound of Barra. To the south of the island is a string of tiny islands, including Sanday, Rosinish, Mingulay and Berneray. The island's airstrip is in fact the beach at **Cockle Bay**, a name which is richly deserved as cockles are still collected there today. The main settlement is Castlebay, the terminal for the Oban ferry. On an island in the bay itself is **Kisimul Castle**, the largest fortification in the Western Isles. It was originally built in about 1030 for the then chief of the Macneils, who had the reputation of being a ruthless pirate. The present building dates

Kisimul Castle, Isle of Barra

form the 15th century, and was restored in the middle of the 20th century.

The chiefs of Clan Macneil had the reputation of being arrogant and proud. A story is told of a Macneil chief at the time of Noah, who was invited aboard the Ark to escape the flood. He is supposed to have haughtily replied "Macneil already has a boat." And in later times, after Macneil had had dinner, one of his servants used to go up to the ramparts of Kisimul Castle and announce: "as the Macneil has dined, the other kings and princes of the world may now dine as well."

The ruined **Cille-bharraidh** (Church of St Barr) is located at the north end of the island, and was the burial place of the Macneils. Also buried here is **Sir Compton Mackenzie**, who wrote *Whisky Galore* (see also Eriskay). The island is predominantly Catholic, and at **Heaval**, a mile north east of Castlebay, is a marble statue of the Madonna and Child called Our Lady of the Sea.

2 VILLAGE

Eriskay, Western Isles PA81 5JL
Tel: 01878 720274

Situated on the truly beautiful island of Eriskay, famous for the hauntingly beautiful song called *The Eriskay Love Lilt*, you will find **2 Village**, a superior self catering establishment owned and managed by Mrs Marion Campbell. It sits close to a wide, sweeping beach with fantastic views, and offers the very best in Scottish hospitality. The place sleeps four people in two comfortable and spotless bedrooms, and there is a shower room, a wc, a well appointed sitting room/kitchen with cooker, automatic washing machine, microwave, TV and so on. There is storage heating throughout the house, and a water heater in the shower room. The minimum stay in this lovely house is one week, and children are more than welcome, with well behaved dogs being allowed by prior arrangement.

It is the ideal place for a relaxing holiday, and also ideal for kids, as it is quiet, peaceful and safe at all times of the year. The island itself is easily reached from South Uist by a causeway, and South Uist itself is connected to the mainland by a car ferry, which runs from Mallaig in the summer months and Oban all the year round. The island boasts a church, a school, a pub and a shop, though Lochboisdale on South Uist, which has more shopping and other facilities, is no more than fifteen minutes away by car. Though it is small, the island is well worth exploring. Eriskay ponies are no more than 12 to 13 hands high, and were used to carry peat and seaweed. It was here, on July 23 1745, that Charles Edward Stuart first set foot on Scottish soil, and it was also here that the *SS Politician* ran aground in 1941, carrying a cargo of whisky. The incident inspired the book *Whisky Galore* by Sir Compton MacKenzie.

13 Orkney and Shetland

In 1469 James III married Margaret, the young daughter of Christian I of Denmark and Norway. Her father pledged Orkney and the Shetland Islands to the Scottish crown until such time as the dowry was settled in full, but as he was crippled with debts, the dowry was never paid. In 1472 therefore, the islands became part of Scotland, and the kingdom's boundaries as we now know them were finally established.

Orkney Cliffs, West Coast

Even today the Norse influences among the islands are strong. Gaelic was never spoken here, and the place names (and many family names) all have Norse derivations. Both sets of islands are nearer Oslo than they are London, and there have even been occasional calls for the islands to be independent of Scotland.

Brough Ness on South Ronaldsay in Orkney is no more than eight miles from the Scottish mainland, while the Shetland Islands sit further out to sea, with the distance between Sumburgh Head and the mainland being over 100 miles. Few people realise the distances involved, as maps of the British Isles invariably put the Shetlands in a box close to the mainland.

Orkney and the Shetland Islands may appear remote nowadays, but in olden times they were at a major communications crossroads, and gained an importance which far outweighed their size. They are rich in historical sites and remains (far too many to mention them all in this book) which show a continued occupation for thousands of years. And because the landscape has never been intensely farmed or cultivated, many of these sites have remained relatively undisturbed.

Shetland Islands

The main difference between the two archipelagos can be summed up in the old saying that an Orcadian (an inhabitant of Orkney) is a farmer with a boat, whereas a Shetlander is a fisherman with a croft. Orkney is therefore the more fertile of the two, though this is relative, as the landscape is nothing like the fertile areas of the mainland, and trees are the exception rather than the rule. One thing has brought prosperity to the islands, however, and that is North Sea oil. It has transformed their economies, but at the same time has remained remarkably unobtrusive, apart from places like Sullom Voe in Shetland, the largest oil terminal and port in Europe.

The Orkney archipelago consists of about 70 islands, only 19 of which are inhabited. The largest island is Mainland, where the islands' capital, Kirkwall, is located. It is a small city as well as a royal burgh, as it has its own medieval cathedral, the most northerly in Britain and the most complete in Scotland. Most of the islands are connected by ferry, and the best way to appreciate the smaller ones is on foot rather than by car. Some of the sites are world famous, such as Skara Brae, and must not be missed.

The Shetland Islands has about 100 islands, with less than 20 being inhabited. Its largest island, and also its most southerly, is again called Mainland, and it is here that Lerwick is situated. It is the islands' capital, and the most northerly town in Britain. Every year in January the ancient "Up Helly Aa" festival is held here, where a Viking ship is paraded through the streets of the town before being ceremonially burnt. Its origins go back to pagan times, when the turn of the year meant that the days started getting longer again.

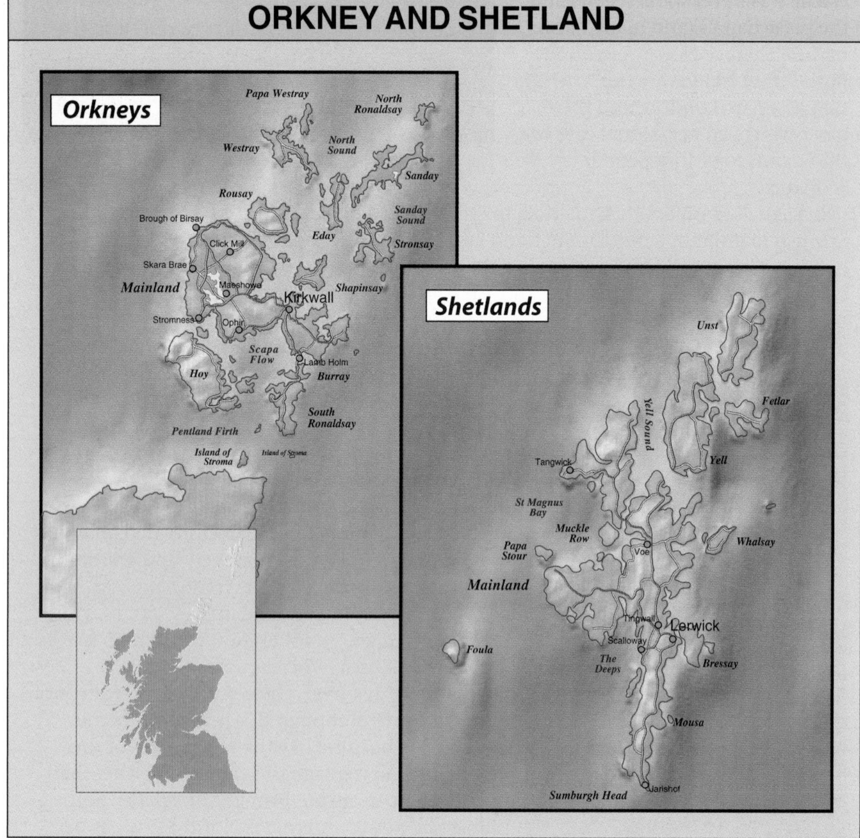

KIRKWALL

The capital of Orkneys has a population of about 4,800, and was granted its charter as a royal burgh and city in 1486. It sits almost in the centre of Mainland, and divides the island into East Mainland and West Mainland. It is a lively, busy place of old stone buildings and streets paved in flagstones, with a shopping centre that serves all of the islands. **St Magnus Cathedral** was founded in 1137 by the saint's nephew Rognvald, though the cathedral as you see it today dates from between the 12th and 16th centuries. The story goes that Magnus was the son of one of two earls who ruled Orkney, and on a raiding expedition to Wales he refused to take part in the usual rape and pillage, deciding instead to sing psalms. The Norwegian king, also called Magnus, was displeased, and young Magnus had to flee.

Kirkwall Harbour

After the king's death, he returned to Orkney and in 1117 arranged to meet with Hakon, the new ruler of the islands, to claim his inheritance. However, on Hakon's orders he was killed by a blow to the skull by an axe. Some people regarded this story as more of a legend than historical fact, but in 1919, during some restoration work, a casket containing human bones was found embedded high up in one of the cathedral's pillars. The skull had been split open with an axe.

The **Bishop's Palace** (Historic Scotland) dates mainly from the 12th century, and is a well preserved ruin. The Round Tower was built by Bishop Reid between 1541 and 1548. The notorious Patrick Stewart, Earl of Orkney, built the adjacent **Earl's Palace** (Historic Scotland) between 1600 and 1607. The Stewart earls were hated in the islands, because they exploited the people and bled them dry. Patrick himself was arrested by James VI and executed for treason in 1615. All that is left of the medieval **St Olaf's Church**, after which Kirkwall (kirkjuvagr, meaning "church bay") was named, is a doorway in St Olaf's Wynd. Within Tankerness House, built as a merchant's house in the 16th century, is the **Tankerness House Museum**, which contains artifacts and exhibits about the island. The **Orkney Wireless Museum** is at Kiln Corner, and has examples of wartime and domestic wireless sets used on the islands.

On a building in Castle Street is a plaque commemorating **Kirkwall Castle**, which was dismantled in 1615 and finally demolished in 1865. It had been built in the 14th century by the Sinclairs of Roslin, who had been created Earls of Orkney by Hakon of Norway in 1379.

AROUND KIRKWALL

LAMB HOLM

7 miles S of Kirkwall on the A961

After the sinking of the Royal Oak by a U-boat in 1939 a string of islands to the south of Mainland were joined by causeways. On Lamb Holm, one of the islands, is the **Italian Chapel**. It was made by Italian prisoners-of-war working on the causeways, and the work is remarkable considering its basis is two

Italian Chapel, Lamb Holm

Nissen huts and various pieces of cast off metal and wood. In 1960 some of the prisoners were invited to return to the islands to restore it.

MAESHOWE

8 miles W of Kirkwall off the A965

Maeshowe is Britain's largest chambered cairn, and is looked after by Historic Scotland. The name comes from the Old Norse and means "great mound". It is 36 feet high and 300 feet in circumference, and was built about 2,700 BC. A long, narrow passage leads into a central chamber with smaller side chambers which are roofed and floored with massive slabs.

Also looked after by Historic Scotland are the **Stenness Standing Stones**, which are close by and date from around the same time, and the **Ring of Brodgar**. Only four of the Stenness Stones remain standing, though Brodgar still has 27 of its original 67 stones.

OPHIR

9 miles W of Kirkwall off the A964

Ophir Church was built by Hakon, who had St Magnus murdered in the 12th century, possibly as an act or penance after a pilgrimage to Jerusalem. Nothing now remains apart from the apse.

Sea Cliffs, Orkneys

HOY

17 miles W of Kirkwall

Hoy is Orkney's second largest island, and sits off the west coast of Mainland. It is connected to Mainland by a passenger ferry which runs between Stromness and Moaness. The **Old Man of Hoy** is a famous stack over 445 feet high off its north west coast, and a constant challenge to climbers. At the south west end of the island is a **Martello Tower**, erected between 1813 and 1815 to protect the island from the French.

The **Dwarfie Stone** is unique - a burial chamber dating from at least 3000 BC cut into a great block of sandstone.

STROMNESS

15 miles W of Kirkwall on the A965

This little burgh faces Orkney's second largest island, Hoy. Though it looks old and quaint, it only received its burgh charter in 1817 , and was founded in the 17th century. The **Stromness Museum** in Alfred Street has displays on **Scapa Flow**, whaling and the Hudson's Bay Company (which had a base here, and employed many Orcadians). Scapa Flow is one of the best natural harbours in the world. After World War I the German fleet was brought to Scapa Flow while a decision was made about it's future. However, the German officers decided the fleet's future themselves - they scuttled the ships.

CLICK MILL

13 miles NW of Kirkwall on the B9057

Click Mill is now owned by Historic Scotland, and is the islands' last surviving example of a horizontal watermill. They were once common throughout Scandinavia. At Harray, a couple of miles south of the mill is the **Corrigall Farm Museum**. Exhibits include a working barn with grain kiln.

SKARA BRAE

17 miles NW of Kirkwall on the B9056

In 1850 a storm uncovered the remains of a village which was at least 5,000 years old - older even than the Pyramids. It is the oldest known prehistoric village in Europe, and the remains are now looked after by Historic Scotland. They show that the people who built it from stone were sophisticated and ingenious, and that the houses were comfortable and well appointed, with beds, dressers and cupboards.

Close by is **Skaill House** (Historic Scotland), the finest mansion in Orkney. It was originally built in 1628 for George Graham, Bishop of Orkney, but extended over the years. It houses a fine collection of furniture, including Bishop Graham's bed, on which are carved the words *GEO. GRAHAM ME FIERI FECIT* ("George Graham caused me to be made").

BROUGH OF BIRSAY

21 miles NW of Kirkwall off the A966

This little island, which is connected to the mainland at low tide, has the remains of a Norse settlement and an early medieval chapel, built on the foundations of a chapel that may date back to the 7th or 8th centuries. The ruins of **Earl Stewart's Palace** overlook the island. This was one of the castles owned by the unpopular Stewarts. The **Kirbuster Farm Museum** has examples of farm implements used on Orkney over the years, and a Victorian garden.

Earl Stewart's Palace

South of the island, at Marwick Head, is the **Kitchener Memorial**. It was erected in memory of Kitchener of Khartoum, who was killed when HMS Hampshire, on which he was travelling, struck a German mine near here in 1916.

LERWICK

The capital of the Shetland Islands was granted its burgh charter in 1818. However, its history goes much further back than that, and it was originally developed by the Dutch in the 17th century to service their fishing fleet. It is the most northerly town in Britain, and, with a population of about 7,000, sits on the island of Mainland. The town is so far north that during the months of June and July, there is little or no darkness.

Every year, on the last Tuesday in January, the festival of "Up Helly Aa" is held. After being hauled through the streets of the town accompanied by men carrying torches and dressed as Vikings, a Viking longboat is set on fire. Though an enjoyable and spectacular sight, it is a ritual which is thought to date back to pagan times, when the perceptible lengthening of the days after the long darkness of winter was greeted with joy and relief.

Like Orkney, all the islands in the Shetland archipelago are rich in ancient remains and small interpretation centres and museums - too rich for all of them to be mentioned in this book. They are said to have "nine months of winter and three months of bad weather", but this is an exaggeration. Certainly the number of days in the year when the temperatures rise above 70 degrees are few, but there are compensations, not least of which is the quality of light. And there is less rain here than in Fort William or even North Devon.

Fort Charlotte was built in

Lerwick Harbour

about 1653 by Cromwellian troops sent to claim the fishing grounds for England, and indeed the fort may have been the first permanent stone building in the town. **Shetland Museum** gives an insight into the history of the islands and its people, and has some marvellous displays on archaeology.

The wonderfully named **Bšd of Gremista** is located north of the town, and was the birthplace of **Arthur Anderson**, co-founder of the P&O line. The building has been restored as a small museum and interpretation centre on the island's maritime history.

One of the highlights of any visit to the Shetland Islands is an organised tour. Several are on offer, led by Elma Johnson in national costume. The Historic Lanes and Lodberries Trail takes you around Lerwick, while the Busta Trail takes in Busta House (now a hotel) beside Busta Voe, and tells the tale of Barbara Pitcairn. The Crofthouse Trail centres on the Crofthouse Museum (see separate entry). They concentrate on the people and stories of the islands rather than on architecture, and run from May until September.

AROUND LERWICK

BRESSAY

1 mile E of Lerwick

The island of Bressay sits opposite Lerwick, and shelters its harbour. The **Bressay Heritage Centre**, close to the ferry terminal, illustrates through displays and exhibits what life was like on the island in former times.

MOUSA

13 miles S of Lerwick

There are about 70 confirmed broch (a round, fortified tower) sites in Shetland, and one of the best preserved is at Sandwick on this tiny island off the east coast of Mainland. The **Broch of Mousa** (Historic Scotland) was built sometime between the 1st and 3rd centuries, and is over 40 feet high. It has lost its uppermost courses, but is still in a remarkable state of preservation, and shows the the typical layout of these curious buildings, which are found nowhere else but in Scotland. The double walls slope inwards as they get higher, and embedded in them are staircases and defensive galleries.

JARLSHOF

25 miles S of Lerwick on the A970

Lying close to Sumburgh Airport on Mainland, Jarlshof is one of the most important historical sites in Europe, and has been continuously occupied from the Bronze Age right up until the 17th century. There are Bronze Age huts, Iron Age earth houses, brochs, wheel-houses from the Dark Ages (possibly Pictish), Norse longhouses and medieval houses. It is managed by Historic Scotland, and there is a small museum and interpretation centre.

At **Old Scantess**, north of Jarlshoff, is an archaeological site centred on a number of ancient brochs, wheelhouses and dwellings. There is a living history area with demonstrations which reproduce ancient technologies using authentic materials.

FAIR ISLE

46 miles S of Lerwick

The most southerly of the Shetland Islands lies almost half way between Shetland and Orkney. It is owned by the National Trust for Scotland, and is one of the remotest inhabited islands in the country, with a population of about 70. The island was once owned by

George Waterston, who was the Scottish Director of the Royal Society for the Protection of Birds, and who founded a bird observatory in 1948. **The George Waterston Memorial Centre and Museum** has displays about the history and wildlife of the island.

SCALLOWAY

6 miles W of Lerwick on the A970

Though only six miles from Lerwick, it is said that this small village sits on the Atlantic seaboard while its larger neighbour sits on the North Sea. It was once Shetland's capital, but as Lerwick expanded so the centre of power shifted eastwards. **Scalloway Castle** dates from around 1600, and was built by Patrick Stewart, who was executed 15 years later in Edinburgh (see also Kirkwall).

During World War II the village was a secret Norwegian base, and from here native Norwegians used to be ferried across to their country in fishing boats to mount sabotage operations and bring back resistance fighters who were on the run. The small **Scalloway Museum** tells the story of these men, as well as the story of Scalloway itself.

TINGWALL

6 miles NW of Lerwick on the A970

Law Ting Holm near Tingwall was where the ancient Shetland Islands parliament, or Althing, used to meet. It sits on a small promontory jutting out into the Loch of Tingwall which in Norse times was an island. The **Tingwall Agricultural Museum** at Veensgarth is housed in an old 18th century granary, and has displays on crofting and fishing.

TANGWICK

35 miles NW of Lerwick on the B9078

The **Tangwick Haa Museum**, based in Tangwick Haa, has displays and artefacts about the local history of the northern part of the island of Mainland. The haa ("hall") itself dates from the 17th century, and was built by the Cheyne family, the local landowners. It was restored and opened as a museum in 1988.

Island of Yell

VOE

17 miles N of Lerwick on the A970

The **Crofthouse Museum** comprises a house, steading and water mill, and illustrates what life was like in a 19th century Shetland Islands croft. It would have housed an extended family of children, parents and grandparents, and the men would have earned their living from the sea while the women worked the land.

FETLAR

40 miles NE of Lerwick

The small island of Fetlar is no more than seven miles long by five miles wide at its widest, and sits off the east coast of Yell, to which it is connected by ferry. **The Fetlar Interpretive Centre** at Beach of Houbie has displays on Fetlar history, wildlife, history and folklore, as well as a library of films (all on video) and genealogical archives. It won the 2000 Museum of the Year Award in the Educational Initiative category.

YELL

30 miles N of Lerwick

The second largest island in Shetland is about 20 miles long by seven miles wide at its widest. It is connected to Mainland by a ferry from Toft to Ulsta. The **Old Haa of Burravoe**, at the island's south east corner, is the oldest complete building on the island, and dates from 1637. It now houses a small museum and interpretation centre. The **Lumbister RSPB Reserve** sits almost in the middle of the island, between Whale Firth (said to be the smallest "firth" in Scotland) and Basta Voe. It has some good hill walks, with the coastlines being full of dramatic scenery.

Isle of Unst

UNST
46 miles N of Lerwick

Unst is the most northerly of the Shetland Isles, and **Hermaness** is the most northerly point in Britain. At the south west corner of the island are the gaunt ruins of **Muness Castle**, said to be the most northerly castle in Britain. It dates from 1598. and was built by Lawrence Bruce, a relative of the wayward Stewart dynasty that ruled the islands, and a man every bit as cruel and despotic as they were.

List of Tourist Information Centres

ABERDEEN

Provost Ross's House, Shiprow, Aberdeen
Tel: 01224 288828

Open all year

ABERFELDY

The Square, Aberfeldy PH15 2DD
Tel: 01887 820276

Open all year

ABERFOYLE

Trossachs Discovery Centre, Main Street, Aberfoyle FK8 0TH
Tel: 01877 382352

(Limited winter hours)

ABINGTON

Welcome Break, Motorway Service Area, Junction 13, M74, Abington ML12 6RG
Tel: 01864 502 436

ALFORD

Railway Museum, Station Yard, Alford
Tel: 019755 62052

ALVA

Mill Trail Visitor Centre, West Stirling Street, Alva FK12 5EN
Tel: 01259 769696

Open all year

ANSTRUTHER

Scottish Fisheries Museum, Harbourhead, Ansthruther KY10 3BA
Tel: 01333 311073

ARBROATH

Market Place, Arbroath DD11 1HR
Tel: 01241 872609

Open all year

ARDGARTAN

Clen Croe, by Arrochar G83 7AR
Tel: 01301 702432

AUCHTERARDER

90 High Street, Auchterarder PH3 1BJ
Tel: 01764 663450

Open all year

AVIEMORE

Grampian Road, Aviemore PH22 1PP
Tel: 01479 810363

AYR

22 Sandgate, Ayr
Tel: 01292 678100 (central number)

Send all written enquiries to:

Ayrshire & Arran Tourist Board,
15A Skye Road, Prestwick KA9 2TA

Open all year

BALLATER

The Old Royal Station, Station Square, Ballater
Tel: 013397 55306

BALLOCH

Balloch Road, Balloch G83 8LQ
Tel: 01389 753533

BANCHORY

Bridge Street, Banchory
Tel: 01330 822000

BANFF

Collie Lodge, Banff AB45 1AU
Tel: 01261 812419

BARRA

Main Street, Castlebay
Tel: 01871 810336

BIGGAR

155 High Street, Biggar ML12 6DL
Tel: 01899 221066

BLAIRGOWRIE

26 Wellmeadow, Blairgowrie PH10 6AS
Tel: 01250 872960

Open all year

BO'NESS

Car Park, Seaview Place, Bo'ness EH51 0AJ
Tel: 01506 826626

BOWMORE

The Square, Bowmore, Isle of Islay PA43 7JP
Tel: 01496 810254

Open all year

BRAEMAR

The Mews, Mar Road, Braemar
Tel: 013397 41600

Open all year

BRECHIN

Brechin Castle Centre, Haughmuir,
Brechin DD9 6RL
Tel: 01356 623050

BRODICK

The Pier, Brodick, Isle of Arran
Tel: 01292 678100 (central number)

Send all written enquiries to:
Ayrshire & Arran tourist Board,
15A Skye Road, Prestwick KA9 2TA

Open all year

CALLANDER

Rob Roy & Trossachs Visitor Centre,
Ancaster Square, Callander FK17 8ED
Tel: 01877 330342

(Limited winter hours)

CAMPBELTOWN

MacKinnon House, The Pier,
Campbeltown PA28 6EF
Tel: 01586 552056

Open all year

CARNOUSTIE

1b High Street, Carnoustie DD7 6AN
Tel: 01241 852258

CASTLE DOUGLAS

Market Hill Car Park,
Castle Douglas DG7 1AE
Tel: 01556 502611

COLDSTREAM

Town Hall, High Street, Coldstream TD12 5JE
Tel: 01890 882607

CRAIGNURE

The Pier, Craignure, Isle of Mull PA65 6AY
Tel: 01680 812377

Open all year

CRAIL

Crail Museum & Heritage Centre,
62-64 Marketgate, Crail KY10 3TL
Tel: 01333 450869

CRATHIE

The Car Park, Crathie
Tel: 013397 42414

CRIEFF

High Street, Crieff PH7 3HU
Tel: 01764 652578

Open all year

DORNOCH

The Square, Dornoch IV25 3SD
Tel: 01862 810400

Open all year

DRUMNADROCHIT

The Car Park, Drumnadrochit IV63 6TX
Tel: 01456 459076

DRYMEN

Drymen Library, The Square,
Drymen G63 0BD
Tel: 01360 660068

DUFFTOWN

The Clock Tower, The Square, Dufftown
Tel: 01340 820501

DUMBARTON

(Milton) A82 Northbound, Milton G82 2TZ
Tel: 01389 742306

Open all year

DUMFRIES

64 Whitesands, Dumfries DG1 2RS
Tel: 01387 253862

Open all year

DUNBAR

143 High Street, Dunbar EH42 1ES
Tel: 0131 473 3800 (central number)

Open all year

DUNBLANE

Stirling Road, Dunblane FK15 9EP
Tel: 01786 824428

DUNDEE

21 Castle Street, Dundee DD1 3AA
Tel: 01382 527527

Open all year

DUNFERMLINE

13/15 Maygate, Dunfermline KY12 7NE
Tel: 01383 720999

DUNKELD

The Cross, Dunkeld PH8 0AN
Tel: 01350 727688

Open all year

DUNOON

7 Alexandra Parade, Dunoon PA23 8AB
Tel: 01369 703785

Open all year

DUNVEGAN

2 Lochside, Dunvegan, Isle of Skye IV55 8WB
Tel: 01471 822361

(Limited winter hours)

DURNESS

Durine, Durness IV27 4PN
01971 511259

(Limited winter hours)

EDINBURGH

3 Princes Street, Edinburgh EH2 2QP
Tel: 0131 473 3800 (central number)

Open all year

EDINBURGH INTERNATIONAL AIRPORT

Edinburgh International Airport,
Edinburgh EH12 9DN
Tel: 0131 473 3800 (central number)

Open all year

ELGIN

17 High Street, Elgin
Tel: 01343 542666

Open all year

EYEMOUTH

Auld Kirk, Manse Road, Eyemouth TD14 5HE
Tel: 01890 750678

FALKIRK

2/4 Glebe Street, Falkirk FK1 1HX
Tel: 01324 620244

Open all year

FORFAR

East High Street, Forfar DD8 2EG
Tel: 01307 467876

FORRES

116 High Street, Forres
Tel: 01309 672938

FORT AUGUSTUS

Car Park, Fort Augustus PH32 4DD
Tel: 01320 366367

FORTH BRIDGES

c/o Queensferry Lodge Hotel,
St Margaret's Head,
North Queensferry KY11 1HP
Tel: 01383 417759

Open all year

FORT WILLIAM

Cameron Square, High Street,
Fort William PH33 6AJ
Tel: 01397 703781

Open all year

FRASERBURGH

3 Saltoun Square, Fraserburgh
Tel: 01346 518315

GALASHIELS

3 St John's Street, Galashiels TD1 3JX
Tel: 01896 755551

GATEHOUSE OF FLEET

Car Park, Gatehouse of Fleet DG7 2JQ
Tel: 01557 814212

GIRVAN

Bridge Street, Girvan
Tel: 01292 678100 (central number)

Send all written enquiries to:
Ayrshire & Arran Tourist Board,
15A Skye Road, Prestwick KA9 2TA

GLASGOW

11 George Square, Glasgow G2 1DY
Tel: 0141 204 4400

Open all year

GLASGOW INTERNATIONAL AIRPORT

Tourist Information Desk, Glasgow
International Airport, Paisley PA3 2ST
Tel: 0141 848 4440

Open all year

GRANTOWN ON SPEY

54 High Street, Grantown on Spey PH26 3EH
Tel: 01479 872773

GRETNA GREEN

Old Headless Cross, Gretna Green DG16 5EA
Tel: 01461 337834

HAMILTON

Road Chef Services, M74 Northbound,
Hamilton ML3 6JW
Tel: 01698 285590

Open all year

HARRIS

Pier Road, Tarbert
Tel: 01859 502011

Open all year

HAWICK

Drumlanrig's Tower, Tower Knowe,
Hawick TD9 9EN
Tel: 01450 372547

Open all year

HELENSBURGH

Clock Tower, The Pier, Helensburgh G84 7NY
Tel: 01436 672642

HUNTLY

9a The Square, Huntly
Tel: 01466 792255

INVERARAY

Front Street, Inveraray PA32 8UY
Tel: 01499 302063

Open all year

INVERNESS

Castle Wynd, Inverness IV2 3BJ
Tel: 01463 234353

Open all year

INVERURIE

18 High Street, Inverurie
Tel: 01467 625800

Open all year

IRVINE

New Street, Irvine
Tel: 01292 678100 (central number)

Send all written enquiries to:
Ayrshire & Arran Tourist Board,
15A Skye Road, Prestwick KA9 2TA

JEDBURGH

Murray's Green, Jedburgh TD8 6BE
Tel: 01835 863435/863688
Open all year

KELSO

Town House, The Square, Kelso TD5 7HF
Tel: 01573 223464

KILCHOAN

Pier Road, Kilchoan, Acharacle PH36 4LH
Tel: 01972 510222

KILLIN

Breadalbane Folklore Centre, Falls of Dochart,
Killin FK21 8XE
Tel: 01567 820254

(Limited winter hours)

KINROSS

Adjacent to the Service Area, Junction 6,
M90, Kinross KY13 7NQ
Tel: 01577 863680

Open all year

KIRKCALDY

19 Whytescauseway, Kirkcaldy KY1 1XF
Tel: 01592 267775

Open all year

KIRKCUDBRIGHT

Harbour Square, Kirkcudbright DG6 4HY
Tel: 01557 330494

KIRKWALL

6 Broad Street, Kirkwall, Orkney KW15 1NX
Tel: 01856 872856

Open all year

KIRRIEMUIR

Cumberland Close, Kirriemuir DD8 4EF
Tel: 01575 574097

LANARK

Horsemarket, Ladyacre Road,
Lanark ML11 7LQ
Tel: 01555 661661

Open all year

LARGS

Railway Station, Main Street, Largs
Tel: 01292 678100 (central number)

Send all written enquiries to:
Ayrshire & Arran Tourist Board,
15A Skye Road, Prestwick KA9 2TA

LERWICK

Market Cross, Lerwick, Shetlands ZE1 0LU
Tel: 0195 693434

Open all year

LEWIS

26 Cromwell Street, Stornoway HS1 2DD
Tel: 01851 703088

Open all year

LINLITHGOW

Burgh Halls, The Cross,
Linlithgow EH49 7AH
Tel: 0131 473 3800 (central number)

LIVINGSTON

McArthurGlen Designer Outlet, Livingston
Tel: 0131 473 3800 (central number)

LOCHCARRON

Main Street, Lochcarron IV54 8YB
Tel: 01520 722357

LOCHGILPHEAD

Lochnell Street, Lochgilphead PA30 8JN
Tel: 01546 602344

LOCHINVER

Assynt Visitor Centre, Lochinver IV27 4LX
Tel: 01571 844330

MALLAIG

The Pier, Mallaig PH41 4SQ
Tel: 01687 462170

(Limited winter hours)

MELROSE

Abbey House, Abbey Street, Melrose TD6 9LG
Tel: 01896 822555

MILLPORT

28a Stuart Street, Millport, Isle of Cumbrae
Tel: 01292 678100 (central number)

Send all written enquiries to:
Ayrshire & Arran Tourist Board,
15A Skye Road, Prestwick KA9 2TA

MOFFAT

Ladyknowe, Moffat DG10 9DY
Tel: 01683 220620

MONTROSE

Bridge Street, Montrose DD10 8AB
Tel: 01674 672000

NATIONAL WALLACE MONUMENT

Abbeycraig, Stirling FK9 5LF
Tel: 01786 472140

Open all year

NEWTONGRANGE

Scottish Mining Museum,
Newtongrange EH22 4QN
Tel: 0131 473 3800 (central number)

NEWTON STEWART

Dashwood Square, Newton Stewart DG8 6EQ
Tel: 01671 402431

Open all year

NORTH BERWICK

Quality Street, North Berwick EH39 4HJ
Tel: 0131 473 3800 (central number)

Open all year

NORTH UIST

Pier Road, Lochmaddy
Tel: 01876 500321

OBAN

Argyll Square, Oban PA34 4AN
Tel: 01631 563122

Open all year

OLD CRAIGHALL

Old Craighall Junction, A1,
Musselburgh, EH21 8RE
Tel: 0131 473 3800 (central number)

Open all year

PAISLEY

9A Gilmour Street, Paisley PA1 1DD
Tel: 0141 889 0711

Open all year

PEEBLES

High Street, Peebles EH45 8AG
Tel: 01721 720138

Open all year

PENICUIK

Edinburgh Crystal Visitor Centre,
Penicuik EH26 8HB
Tel: 0131 473 3800 (central number)

PERTH

Lower City Mills, West Mill Street,
Perth PH1 5QP
Tel: 01738 450600

Open all year

PIRNHALL

M9/M80 Junction 9, Stirling FK7 8ET
Tel: 01786 814111

PITLOCHRY

22 Atholl Road, Pitlochry PH16 5BX
Tel: 01796 472215/472751

Open all year

PORTREE

Bayfield House, Bayfield Road, Portree,
Isle of Skye IV51 9EL
Tel: 01478 612137

Open all year

ROTHESAY

13 Argyle Street, Rothesay,
Isle of Bute PA20 0AT
Tel: 01700 502151

Open all year

ST ANDREWS

70 Market Street, St Andrews KY16 9NU
Tel: 01334 472021

Open all year

SELKIRK

Halliwell's House, Selkirk TD7 4BL
Tel: 01750 20054

SOUTH UIST

Pier Road, Lochboisedale
Tel: 01878 700286

STIRLING

41 Dumbarton Road, Stirling FK8 2QQ
Tel: 01786 475019

Open all year

STIRLING

Royal Burgh of Stirling Visitor Centre,
Castle Esplanade, Stirling FK8 1EH
Tel: 01786 479901

Open all year

STONEHAVEN

66 Allardice Street, Stonehaven
Tel: 01569 762806

STRANRAER

28 Harbour Street, Stranraer DG9 7RA
Tel: 01776 702595

Open all year

STROMNESS

Ferry Terminal Building, Ferry Road,
Stromness, Orkney KW15 1BH
Tel: 01856 850716

Open all year

TARBET

Main Street, Tarbet G83 7DE
Tel: 01301 702260

TARBERT

Harbour Street, Tarbert PA29 6UD
Tel: 01880 820429

TOBERMORY

Main Street, Tobermory,
Isle of Mull PA75 6NU
Tel: 01688 302182/302610

TOMINTOUL

The Square, Tomintoul
Tel: 01807 580285

TYNDRUM

Main Street, Tyndrum FK20 8RY
Tel: 01838 400246 / 400324

ULLAPOOL

Argyle Street, Ullapool IV26 2UB
Tel: 01854 612135

(Limited winter hours)

WICK

Whitechapel Road, Wick KW1 4EA
Tel: 01955 602596

(Limited winter hours)

Index of Towns, Villages and Places of Interest

A

Abbey St Bathans 4
- *Cockburn Law 4*
- *Edinshall Broch 4*
- *Southern Upland Way 4*

Abbotsford 9
- *Sir Walter Scott 9*

Aberdeen 256
- *Aberdeen Art Gallery and Museums 257*
- *Aberdeen Maritime Museum 257*
- *Blairs Museum 258*
- *Bridge of Dee 256*
- *Brig o' Balgownie 256*
- *Cathedral Church of St Machar's 256*
- *Church of St Nicholas 257*
- *Cruickshank Botanic Gardens 256*
- *Duthie Park 256*
- *Footdee 258*
- *Glover House 256*
- *Gordon Highlanders Museum 258*
- *Hazelhead Park 256*
- *James Dun's House 257*
- *Johnston Gardens 256*
- *King's College 257*
- *King's College Centre 257*
- *Marischal College 257*
- *Mercat Cross 257*
- *Planetarium 257*
- *Provost Ross's House 257*
- *Provost Skene's House 257*
- *Rubislaw Quarry 258*
- *Union Street 257*
- *Union Terrace Gardens 256*
- *William Elphinstone 256*

Aberdour 141
- *Aberdour Castle 141*
- *St Fillan's Parish Church 141*

Aberfeldy 249
- *Aberfeldy Water Mill 250*
- *Black Watch Memorial 250*
- *Castle Menzies 250*
- *Dewar's World of Whisky 250*
- *General Wade's Bridge 250*

Aberfoyle 176
- *Duke's Road 176*
- *Queen Elizabeth Forest Park 176*
- *Rev. Robert Kirk 176*
- *Scottish Wool Centre 176*
- *Trossachs 176*

Aberlady 128
- *Aberlady Bay Nature Reserve 128*
- *Aberlady Parish Church 128*
- *Luffness Castle 128*
- *Myreton Motor Museum 128*
- *Nigel Tranter 128*

Aberlemno 237
- *Aberlemno Sculptured Stones 237*

Abernethy 244
- *Abernethy Round Tower 244*

Abington 115

Aboyne 263
- *Aboyne Highland Games 263*
- *Culsh Earth House 263*
- *Glen Tanar 263*

Achnacarry 286
- *Cameron Museum 286*
- *Loch Arcaig 286*

Ae 27

Ailsa Craig 69

Airdrie 109
- *John Reith 109*
- *Monkland Canal 109*
- *Summerlee Heritage Centre 109*
- *Time Capsule 109*

Airth 167
- *Airth Castle 167*
- *The Pineapple 167*

Alexandria 103, 104
- *Antartex Village Visitor Centre 103*
- *Loch Lomond Factory Outlets and Motoring Memories 103*
- *Old Kilpatrick 103*
- *Overtoun Estate 103*

Alford 261
- *Alford Valley Railway and Railroad Museum 261*
- *Craigievar Castle 263*
- *Grampian Transport Museum 263*

Alloa 165
- *Alloa Museum and Gallery 166*
- *Alloa Tower 165*
- *St Mungo's Parish Church 165*

Alloway 79
- *Alloway Kirk 79*
- *B ' Doon 79*
- *Burns Cottage 79*
- *Burns Monument 79*
- *Burns Museum 79*

Mount Oliphant Farm 81
Tam o' Shanter Experience 81

Altnaharra 319
Loch Naver 319

Alva 165
Alva Glen 165
Ben Cleuch 165
Mill Trail Visitor Centre 165
St Serf's Parish Church 165
The Mill Trail 165
The Ochil Hills Woodland Park 165

Ancrum 18
Battle of Ancrum Moor 18
Harestanes Countryside Visitor Centre 18
Waterloo Monument 18

Annan 33
Annan Parish Church 34
Haaf Net Fishing 34
Historic Resources Centre 34
Solway Viaduct 34
Thomas Blacklock 34

Anstruther 155
Isle of May 155
Scottish Fisheries Museum 155

Arbroath 236
Arbroath Abbey 236
Arbroath Museum 236
Arbroath Smokie 236
Auchmithie 237
Cliffs Nature Trail 237
Declaration of Arbroath 236
Kerr's Miniature Railway 237

Arbuthnott 260
Arburthnott Missal 260
Arbuthnott Collegiate Church 260
Lewis Grassic Gibbon 260
Lewis Grassic Gibbon Centre 260

Ardchattan 214
Archchattan Priory 214
Ardchattan Priory Garden 214

Ardfern 199
Kilmarie Old Parish Church 199

Ardishaig 195
Crinan Canal 195

Ardnamurchan 289
Castle Tioram 289
Glenborrodale Castle 289
Mingary Castle 289
Seven Men of Moidart 289

Ardrossan 85
Ardrossan Castle 85
St Peter in Chains 85
The Obelisk 85

Arduaine 217
Arduaine Gardens 217

Ardwell 59
Ardwell Gardens 59

Arisaig 289
Loch nan Uamh 289

Arniston 124
Arniston House 124

Arnprior 174
King of Kippen 174

Arrochar 201
Ben Ime 201
Ben Narnain 201
Cruach Tairbeirt Walks 201
Rest and Be Thankful 201
The Cobbler 201

Athelstaneford 128
National Flag Centre 128
Saltire 128

Auchindrain 201
Auchindrain Township 201

Auchinleck 78
Auchinleck House 78
Auchinleck Kirk 78

Auchterarder 244
Auchterarder Heritage 244
Tullibardine Chapel 244

Auchtermuchty 159
Tolbooth 159

Aviemore 305
Boat of Garten 305
Cairngorm Funicular Railway 305
Cairngorm Reindeer Centre 305
Caledonian Pine Forest 305
Rothiemurchus Highland Estate 305
Strathspey Steam Railway 305

Ayr 71
Auld Brig o' Ayr 73
Auld Parish Kirk 71
Ayr Citadel 71
Camelot 73
Greenan Castle 73
John's Tower 71
Kirkyard Lychgate 73
Lady Cathcart's House 73
Loudoun Hall 73
New Bridge 73
Newton Tower 73
Newton upon Ayr 73
Tam o' Shanter Inn 73
Town Hall 71

Ayton 5
Ayton Castle 5

B

Balerno 126
Malleny Garden 126, 127

Balfron 178
Ballachulish 287
Aonach Eagach 288
Colin Campbell 288
Glencoe Visitors Centre 288
Information and Interpretation Centre 288
James of the Glen 288
Three Sisters 288
Ballantrae 67
Ardstinchar Castle 67
Bargany Aisle 67
Carleton Castle 67
Sawney Bean's Cave 67
Ballantrushal 331
Clach an Trushal 331
Ballater 263
Birkhill 265
Glen Muick 263
Lochnagar 263
Ballindalloch Castle 273
Glenfarclas Distillery 273
Glenlivit Distillery 275
Balloch 103
Balloch Castle Country Park 104
Leven Valley Heritage Trail 104
Loch Lomond 103
Loch Lomond and the Trossachs National Park 104
Loch Lomond Shores 104
Balmaclellan 43
Robert Paterson 43
The Clog and Shoe Workshop 43
Balmaha 178
Balmoral 265
Braemar Castle 266
Braemar Highland Games 266
Crathie Church 265
John Brown 265
Mar Lodge Estate 266
Royal Lochnagar Distillery 265
Victorian Heritage Trail 265
Balquidder 181
Breadalbane 181
Loch Voil 181
Rob Roy MacGregor's Grave 181
Banchory 261
Banchory Museum 261
Crathes Castle 261
Horn of Ley 261
J. Scott Skinner 261
Banff 279
Banff Museum 279
Duff House 279
Barr 66
Kirkdandie Fair 66
Laird of Changue 66
Barra 335
Cille-bharraidh 336
Cockle Bay 335
Heaval 336
Kisimul Castle 335
Sir Compton Mackenzie 336
Barvas 329
Arnol Blackhouse 329
Bathgate 135
Bennie Museum 135
Cairnpapple Hill 135
James "Paraffin" Young 135
Polkemmet Country Park 135
Sir James Simpson 135
Bearsden 102
Antonine Wall 102
Roman Bathhouse 102
Beauly 307
Beauly Priory 307
Moniack Winery 311
Wardlaw Mausoleum 311
Beith 87
Eglinton Street 87
High Church 87
Ben Lomond 104
Ben More 182
Ben Nevis 285
Benbecula 333
Balivanich 333
Borve Castle 333
Nunton Chapel 333
Rueval 333
Benmore 191
Younger Botanic Garden 191
Biggar 115
Albion Motors Archives 115
Biggar Gas Works Museum 115
Biggar Puppet Theatre 115
Gladstone Court Museum 115
Greenhill Covenanter's House 115
Hugh McDiarmid 115
Moat Park Heritage Centre 115
St Mary's Church 115
Blackness 134
Blackness Castle 134
Blair Atholl 252
Atholl Highlanders 252
Blair Castle 252
Clan Donnachaidh Museum 252
Falls of Bruar 252
House of Bruar 252
St Bride's Kirk 252
Blair Drummond 178
Blair Drummond Safari and Adventure Park 178

Blairgowrie 243
Cargill's Visitor Centre 243
Cateran Trail 243
Keithbank Mill 243
Rattray 243
Blairlogie 165
Dumyat 165
Blantyre 113
David Livingstone Centre 113
Boat of Garten 305
Bo'ness 134
Birkhill Fireclay Mine 134
Bo'ness and Kinneil Railway 134
Kinneil House 134
Kinneil Museum 134
Borthwick 124
Borthwick Castle 124
Borthwick Parish Church 125
Bothwell 112
Battle of Bothwell Bridge 112
Bothwell Castle 112
Joanna Baillie 112
St Bride's Parish Church 112
Bowhill 14
Aikwood Tower 14
Bowhill Little Theatre 14
Bowmore 205
Bowmore Distillery 208
Braemar 265
Breadalbane 181
Brechin 237
Brechin Castle 237
Brechin Castle Centre 237
Brechin Cathedral 237
Brechin Museum 237
Caledonian Railway 237
Caterthuns 237
Glen Lethnot 237
Maison Dieu Chapel 237
Pictavia 237
Round Tower 237
Whisky Trail 237
Bressay 342
Bressay Heritage Centre 342
Bridge of Allan 171
Airthrie Estate 171
Bridge of Allan Brewery Company 171
Fountain of Ninevah 171
Holy Trinity Church 171
Broadford 292
Brough of Birsay 341
Earl Stewart's Palace 341
Kirbuster Farm Museum 341
Kitchener Memorial 341
Broughton 21
John Buchan Centre 21
Buckhaven 150
Buckhaven Museum 150
Buckie 271
Buckie Drifter 271
Deskford Church 273
Peter Anson Gallery 271
Bunessan 225
Burntisland 150
Authorised Version of the Bible 151
Burntisland Edwardian Fair Museum 151
St Columba's Parish Church 150
The Binn 150
Bute 188
Kerrycroy 189
Kilmichael 189
Loch Fad 188
Port Bannatyne 189
Rothesay 188
Straad 189

C

Caerlaverock 37
Caerlaverock Castle 37
Caerlaverock Wildfowl and Wetlands Trust 38
Solway Coast Heritage Trail 38
Cairndow 201
Arkinglas Woodland Garden 201
Clachan Farm Woodland Walks 201
Cairnholy 48
Carsluith Castle 48
Cairnryan 51
HMS Ark Royal 51
Caledonian Canal 286
Calgary 223
Callander 179
Hamilton Toy Museum 180
Rob Roy and Trossachs Visitor Centre 179
Callanish 327
Callanish Stone Circle 327
Campbeltown 191
Campbeltown Cross 193
Campbeltown Museum 193
Davaar 193
Canna 290
Canonbie 36
Debatable Lands 36
Gilnockie Castle 36
Hollows Bridge 36
Hollows Mill 37
Hollows Tower 37
Johnnie Armstrong 36
Cape Wrath 315

Carloway 329
Dun Carloway Broch 329
Carluke 115
Carmichael 115
Carmichael Parish Church 115
Discover Carmichael Visitor Centre 115
Carnoustie 239
Barry Mill 239
Carlungie and Ardestie Souterrains 239
Carrbridge 305
Landmark Forest Heritage Park 305
Speyside Heather Centre 305
Carsphairn 43
Carsphairn Heritage Centre 43
Castle Douglas 44
Carlingwark Loch 44
Castle Douglas Art Gallery 44
Sulworth Brewery 44
Cawdor Castle 301
Ceres 158
Bishop's Bridge 158
Fife Folk Museum 158
Parish Church 158
Chapel Finian 56
The Machars 56
Charlestown 143
Limekilns 143
Chirnside 5
Parish Church 5
Clackmannan 163
Clackmannan Tower 163
Gartmorn Dam Country Park 163
Mannau Stone 163
Parish Church 163
Tolbooth 163
Click Mill 340
Corrigall Farm Museum 341
Closeburn 28
Closeburn Castle 28
Lock Ettrick 28
Mother Buchan 28
Parish Church of Closeburn 28
Clovenfords 10
School of Casting, Salmon and Trout Fishing 10
Clydebank 101
Clydebank Blitz 101
Clydebank Museum 101
Coatbridge 109
Cockburn Law 4
Edinshall Broch 4
Cockburnspath 4
Cockburnspath Tower 4
Parish Church 4
Pease Bridge 4
Pease Dean 4
Coldingham 4
Coldingham Priory 4
Coldstream 7
Coldstream Bridge 7
Coldstream Guards 7
Coldstream Museum 7
Henderson Park 7
Old Toll House 7
The Hirsel 7
Coll 227
Breachacha Castle 227
Great Exodus 227
Colmonell 67
Kirkhill Castle 67
Colonsay 227
Colonsay House 227
Kiloran Valley 227
The Strand 227
Comrie 245
De'ils Cauldron Waterfall 247
The Earthquake House 247
Coupar Angus 243
Coupar Angus Abbey 243
Cowdenbeath 141
Cowdenbeath Racewall 141
Coylton 77
Old King Cole 77
Craigellachie 273
Craigellachie Bridge 273
Glen Grant Distillery 273
Malt Whisky Trail 273
Speyside Cooperage 273
Crail 154
Crail Museum and Heritage Centre 155
Tolbooth 155
Cramond 125
Parish Church 126
Roman Fort 126
Crarae 201
Crarae Garden 201
Crawford 115
Creetown 48
Creetown Country Weekend 48
Creetown Exhibition Centre 48
Creetown Gem Rock Museum 48
Crianlarich 182
Ben More 182
Falls of Falloch 182
Stobinian 182
Crichton 125
Collegiate Church 125
Crichton Castle 125
Vogrie Country Park 125
Crieff 245
Crieff Visitor Centre 245

Falls Of Turret 245
Glenturret Distillery 245
Crinan Canal 195
Crocketford 39
Cromarty 301
Cromarty Courthouse Museum 301
Dolphin Ecosse 301
Hugh Miller's Cottage 301
Crook of Devon 146
Crossford 116
Craignethan Castle 116
Crosshill 65
Crosshouse 82
Andrew Fisher 82
Crossraguel Abbey 68
Baltersan Castle 68
Cuillins 291
Cullen 273
St Mary's Church 273
Culloden 303
Clava Cairns 303
Culloden Visitors Centre 303
Leonach Cottage 303
Culross 143
Culross Abbey 144
Culross Palace 144
Longannet Power Station 144
Mercat Cross 143
The Study 144
Torry Bay Local Nature Reserve 144
Town House 144
Culzean Castle 70
Culzean Country Park 70
Eisenhower Presentation 70
Gasworks 70
Cumbernauld 100
Palacerigg Country Park 100
Cumbraes 87
Cathedral of the Isles 87
Great Cumbrae 87
Little Cumbrae 87
Millport 87
University Marine Biological Station 87
Cumnock 78
Bello Mill 78
Cumnock Old Parish Church 78
Dumfries House 78
Cupar 157
Douglas Bader Garden 158
Hill of Tarvit Mansionhouse 158
Mercat Cross 157
Old Parish Church 158
Raptor World 158
Scottish Deer Centre 158

D

Dalavich 217
Dalavich Oakwood Trail 217
Dalbeattie 46
Buittle Castle and Bailey 47
Motte of Urr 48
Murdoch Memorial 47
Dalgety Bay 141
2nd Earl of Moray 141
St Bridget's Church 141
Dalkeith 123
Dalkeith Palace 123
St Nicholas Parish Church 123
Dalmellington 65
Dunaskin Open Air Museum 65
Iron Works 65
Loch Doon 65
Loch Doon Castle 65
School of Aerial Gunnery 65
Scottish Industrial Railway Centre 65
The Brickworks 65
Dalry 86
Blair 86
Parish Church of St Margaret 86
Dalrymple 78
Cassillis Castle 79
Parish Church 79
Dalserf 111
Dalserf Parish Church 111
Rev. John Macmillan 111
Dalswinton 27
Dalswinton Loch 27
Darvel 84
Distinkhorn 84
Loudoun Hill 84
Sir Alexander Fleming 84
Deanston 179
Deanston Distillery 179
Denholm 17
Fatlips Castle 17
John Leyden Memorial 17
Sir James Murray 17
Dervaig 223
Dingwall 311
Dingwall Canal 311
Dingwall Museum 311
Mitchell Tower 311
Sir Hector MacDonald 311
Dirleton 127
Dirleton Castle 127
Dollar 164
Castle Campbell 164
Dollar Academy 164
Dollar Glen 164
Dollar Museum 164

Dornoch 299
Dornoch Cathedral 299
Douglas 116
Bell the Cat 116
Castle Dangerous 116
James, Earl of Angus 116
The Sun Inn 116
Doune 178
Doune Castle 179
Mercat Cross 179
Dreghorn 84
Dreghorn Parish Church 84
John Boyd Dunlop 84
Drum Castle 260
Drumelzier 20
Drumelzier Castle 20
Drumnadrochit 307
Loch Ness 307
Loch Ness 2000 307
Original Loch Ness Exhibition 307
Urquhart Castle 307
Dryburgh 13
Abbeys Cycle Route 13
Dryburgh Abbey 13
Field Marshall Earl Haig of Bemersyde 13
Mertoun House and Gardens 13
Mertoun Kirk 13
Scott's View 13
St Modan 13
William Wallace Statue 13
Drymen 178
Buchanan Castle 178
Dufftown 273
Balvenie Castle 273
Glenfiddich Distillery 273
Dumbarton 102
College Bow 103
Denny Tank Museum 102
Dumbarton Castle 102
Dumfries 25
Archibald the Grim 26
Burns' House 25
Burns Mausoleum 25
Camera Obscura 26
Crichton Royal Museum 27
Devorgilla's Bridge 26
Dumfries Academy 27
Dumfries and Galloway Aviation Museum 26
Dumfries and Galloway Family History Research Centre 27
Dumfries Museum 26
Greyfriar's Kirk 25
Lincluden College 26
Lincluden Motte 26
Maxwelltown 26
Midsteeple 25
Old Bridge House 26
Robert Burns Centre 25
St Michael's Parish Church 25
Theatre Royal 26
Dunadd 196
Dalriada 196
Dunbar 131
Battle of Dunbar 131
Dunbar Castle 131
John Muir 131
John Muir Centre 131
John Muir Country Park 131
Torness Nuclear Power Station 131
Town House 131
Dunblane 171
Battle of Sheriffmuir 173
Bishop Leighton's Library 173
Cathedral Church of St Blane and St Lawrence 171
Dean's House 172
Dunblane Hydro 172
Dundee 231
Broughty Ferry 232
Broughty Ferry Museum 232
Camperdown Wildlife Centre 232
Carse of Gowrie 232
Discovery Point & RSS Discovery 231
Dudhope Castle 232
Dundee Law 232
HM Frigate Unicorn 231
McManus Galleries 232
Mills Observatory 232
N'erday Dook 232
Old Steeple 231
Sensation 232
Shaw's Dundee Sweet Factory 232
Tay Rail Bridge 231
Tay Road Bridge 231
Tealing Souterrain 232
The Verdant Works 232
William Topaz McGonagall 231
Wishart Arch 231
Dundonald 75
Dundonald Castle 75
Dundrennan 48
Dundrennan Abbey 48
Dunfermline 139
Abbot House Heritage Centre 140
Andrew Carnegie 140
Andrew Carnegie Birthplace Museum 140
Carnegie Hall 141
Dunfermline Abbey and Palace Visitors Centre 140
Dunfermline Museum 141
Louise Carnegie Gates 141
Malcolm's Tower 140
Pittencrieff House Museum 140
Pittencrieff Park 140
Scottish Vintage Bus Museum 141

St Margaret of Scotland 139
St Margaret's Cave 140

Dunkeld 249
Battle of Dunkeld 249
Beatrix Potter Ehibition and Gardens 249
Count Rohenstart 249
Dunkeld Cathadral 249
Ell Shop 249
William Cleland 249
Wolf of Badenoch 249

Dunlop 83
Clandeboyes Hall 83
Hans Hamilton Tomb 83

Dunnet Head 320

Dunnichen 235
Battle of Nechtansmere 235
Letham 236

Dunning 244
Maggie Wall 244
St Serf's Parish Church 244

Dunoon 189
Castle House Museum 189
Cowal Highland Gathering 189
Dunoon Ceramics 191
Highland Mary 189
Holy Loch 191

Duns 4
Covenanters Stone 4
Duns Castle 4
Duns Law 4
Jim Clark Memorial Trophy Room 4
John Duns Scotus 4
Manderston House 4
Tolbooth House 4

Dunscore 39
Jane Haining 39
Parish Church 39

Dunstaffnage 213
Dunnstaffnage Castle 213
Dunstaffnage Chapel 213
Ell Maid 213

Dunure 71
Dunure Castle 71
Roasting of the Abbot 71

Durisdeer 29
Durisdeer Marbles 29
Parish Church 29

Durness 315
Smoo Cave 315

E

Eaglesham 112
Parish Church 112
Rudolph Hess 112

Earlsferry 157

Earlston 11
Black Hill 11
Thomas Learmont of Earlston 11

Easdale 218

East Kilbride 111
Calderglen Country Park 112
Hunter Hous 112
James Hamilton Heritage Park 112
Mains Castle 112
Olympia Centre 112
Princes Mall 112
Scottish Museum of Country Life 112
The Plaza 112

East Linton 130
Hailes Castle 130
John Rennie 130
Phantassie 130
Phantassie Doocot 130
Preston Mill 130
Prestonkirk 130
Scottish Museum of Flight 131

Eastriggs 35
Eastriggs Heritage Project 35

Ecclefechan 34
Carlyle's Birthplace 35

Edinburgh 119, 122
Adam Smith 121
Agnes McLehose 121
Canongate 121
Canongate Church 121
Canongate Tolbooth 121
Castle Esplanade 119
Craigmillar Castle 122, 123
Crown Chamber 119
Edinburgh Book Festival 122
Edinburgh Castle 119
Edinburgh City Chambers 120
Edinburgh International Festival 120
Edinburgh Military Tattoo 119
Edinburgh Zoological Gardens 123
Fringe 120
Georgian House 122
Gladstone's Land 120
Greyfriars 122
Greyfriar's Bobby 122
Half Moon Battery 119
Honours of Scotland 119
John Knox's House 121
John Napier 123
King's Lodging 119
Lauriston Castle 123
Magdalen Chapel 122
Mary King's Close 120
Most Ancient and Noble Order of the Thistle 120
Museum of Childhood 121
Museum of Edinburgh 121
Museum of Scotland 122
National Gallery of Scotland 122

National Museum of Scotland 122
National War Memorial 119
National War Museum of Scotland 120
New Town 122
Newhaven Heritage Museum 122
No 28 Charlotte Square 122
Ocean Terminal 122
Our Dynamic Earth 121
Palace of Holyroodhouse 120, 121
Parliament House 120
Princes Street 122
Princes Street Gardens 122
Queen Mary's Room 119
Register House 122
Robert Fergusson 121
Royal Botanic Gardens 122
Royal Mile 120
Royal Observatory 123
Royal Yacht Britannia 122
Scotch Whisky Heritage Centre 120
Scott Monument 122
Scottish National Gallery of Modern Art 122
Scottish National Portrait Gallery 122
Scottish Parliament Building 121
St Gile's Cathedral 120
St Margaret's Chapel 119
St Mary's Cathedral 122
Stone of Destiny 119
Thistle Chapel 120
White Horse Close 121
Writer's Museum 120

Ednam 13
Henry Francis Lyte 13
James Thomson 13

Edzell 238
Dalhousie Arch 239
Edzell Castle 238
Glen Esk 239
Glen Esk Folk Museum 239

Eigg 290
An Sgurr 290
Cathedral Cave 291
Massacre Cave 290

Elgin 270
Church of St Peter 271
Duffus Castle 271
Elgin Cathedral 270
Elgin Museum 270
Gordonstoun 271
Moray Motor Museum 270
Old Mills 271
Panns Port 271
Parish Cross 271
Spynie Palace 271
St Giles Church 270

Elie 157
Gillespie House 157

Ellisland 27
Hermitage Cottage 27

Ellon 269
Forbes Tomb 269
Formartine Buchan Way 269
Haddo House 269
Kelly Lake 270
Museum of Farming Life 269
Parish Church 269
Tolquhon Castle 269

Eriskay 335

Errol 244
Carse of Gowrie 244
Parish Church 244

Eskdalemuir 32
Eskdalemuir Observatory 32
Samye Ling Centre 32

Eyemouth 6
Eyemouth Museum 6
Gunsgreen House 6
Herring Queen Festival 6

F

Failford 77
Failford Monument 77
King Cole's Grave 77

Fair Isle 342
George Waterston Memorial Centre and Museum 343

Falkirk 166
Antonine Wheel 166
Bonnybridge Triangle 166
Callendar House 167
Callendar Park 167
Old Parish Church 166
Park Gallery 167
Rough Castle 166
Town Steeple 166

Falkland 148
Falkland Palace 148
Lomond Hills 148
Royal Tennis Court 149
Town Hall 149

Fenwick 82
Fenwick Parish Church 82
Jougs 82

Fetlar 343
Fetlar Interpretive Centre 343

Fettercairn 260
Fasque 260
Fettercairn Arch 260
Kincardine Cross 260

Findhorn 277
Dallas Dhu Distillery 277
Findhorn Foundation 277
Findhorn Heritage Centre and Museum 277

Findochty 271
Fintry 173
Campsies 173
Carron Valley Reservoir 173
Culcreuch Castle 173
Loup of Fintry 173
Fionnphort 225
Floors Castle 13
Fochabers 271
Baxter's Highland Village 271
Bellie Church 271
Milne's High School 271
ochabers Folk Museum 271
Fordyce 273
Fordyce Joiner's Workshop and Visitor Centre 273
Forfar 234
Balgavies Loch 235
Forfar Bridie 234
Meffan Museum and Art Gallery 234
Restenneth Priory 235
Forres 275
Brodie Castle 277
Culbin Sands 277
Falconer Museum 275
Kinloss 277
Nelson Tower 275
Sueno's Stone 275
Fort Augustus 287
Caledonian Canal Heritage Centre 287
Fort Augustus Abbey 287
Fort George 301
Queen's Own Highlanders Museum 301
Fort William 283
Aonach Mor 285
Ben Nevis 285
Ben Nevis Distillery and Whisky Centre 285
Caledonian Canal 286
Commando Memorial 286
Glen Nevis 285
Glen Nevis Visitors Centre 285
Inverlochy Castle 285
Jacobite Steam Train 286
Neptune's Staircase 286
Spean Bridge Mill 286
Treasures of the Earth 285
West Highland Museum 285
Forteviot 244
Dupplin Cross 244
Fortingall 250
Fortingall Yew 251
Glen Lyon 251
Meall Luaidhe 251
Pontius Pilate 250
Fortrose 301
Fortrose Cathedral 301
Foulden 6
Fowlis Easter 232
Parish Church of St Marnan 232
Fowlis Wester 245
Parish Church of St Bean 245
Fraserburgh 277
Kinnaird Lighthouse 277
Memsie Burial Cairn 278
Old Kirk 277
Sandhead Meal Mill 277
Wine Tower 277
Fyvie 268
Fyvie Castle 268

G

Gairloch 315
Gairloch Heritage Museum 315
Inverewe Gardens 315
Galashiels 8
Lochcarron of Scotland Cashmere and Wool Centre 8
Mercat Cross 8
Sir Walter Scott 9
Tweed Cycle Way 10
Galston 83
Auld Yew Tree 83
Barr Castle 83
Lady Flora Hastings 83
Loudoun Castle 83
Loudoun Castle Theme Park 83
Loudoun Kirk 83
Parish Church 83
St Sophia's RC Church 83
Garelochhead 105
Gare Loch 105
Linn Botanical Gardens 105
Rosneath Peninsula 105
Gargunnock 175
Garlogie 260
Garlogie Mill Power House 260
Gartmore 177
Cunninghame Graham Memorial 177
Gartocharn 104
Duncryne Hill 104
Highland Boundary Fault 104
Queen Elizabeth Forest Park 104
Garvald 131
Garvald Parish Church 131
Nunraw 132
Gatehouse of Fleet 48
Cardoness Castle 49
Mill on the Fleet 49
Murray Arms 49
Port MacAdam 48

Gifford 132
Goblin Ha' 132
Yester Castle 132
Yester House 132
Yester Parish Church 132
Gigha 195
Achamore Gardens 195
Girvan 69
Ailsa Craig 69
Auld Stumpy 69
Byne Hill 69
Knockcushan Gardens 69
McKechnie Institute 69
Glamis 232
Angus Folk Museum 233
Glamis Castle 232
Glasgow 98
Armadillo 98
Blackadder Aisle 98
Braehead Shopping Centre 100
Buchanan Galleries 100
Burrell Collection 100
Cathedral of St Mungo 98
Charles Rennie Mackintosh 100
City Chambers 99
Clydebuilt 98
Forge 100
Gallery of Modern Art 99
Glasgow Botanic Gardens 99
Glasgow Green 100
Glasgow Museum of Transport 99
Glasgow School of Art 100
Glasgow Science Centre 98
Glasgow Subway 99
Greek Thomson 100
Holmwood House 100
House for an Art Lover 100
Hunterian Art Gallery 99
Hunterian Museum 99
Hutcheson's Hall 99
IMAX Theatre 98
Italian Centre 100
Kelvingrove Art Gallery and Museum 98
Kibble Palace 99
Mackintosh House 100
Martyr's Public School 100
Merchant City 99
Necropolis 98
People's Palace 100
Pollok Country Park 100
Pollok House 100
Princes Square 100
Provand's Lordship 98
Queen's Cross Church 100
S.V. Glenlee 98
Scotland Street School 100
Scottish Exhibition and Conference Centre 98
Scottish Football Museum 99
St Enoch Centre 100
St Mungo Museum of Religious Life and Art 98
St Vincent Street Church 100
Tall Ship at Glasgow Harbour 98
Templeton's Carpet Factory 100
Tenement House 99
The Lighthouse 100
Tomb of St Mungo 98
West End 98
Willow Tea Rooms 100
Glenbarr 195
Clan Macalister Centre 195
Glenbervie 260
Glencoe 288
Glencoe Folk Museum 288
Glendaruael 201
Glenfinnan 289
Charles Edward Stuart Monument 289
Loch Shiel 289
Glenluce 51
Alexander Agnew 51
Castle of Park 51
Glenluce Abbey 51
Glenrothes 148
Balbirnie Park 148
Glentrool 51
Bruce's Stone 51
Golspie 299
Bienn a'Bhragaidh 299
Dunrobin Castle 301
Gordon 10
Greenknowe Tower 10
Mellerstain 10
Gourock 107
Cloch Lighthouse 107
Granny Kempock's Stone 107
Royal Gourock Yacht Club 107
Grangemouth 167
Grangemouth Museum 167
Jupiter Urban Wildlife Garden 167
Grantown-on-Spey 303
Inverallan Parish Church 305
Revack Country Estate 305
Great Bernera 329
Bostadh 329
Community Centre and Museum 329
Great Bernera Bridge 329
Great Cumbrae 87
Greenlaw 7
Greenock 105
Cross of Lorraine 105
Custom House 105
Customhouse Quay 105
Highland Mary 105
James Watt 105

McLean Museum and Art Gallery 105
Old West Kirk 106
The Tail of the Bank 105
Gretna Green 35
Gretna Gateway Outlet Village 36
Gretna Hall 35
Lochmaben Stone 36
Old Blacksmith's Shop 35
Old Toll House 35
Gullane 127
Heritage of Golf 127
Muirfield 127

H

Haddington 127
arish Church of St Mary 127
Haddington to Whitekirk Pilgrimage 127
Jane Welsh 127
Lauderdale Aisle 127
Lennoxlove 127
Nungate Bridge 127
Samuel Smiles 127
St Martin's Church 127
Town House 127
Traprain Law 127
Hamilton 107
Cadzow Castle 108
Cadzow Oaks 108
Chateleherault 107
Chatelherault Country Park 108
Clyde Valley Tourist Route 109
County Buildings 108
Hamilton Mausoleum 107
Hamilton Parish Church 108
Heads Monument 108
Iron Age Fort 108
Low Parks Museum 109
Netherton Cross 108
Sir Harry Lauder 109
The Cameronians (Scottish Rifles) 109
White Cattle 108
Hawick 15
Drumlanrig's Tower 15
Hawick Cashmere Company 16
Hawick Common Riding 15
Hawick Museum and Scott Art Gallery 16
Jimmy Guthrie Statue 16
Peter Scott and Company 16
St Mary's Parish Church 15
Wilton Lodge Park 16
Wrights of Trowmill 16
Helensburgh 105
Geilston Gardens 105
Glen Fruin 105
Hill House 105
John Logie Baird 105
PS Waverley 105
St Mahew's Chapel 105
Helmsdale 319
Strath of Kildonan 319
Timespan 319
Holy Island 94
Holywood 27
Holywood Parish Church 27
Twelve Apostles 27
Hoy 340
Dwarfie Stone 340
Martello Tower 340
Old Man of Hoy 340
Huntly 268
Brander Museum 268
George MacDonald 268
Huntly Castle 268
Hutton 5
Hutton Castle 5
Hutton Parish Church 5

I

Inchcolm 141
Inchcolm Abbey 142
Ingliston 126
Royal Showground 126
Innerleithen 20
Robert Smail's Printing Works 20
St. Ronan's Well Interpretive Centre 20
Inveraray 199
Argyll Wildlife Park 200
Church of All Saints 200
Inveraray Castle 200
Inveraray Jail 200
Inveraray Maritime Museum 200
Neil Munro 200
Parish Church 200
Inverbervie 259
Kinneff Church 259
Thomas Coutts 259
Inverewe Gardens 315
Inverkeithing 142
Battle of Inverkeithing 142
Inverkeithing Museum 142
Mercat Cross 142
Old Town Hall 142
St Peter's Churc 142
Inverness 296
Abertaff House 297
Balnain House 297
Dolphins and Seals of the Moray Firth Visitor Centre 297
Dunbar's Hospital 297
Flora MacDonald 296

Inverness Castle 296
Inverness Cathedral 297
Inverness Museum and Art Gallery 297
Kessock Bridge 297
Old Gaelic Church 297
Old High Church 297
Tolbooth Steeple 297
Town House 297
Victorian Market 297
Inverurie 267
Aberdeenshire Canal 267
Battle of Harlaw 267
Bennachie 267
Carnegie Inverurie Museum 267
Monymusk Reliquary 267
Port Elphinstone 267
Iona 225
Iona Abbey 225
Iona Community 226
Irvine 84
Alexander MacMillan 84
Eglinton Country Park 85
Eglinton Tournament 85
Glasgow Vennel 84
Magnum Leisure Centre 85
Marymass Week 84
Parish Kirk 84
Scottish Maritime Museum 85
Seagate Castle 84
The Big Idea 85
Islay 203
Ardbeg 205
Bowmore 205
Bowmore Distillery 208
Bruichladdich Distillery 208
Bunnahabhain 205
Caol Ila 205
Cultoon Stone Circle 208
Dunyveg Castle 205
Islay Natural History Trust 208
Kildalton Cross and Chapel 205
Lagavulin 205
Loch Finlaggan 203
Museum of Islay Life 208
Port Askaig 203
Port Charlotte 208
Port Ellen 205
Isle of Arran 89
Arran Aromatics 89
Arran Brewery 89
Arran Provisions 94
Auchagallon Stone Circle 91
Balmichael Visitor Centre 93
Blackwaterfoot 93
Brodick 89
Brodick Castle 89
Catacol 91
Corrie 89
Drumadoon 91
Giant's Graves 93
Glen Chalmadale 89
Glenashdale Falls 93
Goat Fell 89
Holy Island 94
Isle of Arran Heritage Museum 89
Isle of Arran Whisky Distillery 91
Lagg 93
Lamlash 93
Lochranza 89
Lochranza Castle 89
Machrie Moor Stone Circle 91
Moss Farm Road Stone Circle 91
Pladda 93
Shiskine 93
St Molas Church 93
The King's Cave 91
The String 93
The Twelve Apostles 91
Torrylinn Creamery 93
Whiting Bay 93
Isle of May 155
Isle of Whithorn 57
St Ninian's Cave 57
St Ninian's Chapel 57

J

Jarlshof 342
Old Scantess 342
Jedburgh 17
Carter Bar 18
Jedburgh Abbey 17
Jedburgh Castle Jail 17
Jedforest Deer and Farm Park 17
Mary Queen of Scots House 17
Monteviot House and Gardens 17
Teviot Water Gardens 18
John O' Groats 320
Castle of Mey 320
Dunnet Head 320
Jura 208
Ardlussa 208
Ben a' Chaolais 208
Ben an Oir 208
Ben Shaintaidh 208
Chapel of St Earnadail 208
Corrvrekkan 209
Craighouse 208
Feolin Ferry 208
Jura House Garden 208
Mary MacCrain 208
Paps of Jura 208

K

Keir 28

Kirkpatrick MacMillan 28
Kelso 12
Camelot 13
Floors Castle 13
Kelso Abbey 12
Kelso Civic Week 12
Kelso Race Course 13
Market Square 12
Roxburgh Castle 12
Royal Burgh of Roxburgh 12
Town House 12
Kenmore 250
Ben Lawers 250
Ben Lawers Mountain Visitor Centre 250
Eilean nan Bannoamh 250
Loch Tay 250
Scottish Crannog Centre 250
Kennethmont 269
Leith Hall 269
Kerrycroy 189
Mount Stuart House 189
Kershopefoot 19
Kilbarchan 107
The Weaver's Cottage 107
Kilbirnie 87
Barony Parish Church 87
Place of Kilbirnie 87
Killiecrankie 252
Battle of Killiecrankie 252
Killiecrankie Visitors Centre 252
Soldier's Leap 252
Killin 181
Breadalbane Folklore Centre 181
Falls of Dochart 181
Falls of Lochay 182
Finlarig Castle 182
Loch Tay 181
Moirlanich Longhouse 182
Kilmarie 199
Kilmarnock 81
Burns Monument 81
Burns Statue 81
Dean Castle 82
Dean Castle Country Park 82
Dick Institute 81
Gatehead Viaduct 82
Howard Park 82
James Shaw 82
John Nesbit 81
Johnnie Walker Bottling Plant 81
Lady's Walk 82
Laigh Kirk 81
Old High Kirk 81
Old Sheriff Court 82
Riccarton 82
William Wallace 82
Kilmartin 197
Ballymeanoch Standing Stones 198
Carnassarie Castle 198
Glebe Cairn 197
Kilmartin House Museum 199
Knights Templar 199
Nether Largie Standing Stones 198
Parish Church 197
Temple Wood Circle 198
Kilmaurs 85
Glencairn Aisle 86
John Boyd Orr 86
Parish Church 86
Tolbooth 86
Kilmelford 215
Parish Church 215
Kilmichael 189
St Macaille Chapel 189
Kilmichael Glassary 197
Parish Church 197
Kilmory 199
Castle Sween 199
Keils Chapel 199
Kilmory Scultpured Stones 199
MacMillan's Cross 199
Kilmun 191
Elizabeth Blackwell 191
Kilmun Arboretum 191
Kilmun Church 191
Rev. Alexander Robinson 191
Kilwinning 86
Dalgarven Mill 86
Kilwinning Abbey 86
Papingo Shoot 86
Kincardine on Forth 144
Kincardine Bridge 144
Mercat Cross 144
Tulliallan Castle 144
Tulliallan Church 144
Kincardine O'Neill 261
Kirk of St Mary 261
Old Smiddy Centre 261
Kingcase 74
Kinghorn 150
Pettycur Crags 150
Kingston 273
Kingussie 305
Highland Folk Museum 305
Monadhliath Mountains 305
Kinloch Rannoch 251
Loch Rannoch 251
Rannoch Moor 251
Rannoch Station 251
Schiehallion 251
Kinlochewe 315

Kinlochlaich Gardens 213
Kinlochleven 287
Aluminium Story Visitor Centre 287
Kinross 144
Cashmere at Lochleven 146
Kinross House 145
Loch Leven 145
Lochleven Castle 145
Mercat Cross 145
Scottish Gliding Centre 146
St Serf's Island 145
T in the Park 146
Tolbooth 145
Vane Farm Nature Reserve, 145
Kintore 267
Kintore Parish Church 267
Kintore Tolbooth 267
Kippen 173
Flanders Moss 173
Kippen Parish Church 173
Kippen Vine 173
Kippford 45
Kirk Yetholm 18
Peninne Way 18
Town Yetholm 18
Kirkbean 39
Arbigland 39
Dr James Craik 39
John Paul Jones 39
Kirkbean Parish Church 39
Kirkcaldy 147
Adam Smith 148
an Ha' 147
Dysart 147
John McDouall Stuart Museum 148
Kirkcaldy Museum and Art Gallery 147
Links Market 147
Marjory Fleming 148
Old Parish Church 147
Ravenscraig Castle 147
Robert Adam 148
Sailor's Walk 147
Wemyss Ware 147
William Adam 148
Kirkconnel, Kirtlebridge 35
Adam Fleming 35
Fair Helen of Kirkconnel Lee 35
Kirkconnel, Upper Nithsdale 31
St Connel's Parish Church 31
Kirkcowan 55
Kirkcudbright 40
Auchingool House 42
Billy Marshall's Grave 41
Broughton House 42
Castledykes 42
Dorothy L. Sayers 42
Greengates Close 42
Greyfriar's Kirk 41
Harbour Cottage Gallery 41
High Street 42
Japanese Garden 42
MacLellan's Castle 41
Manxman's Lake 42
Moat Brae 41
Ronald Searle 42
Sir Thomas MacLellan of Bombie 41
St Cuthbert's Parish Church 41
St Mary's Isle 42
St Trinians 42
Stewartry Museum 42
Tolbooth 42
Kirkintilloch 100
Auld Kirk Museum 100
Forth and Clyde Canal 100
Peel Park 100
Kirkmadrine 59
Kirkmadrine Stones 59
Kirkmaiden 59
Mull of Galloway 59
Kirkmichael 65
Kirkmichael International Guitar Festival 65
Parish Church 65
Kirkoswald 68
Kirkoswald Parish Church 68
Old Parish Church of St Oswald 68
Robert the Bruce's Baptismal Font 68
Souter Johnnie's Cottage 69
Kirkpatrick Fleming 35
Robert the Bruce's Cave 35
Kirkwall 339
Bishop's Palace 339
Earl's Palace 339
Kirkwall Castle 339
Orkney Wireless Museum 339
St Magnus Cathedral 339
St Olaf's Church 339
Tankerness House Museum 339
Kirriemuir 235
Backwater Reservoir 235
Camera Obscura 235
Gateway to the Glens Museum 235
Glen Clova 235
Glen Doll 235
Glen Isla 235
Glen Prosen 235
JM Barrie's Birthplace 235
Kirriemuir Aviation Museum 235
Loch of Lintrathan 235
Kyle of Lochalsh 290
Eilean Donan Castle 290
Lochalsh Woodland 290
Skye Bridge 290

L

Ladykirk 6
Parish Church of St Mary 6
Laggan 307
Lairg 301
Falls of Shin 301
Ord Hill 301
Lamb Holm 339
Italian Chapel 339
Lanark 113
Lanimer Day 113
Royal Burgh of Lanark Museum 113
St Kentigern's Church 113
St Nicholas's Church 113
William Smellie 113
Langholm 32
Armstrong Clan Museum 32
Bentpath Library 32
Common Riding Ceremony 33
Hugh McDiarmid 32
Thomas Telford 32
Westerkirk 32
Largo 150
Alexander Selkirk 150
Great Michael 150
Parish Church 150
Scotland's Larder 150
Sir Andrew Wood 150
Largs 87
Battle of Largs 87
Kelburn Castle 89
Largs Museum 89
Skelmorlie Aisle 89
The Pencil 89
Vikingar! 89
Latheron 318
Clan Gunn Heritage Centre 318
Dunbeath Heritage Centre 319
Lhaidhay Caithness Croft Museum 319
Leadhills 115
Allan Ramsay Library 116
John Taylor 116
William Symington 116
Lendalfoot 67
Carleton Castle 67
Gamesloup 67
Lerwick 341
Arthur Anderson 342
Bšd of Gremista 342
Fort Charlotte 341
Shetland Museum 342
Leuchars 159
Earlshall Castle 159
Leuchars Air Show 159
Parish Church of St Athernase 159
Linlithgow 132
Beecraigs Country Park 134
County Buildings 134
Hopetoun House 134
House of the Binns 134
Linlithgow Canal Centre 134
Linlithgow Loch 132
Linlithgow Palace 132
Linlithgow Story 134
Outer Gateway 133
Queen's Bedchamber 132
St Michael's Parish Church 133
Lismore 218
Achadun Castle 219
Achnacroish 218
Barr M—rr 218
Coeffin Castle 219
Kilmoluaig 218
Lismore Cathedral 218
Tirefour Castle 219
Little Cumbrae 87
Livingston 135
Almond Valley Heritage Centre 135
Almondell and Calderwod Country Park 135
Livingston Parish Church 135
Loch Achray 181
Loch Awe 214
Cruachan Power Station 215
Kilchurn Castle 214
St Conan's Kirk 215
Loch Drunkie 181
Loch Katrine 180
Loch Arklet 180
Sir Walter Scott 181
Loch Ken 43
Loch Leven 145
Lochleven Castle 145
St Serf's Island 145
Vane Farm Nature Reserve 145
Loch Lomond 103
Loch Lomond and the Trossachs National Park 104
Loch Lubnaig 181
Falls of Leny 181
Loch Ness 307
Loch Tay 181
Loch Venachar 181
Loch Voil 181
Lochgelly 141
Lochore Meadows Country Park 141
Lochgilphead 195
Ardishaig 195
Crinan Canal 195
Kilmory Woodland Park 195

Lochinvar 43
Lochinver 311
Ardvreck Castle 315
Assynt Visitor Centre 315
Lochmaben 31
Lochmaben Castle 31
William Paterson 31
Lochmaddy 331
Lochnagar 263
Lochwinnoch 107
Clyde Muirshiel Regional Park 107
Lock Ettrick 28
Lockerbie 33
Battle of Dryfe Sands 33
Lockerbie Disaster 33
Remembrance Garden 33
Tundergarth 33
Lossiemouth 271
James Ramsay Macdonald 271
Lossiemouth Fisheries and Community Museum 271
Luing 217
Luss 104
Ben Lomond 104
Parish Church of St MacKessog 105
Lyne 21
Lyne Church 21

M

Macduff 279
Macduff Marine Aquarium 279
Maeshowe 340
Ring of Brodgar 340
Stenness Standing Stones 340
Mallaig 289
Loch Morar 290
Mallaig Heritage Centre 290
Mallaig Marine World Aquarium and Fishing Exhibition 290
Maryculter 260
Drum Castle 260
Mauchline 76
Abbot Hunter's Tower 77
Ballochmyle Viaduct 77
Burns House Museum 76
Burns Memorial 77
Mossgiel Farm 76
Nance Tinnock's Inn 76
Parish Church 76
Poosie Nansy's Inn 77
William Fisher's Grave 77
Maud 278
Maud Railway Museum 278
Maybole 64
Electric Brae 65
Maybole Castle 64
Maybole Collegiate Church 64
Town Hall 64
Meikleour 243
Meikleour Hedge 243
Melrose 10
Eildon Hills 10
Harmony Garden 11
King Arthur 10
Melrose Abbey 10
Old Melrose 11
Priorwood Gardens 11
St Cuthbert 11
St Cuthbert's Way 11
Menstrie 165
Menstrie Castle 165
Sir Ralph Abercromby 165
Sir William Alexander 165
Methil 150
Methil Heritage Centre 150
Mid Calder 135
Calder House 135
Kirk of Calder 135
Milnathort 146
Burleigh Castle 146
Milngavie 102
Mugdock Country Park 102
West Highland Way 102
Mintlaw 278
Aden Farming Museum 278
Moffat 31
Air Chief Marshal Lord Dowding 32
Black Bull Inn 32
Grey Mare's Tail 32
Hartfell 32
John Loudon McAdam 32
Merlin the Magician 32
Moffat House 32
Moffat Museum 32
Star Hotel 32
Station Park 32
Moniaive 39
James Paterson Museum 39
Maxwelton House 40
Poetry Shop 39
Monifieth 239
St Rule's Church 239
Monkton 74
Ladykirk Chapel 75
MacRae's Monument 74
St Cuthbert's Church 74
Montrose 238
House of Dun 238

Montrose Air Station Museum 238
Montrose Basin Wildlife Centre 238
Morebattle 18
Cessford Castle 18
Linton Church 18
Morvern 289
Kinlochaline Castle 289
Moscow 83
Lochgoin Farm 83
Motherwell 109
Motherwell Heritage Centre 109
Roman Bathhouse 111
Strathclyde Country Park 111
Mousa 342
Broch of Mousa 342
Muck 291
Beinn Airein 291
Dun Ban 291
Port Mor 291
Muirkirk 78
Battle of Airds Moss 78
Mull 219
Bunessan 225
Calgary 223
Chapel of St Ronan 226
Columba Centre 225
Craignure 219
Dervaig 223
Duart Castle 219
Fionnphort 225
Fishnish Pier 221
Iona Heritage Centre 227
John Smith 226
Little Mull Theatre 223
Loch na Keal 225
Loch Tuath 223
MacLean's Cross 226
Macquarrie's Mausoleum 221
Mull and West Higland Railway 219
Mull Museum 223
Reilig Odhrain 226
Ridge of the Chiefs 226
Ridge of the Kings 226
Road of the Dead 226
Ross of Mull Historical Centre 225
Salen 221
San Juan de Sicilia 223
St Columba 225
St Martin's Cross 226
St Mary's Nunnery 226
St Oran's Chapel 226
Tobermory 221
Tor Ab 226
Torosay Castle 219
Ulva 223
Mull of Galloway 59
Musselburgh 123
Battle of Pinkie 123
Inveresk Lodge Gardens 123
Tolbooth 123
Muthill 244
Ardunie Signal Station 245
Drummond Castle Gardens 245
Innerpeffray Chapel 245
Innerpeffray Library 244
Muir O'Fauld Signal Station 245
Muthill Parish Church 244

N

Nairn 301
Boath Doocot 301
Cawdor Castle 301
Neidpath Castle 19
New Abbey 38
New Abbey Corn Mill 38
Shambellie House Museum of Costume 39
Sweetheart Abbey 38
The Criffel 38
New Cumnock 78
Glen Afton 78
Knockshinnoch Mining Disaster 78
New Galloway 43
Glenkens 43
Kells Churchyard 43
Scottish Alternative Games 43
New Lanark 113
Annie Mcleod's Story 115
Falls of Clyde 115
Millworker's House 115
Robert Owen 113
Robert Owen's House 115
Robert Owen's School 115
Scottish Wildlife Trust Visitors Centre 115
Village Store Exhibition 115
Visitors Centre 113
Newburgh 158
Laing Museum 158
Lindores Abbey 158
Newcastleton 18
Hermitage Castle 19
Kershopefoot 19
Liddesdale Heritage Centre Museum 19
Newmilns 84
Newmilns Tower 84
Parish Church 84
Town House 84
Newport-on-Tay 159
Balmerino Abbey 159
Wormit 159
Newstead 11
Trimontium Exhibition 11
Trimontium Roman Fort 11

Newton Stewart 55
Newton Stewart Museum 55
Sophie's Puppetstube and Dolls House Museum 55
Newton upon Ayr 73
Newton Tower 73
Newtongrange 123
Scottish Mining Museum 123
Newtonmore 305
Highland Folk Museum 305
Highland Wildlife Park 305
Ruthven Barracks 305
North Berwick 128
Auld Kirk 128
Bass Rock 128
North Berwick Law 128
North Berwick Museum 128
Scottish Seabird Centre 128
Tantallon Castle 129
Witches Coven 129
North Queensferry 142
Deep Sea World 142
Fife Coastal Path 143
Forth Bridges Visitors Centre 142
North Uist 331
Balranald Nature Reserve 332
Battle of Carinish 332
Loch Scadavay 331
Lochmaddy 331
Teampall na Triobad 331
Teampull MacBhiocair 332

O

Oban 209
A World in Miniature 211
Armaddy Castle Garden 213
Cathedral Church of St John the Divine 211
Cathedral of St Columba 211
Connel Bridge 213
Dunollie Castle 211
Falls of Lora 213
Gylen Castle 213
Kerrera 213
McCaig's Folly 211
Oban Distillery 213
Oban Seal and Marine Centre 213
Ochiltree 77
George Douglas Brown 77
The House with the Green Shutters 78
Old Dailly 66
Bargany House 66
Charter Stones 66
Dante Gabriel Rossetti 66
New Dailly 66
New Dailly Parish Church 66
Old Dailly Parish Church 66
Penkill Castle 66
William Bell Scott 66
Old Deer 278
Deer Abbey 278
Old Man of Hoy 340
Ophir 340
Ophir Church 340
Oronsay 227
Oronsay Cross 227
Oronsay Priory 227
Oyne 267
Archaeolink Prehistory Park 267

P

Paisley 101
Coats Observatory 102
Gleniffer Braes Country Park 102
John Witherspoon 102
Paisley Museum and Art Galleries 102
Paisley Abbey 101
Paisley Arts Centre 102
Sma' Shot Cottages 102
Tannahill Cottage 102
Thomas Coats Memorial Church 102
Palnackie 45
North Glen Gallery 46
Orchardton Tower 46
World Flounder Tramping Championships 45
Paxton 6
Paxton House 6
Union Suspension Bridge 6
Peebles 19
Beltane Week 19
Chambers Institute 19
Cornice Museum 19
Cross Kirk 19
Cuddy Bridge 19
Kailzie Gardens 19
Peebles Parish Church 19
Pencaitland 132
Glenkinchie Distillery 132
Pencaitland Parish Church 132
Winton House 132
Penicuik 125
Allan Ramsay Obelisk 125
Edinburgh Crystal Visitor Centre 125
Scald Law 125
St Mungo's Parish Church 125
Peninne Way 18
Pennan 279
Penpont 28
Perth 239
Bell's Cherrybank Centre 242
Black Watch Regimental Museum 241
Elcho Castle 242

Fair Maid's House 242
Fergusson Gallery 242
Huntingtower 242
Kinnoull Hill 242
North Inch 241
Perth Museum and Art Gallery 241
South Inch 241
St John's Kirk 241
St Ninian's Cathedral 241
Peterhead 278
Arbuthnott Museum 278
Bram Stoker 278
Peterhead Maritime Heritage 278
Slains Castle 278
Pitlochry 247
Clunie Arch 248
Edradour Distillery 248
Forestry Commission Visitor Centre 247
Kindrogan 248
Loch Faskally 248
Pitlochry Festival Theatre 248
Pitlochry Visitor Centre 248
Queen's View 247
Salmon Ladder 248
Pittenweem 155
Kellie Castle 157
Parish Church 157
St Fillan's Cave 157
Pladda 93
Plockton 290
Strome Castle 290
Pluscarden 275
Port Bannatyne 189
Kames Castle 189
Port Ellen 205
Port Glasgow 106
Finlaystone Estate 106
Newark Castle 106
Port Logan 59
Logan Botanic Garden 59
Logan Fish Pond 59
Port of Menteith 175
Dog Island 176
Inchmahome Priory 176
Inchtulla 176
Lake of Menteith 175
Port Seton 123
Seton Castle 123
Seton Collegiate Church 123
Portavadie 201
Portnockie 271
Portpatrick 59
Dunskey Castle 60
Knockinaam Lodge 60
Portpatrick Parish Church 60
Portree 292
Portsoy 279
Powfoot 37
Prestonpans 123
Battle of Prestonpans 123
Prestongrange House 123
Prestwick 73
Bruce's Well 74
Elvis Presley 74
Kingcase 74
Parish Church of St Nicholas 74
Prestwick International Airport 73

R

Raasay 292
Ratho 126
Edinburgh Canal Centre 126
Ratho Parish Church 126
Renfrew 102
Battle of Renfrew 102
Renton 104
Rest and Be Thankful 201
Rhynie 268
Anderson Bey Museum 268
Rockcliffe 48
Mote of Mark 48
Rough Island 48
Rodel 327
St Clement's Church 327
Rosemarkie 301
Groam House Museum 301
Rosneath Peninsula 105
Rosslyn 125
Apprentice Pillar 125
Holy Grail 125
Roslin Glen Country Park 125
Rosslyn Castle 125
Rosslyn Church 125
Solomon's Temple 125
Rothesay
Ardencraig Gardens 188
Ascog Hall Fernery and Garden 189
Bute Museum 188
Canada Hill 188
Church of St Mary 188
Isle of Bute Discovery Centre 188
Rothesay Castle 188
St Blane's Chapel 189
Victorian Toilets 189
Rum 291
Bulloch Mausoleum 291
Kinloch Castle 291
Rutherglen 100
Greenbank House 101

Newton Mearns 101
Parish Church 101
Ruthwell 37
Parish Church 37
Rev. Henry Duncan 37
Ruthwell Cross 37
Savings Bank Museum 37

S

Saddell 193
Saddell Abbey 193
Saddell Castle 193
Salen 221, 289
Saltcoats 85
Betsy Miller 85
North Ayrshire Museum 85
Sanquhar 30
James Crichton 30
Richard Cameron 30
Sanquhar Castle 30
Sanquhar Declaration 30
Sanquhar Historic Walk 30
Sanquhar Post Office 30
Sanquhar Tolbooth 30
St Bride's Parish Church 30
Scalloway 343
Scalloway Castle 343
Scalloway Museum 343
Scalpay 327
Scalpay Bridge 327
Scone Palace 242
Moot Hill 242
Scone Abbey 242
Scotlandwell 146
Arnot Tower 146
Holy Well 146
Seamill 87
Seil Island 217
An Cala Garden 218
Bridge Across the Atlantic 217
Cuan 218
Easdale 217
Easdale Island Folk Museum 218
Ellenabeich 217
Heritage Centre 218
Selkirk 14
Common Riding Ceremony 14
Halliwell's House 14
Mungo Park 14
Old Courthouse 14
Robert D. Clapperton Photographic 14
Selkirk Glass 14
Yarrow 14
Shader 331
Steinacleit Stone Circle and Standing Stones 331
Shawbost 327
Shawbost School Museum 327
Shiel Bridge 290
Countryside Centre 290
Five Sisters of Kintail 290
Skara Brae 341
Skaill House 341
Skye 291
Armadale Castle Gardens and Museum of the Isles 296
Broadford 292
Colbost Croft Museum 292
Cuillins 291
Dunvegan Castle 292
Portree 292
Raasay 292
Sghurr Alasdair 291
Skye Road Bridge 291
Smailholm 12
Smailholm Tower 12
Sorn 78
Prophet Peden 78
Sorn Castle 78
Sorn Parish Church 78
South Queensferry 126
Carmelite Friary 126
Dalmany House 127
Dalmeny Church 127
Forth Rail Bridge 126
Forth Road Bridge 126
Hawes Inn 126
Plewlands House 126
Queensferry Museum 126
South Uist 333
Beinn Mhor 333
Eriskay 335
Kildonan Museum 335
Loch Druidibeag Nature Reserve 333
Milton 333
Ormiclate Castle 335
Our Lady of the Isles 333
SS. Politician 335
Southend 193
Keil 193
Southern Upland Way 4
Soutra 125
Soutra Aisle 125
Spittal of Glenshee 248
Cairnwell 249
Devil's Elbow 249
St Abbs 5
St Abb's Head 5
St Andrews 151
Archbishop James Sharp 153
British Golf Museum 153
Cardinal David Beaton 151

Dominican Friary 153
Holy Trinity Parish Church 153
Madras College 153
Martyr's Monument 153
Old Course 154
Partick Hamilton 153
Queen Mary's House 153
Queen Mary's Thorn 153
Royal and Ancient Golf Club 154
Secret Bunket 154
St Andrews Aquarium 153
St Andrews Castle 151
St Andrews Cathedral 151
St Andrews Museum 153
St Andrews Preservation Trust Museum and Garden 153
St Leonard's Chapel 153
St Leonard's College 153
St Mary on the Rock 151
St Mary's College 153
St Rule's Tower 151
St Salvator's Church 153
St Salvator's College 153
Tom Morris 154
West Port 153

St Boswells 14

St Fillans 247
Ben Vorlich 247
Dunfillan Hill 247
St Fillan's Chair 247

St John's Town of Dalry 43
Lochinvar 43
St John's Stone 43

St Mary's Loch 15
James Hogg 15
Loch of the Lowes 15
Tibbie Shiel's Inn 15
William Wordsworth 15

St Monans 157
Parish Church of St Monans 157
St Monans Windmill 157

St Vigeans 237
Parish Church of St Vigeans 237
St Vigeans Museum 237

Staffa 227
Fingal's Cave 227

Stanley 243
Kinclaven Castle 243

Stenhousemuir 166

Stenton 131
Presmennan Lake 131
Pressmennan Forest Trail 131
Tron 131

Stevenston 85
High Church 85

Stewarton 83
David Dale 83
Parish Church of St Columba 83

Stirling 167
Argyll's Lodging 170
Bastion 170
Battle of Bannockburn 170
Battle of Stirling Bridge 170
Beheading Stone 170
Cambuskenneth Abbey 171
Church of the Holy Rude 169
Cowane's Hospital 169
Frenzied Friar of Tongland 168
King's Park 169
Lady's Rock 169
Mar's Wark 170
Martyr's Monument 169
Mercat Cross 170
National Wallace Monument 171
Old Stirling Bridge 170
Old Town Jail 169
Smith Art Gallery and Museum 171
Stirling Castle 168
Stirling New Bridge 170
The Bannockburn Heritage Centre 171
The King's Knot 169
Tolbooth 170
Town Wall 170

Stobinian 182

Stobo 21
Dawyck Botanic Garden and Arboretum 21
Stobo Castle 21
Stobo Kirk 21

Stonehaven 258
Dunnotter Castle 258
Fireball Festival 259
Mercat Cross 258
Steeple 258
Tolbooth Museum 258

Stornoway 325
An Lanntair Arts Centre 326
Free Church 325
Lews Castle 325
Loom Centre 326
Martins Memorial 326
Museum nan Eilean 326
Parish Church of St Columba 325
St Columba's Church 326
St Peter's Episcopal Church 325

Stow 10
St Mary of Wedale Parish Church 10

Straad 189
St Ninian's Chapel 189

Strachur 201
Lachlan Castle 201
Strachur Smithy 201

Straiton 65

Blairquhan 65
Hunter Blair Monument 65
Nick o' the Balloch 65
St Cuthbert's Parish Church 65
Stranraer 49
Castle Kennedy Gardens 51
Castle of St John 49
Glenwhan Gardens 51
Lochinch Castle 51
North West Castle 49
Old Town Hall 49
Princess Victoria Monument 49
Rhinns of Galloway 49
Sir John Ross 49
Soulseat Abbey 51
Strathaven 111
Battle of Drumclog 111
John Hastie Museum 111
John Hastie Park 111
Strathaven Castle 111
Strathglass 311
Strathpeffer 311
Eagle Stone 311
Highland Museum of Childhood 311
Spa Pump Room 311
Stromness 340
Scapa Flow 340
Stromness Museum 340
Stronachlachar 181
Factor's Island 181
Strontian 289
Sweetheart Abbey 38
Symington 75
Barnweil Church 75
Symington Parish Church 75
Wallace Monument 75

T

Tain 299
St Duthus Collegiate Church 299
Tain Through Time 299
Tangwick 343
Tangwick Haa Museum 343
Tarbert 193, 326
Amhuinnsuidhe Castle 326
An Tairbeart 194
Kennacraig 194
Skipness Castle 195
Stonefield Castle Garden 194
Tarbet 201
Tarbolton 76
Bachelor's Club 76
Tarbolton Parish Church 76
Taynuilt 214
Barguillean's Angus Garden 214
Bonawe Furnace 214
Thornhill 28
Boatford Cross 28
Drumlanrig Castle 28
Threave Castle 45
Threave Gardens and Estate 45
Thurso 320
Scrabster Castle 320
St Peter's Church 320
Thurso Heritage Museum 320
Tighnabruaich 201
Tillicoultry 164
Tillicoultry Glen 164
Tingwall 343
Law Ting Holm 343
Tingwall Agricultural Museum 343
Tiree 227
Ben Hough 227
Ben Hynish 227
Ringing Stone 227
Sandaig Museum 227
Scarnish 227
Tobermory 221
Tomatin 303
Tomatin Distillery 303
Tomintoul 275
The Lecht 275
Tomintoul Museum 275
Tongland 42
Tongland Abbey 42
Tongland Bridge 43
Tongland Power Station 43
Tongue 319
Castle Bharraich 319
Strathnaver Museum 319
Torphichen 135
Torphichan Parish Church 135
Torphichen Preceptory 135
Toward 191
Toward Castle 191
Town Yetholm 18
Traquair 20
Bear Gates 20
Traquair House 20
Traquair House Brewery 20
Troon 75
Ballast Bank 75
Dundonald Hills 75
Troon/Kilmarnock Railway 75
Tullibody 166
Robert Dick 166
St Serf's Church 166
Tullibody Auld Brig 166

Turnberry 69
Turnberry Castle 69
Turnberry Hotel 69
Turnberry Lighthouse 69
Turriff 278
Glendronach Distillery 278
Turra Coo 278
Turriff Parish Church 278
Tweedswell 32
Devil's Beeftub 32
Twynholm 48
David Coulthard Museum 48
Tyndrum 182
Dalrigh 182
Strath Fillan 182
Strathfillan Priory 182
Tynron 29
Parish Church 29

U

Ullapool 311
Hydroponicum 311
Leckmelm Gardens 311
Ullapool Museum and Visitor Centre 311
Ulva 223
Unst 344
Hermaness 344
Muness Castle 344
Urquhart Castle 307

V

Voe 343
Crofthouse Museum 343

W

Wanlockhead 29
Beam Engine 29
Leadhills and Wanlockhead Light Railway 29
Lochnell Mine 29
Miners' Library 29
Museum of Lead Mining 29
UK National Gold Panning Championships 30
Wemyss 149
MacDuff Castle 149
West Kilbride 87
Hunterston Castle 87
Hunterston Nuclear Power Station 87
Law Castle 87
Portencross Castle 87
Seamill 87
West Linton 21
Lady Gifford's Well 21
St Andrews Parish Church 21
Whipman 21
Whitekirk 129
Aeneas Sylvius Piccolomini 129
St Mary's Parish Church 129
Whithorn 56
Candida Casa 56
Latinus Stone 57
Priory Museum 57
St Ninian 56
The Pend 57
Whithorn Priory 56
Whithorn Visitors Centre 57
Wick 315
Girnigoe Castle 318
James Bremner 318
Northlands Viking Centre 318
Old Parish Kirk 315
Parliament Square 315
Sinclair Aisle 315
Sinclair Castle 318
Wigtown 55
Bladnoch Distillery 56
Covenanters Monument 56
Martyrs' Graves 56
Martyrs Monument 56
Scotland's Book Town 55
Wishaw 109

Y

Yarrow 14
Yarrow Parish Church 14
Yell 343
Lumbister RSPB Reserve 344
Old Haa of Burravoe 343

List of Advertisers

NUMBERS

2 Village	Eriskay, Western Isles	336
22 Braighe Road	Stornoway, Isle of Lewis	324
5 Hacklete	Great Bernera, Isle of Lewis	329

A

Acarsaid Hotel	Pitlochry, Perthshire	246
Achins Bookshop And Coffee Shop	Inverkirkaig, nr Lochinver, Sutherland	313
Achnacarry Guest House	Perth, Perthshire	241
Achnadrish House	by Tobermory, Isle of Mull	225
Admirals Inn	Findochty, Morayshire	272
The Aizle	Balat Crossroads, nr Balfron, Stirlingshire	179
Allt-Na-Craig	Ardrishaig, Argyllshire	196
Allt-Nan-Ros Hotel	Onich, by Fort William, Inverness-shire	287
Alvermann Guest House	Balloch, Dunbartonshire	103
Am Bothan And The Gille Dubh	Poolewe, Ross-shire	316
Anwoth Hotel	Gatehouse-of-Fleet, Kirkudbrightshire	48
The Arches Restaurant	Stranraer, Wigtownshire	49
Ardbeg Cottage	Lochmaben, Dumfriesshire	31
Ardsheal House	Kentallan of Appin, Argyllshire	288
Ardshiel House	Campbeltown, Argyllshire	190
Argyll Restaurant	Bunessan, Isle of Mull	226
Arisaig Cottage	Ballater, Aberdeenshire	262
Atholl House hotel	Dunvegan, Isle of Skye	294
Aulay's Bar	Oban, Argyllshire	209
Avoriaz	Oban, Argyllshire	210

B

Balavil Sport Hotel	Newtonmore, Inverness-shire	307
Baleloch House	Tigharry, nr Lochmaddy, North Uist	332
Balinakill Country House Hotel	Clachan, nr Tarbert, Argyllshire	194
Ballivicar Farm	Port Ellen, Isle of Islay	202
Balloan House Hotel	Marybank, Ross-shire	310
Balvicar Farm	Isle of Seil, Argyllshire	218
Barcaldine House Hotel	Barcaldine, nr Oban, Argyllshire	213
Beaches Tearoom and Gift Shop	Ayr, Ayrshire	72
Beechwood Guest House Hotel	Ayr, Ayrshire	72
Belle Vue	Dalbeattie, Kirkcudbrightshire	46
Belmont Guest House	Ayr, Ayrshire	72
Belmont House	Largs, Ayrshire	88
The Bentley Hotel	Motherwell, Lanarkshire	110
Birchfield Cottages	Nethybridge, Inverness-shire	303
Birchwood Cottage	Chapelbrae, nr Braemar, Aberdeenshire	264
Birkenside Farm	Earlston, Berwickshire	12
Blackwaterfoot Lodge	Blackwaterfoot, Isle of Arran	94
Blarghour Farm Cottages	Blarghour Farm, by Dalmally, Argyllshire	215

Boars Head Hotel	Colmonell, nr Girvan, Ayrshire	67
The Bower Inn	Bowermadden, by Wick, Caithness	317
The Bowmore Hotel	Bowmore, Isle of Islay	204
Braeburn Cottage	West Auchencarroch Farm, Dunbartonshire	104
Bragleenbeg	Kilninver, by Oban, Argyllshire	217
Brambles Coffee Shop And Restaurant	Perth, Perthshire	240
Breadalbane Hotel	Kildonan, Isle of Arran	92
Bridge House Hotel	Ardrishaig, Argyllshire	196
Bridgeside B&B and Self Catering	Bayhead, Isle of Scalpay	326
Brown Bull	Lochwinnoch, Renfrewshire	106
Burnhouse Manor Hotel	Burnhouse, by Beith, Ayrshire	86

C

Caberfeidh Restaurant	Lochinver, Sutherland	313
The Caddy Mann Restaurant	Mounthooly, nr Jedburgh, Roxburghshire	17
Café Med	Ayr, Ayrshire	72
Cairn Hotel	Carrbridge, Inverness-shire	305
Cairnryan Caravan Park	Cairnryan, nr Stranraer, Wigtownshire	50
Callater Lodge	Braemar, Aberdeenshire	264
Cardross Holiday Homes	Port of Menteith, Stirlingshire	175
Carradale Hotel	Carradale, Argyllshire	192
Carseview	Cambuskenneth, nr Stirling, Stirlingshire	170
Castle Arms Hotel	Mey, Caithness	319
Castleton House Hotel	by Glamis, Angus	233
Cawdor Tavern	Cawdor, Nairnshire	302
Ceol-Na-Mara	Point, Isle of Lewis	325
Chapelbank House Hotel & Restaurant	Forfar, Angus	234
The Chardonnay Restaurant	Carluke, Lanarkshire	113
Cherrybank Inn	Perth, Perthshire	240
Chirnside Hall Hotel	Chirnside, nr Duns, Berwickshire	5
Christina's Bar	Ayr, Ayrshire	71
Clovenfords Hotel	Clovenfords, Selkirkshire	8
Clugston Farm	nr Newton Stewart, Wigtownshire	54
Cnoc Ard Taighean Gorm	Bowmore, Isle of Islay	205
Cobbles Inn	Kelso, Roxburghshire	12
The Coffee Club	Kilmarnock, Ayrshire	80
Columba Hotel	Tarbert, Argyllshire	193
Commercial Hotel	Wishaw, Lanarkshire	109
The Commercial Inn	Dunfermline, Fife	140
Corsewall Lighthouse Hotel	Corsewall Point, nr Stranraer, Wigtownshire	50
Coullabus Keeper's Cottage	Bridgend, Isle of Islay	206
Coulliehare Farm	Udny, nr Ellon, Aberdeenshire	269
Craigard House	Low Askomil, nr Campbeltown, Argyllshire	190
Craigie Inn	Craigie, by Kilmarnock, Ayrshire	80
Craigvrack Hotel	Pitlochry, Perthshire	247
Craigwelder B&B	Kirkcowan, nr Newton Stewart, Wigtownshire	54
Cranford Guest House	Braemar, Aberdeenshire	266
Crannog Seafood Restaurant	Fort William, Inverness-shire	284
Creagan Cottage	Creagan, nr Callanish, Isle of Lewis	328
Creag-Ard House	by Aberfoyle, Stirlingshire	178
Creebridge House Hotel	Minnigaff, Newton Stewart, Wigtownshire	52

Cressfield Country House Hotel	Ecclefechan, Dumfriesshire	34
Crofters Cafe Bar	Rosemarkie, nr Fortrose, Inverness-shire	300
Cross Keys Hotel	Canonbie, Dumfriesshire	36
The Crown Hotel	Inverbervie, Kincardineshire	259
Cuckoo Wrasse	Cromwell Harbour, nr Dunbar, East Lothian	130
Culligran Cottages	Struy, nr Beauly, Inverness-shire	309
Culter Mill Restaurant And Bistro	Coulter, by Biggar, Lanarkshire	114

D

Daleside	Biggar, Lanarkshire	114
Dallmartin Cottage	Douglas, nr Lesmahagow, Lanarkshire	116
Dalshian Chalets	Pitlochry, Perthshire	246
Delnasaugh Inn	Ballindalloch, Banffshire	274
Denburn House	Crail, Fife	154
Dornoch Bridge Inn And Restaurant	Meikleferry, nr Tain, Ross-shire	298
Drumla Farm	Kildonan, Isle of Arran	92
Duisdale Country House Hotel	Sleat, Isle of Skye	292
Dunchraigaig House	Kilmartin, nr Lochgilphead, Argyllshire	197
Duncree House	Newton Stewart, Wigtownshire	54
Dunduff Farm	nr Dunure, Ayrshire	70
Dunvalanree	Port Righ, nr Carradale, Argyllshire	192
Dunvegan House	Brodick, Isle of Arran	88

E

Eagle View Guest House	Newtonmore, Inverness-shire	307
East Challoch Farm	Dunragit, nr Stranraer, Wigtownshire	50
East Lochhead	Lochwinnoch, Renfrewshire	106
East Neuk Hotel	Crail, Fife	155
Eilean	Lennoxtown, Glasgow	101
Eleraig Highland Lodges	Kilninver, by Oban, Argyllshire	216
Elmarglen Hotel	Thornhill, Dumfriesshire	28

F

Flanagan's Bar and Tapas Restaurant	Elgin, Morayshire	270
Ford Bank Country House Hotel	nr Bladnoch, nr Wigtown, Wigtownshire	55
Fordell	Barassie, nr Troon, Ayrshire	74
Fordhead Cottage	Fordhead, nr Kippen, Stirlingshire	173
Fordyce Castle	Fordyce, Banffshire	273
Forth House	Aberfoyle, nr Stirling, Stirlingshire	177
Forth Inn	Aberfoyle, Stirlingshire	176
Fortingall Hotel	Fortingall, Perthshire	251

G

Gallanach	by Oban, Argyllshire	210
Galley of Lorne Inn	Ardfern, Argyllshire	198
Galloway Arms Hotel	Newton Stewart, Wigtownshire	53
Gardener's Cottage	Faskally, nr Pitlochry, Perthshire	248
The Ginger Jar	Galashiels, Selkirkshire	9
Glassford Inn	Glassford, nr Strathaven, Lanarkshire	111
Glen Affric Chalet Park	Cannich, by Beauly, Inverness-shire	308
Glenaden Hotel	Ballater, Aberdeenshire	263

Glenearn House	Crieff, Perthshire	245
Glenegedale House	Glenegedale, Isle of Islay	203
Glenfoyle Cottage	Gargunnock, Stirlingshire	172
Glenisle Hotel	Lamlash, Isle of Arran	90
Glenlivet House	By Ballindalloch, Banffshire	274
Glenluiart Holiday Cottages	Moniaive, Dumfriesshire	40
Glenny Cottages	Port of Menteith, nr Aberfoyle, Stirlingshire	176
Glensanda House	Stanley, Perthshire	243
Goblin Ha' Hotel	Gifford, East Lothian	132
Gordon Arms Hotel	Kincardine O'Neil, Aboyne, Aberdeenshire	261
Granite Villa Guest House	Golspie, Sutherland	299

H

Hannibals Restaurant	Stirling, Stirlingshire	168
Harbour House Hotel	Portpatrick, Wigtownshire	60
Harbour Inn	Garlieston, Wigtownshire	57
Harmony B&B	Castle Douglas, Kirkcudbrightshire	44
Heatherghyll Motel	Crawford, Lanarkshire	116
Hillcrest B&B	Badnaban, nr Lochinver, Sutherland	312
Homeston Farm	Campbeltown, Argyllshire	190
Hotel Seaforth	Arbroath, Angus	236
Huntingtower House	Perth, Perthshire	240

I

Inshaig Park Hotel	Easdale, by Oban, Argyllshire	218
Invercairn House	Brodie, by Forres, Morayshire	276
Island Croft Holidays	Bornish, South Uist	334
Island Encounter Wildlife and Birdwatchers Safaris	Aros, Isle of Mull	220
The Islay Whisky Club	Bowmore, Isle of Islay	204
Isle of Mull Silver and Goldsmiths	Tobermory, Isle of Mull	221
Ivy Bank Cottage	Creebridge, nr Newton Stewart, Wigtownshire	53

J

Jock's Restaurant and Crafts	Kirkmichael, Ayrshire	64
Jokers	Dunfermline, Fife	139

K

Kames Hotel	Kames, by Tighnabruaich, Argyllshire	202
Kerrow House	Cannich, by Beauly, Inverness-shire	309
Kilchoman House Cottages	Kilchoman, by Bruichladdich, Isle of Islay	206
Kildonan Schoolhouses	Kildonan, Isle of Arran	93
Kingask Country Cottages	St Andrews, Fife	152
Kings Arms Hotel	Barr, nr Girvan, Ayrshire	66
Kingsfield House	Kintore, Aberdeenshire	266
Kinlochewe Hotel	Kinlochewe, by Achnasheen, Wester Ross	314
Kinnighallen Farm B&B	Fortingall, Perthshire	251
Kippielaw Farmhouse	East Linton, East Lothian	130
Knockqueen	Carinish, North Uist	332

L

The Lake Hotel	Port of Menteith, Perthshire	174

Lathamor Guest House	Newmarket, nr Stornoway, Isle of Lewis	324
Laurel Bank Tea Room	Broughton, by Biggar, Peeblesshire	21
Lerags House	by Oban, Argyllshire	211
Little Swinton Farm	Swinton, nr Coldstream, Berwickshire	7
Loch Insh Watersports	Kincraig, Inverness shire	306
Loch Ness Backpackers Lodge	East Lewiston, nr Drumnadrochit, Inverness-shire	308
Lochside Cottage	Lochboisdale, South Uist	334
Lochside Lodge And Roundhouse Restaurant	Bridgend of Lintrathen, by Kirriemuir, Angus	235
Lorgba Holiday Cottages	Port Charlotte, Isle of Islay	208
Lyne Farmhouse	Lyne Farm, nr Peebles, Peeblesshire	20

M

MacDonald Arms Hotel	Balbeggie, Perthshire	242
Mains Cottages	Carradale, Argyllshire	192
Mansfield House Hotel	Hawick, Roxburghshire	16
Marine Hotel	Stonehaven, Aberdeenshire	258
Markie Dans	Oban, Argyllshire	210
The Mint	Coatbridge, Strathclyde	108
Moorfield House Hotel	Chapelbrae, nr Braemar, Aberdeenshire	265
The Moorings Hotel	Muir or Ord, Ross-shire	310
The Moorings Restaurant And Thistle Dubh B&B	Fort Augustus, Inverness-shire	286
Morgan McVeigh's	Colpy, Aberdeenshire	268
Morrison's B&B and Caravans	Lochboisdale, South Uist	335
Muasdale Holiday Park	Muasdale, nr Tarbert, Argyllshire	195
Muirfield	Dunbar, East Lothian	131
Mull Pottery	Tobermory, Isle of Mull	223
Munlochy Hotel	Munlochy, Ross and Cromarty	300
Murray Luxury Dumplings & Factory Kitchen	Coulter, by Biggar, Lanarkshire	114

N

Nicols	Kirkcaldy, Fife	147
No 13 B&B	Dalbeattie, Kirkcudbrightshire	46
North Beachmore	Muasdale, nr Tarbert, Argyllshire	194
Norwood	Whiting Bay, Isle of Arran	91
Number 25	Portree, Isle of Skye	293

O

Octomore Cottage	Port Charlotte, Isle of Islay	207
The Old Aberlady Inn	Aberlady, East Lothian	128
The Old Courthouse	Lochmaddy, North Uist	330
The Old Crofthouse	by Portree, Isle of Skye	294
The Old Inn	Flowerdale Glen, nr Gairloch, Ross-shire	317
The Old Manor	Carnoustie, Angus	239
Old Monastery Restaurant	Drybridge, nr Buckie, Morayshire	272
The Old Smiddy	Errol, nr Carse of Gowrie, Perthshire	244
Orasay Inn	Lochcarnan, South Uist	333
The Original Roslin Inn	Roslin, Midlothian	124
Over Langshaw	Langshaw, nr Galashiels, Selkirkshire	9
The Owl and Trout Country Inn	Hillend, nr Airdrie, Strathclyde	109
The Owls Restaurant	Ferniegair, nr Hamilton, Strathclyde	108

P

Petrucci's Pizzeria	Stranraer, Wigtownshire	49
The Pheasant Inn	Sorbie, Wigtownshire	57
Pine Guest House	Inverness, Inverness-shire	296
Point House and Cottages	Kings Cross, Isle of Arran	90
Polfearn Hotel	Taynuilt, Argyllshire	214
Pooltiel	Pitlochry, Perthshire	246
Poppies Hotel	Callander, Perthshire	180

Q

Queen's Arms Hotel	Isle of Whithorn, nr Newton Stewart, Wigtownshire	58

R

Ravenscourt House Private Hotel	Grantown-on-Spey, Morayshire	302
Riverside Lodges	Invergloy, nr Spean Bridge, Inverness-shire	284
Robbies	Hawick, Roxburghshire	15
Rock Cottage	Salen, nr Aros, Isle of Mull	219
Roineabhal Country House	Kilchrenan, nr Taynuilt, Argyllshire	214
Rokeby House	Dunblane, nr Stirling, Stirlingshire	172
Rose Cottage	Gelston, nr Castle Douglas, Kirkcudbrightshire	44
Rosemount Guest House	Low Askomil, nr Campbeltown, Argyllshire	190
Roslin Glen Hotel	Roslin, Midlothian	124
The Rossan	Castle Douglas, Kirkcudbrightshire	44

S

Scaliscro Lodge	Uig, Isle of Lewis	328
Seafield Farm Cottages	Achnamara, nr Lochgilphead, Argyllshire	198
The Seaforth	Ullapool, Ross-shire	312
Seaview Farm House	Hill of Forss, nr Thurso, Caithness	318
Seaview Holiday House	Morven, Berneray, North Uist	330
Sergio's	Sandbed, nr Hawick, Roxburghshire	16
Sgeir Ruadh	Hougharry, nr Longmaddy, North Uist	331
Shawland Hotel and Travel Lodge	nr Stonehouse, Lanarkshire	110
Shawlee Cottage	Chapelhall, nr Airdrie, Strathclyde	108
The Ship Hotel	Eyemouth, Berwickshire	6
The Ship Hotel	Newburgh, nr Cupar, Fife	158
The Shore Inn	Portsoy, Banffshire	279
Shotts Farm	Barrmill, nr Beith, Ayrshire	86
Sleat Holiday Homes	Ardvasar, Isle of Skye	292
The Smoo Cave Hotel	Sutherland	314
The Smuggler's Inn	Anstruther, Fife	156
Speyside Leisure Park	Aviemore, Inverness-shire	304
St Ninian's	Sandyhills, nr Dalbeattie, Kirkcudbrightshire	47
Stable Cottage	Symington, Ayrshire	75
Strachan Cottage	Tarland, nr Aboyne, Aberdeenshire	262
Strathallen House	Dollar, Clackmannanshire	163
Strathaven Gift Shop and Tea Room	Strathaven, Lanarkshire	111
Struan Hall	Aboyne, Aberdeenshire	262

T

Tannochbrae Tearoom	Auchtermuchty, Fife	158
Tarras Guest House	Lockerbie, Dumfriesshire	33
Taste Buds	Dundonald, Ayrshire	76
Thorntree	Arnprior, Stirlingshire	174
Tigh Na Lochan Guest House	Bunessan, Isle of Mull	224
Tigh-Na-Mara Hotel	Sandhead, Wigtownshire	59
Tobermory Hotel	Tobermory, Isle of Mull	222
Toll Bridge Lodge	Bridge of Feugh, Banchory, Aberdeenshire	260
Torlinnhe	Fort William, Inverness-shire	285
Torlochan	Gruline, Isle of Mull	220
Torrisdale Castle	Torrisdale Castle, nr Carradale, Argyllshire	192
Tower House	Kilbarchan, Renfrewshire	106
Town House Hotel	Aberfoyle, Stirlingshire	177
The Trentham Hotel	Dornoch, Sutherland	298

U

Uig Hotel	Uig, Isle of Skye	295
Urquhart Caledonian Hotel	Portree, Isle of Skye	293

V

Village Inn	Kirtle Bridge, nr Lockerbie, Dumfriesshire	32

W

Wallamhill House	Kirkton, nr Dumfries, Dumfriesshire	27
Watergate	Blairlogie, nr Stirling, Stirlingshire	165
Well View Hotel	Moffat, Dumfriesshire	31
Wellhill Farm Cottage No 1	Dyke, nr Forres, Morayshire	275
Wellside Farmhouse	Forres, Morayshire	276
Wemyss Central Hotel	East Wemyss, Fife	149
Wemyss Farm	Forfar, Angus	234
West Loch and Brenfield	Tarbert, Argyllshire	193
The Wheatsheaf Monkton Inn	Monkton, nr Prestwick, Ayrshire	74
White Heather Hotel	Kyleakin, Isle of Skye	291
White Swan Hotel	Earlston, Berwickshire	11
Whitecairn Farm Caravan Park	Glenluce, Wigtownshire	52
Wide Mouthed Frog	Connel, nr Oban, Argyllshire	212

Y

Yacht Corryvreckan	Kilmore, nr Oban, Argyllshire	211

Hidden Places Order Form

To order any of our publications just fill in the payment details below and complete the order form ***overleaf***. For orders of less than 4 copies please add £1 per book for postage and packing. Orders over 4 copies are P & P free.

Please Complete Either:

I enclose a cheque for £ ____________ made payable to Travel Publishing Ltd

Or:

Card No:

Expiry Date:

Signature:

NAME:

ADDRESS:

POSTCODE:

TEL NO:

Please either send, telephone or fax your order to:

Travel Publishing Ltd
7a Apollo House
Calleva Park
Aldermaston
Berks, RG7 8TN

Tel : 0118 981 7777
Fax: 0118 982 0077

	Price	Quantity	Value
Hidden Places Regional Titles			
Cambs & Lincolnshire	£7.99	....	....
Chilterns	£7.99	....	....
Cornwall	£8.99	....	....
Derbyshire	£7.99	....	....
Devon	£8.99	....	....
Dorset, Hants & Isle of Wight	£8.99	....	....
East Anglia	£8.99	....	....
Gloucestershire & Wiltshire	£7.99	....	....
Heart of England	£7.99	....	....
Hereford, Worcs & Shropshire	£7.99	....	....
Highlands & Islands	£7.99	....	....
Kent	£8.99	....	....
Lake District & Cumbria	£8.99	....	....
Lancashire & Cheshire	£8.99	....	....
Lincolnshire & Nottinghamshire	£8.99	....	....
Northumberland & Durham	£8.99	....	....
Somerset	£7.99	....	....
Sussex	£7.99	....	....
Thames Valley	£7.99	....	....
Yorkshire	£7.99	....	....
Hidden Places National Titles			
England	£10.99	....	....
Ireland	£10.99	....	....
Scotland	£10.99	....	....
Wales	£9.99	....	....
Hidden Inns Titles			
Heart of England	£5.99	....	....
Lancashire & Cheshire	£5.99	....	....
South	£5.99	....	....
South East	£5.99	....	....
South and Central Scotland	£5.99	....	....
Welsh Borders	£5.99	....	....
West Country	£5.99	....	....
Wales	£5.99	....	....
Yorkshire	£5.99	....	....
		______	______
		______	______

For orders of less than 4 copies please add £1 per book for postage & packing. Orders over 4 copies P & P free.

Hidden Places Reader Reaction

The *Hidden Places* research team would like to receive reader's comments on any visitor attractions or places reviewed in the book and also recommendations for suitable entries to be included in the next edition. This will help ensure that the *Hidden Places* series continues to provide its readers with useful information on the more interesting, unusual or unique features of each attraction or place ensuring that their stay in the local area is an enjoyable and stimulating experience. To provide your comments or recommendations would you please complete the forms below and overleaf as indicated and send to:

The Research Department, Travel Publishing Ltd,
7a Apollo House, Calleva Park, Aldermaston, Reading, RG7 8TN.

Your Name:

Your Address:

Your Telephone Number:

Please tick as appropriate: Comments ☐ Recommendation ☐

Name of *"Hidden Place"*:

Address:

Telephone Number:

Name of Contact:

Hidden Places Reader Reaction

Comment or Reason for Recommendation:

....

....

....

....

....

....

....

....

....

....

....

....

....